Praise for *Windows Serι*

"Once again, Roberta Bragg proves why she is
field! It's clear that Roberta has had a great deal of experience in real-world security
design and implementation. I'm grateful that this book provides clarity on what is
often a baffling subject!"

—James I. Conrad, MCSE 2003, Server+, Certified Ethical Hacker
James@accusource.net

"Full of relevant and insightful information. Certain to be a staple reference
book for anyone dealing with Windows Server 2003 security. Roberta Bragg's
Windows Server 2003 Security is a MUST read for anyone administering Windows
Server 2003."

—Philip Cox, Consultant, SystemExperts Corporation
phil.cox@systemexperts.com

"Few people in the security world understand and appreciate every aspect of network security like Roberta Bragg. She is as formidable a security mind as I have
ever met, and this is augmented by her ability to communicate the concepts clearly,
concisely, and with a rapier wit. I have enjoyed working with Roberta more than I
have on any of the other 20 some odd books to which I have contributed. She is a
giant in the field of network security."

—Bob Reinsch
bob.reinsch@fosstraining.com

"*Windows Server 2003 Security* explains why you should do things and then tells
you how to do it! It is a comprehensive guide to Windows security that provides the
information you need to secure your systems. Read it and apply the information."

—Richard Siddaway, MCSE
rsiddaw@hotmail.com

"Ms. Bragg's latest book is both easy to read and technically accurate. It will be a
valuable resource for network administrators and anyone else dealing with Windows Server 2003 security."

—Michael VonTungeln, MCSE, CTT
mvontung@yahoo.com

"I subscribe to a number of newsletters that Roberta Bragg writes and I have 'always' found her writing to be perfectly focused on issues I 'need' to know in my workplace when dealing with my users. Her concise writing style and simple solutions bring me back to her columns time after time. When I heard she had written a guide on Windows 2003 security, I 'had' to have it.

Following her guidance on deployment, her advice on avoiding common pitfalls, and her easy to follow guidelines on how to lock down my network and user environments (those darned users!) has me (and my clients) much more comfortable with our Win2k3 Server deployments. From AD to GPO's to EFS, this book covers it all."

—Robert Laposta, MCP, MCSA, MCSE, Io Network Services,
Sierra Vista, AZ
rob.laposta@cox.net

"Roberta Bragg has developed a 'must have' manual for administrators who manage Microsoft Windows 2003 servers in their organizations. The best practices for strengthening security controls are well organized with practical examples shared throughout the book. If you work with Windows 2003, you need this great resource."

—Harry L. Waldron, CPCU, CCP, AAI,
Microsoft MVP - Windows Security
Information Technology Consultant
harrywaldronmvp@yahoo.com

"Roberta Bragg's *Windows Server 2003 Security* offers more than just lucid coverage of how things work, but also offers sound advice on how to make them work better."

—Chris Quirk; MVP Windows shell/user
cquirke@mvps.org

"This book is an invaluable resource for anyone concerned about the security of Windows Server 2003. Despite the amount and complexity of the material presented, Roberta delivers very readable and clear coverage on most of the security-related aspects of Microsoft's flagship operative system. Highly recommended reading!"

—Valery Pryamikov, Security MVP, Harper Security Consulting.
valery.pryamikov@harper.no

"As long as you have something to do with Windows 2003, I have four words for you: 'Order your copy now.'"

—Bernard Cheah, Microsoft IIS MVP, Infra Architect, Intel Corp.
bernard@mvps.org

Windows Server 2003 Security:

A Technical Reference

Windows Server 2003 Security:

A Technical Reference

Roberta Bragg

♠Addison-Wesley

Upper Saddle River, NJ • **Boston** • **Indianapolis**
San Francisco • New York • Toronto • Montreal
London • Munich • Paris • Madrid • Capetown
Sydney • Tokyo • Singapore • Mexico City

Many of the designations used by manufacturers and sellers to distinguish their products are claimed as trademarks. Where those designations appear in this book, and the publisher was aware of a trademark claim, the designations have been printed with initial capital letters or in all capitals.

The author and publisher have taken care in the preparation of this book, but make no expressed or implied warranty of any kind and assume no responsibility for errors or omissions. No liability is assumed for incidental or consequential damages in connection with or arising out of the use of the information or programs contained herein.

The publisher offers excellent discounts on this book when ordered in quantity for bulk purchases or special sales, which may include electronic versions and/or custom covers and content particular to your business, training goals, marketing focus, and branding interests. For more information, please contact:

> U. S. Corporate and Government Sales
> (800) 382-3419corpsales@pearsontechgroup.com

For sales outside the U. S., please contact:
> International Sales
> international@pearsoned.com

Visit us on the Web: www.awprofessional.com

Library of Congress Catalog Number: 2005922434

ISBN 0-321-30501-9
Text printed in the United States on recycled paper at Edwards Brothers, Ann Arbor, Michigan.
First printing, May 2005

This one's for John F. Your success against all odds made my personal struggles seem surmountable. If I hadn't known you, this book would not have been completed.

Contents

PART II   SECURING THE SERVER ITSELF

PART III   SECURING DOMAIN SERVICES

Chapter 7   Active Directory's Role in Domain Security 337

PART IV   PUBLIC KEY INFRASTRUCTURE

PART V   SECURING THE VIRTUAL NETWORK

PART VI   MAINTENANCE AND RECOVERY

Chapter 16   Maintenance Strategies and Administrative Practices 895

Chapter 17   Basics of Data Backup and Restore 957

PART VII   MONITORING AND AUDIT

Chapter 18 Auditing **1007**

Acknowledgments

The more I write, the more I realize that my books are not mine alone. It takes a community to publish a book, and this one is no different. Although my name is the only one that goes directly on the front cover as author, this book is the result of work by a multitude of people. I'd like to thank them. Their names do not appear in any particular order.

Thanks to Sue and Gordon who many years ago encouraged this alternative student during a grueling graduate program in computer science and then told her that her writing style was not really academic enough, but more suited to technology users.

Thanks to past employers. You each taught me something, but mostly you taught me that independent work would be more rewarding.

Thanks to Karen Gettman, AWL editor-in-chief. You didn't know it, but your belief in the value of this book came at a time when it was really needed.

To the whole AWL team, Goodness! I keep wondering how you do it. And this is only one book!

Thanks to Perrin. Your calm companionship and occasional hissy fits perfectly fit my needs.

Luke, your hard times reminded me of my responsibilities and allowed me to choose the correct path. Keep on trucking.

Last but not least, thanks to all of the reviewers of this book: Susan Bradley, Gregg Braunton, Marc Coughlin, Philip Cox, Jeff Daniels, Todd Demers, Ken Howard, Robert Laposta, Men Lim, Mark J. Lucas, Torren Craigie-Manson, David McClure, Valery Pryamikov, Chris Quirk, James Sellwood, Bhargav Shukla, Richard Siddaway, and Michael VonTungeln. Thank you for your time and efforts. I am honored that you literally leapt to the call and helped to make this a better work.

About the Author

Roberta Bragg, CISSP, MCSE: Security, Security +, is a 30-year survivor of IT. From mainframes to mobile systems, punch cards to .NET, dial-up to Internet, she's been there and lived to tell the tale. Current projects include high-level/short-term consulting engagements on Windows security and security evangelism through the technical and trade press. Roberta wrote the monthly *MCP/Redmond Magazine Security Advisor* column for seven years and the weekly 101 Communications Security Watch email-based weekly newsletter for three years. She is the TechTarget SearchWindowsSecurity.com site security expert and is the author of its Security Checklist column. She has also published in numerous national and international periodicals. She is the author in part or in whole of 10 books on network security and Windows security. She is the series editor of the *Hardening* series and author of its *Hardening Windows Systems*. The series consists of practical guides to hardening your network before you are hacked. Her company, Have Computer Will Travel, Inc., provides the medium whereby she can be your security evangelist, security therapist, or security curmudgeon depending on her mood.

About the Technical Editor

Bob Reinsch is a senior technical trainer for Foss Training Center in Leawood, Kansas. He has been a Microsoft Certified Trainer and Systems Engineer for 10 years, and he resides in Lawrence, Kansas, with his wife and three kids. When he is not in the classroom, consulting on messaging or security matters, or spending time with his family, he can be found either strumming a guitar or building a new one. He can be contacted at bob@piercingblue.com.

Preface

Writing a technical book and getting it published are not particularly difficult projects. The primary requirements are dogged determination and persistence.

Writing a technical book that people can use, a book that they keep on their shelf as a reference, a book that becomes the standard in its class—that's quite a bit harder. To do that, you not only have to know the subject matter and be able to present it in a reasonably interesting manner, but you also have to include the information that people need to know and provide the analysis that experience provides. In addition, the technology must be presented in a way that is digestible by the average person responsible for implementing it. Accuracy, of course, must be ensured. Doing all of these things is not easy. It is, however, what I set out to do.

Should You Buy This Book?

My ego and my pocketbook say yes. My conscience, however, tells me that this book is not one that every techie will need. Here are some guidelines:

This book is not designed with the Windows end user, advanced or not, in mind. It is meant for the server administrator, network administrator, security administrator, IT manager, technology specialist, or other individual who must design, implement, troubleshoot, or configure the security of Windows Server 2003 or the networks it is used on.

Although it does provide the details that may help anyone studying for an exam, it is not a resource for those whose only interest is passing an exam. There are no study questions and way too much information on topics that may not be on an exam but that are vital to the understanding and operation of server and network security.

This book does provide important information and the details of securing Windows Server 2003; however, it is not a step-by-step guide on how to harden the server. Instead, it is a technical resource, and it provides much of the rationale behind hardening steps.

If you do not use Windows and don't believe it has a place in your network, why are you reading this? I do believe that if you read this book, you may find that Windows Server 2003 *does* have a place in your network. However, I must warn you— you need to consider the next statement.

If you have no experience or knowledge of Windows, you will need a companion book that concentrates on the technology, a server you can explore on your own, or a willingness to research basic Windows and basic Windows networking on your own. Before you begin studying the more advanced topics, such as securing Active Directory or utilizing Windows Server 2003 resources to provide network security, you will need some understanding of Active Directory. This book assumes that you are not new to Active Directory.

If you are an expert on Windows Server 2003 security, you may learn something new here.

If you are, like most technical Windows users, solidly savvy in some security areas but lacking information in others, I believe you'll be able to find the information you need to become well rounded within these pages.

If you are a programmer, this book can do much to help you understand how Windows server security works and how its security technologies are used on a network. It should not, however, be your source for the intimate details you need if you must program security or program securely. The technical details you need are primarily provided in the Software Development Kit (SDK) available from Microsoft. The sound security knowledge and necessary programming skill are functions of training and experience. I would especially caution you that the algorithms provided within this book to help readers understand how technology works do not provide enough information for you to produce code that can correctly implement the technology. Programming security technologies is especially difficult to get right and is not a subject addressed by this book.

What's Inside and What's Not

Information security is not a new field. What is new is the requirement that every information technology worker emerges from being security-challenged to being security-conscious. Those who are responsible for any facet of production networks have a higher calling. They must not only be aware, but they also must be proactive. They cannot afford to merely react to the latest Internet threat. They must apply the principles of information security through their network. This book can help them.

Chapter 1, "Principles of Information Security," defines these principles and relates them to the content of each chapter. Each chapter deals with a specific Windows Server 2003 security topic and provides both information and instructions for securing the server and for using its security technologies to provide protection for the network. Topics include authentication, user rights and permissions, Software Restriction Policies, Authorization Manager, NTFS, the Encrypting File System (EFS), WebDAV, changes in security technologies introduced with Active Directory, securing Active Directory, trusts in an Active Directory forest between domains in different forests and between forests, Public Key Infrastructure (PKI), using Routing and Remote Access and RADIUS, IPSec and PPTP, SMB signing, a role-based approach to server security, auditing monitoring, and maintenance.

This book often provides a unique approach to its subject. It explains not just how to use the technology but when and why and how to use security technologies in a secure manner. An example of this approach is the two chapters on PKI. The first chapter explains the technology and details what must be done to ensure that this key security technology does increase security and not just provide a false sense of security. The second chapter details precisely how to do this. It provides the implementation details of securely implementing a two-tier Certification Authority (CA) hierarchy, including an offline root CA. This chapter is also an example of the type of value added by this book—it's rare to find a thoughtful security approach to a security technology, and it's even rarer to find such a step-by-step detail all in one document.

While the book starts with basic security information relative to Windows Server 2003 in a workgroup or domain environment, progresses to security in an Active Directory network, and finishes by explaining the details of advanced Windows-based security technologies, an advanced reader can also benefit by jumping right to the material relevant to a specific problem or a current desire for knowledge. This is because with some exceptions, chapters are based on technical issues rather than technologies. Chapters are therefore often focused around topics such as "Securing Remote Access" (RRAS, VPNs, Internet Information Server), "Securing Data in Flight" (IPSec, PPTP), "Controlling Access to Data" (NTFS, EFS, protecting shares, using WebDAV), "Authorization: Limiting System Access and Controlling User Behavior" (user rights and permissions), or "Restricting Access to Software, Restricting Software's Access to Resources" (Software Restriction Policies, Authorization Manager).

This book cannot be your only source for Windows security information. It does not, for example, provide information on securing other versions of Windows. While much of the information on Windows Server 2003 is relevant to the security of earlier versions and will be relevant to future versions, much is unique to Windows Server 2003. You also won't find everything you need to know about securing IIS or securing Windows applications. It is not a book on secure programming, and it does not seek to train you in computer forensics. These topics require book-length discussions of their own. It would be presumptuous to attempt to deliver them along with everything else.

This is also not a sexy book. You won't find cool hacker tricks within or justification for using a security technology based on some exploit that works if you don't utilize the hardening technique. There are far too many "I can hack into your network and here is how to stop me" security books. You should not be relying primarily on securing your network against attacks that are so well known that they are published in a book. Instead, you should be applying the knowledge that not only works against multiple current attacks, but that also may quite possibly secure networks against exploits not yet designed.

An Unusual Approach to Production

The normal technical book production process, the process that is supposed to produce "the" book on "some subject," leaves much to be desired. An author is selected and writes. A technical reviewer is paid a pittance and may or may not actually find errors or step through the instructions to confirm the author's work. Editors, while they may know their grammar and how to improve writing style, are not technically trained. Finally, the process is at times rushed, and compromises have to be made.

This book was done differently. In addition to the normal editorial support, numerous technical volunteers examined each chapter for content, correctness, and usability. These volunteers gave their time freely, many of them doggedly reading the entire manuscript and others concentrating on topics they felt the most comfortable with or the most interested in learning about. Every one of them contributed substantially, providing me with insight that an author usually gets only after the book is published. This book is incredibly better because of them.

That said, the organization of the material is mine, and any errors although unintentional, are mine as well.

Bibliography

The primary references used during the writing of this book were the operating system itself and my experiences with it in test and production use, its documentation, and the many excellent articles and whitepapers available on the Microsoft.com web site. You cannot go wrong using these same resources. However, from these, I would also like to recommend these specific resources to those who want to delve further into different aspects of Windows Server 2003 security.

"Microsoft Windows Server 2003 Security Guide" http://www.microsoft.com/technet/security/prodtech/windowsserver2003/w2003hg/sgch00.mspx

"Public Key Infrastructure for Windows Server 2003," a technology center at http://www.microsoft.com/windowsserver2003/technologies/pki/default.mspx

"Deploying PKI within Microsoft," http://www.microsoft.com/technet/itsolutions/msit/security/deppkiin.mspx

"Microsoft Windows Server 2003 Deployment Kit," http://www.microsoft.com/windowsserver2003/techinfo/reskit/deploykit.mspx

"Windows Server 2003 Tools," http://www.microsoft.com/windowsserver2003/downloads/tools/default.mspx

"Windows Server 2003 Active Directory," a technology center at http://www.microsoft.com/windowsserver2003/technologies/directory/activedirectory/default.mspx

"Internet Information Services 6.0," A guide to securing IIS, http://www.microsoft.com/technet/security/prodtech/IIS.mspx

Microsoft Windows 2003 Server PKI and Certificate Security, Brian Komar, Microsoft Press, 2004, ISBN 0735620210

"Five Key Lessons to Securing Your Active Directory," Roberta Bragg, an e-book at http://redmondmag.com/techlibrary/resources.asp?id=37

PART I

Security Basics

CHAPTER 1

Principles of Information Security

To secure Windows Server 2003, you can start by learning the principles of information security. These principles will not only guide you in selecting technologies, but they also will show you where these technologies are weak. If you understand these dictums, then you can think independently about operating systems, applications, security technologies, hardening guides, and security gurus. You will be better equipped to use the information in this book, in addition to information from Microsoft documentation, from the Internet, and from conferences, personal experiences, and periodicals. You will be able to transfer your knowledge to new features added to Windows Server 2003, to your current network of Windows systems, and to your future responsibilities encompassing other operating systems, the networks they run on, and the applications and data that reside upon them.

Most of all, you will be able to stop reacting to security incidents and start proactively preventing them.

This chapter will get you started by explaining these principles. Because this book is a technical security reference for Windows Server 2003, it will show you how to implement security principles using the technologies and controls that are built into the server.

Principle Number One: There Is No Such Thing as a Secure Computer

This should be evident to most people in computing. By now, every operating system, browser, or application that is exposed to the Internet has been taken to task by malware or attacks perpetrated by using some feature or bug in the product. Like life, computing poses risks depending on what we do, where we are, when we do it, how we do it, and perhaps even why we do it. Our job in information security is to correctly gauge that risk and do what can be done to mitigate it. At the same time, we have to keep in mind that there is no such thing as a secure computer. Computers are more or less securable, though, and the security of the information stored on them (or transferred by them to other computers) depends on how well we understand how to secure them.

Securing computers is a process that is part hardening, part auditing to make sure we did it in the best manner and that configuration stays in place, and part intrusion detection and response. But "securing" is not a process that makes computers secure. Instead, it must be defined as a process that makes a computer as secure as possible, given current knowledge of the threats that the computer will face.

Perhaps a better way to think about security is not as some unattainable goal, but as a continuum. On one end is a computer system that has a poor security design, that has had no hardening, that has non-existent external defenses, and that is used by individuals who purposely practice "unsafe" computing. On the other end is a computer designed by the most knowledgeable security engineers and uncluttered by any marketing requirements to make it user-friendly or to conform to some standard other than security. This computer also has been hardened (there will always be some post-design flexibility that requires that the computer be used for something). The computer has multiple external defenses including firewalls, anti-spam, anti-virus, and anti-spyware perimeter controls, in addition to network access controls, which include security requirements that must be met before a computer can operate on the network. The computer is operated by a highly trained security expert whose ethical behavior is unquestionable. Additional defenses such as intrusion detection, intrusion prevention, and things that we haven't discovered yet are also in operation. Think of the first computer as residing at ground zero, and the second one at infinity. Envisioning several continuums that start at zero and extend to infinity might represent a better understanding. Each one could represent one of these parameters, such as user ethics, knowledge, or secure design. The position of the computer on the composite continuum can then be expressed as a combination of its location on all of the separate continuums. This representation is not static. Think of each point on the continuum as a marker, like the wooden rings on an old abacus—they are meant to be moved.

If you accept this representation, then you can see the definition of your job in securing the computers on your network. Your job is to push these markers as much as you can to the right toward infinity. Which markers you individually push will depend on your current job and abilities, but push you must. Some of the markers can't be pushed at all; you can't change the design of a current operating system (although you may be able to push its manufacturers to make some attempt at dealing with a poor design), and you probably can't change the behavior of people whose purpose in life is to destroy things in the name of figuring out how they work or who simply want the financial reward inherent in doing so.

This book will help you move the markers on one of these continuums—the hardening one—for Windows Server 2003. When you do that, you will also move the marker on the composite continuum, but I don't think you'll be fooled into thinking that your work is the only thing necessary to secure your computing infrastructure. This book will also advise you of things you can do to push the markers a little bit more in some of the other areas, but in the end, the security composite of your network will depend on more than can be represented in this book.

Start here by learning or reviewing basic security principles, and then use the rest of this book to help you understand how to use these principles to secure Windows Server 2003.

Classic Security Principles: Confidentiality, Integrity, and Accounting

The next step in learning about security is understanding and implementing the three classic security principles: confidentiality, integrity, and accounting (CIA). Confidentiality is the ability to keep things secret. Integrity is ensuring that things remain the same unless a change is authorized. Accounting, sometimes referred to as auditing, is the process of making sure that things are the way they are supposed to be.

WHAT ABOUT AVAILABILITY?
Some information security professionals use the A in CIA to stand for availability. In a security context, availability means that information should be available to those who are authorized to use it. This is an important concept. We all have had experience with a computer that is so secure that no one can use the information on it. We all can relate to unrealistic demands for security that make our job difficult, if not impossible, to do. Keep availability in mind whenever designing or implementing security.

Confidentiality

Four major technical controls are used to keep information on computer systems secret: encryption, permissions, user rights, and authentication. Encryption scrambles data so that it cannot be deciphered unless the key is known. Permissions determine who can do what with which information. Can an individual read a file? Change it? Delete it? This is determined by setting permissions. Files, however, are not the only objects controlled by permissions. Applications (who can run them), folders, and printers, and in Windows systems, registry keys and Active Directory objects, are protected by setting permissions. User rights grant users the ability to perform some function. If performing that function is a prerequisite for getting access to the data container, then the user right can be said to be aiding confidentiality. Authentication is the process of proving that we are who we say we are. (Actually, authentication only proves or disproves who we *say* we are. If, for example, you know my password and then use it to log on using my account, you are me on the computer system or network.) User rights and permissions are based on the identity of the user attempting to do or access something. Authentication proves that we have the right to act as that identity.

Windows Server 2003 includes many technical controls to aid in keeping information confidential.

- Chapter 2, "Authentication: Proof of Identity," explores authentication in Windows Server 2003, including a discussion of Kerberos and NTLM. In it, you will learn how authentication works and how to make it operate better.
- Chapter 3, "Authorization—Limiting System Access and Controlling User Behavior," discusses user rights and permissions basics.
- Software Restriction Policies and Authorization Manager, two new tools for software management, are detailed in Chapter 4, "Restricting Access to Software; Restricting Software's Access to Resources."
- Chapter 5, "Controlling Access to Data," details access permissions in NTFS with special attention to permission inheritance. NTFS presents a granular access control system for files and folders, but it is complex. Its nuances can be difficult to understand, and then just when you think you grasp them, a new version of the operating system may change that meaning. This chapter also provides information about protecting shares and using WebDAV.
- An introduction to the Encrypting File System is provided in Chapter 6, "EFS Basics." Encrypting data at rest is a good way to keep unauthorized people from viewing it, but EFS should not be used without a thorough understanding of how it works and where it is vulnerable.

- Chapter 7, "Active Directory's Role in Domain Security," explains how to implement and work with authentication, user rights, permissions, and encryption in a domain environment.
- Chapter 8, "Trust," explains trusts in an Active Directory forest and explains trusts between domains in different forests. New to Windows Server 2003, the forest trust, selective authentication, and the new permission "allowed to authenticate" are also covered. Trusts make possible the assignment of user rights and permissions to objects across domain and forest boundaries. This is a critical issue. Although trusts can make it possible to work with large numbers of users and large numbers of objects and to correctly control access, trusts make the process complex. The more access paths there are to data, the harder it is to keep it secret.
- Chapter 12, "PKI Basics," explains how PKI can be implemented in Windows Server 2003 by building a certification authority (CA) hierarchy and issuing certificates for use in encryption and authentication. Chapter 13, "Implementing a Secure PKI," provides the explicit, step-by-step instructions for doing so.
- In addition to chapters that deal directly with the confidentiality of data that is stored on Windows Server 2003, several chapters explain how to protect the security infrastructure itself by keeping security configuration information accessible to those with the right to know and manipulate it. Chapter 10, "Securing Active Directory," illustrates how. Chapter 13, "Implementing a Secure PKI," addresses securing PKI.
- Chapter 14, "Securing Remote Access," explains how to use Routing and Remote Access Services (RRAS) and Internet Authentication Services (IAS) to lock down remote access. Authentication and authorization aspects of remote access policies are detailed. As part of this chapter, sound principles for secure wireless and Internet Information Server access are also discussed.
- Chapter 15, "Protecting Data in Flight," provides information on the encryption technologies such as IPSec and PPTP that can be used to keep communications between computers secret.

Integrity

Integrity can be provided using special algorithms that include encryption, but not all encryption algorithms provide integrity. Specifically, those algorithms used to encrypt data to keep it private do not also guarantee integrity. One common way in which the integrity of data in flight is violated is by capturing the data, changing it, and then sending it on. It is a common misconception that if data is encrypted during transfer, the data received will be the same as the data sent. Unfortunately, that is not always true. For example, changing the bits in encrypted data changes its meaning. An attacker does not have to know exactly what the data is to change it. If the data stream is organized in a specific order, and it usually is, the attacker may be able to make some guesses and successfully modify the data, causing an unintended action when it is received. Even if the attacker is unsuccessful in creating meaningful data with this method, he or she has made the data unusable. Likewise, an attacker can monkey with encrypted data on disk. Integrity provides some kind of check—a failsafe way to calculate or manipulate the received data and compare the results to some value provided by the use of the same calculation or manipulation wherever the data originated. Cryptographic hashes and digital signatures are typically used for this purpose. These constructs are used in the Windows Server 2003 implementation of IPSec, in SMB signing, and in various uses of certificates. Chapters 12, 13, 14, and 15 include information on these techniques.

Using strong administrative practices and strong access controls also helps provide integrity. Chapter 7, which explains managing users and delegation of authority, describes these practices. Chapter 11, "Securing Infrastructure Roles," provides information on how to centralize strong technical controls that are designed for specialized functions such as DNS, domain controllers, desktop systems, and so forth. Earlier chapters on access controls and authentication can also help you promote data integrity. Protecting the integrity of the operating system is often at least partially accomplished by patching and maintenance practices, as discussed in Chapter 16, "Maintenance Strategies and Administrative Practices." The ability to restore damaged or lost data and various recovery procedures is detailed in Chapter 17, "Basics of Data Backup and Restore."

Accounting

Accounting (or "auditing") is turned on by default in Windows Server 2003, but there is more to auditing than collecting events in the event log. Chapter 18, "Auditing," describes what the Audit policy is about, how to configure auditing not just for the operating system but also for many server-based applications such as PKI and remote access, and how to interpret many of the events. Chapter 19, "Monitoring and Assessment," describes the functions that should be monitored to ensure proper operation of security technologies and to detect security incidents.

Corollaries: Principles That Spring from the Classics

Although the classic three security principles can be used to describe just about every security technology and practice, additional security principles have grown from them and from the experiences of security practitioners. If you examine these principles, you will see how many of your efforts for hardening and defending your information systems and their data fit into the greater picture. Put these principles together with those described earlier in this chapter, and you will be able to anticipate ways to protect your systems now and in the future.

Defense in Depth

No security device or hardening technique alone will protect your information systems. Defense in depth means using multiple layers of security. Although there is no guarantee that layering security will prevent compromise, developing such defenses has proven in the past to be more effective than relying on a single defense.

An example of defense in depth used to protect sensitive files is shown in Table 1-1, as are the Windows Server 2003 technologies that could be used to provide this protection. For this example, assume that the files in question are in a folder on server A on a private network.

WARNING: Defense in Depth Does Not Mean Every Defense Must Be Used

Use common sense when using any one approach to defense in depth. For example, I wouldn't necessarily use *all* of the defense strategies listed in Table 1-1. The defenses that you should use depend on the risk and the nature of the files to be protected, and they should be balanced by the need to administer the server and make the data available to those that are authorized to use it.

Table 1-1   Defense in Depth

Defense	Implementation	Discussion
Perimeter Firewall	Microsoft Internet Security and Acceleration Server (ISA) or other firewall placed at the junction of internal network.	A perimeter firewall can protect the internal network hosts from many types of attack that originate on the external network.
Perimeter anti-virus and other malware destroyer products	Third-party products designed for use at the perimeter. May be on firewall or other device.	By blocking malware at the perimeter, the chance of infection on server A is greatly reduced. Infection might just prevent the server from being available, or it may lead to server compromise. These products must be kept up-to-date and cannot be the only protection from malware.
Local firewall	Windows Server 2003 built-in firewall on server A	A local firewall should never be used in place of an external firewall to protect sensitive files. A local firewall can provide another layer of protection.
Local anti-virus and other malware destroyer products	Third-party products designed for use on servers and installed on server A and throughout the network. Third-party products designed for use on workstations installed on workstations throughout the network.	These products back up the perimeter products. They should be from a different vendor. It's likely that one vendor will be quicker with a signature and thus protect systems where the other might have failed. Protecting all computers individually helps to protect others.
Isolate the server	Place server A on a subnetwork and protect access to it using remote access services or a VPN.	A flat network allows an attacker who is able to gain access to attack other computers on the network. You can segment the network into security areas and limit access between the areas.

Defense	Implementation	Discussion
Network Access control	Establish network access control—that is, screen all servers that connect to the network and ensure that they meet your security policy.	Network access control is a new technology and is currently only provided to screen computers that are remotely connecting to the network. In the future, this technology may be applied to computers connecting to the local network.
Implement PKI	Implement Microsoft Enterprise CA hierarchy.	PKI can provide certificate and key management for those services that require certificates and can provide new, more secure solutions for those services that do not.
IPSec block and permit policy	Implement server A IPSec policies to block traffic to and from server A with the exception of the protocols necessary for network access from the computers authorized to access this computer over the network.	An IPSec policy can be written using two rules: Rule 1 blocks all traffic. Rule 2 permits traffic from specific machines (by using their IP address) using specific protocols.
IPSec negotiate policy	Implement an IPSec negotiate policy on server A and those devices allowed to communicate with server A.	To further guarantee that only approved computers are used, a negotiate policy requires authentication. A negotiate policy can also be used to encrypt data traveling between server A and authorized devices.
Require SMB signing	SMB signing is turned on by default in Windows Server 2003.	SMB signing provides assurance that communications between two computers actually come from those computers.

Table 1-1   Defense in Depth Continued

Defense	Implementation	Discussion
User Rights	Establish user rights on server A.	Both users and computers can be granted and denied rights. Establish rights so that only those authorized to access data on the machines have the right to access the machine and so that depending on the sensitivity of the data, others are explicitly denied. (Those not granted rights will be implicitly denied.) Do not assign elevated privileges to users. Reserve administrative privileges for administrators. Be sure to test solutions.
Security Options	Establish Security Options on server A.	Use options such as `Limit local account use of blank passwords` and those Security Options that tighten anonymous access restrictions or otherwise protect the server.
Establish strong authentication practices in the domain and on the server	Strong authentication practices can mean a strong password policy or the use of smart cards or biometrics.	Requiring long passwords and eliminating the LM hash (on by default in Windows Server 2003) will block most of the password-cracking programs available today. If the server is a domain member, use domain policies, but don't ignore the local user database. Strengthen its authentication policy too.
Use NTFS file permissions	Set local file permissions on server A.	NTFS should be used throughout the server to protect operating system files and data files.

Defense	Implementation	Discussion
Use file encryption	If only a few users require access to files, consider EFS. Investigate third-party encryption products.	EFS is a sound file encryption solution. However, there are risks to using EFS on a server when remotely accessing the encrypted files.

Psychological Acceptability

Psychological acceptability means that the security implementation does not cause fear, distrust, or undue anxiety for its users. Security that is psychologically acceptable will be more likely to be used. Examples of psychological issues with security are as follows:

- Users of hand geometry biometric devices often fear that their hands will get stuck.
- Users required to use a retinal scanner may fear catching some eye disease or injury to their eyes.
- When fingerprint readers are introduced, users may fear that their fingerprints will be shared with some law enforcement agency or kept in a database that might be used for some nefarious purpose.
- An application may seem threatening, abusive, coercive, or hostile because of its language, graphics, or the way it works. Security implementations can also produce this feeling.
- Users may get unduly concerned about having to use very long passwords that they can't write down. They may fear punishment if they forget their passwords.

Do not approach these psychological issues as silly, unwarranted fears, and most especially don't reject these security approaches because they might seem psychologically unacceptable at first glance. Instead, realize that these objections and fears do exist and may be heightened or eliminated depending on the way that these security techniques are implemented. You can overcome fears with awareness and product training and by treating voiced concerns as legitimate. You can obtain acceptance if you don't ignore these concerns.

Evaluate the psychological impact of any current security implementation look for improvement. Always consider this effect when reviewing new implementations.

Least Privilege

The principle of least privilege requires that no one be given more access or rights than are necessary to do his job. Users, for example, do not need to be administrators to do ordinary work. There are applications that will not run without elevated privileges. While you work on eliminating these products, or in configuring systems to limit their privileges, you may have to continue to provide users elevated privileges. When elevated privileges are required, make them machine-dependent. There is no reason to make users domain administrators. Windows Server 2003 provides the ability to assign user rights and object (file, printer, registry, folder and, in a domain, Active Directory) rights in a granular fashion. Use this ability. In a domain, very granular administrative privileges can be designed by using Active Directory object permissions and delegating control over AD objects. Examples of least privilege include:

- Creating a custom Windows group called Help Desk and assigning it permissions such as the ability to reset passwords or create user objects at an organizational unit level. By adding help desk employee user accounts to the Help Desk group, you give them these privileges but do not make them full administrators.
- Limiting database server administrators to the local server administrator role.
- Investigating why an application requires a user to be an administrator and giving users appropriate access to the files, folders, and registry keys that the application actually uses instead of making them administrators.
- Limiting external users (customers, vendors, the public) to special servers and only to certain data and privileges on those servers.

Implement a Security Policy

If you don't establish a security policy, your security status will be subject to the whims of those with the ability to modify it. A security policy is developed based on a risk analysis of the organization and its information system needs, requirements, and assets. It must be approved and backed by management, and there must be consequences for not following it. A security policy is a formal document that expresses the will of the organization, and it should be separate from a discussion of the technology required to implement it (although it may drive technology purchases). The security policy establishes who is responsible for implementing it. Procedures must be written to specify how technology controls and standards will be implemented to enforce the security policy. Windows Server 2003 provides support for technology controls by using Group Policies, local security policies, object permissions, and other technologies.

Separation of Duties

Long before computers existed, organizations realized they must protect themselves from employees and other trusted individuals who might steal from the organization or otherwise engage in fraudulent activities. Separating duties attempts to make this more difficult by ensuring that two or more individuals are required to perform sensitive operations. For example, accounting best practices split the process of ordering supplies and paying for goods received. One group of people is allowed to issue purchase orders, and a different group must approve payment. The idea is that if one individual had both privileges, she could issue a purchase order for goods from a fake company for which she has established a bank account and then write a check in payment for a product never received. If those duties are separated, the dishonest employee would have to collaborate with at least one other individual to commit the fraud. Although this collaboration would not be impossible, it would be harder to accomplish than acting alone, and it would be easier for the company to discover it.

You should also implement separation of duties on computer systems. For example, when PKI is implemented, different groups should be assigned the role of certification authority (CA) administrator (who manages the CA policy) and certificate administrator (who manages the certificates issued by the CA). In an Active Directory forest, you should assign data administrators (those who manage users, servers, and data) and a different group of infrastructure administrators (those who manage network services and the Active Directory). Computer solutions are not always easy to deploy. The necessary distinctions between some roles may not be possible, or your organization's management structure may not allow it. For example, although you can create data administrators who cannot exercise infrastructure administrator duties, infrastructure administrators are able to manage data. More than technical controls will be necessary here.

Complete Mediation

Complete mediation means applying a thorough solution. If, for example, you will use EFS to encrypt files, you should understand that access to EFS encrypted files is available to the user who encrypted them and any user who knows that user's account and password. Training, the use of a strong password policy, and other efforts will be necessary to make the solution robust. As a second example, consider that the use of local accounts to protect a computer becomes useless if an attacker obtains physical access to the computer and is able to use a boot disk to boot to another OS and a password insertion utility to change the Administrator password on the computer. A password insertion utility does not crack passwords; instead, it replaces the current Administrator password with one of the attacker's choosing or makes it blank. Techniques exist to mitigate this type of attack, such as removing the floppy drive and other types of bootable accessible drives such as CD-ROMs. To protect the computer, you must apply physical security. Approach all security solutions with this in mind. Can the security you implement be easily bypassed? What is necessary to close that hole?

Keep Up-To-Date

In today's world, it sometimes seems as if every day brings some new threat to information systems. You must keep up-to-date on these threats and understand your own systems to know if current security provides adequate protection, or if other measures such as applying a patch or changing a configuration must be done. Patching against known vulnerabilities and keeping service packs current is the primary activity here. However, knowledge of current infrastructure and its security hardening status is also an important issue.

Use Open Designs

Open designs are designs that are well documented. This means that anyone can study them and make their own informed decisions on what they can do to offset any actual or perceived vulnerabilities or to reject the use of the design. Encryption technologies were once based on keeping the encryption process secret. It is now believed that the encryption algorithms should be available so that anyone can study them. Instead of secret processes, keeping the encryption keys secret prevents decryption.

Providing open designs is different from providing open source. Open source means that your code is freely available to anyone who wants it. The idea is that many eyes will look at the code and find its flaws so they can be corrected. In reality, much open source code is not reviewed by the necessary people with the knowledge to spot flaws. Administrators, who must make decisions on how best to use operating systems and applications, don't have the time and, in many cases, the knowledge to understand code. However, they can and do use good documentation to help them. When application developers document the workings of their application, more people can study it and understand what is necessary to keep it secure. Knowing, for example, that the NTFS file permission inheritance is different in Server 2003 than it was for Windows NT 4.0 empowers administrators to create appropriate permissions that will protect files. Although the code for NTFS is not generally available, permission inheritance is well documented by Microsoft and available publicly to anyone with Internet access. It is also explained in Chapter 5 of this book.

Reduce the Attack Surface

Take this lesson from military historians and practitioners—the smaller the attack surface available to the enemy, the less chance your attacker has of overcoming you. Not only is there less to defend, but vulnerabilities, even those unknown to you, cannot be used against you if they are not present. In information systems, you can reduce the attack surface by not installing services and applications that are not required, disabling those services that cannot be removed, and configuring applications to provide fewer features. Do not, for example, install IIS on non-web servers. Do not add services offered by IIS unless they are required. (By default, IIS is not installed, and when you install it, it is installed with few capabilities.) In addition, inspect services turned on by default. If they are not required, disable them. This principle can also be applied to other technologies. For example, you should remove drives and disable unnecessary USB and serial ports, and you should teach employees how to respond to social engineering attacks.

Fail-Safe Defaults

Security doesn't always work, but if a security device or application fails, it should not allow open access. The easiest example of this principle is the firewall. If a working, properly configured firewall is disabled, it should prevent access to the internal network. This dictum does not mean that a firewall should fail unless it is configured properly. (If an administrator opens all ports to the Internet, no firewall will prevent him.) It does not mean that when an administrator decides to turn off protections such as anti-virus or remove configuration such as file permissions, the application should somehow protect him from the consequences.

Trust but Audit

To manage information systems, trust must be granted to users and administrators. Privileges of any sort can be abused, either through ignorance or malice. Thus, you should audit information systems to observe the behavior of trusted individuals and groups of users.

Provide Training and Awareness for Everyone

The more that you learn about security, the more you will recognize the importance of people in the security equation. It matters little what security you apply if you have not hardened your users to correctly respond to social engineering attacks and to avoid insecure practices such as sharing account IDs and passwords. Administrators have elevated privileges on systems and yet often lack basic information security training. This is not a sound practice. Instead, develop security awareness appropriate for different groups of users and insist that all of them take advantage of it. Specialized security training may be necessary for those who implement security or those who work with sensitive data and systems. However, specialized training for the few cannot take the place of broad training programs for all.

Economy and Diversity of Mechanism

This principle may appear at first to present a conundrum. How can you use few security mechanisms and yet use many different ones? It also may appear to conflict with other principles—How can you use defense in depth if you must economize? The fact is that you sometimes may have to choose which principle to employ and how far to go with it.

Economy of mechanism does not mean that you should apply the cheapest or least intrusive solution. It simply means that where simple security solutions exist, or where you can do less work for the same or close to the same results, do so. You don't have to read and analyze every bit of code that you run. You define trusted code sources and select applications that can be protected. Correct documentation is far better than millions of lines of actual code that you must digest.

Diversity of mechanism means that you should avoid using the same solution for everything or the same applications and hardware. The intent is to prevent a vulnerability or security failure from allowing an attacker access to everything. For example, if an external firewall and an internal firewall are used to provide a zone in which Internet-accessible computers such as web servers are located, both firewalls provide protection for hosts on the internal network. Best practices indicate that a different firewall should be used at each location. Should the external firewall be compromised, an attacker probably would not be able to use the same vulnerability to compromise the internal firewall. Diversity of mechanism is often interpreted as preventing your network from running only one operating system. Thus, you could apply this principle to Windows networks by using other types of clients and servers on the network. You can also make a strong argument in both the firewall and operating system examples for the need for technical experts in different firewalls and OSs. If they are not available, then the networks will actually be more vulnerable because security may be improperly applied or not applied at all.

PART II

Securing
the
Server Itself

CHAPTER 2

Authentication: Proof of Identity

The most important thing that you can do to manage information access is to require that those who want to access information provide proof of identity. If you require all potential users of your information system resources to authenticate themselves, that is, to prove they are who they say they are, then you can restrict system and resource access to approved identities. Authentication can be a precursor to authorization and accountability. Authorization determines the type of access the authenticated users are allowed and the rights they have on the system. Accountability is the ability to determine who did what. It is based on your ability to record the systems and resources that users have accessed and the things they have done while connected to these resources. Requiring authentication facilitates both authorization and accountability. However, if you know nothing about processing credentials and verifying identities, and if you do not harden and manage these processes, you can support neither authorization nor accountability. You may as well have required no proof of identity at all. The content in this chapter will provide the knowledge and best practices you need to successfully harden authentication.

The process of authentication is familiar to most people. In the real world, we are often required to authenticate ourselves. We present a driver's license before we can board a plane, a passport before we can enter a different country, or a company ID to enter business offices. These documents are validated, in many cases, by the simple process of comparing the picture on the document with the person presenting it, and comparing the features of the credentials (official stamps, seals, and signatures) with those we know to be valid. In legacy versions of the Windows operation system, authentication is optional. However, authentication is required to access Windows systems based on Windows NT technologies (Windows NT 4.0, Windows 2000, Windows XP

Professional, and Windows Server 2003). Authentication occurs when each user logs on, and again when that user attempts to access resources such as files, remote computers, printers, and so forth. The credentials required consist of a valid account and some factor such as password, biometric, token, or certificate. The process used to authenticate the user will vary depending on the specific authentication algorithm used and how it is configured. An important part of authentication management is knowing what's possible, what's practical, and what's allowed and then knowing how to use that information to make your systems as secure as they can be.

TIP: Monitor Security Logs During Times of Normality
Failed logons and other authentication anomalies may be user errors, improper system configurations, or network problems, or they may be indications of an attack. If you monitor the authentication process and learn to determine the cause of errors, you will be able to better respond—whatever the real cause.

Stop! Think Before Changing the Authentication Process

Before you make changes to your authentication process, such as modifying the password policy, configuring authentication protocols, or hardening authentication process-related settings, you must evaluate the impact of these changes, and you must review your organization's security policy for the appropriateness of the change. Your security implementation decision should always be based on fulfilling the organization's security policy. Not only is this a standard that governs your actions, but changing authentication requirements or processes also can inadvertently damage your organization by making it impossible for people to do their jobs. Users can find themselves unable to log on, processes may halt, resources can become inaccessible, and actual work can be reduced to a trickle.

This chapter will assist you in meeting the goal of effectively managing and securing authentication processes. It will:

- Explain the logon process
- Define network and domain authentication
- Introduce forest and cross-forest authentication

- Describe authentication algorithms and their configuration
- State best practices for authentication management

This chapter will not provide the details of the remote or web authentication process; these will be detailed in Chapter 14, "Securing Remote Access." Nor will it describe Group Policy processing. You will find additional information on Group Policy and the management of authentication in a Windows domain in Chapter 7, "Active Directory's Role in Domain Security." Information on auditing authentication is detailed in Chapter 19, "Monitoring and Assessment."

Logon Process

To access most resources on Windows computers based on NT technologies, a user must know a valid account name in the account database of the computer or domain and the password for that account. Then she must use this information to log on. Users are not the only security principals (objects that can be granted rights and permissions on Windows systems). In a Windows domain, those computers (Windows NT 4.0, Windows 2000, Windows XP Professional, and Windows Server 2003) that can become domain members are also considered security principals and, like users, must be provided a domain computer account.

Both users and computers use the logon process to authenticate. The details of the logon process may vary based on operating systems, account type, logon type, and credentials, but the basic steps are similar. The process includes three steps:

- The security principal (user or computer) must present a user ID or other identity symbol such as a smart card.
- When requested, the security principal must present credentials. Credentials may be a password, biometric, token, or PIN.
- The combination of identity symbol and credentials are validated or rejected. The validation process consists of identifying the account as legitimate, satisfying account restrictions (logon hours, for example), and evaluating the proof of identity (password or other factor) provided. If the logon is not local, (based on an account database on the same computer), a network authentication protocol is used.

Password Storage

Passwords are not stored in the Windows password database in clear text. Instead, a hash of each password is stored. A hash is the result of taking a variable-length binary input and processing it to produce a fixed-length binary output. When a good hashing algorithm is used, it is statistically infeasible that two different inputs will produce the same output. This also means that the same input will always produce the same output. A cryptographic hash uses a secret key to protect the results of the process. Cryptographic hashing is a one-way function (OWF); that is, the process is irreversible. Unlike the results of secret key encryption, the cryptographic hash cannot be decrypted.

The hash used in Windows is a cryptographic hash, and thus the process is irreversible. This is why a comparison process is used during authentication. A sound hash algorithm will never reduce different bits of data to the same result, so if the result of hashing the entered password matches the stored password hash, then the password has been validated, and the user has proved his or her identity to the system.

NOTE: Reality Check
In reality, no existing hashing algorithm is perfectly sound. That is, mathematically there is the possibility that two different passwords might hash to the same result or produce a collision. The question to ask here is not whether we should throw out hashing algorithms as security tools for password storage, but rather how likely the collision is and how easy it would be for someone to use this possibility to crack passwords. At this point, the possibility of collision is considered slight enough and the difficulty of exploiting this flaw is high enough to justify continuing to use current hashing algorithms while seeking better ones and alternative mechanisms. (Current password cracking tools do not crack passwords by using this flaw.)

Password hashes for local accounts are stored in the local account database, the security accounts manager (SAM), on the local computer, or, when accounts are domain accounts, in the domain password database in the Active Directory. During local logon, when a user presents a password, the hash cannot be decrypted, so the same cryptographic hashing process is used on the entered password, and the results are compared to the stored hash. If both hashes match, then the passwords match, and the user is authenticated.

Logon Types

The exact process used during authentication is dependent on the logon type. Logon types are as follows:

- **Interactive**—In most cases, the user provides credentials at a console. Exceptions are some types of remote logon such as web server access that require interactive logon permissions but for which the user does not have to log on from the console. The user's credentials are checked against the user account database either in the SAM if the account is local or in the Active Directory if it is the domain account. If the account is a domain account, Kerberos is used by default. In an Active Directory forest, a user's domain account can be used for approved access to resources in any domain in the forest. Cross-forest trusts can extend this access to other external domains. The ability to use a single account for such wide-reaching access is known as single sign-on.
- **Network**—Provides proof of the user's identity to a network service or resource that the user is attempting to access. Many types of network authentication are available, such as Kerberos V5, Secure Socket Layer/Transport Layer Security (SSL/TLS), and, for compatibility with Windows NT 4, NTLM. Network authentication occurs when a domain account (an account stored in a domain database) is used or when a remote resource is accessed.
- **Anonymous**—No user account or credentials are required.

NOTE: Variations on Logon Types

Microsoft extends these definitions with additional types of logon, including batch (executing on behalf of a user), service (a service starts), unlock (a locked computer was unlocked), network clear text (password passed in clear text across the network), new credentials (new credentials are used for other network connections), remote interactive (Terminal services or Remote desktop), and cached interactive (locally cached credentials are used and no domain controller was contacted.) However, these are only slight variations of the following explanations.

Interactive Logon Process Details

When the logon process is interactive (a user is sitting at a Windows computer), the following steps are used:

1. The user provides an attention signal, such as the CTRL+ALT+DEL key combination, the insertion of a smart card, or the presentation of a biometric.
2. The Winlogon service calls the Graphical Identification and Authentication (GINA) dynamic link library (dll), and the logon screen is presented. (When the logon process involves something other than passwords, the GINA may be altered or replaced and a different screen may appear.)
3. The user provides credentials in the form of a user ID and password or, in the case of a smart card, a PIN. After entering the data, the user may need to click an OK button.
4. The Local Security Authority (LSA) processes the credentials.
5. If a user ID and password are used, the LSA user function converts the credentials into the same form in which they are stored in the account database (either the local SAM or domain controller resident Active Directory). In an unmodified Windows Server 2003 server, two storage forms are prepared and stored—an LM hash and an NTLM hash. If a smart card is used, the LSA uses the entered PIN (if it is valid) to obtain the private key of the user's smart card certificate from the smart card.
6. Account restrictions are checked. Account restrictions are things such as `Account is disabled` or `Smart card is required for interactive logon`.
7. User logon rights, such as the right to log on locally, are checked and the credentials are validated.
8. If the logon is local, the LSA compares the result of step 5 with the hashed password data stored in the local SAM. If the result is a match, the user is authenticated and access is provided.
9. If the logon is to a domain, the authentication package MSV_0, which includes Kerberos, LM, and NTLM, is used to validate the credentials.

Smart Card Processing
Native Windows Server 2003 smart card processing is integrated into Windows Server 2003 certificate services and is available only in an Active Directory domain. Smart card authentication also uses certificates for the initial Kerberos processing. More information is provided in the "Certificates, Smart Cards, Tokens, and Biometrics" section later in this chapter and in Chapter 13, "Implementing a Secure PKI."

Domain and Network Authentication

Local interactive logon simply compares a password hash to the hash stored in the local account database, the SAM.

When a domain account is used, the process is different. A network authentication protocol, such as Kerberos, LAN Manager (LM), NT LAN Manager (NTLM), or NTLM version 2 (NTLMv2), is used. A network authentication protocol is also used when a user requests access to a network resource. For example, if a user attempts to access files on a network file server, he must first authenticate to the file server. The remote authentication process is transparent to the user when the process is able to use currently cached logon credentials (password hash or Kerberos tickets). If the ticket has expired and cannot be renewed, or if the credentials for the account on the remote system do not match those used by the logged-on user, a prompt for new credentials may appear.

Network Authentication Processes

Some network authentication algorithms use the password hash as an encryption key. Instead of sending password credentials across the network, challenge/response-type algorithms such as NTLM use the hash to encrypt the nonce, or challenge. The challenge is a string sent by the domain controller (DC) to the client. The client generates and returns a response by encrypting the challenge using a cryptographic hash of the password entered by the user. Because the DC knows the challenge and the user's password hash is stored in its account database, the DC can create its own response. If its response matches the client's, then the user is authenticated.

Various authentication algorithms are used to provide authenticated access to Windows domains and resources. The algorithm used is based on the application employed on the client computer. For example, logging on to a domain using an account and password entered in the GINA's credentials dialog box will use either Kerberos or some version of LM or NTLM authentication. Other applications, such as dial-up, VPN services, or a web server, can use other authentication choices. An administrator cannot select one authentication algorithm for all of the processes that require authentication. Instead, she must select the best authentication choice in each category. Table 2-1 provides a list of authentication types available in Windows Server 2003 and explains where they can be used. Chapter references where you can find more information on each subject are also included.

Table 2-1   Windows Server 2003 Authentication Types

Type	Where It Is Used: Authentication Category	Chapter
Anonymous	Local and domain authentication	2
Local logon	Local authentication	2
Kerberos	Domain authentication, interactive and network	2, 7
LM, NTLM, NTLMv2	Domain authentication, interactive and network for downlevel clients	2
Basic, Windows Integrated, Digest, Advanced Digest, Anonymous Web Access, .Net Passport	Web server authentication	14
Secure Sockets Layer/Transport Layer Security (SSL/TLS)	Web server authentication	14
Certificates	IPSec, client and computer authentication, SSL/TLS, smart cards	12, 13, 14
PAP, CHAP, MS-CHAP, MS-CHAPv2	Remote Access via Routing and Remote Access Services, including VPN connections	14
Smart cards	Certificates and Kerberos used for domain logon	2, 6, 12
802.1x, PEAP, WPA	Primarily authentication to 802.11b wireless networks; however, 802.1x can also be used to authenticate to wired networks	14

In some cases, an administrator may not be able to directly implement her choice. For example, she might prefer Kerberos rather than NTLM for network authentication, but there is no absolute way to prevent NTLM from being used. She can only strongly support the use of Kerberos by removing machines that rely on NTLM, or she can promote the use of NTLM by continuing to use legacy systems; however, she cannot flip a switch and limit network authentication to a single protocol.

An administrator may not be able to implement what he knows is the most secure option or configure what must be available in the most secure manner. The organization's security policy, possible detrimental results, or the impracticability of the choice may hinder his efforts. Security implementation should be based on risk, which must consider security and usability.

LM

The LM protocol was originally developed to provide a network authentication scheme that could be used with MS-DOS and Windows 3.1. It is the native algorithm used by Windows 95/98 and Windows ME. It may be used by Windows Server 2003 to authenticate users whose computers use these earlier versions of Windows on the network. Later, more secure versions of the protocol were developed: NTLM and NTLMv2. NTLM addresses the weaknesses in LM and was introduced with Windows NT. NTLMv2 addresses the weaknesses of NTLM and was introduced with service pack 3 for Windows NT 4.0. Although all three protocols are authentication protocols, using NTLMv2 for session security improves the level of protection applied to the data being communicated after authentication.

LM Authentication Algorithm

In all three protocols, the authentication process consists of a challenge/response composed of four parts:

1. The entered password is encrypted with a one-way function (OWF), and an authentication request is issued to the domain controller.
2. The domain controller responds with a challenge—a random number often called a nonce.
3. The client uses the password hash to encrypt the nonce, produce the "response," and return it to the domain controller.
4. The domain controller uses a stored copy of the user's password hash to encrypt the nonce and compares the result to the response. If both results match, the user is authenticated.

Differences in processing between the versions of LM are presented in Table 2-2.

Table 2-2   Variations of the LM Protocol

	LM	NTLM	NTLMv2
Maximum password length	14	14 in GUI; 128 possible programmatically	128; GUI not restricted in Windows Server 2003
Character set	OEM	Unicode	Unicode
Case-sensitive?	No	Yes	Yes
Time sensitivity between client and server	No	No	30 minutes
Password storage	LM OWF: convert to uppercase, break into 7-character halves	NTLM OWF MD4 hash (16-byte digest) (not broken into two parts before hash)	NTLM OWF MD4 hash (16-byte digest) (not broken into two parts before hash)
Nonce encryption algorithm	DES using the LM OWF hash	DES using NTLM OWF hash	DES using the NTLM OWF hash
Session Security enhanced?	No	No	If client and server support NTLMv2, session security negotiated. Separate keys for message integrity and confidentiality. Client input into the challenge (prevent chosen plaintext attacks). HMAC-MD5 for message integrity checking.

Still Confused After So Many Years

The LM password hash is created by converting the password to uppercase, breaking it into two 7-character halves, adding padding for passwords of fewer than 14 characters, and encrypting each half independently. This makes the password easier to crack, first because fewer characters must be tried in a brute force attack, and second because anything over 7 characters was no more difficult to crack than a 7-character password. The NTLM protocol available since the release of NT and available to Windows 9x computers on which the Active Directory client extensions are installed and NTLM configured allows a larger character set and does not break the password into parts before hashing. Still, many computer experts and those new to Windows do not understand the improvements and increased security available by using NTLM and NTLMv2. They incorrectly describe the authentication process and bemoan its weaknesses. Fortunately, some of them even write password-cracking tools and tables. You can easily defeat these tools by using NTLM and by creating long or complex passwords. However, you should realize that not all tool makers and tools are so confused—NTLM password-cracking tools are available, and given enough time, they should be able to crack all passwords. Don't make their job easier—use long, complex passwords, configure Windows computers to use NTLM/NTLMv2, and remove the LM password hash from the password databases.

LM Password Requirements

Although in most cases the user determines the characteristics of the password, the LM algorithm used and the password policy restrictions limit choices. An LM password can be composed of up to 14 characters, and the available character set is limited to uppercase letters, the numbers 0 to 9, and the special characters or punctuation marks. (If the user enters lowercase letters, the letters are converted to uppercase before the password is hashed.)

TIP: Use Unicode Characters in Passwords

NTLM and NTLMv2 passwords can include Unicode characters. Unicode characters can be good choices for passwords because common password-cracking programs do not include them in their brute force algorithms. Password-cracking programs could be extended to test for Unicode characters, but the larger the character set that the program has to test for, the longer the program will take to work. To include Unicode characters, hold down the ALT key and enter a three- or four-digit number using the numeric keypad. Not all Unicode characters will improve security, as some may simply represent characters that can be entered from the keyboard. ALT+0100, for example, is converted to "d." To determine if your favorite Unicode character translates into a common keyboard character, entering it in Notepad to see the results.

The Microsoft document "Selecting Secure Passwords" at http://www.microsoft.com/smallbusiness/gtm/securityguidance/articles/select_sec_passwords.mspx includes a table of numbers that will create Unicode characters that do not translate into ordinary characters.

LM/NTLM Configuration

The LM legacy weakens security in a Windows domain in two ways. First, passwords hashed for use with the LM algorithm are easier to crack, and several tools exist that capitalize on this weakness. When LM is used for network authentication, the authentication material can be captured and the password may be deduced. Second, even if LM is not used to authenticate network clients, a password hash that might be used by the LM algorithm may be stored in the password database. An attacker who is able to obtain access to the weaker LM-compatible hash may be able to crack it and use the results to obtain the NTLM password required for authentication. If no LM password hash is available, it will be more difficult for passwords to be cracked. Where all clients can be configured to use NTLM, you should prevent the storing of the LM password hash in the database, as described in the following. To ensure no storage of an LM password hash, use passwords longer than 14 characters. If the password is longer than 14 characters or contains characters not allowed in the LM character set, no LM-compatible password hash will be stored.

By default, a Windows Server 2003 domain does not allow the use of the LM network authentication algorithm, but it does not prevent the storage of the LM-compatible password hash. If Windows 95 or Windows 98 clients must be used by users who need to log on to a

Windows Server 2003 domain, you can weaken authentication by allowing use of the LM algorithm in the domain, or you can update clients to enable them to use NTLM or NTLMv2. The domain may be made more secure by eliminating the storage of the LM-compatible hash.

To update Windows 95 and Windows 98 clients so that the more secure NTLM algorithm can be used, you must load the Active Directory client and configure the client to use NTLM or preferably NTLMv2. Depending on your choice, you may also be able to tighten security on the server by requiring the use of NTLMv2. If this is not possible, you will either have to upgrade these clients to Windows 2000 Professional or XP Professional or weaken domain security by making a change to Group Policy. Before you tighten or weaken security, you must understand the NTLM configuration options, how they are configured on each operating system, and how some legacy applications may prevent you from applying the most secure version of LM.

Reduce Security

It is possible to weaken security by accepting LM authentication in a Windows Server 2003 domain. Because the default domain controller setting does not allow the use of LM authentication, if you cannot configure the client, you must change the NTLM/LM configuration settings on the domain controller. This is not advised. To do so, adjust the default domain security policy by changing the Security Option `LAN Manager Authentication Level to Send LM And NTLM Responses`. Security Options are located in the Windows Configuration, Security Settings, Local Policy section of the Group Policy object. Verify that the Security Option `Network Security: Do Not Store LAN Manager Hash Value On Next Password Change` is set to `Disabled` (the default). This means that the LM-compatible hash will be stored and available for use. If you will be allowing LM authentication, you want the LM hash to be present in Active Directory.

Improve Security on Legacy Clients

To improve security on legacy clients (Windows 95, Windows 98, and Windows NT 4.0 post service pack 4), you may need to install the Active Directory client and/or make registry changes that enforce the use of the stronger NTLM or NTLMv2 authentication protocols on every Windows 95 and Windows 98 computer used to authenticate to the domain. The Active Directory Client software is available for download from Microsoft.com at http://support.microsoft.com/default.aspx?kbid= 288358#2. Although a copy is available on the Windows Server 2000 installation CD-ROM, you should obtain the latest version from Microsoft. Make registry changes on all legacy clients.

NOTE: The Windows NT 4.0 Active Directory Client is Not Necessary for NTLM Configuration

A Windows NT 4.0 version of the Active Directory client is available. However, it is not necessary to install it to make Windows NT 4.0 require the use of NTLM or NTLMv2. You may want to install it to provide other advantages such as site awareness (the ability to log on to the domain controller closest to the client rather than to the Primary Domain Controller (PDC) emulator), availability of a DFS fault-tolerant client (NT 4.0 clients will be able to use Windows 2000 fault-tolerant and fail over file shares specified in Active Directory), and to provide a common programming interface for programmers developing Active Directory scripts.

Warning: Editing the Registry Can Produce Catastrophic Results

The registry editing tools allow changes to system and application configuration without requiring confirmation and without warning of the results. Caution should be used whenever editing the registry, and it is always appropriate to make a backup of the registry before making changes.

Registry changes for NTLM are made by doing the following:

1. From the Start menu, click Run and then type Regedit.exe to start the Registry Editor.
2. Locate and select the following key in the registry:
   `HKEY_LOCAL_MACHINE\System\CurrentControlSet\Control\LSA`
3. To add a value to the LSA key, click Add Value on the Edit menu, select New, select DWORD value, and then add the following data, as shown in Figure 2-1.
4. Add the Value Name: LMCompatibility.
5. Select the Base: Decimal.
6. Enter the Value: 2 or 3. (Level 2 requires the use of NTLM; 3 requires the use of NTLMv2.)
7. Exit the Registry Editor.

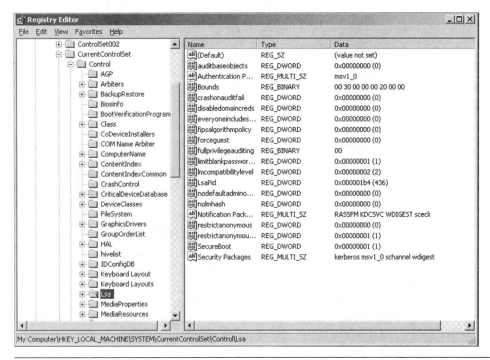

Figure 2-1 The registry value LMCompatibilty must be configured to configure LAN Manager Compatibility Level for Windows 95, Windows 98, and Windows NT 4.0 computers in a Windows Server 2003 domain.

Improving Security on the Windows 2000, Windows XP Professional, and Windows Server 2003 Servers and Domain Controllers

Newer versions of Windows based on Windows NT technologies can be configured to require NTLM or NTLMv2 by adjusting Group Policy LAN Manager Security Option settings, as shown in Figure 2-2.

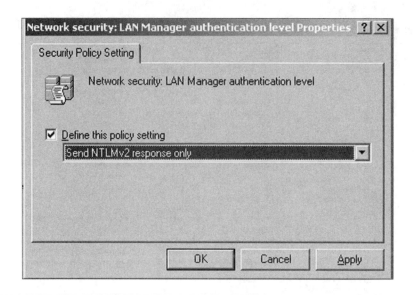

Figure 2-2   Group Policy is used to configure LAN Manager Compatibility Level for Windows 2000, Windows Server 2003, and Windows XP systems in a Windows Server 2003 domain.

Table 2-3 describes the use of each of the available Security Option settings and the corresponding registry key values.

Table 2-3   Security Option Settings and Registry Key Values

Registry Key Value	Value	Description
Send LM & NTLM Response	0	LM & NTLM will be used by servers. Servers will not respond to NTLMv2. (Domain controllers will respond to NTLMv2.)
Send LM & NTLM—use NTLM v2 session security if negotiated	1	LM & NTLM are used, as is session security if configured.
Send NTLM Response Only	2	Use this setting on Windows 95, Windows 98, and Windows NT 4. NTLMv2 session security is negotiated if configured. Clients use NTLM only while domain controllers accept NTLM, LM, and NTLMv2.

Registry Key Value	Value	Description
Send NTLMv2 Response Only	3	Clients use NTLMv2 and session security, if the server supports it. The domain controllers accept NTLM, LM, and NTLMv2.
Send NTLMv2 Response Only/Refuse LM	4	Use this value for the Windows NT 4 domain controller. Clients can use NTLM or NTLMv2, but a domain controller will refuse LM. This setting can cause authentication issues with some programs.
Send NTLMv2 Response Only/Refuse LM and NTLM	5	Use this value for the Windows NT 4 domain controller. Clients will use NTLMv2. Domain controllers will accept only NTLMv2.

Considerations

Before making changes that will reduce or improve security, you should evaluate the possible negative impact of doing so. There are three LM issues to consider:

- All clients in the domain may need to be adjusted to use the more secure protocol when domain controllers are configured to reject the weaker ones. If you leave out any clients, they will not be able to communicate with the domain controller. Users will not be able to log on.
- All domain controllers in the domain must be configured the same way. If you leave out any, some clients will not be able to communicate with the domain controller. Users will not be able to log on. Use Group Policy to ensure that changes are implemented on all domain controllers.

- Some services might not work when the LM controls are configured—specifically, legacy services including RAS and RRAS on Windows NT 4.0, the print spooler service on some systems, and browsing services in Windows NT. If you must use these services, you will have to wait until these services are updated before modifying these settings past the elimination of LM. Of course, as you upgrade servers and migrate users to Windows 2000 Professional, Windows XP Professional, Windows Server 2003, and operating systems that can use Kerberos for authentication, you will ultimately improve the authentication security for your domain.

Remove the LM Hash from the Account Database

For additional security, you should remove the LM hash from the account database. To do so, you must change the Security Option `Network Security: Do Not Store LAN Manager Hash Value On Next Password Change` to `Enabled` and require all users to change their passwords. Alternatively, you can modify a registry key. To modify the registry entry, follow these steps:

1. On a domain controller, open the Start menu, click Run, and then enter Regedit.exe to start the Registry Editor.
2. Navigate to the key
   `HKLM\SYSTEM\CurrentControlSet\Control\Lsa`.
3. Add or modify the REG_DWORD value NoLMHash.
4. Change its value to 1 to remove the hash.
5. Repeat at every domain controller in the domain.

Change the user account setting `User must change password at next logon` so that users will be required to do so. The LM hash will remain in the database until the user next changes his password.

Session Security

Enhanced session security can increase the likelihood that attacks fail. If client and server support NTLMv2, two Security Options can be used to configure session security; alternatively, a registry entry may be set.

The Security Options `Network Security: Minimum Session Security for NTLM SSP based (including secure RPC based) clients` and `Network Security: Minimum Session Security for NTLM SSP` based (including secure RPC based) servers include choices that set session security. The choices are listed in the "Options" column of Table 2-4. Registry key values are also listed.

Table 2-4 NTLMv2 Session Security

Option	Registry Value	Discussion
Require Message integrity	0x00000010	The data is checked and verified upon receipt to guarantee that the data sent has not been altered in transit. HMAC-MD5 algorithm is used.
Require Message confidentiality	0x00000020	Data is encrypted to ensure privacy.
Require NTLMv2 session security	0x00080000	Connection will fail if NTLMv2 authentication is not negotiated.
Require 128-bit encryption	0x20000000	A larger keyspace is used. Keyspace is the result of the number of characters used. When more characters are possible, there are many more possible key combinations to check. When brute force algorithms are used in an attempt to crack passwords, a larger keyspace is better—it will take a much longer time to crack the password because many more options must be tested.

To configure session security, select the required options or configure the registry key.

1. From the Start menu, click Run, and then enter Regedit.exe to start the Registry Editor.
2. Navigate to the key
   HKLM\SYSTEM\CurrentControlSet\Control\Lsa\MSV1-0\.
3. Add or modify the following registry value: NtlmMinClientSec (or NtlmMinServerSec value for servers).
4. To select a single value, enter the hexadecimal number from Table 2-4.
5. To select multiple values, combine the registry values from Table 2-4 using a logical OR, as shown in Figure 2-3.

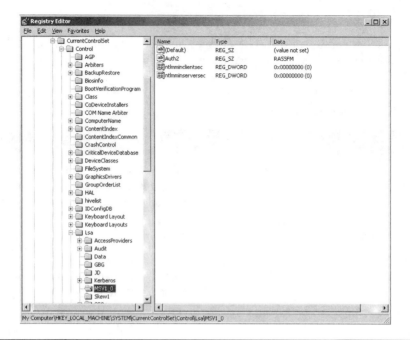

Figure 2-3   To combine multiple values, use a logical OR.

TIP: Combine Session Security Options Using Hexadecimal Numbers
The advantage of using the registry key is the ability to combine the session security options. You can do so by using the Windows Calculator program. Simply change the calculator to scientific view and use the logical OR button. You can combine any number of hexadecimal numbers quickly by entering the number for the first value you want, clicking the OR button, and repeating this process until the last number has been OR'd. Click the = button to get the final result. For example, combining the values for integrity and confidentiality from Table 2-4 results in the hexadecimal number 0x00000030. Enter this value in the registry key NtlmMinClientSec or NtlmMinServerSec to require that confidentiality and integrity be used in an NTLMv2-based session.

Kerberos

Kerberos is the default network authentication protocol for Windows 2000, Windows XP Professional, and Windows Server 2003 computers that are joined in a Windows 2000 or Windows Server 2003 domain. These systems will use NTLM if they are not in a domain and are attempting to access remote resources. They may also fall back to NTLM when Kerberos can't be used. An example is that drives mapped from domain members using the IP address of the file server will use NTLM, while the same drive mapping using the computer name of the file server will use Kerberos. Domain members may also use NTLM when mapping drives using computer names if the client or server does not have network connectivity with a DC.

The use of Kerberos for authentication in Windows systems starting with Windows 2000 is an important development on two fronts. First, Kerberos is an IETF standard (RFC 1510), and versions exist for multiple operating systems. Security algorithms of any type are usually judged to be more secure if they are public standards in use by many people. The rationale is that many people can inspect the algorithm, increasing the chance that flaws will be found and corrected. Over time, a hardened, tested security algorithm is developed, as is experience in coding it. Therefore, there is a smaller chance that vulnerabilities exist that an attacker could use to compromise the systems that use them. Second, because it is a standard in wide use, interoperability between operating systems is possible. It is possible to configure Kerberos authentication between Windows and other operating systems.

NOTE: Will the Use of Kerberos Create a Dangerous Monoculture?
When only one process is used throughout many systems, it is often referred to as a monoculture. The extraordinary number of Windows desktops in use is often so defined. Although it is true that well-known standards tend to provide more secure processes because it is more likely that their flaws will be found and corrected, it is also possible that if a flaw is discovered and not reported, more machines will be susceptible to compromise. If most computers use one security protocol for authentication, a directed attack against some flaw in that authentication protocol could impact more than one operating system.

Kerberos offers security functionality far beyond that offered by the challenge/response-type authentication processes such as NTLM. Kerberos offers the following security characteristics:

- **Secure transmission**—All Kerberos messages are encrypted using a variety of encryption keys. The password is never sent across the network; instead, the password hash may be used as an encryption key.
- **Mutual authentication**—The client verifies a server's identity; the server verifies the identity of the client.
- **Replay protection**—When authentication messages cross the network, they can be captured. It might be possible for an attacker to reuse them to compromise the system. Kerberos provides protection against these replay-type attacks. To do so, it requires that each message include an authenticator—an encrypted timestamp. The time on the client can be compared to the time on the server, and delayed messages (those possibly captured and replayed) are rejected.

Windows 2000, Windows XP Professional, and Windows Server 2003 computers joined in Windows 2000 or Windows Server 2003 domains may use Kerberos as their authentication protocol of choice.

When is Kerberos Used?

Although Windows 2000, Windows XP, and Window Server 2003 computers joined in a Windows 2000 or Windows Server 2003 domain prefer the use of Kerberos for authentication, Kerberos may not always be used for authentication in these domains. The following list of authentication rules should be kept in mind when considering authentication in these domains. Pay special attention to the use of "will" and "may." When attempts at Kerberos authentication fail, authentication may fall back to some version of LM.

- User and computer authentication from Windows 2000, Windows XP, and Windows Server 2003 computers joined in a Windows 2000 or Windows Server 2003 domain will attempt to use Kerberos.
- User domain authentication from Windows 2000, Windows XP, and Windows Server 2003 computers not joined in a Windows 2000 or Windows Server 2003 domain will use NTLM by default. In this case, the user may have a Windows 2000 or Windows Server 2003 domain account, but the computer itself is not joined in the domain.

- User domain authentication from Windows 95/98 computers will use LM by default.
- User domain authentication from Windows NT 4.0 computers will use NTLM by default.
- Windows NT 4.0 computers joined in a Windows 2000 or Windows Server 2003 domain will use NTLM by default.
- Authentication for access to resources in a Windows 2000 or Windows Server 2003 domain will always use NTLM if an IP address is used to identify the source of the server (for example, if a share resource is entered in the form \\192.168.5.55\sharename).
- Authentication for access to resources in a Windows 2000 or Windows Server 2003 domain from users or computers joined in a Windows 2000 or Windows Server 2003 domain will attempt to use Kerberos if the name of the server identifies the server (for example, if a share resource is entered in the form \\anyserver\sharename).

Kerberos Components

The Kerberos algorithm is complex but easily understandable if broken into the separate processes that it is used for: logon, resource access, access to resources in other domains, and delegated authentication. The components of the Kerberos process are as follows:

- **Key distribution center (KDC)**—Manages shared secrets for client and server and supplies ticket granting tickets (TGT) and service tickets to users and computers on the network. The Windows Server 2003 KDC service exists on every domain controller.
- **Kerberos tickets**—The Kerberos process identifies specific data structures as tickets to make them easier to talk about. In reality, each ticket is a collection of data and includes information about the client, the user, the request, and the KDC. Parts of the ticket are encrypted using the password hash of the user/client, which may be inspected by the user, and parts of the ticket are encrypted using the password hash of the KDC so that the KDC can recognize it as its own. Two types of tickets and a variation are used in Windows Server 2003 Kerberos.
- **Ticket Granting Ticket (TGT)**—Provided to the authenticated user when he or she first logs on to the network. The TGT is used to request a service ticket when access to a new service is required.

- **Service Ticket**—Required to obtain access to a service or resource.
- **Referral ticket**—When a service ticket is required to access a resource that exists outside of the user's logon domain, the user's KDC issues a special kind of TGT: a TGT for another KDC. If the resource is not in that domain, that domain can issue a referral ticket to another domain and so on until the appropriate domain has been reached.
- **Authenticator**—An extra piece of information that enables authentication. A small piece of unique data (the time stamp at the client computer) is encrypted using a password hash. A fresh authenticator always accompanies the ticket whether the ticket is a TGT, a service ticket, or a referral ticket. Although a ticket could be captured and used in a replay attack, because the authenticator is created fresh each time a ticket is used, the tickets can be validated for their authenticity.

User Logon

User logon consists of an authentication request, validation, TGT issue, request for a service ticket for access to the user's desktop, and issuance of the service ticket, after which, if the user is authorized to log on from this machine, the user gets her desktop.

One way to think about this two-ticket transaction is to think about the process you follow when traveling by air. When you purchase a ticket over the Internet, you receive an electronic receipt, or if you request it, perhaps a paper ticket. This alone will not get you on board the plane. The receipt or the paper ticket may be compared to the TGT. You have to present credentials as part of the process. At the airport, you present the receipt or paper ticket and your photo ID (or if your original purchase was done electronically, it should be in the ticket agent's database, and it will not be necessary to present a receipt at all). In exchange, you receive a boarding pass. The boarding pass may be compared to the session ticket. It's a ticket that can be presented to go through security checkpoints and board the plane. At security, you present the boarding pass and your photo ID (the authenticator) to get through to the gate. At the gate, you use this "session" ticket to board the plane. You may also be required to present your authenticator at boarding to ensure that the service ticket is valid. Figure 2-4 illustrates the Kerberos logon process, as listed in the following.

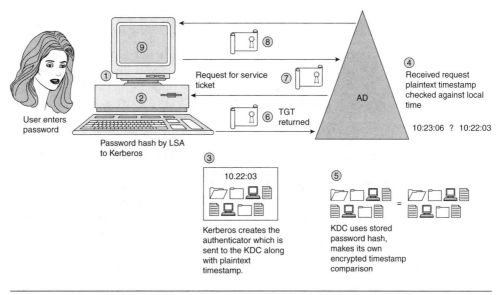

Figure 2-4 The Kerberos logon process.

1. The user enters his user ID and password.
2. The LSA subsystem prepares the appropriate password hash and passes it to the Kerberos process.
3. The Kerberos process uses the hash to encrypt the client's timestamp and to create the authenticator. The authenticator and a plaintext copy of the timestamp are sent to the KDC.
4. The KDC receives the request for authentication and checks the plaintext timestamp against its own clock. If the difference between the two times is more than the Kerberos policy clock skew time (five minutes by default), then the user request is rejected.
5. If the difference is less than the clock skew time, the KDC uses the Active Directory stored password hash to encrypt the plaintext timestamp. The result is compared to the authenticator. If there is a match, then the user is authenticated.
6. The KDC returns a TGT to the Kerberos process on the user's computer. Part of the TGT is encrypted using the user's password hash, and part is encrypted using that of the KDC.
7. A copy of the TGT is cached for later use, and the TGT is used to request a service ticket from the KDC for the user's access to the desktop.

8. The KDC uses its own credentials to decrypt its portion of the TGT, determines that it signed the TGT, checks the authenticator, and if all is valid, issues a service ticket to the user's desktop.
9. The service ticket is received, cached and, the user's authorization for access to the desktop is evaluated. If all is in order, access is granted, and the user gets his desktop.

Resource Access

In the previous example, Kerberos was used to authenticate the user to the domain. However, another process also occurred—the user was authorized to log on to the domain from that specific computer during that time frame and was granted access to resources on the computer. As a user uses the computer to do work throughout the day, she will request access to resources both on the local computer and on servers and systems connected to the local network and elsewhere. That process, authorization, is described in Chapter 3, "Authorization: Limiting System Access and Controlling User Behavior." For now, simply remember that Kerberos plays a role in authorization. During the logon process, information about the user's membership in groups and rights on systems is collected and recorded as part of the Kerberos ticket. This information, the user's domain credentials, is therefore available and can be used for authorization by processes that the user may run. The credentials are used to authorize use of system(s) resources.

The user's credentials are added to the authorization data field of the TGT at the time it is created at the KDC. The authorization field data is copied to each service ticket. On each machine the user visits, data specific to her rights and privileges on that local machine is combined with that in the authorization field to create the access token used during the authorization process. The user's credentials are her SID, the SIDs of the groups of which she is a member, and the user rights that belong to her. This data can be compared to the rights and membership required for resource access. The approval or authorization process is not part of the Kerberos algorithm. An example of the authorization process when Kerberos is the network authentication protocol is shown in Figure 2-5 and listed in the following.

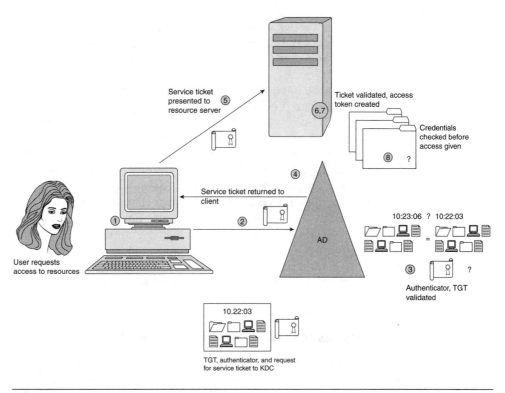

Figure 2-5 Kerberos and remote file access.

1. The user requests access to the resources (maps a drive, selects a folder on a mapped drive, and so on).
2. A cached TGT is retrieved. It includes the user's credentials in the authorization field. The TGT, an authenticator, and a request for a service ticket for the resource are sent to the KDC.
3. The KDC examines the authenticator for its timeliness and the TGT to verify that it was issued by itself.
4. If all is in order, the KDC issues a service ticket for the requested resource. The data in the authorization field of the TGT is copied to the authorization field of the service ticket. A portion of the service ticket is encrypted using the password hash of the server on which the resources reside.
5. The service ticket is returned to the client.

6. The client caches a copy of the service ticket (it can be used again to access the same resource) and presents the service ticket to the resource computer on which the required resources reside.

7. The resource computer, the file server, decrypts the portion of the ticket encrypted with its password hash. Because only the computer and the KDC have knowledge of the resource computer's password, the computer knows the service ticket was granted by the KDC. The resource computer accepts the KDC's word for the validation of the user's identity. The server does not do its own check on the user's credentials.

8. An access token is created for the user that consists of the data provided in the authorization field, and any local group membership SIDS and any local user rights granted to the user or local groups she is a member of.

9. The requested resource is examined to determine if the user has the authorization to access it in the manner requested.

Accessing Resources in Other Domains in the Forest

If a resource does not exist in the local domain, the local KDC provides a referral ticket for another KDC. This is possible because each Windows domain shares a domain password with its parent and child domain. Before issuing such a ticket, the KDC will determine the trust path required to reach the domain in which the desired resource resides. The trust path is a list of domains that must be traversed to reach the resource domain. When this path is known, the client begins the process of obtaining a TGT for the resource domain by obtaining, one after another, referral tickets from domains along the trust path. Figure 2-6 illustrates a trust path between the west.indiania.fizzrep.org domain where user JoeyP's account resides and the fachunk domain where the file share \\vegas\motel6 exists. In the drawing, dotted lines represent domain relationships, wheras arrows represent the steps along the trust path.

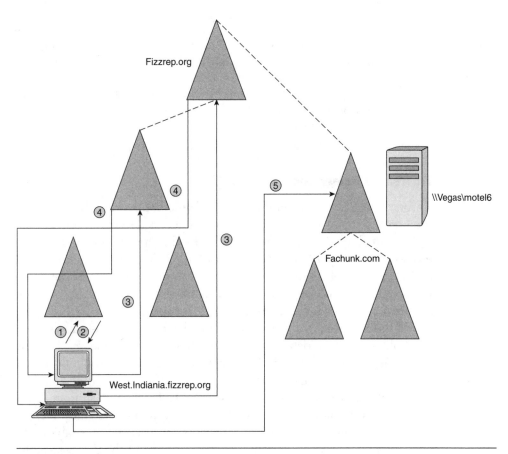

Figure 2-6   Illustration of trust path.

The process can be described simply as:

1. The client sends the user's TGT, an authenticator, and a request for the remote resource to its local KDC.
2. The KDC validates the request and recognizes that the resource does not exist in its domain. It requests information from DNS to determine which domain controller, one of its child domains or its parent domain, is the first domain on the trust path that must be traversed. It then prepares a referral ticket for that domain and returns it to the client.
3. The client presents this referral ticket, an authenticator, and a request for the resource to the new domain. If this is not the resource domain, the new KDC follows the process in step 2, and the client receives a referral ticket for the next domain along the trust path.

4. Eventually, the client obtains a referral ticket for the domain within which the resource resides. When the client presents this referral ticket to the KDC in that domain, if all is correct, a service ticket for the resource is issued.

5. The client presents this ticket to the resource server and is either given access or denied access based on rights and privileges assigned to the user.

Trusted for Delegation

Kerberos works well when the security principal that needs access to a remote resource is making the request for access. However, some applications are built in tiers, and sometimes the application is making a request for resources at a remote location. One such application is the typical web application that requires access to a remote database. Kerberos-delegated authentication can be used to solve this two-tier application issue. This scenario is illustrated in Figure 2-7. In the figure, a user authenticates to the web server; however, the web application must obtain or store data in a database on a third machine. Prior to the Kerberos implementation in Windows 2000, there was no built-in way for Windows web applications to impersonate or use the user's credentials to obtain access to the database. (NTLM does not support "two-hop" authentication.) This lack of capability to impersonate a user's credentials limited the granularity of access controls on the database and the capability to provide accountability—an audit of the database activity could not provide specific records that would indicate which user accessed the database. Using Kerberos and Windows 2000, the web server can be "trusted for delegation," and the user's credentials can be used to access the database. The web server application, in essence, "impersonates" the user.

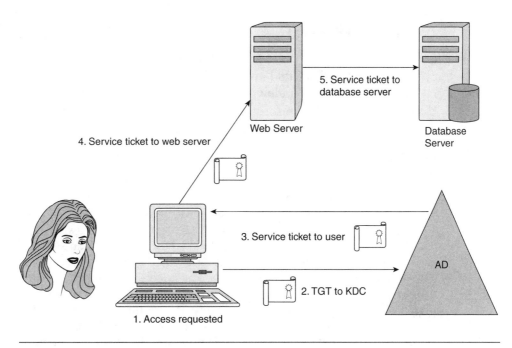

Figure 2-7   Illustration of web application/database authentication.

Delegation can be configured by checking the `Trusted for delegation` check box in the server's properties in Active Directory. The user whose account will be impersonated must also be Trusted for delegation and not have the `This account is sensitive and must not be trusted for delegation` selection made in his or her Account properties.

However, trusting a server for delegation can create a serious security issue. The problem is that by default, no limit is placed on the delegation. (Windows Server 2003 delegation can be constrained; Windows 2000 delegation cannot be.) Although the purpose of the delegation may be to provide granularity in access control to a database, when delegated, the credentials could be used to provide access anywhere that the user has been assigned access. A malicious person might take advantage of this. For this reason, unconstrained delegation of Administrator accounts is not recommended. If delegation is a requirement for web or other multitier applications, the risks should be evaluated before delegation is considered. If delegation is required, where possible, constrained delegation should be used.

Constrained Delegation

Constrained delegation provides the ability to limit the use to which the server can put the delegated user's credentials. (Constrained delegation is only available on a Windows Server 2003 server and only when the Windows Server 2003 domain functional level is set to Windows Server 2003—a functional level that can only be set when no NT 4.0 or Windows 2000 domain controllers are part of the domain—see Chapter 7, "Active Directory's Role in Domain Security.") An example of constrained delegation would be to limit the credentials for use in accessing SQL server database services.

Constrained delegation uses a new Kerberos request type called Service-for-User-to Proxy (S4u2Proxy) Extension. This request type, if enabled by constrained delegation, is used when a service 1 on server A uses the client's credentials to request a ticket for service 2 on server B. The domain controller will check to see if service 1 is allowed to use the user credentials to obtain access to service 2; it checks to make sure the service is allowed to delegate credentials. In our web application example, a Windows 2000 server trusted for delegation gets a copy of the client's TGT and uses it to obtain its own session ticket for the database server. In Windows Server 2003, the server trusted for delegation can request on its own, a user's session ticket if the user account is trusted for delegation. When constrained delegation is configured, the capability of the server to use this request can be limited to those services approved for its use.

Configuring constrained delegation is usually part of a complex multitiered web-based application that includes server configuration and application development efforts. The proper development and implementation will depend on understanding both the new technology and the application requirements. For example, a service running on the web server may need to impersonate the account of a user to access data in a Microsoft SQL Server database. Constrained delegation is configured on the property pages for the web server computer in Active Directory Users and Computers, and user accounts that may be impersonated must not be marked Account is sensitive and cannot be delegated in the user Account properties. In addition, if special user accounts are created for services that must be delegated; a server principal name (SPN) must be registered for the account. Application and configuration need to be developed hand-in-hand.

Constrained delegation can be configured to provide delegated access to any services running on the target computer.

To configure constrained delegation:

1. Open `Active Directory Users and Computers`.
2. From the `View` menu, select `Advanced`.
3. Navigate to the computer account of the server that will require the delegated credentials.
4. Right-click the computer and select `Properties`.
5. Select the `Delegation` tab, as shown in Figure 2-8.

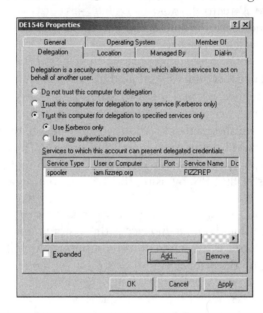

Figure 2-8   Use the delegation tab of the computer account to configure constrained delegation.

6. Select `Trust this computer for delegation to speci ed services only`.
7. Select `Use Kerberos only`.
8. Click the `Add` button.
9. Click the `User or Computer` tab.
10. Use the object picker to select a computer, and then use the `Add Services` dialog to select a service that the original computer may obtain delegated access to.
11. Click `OK` to add the service. The service will be displayed on the Delegation page in the `Services to which this account can present delegated credentials` window, as shown in Figure 2-8.
12. Click `OK` to close the Properties page.

The user account property `Account is sensitive and cannot be delegated` is not selected by default. If it is, access using this user's credentials cannot be delegated. To check the status of a user account, do the following:

1. Navigate to the user account and double-click it to open its properties page.
2. Select the `Account` tab.
3. Make sure the `Account is sensitive and cannot be delegated box` is deselected.
4. Click OK to close.

If special user accounts are created for services that will be used, an SPN must be registered, and the user account must be marked as delegated to specific services only. Restricting the account in this way makes its use in other unauthorized delegation scenarios less likely because an administrator would have to reconfigure the account. The ability to restrict the account is only configurable if an SPN has been registered for it.

Register an SPN by using the `setspn` command with the following syntax:

```
Setspn —A nameofservice/useraccount computername
```

In the command, *nameofservice* is the system name for the service, and *computername* is the name of the computer. The following line registers an SPN for the user account *User1* on the computer *reaglinn* in the domain *chicago.local* for the Themes service.

```
Setspn -A shsvcs/user1 regalinn
```

Protocol Transition

Constrained delegation requires the service to use the client's user's Kerberos session ticket to obtain a TGT using the client's user's credentials. But many web browsers and web applications are not configured to use Kerberos authentication. In this case, another Kerberos extension, S4U2Self (Service-for-User-to-Self) allows the service to obtain a user's service ticket. Delegation can occur even if the original client authentication is some protocol other than Kerberos. This process is known as protocol transition. To configure protocol transition, do the following:

1. Open `Active Directory Users and Computers`.
2. Navigate to the computer account that will require the delegated credentials.
3. Right-click the computer and select `Properties`.

4. Select the Delegation tab.
5. Select Trust this computer for delegation to speci ed services only.
6. Select Use any authentication protocol.
7. Click OK to close the property pages.
8. Open the Builtin\Windows Authorization Access Group property pages and then select the Members tab.
9. Click the Add button and then use the object picker to select the service account for the service to whom delegation ability is granted. This gives the account permission to enumerate the group membership for a user account when obtaining a session ticket for its use. Members of the Windows Authorization Access Group can do so because they are granted read permission on the Token-Groups-Global-And-Universal object attribute of user accounts.

This extra step is necessary to ensure that not just any service can obtain this information. A second check is placed on the service. During the process, both S4u2Self and S4u2Proxy are used. If the user's account is set as Sensitive and cannot be delegated, then S4u2Proxy cannot be used. If the client's account is not so marked, the process is still governed by the list of services added to the server's properties page.

Additional steps may be necessary to configure the web server. More information on S4U2Proxy and S4U2Self is contained in the MSDN Magazine article, "Exploring S4U Kerberos Extension in Windows Server 2003" at http://msdn.microsoft.com/msdnmag/issues/03/04/ SecurityBriefs/ and in the article "Kerberos Protocol Transition and Constrained Delegation" at http://www.microsoft.com/technet/ prodtechnol/windowsserver2003/ technologies/security/constdel.mspx.

Configuring Kerberos—The Kerberos Policy

Although you cannot turn Kerberos "off" or "on," you can influence how Kerberos works. These configuration parameters are located in the Group Policy, Account Policy, Kerberos Policy. They can also be manipulated via the registry on domain controllers. The Kerberos policy can only be adjusted in the domain security policy. More information on the domain security policy and policy processing can be found in Chapter 7.

Kerberos policy consists of five elements. Table 2-5 lists the parameters, discusses their meanings, and provides the default settings.

Table 2-5 Kerberos Policy

Policy	Description	Default
Enforce User Logon Restrictions	Determines whether the KDC validates every request for a session ticket against the user rights of the account. Specifically, the KDC looks to determine the user's logon rights. This policy is sometimes disabled to improve performance, but it should not be disabled because it weakens security.	Enabled
Maximum Lifetime for Service Ticket	Time in minutes that a granted session ticket can be used to access resources. The range is from greater than 10 minutes to less than or equal to the setting for Maximum lifetime for user (TGT) ticket. If a server is presented an expired ticket, the server will refuse the ticket. A new service ticket can be requested from the KDC by using a valid TGT. However, when a resource access is authorized, if the service ticket expires, nothing will happen.	600 minutes (10 hours)
Maximum lifetime for User° Ticket	Time, in hours, that a TGT may be used. When the ticket expires, a new one can be requested or the current one renewed.	10 hours
Maximum lifetime for User° Ticket Renewal	The number of days during which a TGT may be renewed.	7 days

Policy	Description	Default
Maximum tolerance for computer clock synchronization	If the time difference between client and KDC computers is greater than this time, authentication will not occur, even if the user's credentials would have later been found valid. The difference is expressed in minutes. If this setting is changed and the computer is rebooted, the time will revert back to the default of 5 minutes.	5 minutes

°The Kerberos policy refers to a TGT as a "user" ticket.

Certificates, Smart Cards, Tokens, and Biometrics

Certificates and biometrics can also be used for network authentication. Several certificate uses are defined in other chapters, including the use of certificates in IPSec for machine authentication in Chapter 15, "Protecting Data in Flight," and in web server and web client authentication using SSL/TLS in Chapter 14, "Securing Remote Access." A discussion of the specifics of certificate authentication is reserved until that time, as a background in Microsoft Certificate Services is required. Certificate Servers are discussed in Chapter 12, "PKI Basics" and in Chapter 13, "Implementing a Secure PKI."

Built-in support for smart cards is present in Windows Server 2003. Certificate Services must be available. In addition, many other token-based authentication systems that are built for Windows Server 2003 rely on the use of certificates. Application Programming Interfaces (APIs) are available for the use of biometric forms of authentication. Biometric authentication relies on some physical proof, such as fingerprints, voiceprints, retinal or iris scans, and so on. No default application support is available, but the hooks, in the form of APIs, are available. Third-party biometric-based authentication packages are available for both local and network authentication. They may or may not be fully integrated with Active Directory.

Network Authentication Protocols Selection and Cached Logon Credentials

Previous sections outlined how the type of network authentication protocol used depends on these elements:

- The client operating system
- The domain controller or network server operating system

Configuration of Both Client and Server Operating Systems

Table 2-6 lists possible clients in a Windows Server 2003 domain, the default authentication process they will attempt to use, whether they can use this to authenticate to a Window Server 2003 domain, and what configuration choices are available to secure network authentication.

Table 2-6   Network Authentication Protocols in Windows Server 2003

Client	Default	Desired	Suggested Client Configuration
Windows 95 and Windows 98	LM	No	Install Active Directory client and configure for NTLM. Use NTLMv2 where possible.
Windows NT 4.0	NTLM	No	Use NTLMv2 post service pack 4 where possible.
Windows 2000, Windows XP Professional, Windows Server 2003	Kerberos	Yes	Configure to use NTLM when Kerberos isn't accessible. Configure to use NTLMv2 where possible.

All of these possibilities are dependent on the ability of the client to connect to a domain controller. If no connection is possible, network authentication is impossible. This can occur when the domain controller is down or unavailable for some other reason, or when the client computer has been removed from the network. For example, a laptop can be removed from the network when it is carried away from the building. In this case, the user may be able to authenticate locally using a domain account if that account's credentials are cached.

By default, the last 10 logon credentials are cached. This number can be changed using the Group Policy Security Option `Interactive Logon: Number Of Previous Logons To Cache`. Valid settings are 0 through 50. When set to 0, this feature is disabled. Do not set this option to 0 when it might affect laptops, when users must log on to a domain controller across a WAN, or where the domain controller is often not available. If you do, users will not be able to log on. This can be more serious than you think. A laptop user may be miles from the office and unable to access her laptop, and hence email and other company resources, until she can return to the office.

Windows Time Service

Maintaining a correct computer time is important to security for two reasons. First, it is important that security events are recorded with the correct timestamp. If it is necessary to determine when something happened, or to match user logon times to events, it is important to be able to prove that the computer clock is accurate. Standalone Windows 2003 servers can be synchronized with an external timeserver using the Date and Time applet in the Control Panel or by using the net time command at the command line. (The time on Windows 2003 servers joined in a domain cannot be synchronized using this applet.) An external timeserver can be a reliable source on the network or a public timeserver on the Internet. If one Windows Server 2003 computer is synchronized with an external source, the rest of the Windows Server 2003 computers can be synchronized with it.

To set the server to synchronize with an external time source, follow these steps:

- Open the `Date and Time` applet in the Control Panel.
- Select the `Internet Time` tab.
- Enter the Internet address for an accurate time source. The default is time.windows.com, a timeserver that is operated by Microsoft. You can change the timeserver name, but the timeserver must use NTP (RFC 1305). A timeserver that uses HTTP will not work.

WARNING: A Local Hardware-Based Time Clock May Be Required
It may be possible to spoof timeservers on the Internet. If your time service obtains the time from a fraudulent timeserver, no time-based process on the machine can be depended upon. To lessen the possibility of this happening, a hardware clock on the local network can be used. These clocks receive their time synchronization via radio waves and can become the source for computer time on your network. A list of these clocks can be found at http://www.boulder.nist.gov/timefreq/general/receiverlist.htm.

The time service will attempt to synchronize once a week with the timeserver; however, if it is not connected to the Internet at this time, it will be unable to do so. To force synchronization of non-domain member Windows computers, click the Update Now button on the Internet Time tab of the Date and Time applet, as shown in Figure 2-9. (The Update Now button will not be available if your computer is a member of a domain.)

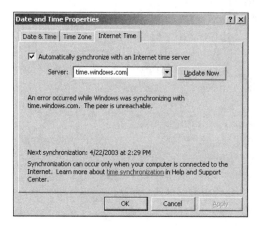

Figure 2-9   The Internet Time tab.

Synchronization failure can mean authentication failure, so be sure to determine why this is occurring and correct it. Synchronization failure may be due to several reasons:

■ The check box Automatically synchronize with an Internet time server is not checked.
■ The timeserver is busy or unavailable.

- A firewall is blocking the use of the NTP.
- The computer date is incorrect. Many Internet timeservers will not synchronize if the computer date is incorrect

You can also use the net time command or the W32tm command to establish the use of a specific timeserver. In the following command, *computername* stands for the name of the computer and *timeserverlist* represents a list of timeservers that can be used to obtain the correct time:

```
Net time \\computername   /setsntp:timeserverlist
```

Here, *computername* specifies the name of the computer to synchronize with and *timeserverlist* is the list of IP addresses or fully qualified domain names (separated by spaces) of servers to be used. If multiple timeservers are listed, the list must be enclosed in quotes. A list of time-servers available on the Internet can be located at http://boulder.nist.gov/timefreq/service/time-servers.html. Both IP address and computer name are listed. For best results, use the IP address instead of the computer name in your configuration.

The following command, where *domainname* is the name of the domain, will synchronize the current computer with the time of the domain:

```
Net time /domain:domainname
```

The Windows Server 2003 time service is used to synchronize computer clock time for all computers in the forest. All computers in the forest will attempt to synchronize their clocks with the domain controller that holds the role of PDC emulator for their domain or with another domain controller. Domain controllers, in turn, attempt to synchronize with the PDC emulator in the root domain of the forest, although they can synchronize with other domain controllers. The PDC emulator in the root domain for the forest should be set to synchronize with an external time source or with a valid timeserver on the LAN.

Group Policy can be used to configure the time service of domain computers to use an alternative timeserver and to use the Windows server as a timeserver. For more information on the time service, see the white paper "Using Windows Time Service in a Managed Environment" at http://www.microsoft.com/technet/prodtechnol/windowsserver2003/technologies/security/ws03mngd/26_s3wts.mspx.

Computer Accounts and Authentication Controls

Computer accounts are also security principals. Therefore, no study of Windows authentication or Windows administrator should ignore them. You should understand how computer accounts are created, how their passwords are modified, and what you can do to affect account processing.

Computer Account Creation and Passwords

If a computer account has not been prestaged (created in the Active Directory prior to the computer joining the domain), an account is created for the computer when a Windows NT 4.0, Windows 2000, Windows XP Professional, or Windows Server 2003 computer is joined to a Windows domain. The computer account is placed by default in the computer's Organizational Unit (OU) but can be moved to another OU. (Windows 95 and Windows 98 computers cannot join a domain, although users with valid domain accounts can log on to the domain from these computers.) The domain controller creates a password for the computer account, provides it to the computer, and places its hash in the Active Directory database. At all future restarts, these credentials are used to authenticate the computer to the domain and download its security policy. The password is ordinarily changed every 30 days by the computer and sent to the domain controller.

Computer account passwords are very strong. They are created and managed by the operating system. You cannot directly modify them. However, I also have not found an application that can crack or otherwise deduce them, and even if you could determine a computer account password, you could not use this credential to "log on."

Computer Account Processing Manipulation

You can manipulate three controls that affect the computer account processing. First, by default, domain users have the right to join up to 10 computers to the domain. This user right can be extended in Group Policy by giving a group of specific users the right to join any number of computers to the domain. Second, by prestaging computer accounts, you can restrict which users can join which computers. By moving computer accounts to specific OUs, you control the security settings for the computer. Finally, you can prevent computer account passwords from changing. Although this is not a good security practice, if you have computers that are not in constant communication with their domain controllers, the computers may eventually find that they no longer have a valid password and cannot authenticate to the domain.

In addition to manipulating controls, you can affect computer account processing by placing the computer account in an OU. The computer account OU location determines the GPO that will apply to it. GPOs set specific security policies for the objects within the container that the GPO is linked to.

To manage the right to join computers to the domain, you add or remove user groups from the Group Policy-based `User Right: Add Computers to a Domain`. User rights are located in the Computer Configuration, Windows Settings, Security Settings, Local policy section. This change should be made in the Default Domain Controller Policy for each domain you want to manage.

To prestage computer accounts, follow these steps:

- Choose `Active Directory Users And Computers` from the Administrative Tools menu.
- Navigate to the container (OU or Computer) where the computer account should reside.
- Right-click the container and select `Add Computer Account`.
- Type the Computer Name and the User Or Group account that is allowed to add this computer to the domain, as shown in Figure 2-10, and click `OK`.

To prevent computer passwords from changing, perform these steps:

- Open the Group Policy Object linked to the container that manages this computer account.
- Change the security option `Domain Member: Disable Machine Account Password Change` to `Enabled`. The computer will not attempt to change its password.

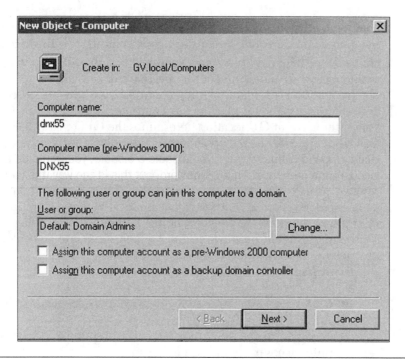

Figure 2-10 Prestaged accounts provide greater control over who is authorized to join the computer to the domain.

WARNING: Don't Disable the Machine Account Password Change Security Option

Ordinarily, you should not change this option! It is a good security practice to ensure that computer account passwords are frequently changed. If you have issues with password synchronization, you should first try to resolve the issue by modifying the number of days between password changes using the Domain Member: Maximum Machine Account Password Age security option.

TIP: Don't Be Confused
The language used in many security settings can be confusing. Make sure that you read them and understand them in context. For example, if you want to use the security option `Domain Member: Disable Machine Account Password Change` to prevent computer account passwords from being automatically changed, you might think you should select `Disabled`. However, if you read the Security Option statement carefully, you'll see that this isn't the case. Instead, you enable the disablement of computer account password change. If you disable a disable, you would be enabling account maintenance. This is awkward, but this is the way it is.

Anonymous Access

When authentication is required, access to computer resources can be restricted. The ability of any individual, computer, or process to obtain, manipulate, or delete data or to configure systems can be specified according to permissions and rights assigned to specific objects or groups of objects. Unfortunately, it is not possible always to require authentication. Anonymous, unauthenticated access is part of Windows operation. Null sessions (sessions obtained anonymously) are used to provide access to printers, to determine which computers and shares are available on the network, and to make possible the operation of various applications.

Anonymous access, however, can be restricted and is by default in Windows Server 2003. Many registry settings can be managed via Group Policy and are described in Chapter 3.

Authentication Management via Group Policy

Group Policy can be used to strengthen authentication practices for Windows. Password, account lockout policy, and Kerberos policies should be used, and many restrictions are also set in Group Policy Security Options. NTLM process restrictions, for example, are tightened via the Security Options, as described previously in this chapter in the section "LM/NTLM Configuration." Individual user account restrictions can be used to further manage and secure the authentication process.

Account Policy

The Group Policy Account Policy options determine the specifics of the Domain Password policy (see Figure 2-11 and Table 2-7), the Account Lockout policy (see Figure 2-12 and Table 2-8), and, in a domain, the Kerberos policy. Individual User Account policy determines the specific restrictions placed on an individual account. If a conflict exists, the individual user account policy has precedence.

Account Policy for a domain must be configured in the Default Domain Security Policy. There can only be one Account Policy per domain. However, when local accounts are used, the local account policy settings are used unless the account policy has been configured for the OU in which a domain member computer account resides.

Local Logon Versus Domain Logon

Local accounts exist in the local account database of every Windows computer based on NT technologies. Domain accounts exist in the domain database of a Windows NT 4.0 domain controller and in the Active Directory of Windows Server 2003 and Windows 2000 domains. When a Windows 2000 or Windows Server 2003 computer is promoted to DC, the local account database is not directly accessible, and during normal operation, the only accounts that have access to the computer's resources are domain accounts.

Windows computers that are member computers in a Windows domain, however, retain their local account database, and the user accounts in this database may be used for logon and access to the local computer's resources. This is important because either the local account or the domain account may be granted access to the local computer's resources, and the local accounts may be used to do so, but administrators often ignore the local computer account policy.

This is a significant, avoidable vulnerability.

Recently I was asked to provide a security review of an organization's Windows domain. It did not take long to discover that the password of the local Administrator account of some member servers was blank and that many member computer systems had weak or non-existent controls over the local account database. Consequently, a large number of computers contained numerous administrative-level accounts of which domain administrators were unaware. Many users had created workarounds to restrictive domain controls by using local accounts on servers to gain network access to resources.

To prevent such unmanaged access and close holes that an attacker might use to obtain unauthorized access, you should set restrictions on member computer account databases by using Group Policy at the organizational unit level. Remember, it is only possible to restrict domain account policy in the domain Group Policy, but it is possible to restrict member computer account policy at the OU level. When users log on using their domain account, the domain account policy governs the logon process, and the restrictions on their domain account are in effect. However, if users log on to a computer using a local computer account, the computer account policy and the restrictions on that local account govern logon. For more information on managing local account databases using Group Policy, see Chapter 7.

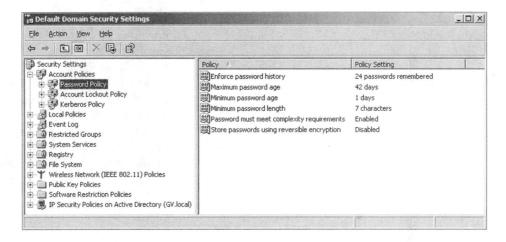

Figure 2-11   The Domain Password policy.

The Password Policy

Password policy establishes restrictions that control password composition and modification.

Table 2-7   Password Policy

Option	Description	Recommendations
Enforce password history	Determines the number of unique passwords associated with a user account before a password can be reused. Default: 24.	Retain this setting to prevent password reuse. It does no good to change a password if a user changes it back to the same thing.
Maximum password age	Number of days before which a user must change his password (1–999). Default: 42.	Reduce the number of days to tighten the policy.
Minimum password age	Number of days before a password can be changed (0–998). Default: 1 on domain controllers, 0 on servers.	Enforce this policy to make password history work. If users can immediately change their passwords, many will do so as many times as necessary to get back to their old passwords. If the minimum password age is set, it is unlikely that users will wait a day or more between password changes.
Minimum password length	The least number of characters a password must contain (0–128). Default: 7 on domain controllers, 0 on servers.	Although a longer password is more secure, you must remember that longer passwords are harder to remember and may result in more of them being written down where anyone can see them. Each added character in length requires geometrically increasing times for brute force password attacks to work. A password of 15 characters is resistant to most brute-force password crackers because of its length and because an LM version of the password cannot be created.

Option	Description	Recommendations
Passwords must meet complexity requirements	If enabled, a password must not contain any part of a user's name, must be at least 6 characters, and must be composed of three or four categories (uppercase and lowercase letters, numbers, and special characters). Default: enabled on domain controllers, disabled on standalone servers.	Enforce this setting but train users in how to create strong passwords. A password such as Dogs32 meets this requirement but will be cracked in seconds by readily available cracking tools. Putting numbers within the password, not having any part of password be a word, making the password longer, and including special characters will make it harder to crack. Many argue that password length is more important than complexity and advise teaching users how to create passphrases in order to make long passwords easier to remember.
Store passwords using reversible encryption	If enabled, passwords are stored for all practical purposes in plain text. This setting is required by some applications that do not understand the Microsoft algorithms and need to be able to determine if a correct password was entered. Examples are CHAP and Digest authentication. Disabled by default.	Do not enable this setting. Seek workarounds for applications that require this setting or do not use these applications. If you must use these applications, restrict their use to only those users necessary and instead of setting this here, do so within individual user account restrictions.

TIP: New Account Gotcha

When new accounts are created, a password should be configured and provided to the user. The user should be advised to change his or her password immediately, but if no other configuration is applied and the password policy is set to require a minimum password age, the user cannot change his or her password until that time has elapsed. All new user accounts should be configured to require that the `User must change password at next logon`. This setting is configured in the user Account property page in the Account options box and will override the password policy minimum password age setting.

In addition to password policy, the Group Policy Security Option `Accounts: Limit local account use of blank password to console logon only` is `Enabled` by default. If the local password policy allows blank passwords, local accounts can be configured with no password. However, if this option is enabled, as it is by default, then these accounts cannot be used over the network as authentication to access resources. A user may sit at the console and use the account to log on to the computer, but if access from another computer is attempted to resources on the computer that allow access by this account, the attempt will be blocked.

Creating Strong Passwords: Bigger is Better

Modern password-cracking tools are available that can be used to crack even passwords that you may have been led to believe are strong. To break false assumptions about password strength and to assist all users in creating more crack-resistant passwords, I often demonstrate one of these tools. The activity usually consists of having available a test domain controller with default configuration, but with a small number of existing user accounts and different password configurations. I ask participants to submit a strong password and then have a volunteer enter a user account for each individual and enter their password, or if the group is small enough, I have each user create his account and enter his or her own password. Then I load the password cracker and explain how it works. I start it running and move on to other topics.

Periodically, we return to the program to see how it is doing. Because passwords that are cracked are displayed on the screen along with the time it took to crack them, we can judge each password's strength by the time it took to crack. Participants are often surprised to see that their "strong" passwords—composed of upper- and lowercase letters, numbers, and special characters—are often cracked in minutes or seconds on a three-year-old laptop.

They also learn that passwords greater than 14 characters are not easily cracked because no LM password hash is stored and the cracker works by first attacking this weak hash.

The lesson to be learned from this demonstration is that requiring strong passwords means more than selecting the password policy that requires password complexity. When the LM hash is not available in the password database, and when users are taught how to create truly strong passwords, passwords can be made more secure for authentication. If you adopt this practical exercise in security awareness, be sure to emphasize that cracking truly strong passwords is also possible, but it takes longer. You should also be clear that the attack you ran required administrative access to the account database. When strong passwords are used in tandem with account policy settings such as the requirement to frequently change passwords and not repeat them, then password cracking programs can be deterred. An attacker may be able to crack a password, but if it takes him a long time, it may be useless because the password will have already changed, or the data he wanted to obtain will have become obsolete. You might also introduce the concept of passphrases—creating a password that is a phrase instead of a meaningless arrangement of letters and characters. This is a way that users can create long passwords that are easier to remember.

Truly, where passwords are concerned, bigger is better.

The Account Lockout Policy

An Account Lockout Policy can be configured to prevent online brute force cracking attacks from succeeding. Unfortunately, this may also lock out legitimate users. In the typical Account Lockout Policy, an account is locked out after some number of unsuccessful attempts. If the number of attempts is low, an attacker attempting to guess passwords or a legitimate user who has forgotten his password will quickly lock out an account. An automated attack, in which many accounts are targeted, can quickly lock out an entire population of users. Although accounts can be easily reset, there is no quick way to reset a large number of accounts with Active Directory Users and Computers. It is possible, however, to script the resetting of many accounts.

For this reason, account lockout policies are often not established. However, a better approach would be to evaluate the risk of such an attack against the need to prevent unauthorized access. In some circumstances, it may be better for legitimate users to be locked out than for unauthorized attackers to be allowed in. In many cases, setting the required number of incorrect attempts to a large number may provide a compromise. If systems are monitored, large numbers of invalid logon attempts should trigger investigations and countermeasures long before legitimate users are locked out. Should this detection fail, the account lockout policy has a good chance of locking accounts before an attacker gains access.

Figure 2-12 displays the Account Lockout Policy, and Table 2-8 describes the function of each of its settings.

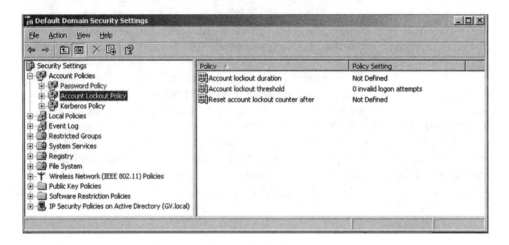

Figure 2-12   Account Lockout Policy.

Table 2-8   Account Lockout Policy

Option	Description	Recommendation
Account Lockout Duration	Set the number of minutes an account will remain locked out. Range: 0–99999 minutes (10 weeks). A setting of 0 means the account must be manually unlocked by an administrator. Default is none.	Must be greater than or equal to the reset time. Set the time low enough that a user can get back to work within a reasonable time. However, making the time too short might allow an automated attack to take advantage of it. A time of 15 to 30 minutes is probably adequate. Require administrative reset in high-security situations.

Option	Description	Recommendation
Account Lockout Threshold	The number of times a bad password may be entered before an account is locked out. Bad password entry at screen saver logons also counts toward this total. Range 1–999. Default is none.	Set at 30 or so. This is high enough that most users will never have their account locked out, yet low enough that a brute force attack will lock the account before successfully deducing the password in most cases. Setting a high number for the threshold also avoids the problem created due to the way password attempts are evaluated. A single incorrect password may trigger a number of recorded bad password attempts because the password attempt is forwarded to the PDC emulator for the domain. Windows Server 2003 and Windows 2000 SP3 limit this effect (see KB article 272065), but even so, up to 10 requests may be forwarded.
Reset account lockout counter after	Determine how long a time in minutes must pass between bad logon attempts before the lockout counter is reset. For example, if the threshold is set to 4, the reset is set to 5, a single bad password is entered, and then no additional attempt to log on is made for 5 minutes, the user will again have 4 possible attempts to enter the correct password. Must be <= account lockout duration. Range 0–99999	Set to some number less than the account lockout duration.

User Account Restrictions

Setting account properties further restricts accounts. These account restrictions, some of which can be seen in the Account Options section of the User properties Account tab shown in Figure 2-13, are listed and defined in Table 2-9.

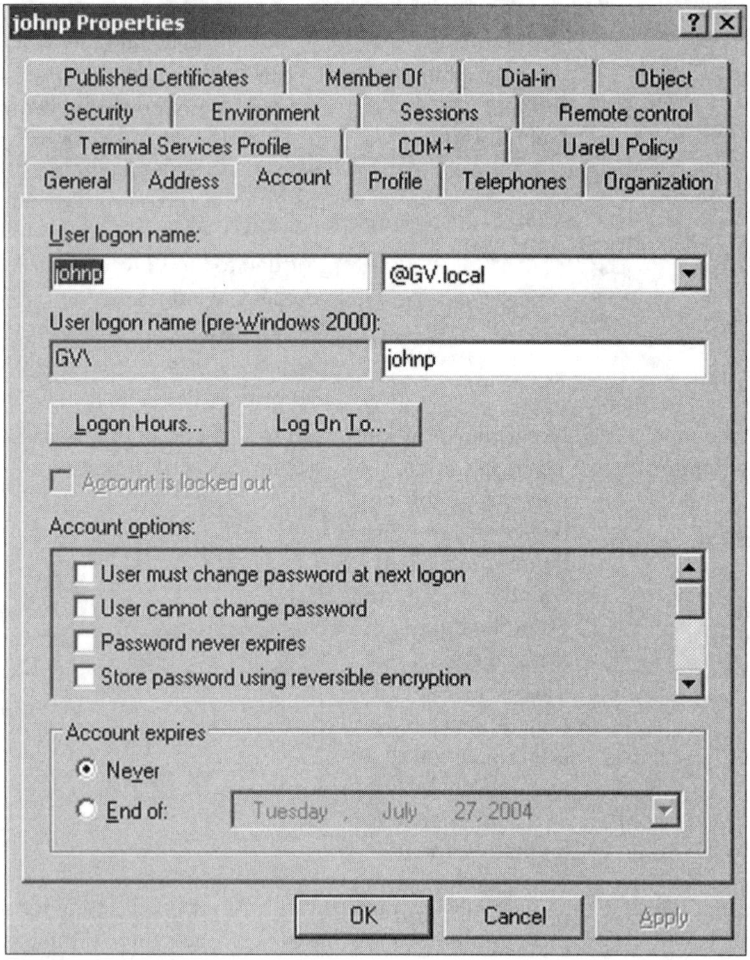

Figure 2-13   User account restrictions.

Individual User account restrictions can be set for each user account.

Table 2-9 User Account Restrictions

Restriction	Description	Recommendation
Logon Hours	By default, the user has unrestricted logon hours. A more limited schedule can be set.	At least restrict logon hours for temporary workers and contractors. Users should not be able to return and access computer systems outside of regular business hours, and those able to access computers in the evening should not be able to take advantage of found passwords.
Log On To	Users may be restricted to a set of computers from which they can log on. Using a different computer will result in logon failure. NetBIOS names for the computers must be entered, not DNS names.	Set restricting for temporary workers, contractors, and so on to reduce attack surface.
User must change password at next logon	When a user logs on, he will be prompted to change his password.	This should be set on new accounts. As a first password is provided to the user, setting this will ensure that the password quickly becomes known only to the user. Set this if attempting to remove LM hashes from the registry.
User cannot change password	A user may log on to this account but cannot change the password. An administrator must reset the password if this is required.	A good setting for service accounts. If the password is deduced, an attacker cannot change it while logged on.

Table 2-9   User Account Restrictions Continued

Restriction	Description	Recommendation
Password never expires	Overrides password policy and enables a service account to retain its password until reset by an administrator.	Set for service accounts. Do *not* set for user accounts.
Store password using reversible encryption	Effectively places a plaintext password in the account database. May be necessary for legacy authentication protocols used in remote access.	If this must be set, set it here for a single user or small number of users, not in the password policy where it would affect all user accounts.
Account is trusted for delegation	Account credentials may be delegated.	Set if establishing delegation for specific services to be delegated in a multitier application.
Account is sensitive and cannot be delegated	An account cannot be delegated.	Do not delegate administrator accounts or other sensitive accounts.
Use DES encryption types for this account	Some clients may require this encryption type. This will change the way the password is stored in the account database.	Set only if necessary.
Do not require Kerberos preauthentication	The credentials testing before issuing the TGT will not be done.	Clients authenticating to a non-Windows Kerberos realm may not need to pre-authenticate. Set this for them.
Account expires	Never is the default, but a day, month, and year may be set.	Set for temporary and contract workers.

Local Account Policy and the Password Reset Disk

A Windows Server 2003 computer's local account policy can be configured through its local Group Policy. These settings will affect only local accounts. If the server is not joined in a domain, a password reset disk can be made for local user accounts. The password reset disk can be used to recover access to the server using an account whose password has been forgotten.

Although local accounts on the server should not be used interactively for end-user tasks such as web browsing, email, or EFS file encryption, it is true that resetting a local user account password on a standalone Windows Server 2003 computer will destroy access to encrypted email, EFS encrypted files, and Internet passwords saved on the disk. This is the same behavior seen on a standalone Windows XP computer. A password reset disk can be used to recover access to local accounts and thus return access to the encrypted data.

NOTE: Linux/Other OS Password Reset Disks
Numerous utilities are available that can be used to boot a Windows computer to another OS and attack the computer by resetting passwords. If the files have been encrypted using EFS, and the password is reset using any of these utilities, access to the EFS encrypted files is lost.

The Password Reset utility is used to make the Password Reset disk. When the utility is used, a public key/private key pair is created, and the user's current password is encrypted using the public key. The encrypted password is stored only on the local computer disk, not on the reset disk. The private key is stored on the password-reset disk. To recover the password, the Password Reset utility can use the private key from the disk to decrypt the encrypted password; the user will then be able to use the change password utility to change her password and log on to the system. The new password is encrypted with the same public key and is accessible with the same password reset disk, should it be necessary again.

To create a password reset disk, follow these steps:

1. Press Ctrl+Alt+Del, and then click Change Password.
2. In the User name box, enter the user name that the reset disk will be created for.
3. Select the local computer in the dropdown list Log on to.
4. Click the Backup button.
5. Click Next from the welcome page of the Forgotten Password wizard.
6. Insert a blank, formatted disk in the A:\drive and click Next.
7. Enter the current password and click Next.
8. When the progress bar indicates that the disk is 100% complete, click Next.

9. Click `Finish` to complete the wizard.
10. Remove the disk and store it in a safe place.
11. Click `Cancel` twice to return to your current session.

To use a password reset disk:

1. At the logon prompt, enter the user account name and click OK.
2. If a password reset disk was created, the `Logon Failed` box will appear.
3. Click `Reset`.
4. Insert the password reset disk.
5. The Create New Password wizard will start. Enter a new password for the account and confirm it.
6. Enter a new "password hint" and click `OK`. The password is then reset.

Forest and Interforest Authentication

Within a Windows 2000 or Windows Server 2003 forest, trusts between domains are based on Kerberos version 5 and are both two-way and transitive. Transitive trust means that every domain within the forest trusts every other domain in the forest. A user with a valid domain account in one of the domains in the forest can authenticate from a computer in any of the other domains in the forest. In a Windows NT 4 domain, trust with another domain is one-way and nontransitive, although two one-way trusts can be created to establish bi-directional trusts. The authentication protocol used across trusts within a forest depends, as it does within a domain, on the client and server operating systems and their configurations.

Trust may also be created between a domain in a forest and a Windows NT 4.0 domain or between domains in two different forests. Windows Server 2003 forests can also create forest trusts, in which every domain in the forest trusts every domain in another forest. More information on trusts in Windows Server 2003 is contained in Chapter 8, "Trust." At this point, however, you should be aware that the authentication algorithm used between trusts can be deduced by considering the operating system of the domains. Table 2-10 provides this information. To read the table, match the domain types in the trust, one from column one and one from the first row, and find the cell that is the intersection of the row and column they begin. The listed protocol is the one used for authentication between the two domains.

Table 2-10 Authentication Protocols Between Trusted Domains

Operating System	NT 4.0	Windows 2000	Windows Server 2003
NT 4.0	NTLM	NTLM	NTLM
Windows 2000	NTLM	Kerberos or NTLM	Kerberos or NTLM
Windows Server 2003	NTLM	Kerberos or NTLM	Kerberos or NTLM

It is important to keep in mind a major distinction: It is not possible to have a Kerberos-style trust between Windows 2000 domains in separate forests or between a domain in a Windows 2000 forest and a Windows NT 4 domain. Authentication will be via NTLM and will be Windows NT-style. If trust is required between multiple domains in one forest and those in another forest, separate one-way trusts must be established. Windows Server 2003 forests can establish Kerberos-style transitive two-way trusts with another Windows Server 2003 forest. Kerberos will be the authentication protocol of choice, and trust is established between all domains in both forests.

Inter Realm Trust

Kerberos is an authentication standard, and an implementation for many operating systems can be purchased or obtained at little to no cost. When an operating system or application is provided with the ability to use Kerberos, it is said to be Kerberized. In the standard, and in many implementations, the logical grouping of Kerberized clients and servers is called a "realm." In the Microsoft implementation, the word "domain" is used.

To share resources between a Kerberos realm and a Windows domain, a realm trust can be created. This allows users to have a single account name and password. It is also possible to configure Windows 2000, Windows XP, and Windows Server 2003 computers to be clients in a Kerberos realm or to configure Kerberized, non-Windows clients to allow their users to authenticate to a Windows 2000 or Windows Server 2003 domain. In many cases, a one or two-way trust can be established. Authentication will always be via Kerberos.

To create a realm trust with a Unix-based Kerberos realm or to otherwise establish authentication between Windows and Unix systems, obtain Windows Services for Unix (SFU). The SFU home page is at http://www.microsoft.com/windows/sfu/default.asp.

Best Practices for Securing Authentication

This chapter describes Windows authentication and provides instructions for configuring Windows authentication. It details practices that can make Windows systems more secure. However, it does not always point out which practices are considered best, and it doesn't support authentication practices by detailing auxiliary practices that support and protect authentication practices. You should use the information in this section to evaluate and strengthen your current authentication practices:

- Create a strong account policy.
- Configure user account restrictions when individual restrictions vary. In general, use account restrictions if it is necessary to weaken security.
- Teach users how to create strong passwords. Options include creating long passphrases and adding numbers and special characters in the middle of passwords.
- Require administrators to use password requirements that exceed those set in the domain password policy. For example, administrators might be required to use passwords longer than 14 characters, while the domain policy only requires passwords to be 8 characters. Another option administrators might use is Unicode characters. You cannot technically enforce the administrator requirement without writing or purchasing custom code; however, you can still create the requirement and audit its implementation.
- Set Security Options that enforce secure authentication practices such as requiring NTLMv2 and maintaining or improving anonymous connection restrictions.
- Use a Password Auditing Tool to audit compliance with password policy. Be sure to have written authorization to do so.
- Understand the role of defense in depth. Security practices such as physical security, authorization controls, and others can stop attacks that breach authentication controls or prevent attempts at authentication attacks.

- Train users to resist social engineering attacks. All of the strong passwords and secure authentication practices can do no good if users can be tricked into revealing their passwords to others.
- Train users in good credential management practices. If users leave passwords where others can see or find them, or if users use domain passwords for website registration or lend passwords or other credentials to others, then it won't matter if authentication controls are in place.
- Understand all of the administration tools and methods by which authentication can be manipulated, and ensure that access to these tools is permitted only to those authorized to use them.

Summary

Authentication is the process of proving you are who you say you are. In Windows Server 2003, some default settings are stronger than in previous versions of the OS. However, it is still possible to strengthen authentication and ensure that the process is attack-resistant. Numerous default settings fulfill the goal of "secure by design," including the elimination of the use of the LM protocol for authentication, the default use of the Kerberos protocol for network authentication between Windows 2000, Windows XP Professional, and Windows Server 2003 computers, the availability of constrained delegation and Protocol transition, and more secure default settings on Security Options in Group Policy. In addition, tools that ease security configuration abound.

But default settings and the availability of more secure processes will not raise the security bar in your network if you do not understand and use them, increase security by configuring a strong Password Policy and Account Lockout policy, and train users in security practices.

CHAPTER 3

Authorization—Limiting System Access and Controlling User Behavior

Imagine you've come to my house for a visit. We've met and talked before, worked on a project together, or perhaps we know each other from church or because our boys attend the same high school. At the door, I greet you and invite you inside. What is it that keeps you from immediately going wherever you want? What prevents you from grabbing a beer from my refrigerator, knocking over the china cabinet, and kicking my dog?

Surely you're grinning now; you've recognized my ploy—you've equated my recognition of you as authentication and the use of biometrics (I recognize you by your appearance). And you've recognized my inviting you inside as authorization to enter the house, and the other activities as things you are not authorized to do. But I repeat: What prevents you from doing those things?

I suspect that you won't have to think very long before you respond that our common cultural background instilled in us a set of common beliefs that tells us what is acceptable behavior when visiting someone for the first time.

When we provide access to our information systems, computers, and networks to others, we cannot afford the luxury of making assumptions about their code of ethics or their understanding of what's considered appropriate. Instead, we must develop access control systems that prevent unwanted behavior. Our access control systems should transparently determine user behavior on the system or systems in our networks. Access controls define what someone is authorized to do after he has been authenticated. Windows Server 2003 authorization is determined by the evaluation of assigned rights, permissions, and restrictions. This chapter introduces the authorization process and defines users, groups, rights, permissions, and restrictions that determine access on a stand-alone Windows Server 2003 server. Later chapters expand on this introduction to provide the detail behind complex object permission structures and the options available within a Windows Server 2003 domain.

How to Approach This Chapter

The access control systems available in Windows Server 2003 allow you to develop a granular system of control that enforces your organization's policy. You need to consider the access control mechanisms that are used, the rights and permissions that can be assigned, the types of security principals that can be granted to them, and the tools that are used to manage access. The time you spend exploring this information will depend on your experience with Windows.

- If you are new to Windows, then there is a wide range of information to learn and consider. Access control mechanisms are extremely important security controls, and you will want to dedicate a significant amount of time to understanding them. Your ability to understand advanced security paradigms such as Group Policy, IPSec, and certificate services will depend upon how well you grasp the basics developed here and in the next few chapters.

- If you are familiar with rights and permissions as used in Windows NT 4.0, you will find some subtle yet significant differences. There are new default groups and user rights. Areas to study include a new model of permission inheritance, the effective permissions model, and new tools for managing access control. You will also need time to adjust to object permissions as they apply to objects in the Active Directory.

- If you have been working with Windows 2000, you should be familiar with most of the processes, groups, user rights, and permissions in Windows Server 2003; however, you will find new groups, rights, and a few new concepts such as the ability of Windows Server 2003 domains to cache Universal Group membership and avoid the need to access Global Catalog Servers before authenticating users. Use the basic information presented here to ensure that your knowledge is complete.

Wherever you are in your understanding, take some time to ensure that you are aware of how these controls work in Windows Server 2003.

Windows Security Architecture and the Authorization Process

The Windows security architecture model is based on multiple inter-related components. You have already been introduced to one aspect of the design: the authentication component. In Figure 3-1, these areas of the architecture are circled and labeled. Authentication is the first hur-dle a potential system user must pass. After logging on, the user's ability to do anything depends on the evaluation done by the Security Refer-ence Monitor (SRM). The SRM resolves each request the user makes for access by comparing the request to his rights on the system and/or the permissions that he has been granted on the resource. If you are charged with assigning rights and permissions on systems, your first obli-gation is to understand how this process works.

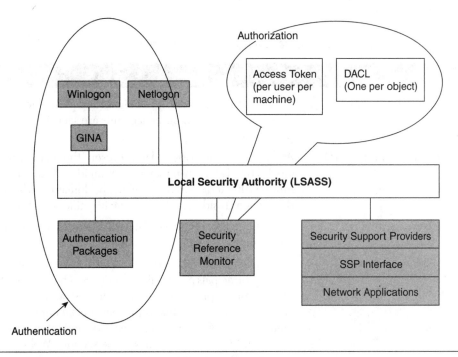

Figure 3-1 Windows security architecture.

WARNING:
Exceptions to the Account Required for Access Rule
The Windows security architecture is based on the rule that an account is required for access. A prospective user of a system must first have a valid account and password or other credentials to authenticate, and then she must have the rights and permissions assigned to do what she wants, such as reading a file or running a program. However, there is an exception to this rule that must be managed. This exception is the ability to access certain resources and obtain system information without using a valid account and password. This weakness can be mitigated and is less pronounced in Windows Server 2003 than in earlier versions of Windows. More information is provided in the section "Anonymous Access" later in this chapter.

The components that play a part in authorization are defined in Table 3-1.

Table 3-1   Components That Have a Role in Authorization

Component	Description
Security Principals	Accounts that can be assigned rights and permissions. User, group, and computer accounts are security principals.
Security identifier (SID)	A character string assigned to represent the security principal. The SID has two major parts: an identification number that indicates the machine or domain in which the account resides, and a Relative identifier or RID.
Relative identifiers	The unique part of the SID that enables it to represent the account.
Well-known SIDs	Security identifiers that contain RIDs that represent security principals common to Windows. The RID 500, for example, represents the local Administrator account, and well-known SIDs that represent special implicit identities such as anonymous, network, and interactive also exist. More information is in the section "Well-Known SIDs."

Component	Description
Local Security Authority (LSA)	The component that controls user logon and access permission. It is made up of user mode services, the Local Security Authority Subsystem (LSASS), Winlogon, and other kernel mode components. The local security authority can also be thought of as the database of password rules, system policies, and trust accounts for the computer.
Local Security Authority Subsystem (LSASS)	Hosts the Kerberos KDC on a domain controller, the NTLM security support provider, the Security Account Manager (SAM), Netlogon, IPSec, and Protected Storage.
Security Support Providers (SSP)	These are protocols such as Kerberos, NTLM, Digest, Schannel, basic authentication (Clear text password authentication), and Passport support. SSPs manage credentials, determine access, protect data, and secure client-server communications.
Winlogon	Obtains credentials from users interactively.
Netlogon	Obtains credentials over the network.
Security Support Provider Interface (SSPI)	Provides the interface between the SSPs and the application processes (IPSec, CIFS/SMB, LDAP, and so on).
Security Reference Monitor (SRM)	The arbitrator of access on the system. The SRM examines SIDs in the access token and security descriptors placed in an ACL on an object to determine whether requested access should occur.
Security Descriptors	Data structures that contain the discretionary access control list and system access control list for an object.
Discretionary Access Control Lists (DACLs)	Sometimes referred to as access control lists (ACLs), these are linked to objects. The DACL provides information including the security principals that have explicit permission to access the objects and those that are explicitly denied. This information is included in Access Control Entities and is used during authorization.
System Access Control List (SACL)	Contains information that specifies the type of audit records that should be recorded during access attempts. The information is contained in ACEs, which contain the SID of the security principal and the type of audit record that should be produced if the SID is used to access the object.

Table 3-1 Components That Have a Role in Authorization Continued

Component	Description
Access Control Entities (ACEs)	Contains a user or group SID, a permission (such as read or write), and the Allow or Deny designation. Figure 3-2 displays the Permission page of the Advanced Security settings property page. The first three columns—type, name, and permission—represent the ACE. The ACEs of an SACL are sometimes referred to as audit control entries and are composed of a user or group SID, the type of access (read, write, and so on) that should be recorded, and whether or not the access was successful.
Access Token	Built by the LSASS when a user logs on. It contains the user's SID, the SIDs for any groups of which the user is a member, and security policy settings, including the rights assigned to the user. The access token is built on the local machine when the user logs on. Another access token is built when the user attempts to access a network resource. During authentication, the list of information necessary to build an access token is collected and stored in the authentication material produced. When Kerberos is utilized for network authentication, the SIDs and other authorization information are stored in the authorization field of the TGT and session tickets. NTLM authentication returns this information when the user is authenticated at logon and when a server confirms a user's credentials after the user requests access. Access tokens are built for each unique computer on which the user requests access. Access tokens do not traverse the network. After an access token is created, it is attached to every process that the user runs so that the process has it available when it needs to request access to resources or exercise a right.

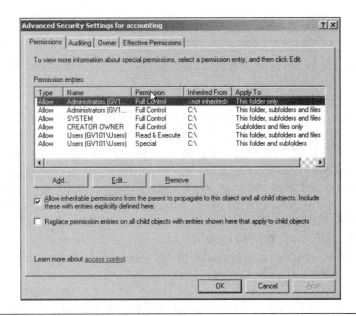

Figure 3-2   The Advanced Permissions page.

In spite of the large number of components, the access control process can be easily explained by focusing on four components: SIDs, access control lists (ACLs), access tokens, and the SRM. A more complex explanation with examples is provided in the section "The Access Control Process" and in Chapter 5, "Controlling Access to Data." Following are the basic steps that occur:

1. An access token is created for each logged on user. The access token consists of the user's SID, the SIDs of all of the groups she is a member of, and the rights she has on the specific machine.
2. Each resource has an ACL. Within the ACL, ACEs detail who can do what with this resource. Each ACE includes a SID.
3. A logged on user makes a request to access an object (read a file, run a program, and so on).
4. The SRM compares the user's access token information and the ACL on the object the user is attempting to access and determines if that user can do what she has asked to do. The request is either granted or denied.

Rights, Privileges, and Permissions

As you read about Windows access controls, you may find that the words "rights," "privileges," and "permissions" are used interchangeably. Don't get confused. One author often uses the term "privilege" when another will use the word "rights." Some discussions, especially those talking about Windows NT access controls, make the distinction that privileges are divided into Logon Rights and user privileges. The Windows 2000 and Windows Server 2003 interface, however, includes privileges and logon rights in the section of Local Policy called User Rights. Permissions are sometimes called "object permissions" and sometimes just "permissions." The real distinction is that rights and privileges are something that you can do system-wide, such as create users or shut down the server, and permissions are things you can do to an individual object, such as read a file.

In this book, user rights are those defined in the User Rights section of Local Policy and the implicit rights that default accounts are given. User rights are granted to users, groups, and computers. Permissions are the access controls defined on a specific object, whether it is a file, folder, printer, registry key, or Active Directory object. Rather than introduce a long list of rights and detail all of the object permissions that are available in Windows Server 2003, rights and permissions are defined as appropriate to the discussion. In this chapter, those rights that impact the ability of a user to log on and those that broadly restrict access will be detailed. Whenever implementing modifications to user rights, best practices advise doing so by using security groups, not individual user accounts.

Implicit Rights

The built-in accounts, which are created during Windows Server 2003 installation, and accounts created when an application or service is installed are granted a set of rights on the system. Some of these rights are defined in the User Rights Assignment section of Group Policy, and some of them can be removed. (Reducing the rights of a default account will reduce the ability of the account to function on the system.)

However, other user rights, such as the right of a member of the Administrators group to take ownership of any object, cannot be removed. Such rights are implicit rights.

Logon Rights

Even though logon rights are included in the broader category of user rights, it is convenient to group them for purposes of discussion. Logon rights are those rights that define a user's right to log on. A user may present valid credentials such as a user account name and password and therefore be authenticated but still be denied access to a specific system because the user has or doesn't have one of these logon rights. Ordinary users, for example, do not have authority to log on to a Windows Server 2003 domain controller from the console, while members of the Administrators group, members of other administrative groups, and those explicitly assigned this right do.

Allow Logon Locally

The `Log on Locally` right allows the user to start an interactive session. An interactive session is initiated by entering credentials at the console, remotely by using Terminal Services, or possibly by using web-based applications. Terminal Services interactive sessions, however, should be controlled through the two logon rights: `Allow Logon Through Terminal Services` and `Deny Logon Through Terminal Services`. If you use those two rights, you do not need to assign the terminal services users the `Allow Logon Locally` right. If you give terminal services users the `Allow Logon Locally` right, you also allow them to use the console of the terminal services computer, which presents a security risk.

On a domain controller (DC) and servers, you should restrict this right to Administrators, Backup Operators, and Server Operators. Alternatively, in areas of high risk or in large enterprise environments, you may want to consider limiting this right to a subset of administrators, or limiting this right on specific servers or groups of servers to different subsets of administrators.

If users are denied logon using one of the `Deny` logon rights, those rights supersede the `Allow` logon rights—the user will not be able to log on.

Allow Logon Through Terminal Services

The `Terminal Services` logon right allows the user to use a Remote Desktop connection to log on. Users in the Remote Desktop Users group will also be able to log on using a Remote Desktop connection; it is not necessary to explicitly give them this right. On a domain controller, you should only grant this right to Administrators. If a computer is not running Terminal Services in application mode, do not assign this right, and do not assign membership in the Remote Desktop Users group to anyone who does not need it to perform remote administration. If a server is providing application mode terminal services, only provide membership in the Remote Desktop Users group to those who should have it.

Deny Logon as a Batch Job

The Logon as a Batch Job right is needed to schedule jobs run by the Task Scheduler, a batch-queue facility. This right might be used to launch denial of service (DoS) attacks or to run malicious programs. Best practices are to at least deny this right to the local Guest account. Only administrators tasked with scheduling jobs to run should have the right to log on as a batch job.

Deny Logon as a Service

An account used to run a service requires the Logon as a Service right. Accounts given this right could be used to launch Trojans and other malicious programs as services. Use this right to prevent accounts from logging on as a service.

Deny Log on Locally

Users will not be allowed to log on using an interactive session.

Deny Logon Through Terminal Services

Users are not permitted to establish an inbound terminal server connection. This includes denying the ability to make a Remote Desktop connection.

Log On as a Batch Job

The user can log on using a batch-queue facility such as Task Scheduler. This right is required for accounts used as the identity of DCOM servers and COM+ applications. By default, the system manages this right. If an administrator schedules a job to run under another account or uses DCOM configuration or the Component Services management console for assigning user account as identity of DCOM server/COM + applications, that account is given this right automatically by the system. If you give this right to accounts (manage this right via domain-based group policies, for example), you will not be able to allow the system to manage it, and you should ensure that the right is given to the Local Service account. On an IIS 6.0 server, the IUSR_computername and IWAM_computername accounts should have this right. (If they do not, they will not be able to run some necessary COM objects.)

Log On as a Service

The account can log on as a service. The Local System, Local Service, and Network Service accounts have this right. If user accounts are used as service accounts, they must be given this right.

User Rights

Additional rights define specific access to the system. Rights that only make sense in the context of a domain controller are discussed in Chapter 7, "Active Directory's Role in Domain Security."

Access This Computer from the Network

This right allows connections to a computer from the network. Connections made using protocols such as SMB, CIFS, NetBIOS, and COM+ require this right. Although it is possible to remove this right by changing its status to Not Defined, doing so prevents necessary connections and malicious ones. For example, removing this right on a domain controller will prevent the DC from being used for logon and will therefore hamper access to network resources. You can, however, change the defaults and restrict access to administrators and users for Domain Controllers, and you can restrict access to specific groups on servers. For example, if a file server should only be used by members of the Human Resources department, you could create a custom group that has as members all Human Resources department members. Then you could remove authenticated users from this right and add administrators and Human Resource groups.

NOTE: Lock Down Versus Lock Out

In their eagerness to lock down systems, administrators new to Windows may attempt to restrict the `Access this computer from the network` right. They may define it too narrowly. This was the case at a junior college I visited recently. They had removed all groups except the Administrators group from this right, and then they wondered why users could not remotely access resources. When they gave the right back to the groups, the problem was solved.

Act as Part of the Operating System

The operating system has access to every user's information and can perform any task that an individual user can. Assigning this right to a user allows the user to do anything the operating system can. He will be able to impersonate any user without explicit permission or to ask that additional explicit rights be added to the access token used by some process they are running. It is also possible that the user might create a token to which no identity is attached—thus effectively hampering any auditing or forensics. You might, for example, be able to tell that something did take place but not be able to determine who performed the action. In essence, a user who has this right can take over the system and leave no evidence of what he has done with it. This is not a situation that you want to have. The LocalSystem account has this right by default, and it is recommended best practice that if the right is required by a service account, you assign the Local System account to that service for logon instead of creating a new account and granting it that right.

Adjust Memory Quotas for a Process

This right determines who can change the maximum memory that a process can consume. This right can be used in application tuning, but if misused, it can result in a Denial of Service (DoS) attack. If a user reduces the amount of memory available to business-critical applications, he might cause them to cease responding. On the other hand, increasing the memory available to other operations might also have a similar impact. This right may be required by some service accounts, such as the service account used by the cluster service. By default, only administrators and the Network and Local Service group have this right. You may want to further restrict this right only to administrators who may need it to perform their job, such as those in charge of the Active Directory and its infrastructure, and those managing database management systems.

Backup Files and Directories

This right determines which users can bypass file, directory, registry, and other object permissions for the purpose of backing up the system. This right is only usable by applications, such as the native NTBACKUP.exe program, that use the NTFS backup application programming interface (API). It does not allow the user to read the file by using an application such as Word or a program that does not use the backup API, in this case. When the user uses these other techniques to access the file, normal permission settings apply. If the user has permission to read the file, he will be able to read it. If he does not, then he will not be able to. There is no way, however, to know if an authorized user is using this right to obtain a copy of files or is just making an authorized backup. This right does provide the bypass traverse checking right; however, this is the default access control status for all users. If the bypass traverse checking right is removed but is given to some users, administrators should understand that this right also grants bypass traverse. By default, Administrators and Backup Operators groups have this right.

Bypass Traverse Checking

Bypass traverse checking allows a user to traverse directory trees even if the user does not have permissions on the directory. The user cannot list the contents of the directory, but if he has permissions to access a file within a directory, he may programmatically access the file, even if he has no permission on the folder that the file lies within. In Figure 3-3, user Joe has read access to the file Document 1 but does not have permission to the Folder1 folder within which the file resides. Joe cannot use Windows Explorer to browse to the file and open it; however, he can use a program that identifies the path of the file. By default, all users of Windows systems have this right. If you remove this right, you may break applications. (Many Windows applications, including the operating system, are designed on the premise that everyone has this right.)

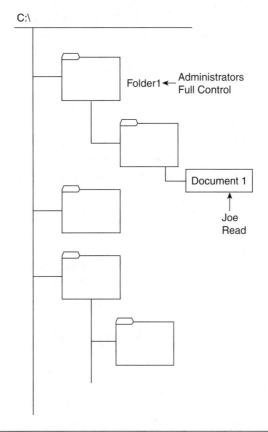

Figure 3-3 Visualizing Bypass traverse checking.

Change the System Time

This right determines which users and groups can change the time and date on the internal clock of the computer. If a user can change the time, he can make the time on events in the event log appear to be different from what they really are and then can create and modify timestamps on files and folders. Users may also be unable to authenticate because Kerberos is time-sensitive. However, automatic time synchronization in a domain may mitigate this effect. Nevertheless, event time is critical to auditing, and being able to demonstrate that a user might have modified it may be sufficient to establish doubt that your audit trail is accurate—an accused perpetrator may be proven innocent. It's also important to think of the impact here if the Time service itself were manipulated, either by turning it off or by pointing it to an inaccurate timeserver.

Create a Page File

This right determines who can create and change the size of a page file. The page file is used to temporarily store system and user data. Even a system with a very large memory requires a page file. The operating system will create a page file at boot if one does not exist. With this right, however, a user can change the location and size of the page file and can create additional page files on different drives. User management of page files can be done from the Systems applet in the Control Panel. A user might maliciously or accidentally use this right to create a too-small page file that might result in system instability. By default, only administrators have this right.

Create a Token Object

This right determines an account that a process can use to create a token. Tokens are used to obtain access to local resources. A user's rights are determined by inspecting the access token attached to processes she is running on the system. The token is created by the operating system when the user logs on to a Windows computer or accesses it over the network. A user with this right could change another user's rights or grant him access to resources on the computer by making it appear as if he had membership in a group given that access. By default, this user right is not assigned, and it should not be. If a process requires this right, have the service log on using the local system account.

Create Global Objects

Global objects are those that are available to all sessions running on the system. If a user can create a global object, he may impact other processing, including causing processes to fail or causing data corruption. Users do not need this right to create objects for use in their own sessions.

Create Permanent Shared Objects

Permanent shared objects are things like shared printers, folders, and other objects in the directory. This right is not assigned by default and should not be assigned. The local system account has this right. Administrators will be able to create, modify, and delete shared folders and printers.

Debug Programs

This right gives the user the right to attach a debugger to a process and therefore debug programs. If a user with this right uses specific attack code, she can obtain password hashes and other security information. By default, only administrators have this right. You can further restrict this right by removing the Administrators group. Debugging should be done on test systems, not production systems. However, should the need arise, an administrator can temporarily be granted this right. Be aware, however, that some software usage requires this right, such as the implementation of some Microsoft patches.

Deny Access to This Computer from the Network

If an account can access a computer over the network, it may be able to obtain information, such as user account lists, or connect to shares that are not restricted. Denying that right by using this user right can provide another layer of protection. Deny this right to the ANONYMOUS LOGON, the built-in local Administrator account, the local Guest account, and those service accounts that do not require access over the network to this computer.

Force Shutdown from a Remote System

This right allows a user to remotely shut down a system. This right should be restricted to the Administrators group.

Generate Security Audits

This right gives a process the right to put records in the audit log. An attacker could use this right to write to the log events that did not happen. Depending on the settings in the audit log, an attacker with this right could fill the log and create a DoS condition. The LocalService and NetworkService groups should have this right assigned.

Increase Scheduling Priority

This right allows a user to increase the base scheduling priority of a process. This right is not ordinarily required, but some programming tools may require it. A user with this right could elevate the scheduling priority of a process to real time and therefore prevent other processes from functioning normally, thereby causing a DoS attack.

Load and Unload Device Drivers

This right determines who can dynamically load and unload device drivers. Because device drivers run as privileged code (they run in the kernel), a user with this right can inadvertently or maliciously load a Trojan or other malicious code that is purported to be a device driver. This right, plus membership in the Administrators or Power Users group, is required before you can load a new driver for local printers or manage a printer. (This requirement for both membership and user right is new to XP and Windows Server 2003.)

Lock Pages in Memory

Most system and user data is paged in and out of memory as necessary. However, some system data is never paged. Use of this right allows a user to lock other pages in memory and thus may restrict the ability of the system to manage memory appropriately, resulting in performance problems or DoS attacks.

Manage Auditing and Security Log

This right allows a user to assign object access auditing for files, AD objects, and registry keys. The user can also view and clear the security log from the Event Viewer.

Modify Firmware Environmental Values

This right allows a user to configure firmware environmental variables either through a process or through System Properties. Abuse of this right could cause the system to fail, resulting in a DoS attack.

Perform Volume Maintenance Tasks

This right allows a non-administrator to manage disks. Abuse of this right might mean the user could delete a volume, resulting in loss of data or a DoS attack.

Profile Single Process

This right allows a user to observe the performance data of an application. An attacker might use this information to determine which processes are running on the system and therefore choose specific attack methods. A user might also identify countermeasures, such as intrusion detection systems or anti-virus products, that might be running and use this information to avoid detection by attempting to disable these systems or performing attacks that cannot be detected by them. This right is not necessary to run the Performance Monitor snap-in. It is required if the System Monitor is managed by Windows Management Instrumentation (WMI).

Profile System Performance

This right allows a user to sample system performance. The attacker might learn information that would assist him in an attack. This right is not needed to run the Performance Monitor snap. It is required if the System Monitor is managed by WMI.

Remove Computer from Docking Station

This right is only required to remove a computer from the docking station by selecting the Eject PC choice from the Start menu. The computer can be removed without this right if the system is shut off or if the Windows system has not booted. Also, there is nothing to prevent a thief from also stealing the docking station. Users of portable systems with docking stations should have this right so they do not have to shut systems down to remove them from the docking station. This right is, in most cases, irrelevant to Windows Server 2003 because servers are not run on portable laptop computers.

Replace a Process Level Token

This right allows a parent process to replace the token used by a child process. An attacker with this right and the Change Memory Quota Process right could launch processes as other users and even hide what he is doing on the system. Only the Local Service and the Network Service groups need to have this right.

Restore Files and Directories

A user with this right can restore files and set any valid users as owners of objects. An attacker could use this to overwrite current data with old data. The current data would therefore be lost.

Shut Down the System

This right allows a user to shut down the local system. Restrict this right on servers and especially on domain controllers. Shutting down critical systems can mean a DoS attack.

Synchronize Directory Service Data

This right allows a process to read all objects and properties in the directory, regardless of protection on the objects and properties. It is required to use LDAP directory synchronization services. Only domain controllers should be able to synchronize directory service data. The synchronization process runs in the context of the Systems account, and it has this right. An attacker with this right could view sensitive data, such as employee phone numbers or addresses, or information that might allow him to mount a successful attack.

Take Ownership of Files or Directories

This right allows a user to take ownership of any securable object in the system, regardless of the permissions on that object. He could then give himself the necessary rights to view, change, or delete the objects.

WARNING:
Protect Systems from Power Users Group Elevation of Privilege Attack
Membership in the Power Users group is often granted to users who need privileges beyond ordinary users but who do not require full administrative privileges. However, because of the rights granted to power users, a malicious user with membership in this group might be able to elevate their privileges to that of administrator. Power users can install programs and dlls that might elevate their privileges or add them to the Administrators group. Although the Power Users group does not have the right to run such a program, if they could trick an administrator to run the program, the power users would receive the rights or membership granted by the program. The only way to prevent this possible elevation of privilege is not to assign membership in the Power Users group.

Adding and Removing Predefined User Rights

User rights determine what a user can do on an entire system. Object permissions define what a user can do with a specific object or a collection of objects; rights operate at a broader level. Rights are assigned by adding a user account or a group account to the User Rights section of the Local Security Policy of a standalone server. If the server is joined to a domain, then user rights can be defined through the use of Group Policy.

Complete the following steps to add local user rights. You can also remove a user or group by following this procedure:

1. Open the `Administrative Tool, Local Security Policy` console.
2. Expand the `Local Policies` node and select `User Rights Assignments`.
3. In the detail pane, double-click the right you want to modify. To add a user or group, click the `Add User Or Group` button.
4. To remove a user or group, select the user or group and click the `Remove` button.
5. When adding users or groups, use the object picker from the `Select Users Or Groups` dialog box, as shown in Figure 3-4, to select users or groups.
6. Click `OK` to close the rights dialog box.

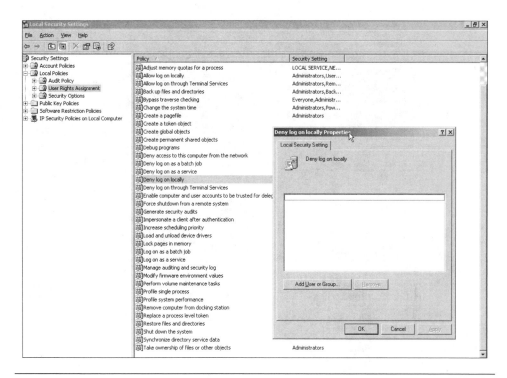

Figure 3-4   The Select Users or Groups dialog box.

Many operations require the use of the object picker to select users or groups. To do so, use one of the following techniques:

- Type the name in the `Enter the Object Name to Select` text box and then click `Check Names` to verify that the name exists as an object.
- Click `Advanced` and then click `Find Now` if you are unsure of the name. As illustrated in Figure 3-5, this action displays a list of users and groups on this computer. Select the accounts to be added.

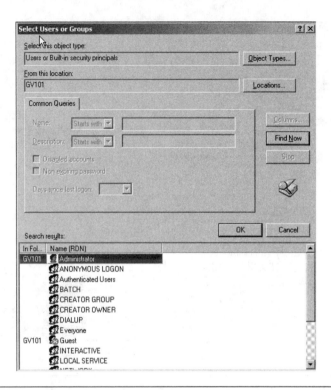

Figure 3-5   The Select Users or Groups dialog box with search results.

Recommendations for Lockdown

The default settings for user rights are reasonable. However, Microsoft recommends several modifications to user rights in the document "Threats and Countermeasures: Security Settings in Windows Server 2003 and Windows XP." Table 3-2 lists these changes, including an abuse potential rating and the impact of making the recommended change. The impact of making a change should always be considered. The operating system manufacturer should not be allowed to determine security settings. Instead, organizations should do a risk assessment and modify security settings to mitigate that risk. However, even if a change would have a severe impact, you may want to consider it if the security risk is large enough.

Table 3-2 Recommended User Rights Modifications

Right	Abuse Potential	Recommended Setting or Change	Impact of Change
Access this computer from the network	Low to moderate. May have higher impact where systems are upgraded from systems with loose folder share access controls.	Assign to users who need access.	Unintended Dos. Prevent authorized users from logon and access of network resources.
Add workstations to the domain	Moderate	Assign only to those authorized.	If you remove authenticated users will not be able to join their computers to the domain.
Adjust memory quotas for a process	Moderate	Assign only to administrators in charge of databases or directory infrastructure.	Should have little impact because it is not widely assigned or needed by default.
Allow to log on locally	Moderate to severe	Assign on DCs only to administrators and on servers only to those necessary, such as backup operators and power users. However, by default, even users have this access. The Users group should be removed and should not be allowed to log on locally to servers. Also question the right of power users to log on to servers because power users can install applications and thus might install an application that adds them to the Administrators group, thus successfully performing an elevation of privilege attack.	May restrict ability of some to do the job.

Table 3-2   Recommended User Rights Modifications Continued

Right	Abuse Potential	Recommended Setting or Change	Impact of Change
Allow logon through terminal services	Moderate to severe	Assign only to administrators who need to administer servers using this service.	May restrict ability of some to do job.
Change the system time	Severe	Assign only to members of the administrative team who need it.	None to little; default is restricted to administrators and server operators.
Debug programs	Severe	Remove all groups. Do not assign.	No one can debug programs, but not usually needed.
Deny access to this computer from the network	Moderate to severe	Assign to ANONYMOUS LOGON, Administrator account, Guest account, Support_388945a0.	Could prevent some required access.
Deny logon as a batch job	Moderate	Assign to Support_388945a0.	Could prevent use of scripts designed to provide support.
Deny logon locally	Moderate	Assign to Support_388945a0.	None; not necessary for this account to be used interactively.
Deny logon through terminal services	Moderate	Assign to built-in local Administrator account and all service accounts.	Could prevent remote administration support.
Force shutdown from a remote system	Moderate to severe	Assign only to administrators.	Removing server operator could limit administrative roles.

Right	Abuse Potential	Recommended Setting or Change	Impact of Change
Load and unload device drivers	Moderate to severe	Limit assignment to Administrators group.	Removing print operators limits administrative roles.
Profile single process	Moderate to severe	Limit assignment to Administrators group.	Removing power users could prevent administrative role.
Remove computer from docking station	Low	Assign as necessary.	Little.
Restore files and directories	Moderate to severe	Assign only to Administrators group.	Removing backup operators may limit administrative role.
Shut down system	Moderate to severe	Assign only to administrator and backup operators on member servers and administrators on domain controllers.	Can restrict administrative roles.

Table 3-3 lists Microsoft recommendations that are implemented by default.

Table 3-3   Microsoft Recommendations That Are Implemented by Default

User Right	Abuse Potential	Recommended Setting
Act as part of the operating system	Extreme	Do not assign.
Backup files and directories	Moderate	Limit to those necessary: backup operators and administrators.
Bypass traverse checking	Low	Leave at default.
Create a page file	Moderate	Restrict to administrators.

Table 3-3 Microsoft Recommendations That Are Implemented by Default Continued

User Right	Abuse Potential	Recommended Setting
Create a token object	Severe	Do not assign.
Create global objects	Moderate to severe	Restrict to local administrators and service groups.
Create permanent shared objects	Moderate to severe	Do not assign.
Deny logon as a service	Moderate to severe	Do not assign.
Generate security audits	Severe	Limit to local service and network service.
Increase scheduling priority	Moderate to severe	Limit to Administrators group.
Lock pages in memory	Moderate to severe	Do not assign.
Log on as batch job	Moderate to severe	Allow system to manage.
Log on as a service	Severe	Restrict to Network Service group.
Manage auditing and security log	Severe	Restrict to Administrators group.
Modify firmware environmental values	Moderate to severe	Restrict to Administrators group.
Perform volume maintenance tasks	Moderate to severe	Restrict to Administrators group.
Profile system performance	Moderate to severe	Restrict to Administrators.
Synchronize directory service data	Moderate to severe	No accounts should have this right.
Take ownership of files or other objects	Severe	Restrict to Administrators group.

Going Beyond Existing User Rights

Network administrators often ask me how they might further extend the use of user rights. Administrators ask how they can give some users the ability to perform some tasks that only an administrator can perform. They reason (correctly) that Help Desk personnel ought to be able to reset passwords without becoming administrators on computers or in domains. This specific right is not defined in the user rights section of group policy and cannot be granted. In a Windows Server 2003 domain, Active Directory object permissions can be delegated. Instructions on how to use the Delegation of Control Wizard can be found in Chapter 7, "Active Directory's Role in Domain Security."

The Delegation of Control Wizard is just a simple way to assign users permissions on Active Directory objects. These permissions may allow users to do something often only allowed to administrators or to combine unique permissions to assist you in assigning roles. The ability to reset the passwords of a collection of users, for example, can be delegated. The `reset password` permission on the user object in Active Directory can be granted to a user or group. An ordinary user who is granted the `reset password` permission can reset passwords, but only for those users to whom the permission has been given.

Best Practices for Assigning User Rights

Those new to Windows or new to thinking about Windows security often jump in and begin restricting user rights or granting user rights that sound as if they should be available to groups such as administrators. Do not follow that practice. Instead, make sure you understand the impact of user rights, especially how they may be combined either to deny access to those who require it or to allow access to those who should not require it. Review the default rights assigned to default groups and don't attempt to remove them until you know why it may or may not be a good idea. In addition, do the following:

- Assign user rights to groups, not to individual users.
- Leave rights at default assignments, or restrict them cautiously. A number of rights can prevent further administration of the domain.
- Test modifications on a test system.
- Use Deny rights to apply to subsets of groups already given Allow rights. Hence, deny specific accounts or groups where the Users group has the Allow rights.

- Do not deny the Everyone group a right. If you do, you have denied all users the right. You cannot deny Everyone and then "allow" some. You can, however, allow the group Everyone and then deny some.
- Use caution when removing rights on well-established domains. A number of rights may provide necessary administrative rights to legitimate valid users. Rashly removing them can result in the inability of administrative staff to perform their duty. Also don't rashly add rights to user groups. Do not provide rights to a larger number of individuals without good reason, and don't give too many rights to users who do not need them.

Using Object Permissions to Control Access

Object permissions determine the type of access that is granted to an object or an object property. Objects are files, folders, registry keys, printers, and Active Directory objects. The type of access granted is dependent on the type of object. File permissions, for example, include permissions such as `read`, `write`, `execute`, and `delete`, while Active Directory object permissions might include things such as `Reset Password`, `Create Object`, or `Modify the Membership of a Group`. This chapter includes a general discussion about how permissions are defined and how inheritance affects permissions, and it includes an example of defining printer permissions.

Object permissions on Active Directory objects often sound like rights instead of permissions. They are, however, restricted to modifying properties in some area of the Active Directory, not on a specific computer. A detailed discussion on specific object permissions can be found in chapters dedicated to object types, such as Chapter 5 and Chapter 7.

Permission Basics

Who can assign object permissions? Administrators, object owners, and any user or group given the `Permission` right on an object can assign permissions. Users given object control over objects in the Active Directory can assign permissions on those objects.

In addition to explicit (those assigned directly on an object) object permissions, inherited permissions are also used to determine the effective permissions on an object. Inherited permissions are permissions that are not assigned directly to an object; instead, they are assigned to a parent object and passed on to their children. Inheritable permission can be blocked, so it may be quite confusing to attempt to figure out exactly what permissions are applied to an object. A child object is one that exists in a subcontainer. For example, files are child objects of folders, and subfolders are child objects of other folders. In the file system, all first-level folders are considered child folders of the root.

For example, file and folder permissions and Active Directory object permissions can be inherited from the object above them in the hierarchy. So a file in a subfolder of the volume root may inherit the permissions placed on the root. Figure 3-6 shows the C:\Accounting folder security property page. Notice that the permission boxes are shaded. This means that they are inherited permissions.

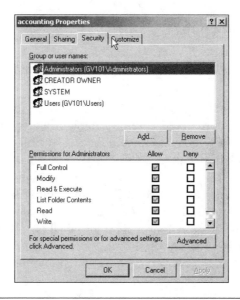

Figure 3-6   The accounting folder inherits its permissions from the drive root permissions.

Clicking the `Advanced` button on the Security page of an object's properties exposes the selection boxes that can enable or disable inheritance. In Figure 3-7, you can see that the check box is selected for `Allow Inherited Permissions for the parent to propagate to the object and all child objects. Include these with entries explicitly defined here.` This folder happens to be a top-level folder—that is, its only parent is the root of the drive. If the permissions on the root are changed, the permission on this folder also will change.

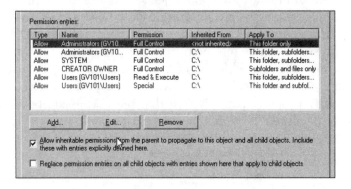

Figure 3-7   Selection of a check box controls inheritance on a folder.

On the other hand, the F:\WONT\system 32 folder in Figure 3-8 and Figure 3-9 is protected from permission inheritance. The check boxes are not shaded gray, and on the `Advanced` property page, the `Inheritance` check box is not selected. Instead, explicit permissions have been set. If root permissions are changed, permissions here will not change. This is an important concept. Because of inheritance, administration of permissions is simplified—you can set permissions once and be assured that the same permissions will be set on all objects below. However, you can also protect sensitive subfolders' permission sets; they will not be changed when the parent object permissions change.

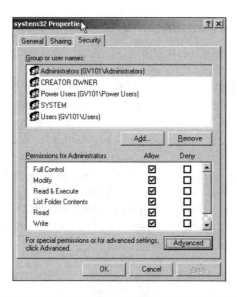

Figure 3-8   Folders can be protected from inheritance. Unshaded boxes mean that the permissions shown are not inherited but explicitly set on the object.

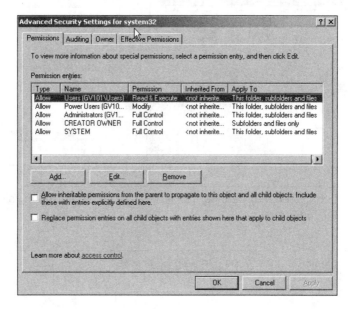

Figure 3-9   The Advanced property page will show you what permissions are inherited, and the Apply To column of the page shows if and when the current permissions will be inherited.

Combining Permissions

A folder or file can have both inherited and explicit settings. Figure 3-10 indicates that permissions on *myfolder* for Joe Smith are "not inherited." Figure 3-11 shows the special permissions page for the user Joe Smith of the *myfolder\temp* folder, indicating that he has been given the `Create Files/Write Data` permission on this folder. He has inherited the `Read` and `Execute` permissions from the *myfolder* folder. The effective permissions on any folder are calculated for any user by combining explicit and inherited permissions. You can see in Figure 3-12 the effective permissions on the *myfolder\temp* folder for the user Joe Smith. Note that the effective permissions are a combination of the permissions explicitly given Joe on the *temp* folder and those inherited from the *myfolder* folder.

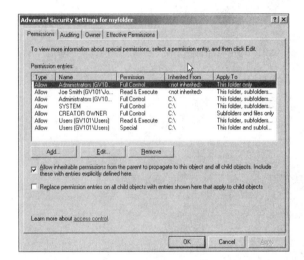
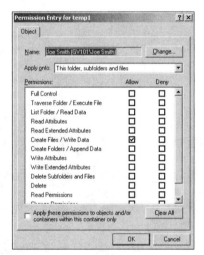

Figure 3-10   Permission may be inherited or, as is the case for the *myfolder* folder for Joe Smith, not.

Figure 3-11   Explicit permissions can also be granted.

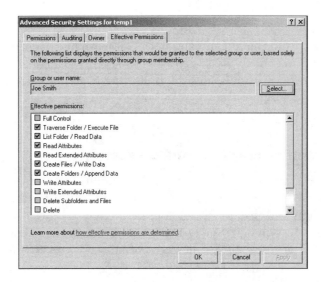

Figure 3-12   Effective permissions are the combination of inherited and explicit permissions.

Permissions can be directly configured on an object—instructions are provided in the chapters where each type of permission is discussed in detail. However, permissions on files, folders, registry keys, and service accounts can also be set in Group Policy and in security templates. This allows you to automate the setting of permissions across multiple machines.

Using these automated methods to apply permissions can be time-savers when large numbers of permissions must be applied to many machines. They are also useful in auditing; you can determine if permissions for a large number of files or registry keys are set the way they are supposed to be.

Best Practices for Assigning Object Permissions

Assigning object permissions requires careful planning to ensure that the access a user ultimately has is correct. Best practices for object permissions are as follows:

- Use deny permission to exclude a subset of a group that has allowed permissions or to exclude a special permission when full control has been granted.

- Use security templates.
- Avoid chaining default permissions on file system objects.
- Don't deny the Everyone group access to an object.
- Apply permissions high in the tree and use inheritance to propagate.

Printer Permissions and Ownership

A logical printer is the GUI representation of the physical device, and you can create as many as you want for each physical printer. Printer permissions and printer ownership are configured directly on the printer object. In Windows Server 2003, as in Windows 2000 and Windows NT, printer permissions are allowed or denied. Permissions are discussed in the next sections:

Print

Print documents; read permissions.

Manage Printer

Stop, pause, or start printing; delete an item from the printer queue; change the priority of print jobs; read and change permissions. In other words, this permission gives the owner complete control.

Manage Documents

Pause printing; delete an item from the printer queue.

To set printer permissions, follow these steps:

1. Open the Printers and Faxes console.
2. Right-click on the printer you want to manage and select `Prop-erties` from the shortcut menu.
3. Select the `Security` tab, as shown in Figure 3-13.

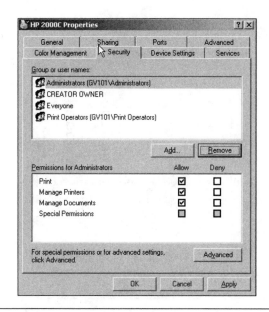

Figure 3-13   The Security tab of the printer object.

4. Add or remove a group using the Add or Remove buttons or select a group to assign permissions.

5. To assign permissions, select the permission from the Permissions box or click the Advanced button.

6. If you click the Advanced button:

   ■ Use the Apply Onto drop-down box to select This printer only, Documents only, or Printer and documents.

   ■ Select the user group, as shown in Figure 3-14. Click the Edit button and then select the desired permissions.

   ■ Click OK twice to return to the Security page.

7. Click OK to close the property pages.

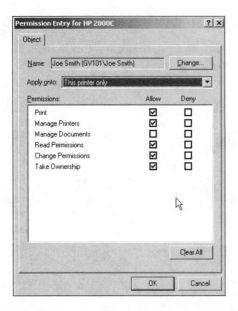

Figure 3-14   Additional "special" permissions are set from the Advanced properties page.

Making Choices and Restricting Permissions

The default permissions applied to printers may be okay in some environments. While printer access is not generally perceived to be an area for security concern, you need to evaluate the risk based on what the printer is used for and whether or not you believe the printer is accessible to a hostile environment.

Restrict Printer Access

If a printer is used to print checks, securities, or other documents with monetary value, it may be appropriate to restrict the ability to print to authorized personnel. Color printers and plotters and other printers that are expensive to operate are another class of devices to which access should be restricted. If these printers are expensive to operate, then it makes sense to restrict print access to reduce cost.

Modify Default Permissions

The CREATOR OWNER group (meaning the one who created the object and owns it) has, by default, the `read`, `manage documents`, and `change` permissions and takes `ownership` permission on documents only.

This is a reasonable setting because it allows the person sending a document to the printer to see the document in the queue and delete the document, pause, and restart printing of the document. They cannot manage documents that are not theirs. They cannot change the document's priority, either—that is, they cannot make their document print before another in the queue. However, users do not need this setting to print, so you could argue that they should not have it. In this case, a print operator takes responsibility for managing all documents.

The Everyone group has the right to print. This is fine in a trusted environment for generic document printers, but in an untrustworthy or hostile environment, it should be removed. However, you must ensure that all groups of users that do need to print have permission to do so.

Administrators, server operators, and print operators have the manage printer right. They can manage all documents, change priority, load new drivers, and so forth. In a restricted environment, create custom groups for classes of printers, assign these groups the right to manage printers, and remove the defaults. For example, just as you may not want all users to be able to print to the check printer, you may not want all administrators, server operators, and print operators to be able to manage the check printer.

Rights and Permissions Factoids

To evaluate rights and permissions, keep these facts in mind:

Rights may override permissions. You may have `Allow` permissions on a file, but if you do not have the right to access this computer from a network and cannot log on locally, you will not be able to access the file.

Explicit permissions take precedence over inherited permissions, even inherited `Deny` permissions. Inherited `Deny` permissions do not prevent access to an object if the object has an explicit permission entry.

While permissions applications, inheritance, and general practices are the same, each object type, file, folder, registry key, printer, and Active Directory object has differences.

Built-in groups represent administrative roles. However, some user rights assigned to these groups can be removed, and others can be added. Do not rely on your understanding of what a member in these groups can or cannot do. Check the Local Security Policy.

Build custom roles by following the model used for built-in roles. Create a group, assign the group rights and permissions, and add user accounts to the group.

Assign rights and permissions to groups, not individual accounts.

Computers also have rights, and access to resources can be managed by modifying these rights. For example, you can deny a computer access to another computer over the network.

Role-based access control is supported by creating and managing roles composed of user rights and object permission settings.

Rule-Based Versus Role-Based Access Control Systems

Computer access control systems can be defined according to the way that they are used. The two most often specified access control systems are rule-based access control and role-based access control. Rule-based access control requires that specific rules be written that determine who can access what. An example of rule-based access control is the Access Control Lists (ACLs) written for firewall and router configurations that allow or deny access to networks. A rule-based system for users would include a multitude of rules or statements that would indicate which files, printers, or other resources a specific user could use. Rules might state things such as "JohnP can read the chapter_5.txt file, MaryJ can read and write the Septaccount.txt file, and AndrewJ can configure TCP/IP." Rule-based access control is difficult to implement as a management control for large numbers of users.

NOTE: MAC and DAC

Another way of looking at access control is by specifying the implementation of rules using either Discretionary Access Control (DAC), where access to resources is determined by resource owners, or Mandatory Access Control, where access to resources is determined by matching one's assigned level to the level assigned to the resource. Windows systems natively use DACs.

Role-based access control is based on the assumption that people use computer systems to do a job. If you can translate the job needs into computer-speak, you have defined a role and can implement it on a computer. For example:

- The need to access a records room is translated into accessing a file server over the network.
- The need to issue a check in payment is translated into the ability to run a specific computer program.
- The need to access a group of documents is translated into granting file access permissions for the group of documents.

Implementing Role-Based Access Control in a Windows Server 2003 Network

A strict definition of role-based access control requires implementing the role by writing a script that assigns the rights and permissions needed by the role. Then, to give users the access they require, you administratively assign users to the role. While this method can be used in Windows Server 2003, role-based access control is more frequently implemented by using the following:

- *Application roles* are provided by software applications. Microsoft SQL Server, for example, defines server roles such as dbCreator (which can create databases) and Security Administrator (which can create and manage logins, and so forth) and database roles such as db_datawriter (which can change the database information) and db_reader (which can read information in the database). You can also define roles for a specific database by developing them in your SQL Server application. Another example is provided by Windows Server 2003 Certificate Services. Two Certificate Services roles are Certificate Manager and Certification Authority Administrator. The application-centric process is also facilitated in Windows Server 2003 by the use of the Authorization Manager, a new management console-based tool. Applications designed for the Authorization Manager allow Windows administrators to assign user accounts to roles. More details on the Authorization Manager can be found in Chapter 4, "Restricting Access to Software; Restricting Software's Access to Resources."
- *Operating system roles* are represented in Windows Server 2003, like its predecessors Windows NT and Windows 2000, by predefined user accounts and groups: Administrator, Server Operator, DNSAdmins, Domain Users, and so on. Operating system

roles are further defined in the section "Default Operating System User Roles." Each default Windows group has assigned rights and predefined object permissions. To assign an individual user to one of these roles, you simply make that person a group member.

- *Computer roles* represent the rights and permissions that define the computer role on the network. Examples of computer roles include a DNS server, a DHCP server, and a domain controller. In a Windows Server 2003 domain, you can manage and control these computers by developing specific sets of security controls for each computer role. Chapter 11, "Securing Infrastructure Roles," provides information on how to secure these roles. Chapter 13, "Implementing a Secure PKI," defines Certificate Services roles and additional methods for securing a Certification Authority.

- *Custom roles* are useful when the existing operating system roles may not be granular enough for your purposes. Perhaps you want a role, such as Help Desk Operators, that can reset users' passwords but that does not have full Administrator rights. Or perhaps applications that you need to run do not present defined roles for their use. For completeness, you can build additional roles either by creating custom groups or by writing applications that create their own roles.

Chaos Rules

There are other methods of managing access control for Windows systems. While doing a security review for a large enterprise, I found that access to systems and to resources was granted based on the last call to IT. In other words, if access to a resource was needed, a manager would call IT and ask for it. That was all that was necessary.

If someone found that he could not read a file, connect to a specific server, access systems remotely, or otherwise do something on the network, he simply requested the ability to do so. In most cases, his requests were granted without review. In a few cases, an ordinary user's request was ignored, but any management request was granted. Large numbers of ill-named (no idea what they were for) and ill-conceived groups existed, and there was no control over the rights and privileges granted to these groups. Some privileges and file access were also granted to individual accounts.

To be fair, in most cases, the owner of the resource was the one requesting access, and so the access was most likely granted to legitimate valid users.

However, because there was no real control over the process and no standard procedures for granting or applying permissions, there was really no good way to determine this. In addition, there was no reasonable way to remove access when an individual left the company or transferred to another job within the company.

Having no control, no approved policy or procedure, and no documentation that details what was done and by whose authority is not all that unusual.

Default Operating System User Roles

It is much easier to administer users on a system if the roles that a user may perform on the system are defined, and each user is provided membership in a role. It is easier because it reduces the number of different access definitions that must be managed and because it removes these definitions from the dynamics of employee changes. When roles are defined and used, it is easy to provide the required access to a new employee; he can simply be given that role. It is also simple to remove someone's access by removing him from that role. Auditors can also more easily determine if access is defined correctly (the right access is granted for each role) and assigned correctly (the right individuals are given the correct access). Finally, roles can be more easily modified (granted or denied access) because there are fewer of them.

In addition to user roles, computer roles can also be defined. Just as a user role defines the rights and permissions a user has on a system, computer roles define these things for computers.

Windows Server 2003 roles are defined by creating groups and assigning them user rights and adding them to the ACLs on objects. Default operating system user and computer roles exist. The following information further defines default user and computer roles:

- A few of these default roles are explicitly assigned to a user account, while most of them are defined by default groups.
- These users and groups have inherent rights.
- You can use these groups and users to assign administrative roles.
- Some default rights that these roles have can be removed or assigned to other users. Other default rights, such as the right for an administrator to take ownership, can be assigned to other users but cannot removed from the Administrator account.

- Some groups exist only after a Windows Server 2003 is promoted to domain controller or after a specific service is installed.

Before creating custom groups, examine the default groups to determine if they fit the required need. However, before using default groups, review the rights and permissions granted to group members. Best practices dictate that you assign only the rights and permissions necessary for a user to fulfill her duties. If a default group gives her more power than she needs, create a custom group and use that instead. Follow the model provided by default groups—custom groups do not have to exist in every domain in the forest, and they do not have to exist on every computer in the domain if they are local groups.

Default User Accounts

Default user accounts on a Windows Server 2003 server are as follows:

- The Administrator account is the most powerful user accessible account on the system.
- The Guest account is the least privileged account on the system. If enabled, the guess account can be used by anyone to log on to the server. Authorized users whose accounts are locked out but not disabled could also use it. By default, this account is disabled.

System User Accounts

In addition to default user accounts and built-in groups, three system user accounts are provided that can be used as logon accounts for services. These accounts are not listed in the Users list in the Computer Management console, but, like implicit groups, they are available for assignment as the logon account for a service. Two of them, Network Service and Local Service, are accounts with limited system access. The three system user accounts are as follows:

- The Network Service account has limited access to the local computer and access rights to the network using the computer account for authorization. If assigned as the logon account for a service, you can restrict its access to other network resources by adding the computer account to the right `Deny Access to this computer from the network` on the remote computer.

■ The Local Service account has limited access to the local computer and can only access network resources that can be accessed anonymously.

■ The Local System account is a very powerful account. It can do anything the operating system can do with its own server processes. Do not use this account when selecting an account to use for service logon; however, if this account is assigned to an operating system service, do not change it.

TIP: Do Not Change Default Service Account Assignments
Many default Windows Server 2003 services use the more restrictive accounts. However, some use the Local System account. It is recommended that you not change the service accounts assigned to default services because you may cause them not to start, to stop, to hang, or to otherwise become unstable. Likewise, if more limited accounts are assigned, do not replace them with the Local System account.

Groups

Managing large numbers of anything is difficult, which is why it is intuitive to classify similar objects and then work with the object definition instead of the individual. This is the only practical way to provide access control for complex systems. Even smaller institutions will benefit from an organized approach. This approach is possible in Windows Server 2003 by using built-in and custom groups. Instead of addressing each user's needs, define typical user roles in the organization and create a set of access rights and object permissions for each role. Create a user group to represent the role and then give that group the defined rights and object permission. Assign users to group memberships that represent the roles they have been assigned.

Group Types and Membership

Group types are the group roles that exist on the server. On a standalone server, a server that is not joined in a domain, all groups are local groups and can only give rights and privileges on the local server. Groups created on a standalone server or as local groups on a member server are also local groups. The local group account is stored in the local Security Account Manager (SAM). The following group types are found in Windows Server 2003:

- Default or built-in groups are those groups that exist on the server when it is installed.
- Service-related groups are those that are created when a service is added, such as the DNSProxy group, which is added when the DNS service is installed.
- Domain groups are groups such as Domain Admins and Enterprise Admins that are added when a server is promoted to domain controllers. They can contain domain accounts.
- Local groups are groups whose accounts lie in the local SAM of a server. They are local to that server.
- Universal groups are groups that can only be created in a forest and may contain accounts from any domain in the forest.
- Special identities or implicit groups are those groups that represent some activity. For example, the Network group is composed of all users who are connected to the computer over the network, while the Interactive group is the group composed of all users logged on at the console.

Group scope defines where a group may be granted access and what user and group types may be granted group membership. Group scope and group membership type can change based on the domain functional mode. The domain functional mode defines the operating system type allowed for domain controllers. More information on domain functional mode is available in Chapter 8, "Trust."

Built-In Groups on a Standalone Server

On a standalone server, the built-in group accounts divide the administrative role on the computer. Each group has its own assigned user rights. Table 3-4 lists and defines user groups.

Table 3-4 Built-In Groups on a Standalone Server

Group	Definition
Administrators	Assign user access rights and permissions to all objects. Has access to all aspects of the computer and all the data on it. Administrators can create new users and new groups. By default, the local Administrator account is a member of this group. When a server joins a domain, the Domain Admins group becomes a member of this group.
Backup Operators	Backs up and restores files on the server. Access this computer from the network, `Allow log on locally`, `Backup files`, `Bypass traverse checking`, `Restore Files and directories`, and `Shut down the system`. There are no default members to this group.
Guests	No default rights except the right to log on. If a member of this group is used for logon, a temporary profile is created. The profile is removed when the user logs off. The default member is the Guest account.
Network Configuration Operators	Can make changes to TCP/IP settings and renew and release TCP/IP address. There are no default members and no default user rights.
Performance Log Operators	Can manage log counters, logs, and alerts remotely and locally without being members of the Administrators group. They have no default user rights and no default members.
Performance Monitor Users	Can monitor performance counters on the server remotely and locally without needing to be members of the Administrators group. They have no default user rights and no default members.
Power Users	Create users. Modify and delete accounts they have created. Create local groups and add or remove users from these groups, Power Users, Users, and Guest default groups. Create shared resources and administer the ones they have created. They have the following user rights: `Access this computer from the network`, `Logon locally`, `Bypass traverse checking`, `Change the system time`, `Profile a single process`, `Remove the computer from the docking stations`, `Shut down the system`, `Run legacy applications` (that ordinary users often can't), `Install programs that don't install services` or `modify operating system files`, and `Customize some Control Panel items such as time, printers, power options`. They can also start and stop services.

Table 3-4   Built-In Groups on a Standalone Server Continued

Group	Definition
Print Operators	Manage printers and print queues (a list of documents waiting to be printed). They have no default user rights and no default members.
Remote Desktop Users	Can remotely log on to the server. These users can use the Remote Desktop console to connect to other servers. They have the default right to log on through terminal services.
Replicator	Supports replication functions. Should not be assigned to users, only to an account used for this purpose.
Users	Perform common tasks such as running applications, and using printers. Access this computer from the network. Bypass traverse checking. Authenticated users and interactive users become members of this group. When the computer joins a domain, the Domain Users group becomes a member of this group.

Implicit Groups

Implicit groups are those groups that are composed of users or computers that are performing some function on a system. A user becomes a member of one of these groups, not because he explicitly has his account entered in the group by an administrator, but because of his current activity. Many of these groups are present in all versions of Windows based on NT technologies, and their membership is defined the same. However, the Windows Server 2003 Everyone group no longer contains the anonymous user. In Windows Server 2003, however, while not recommended, it is possible to add the Anonymous user to the Everyone groups. Adding the Anonymous group to the Everyone group provides access that should not be given to an entity that has been able to access the computer without credentials. Implicit groups are defined in Table 3-5.

Table 3-5   Windows Server 2003 Implicit Groups

Group	Definition
INTERACTIVE	Users who are logged on from the console.
NETWORK	Users who are connected over the network.
REMOTE INTERACTIVE	Users who are using local logon but doing so over the network.
TERMINAL SERVICE USER	Those users who are logged on and using terminal services. When terminal services are used in administrative mode, users are not made members of this group. This group has no default user rights.
EVERYONE	All users who are logged on to this computer. (Anonymous users are not logged on, and in Windows Server 2003, they are not included by default.)
ANONYMOUS	Users who connect without using a valid username and password. These users' rights are severely restricted. They no longer have membership in the Everyone group (as they did in Windows 2000 and below). Therefore, access to resources and rights given to the Everyone group does not apply.

NOTE: EVERYONE Includes ANONYMOUS
Earlier versions of Windows included the EVERYONE group in the access token created for the ANONYMOUS logon. This created a security vulnerability because many folder, file, and other object permissions are granted to the group EVERYONE. Windows Server 2003 does not include the ANONYMOUS logon in the EVERYONE group and therefore reduces the attack surface. However, because some legacy application may require this setting, you can change it by using a Security Option or editing the registry. If you need to evaluate this setting, you can access it by viewing the registry value HKLM\SYSTEM\CurrentControlSet\Control\LSA EveryoneIncludesAnonymous. If this value is set to 0 (the default), the EVERYONE SID is not included in the ANONYMOUS access token. If the value is set to 1, it is.

Group Scope

Group scope determines where the group can be given authority and what type of membership it can have. On a single, standalone Windows Server 2003 server, all groups have local scope. That is, they can only be assigned user rights and access to local objects, and only user accounts that are local to the server can be added to these groups. A local user account on one computer cannot be given rights or granted access to objects on another computer. To access resources on a remote computer, a user needs an account on that remote computer.

When a Windows computer becomes a domain member, domain groups (groups that live in the domain partition of Active Directory) can be given access to member computer local resources and can be granted rights on the system. Additional group types are defined in an Active Directory environment. These domain and forest groups are granted access to resources within the forest by following explicit rules. If trust relationships are developed between forests, users and groups in one forest can be granted rights and access to resources in other forests. More information on Group scope can be found in Chapters 7 and 8.

Figure 3-15 shows the Locations dialog box reached from the `Security` tab on a folder of a standalone server. The `Security` tab is used to assign access to users and groups. You can only choose the local computer as the source for groups and users on a standalone server. If, however, the server is joined to a domain and the `Security` tab is reviewed, the `Locations` box can be changed to show the local server or the domain as the source for groups and users who may be granted access.

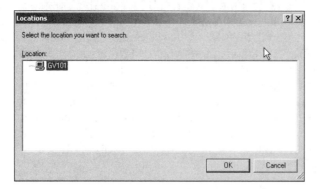

Figure 3-15   The only location that can be used to select groups or users on a standalone computer is the local database.

Managing Users and Groups

On a standalone server, users and groups are managed from the Computer Management console. Users and groups can be added, modified, and removed. Users can be granted group membership and can have their passwords reset, and user account properties can be modified.

User and Group Procedures

Performing modifications to users and groups is simple. Understanding when to add, remove, or edit groups and users is not. While it is important to know how to work with users and groups, it is more important that you understand how to use them properly.

Create a New Group

To create a new group, follow these steps:

1. Open the `Computer Management` console.
2. Expand the `Local Users and Groups` container.
3. Right-click on the `Group` container and select `New Group` from the shortcut menu.
4. Enter the name of the group in the `New Group` dialog box, as shown in Figure 3-16.

Figure 3-16   The New Group dialog box.

5. Enter a description.
6. If you want to add members to the group, click Add, as shown in Figure 3-17.

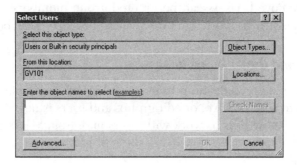

Figure 3-17   Use the Add button to add users to a group.

7. Click the Advanced button (to open the object picker), and then click Find Now.
8. Select usernames from the Search results window.
9. Repeat step 6 until all users have been added to the group, and then click OK to close the group.
10. Continue adding groups until you are done.
11. Click the Close button to stop.

Adding a New User

To add a new user, follow these steps:

1. Open the Computer Management console (Start, Administrative Tools, Computer Management).
2. Expand the Local Users and Groups container.
3. Right-click on the Users container and select New User from the shortcut menu.
4. Enter the new username, a full name for the user, and a description.
5. Enter a password and confirm the password by entering it a second time. The password entry will be represented by dots, as shown in Figure 3-18.

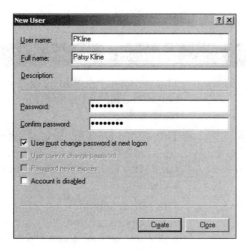

Figure 3-18   A password must be entered at the time of account creation.

6. Select the appropriate check boxes to define the initial account configuration, as displayed in Figure 3-19. This information is defined in Table 3-6.
7. Click OK to create the new account.
8. Repeat steps 4 through 7 to create multiple accounts.
9. Click the Close button to stop creating accounts and then click OK to close the dialog box.

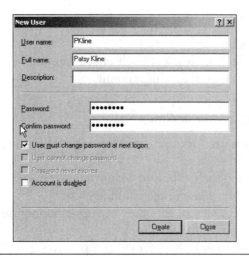

Figure 3-19   New User account information.

Table 3-6 Account Information

Selection	Definitions
User Must Change Password at Next Logon	This setting is selected by default. The user can logon but will be immediately prompted to change his password.
User Cannot Change Password	This setting is useful for controlling user accounts that are used by service accounts. It is available when the User Must Change Password at Next Logon check box is cleared.
Password Never Expires	This setting should be used for a user account that is also a service account. Set the password policy to expire for the user account password, but manually reset the service account password according to your own schedule. This setting is available when the User Must Change Password at Next Logon check box is cleared.
Account Is Disabled	This setting should be selected when setting up new accounts that will not be used immediately.

To change account information, make changes to the General page of the user account property pages.

1. Double-click on the user account to open the account property pages.
2. Select or deselect each check box until the correct properties are created for this account.

Removing a User or Group

To remove a user or group, complete the following steps:

1. Open the Computer Management console and expand the Users and Groups container.
2. Select the User and Group container to show the users or groups in the details pane.
3. Right-click the user or group account in the details pane and choose Delete from the shortcut menu.

Restricting and Provisioning a User Account Using a Logon Script

A logon script can be written to further restrict a user's actions, to configure registry settings on the computer, or to provide additional access by mapping drives or printers. When properly configured, the logon script will run when a user logs on to a computer using a local account. (When a domain account is used, the local account logon script does not run because there is no association with the local account. Local and domain accounts are separate entities.) To utilize logon scripts, configure the user's profile and logon script location on the server.

1. Double-click on the user account in the `Computer Management` console.
2. Select the `Profiles` tab.
3. In the home folder box, enter the path for the folder that will contain the script.
4. In the Login script path box, enter the name of the script.

In a domain, logon scripts must be stored in the shared NETLOGON folder or in subfolders beneath that share. When logon scripts are implemented using GPOs, the scripts are stored in the NETLOGON share located at Windows\SYSVOL\sysvol*domainname*\SCRIPTS.

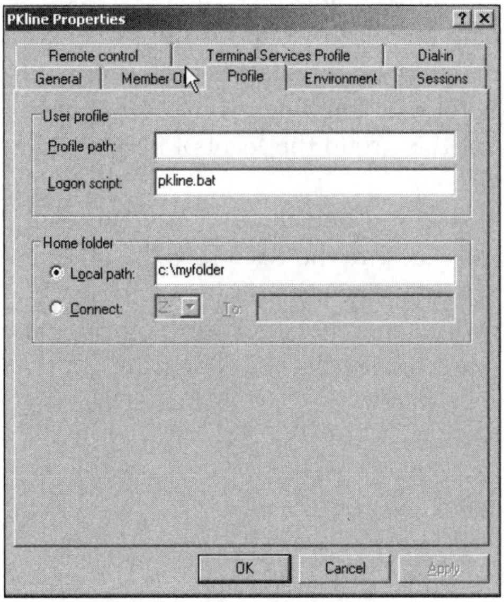

Figure 3-20   The Profile tab can be used to indicate a location for logon scripts.

Creating Custom Roles

The default roles available on Windows Server 2003 will not fulfill the needs of the organization to match access to the role a user plays. To simplify the management of computer resources and create custom roles, use these steps:

1. Determine which custom roles are necessary. Custom roles may be administrative, such as a Help Desk role to assist in managing computers and instructing users, or they may relate to job functions in individual departments, such as Accountants or Accounting Clerks.

2. Determine the computer access and the resource access required by each group to perform its role. Use these questions to help you do so. Do its members need access to every computer? Do they need access to specific resources on the computer? What are these resources? Files? Printers? Folders? What type of access do they need? Print? Read? Write? Execute? Are there resources that they should be explicitly forbidden from using? Are there mutually exclusive roles? That is, if a user has one role, should he be excluded from the other? (An example of mutually exclusive groups are accounts payable clerks and accounts receivables clerks.)

3. Create one user group on the server for every distinct role. If two roles need the same access, then perhaps you need to refine your roles or combine two roles into one.

4. Grant this group the level of access required, as determined in step 2.

5. If this group and another are mutually exclusive, deny each group access to the resources the other group has privileges for.

6. Create one user account for each user.

7. Give user memberships in the groups that represent the roles that users must play.

Creating Custom Group Roles

To successfully develop and use custom groups for role-based access control, you should thoroughly understand the following:

- Predefined user rights
- Predefined access permissions associated with specific object types
- Windows access control mechanisms
- Default operating system roles—the default user groups and users
- How to create custom roles by directly assigning rights to groups and giving these groups access to objects
- How to use tools that provide another way to grant authority, including the Delegation of Control wizard and Authorization Manager
- How to audit user and group use of rights and access

Using custom groups to provide role-based access control is as much a function of administrative and programmer understanding as it is operating system enforcement. To ensure that custom group role development is properly applied on your systems, you should establish a policy that specifies how each custom group role is authorized, defined, implemented, maintained, and audited and how membership in the group is authorized. Executive management must back and enforce this policy. Train programmers and administrators in its concepts and the rules of its application, implement it methodically, and audit it to ensure compliance.

NOTE: Writing Information System Policies

While this book recommends many items that should be included in information system security policies, policy writing is beyond this book's scope. For an excellent introduction to policy writing, see Scott Barman's book *Writing Information Security Policies* (Que, 2001).

Best Practices for Local Users and Local Groups

One of the most important uses of groups is that of providing access to objects in an orderly, scalable, sustainable, and auditable fashion. There are options for doing so. Following sound practices on the single stand-alone computer is important. Good habits here will enable best practices at the domain and forest level if and when the server is joined to a domain. Use these best practices:

- Assign rights and permissions to groups, not to individual users. This makes things far easier to manage. If groups represent the role a user can play, then adding a user account to a group allows the user to play that role, and removing the user prohibits him from playing that role.
- Add users to groups to provide them the access and rights they need on the computer.
- Keep the number of users assigned to the Administrators group small.
- Assign users to groups in a manner that only provides them the access they require and not a bit more.

The Access Control Process

Now that you are familiar with users, groups, and permissions, take another look at the access control process. The access control process examines a request for access and grants or denies access. The following steps take place:

1. Resource access is requested.
2. The Security Reference Monitor compares the contents in the access token one at a time to see if there is any match between the SIDs in the token and those in the ACL on the object. Access is allowed or denied based on the results.
3. If a match is found, the Allow or Deny information in this access control entry is compared to the requested access. If there is an Allow match, then the access is granted.
4. If there is a Deny match, then access is denied, and the process is ended.

5. If the access information is incomplete—that is, both read and write are requested, and the successful comparison indicates read is allowed—then the comparison will continue until write is either explicitly allowed or denied, or until it is implicitly denied because there is no match.

6. Unless a Deny match is found or an Allow is completed, if there are still ACEs in the ACL, the process continues.

7. If the list of ACEs in the ACL is exhausted, and no match has been found, then access is denied.

Let's look at an example of this in practice. User Joe wants to open a Word document, budget.doc, for reading and writing. He double-clicks the file in Windows Explorer. The access control list on the file and the SIDs in his access token are listed in Figure 3-21. The ACL on budget.doc contains the ACEs as listed in the box labeled "Access Control List," while Joe's access token contains the SIDs in the box labeled "Access Token." Because it's easier for us to look at names instead of SIDs, no actual SIDs or other numerical representations are listed. The real access token and ACL would look much different but would evaluate to the same information and produce the same result. The ACL contains ACEs that are composed of SIDs and the access rights granted. The access token includes the account SID and the SIDs of groups of which the account is a member.

Access Control List

Administrators	Full Control	Allow
Accounting	Read	Allow
Accounting Clerks	Write	Allow

Access Token

Joe
Accounting
Accounting Clerks
Users
Authenticated User
NETWORK

Figure 3-21 An example ACL and Access Token for comparison.

While you may be able to quickly determine if Joe will be granted the access he desires by just looking at the figure, take the time to step through the SRM process:

1. The first ACE in the file ACL is examined. It contains the group "Administrators."
2. Joe's access token does not include the Administrators group.
3. The next ACE in the ACL lists the Accountants group. Joe's access token does list this group. The ACE grants the `Read Allow` permission. But this is not enough, because Joe requested `Read` and `Write`.
4. The next ACE is examined. This ACE lists the Accounting Clerks group. Joe's access token also includes this group. The ACE grants the `Allow Write` permission.
5. The requested access is granted, and the process stops, even though there are more ACEs in the ACL and more groups in Joe's access token.

Use the resource kit tool Show Privilege to determine what rights and privileges a user has on a computer. Use the resource kit tool whoami to show the contents of the access token for the currently logged on user.

Managing Proprietary Information

A new component, Rights Management Solutions (RMS), can be used to influence management of proprietary information on Windows systems. RMS is a client/server application development environment. On Windows Server 2003, the core elements of the RMS service manage licensing, machine activation, enrollment, and administrative functions. Client-side development uses native APIs for Windows 98 Second Edition and later clients. Applications that restrict authorization to copy, use, download, and otherwise manipulate licensed software and digital documents and recordings can be centrally controlled. For more information, the document "Microsoft Rights Management Solutions for the Enterprise: Persistent Policy Expression and Enforcement for Digital Information" can be downloaded from http://www.microsoft.com/windowsserver2003/techinfo/overview/rm.mspx.

Authorization Using Security Options and Registry Settings

In addition to user rights and object permissions, other types of controls also affect authorization. Many registry entries can restrict the access that a user or application has to a specific network connection, software, resource, or process. Some registry entries are easy to edit because they are represented in the Security Options section of Group Policy. Others can be found in the Administrative Templates section of Group Policy. In addition, Authorization Manager, Software Restriction Policies, and IPSec Policies can all be used to control user activity and resource access on the network. Administrative Templates, Software Restriction Policies, and Authorization Manager are discussed in Chapter 4.

Security Options can impact authentication and authorization. When set in local group policy, they impact the local computer. They can also be set in a group policy that is applied to many computers. The following Security Options should be considered when building an authorization model.

Accounts: Limit Local Use of Blank Passwords to Console Logon

When this option is enabled, as it is by default, and a user account has a blank password, the user will be able to log on only from the console. Attempts to access the computer over the network using the account with a blank password will fail. This option has no impact on domain accounts.

Devices: Allow Undock Without Having to Logon Only

When enabled, as it is by default, if a server is running on a portable computer docked in a docking station, the server can be removed from the docking station without logging on.

Devices: Allowed to Format and Eject Removable Media

This setting specifies who can format or eject removable drives. Choices are `administrators`, `power users`, or `administrators and interactive users` or `not defined`. By default, the local Administrators group is selected.

Devices: Prevent Users from Installing Printer Drivers

If enabled, as it is by default, users cannot install printer drivers. Printer drivers run in the kernel and are therefore able to do more harm. A malicious individual might provide malicious code in the form of a free printer driver and persuade users to download and install his malware by advertising it as making printers work better. If users are able to install printer drivers, then they might install such malware without knowing they are doing so. Alternatively, an unsupported printer driver that is buggy might be installed and cause problems. Leaving this setting at the default may prevent users from downloading and installing potentially harmful drivers and prevents users from installing and sharing a network printer. By default, administrators, power users, and server operators can install printer drivers. This setting has no impact on them.

Device: Restrict CD-ROM to Locally Logged On User Only: Disabled

If enabled, this setting prevents network access to the server's CD-ROM drive while a user is logged on locally to the server. This setting might prevent access to installation CD-ROMs over the network, thus preserving license compliance, preventing users from obtaining access to software they should not have, and protecting them from access to potentially harmful code on CD-ROMs loaded on the server. The setting is disabled by default. If enabled, however, it may interfere with installer programs that do not run in the context of the current user but in their own user context.

Device: Restrict Floppy Use to Locally Logged On User Only: Disabled

If enabled, this setting prevents network access to the server's floppy drive if there is a locally logged on user. This setting is disabled by default.

Device: Unsigned Driver Installation Behavior: Warn But Allow Installation

When a driver is installed, this setting determines one of three actions: `Warn but allow installation` (the default), `Silently succeed`, or `Do not allow installation`. Drivers may be submitted to the Windows Hardware Quality Lab for testing and approval. Once approved, Microsoft signs the driver. An unsigned driver will cause the action selected here. If a driver is not approved, that does not mean it is bad, just that it hasn't been tested. When an attempt is made to install a driver, the system looks for a signature. If the signature is good, then even if the security option is set to `Do not allow installation`, the driver installation will succeed. If no signature is present, then this setting must be set at the `Warn` designation or the `Silently succeed` setting, or else it will not be installed. By setting this option to the warning, a pop-up will query for approval to install the driver. The hope is that the warning will alert the user that an unapproved driver is about to be installed. Perhaps if problems occur after the installation, the connection with the unapproved driver will lead to a problem resolution. Unfortunately, not every "good" driver is approved, so best practices dictate to set this option to Warn. In a high-security installation, set the option to `Do not allow installation`. If an unsigned driver must be used, an authorized administrator can temporarily change the setting to allow the driver to be installed, and then switch the setting back to `Do not allow installation`.

Network Access: Named Pipes That Can Be Accessed Anonymously

Named pipes are communication processes. Security can be established for named pipes, but some applications create named pipes that do not need authentication. If the server needs access to these types of named pipes, add their name to this Security Option. Several default pipes are listed, and you may want to remove those names if access to those pipes is not necessary.

Network Access: Remotely Accessible Registry Paths

This option allows you to list registry paths that may be accessed remotely, while denying access to all others. This is important. If an attacker can remotely access the registry, much damage can be done. Restricting access limits the risk. Several paths are listed.

Network Access: Remotely Accessible Registry Paths and Subpaths

Additional paths are listed. The system will inspect the WinReg key to determine access permissions for these paths.

Network Access: Shares That Can Be Accessed Anonymously

Anonymous access to shares makes the computer more vulnerable to attack. The shares that you create should have access controlled via share permissions, as defined in Chapter 5. However, blocking anonymous access to all shares may prevent some applications from running. Use this option to list shares that must allow anonymous access.

Allow Systems to Be Shut Down Without Having to Log On:

If this option is enabled, anyone can shut down the server from the logon screen. Servers should only be shut down for maintenance, and you should account for all system shutdowns. The system records the user account and the entered reason for the shutdown in the system log when a logged on user shuts down the system. Requiring a user to log on to shut down a server also ensures that a server is not inadvertently shut down, removing its services from the network. Best practices require that, for a system to be shut down, you must log on and have the authority to shut the system down. In Window Server 2003, this also means that, by default, you are required to enter a reason for the shutdown. This security option would allow you to modify this behavior and present the option in the GINA to shut the system down—no logon required. (The computer can, of course, be shut down by pulling its plug or otherwise interrupting electrical service. However, this will be recorded as an unexpected shutdown.)

System Objects: Strengthen Default Permissions of Internal Systems Objects (e.g. Symbolic Links):

> When enabled, as it is by default, this option increases security on internal system objects. Internal systems objects are those used by the operating system to manage critical operations. Using this setting increases security on those objects but may prevent legacy applications from working.

Computer Roles

Each computer in the network plays a specific role. Computer roles are operations such as DHCP server, file and print server, database server, domain controller, and desktop. Computers themselves are authorized to perform certain functions or are restricted from doing so based on the role that they play. Domain controllers, for example, are the only computers in the domain that can host the Active Directory, while any server can be utilized as a print server by defining a logical printer, adding the correct printer driver, and sharing the service. You could alter this role by removing the printer or by disabling some services, blocking access from the network, and so on.

To create a computer role, you add a service(s) and configure the system. Three options may be used to create a computer role:

- The `Manage Your Server` console can be used to select a computer role. A wizard will then install and configure the services required to implement the role.
- You can manually add applications or additional services by using the `Add/Remove Windows Applications` in the Control Panel.
- Some roles can be added via the command line. For example, entering the `dcpromo` command will promote a server to the domain controller role or demote an existing domain controller.

You must have the appropriate authority to add a computer role to a server. For example, a Windows 2003 DHCP server will shut itself down if it is not authorized in the Active Directory. Computer roles are discussed further in Chapters 11, 12, "PKI Basics" and Chapter 14, "Securing Remote Access."

Anonymous Access

Anonymous access does not require a user account or password. Older versions of Windows required anonymous access for many applications and services to run. As these versions of Windows were updated and as new versions of Windows were introduced, fewer operating system services and fewer server applications required anonymous access. The following options for managing anonymous access are available in Windows Server 2003.

Security Principals, Authorization, and Anonymous Access

Security principals are entities that the security subsystem recognizes and that can be granted rights and permission on the computer. Users, groups, and computers are security principals. Access to computer and network resources is granted directly to user and computer accounts or indirectly via their group membership. Access or authorization can therefore be restricted. User accounts can also be created for use by services, or services may be assigned to use the Local System account, Network, or Local Service account. This enables software that must run in the background to run and be controlled by granting its logon account authorization in the form of rights and permissions. Both user and computer accounts can be explicitly granted membership in Windows groups and can become members of implicit groups based on the actions of the account.

Anonymous connections, connections that do not use accounts or passwords, are often authorized access to resources via explicit access granted to the implicit anonymous group or by the inclusion of the implicit anonymous group in some other group, such as the Everyone group. Anonymous access, however, can be abused. Anonymous access might be used to find out information about a system, such as its user list, SIDs, or security policy, to better attack it. Anonymous access also might be used to launch an attack.

The anonymous connection has been used in several attacks against Windows computers. Windows Server 2003 provides several Security Options that can be used to configure better control over anonymous connections. Windows Server 2003 also requires fewer anonymous connections to function and is by default more secure against attacks based on anonymous access. One of these restrictions is that the anonymous SID, the identifier granted to a user or process connecting anonymously, is not part of the Everyone group on Windows Server 2003. Therefore, the anonymous connection does not provide as much access as can be gained in earlier versions of Windows. You will need to learn more about anonymous connections to protect systems from attacks that use them.

Anonymous Access to Resources

Some shares are created during installation for the purpose of supporting remote administration. In general, these shares should not be modified or deleted. Shares that you create, however, should be protected from anonymous access. One of the default shares is IPC$, which is required for remote administration when shared resources are viewed.

The IPC$ service, by default, provides for anonymous access to support various Windows services. This support makes it possible to connect to the IPC$ share on a Windows computer without providing a user name and password. The IPC$ share is used in the following scenarios:

- To share named pipes.
- For remote administration and when viewing shared folders.
- By some legacy services to enumerate user information. For example, on Windows NT 4, RAS uses this share to determine whether the user has the right to log on remotely.
- By some downlevel computers to complete password changes; access to this share is required.
- To configure access to resources in a trusting domain; the administrator needs access to this share.

Do Not Attempt to Delete the IPC$

You cannot delete the IPC$ share because it is essential in a network environment. Anonymous access to this share may be necessary for certain types of processing. You must understand the dangers of unrestricted anonymous access and use appropriate action to protect your systems from them, but you must be aware that at this time, it is not possible to eliminate all anonymous access. Locally, you know that this is not possible. If you understand how access is gained, you will understand that an anonymous connection must take place before credentials can be exchanged that will authenticate the user.

The danger is that unmanaged anonymous access may provide unauthenticated access to a computer's file system, or worse. Anonymous access also bypasses accountability efforts because the user's identity cannot become part of the log. There is no way to tell who has accessed information when an anonymous access is allowed. If an attacker is able to make an anonymous connection, she might be able to obtain information that might be used in an inappropriate or illegal way, such as compromising the system. Anonymous connections to Windows Server 2003 are restricted by default. You can examine and modify these controls.

Pre-Windows 2000 Compatible Access Group Membership

The Pre-Windows 2000 compatible access security group is a local group only present on Windows 2000 and Windows Server 2003 domain controllers. By default, this group has read access to user and group objects in Active Directory. Membership in this group is configured when a Windows 2000 or Windows 2003 server is promoted to domain controller. The installer is asked if all computers in the domain will be at least Windows 2000; if the answer is yes, no user or group is added to the Pre-Windows 2000 compatible access security group. However, if you have pre-Windows 2000 computers from which domain users will need to log on, you should add the anonymous group to the Pre-Windows compatible access security group. Hence, anyone obtaining anonymous access could potentially also browse the user and group objects in Active Directory.

If necessary, you can add or remove the anonymous group from the Pre-Windows 2000 compatible access security group. This group is listed in the Active Directory Users and Computers console, and its membership can be modified by opening its properties and adding or removing users and groups from the Member page.

The Pre-Windows 2000 compatible access security group also has access to folders, files, and registry keys that are sometimes required by legacy services. Adding the anonymous group to the Pre-Windows 2000 compatible access security group also provides anonymous users access to these resources. If you understand which access is required in your environment, you can restrict access to resources by anonymous users by modifying the ACLs on resources.

Well-Known SIDs

Well-known SIDs are those SIDs that are the same on every system. The name is often a bit misleading. Some well-known SIDs are actually a local representation of a well-known RID. For example, the RID of the local Administrator account is 500, but each system will have a unique local Administrator account SID because the SID includes some unique information that identifies the computer on which is exits. Well-known SIDS represent common entities and even implicit groups (groups whose membership is defined by the actions a security principal takes versus being explicitly added to the group). Well-known SIDs are important for two reasons. First, because they are well-known, an attacker might be able to use them to discover information about the system, or simply use them in an attack. An example of this might be the use of the well-known local Administrator account SID. While an attack that references the Administrator account by name may fail if the account name has been changed, an attack using the well-known Administrator SID will not. Note, however, that the attacker must discover the unique portion of the SID that identifies the machine before she can compose the local Administrator's SID and use it in an attack. (See the section on anonymous access to see how this might be possible and how to protect against it.) The second important thing about well-known SIDs is that they may be added to the access token of a security principal. If the security principal is, for example, attempting to access a network resource and is able to authenticate, then the well-known SID for the implicit NETWORK group will be added to their access token. If this SID has been used to grant access to system resources, then its inclusion in the access token will provide that access.

Table 3-7 lists and defines well-known SIDs for Windows Server 2003.

Table 3-7   Well-Known SIDs

Identity	SID	Description
Administrator	(S-1-5-*domain*-500)	The local Administrator account.
Anonymous Logon	(S-1-5-7)	User who connected without a user-name or password.

Identity	SID	Description
Authenticated Users	(S-1-5-11)	All users and computers who have been authenticated on the system. Does not include Guest even if the guest account includes a password.
Batch	(S-1-5-3)	All users who logged on using a batch queue facility such as task scheduler.
Creator Owner	(S-1-3-0)	Used as a placeholder in inheritable ACE. If the ACE is inherited, this SID is replaced with the SID for the current object's owner.
Creator Group	(S-1-3-1)	Used as a placeholder in inheritable ACE. If the ACE is inherited, this SID is replaced with the SID for the primary group of the object's current owner.
Dialup	(S-1-5-1)	All users who logged in using a dial-up connection.
Everyone	(S-1-1-0)	On Windows Server 2003 systems, includes Authenticated Users and Guest. On earlier Windows systems, the Anonymous Logon is also included.
Interactive	(S-1-5-4)	All users who log on locally or through a Remote Desktop connection.
Local System	(S-1-5-18)	The service account that is used by the operating system.
Network	(S-1-5-2)	All users who are logged on through a network connection.
Self (Principal Self)	(S-1-5-10)	Placeholder in an ACE on user, group, or computer object in Active Directory. It gives access to the security principal. When an access check is performed, the SID is replaced with the SID of the security principal (the one seeking access).
Service	(S-1-5-6)	All who have logged on as a service.
Terminal Server	(S-1-5-13)	All users logged on to a Terminal Services server that is in Terminal Services mode.

Table 3-7 Well-Known SIDs Continued

Identity	SID	Description
Other Organizations	(S-1-5-1000)	A check to ensure that a user from another forest or domain is allowed to authenticate to a particular service.
This Organization	(S-1-5-15)	Added to a user's data if the Other Organizations SID is not already present.

Anonymous SID and Name Translation

A security identifier (SID) is a character string used to represent Windows accounts and groups. When a new user account or new group is added to the account database, a unique SID is assigned. Those accounts and groups created by the system during installation are assigned SIDs at that time. These SIDS are known as "well-known SIDs" because they are either exactly the same or have the same ending for every installation of Windows. One well-known SID is the Administrator account.

To the operating system, it's not the account name that matters, but the SID. In many attacks, an attempt is made to obtain administrative privileges by obtaining the account name and password of an account in the local Administrators group. When an attempt is made to access a resource, the SIDs are compared to Access Control lists that include SIDs and the permissions assigned to them. It's understandably more desirable for an attacker to obtain the username and password for an administrative-level account than for an ordinary user account. Hence, an attacker will attempt to crack the password for the Administrator account. A common security practice is to obscure the local Administrator account by changing its name, thus foiling or at least delaying the attacker who now has to crack all accounts and try them one-by-one. However, because the Administrator account has a well-known SID, an attacker might be able to deduce it if he can gain anonymous access to the computer. He then could write code, or use code written by another, to determine the name of the Administrator account by first listing all SIDs and looking for the one using the well-known RID of the Administrator account. Likewise, if an entire account list cannot be accessed but the name of one account is known, an attacker with anonymous access might be able to construct the SID of the administrator account by translating the known user account to its SID to obtain the machine portion of the SID and then composing the administrator account by adding the well-known Administrator account RID, 500, to the machine portion and then translating this SID to a username.

By default, Windows Server 2003 is protected against anonymous SID name translation. The Group Policy security option Network Access: Allow Anonymous SID/Name Translation is set to Disabled and prevents the use of tools that might translate well-known or other SIDs to usernames. Maintain this security setting as Disabled to prevent the use of such tools and thus the exposure of these accounts. If the list of user accounts is known, an attacker can attempt to run password-cracking attacks against the each account. The following Security Options can be used to close holes provided by anonymous access.

Network Access: Do Not Allow Anonymous Enumeration of SAM Accounts

After an anonymous connection has been made, an unprotected Windows computer may allow enumeration of the accounts in the SAM database. To prevent this, this security option should be enabled. (The default is `disabled` in Windows Server 2003.) If the security option `Network Access: Do Not Allow Anonymous Enumeration of SAM Accounts and Shares` is `Enabled`, this setting is ignored. If the list of user accounts is known, an attacker can attempt to run password-cracking attacks against each account.

Network Access: Do Not Allow Anonymous Enumeration of SAM Accounts and Shares

This security option is `Enabled` by default, so it prevents enumeration of SAM accounts and shares via an anonymous connection. If accounts can be enumerated, password-cracking attacks can be launched against them. If shares are known, connection attempts can be launched.

Network Access: Let Everyone Permissions Apply to Anonymous User

By default, the anonymous group (an implicit group that contains all current anonymous connections) is not a member of the Everyone group. Thus, any rights or permissions of resource access that are granted to the Everyone group are not available to anonymous users. This security option is set to `Disabled` by default. If you enable this setting, you could reverse this security control and reduce security on your Windows Server 2003 system. This should not be done.

You might think it necessary to enable this option to improve compatibility with legacy software. However, you should first attempt to deal with the permission issues of legacy applications by seeking out just the access they need, not by granting widespread access to everything.

You can learn more about safer ways to deal with the permission issues of legacy applications in Chapter 5.

Limit Anonymous Access to Named Pipes

Named pipes provide a transport for communications between the client and server processes of a software application. This inter-process communication can be written to require authorized and authenticated connection. For example, a security descriptor—a list of which users and groups can access a resource and what they can do with it—can be applied. However, if the security descriptor grants full control to the LocalSystem account, to administrators, and to the creator owner or read permission to members of the Everyone group, and the anonymous account, it may provide undesirable access, including elevation of privileges if the pipe has privileged access to a database or other resource. You should seek to prevent anonymous connections to named pipes or restrict them. However, this may prevent applications from running or from running correctly.

If you must provide anonymous access to named pipes, use the security option `Network Access: Named Pipes That Can Be Accessed Anonymously` to list those named pipes that can be accessed anonymously. The default entries for this security option are listed in Figure 3-22. If a named pipe is not listed here, and anonymous access is required, the application may be broken. You can add or delete the names of named pipes from this security option.

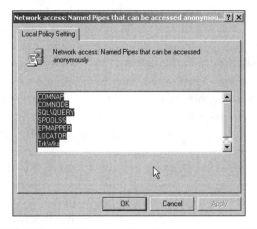

Figure 3-22   Manage named pipes.

Before modifying this setting, you should understand how named pipes may be used in the applications used on specific computers. Use this security option to allow or prevent this type of anonymous access. By default, several named pipes are listed as approved for anonymous access. For increased security, you should determine which of these are not used by specific computers and remove those that are not necessary.

Removing unnecessary connection paths reduces the attack surface. Every anonymous connection could be used in some sort of attack, either known or as yet to be developed, so if you do not need to use these connections, remove them and reduce the potential for compromise.

In many cases, you will find you can remove some of these connection opportunities. The default approved named pipes, their uses, and recommendations about their use can be found in Table 3-8.

Table 3-8   Name Pipes That Can Be Anonymously Accessed by Default

Pipe	Use For	Recommendation
COMNAP	The SNA Server Base connection. Used by SNA Server and Host Integration Server 2000 clients to find a list of available servers. These Microsoft server products are used to facilitate communications with IBM mainframe computers.	Remove unless you have installed SNA Server or Host Integration Server.
COMNODE	The SNA Server Service connection. Used by SNA server and Host Integration Server 2000 clients to connect to the service.	Remove unless you have installed SNA Server or Host Integration Server.
SQL\QUERY	Used by Microsoft SQL Server clients.	Remove unless SQL Server is installed.
SPOOLSS	Used by print clients.	Remove unless this server is a print server.
LLSRPC RPC	Interface of the License Logging Service.	Required.

Table 3-8 Name Pipes That Can Be Anonymously Accessed by Default Continued

Pipe	Use For	Recommendation
EPMAPPER	Lists the services that are available and listening using RPC, and defines the ports used by these applications. For example, Exchange Server has multiple services. When Exchange starts, these services are registered with the end point mapper, which assigns them a port number. The endpoint mapper listens on port 135. If another Exchange server or a client needs to connect with one of the services, it will make a connection using port 135 to the endpoint mapper to determine which port is used by the service it requires. It then can connect to that specific port. For more information, see the Knowledge Base article 159298.	Required by many services that use RPC.
LOCATOR	Name service provided service. An application that uses remote procedure calls (RPCs) or program function calls from an application on one computer to another provides its information to a provider service. The Microsoft locator service is used by default— it maps logical names to specific network names. For example, if a printserver name (the printer name, not the name of the server) is known, the locator service may be able to map this print server name to the IP address of the server that hosts the printer (Knowledge Base article 142024).	Required.

Pipe	Use For	Recommendation
TRKWKS and TRKSRFV	The Distributed Link Tracking Client and Server Services, respectively. These services keep track of link sources that have been moved, such as shortcuts and OLE links. A client, for example, can continue to connect to a database on another computer, even after the database has been moved.	If the link tracking service is not used, delete this named pipe from the list.

If you determine that you can remove specific named pipes, be careful in doing so. Use the security option to ensure success. If you must edit the registry, use the following instructions and be sure to leave each connection name on a separate line. A return should also be entered after the last entry in the list. To edit the registry:

1. Start the Registry Editor.
2. Under the HKEY_LOCAL_MACHINE subtree, go to the following subkey:
   ```
   System\CurrentControlSet\Services\LanmanServer\
   Parameters\
   ```
3. Double-click NullSessionPipes.
4. Add or remove the named pipe name from the list, as shown in Figure 3-23. Remove any extra line spaces; add a return if this is the last named pipe name in the list.
5. Click OK.
6. Perform a shutdown and restart of the server for the change to take effect.

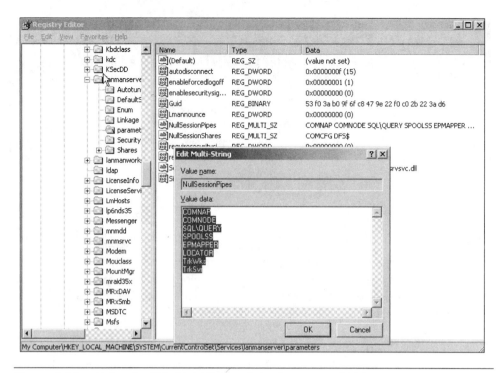

Figure 3-23   Using the Edit Multi-String dialog box to modify the registry.

Restrict Anonymous Access to Shares

The security option `Network Access: Shares That Can Be Accessed Anonymously` lists two shares by default. If they are not used, they should be removed. The shares are listed in Table 3-9.

Table 3-9   Permitted Anonymous Shares

Share	Description	Recommendation
COMCFG	This is the configuration share for Microsoft Host Integration Server 2000 and SNA Server. Users who have read or read and write permissions to the configuration file are able to administer Host Integration Server 2000. Consult product documentation to determine the necessary management of this share and access to the configuration file. Microsoft Host Integration Servers use this share to talk to one another.	Delete unless these products are used.
DFS$	Used to access the Distributed File System (DFS). The Distributed File System is used to aid users in connecting to distributed resources. Resources available from multiple computers appear to be located at one place and users no longer need to understand the physical location for a resource.	Delete unless DFS is used.

Protect the Account Database with Syskey

Passwords in the password database are encrypted. Syskey is a utility that is used by default to provide additional protection. The Syskey utility does the following:

- Encrypts the password database with a 128-bit cryptographically random encryption key.
- Encrypts the password encryption key with a system key.
- Allows storage of the system key in three different ways.
- If configured in "not stored" or "stored on floppy disk" mode, Syskey can protect the system from unauthorized reboot.

There are three options for the storage of the system key:

- **Locally**—A system key is generated by the system and stored on the hard drive using a complex obfuscation algorithm. No intervention is needed at startup. This is the system default.
- **Not stored**—The password must be entered at startup. The administrator implementing this option chooses a system key. If the key is forgotten, the system cannot be started. Password length can be up to 128 characters.
- **Stored on a floppy disk**—A system key is generated by the system and stored on a floppy disk. The floppy disk must be present for the system to start up. If the disk is lost or damaged, the system cannot be started. (Backups, of course, are recommended.)

The Syskey utility, which is an option in Windows NT 4.0, is used by default on Windows 2000 and Windows Server 2003 and cannot be disabled. An administrator, however, may change the storage location of the system key. Without the system key, the system cannot function because the password database will be inaccessible.

If the storage option for the system key is changed and the password is forgotten or the floppy disk is not available, the passwords in the SAM and other information will not be available. To recover, you will have to restore the SAM and SYSTEM hives of the registry to the condition they were in before the storage location was changed. Therefore, the best practice is to make a backup of the system state prior to changing the storage location of the system key. You should also be aware that other system-based changes and local account changes made since the storage location change will also be lost when these hives are restored.

To modify the system key storage location follow these steps:

1. At the Start, Run prompt, type the word syskey and press Enter.
2. As shown in Figure 3-24, the use of Syskey is already enabled. To change the storage location, click the Update button.
3. Select an option as shown in Figure 3-25 to Store Startup Key on Floppy Disk or the option to use Password Startup or leave the option at Store Startup Key Locally.

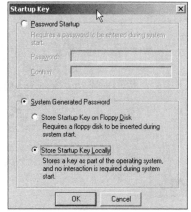

Figure 3-24 The Syskey storage location can be changed by running the utility and clicking the Update button.

Figure 3-25 Three choices for storage location can be used.

4. Either provide a floppy disk or enter a password, depending on your selection in step 3.
5. Click OK.
6. Restart the system.

Although the main purpose of the Syskey utility is to protect the SAM, additional Windows components are affected. Specifically the following steps occur:

■ The SYSTEM and the SAM hives of the registry are changed. (The SAM is encrypted, and the SYSTEM hive now contains information on the option used.) If you need to recover (if you lost the key or floppy disk), both hives should be repaired. If they are not, the system may attempt to boot using the wrong information—it may think a floppy disk is required, for example, when the password is actually stored locally.
■ A master key is created to protect private keys.
■ Protection keys for user passwords are stored in the Active Directory.

- A protection key is created for the Administrator password used to start the system in Safe Mode.
- Protection keys for the LSA Secrets storage area are created. LSA Secrets is an area where sensitive cryptographic information such as users' EFS keys and the passwords of service accounts are stored.

Summary

Authorization is the security principle that determines what can be done on a system once authentication has occurred. Windows Server 2003 has a rich set of user rights, object permissions, and additional methods for controlling access to systems and the data and services that they represent. The wily administrator will learn what these built-in facilities are and will exploit them to maintain tight control over Windows-based services and data. This chapter introduced those facilities and laid the groundwork for information that will permeate the rest of this section and be examined for each succeeding service, application, or process covered throughout the rest of the book. Chapter 4 will continue the theme by exploring methods that can be used to restrict access to software.

Restricting Access to Software; Restricting Software's Access to Resources

Many of today's successful attacks are application layer attacks, which are the result of an exploit based on vulnerabilities in applications other than the operating system. While these attacks do cause enormous problems, many other problems are caused by accidental user actions such as clicking on email attachments, downloading software from the Internet, and misusing applications. These actions can result in accidental deletions, loss of data integrity, and loss of access to encrypted data. While we must strengthen defenses to protect applications from malicious attack, write applications that do not include vulnerabilities, and train users to make better decisions, we must also consider if we can design and manage applications better.

Perhaps the answer is blocking the use of specific software, or perhaps we should configure systems so that only approved software will run. Doing either may help. After all, if malware cannot run, it cannot cause harm. In addition to securely coding applications, perhaps we can do a better job of embedding control within the application to manage user rights and access to resources at the application level. We can accomplish these things by using the following components in a Windows Server 2003 network:

- **File, registry, printer and Active Directory access control lists (ACLs)**—Setting appropriate file ACLs on an executable program prevents unauthorized individuals from running it. Setting file, Active Directory, and registry ACLs can prevent unauthorized individuals from performing specific tasks with the software and can prevent them from copying files to areas of the hard drive. File and registry ACLs were introduced in Chapter 3, "Authorization: Limiting System Access and Controlling User Behavior," and are explored in depth in Chapter 5, "Controlling Access to Data."
- **Authorization Manager Framework**—New in Windows Server 2003, Authorization Manager allows developers to build role-based security into their applications. Administrators manage the use of this software by adding users into Windows groups, Application Groups, Application Basic Groups, and LDAP Groups. Authorization Manager also permits control over who can run specific parts of software running on a system.
- **Software Restriction Policies**—New in Windows XP Professional and new to the server in Windows Server 2003, Software Restriction Policies can be used either to selectively prevent software from running or to only allow identified software to run on a computer.
- **Component Services: Permissions and Roles for COM+**—Applications can be managed using the Component Services tool. To be fully effective, COM+ applications must be developed with defined roles. Otherwise, the administrator is restricted to making changes in launching permissions and authentication levels. New in Windows Server 2003, you can set the Software Restriction security level directly in the COM+ properties pages of the application.
- **Group Policy**—Many applications can also be managed through Group Policy. Specific controls for managing system applets are contained in the Administrative Templates section of Group Policy. Special Administrative Templates are available for products such as Microsoft Office. The use of Administrative Templates in Group Policy is discussed in Chapter 7, "Active Directory's Role in Domain Security."
- **EFS**—Application files can be encrypted using the Encrypting File System (EFS). EFS basics are described in Chapter 6, "EFS Basics."

Three major software management tools are available in Windows Server 2003: Authorization Manager, Software Restriction Policies, and the Component Services console. This chapter will describe them and how they can be used.

Authorization Manager Framework

The Authorization Manager Framework enables the development and administration of Role-Based Access Control (RBAC) programs. Developers use the Authorization Manager Framework's Authorization Manager RBAC application programming interface (API) to develop the application, including the definition of user roles. Administrators use the Authorization Manager Microsoft Management Console snap-in to manage the applications by assigning user groups to role definitions.

Before you can administer these applications, you must understand how they are developed and how they work. The secret to understanding and championing Authorization Manager is to understand that it moves the responsibility for partitioning access to information resources from the administrator to the application.

The Authorization Manager application is pre-programmed to respond to the role of the user interacting with the program. The role, defined as part of the application, is explicitly designed to provide rights and permissions that allow the role holder to do her job and no more. The role might be allowed, for example, to run only certain parts of the program and only read some data while having permission to write, delete, or otherwise manipulate other data. At first glance, this may appear to provide control over computer system resources to the developer. However, in a properly managed development environment, developers work from and are held accountable to specifications developed by the data owners. An application developed to print payroll checks, for example, might have roles such as payroll clerk and payroll manager. Payroll department staff must develop the specifications that define what each role is allowed to do within the program and what files and printers role users may access. Payroll management approves the design and tells IT which employees should be assigned which roll. The system administrator maintains application control by assigning the correct users to the application roles.

The ordinary application, by comparison, does a poor job of granting and denying access to resources. The ordinary application sees data storage as a gray landscape of objects that it can or cannot manipulate depending primarily on the security context of the user. If it needs to interact with the internal processes of the computer, the ordinary application switches context and operates as programmed in ignorance of the security context of the user. Thus, management of the ordinary application is fractured. Authorization to run the application is separate from the right to access resources. To manage ordinary applications, the system administrator must only decide who is authorized to run the application. She manages resources that the application might use separately. The administrator protects resources by determining what rights a user should be granted or denied and which objects a user should have permission to access. Application authorization and resource authorization are disconnected. In addition, while the administrator may grant a user permission to execute a specific program, she may not grant the user the right to run some part of the application while denying the user access to other parts of the application. There are exceptions to this. Both database applications and COM+ applications may have roles defined within their structure. Database administrators assign users to database roles.

In a well-defined and relatively static environment, the system administrator can manage the ordinary application and the burden of assigning rights and permissions. In the well-managed environment, data owners define who should do what with their data, and the administrator can mold the operating system authorization design to fit these requirements. In a relatively static environment, change is slow, so there is time to make these decisions for new applications and weigh the impact on older ones. Many organizations do not provide a well-defined or relatively static environment, though. Change often occurs rapidly, data owners and administrators sometimes don't communicate well, and applications are often adopted that require elevated privileges to run, not because of the way they must function, but because they were poorly written.

The secret to successfully adopting Authorization Manager is to realize that it will not solve the problems created by the past. It cannot be put to use to manage wayward applications or magically relieve the administrator of the burden of assigning rights and permissions. What Authorization Manager can do is provide the infrastructure for which applications can be developed to change the paradigm for the system administrator. For all Authorization Manager applications, the administrator does not need to assign individual users or groups access to objects; she merely has to respond to application owners' identification of which users should play what role in the application.

If this concept appeals to you, you will need to work with data owners and application developers to produce applications that can be managed by Authorization Manager. Writing applications that support RBAC is not within the scope of this book; however, managing such applications with Authorization Manager is. You may be asked to administer such an application, or you may be key in recommending that applications be written that are Authorization Manager-enabled and thus can provide RBAC.

NOTE: Authorization Manager on Other Platforms

The Authorization Manager RBAC API can be obtained for Windows 2000 from http://www.microsoft.com/downloads/details.aspx?FamilyID= 7edde11f-bcea-4773-a292-84525f23baf7&displaylang=en and can be used to develop Authorization Manager applications. Authorization Manager applications can only be administered using the Authorization Manager snap-in from a Windows Server 2003 server or a Windows XP Professional computer on which the Windows Server 2003 Administration Pack for XP has been installed. However, to create Authorization Manager stores in the Active Directory, the domain must be in Windows Server 2003 functional mode.

The following information can help you understand the basics of Authorization Manager and the steps that will need to be taken to use it.

Role-Based Access Control in Windows

Role-based access control is available without Authorization Manager for Windows systems based on NT technologies. Implementing RBAC in previous versions of Windows required administrators to develop roles by doing the following:

- Creating Windows groups.
- Assigning appropriate user rights to these groups.
- ACLing resources such as files, folders, registry keys, and Active Directory objects.
- Adding Windows accounts into and removing them from these Windows groups as individuals joined or left the company or changed roles within the company.
- Working with developers to introduce custom roles into applications. This includes working with .NET applications, COM+ applications, and applications based on prior programming paradigms.

There is nothing wrong with this model. However, much of its success relied upon the administration of permissions on a large number of objects. Get it right, and people can do their jobs, nothing more. Get it wrong, and the wrong people often have access they shouldn't, and those who officially require rights and permissions may be blocked from doing their work. Frustration becomes part of every administrator's and user's day. Eventually, wide holes in security may be created just so that users can do their jobs. It's especially difficult to scale this model when there is high turnover in personnel and rapidly changing job functions. In addition, although the model is highly flexible and offers granular control when it comes to object permissions, it cannot manage the use of software at a granular level.

The issue has not been that a way was needed to do RBAC control, but rather how the following details should be handled:

- Defining the roles. Who does what on which computer systems with what applications? What do people do?

- Translating the job into a set of object permissions. For each role, what programs do they need access to? Which files? Printers? Registry keys?

- Assigning the responsibility for creating the job/rights/permissions mapping. Who should be figuring all this out?

- Determining responsibility for implementation, maintenance, and audit of roles and role assignment. Who should actually configure the computer, make sure it's working the way it's supposed to, and audit the role and role assignments? Are the right people in the right roles? Are the roles defined correctly?

Authorization Manager removes the granular details of role development from the system administrator. Developers create the applications that define the roles based on specifications provided by those who know how the new applications should run. Developers assign object permissions and rights of code execution within the role definition in their application. Once a role is defined, it can be assigned to a group. Administrators simply add Windows users or groups to these groups to allow users or group members to perform the role. Administrators and data owners can participate in the design of the application and its roles. Data owners determine which individuals within the organization should play which role.

By comparison, ACLs attempt to manage software restrictions by setting permissions such as "execute" or "deny execute," and software restriction policies are based on the use of special designations that prevent or allow software to run. Authorization Manager-enabled applications define roles, which are then limited to certain operations within the application. With authorization, you define not only who can run an application, but also what role they can play within that software. This means that users are not only restricted to using only specific applications, but also to only executing some of the code within an application. Roles can also be confined to the use of a subset of the resources used by the application and limited with permissions as to what they can do with the resource. Authorization Manager is the administrative tool used to expose the underlying application, role, and resource partitions, and to assign users to roles. The use of well-defined roles to control system access is known as role-based security.

Authorization Manager Basics

Authorization Manager provides a single interface that administrators can use to manage multiple applications. Authorization Manager-enabled applications, however, must be written to contain the necessary components to provide a deeper level of access control.

Application developers define the components that define the roles within the application. The application installation program populates the authorization policy, a set of rules that define the application roles. The authorization policy is stored in the authorization store and exposed in the Authorization Manager snap-in for use by the administrator. If the installation program does not deliver the authorization policy, components can be created directly in the Authorization Manager.

NOTE: Administrator's Role
The administrator's main responsibility is to assign Application Groups, Windows Groups, and Users to roles and to add users to groups, thus conferring upon them the appropriate role. However, administrators should understand how the process works so that they may understand the rights and permissions granted on their systems when a user is given a role.

To aid your understanding of how Authorization Manager applications work, the sections that follow both define the components and provide instructions on how they can be created in Authorization Manager. To perform many of these operations, you will need to change the operation mode of the Authorization Store from Administrator mode to Developer mode. Administrators cannot create applications, authorization stores, or operations and cannot change application names or version numbers. To change to Developer mode, add the Authorization Manager to an MMC console, and then do this:

1. Right-click on the Authorization Manager node and select `Options`.
2. Select `Developer mode`, as shown in Figure 4-1.
3. Click `OK`.

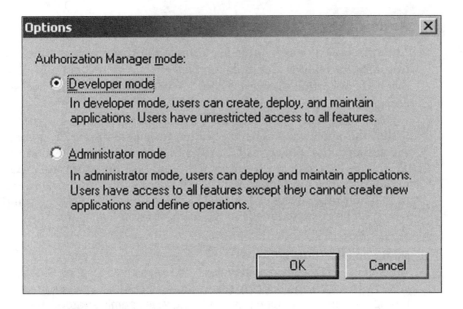

Figure 4-1   The operations available in Authorization Manager depend on the mode that is set.

A complete Authorization Manager application requires the development of the following components:

- **Authorization Store**—The repository for the security policy.
- **Groups**—Entities that can be assigned roles.
- **Application**—Defines the relationship between the applications written to be managed by Authorization Manager and the authorization store.
- **Scope**—A file folder or other resource used by an application.
- **Roles**—A collection of related tasks that must be accomplished.
- **Tasks**—A collection of operations.
- **Authorization Scripts**—Scripts that check a user's authorization to perform a task.
- **Operations**—Lower-level operating system.

Authorization Store

An Authorization Manager-based application reads its security policy from its Authorization Store during startup. The security policy consists of rules that indicate what a specific role can do. There is no default Authorization Store; instead, an Authorization Store is created for a specific purpose. Authorization Stores can reside in the Active Directory or in the NTFS file system (local or remote) in an XML file. Secure the file using ACLs. Table 4-1 illustrates the differences between the two types of stores.

Table 4-1 Authorization Store Definition

	Active Directory	XML
Delegation support	At the Authorization Store, application, and scope level	Not supported. Secured by its ACEs.
Authorization specification	URL with the prefix MMSLDAP:// or LDAP distinguished name (DN) like CN=store, CN=data, DN=mycompany, or DN=com	URL with the prefix MSXML:// or path such as C:\stores\thisstore.xml or \\servera\sharea\thisstore.xml
Windows Support	Windows Server 2003 domain functional level only	NTFS partition (including one on Windows 2000 servers)
Audit Support for Runtime auditing	Authorization Store level and application level	Authorization Store level and application level
Audit Support for Authorization Store change auditing	Authorization Store, application, and scope	Authorization Store level only

An Authorization Store can be created programmatically, or manually in the Authorization Manager. When items such as groups, roles, operations tasks, and so forth are created in the Authorization Manager console, their information is added to the Authorization Store. To create a store, follow these steps:

1. Open Authorization Manager.
2. Right-click on the computer container and select `Create New Authorization Store`.

3. Select XML or Active Directory for the store location and enter the name and location of the store.
4. Enter a description, as shown in Figure 4-2.
5. Click OK to add the store. Figure 4-3 shows the store added to the Authorization Manager console.

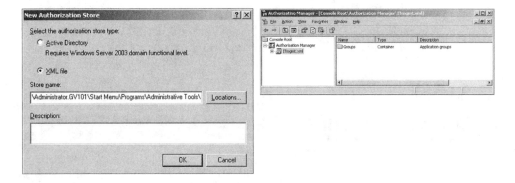

Figure 4-2 The Authorization Store is created by specifying a name and location for its storage.

Figure 4-3 After creation, the store is displayed in the Authorization Manager console.

NOTE: Delegation
Delegation in the Active Directory is a way of assigning administrative responsibility to users who are not members of the Administrators group. Delegation is accomplished by assigning user group permissions on Active Directory objects. Because an Authorization Store that is stored in the Active Directory is an object, you can delegate authority over the store and the objects within it. XML-based Authorization Stores are not in the Active Directory and do not support delegation.

Groups

Groups are used to assign roles to users. Roles are assigned to groups, and administrators place user accounts in groups. Special groups can be created in Authorization Manager, or Windows groups can be used. If

Authorization Manager groups are used, they can be created just for use by an application or even a scope within the application. The group nomenclature is as follows:

- **Application Groups**—A group of users in an Authorization Manager application. They can be created at all three levels in the console: Authorization Store, Application, and Scope. A group created in an upper level can be used at a lower level, but a group created at a lower level cannot be used at an upper level. Application groups are either Application Basic Groups or LDAP Query Groups.
- **Application Basic Group**—Includes a list of members and a list of non-members. A list of non-members is used to deny access to some subset of the larger, allowed access group. A group, therefore, might be provided access to the application but denied access to some subset of the application. Non-membership takes precedence over membership. Basic groups can be Windows Users and Groups or LDAP Query Groups.
- **Lightweight Directory Access Protocol (LDAP) Query Groups**—This is a dynamic group defined by an LDAP query. Any user attribute can be part of the LDAP query. For example, a query group could consist of all those users who live within the city limits of Chicago. Over time, this group might change. Other groups may be more volatile. An example would be all those users who had a birthday during the current month.
- **Windows Users and Groups**—These are standard user accounts and groups, either default or custom. When a role is assigned to a group, you can choose Windows Users and Groups or an Application Group.

To add a group:

1. Right-click the Groups node of the Authorization Store, Application, or Scope and select New Application Group.
2. Enter a name and description for the Application Group.
3. Select either LDAP query or Basic group type, as shown in Figure 4-4.
4. Click OK and view the created group, as shown in Figure 4-5.

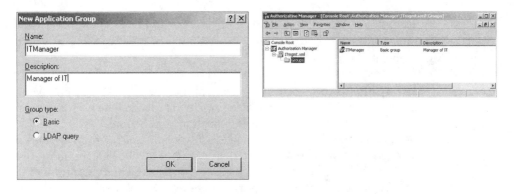

Figure 4-4   The group type is selected during group creation.

Figure 4-5   Groups live within the Groups container.

Application

The development of each Authorization Manager-based application determines how roles will function within the application. The assignment of roles and users to groups defines who can perform which roles. The application object in Authorization Manager is created within its Authorization Store and contains the objects that define the RBAC present in the application. An application can exist in only one Authorization Store, but an Authorization Store can contain multiple applications. Table 4-2 lists common tasks the Authorization Manager application supports and compares them to the processing within an ordinary application.

Table 4-2   Application Tasks Comparison

	Authorization Management	Ordinary Application
1	During application development: define roles, implement operations, and roll operations into tasks.	May define roles, but typically does not. Role definition may mean that administrators can run some applications or operations while both users and administrators can run others.

	Authorization Management	Ordinary Application
2	The installation process creates the Authorization Store, operations, tasks, and application-based roles, in addition to defining files or databases used for application data.	The installation process defines files or databases to hold application data and places configuration data in the registry or in a file.
3	At runtime, the application uses the Authorization Manager to connect to the Authorization Store and read the security policy.	At runtime, the application may check configuration information in files or registry hives. During processing, authorization for access to objects is determined by user rights and permissions assigned by administrators.
4	When clients connect to an application, an application context is created.	When a user starts an application, the application runs in the user's security context.
5	Before a client uses an application, custom application behavior is developed based on roles. During operation, each user role may present a different UI based on his role.	Before a client can use the application, custom behavior is defined primarily by the user's rights and permissions on objects. The user interface may show error messages if a user's rights and permissions do not match those required to run the application.
6	When a client attempts to perform an operation, an access check is performed to see if the user's role includes the right to perform the operation.	When the application attempts to perform an operation, an access check is performed to see if the user has the right or permission needed to perform the operation.

When you manage or participate in the development of an Authorization Manager application, you can manage roles in a different and very natural way. To create an Application object in the Authorization Manager, follow these steps:

1. Right-click on the `Authorization Store` node and select `Create New Application`.
2. Enter a name, description, and version number for the application, as shown in Figure 4-6.
3. Click `OK` and view the application in Authorization Manager, as shown in Figure 4-7.

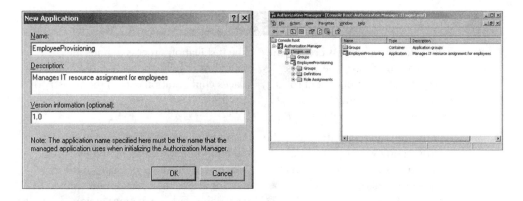

Figure 4-6   Applications are containers created to hold the security policy as defined in roles, groups, operations, and tasks.

Figure 4-7   Applications are created within their Authorization Store.

Scope

Scopes are created within each application to restrict access to resources. A scope specifies resources such as file system folders, Active Directory containers, types of files (such as all *.doc files), URLs, and registry hives. You create Authorization Manager groups, role assignments, role definitions, or task definitions and assign them to the application scope rather than the application. (Operations, however, cannot be defined at the scope level.)

The groups created within the scope have access to the resources they define, while groups created in the application can be assigned access to resources in the entire application including the scope. Using scopes is a good way to restrict the access of some users while empowering others.

A scope can be an NTFS folder, an Active Directory container, a collection of files identified by a mask such as *.doc (a file-masked collection), a URL, and so on. These containers are identified in the Authorization Manager within the Application container.

To create a scope:

1. Right-click on the `Application` node and select `New Scope`.
2. Enter a name and description for the scope, as shown in Figure 4-8. Note that the name is a folder path. Names must represent real locations.
3. Click OK.

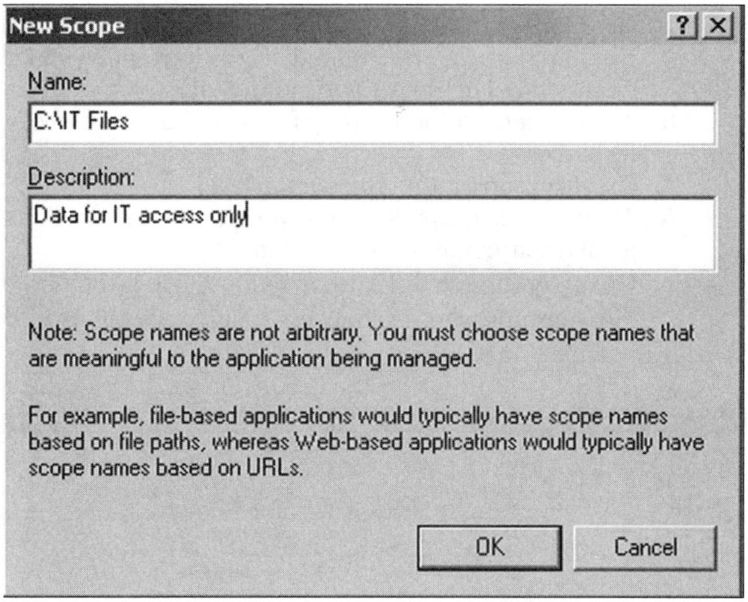

Figure 4-8   Scope names must represent real locations.

You must be careful when creating scopes to make sure they identify resources in a manner that the application can understand. Two things are important here. First, the resource should be identified by location, such as by using file paths, registry hives, or complete URLs, or by identifying existing Active Directory Organizational Units. Second, the application itself must be able to understand the resource. Web-based applications might have URLs as scope identifiers, while file-based applications might use file paths.

To effectively limit access to resources by using their location, follow these steps:

1. Create scopes for resources that need more granular protection.
2. Create application groups in these scopes. Figure 4-9 shows the C:\IT Files scope created within the Itmgmt application. Note how group containers are created at the Authorization Store, Application, and Scope level and how definitions and role assignments are created at both the Scope and Application level. In the figure, any groups created in the Groups container of the C:\IT Files scope can only be granted access to files at that level. Groups created at the Application level may be granted access to

all resources in the application, and groups created in the Authorization Store can be granted access to resources in all applications defined in the Authorization Store.

3. Assign users to these groups who should have access to these resources.

4. Create groups at the Application level.

5. Assign users to Application-level groups that should have access to all resources in the application.

6. Create groups at the Authorization Store level. Assign users to these groups who need access to all applications in the Authorization Store.

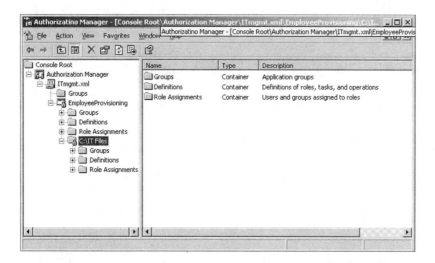

Figure 4-9   The group location determines the resources that may be accessed by its members.

NOTE: Reasons to Use Authorization Manager Groups
You should use Authorization Manager groups for two reasons. First, using these groups provides more control over object access. Second, when Authorization Manager groups are used, the application may be more easily used in both workgroup and domain situations. This is because workgroup machines have different Windows groups from those that are available in the Active Directory. An application designed using Active Directory-based groups could not be used in a workgroup. Note, however, that an application developed specifically for an Active Directory environment may have no useful purpose in a workgroup. You should make your decisions on the types of groups to use based on the application requirements.

Roles, Tasks, Authorization Scripts, and Operations

In an Authorization Manager application, tasks, operations, and authorization scripts define roles. Tasks are composed of lower-level tasks, operations, and authorization scripts. Operations are single units of lower-level operating system functionality. For example, a Help Desk task might be "reset password" for users within a specific organizational unit (OU). A task created within the application might be named ResetPassword. An operation, also created in the application, includes a reference to a number identifying the actual code within the application that allows the user to reset passwords for users within his assigned OU. The operation is assigned to the task, and the task is assigned to the help desk role. Finally, when the role definition is complete, it is assigned to the group created to identify users who will be assigned the help desk role.

When the application is written, operations are programmed. During the development of an Authorization Manager application, the elements for each role are written. During the application's installation, the tasks and operations that define the role populate the Authorization Manager, along with the groups and other application components.

You may have to manually add roles, authorization scripts, tasks, and operations to the Authorization Manager. Just remember that they must correspond to the programmed application, and the numbers defined in the operations forge the links between the Authorization Manager and the application code.

Roles

Before you can control authorization by using roles, the roles must be defined. You do this by adding defined tasks and operations to the roles. Roles can be defined across multiple applications but managed from a single location. Roles can also be confined to specific applications and even to limited resources within the application.

The first step is to identify the roles required. To define roles, think of each one as an abstraction that corresponds to real-world operations and tasks. Help desk operator and systems administrator are roles that might be defined if the application were built to control systems operations. Payroll clerk, accountant, and accounting manager are roles that might be defined for an accounting application. During the development process, a specification based on the real-world tasks of each type of employee is identified. Each task is further broken down into smaller steps or operations.

A well-designed role is one that maps to a job category or responsibility. You can easily find loose role definitions in job titles, but you will need to search beyond the title to determine what it is that the individual actually does. Remember that many employees participate in discrete business functions, and job titles do not always map to specific roles within an application. The process of building a role within an application consists of the following tasks:

- Selecting a name
- Providing a definition
- Specifying lower-level tasks, roles, and operations that are part of the new role. Authorization rules may be written in scripts such as VBScript. Tasks become part of a role definition and can be added or viewed in the Role Definition container.

While the approval for membership in a specific application role is not an administrative task, the actual assignment of a user account to a role is. As usual, understanding what access and rights you are conferring with this assignment is critical. You need to know when a user's access or activity is normal and approved, and when it might represent a breach of conduct, such as an attack upon the system.

NOTE: There's More Than One Way to Create the Role
You can, of course, create all operations first, and then create each task and assign operations to the tasks as you create them. You'd follow this operation by creating roles and adding tasks to them as you create them.

To create and define a role in Authorization Manager, you must create tasks and operations and assign them appropriately. The first step in creating a role in the Authorization Manager is to create the role definition. To do so, follow these steps:

1. Expand the `Application` container, and then expand the `Definitions` container.
2. Right-click `Role Definitions` and select `New Role Definition`.
3. Enter a `name` and `description` for the role, as displayed in Figure 4-10.
4. If lower-level roles, tasks, or authorization scripts have been defined for this role, add them to the role definitions using the `Add` button.
5. Click `OK`.

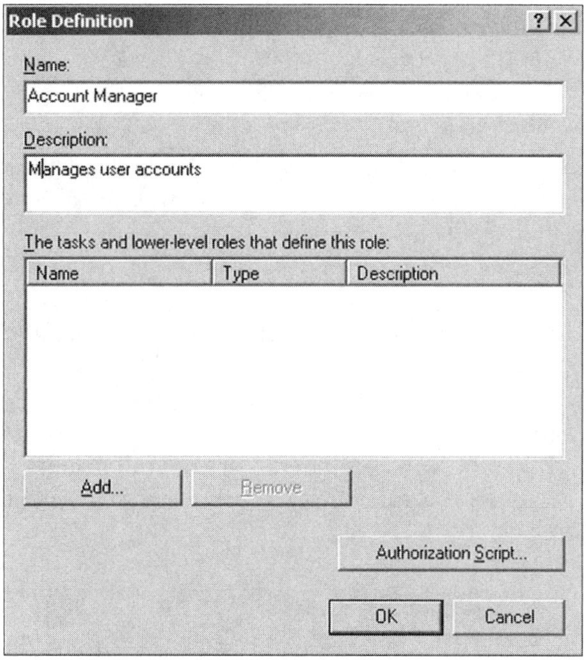

Figure 4-10 Roles are defined by the tasks defined for them and the authorization scripts written for them.

Tasks

Roles are composed of tasks. Tasks are collections of operations, authorization scripts, and possible other tasks. Tasks must be well defined and must be associated with roles. Well-designed tasks represent recognizable work items. Examples of well-defined tasks are as follows:

- Change password
- Enable an account
- Create a user
- Submit an expense
- Approve an expense
- Sign a check

Examples of tasks that are not well defined are:

- Manage employees
- Supervise the accounting department
- Help users with their computers

To determine which tasks should be defined for a specific role, you will need to identify the things that might define what a person performing a role does. For example, a network administrator might change the ACLs on a router. A help desk person might change passwords or reset locked out accounts. Like roles, tasks are defined in the Authorization Manager by identifying a name and description. A task consists of lower-level tasks or operations and authorization scripts.

To create a task, perform the following steps:

1. Right-click the Task Definitions container and select New Task Definition.
2. Enter a name and description for the task, as displayed in Figure 4-11.
3. If lower-level tasks, operations, or authorization scripts have been built for this role, then they can be added using the Add button.
4. Click OK.

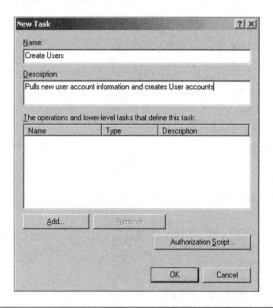

Figure 4-11   Tasks are defined by operations and authorization scripts.

Operations

Operations are a set of permissions associated with system-level or API-level security procedures. Examples would be WriteAttributes or ReadAttributes. Operations are building blocks for tasks. Operations are set only at the application level, not at the Authorization Store or scope level. The definition of an operation includes a name, description, and an operation number. The operation number is used within the application to identify the operation. The operation number is critical because it ties all actions between the Authorization Manager and the application. Because tasks include operations, roles specify the tasks that can be accomplished, and groups are assigned roles, when you add a user to a group, you are giving the user whatever low-level operations make up the tasks assigned to the role.

WARNING: Prevent Operations Number Errors
The number must be an integer from zero to 2147483647. If you must manually enter the number, be sure that it is correct; an incorrect number will cause a bug in the application.

For example, if a number of operations defines the lower-level actions necessary to format the hard drive, and the operations make up the "format disk" task, which in turn is assigned to the Server Manager role, which is assigned to the Application Group ServerManager, then by putting a user in the ServerManager Application Group, you have given her the right to format the hard drive.

To create an operation, do the following:

1. Right-click the Operation Definitions container and select New Operation Definition.
2. Enter a name, description, and operation number, as displayed in Figure 4-12. The operation number must exist within the application code.
3. Click OK.

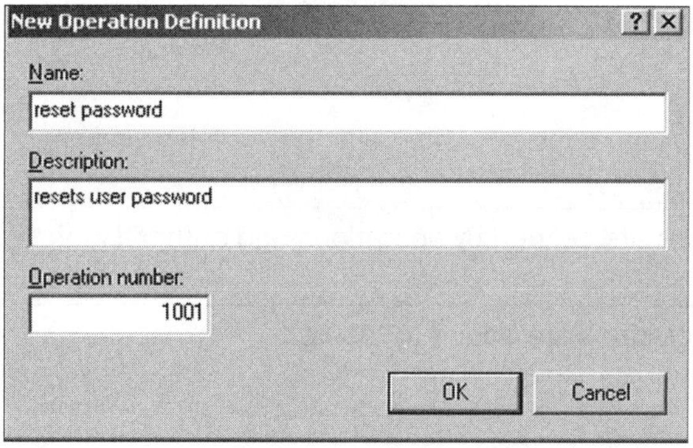

Figure 4-12   Operations are defined by an operation number.

Create Authorization Scripts

Authorization scripts are created to implement authorization rules. An authorization rule tests conditions to determine if a user has the right or permission required to perform a specific task. For example, users may belong to a group that has been assigned a role. The role is defined by tasks that empower a role member to complete some task, such as reading a file. An authorization rule can be used to take into consideration the operating systems rights and object permissions assigned to the user. If the file permissions do not allow the user to read the file, then he will not be allowed to, even though the members of his Application Manager Application group may normally do so. Scripts can be written in VBScript or Jscript and are usually written by programmers.

Define Tasks

Define the task by assigning operations:

1. Double-click the task you want to define.
2. Select the Operations tab.
3. Click to select the operations necessary to define this task, as shown in Figure 4-13.
4. Click OK.

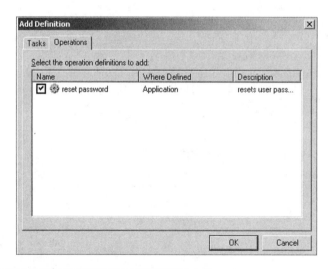

Figure 4-13   Operations are added to tasks.

Define Roles

Finally, you must define the role by assigning it a list of tasks it may perform:

1. Double-click on the role you want to define.
2. Click on the Definitions page.
3. Select the tasks that define the role, as shown in Figure 4-14.
4. If there are authorization scripts that should be added, click the Authorization Scripts button. Enter the script or a path to its location and then click OK.
5. Click OK.

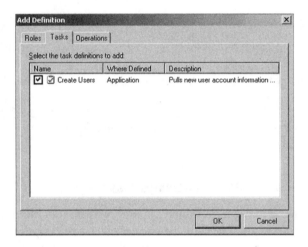

Figure 4-14 Tasks are added to roles.

Assign Roles to Groups

Finally, assign roles to groups:

1. Right-click the Role Assignments container and select Assign Roles.
2. Select roles from the Add Role dialogbox, as shown in Figure 4-15, and then click OK.
3. The role(s) will be added to the Role Assignments container. Right-click on the role you wish to assign and select Assign Groups or Assign Windows Users and Groups.
4. If Assign Groups is selected, select the application group, as shown in Figure 4-16.

5. If `Assign Windows Users and Groups` is selected, use the object picker to select the group or users to be given this role.

6. Click OK.

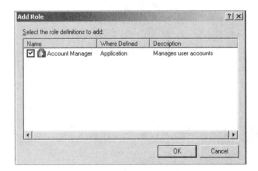 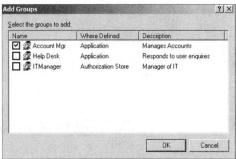

Figure 4-15   Add defined roles to the Roles Assignment container.

Figure 4-16   Assign the appropriate groups to each role.

Authorization Manager Basics Summary

Within Authorization Manager and within specific applications, each role is assigned the right to exercise tasks and operations. The role is assigned to a group, and the group becomes the interface that you, as administrator, will use to assign Windows accounts or groups authorization to use an application and work with resources. Instead of managing resources for the application, you will manage actions and workflow. For example, instead of using the Delegation of Control wizard or directly assigning a user account or group the `reset password` permission on the OU, you will simply add the user's account to the group in Authorization Manager that has been assigned the help desk role.

If access to objects and the rights to run parts of the application are defined, then the administrative role is simple. Instead of hundreds of discrete actions in which you create Windows groups and assign them rights, permissions on Active Directory objects, file objects, registry hives, and other resources, you simply place user accounts or Windows groups into the groups that define the roles.

NOTE: Administrators Need to Know
Administrators are not responsible for building Authorization Manager applications, defining roles, scripting tasks, or authorizing operations. These are developer functions and can be carried out programmatically or by using the Authorization Manager in Developer mode. The administrator's main responsibility is to assign Application groups and Windows groups and users to roles and to add users to groups, thus conferring upon them the appropriate role. However, administrators should understand how the process works so that they may understand the rights and permissions granted on their systems when a user is given a role.

The Authorization Store contains the information required to build the security policy for the application and physically represent it in the Authorization Manager. When the Authorization Store is located in the NTFS file system, it is represented in an XML file. Figure 4-17 is the XML file created by adding the objects defined in the exercises in this section.

Figure 4-17 The Authorization Store XML file holds the security policy for the application.

Auditing Authorization Manager

Event auditing for Authorization Manager Applications can be configured and events will be recorded in the Security event log. Two types of auditing of Authorization Manager are possible:

- **Runtime Auditing**—Audits are generated when policy defined in the Authorization Store is used. Auditing can report success, failure, or both. Client context and access checks are audited. Runtime auditing can be defined for the Authorization Store and the application. It cannot be defined at the scope level.
- **Authorization Store change auditing**—Audit records are generated when the Authorization Store is modified, regardless of location. Active Directory-based Authorization Store change auditing can be defined for Authorization Store, application, and scope. XML Authorization Store change auditing can only be defined at the Authorization Store level.

To turn on auditing, use the check boxes on the Auditing tab, as displayed in Figure 4-18. If auditing of a specific type is not available, the check box will not appear. If the success and failure boxes do not appear, auditing is being managed at a higher level. To change it, you will have to find where it is being managed (locally or Group Policy at the domain or OU level) and modify it there first. All applicable object auditing will be inherited. For example, object access auditing specified on a file in the file system that is a resource in an Authorization Store is inherited. To define auditing the following must apply:

- You must have the Generate security audits privilege.
- You must have the Manage auditing and security log privilege.
- Object access auditing must be turned on either using Group Policy or Local Security Policy as appropriate.

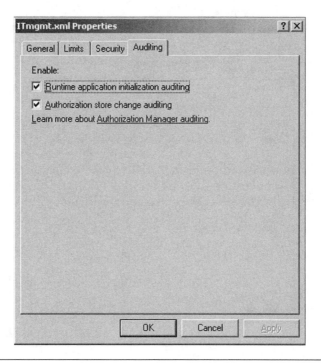

Figure 4-18 Auditing is defined in the properties of the Authorization Store and the application.

Authorization Manager Administration

The administration of Authorization Manager-enabled applications is an easy task if administrators understand how it works and how Authorization Manager applications work. The primary task is to assign users to the groups used in the roles. The administrator may have to participate in the assignment of groups to roles and other tasks if the applications do not programmatically do so. However, like most administrative tasks, simple actions disguise complex operations. The knowledgeable administrator will understand these consequences, audit the activity, and restrain from duplicating or obviating the results by using her power to distribute access to resources and rights that should be left managed by the application.

It may be prudent to limit the number of administrators who can work with Authorization Manager. You can do so by defining the groups and users that may have Administrative access to Authorization Manager. Add or remove groups and users from the `Security` tab of the Authorization Store properties, as shown in Figure 4-19.

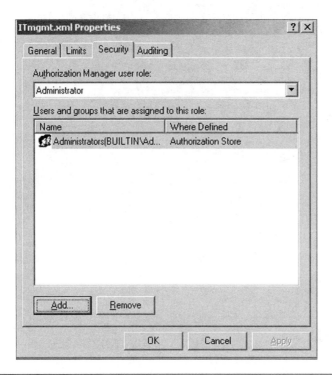

Figure 4-19   Adjust the number of administrators who can administer Authorization Manager applications.

Software Restriction Policies

Imagine if you could prevent a new virus from running on your systems even before your anti-virus vendor had prepared and made public a signature. Imagine if you could prevent well-known but forbidden software such as games or administrative tools from being run by anyone on your system. Imagine if you could prevent as-yet-unknown malicious software from running at all. Would you buy the product that allowed you to do so?

You don't have to. If you have Windows Server 2003 or Windows XP Professional, you already have such a product. Software Restriction Policies is a component that was introduced with Windows XP Professional for the management of a single computer. You can use Windows Server 2003 to write group policies that impact a single server or desktop or thousands of XP Professional and Windows Server 2003 computers. Here's how.

Software Restriction Policy Limitations

If you do not fully understand Software Restriction Policy scope—that is, what it can and cannot do to various things—you may either configure it incorrectly or rely on it for a level of security that it cannot provide. In either case, policies may not work the way you think they do, or worse, you may develop a false sense of security—you may believe you have protected computers from malicious software or prevented anything but authorized programs from running only to find out that this is not so. Properly designed Software Restriction Policies can provide improved security if you understand and work with Software Restriction Policy limitations. The following limitations should be understood.

Software Restriction Policies Have No Effect in Safe Mode

When a computer is booted in Safe Mode, Software Restriction Policies have no effect.

WARNING: Safe Mode
Software Restriction Policies have no effect in Safe Mode. If the user can boot to Safe Mode, she can get around any Software Restriction Policies.

Local Security Policy Affects Every User of the Computer

Software Restriction Policy created in the Local Security Policy will only affect that computer. Because it is a computer-wide policy, it affects every user unless its properties are set to exclude members of the Administrators group. If, however, you use a Group Policy-based Software Restriction Policy, you can create Software Restriction Policies in either the Computer or User Security settings of the GPO. You can determine whom the policy will impact by only applying it to OUs within which specific user or computer accounts lie, or you can filter the GPO's application by removing the Apply Group Policy permission for the desired user groups.

Some Software Is Not Affected by Software Restriction Policies

Software Restriction Policies do not apply to the following:

- Drivers or other kernel mode software
- Programs run by the SYSTEM account

- Macros in Microsoft Office 2000 or Office XP documents (manage macros in Office with the Office Macro security settings)
- Programs written for the common language runtime (these programs use Code Access Security Policy)

There Are Ways to Get Around Rules

Software restriction policies include individual rules that prohibit or allow the use of specific software. However, there are limitations to the effectiveness of each rule. This does not mean that you cannot create effective rules that prohibit use of software; it just means that you must understand each rule's limitations and use it appropriately. Examples of rule limitations are as follows:

- If the code of an application changes, a hash rule no longer applies.
- If the path of an application changes, a path rule no longer applies.
- Internet zone rules apply only to applications created with the Windows Installer.
- Certificate rules rely on the trust you place in the certificate.

For information about these rules, see the section "Creating and Using Software Restriction Policies."

Software Restriction Policy Basics

Restricting access to software doesn't seem like a difficult task. All you have to do is not install it and not allow others to do so either. The problem is that you may lack the ability to control exactly what software should be installed, to control who can install it, and to control who can run software that is already installed on the computer. Some Windows default rights assignments help. A user needs administrative rights to install software that installs a service. But many applications do not do this and therefore do not require administrative rights to be installed. If a user has the right to copy a file to the disk, that simple process may be all the application requires to be installed. Finally, many applications such as Administrative Tools must be present on systems, yet we should deny ordinary users the right to use them. Access to these programs is controlled by user rights assignments and permissions and those you impose. Ordinary users, for example, cannot create or edit Group Policy

Objects (GPOs). Other system applications and their associated registry values are protected by default from some types of users. Group Policy, object ACLs, careful control over user rights—all these things can be used to control access to objects. However, because of poorly coded applications, you may have had to give users administrative rights on their computers.

If you limit user access to resources such as files and registry settings, you may be able to mitigate the harm that might be done by running unauthorized applications. If you provide users awareness training and strictly enforce security policies, you may also prevent applications from being installed. However, none of these techniques will totally prevent the installation and use of rogue or malicious software.

NOTE: Software Restriction Policy Design
An excellent paper that includes information on designing software restriction policies is "Using Software Restriction Policies to Protect Against Unauthorized Software," available at http://www.microsoft.com/technet/ prodtechnol/winxppro/maintain/rstrplcy.mspx. The paper includes design scenarios for Terminal services, line-of-business PC, and the use of different policies for different users.

When you use Software Restriction policies, however, you supplement default settings and hardening steps and provide a solution for controlling things that defaults and other operations cannot control. With Software Restriction Policies, you can do the following:

- Prevent any software from running and then authorize each piece of necessary software individually.
- Allow all software to run and then restrict specific software from running.

These basic security levels determine initially whether software will run or not. After a security level has been chosen, software restriction policies can identify software via hash, path, URL, or code signing certificate and prevent or allow the software to run based on its identification. The software does not have to exist on the system before a policy can be written to prevent or allow its use.

WARNING: Automatic Path Rules

Automatic path rules are created as a protection against locking all users out of the system. These path rules are always visible in the Additional Rules folder and are as follows:

```
%HKEY_LOCAL_MACHINE\SOFTWARE\Microsoft\Windows
NT\CurrentVersion\SystemRoot%
%HKEY_LOCAL_MACHINE\SOFTWARE\Microsoft\Windows
NT\CurrentVersion\SystemRoot%\*.exe
%HKEY_LOCAL_MACHINE\SOFTWARE\Microsoft\Windows
NT\CurrentVersion\SystemRoot%\System32\*.exe
%HKEY_LOCAL_MACHINE\SOFTWARE\Microsoft\Windows\Current
Version\ProgramFilesDir%
```

As a general rule, you should not modify these rules unless you are very knowledgeable about the registry and the access that the System requires to itself.

Creating and Using Software Restriction Policies

To establish a Software Restriction Policy, you must first create the basic policy and then write rules. To establish the policy follow these steps:

1. Create a Software Restriction Policy.
2. Set the security level.
3. Determine enforcement.
4. Establish file types that define what an executable file is.

Create a Software Restriction Policy

A Software Restriction Policy is created in the `Software Restriction Policy` container of a local policy or Group Policy Object (GPO) in the Active Directory. Local policies only affect the machine that they are developed on, while Active Directory-based policies can be linked to domains and organizational units and can impact a multitude of systems and users in a uniform manner. Deciding where to link a GPO requires much thought and will depend on your Active Directory design. More details are available in Chapter 7. Regardless of where a policy is created, you should test its implementation on a single test computer that is configured in the manner typical for its use. If the policy is to be deployed on many machines in a domain, careful testing in a test domain or OU is required. Remember: Software Restriction Policies are power-ful. It is possible to develop a policy that prohibits the use of software on a computer. Imagine what that would do if introduced into thousands of computers in your organization. As usual, deployment issues are the most complicated ones of this task; creating a policy for a single machine is simple. To create a Software Restriction Policy in the Local policy:

1. Click `Start`, `Run`, and in the `Run` box, type `secpol.msc`
   OR
   Click `Start`, `Programs`, `Administrative Tools`, `Local Secu-`
   `rity Policy`.
2. Select the `Software Restriction Policies` container.
3. If no policy exists, as shown in Figure 4-20, right-click the `Soft-`
   `ware Restrictions Policy` container and select `New Software`
   `Restriction Policy`.
4. The default containers and objects will be created, as shown in Figure 4-21.

Figure 4-20   By default, no Software Restriction Policy exists.

Figure 4-21   Creating a policy populates the node.

Set the Security Level

The security level determines whether all software is allowed to run unfettered (in which case some software will be identified as not allowed) or no software is allowed to run (in which case some software will be identified as allowed). Sounds simple, doesn't it? It will take a bit of work, regardless of your decision. The interface may also be a bit confusing.

To allow all software to run and restrict some, the security level is "Unrestricted." Not "allowed," or "ok," or "let all software run unless otherwise identified"—nope, the security level you must choose (it happens to be the default, so we're okay at first) is "Unrestricted." Well, you might say, perhaps that makes sense; after all, the policies are called "Software Restriction Policies," so we want to indicate that unless software is restricted, it's unrestricted. However, the alternative security level is not "restricted," it's "disallowed." If all software is restricted, then it's "disallowed."

You'll find this funkiness repeated when you build the rules. Each rule has its own security level—it's either disallowed or unrestricted. We'll talk more about this use when we discuss each rule type; just keep this official naming convention straight at the policy level so you don't freeze thousands of user machines, okay? Remember: *Unrestricted* means anything can run unless you somehow restrict it. *Disallowed* means nothing can run unless it's allowed. A good rule of thumb is that you should set the security level to "disallow" only if you know all of the applications that must be run. Otherwise, set the security level to "unrestricted" (the default). Paradoxically, setting the level to "disallow" and then only unrestricting the software that is allowed to run can create the more secure environment. This, however, is more difficult than it might sound at first.

To set the security level for the policy, do the following:

1. Expand the Software Restriction Policy.
2. Double-click on the Security Levels Folder.
3. The detail pane shows both possibilities. The current default is marked with a check. If this is not what you want, double-click on the security level you desire: either `Disallowed` or `Unrestricted`.
4. Use the `Set as Default` button to set your choice to the default security level, as shown in Figure 4-22.
5. Click `OK`.

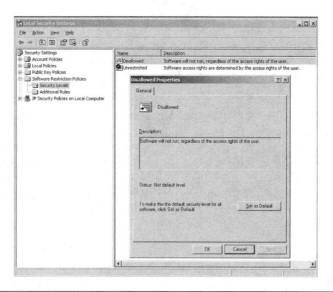

Figure 4-22   The security level can be changed.

Determine Enforcement

Local Software Restriction Policies are computer-based, while Group Policy-based Software Restriction Policies can be computer- or user-based. You can prevent administrators from being affected by policies by using the All users except local administrators enforcement rule. Alternatively, select All users to make sure the policy applies to all users—including members of the Administrators group. If users must be members of the local Administrators group on their own machine, be sure *not* to set enforcement for All users except local administrators.

A second enforcement choice determines if software libraries are restricted. Software libraries are code files that are not executable but are used by executable files. In most cases, this means a file type of DLL. Set either All software files except libraries (such as DLLs) or All software files. Choosing All software files except libraries simplifies policy writing and prevents performance degradation. It assumes that if you want to allow software to execute, you want its libraries to be accessible. It also assumes that if you want to disallow software, its DLLs won't be executed. It doesn't manage the libraries. However, you may want or need tighter control. Remember, however, that DLL checking can reduce performance. Each program the user runs causes a software policy evaluation. If I run 10 programs, 10 checks are done. If each program uses 15 DLLs, and I am enforcing DLL checking, there are 160 checks done. Libraries contain code that could be accessed by other applications that we may not be managing. If harm, either accidental or malicious, might be possible using these libraries, you may want to control them by changing enforcement to `All software files`.

WARNING: The All Software Selection Means Extra Work Identifying DLLs and Writing Rules

Be aware that if you chose the software security level of "disallowed" and an enforcement level of "All software," then to allow a specific software application to run, you must explicitly identify all of its libraries and give them the level of "unrestricted." This could prove to be an onerous task.

To configure enforcement, do the following:

1. Select and expand the Software Restriction Policy.
2. Double-click on the Enforcement object in the detail pane to open its properties, as shown in Figure 4-23.
3. Select the software enforcement level.
4. Select the user enforcement level.
5. Click OK to close the enforcement object.

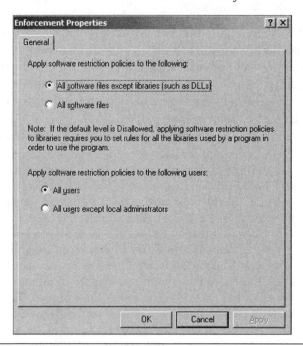

Figure 4-23   Set enforcement rules for the policy.

Establish Designated File Types

What constitutes an executable? What types of files will be restricted if you set the Security Level to "disallowed?" These questions can be answered by viewing the properties of the Designated File Types object within the policy, as shown in Figure 4-24.

On this page, you review, add, or remove the file types that you want to designate as software for purposes of this policy. By doing so, you can keep policies updated if new software introduces new executable file types. You should guard access to this configuration page, because a malicious user might get around software restriction policies by removing a file extension from the list.

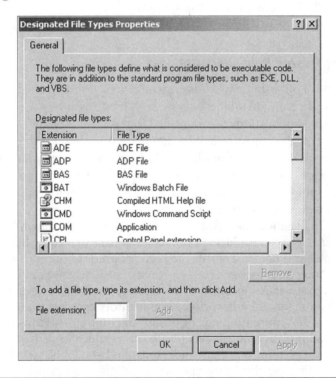

Figure 4-24   Designated file types define "software" to the policy.

To inspect or modify designated file types, follow these steps:

1. Select the `Software Restriction Policies` container.
2. Double-click the `File Types` object in the details pane of the `Software Restriction Policy` container.
3. Scroll through the window, as shown in Figure 4-24, to see which file types are identified as being software.
4. To remove a file type, select it and click the `Delete` button. Click `OK` to dismiss the warning.
5. To add a file type, enter its extension in the `Extension` box and click the `Add` button.
6. Click `OK` to close the window.

Set Trusted Publishers Options

Trusted publishers are those organizations that you trust to publish safe code. This option affects only ActiveX controls and other signed content. Trusted applications are identified to the system by their certificate, and they use their private key to sign code that they produce. By selecting approved, trusted publishers, you can control whether or not signed software can execute on the computer. Add trusted publishers by importing their certificate into the Trusted Publishers container of the computer certificate store.

You can use the Trusted Publisher options, as shown in Figure 4-25, to manage who can accept publisher certificates and what things should be checked before a certificate is considered valid.

You can select `End users`, `Local administrators`, or `Enterprise administrators` as authorized Trusted Publisher selectors. By default, only domain and enterprise administrators can determine Trusted Publishers for entire domains or groups of computers. However, local users and administrators can accept offered certificates as trusted certificates on local systems if policy is not controlled at a higher level. The value of restricting certificate acceptance to administrators is that users cannot simply click `OK` when offered a certificate while downloading or installing software. By setting this level, you prevent them, for example, from making decisions about trusting ActiveX controls that they may download from the Internet or receive as attachments in email. After all, no one has to pass an ethics test to purchase or obtain a code-signing certificate. The only thing the certificate can do is to authenticate the signer in some fashion. You can further extend the concept of using certificates to control software by writing certificate rules.

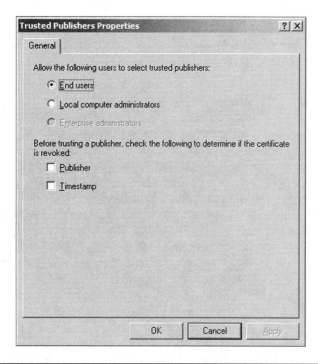

Figure 4-25   Trusted Publisher options allow you to determine who can accept the publishers that will be trusted.

You can require that Publisher, Timestamp, or both characteristics be used to determine the validity of a certificate. Selecting Publisher requires that the certificate be checked for revocation. Checking the Timestamp requires that the certificate be checked for expiration.

Creating Software Restriction Policy Rules

Software restriction policy rules are applied to specific software (using hash rules, certificate rules, computer path, and URL rules), to its location (using path rules and URL rules), and by referring to a registry path that controls it. Each type of rule has its own advantages and disadvantages. Path rules, for example, can unrestrict or disallow a large group of software in one simple rule. However, if a user can copy the file(s) to another path, she can execute the code. Hash rules can be applied only to a single executable per rule but will prevent a user from running that software, no matter its source, path, or name. However, if the software changes (the virus mutates or a new version of the game is produced), then you must write another rule. The best approach is not to rely on one type of rule, and especially not to set rules and then believe you will never have to set them again. The best approach even includes using file ACLs to further control a user's access to the executable objects.

Software Restriction Example

At a company I worked with, Sally was used to controlling her own computer. She downloaded cool tools and drivers from the Internet, brought software from home, and whiled away the hours playing Solitaire and FreeCell. She'd even convinced the powers that be that she needed to have local administrator group membership on her Windows XP Professional system. Then her organization implemented Software Restriction Policies. The first thing Sally noticed was that she couldn't play Solitaire. She'd double-click on the sol.exe shortcut on her desktop and get the warning message in Figure 4-26. So she copied the sol.exe program to another folder to play it. Next, that stopped working, too. Sally was getting mad. She found that many of her other pastimes were disappearing. She could no longer download just any software, and she no longer seemed to have full administrative privileges on her computer. She was losing control. Finally, frustrated and unable to find a way around the restrictions, Sally discovered that the reason for her troubles was the new administrator who'd convinced management to use Software Restriction Policies. Sally tried to sabotage the policies and the new administrator. She began to delete the program files of applications she was supposed to run and moved the location of others to paths that were restricted. When her programs would not run, she reported this and any error message she was able to trigger about policies.

The new administrator almost lost his job, and Software Restriction Policies were blamed for the trouble. Fortunately, the administrator was able to turn on auditing for Sally's computer and figure out what she was doing. With this proof, it was Sally who had to leave.

Since then, all Software Restriction Policies have been backed up by appropriate file ACLs, which prevent harmful action, support the restriction (deny execute), and track user attempts at access and possible attacks.

Figure 4-26   When a user attempts to execute restricted software, a warning message is displayed.

Four types of rules can be created:

- Hash rules
- Certificate rules
- Path rules, including file path rules and registry path rules
- Internet zone rules

To complete your Software Restriction Policy, you must create rules. To begin, determine which software must run and which must not. Next, determine the type of rule to use, and finally, write the rules. The task of determining which software should run and which shouldn't is not easy. You will need to review your security policy and the jobs held by users of the computers, and you will need to consult with management. The suggestions in Table 4-3 may help you decide which type of rule to use.

Table 4-3   Best Practices for Selecting Rule Types

Rule	Purpose
Hash	Allow or disallow a specific version of a program
Zone	Allow software to be installed from Trusted Internet zone sites
Path	Allow or disallow a program that is always installed to the same location
Certificate	Identify a set of scripts that can be run
Registry path	Allow or disallow a program whose path is stored in the registry
Path using UNC format share (\\SERVER\share)	Allow or disallow a set of scripts located on a server
Two path rules *.vbs set to disallowed, and \\LOGIN-XRV\share*.vbs set to unrestricted	Disallow all VBS files except those in a login script—use two path rules
An flcss.exe path rule set to disallowed	Disallow a new virus that is always named flcss.exe

When multiple rules affect the same software file, the precedence rule determines which rule will win by examining the rules against the precedence order. The order of precedence from top to bottom is as follows:

- Hash
- Certificate
- Path
- Internet zone

For example, if the security level of the policy is unrestricted, and a path rule disallows (prevents from running) the software, but a hash rule allows it, the hash rule wins, and the software can run. In the case of multiple path rules, the most restrictive rule will take precedence. For example, if a path rule is set on the C:\mysoftware folder that prevents software from running (the security level of the path rule is "disallowed"), but another path rule names the C:\mysoftware\approved folder and sets the security level to "unrestricted," then software in the C:\mysoftware\approved folder can run.

NOTE: Virus Rules

Software Restriction Policies are not meant to take the place of anti-virus products. Remember that hash rules don't work when files change (and viruses often mutate). Recall that virus names also can change. Anti-virus programs work to recognize patterns or signatures that the viruses have and are more effective in preventing infection. However, a software restriction policy could be written that could add some protection when a new virus is identified but a signature pattern is not yet available from your anti-virus product vendor.

You should test each rule on test systems before putting them on production systems. After configuring rules but before testing, reboot the system to ensure the rule is in effect.

Hash Rules

Hash rules work by creating a hash of the executable file. A hash can take a variable amount of information and reduce it to a unique digest of a standard size. Ideally, no two software files hashed by the same algorithm will ever produce the same hash. Signed and unsigned programs can be restricted with hash rules. The signed program may have a hash produced by either the MD5 or SHA-1 algorithm. When a hash rule is created, it will use whichever hash is present. If a file is not signed, the MD5 hashing algorithm will be used. The hash rule contains the hash, the file length, and an ID that identifies the hash algorithm.

NOTE: Always Choose Collision-Resistant Hashing Algorithms
While the possibility of collision (the production of the same hash from different data) is always present, it is unlikely to occur. When choosing hashing algorithms, developers should choose those currently considered to be less prone to collision. When considering choices between applications, administrators also should consider this. For more information, read http://www.rsasecurity.com/rsalabs/node.asp?id=2738, in which the 2004 results of research on collisions in MD5 are examined.

When a user attempts to run a program and there is a policy in place, a new hash is made and compared with the hash available in the hash rules. If there is a match, and the related hash rule specifies "disallowed," then the software will not run, no matter where the attempt to execute it is made. For example, if a hash rule is made for the sol.exe program, then it will apply to the program, no matter where the executable is stored or run from, even if it has been renamed. Users cannot get around the rule by copying the file to another folder. However, if the executable file changes, the hash made at attempted execution will not match any stored in the rules, and the software will run. To create a hash rule, follow these steps:

1. Open the Software Restriction Policy.
2. Right-click on the Additional Rules folder and select Create New hash rule.
3. In the New Hash Rule dialog box, click Browse.
4. Browse to and select the file you want to create a hash rule for.
5. Click Open to confirm this file and return to the dialog box.
6. The file hash is created and placed in the hash text box, and the information windows are automatically filled, as shown in Figure 4-27.
7. Select "disallowed" or "unrestricted." If the Security Level is unrestricted, to disallow this particular program, select "disallowed." If the Security Level is disallowed, then select "unrestricted" to allow the program to run. Remember: "Disallowed" will prevent the program from running, and "unrestricted" will permit the program to run.
8. Enter a description for the rule.
9. Click the OK button to finish the rule and return to the policy.

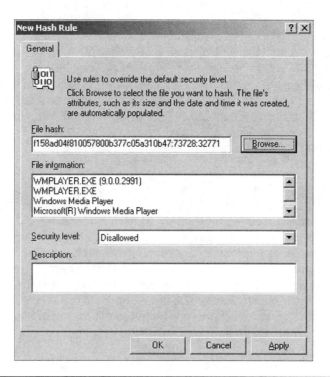

Figure 4-27   After you browse to a file, the hash is copied from the digital signature of the file or is created for you.

NOTE: If the Executable Changes, the Hash Rule Is No Longer Valid
Remember: If the executable changes, the hash rule is no longer valid. It does not matter how significant the change is, and there are simple, freely available tools that can be used to make minor modifications. Reshack.exe is such a tool. It is often used to modify the resources (such as the icon) in a Windows executable file. A determined user may easily discover this tool and learn how to use it. This points out the need for security awareness education, not to teach users how to do such a modification, but rather for administrators to recognize that it is possible and to develop alternatives to technical controls. It also makes a better case for establishing the use of "disallow all" and then only allowing approved executables.

Certificate Rules

Certificate rules can restrict or allow software based on the digital signature applied to the file. A certificate rule specifies a code-signing software publisher certificate. The rule uses the signed hashes from the signature of the signed file to match files. The location of the file does not matter. If the software is signed by one of the certificates identified in a certificate rule, then the security level specified will be applied to the file. This type of rule might be used if a company's policy is to require that all ActiveX scripts are signed by a specific digital signature.

Certificate rules apply only to the file types identified in the Designated Files types folder. To write a certificate rule, you must have a copy of the certificate associated with the signed files. The use of certificate rules must also be enabled using Group Policy. For example, to use a certificate rule to allow only those VB scripts that are signed by your organization's code-signing certificate, you must do the following:

- Enable Certificate Rules in Group Policy.
- Sign your VB scripts.
- Extract a copy of the certificate to an accessible file location.
- Add a path rule that disallows all scripts of this type, such as *.VBS.
- Create a certificate rule that identifies your certificate and set the security policy to "unrestricted."

To enable the use of certificates rules, do this:

1. Open the Group Policy that affects this machine (Group Policy Object in Active Directory or Local Security Policy).
2. Navigate to Local Security Policy, Security Options.
3. Double-click on the option System Settings: Use certificate rules on Windows executables for Software Restriction Policies.
4. Select Enabled.
5. Click OK to close and assign the new security settings.

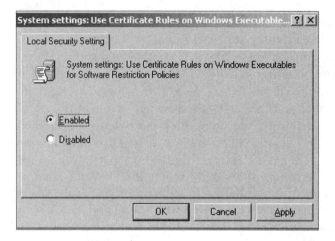

Figure 4-28   To enable certificate rules, you must enable a Security Option.

To create a certificate rule, follow these steps:

1. Open the Software Restriction Policy.
2. Right-click on the `Additional Rules` folder and select `Create New certificate rule`.
3. Browse to select a certificate.
4. Select a security level.
5. Click `OK` to complete the rule.

Internet Zone Rules

Internet zone rules only apply to applications that use the Windows Installer packages to install. Internet zone rules determine if an application from a site in that zone can be installed. All zones can be selected, including Local Computer, Internet, Local Intranet, Restricted Sites, and Trusted Sites.

To create an Internet zone rule, do the following:

1. Open the Software Restriction Policy.
2. Right-click on the `Additional Rules` folder and select `Create New Internet Zone rule`.
3. Select the zone to control.
4. Select a security level for the rule, as shown in Figure 4-29.
5. Click `OK` to complete the rule.

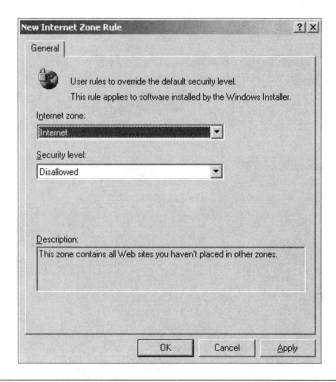

Figure 4-29   Zone rules determine if software can be installed from sites in these zones.

Path Rules and Registry Path Rules

Path rules set restriction policies for software that is stored in or below that path. There are file path rules and registry path rules. You may use wildcards, such as * and ?, and environmental variables, such as %program files% or %system root%, in defining your file system path. If the location in the file system may vary from computer to computer and you know the registry path that specifies its location, then write a registry path rule. Registry paths must be enclosed in percent "%" signs and must be of a REG_SZ or REG_EXPAND_SZ value. You may not use abbreviations such as HKLM or HKLU.

If you have programs that must run at startup and you use the Run registry key to make it happen, create a registry rule for the path `HKEY_CURRENT_USER\Software\Microsoft\Windows\CurrentVersion\Run` and set it to "unrestricted."

Alternatively, if you do not want to have programs run at startup by using this path, you should create a registry rule for the path and set it to "disallowed."

To create a path rule follow these steps:

1. Open the Software Restriction Policy.
2. Right-click the `Additional Rules` container and select `Create a new path rule` or `Create a new registry path rule`.
3. Enter the path, as shown in Figure 4-30.
4. Click OK to close the windows and create the policy.

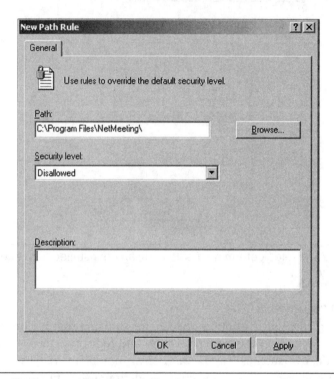

Figure 4-30   Registry and file paths define locations where software is disallowed or unrestricted.

Hacking Software Restriction Policy Security Levels

As administrators, we are often gently suckered into reliance on the visible administrative controls presented in the GUI and in public documentation for command-line tools and registry modification. We often forget that acres of code lie underneath the public presentation provided to us, acres of code that might be used just as much for good as for evil. Don't let my use of the word "hacking" in the title here make you think of illegal activities or wanton disregard for proper testing and planning. Instead, think of it as a warning. I am not suggesting that you attempt to illegally obtain Windows source code or reverse engineer Windows to secure it. Like any good hack, this suggestion is not for use by every Windows administrator or in all circumstances, and it requires extensive testing in your environment to determine if it's suitable. Be forewarned: This hack may break applications. I suggest you thoroughly read documentation http://msdn.microsoft.com/library/default.asp?url=/library/en-us/dncode/html/secure11152004.asp and continued at http://msdn.microsoft.com/library/default.asp?url=/library/en-us/dncode/html/secure01182005.asp. The documentation discusses other ways to reduce user rights without using a separate user identity and includes the warning that this technology may change in future versions of Windows.

The hack consists of modifying the registry so that three new security levels are available in Software Restriction policies. The new levels are as follows:

- **Normal User (or Basic User)**—User does not have Administrator or Power user rights.
- **Constrained (Restricted User)**—HKEY_CURRENT_USER is read-only. %USRPROFILE% is inaccessible. Some crypto operations such as SSL negotiation do not work.
- **Untrusted**—Further constraints beyond Constrained but not documented.

Each level allows the execution of software identified as unrestricted but restricts what the user can do by successively reducing the privileges the user has. This is important because users may need some rights for some applications but may be able to run others successfully without them. It is always considered a good security practice to run any application with the least amount of privileges. For example, running Internet Explorer as an administrator while browsing the Internet is not a good idea. Use Software Restriction Policies and the Normal User Security level to restrict use of IE.

To make the new Basic User Security level available in Software Restriction Policies, you must edit the registry. Open the Registry Editor and navigate to `HKEY_LOCAL_MACHINE\SOFTWARE\Policies\Microsoft\WIndows\Safer\CodeIdentifiers`. Then add a DWORD value named Levels and set it to 0x20000.

Troubleshooting Software Restriction Policies

Many problems with Software Restriction Policies are the result of administrators or users not understanding how and why policies are created. A number of common issues may occur, such as these:

- Users complain they received the message `Windows cannot open this program because it has been prevented by a software restriction policy`. This may be the expected result, because they are not supposed to run the program. Before changing the policy, ask the question, "Why is there a software restriction policy in place?" If the user should be able to run the application, look for possible conflicts between policies (inspect the precedence rule) and identify whether the policy is being applied to the correct Organizational Unit or domain in Active Directory or to the correct computer if Local Security Policy is being used.
- A user complains that he cannot run an application that he has permission to run, and has correct. There are numerous software restriction policies in the domain that may affect the user. You can find the policy that is the problem by inspecting the GUID assigned to the policy rule that is causing the problem. Each software restriction rule is assigned a unique GUID. An event in the user's log will contain the GUID. Running gpresult, a Windows resource kit tool, or Resultant Set of Policy (RSOP) identifies the GPO policy that contains this GUID, and thus this rule. Inspecting the Software Inspection Policy may reveal a mistake, which can then be corrected.
- Administrators complain that when running a utility from the command line, they get the message, "The system cannot execute the specified program." This may be a software restriction policy, because this is the message given if a policy prevents a program from running, and it is executed from the command line. Determine the administrator's right to run the utility, and look for possible conflicts. If the administrator should be able to run the program, but users should not, you may be able to set enforcement on that machine to "All users but Administrators."
- A Local Security Policy Software Restriction Policy is not taking effect. Software Restriction Policies created in Active Directory will take precedence over those created locally. Check to see if a policy exists in the AD.
- A Local Security Policy is taking effect, even though a domain policy exists. Check to ensure that the AD policy has refreshed. Check to ensure that the local computer is downloading the policy from the domain controller.

- A change to Software Restriction Policies is now preventing anyone from logging on at the computer. It is possible to create a rule that prevents some software necessary for successful boot, including logon. You can recover by booting in Safe Mode, logging on as the local administrator, and fixing the policy. Software Restriction Policies do not take effect in Safe Mode.
- A rule created to restrict a specific application is not taking effect. It is possible that the file type for the application is not included in the `Designated File Types` container for Software Restriction Policies. You can add the file type to this list.

You will often be able to determine why a Software Restriction Policy is having a problem by exercising common sense, reviewing settings, and referring to the common problems listed previously. However, when these options do not help, enabling advanced logging will allow you to record every software restriction policy evaluation. Advanced logging is enabled by doing the following:

1. Create the registry key:
   ```
   HKLM\SOFTWARE\Policies\Microsoft\Windows\Safer\
   Codeidentifiers
   ```
2. Add the string value LogFileName.
3. Give the string value the path to a log file.

To disable logging, delete the key.

Best Practices for Software Restriction Policies

When developing Software Restriction Policies, you will want to ensure that you get the best result. These policies can be a powerful agent in controlling what software can run on a computer, or they can hinder productivity and prevent work from getting done. Microsoft recommends the following best practices for software restriction policies.

- If used in a domain, never set software restriction policies in the domain policy. Always create a separate GPO for software restriction policies. Because no software restriction policies are set by default, you have the option of recovering from an incorrect software restriction policy by removing or disabling a created software restriction policy and allowing the domain policy to be reapplied.

- Never link to a software restriction policy in another domain, because it will result in poor performance.
- Use WMI filtering. You can create a filter that restricts the application of a GPO to, say, computers with a specific service pack. WMI filters are set in the property pages of the GPO.
- Use Security Filtering. You can filter which groups of users the policy will apply to. This is done by adding the group to the `security` tab of the GPO property pages and (if you want the group to be exempt from the Software Policy) making sure they do not have the "apply group policy" permissions. You can also improve performance by making sure they do not have the `read policy` permission. If they do not have the `read policy` policy permission, the GPO will not be downloaded to their computer.
- If you have problems with software restriction policies, reboot into Safe Mode. Software restriction policies have no effect in Safe Mode, so you can log on as administrator, change the policy, refresh the policy using gpupdate, and reboot.
- If you are going to change the default security level setting to "disallowed," change the Enforcement setting to "All users except administrators" at least until you can troubleshoot the system. Setting the security level setting to "disallowed" will mean you must write a policy to allow each bit of software to run.
- Use access controls (file and registry access control lists) in concert with software restriction policies. Users will attempt to go around policies by moving files, overwriting files, or adding other copies to other locations. You can deny them the ability to do so.
- Before implementing policies, test them in a test network. If policies are to be used in a domain, test them in a test domain.
- Do not guess about the effects of setting restrictions on files. Disallowing some files to run can prevent the system from running or can make it unstable.
- Filter software restriction policy application when applied in a domain policy by denying read and apply policy permissions on the GPO.
- Manage the designate file types container. This defines what file types besides EXE and DLL are considered to be programs. If you use "disallow" rules, which disallow all programs, and the file type is not defined here, the software will run. Path rules are also affected by this policy.

- Change the default on the trusted publishers from "user" to local computer administrators for standalone servers and either the local administrator or enterprise administrators if the server is in a domain.
- Ensure that users must periodically log off and log back on to systems. (When a new software restriction policy is implemented or there are changes to an existing software restriction policy, the user must log off and log back on again before the policy will take effect.)
- If users are members of the local administrator group on their computer, change enforcement settings so that the policy applies to administrators.
- Write a path rule for the attachment folder of email programs (the folder where attachments are temporarily placed and from which they can be run). If the path is disallowed, attachments cannot accidentally be run, and perhaps you will avoid the next attachment virus. If the attachment is a program that is okay and desired by the recipient, he must save it to another folder, one from which software is allowed to run.

Securing COM, COM+, and DCOM Applications Using Component Services

Component Object Model (COM), COM+, and Distributed COM (DCOM) applications are managed from the Component Services console, as displayed in Figure 4-31. You can manage security for these applications inasmuch as the application provides interfaces for doing so. COM+ applications, for example, may define roles that have specific privileges and permissions within the application. You can manage roles using the console if roles have been defined in the application.

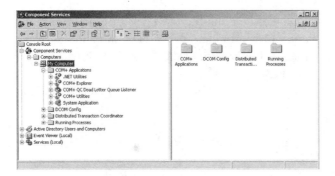

Figure 4-31　　The Component Services console is used to manage security for COM+ and COM applications.

Security for all COM, COM+, and DCOM applications consists of the following:

- Setting user rights, audit, and resources permissions such as those set on NTFS folders and files.
- Setting system-wide properties that will be used by all applications that you do not manage explicitly.
- Setting Application properties for each application that you want to manage explicitly.
- Adding users and groups to roles in role-enabled COM+ applications.
- Ensuring only administrators can modify application settings and add users to roles.
- Limiting the number of administrators who can modify COM+ security.

WARNING: Don't Adjust Existing COM+ Application Properties

It is not recommended that you adjust application properties because applications may contain code that requires the default settings to be in place. Modifying settings may cause an application to fail, become unstable, or behave less securely. Unless you thoroughly understand the application and know why modifying settings can improve security, you should leave settings as they are. The best time to question the default settings used on an application is during its development.

Configuring Security for COM and COM+ Application Interaction

A number of properties can be configured:

- Authentication level for calls
- Authorization
- Security Level
- Impersonation
- Identification
- Launch Permissions
- Access Permissions

Authentication Level for Calls

An identity is a characteristic such as a user ID or computer name. Authentication is the process by which an identity proves it is who it claims to be. Calls to COM+ components may be restricted to users with a specific role, in which case authentication is used to determine if the user is who they say they are, and then their membership is checked.

NOTE: Resource

You can learn more about managing COM+ applications from the platform Software Development KIT (SDK). You can locate a copy online at the MSDN site, http://msdn.microsoft.com.

Authentication level is specified in the Component Services tool, or it can be managed programmatically using Administrative SDK functions. COM+ server and client applications can require authentication. Authentication can be set to a range of degrees, from none to encryption of every packet and all method call parameters. The following list is ordered from no authentication to the highest level. Authentication is negotiated between the client and the server, and the more secure setting of the two is used. You can control authentication from the server side by setting authentication to the highest level you desire. Machine-wide settings (the default is connect) are used if the authentication level is not set for an application. Authentication levels are as follows:

- **None**—No authentication occurs.
- **Connect**—Credentials are checked only when a connection is made.
- **Call**—Credentials are checked at the beginning of each call.
- **Packet**—Credentials are checked, and verification that all called data is received takes place.

- **Packet integrity**—Credentials are checked, and verification that call data has not changed in transit takes place.
- **Packet privacy**—Credentials are checked, and verification that all information in the packet, including sender's identity and signature, are encrypted

To set machine-wide authentication level, follow these steps:

1. Open the Component Services administrative tool.
2. Right-click on the `Computer` container and click `Properties`.
3. Select the `Default Properties` tab, as shown in Figure 4-32.

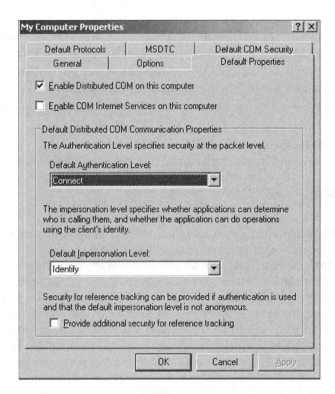

Figure 4-32   The default properties of the application can enable the use of application-defined roles.

4. Ensure that the `Enable Distributed COM on this computer` option is checked.
5. Use the `Default Authentication Level` box to select a value.
6. Click `OK`.

Authorization

If role-based security is available in the COM+ application, enable authorization checking. Users who access the application are checked for role membership before being authorized to do anything in the application. To enable authorization checking, follow these these steps:

1. Open the Component Services console.
2. Right-click on the COM+ application, and then click Properties.
3. Select the Security tab.
4. In the Authorization box, select the Enforce access checks for this application check box, as shown in Figure 4-33.
5. Click OK.

Security Level

The security level sets the level at which access level checks are performed in role-enabled COM+ applications. Access checks can be set at the component level or at the process level. Setting access checks at the component level enables roles. Roles can be assigned to components, interfaces, and methods within the COM+ application. Process-level access checks apply only to application boundaries.

To set a security level, follow these steps:

1. Open the Component Services console.
2. Right-click the application and click Properties.
3. Select the Security tab.
4. Under Security level, as shown in Figure 4-33, select either

   Perform access checks only at the process level

   or

   Perform access checks at the process and component level
5. Click OK.
6. Restart the application for the checks to take place.

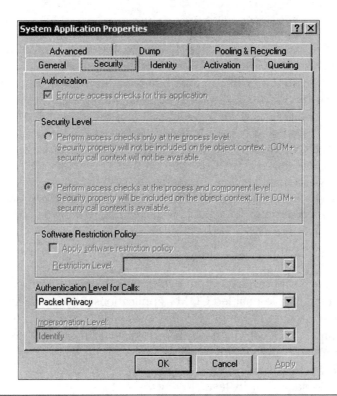

Figure 4-33   Use the Security tab to set authorization level, security level, and impersonation level.

Impersonation and Delegation

When a server makes a call on behalf of a client and uses the client's credentials instead of its own, it is performing impersonation. Resource access is thus expanded, or restricted, depending on what the user can do. For example, you may need the server application to access data in a database, in which case you would want it to be able to get any data that the client has permission to access.

Impersonation levels are as follows:

- **Anonymous**—Client is anonymous as far as the server is concerned. The server can impersonate the client, but no information about the client is in the impersonation token.
- **Identify**—The default; the server can obtain the client's identity and can impersonate. Used for determining access-checking levels.

- **Impersonate**—Default for COM+ server apps. The server can impersonate the client but is restricted. The server can access resources on the same computer as the client. If the server is on the same computer as the client, it can access network resources on the client's behalf. If it is not, it can only access resources on the computer it resides on.
- **Delegate**—The server can impersonate the client, whether or not it is on the same computer as the client. Client credentials can be passed to any number of machines.

To set the impersonation level, follow these steps:

1. Open the Component Services console.
2. Right-click the application and click Properties.
3. Select the Security tab.
4. Use the Impersonation Level box, as shown previously in Figure 4-32, to set the impersonation level.
5. Click OK.
6. Restart the application for the checks to take place.

Delegation is a special type of impersonation used over the network. The server and client applications do not reside on the same computer, and yet the server uses the client's identity to access resources on a third remote machine. Delegation is controlled with the Active Directory Service. To set delegation, see Chapter 8, "Trust." Two requirements must be met:

- The identity the server is running under (the account it uses to run its service) must be marked "Trusted for delegation."
- The client application must be running under an identity that is not marked as "Account is sensitive and cannot be delegated."

Identification

COM and COM+ applications may run as a service. When they do, they run within the security context of an account or the Local System. If they are not implemented as a service, they may impersonate or act on the authority of the user account used to run them.

Application identity is set during application installation and is only relevant for server applications. Identity is the user account that the application runs under and uses when it calls other applications and resources. Library identity is not set. Library COM+ applications use the identity of the host. Using a specific account, either Local service or an assigned user account is more secure than allowing the identity to be interactive. Interactive means that the COM+ application runs with the authority of the logged on user. If, for example, the local administrator is logged on, COM+ applications could be running with his authority and could be used to make calls and access resources, even for clients. If no one is logged on, then the application cannot be run. Identity can be set to this:

- **Interactive**—The user who is logged on
- **Local service user**—An account with minimal permissions to run a locally accessible service
- A specific valid user account

WARNING: Password Storage for COM+ Identity
COM+ stores passwords in LSA secrets, and thus an administrator can obtain them. Be sure to use an account created just for the COM+ application and deny the account the right to log on locally.

Launch Permissions

Launch permissions specify a list of users who can be granted or denied permission to run or launch component model applications. When set in the properties of the computer, permission to launch is conferred for all applications that do not set their own launch permissions list. The default list is INTERACTIVE (anyone logged on locally), SYSTEM, and Administrators.

To set launch permissions:

1. Open the Component Services console.
2. Right-click the computer you want to set system-wide launch permissions for and click `Properties`.
3. Select the `Default COM Security` tab.
4. In the `Launch Permissions` box, select `Edit Default`, as shown in Figure 4-34.
5. Add user groups and assign them the launch permissions, either Allow or Deny.

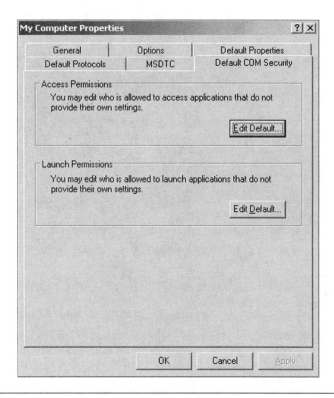

Figure 4-34   Launch Permissions are set from the Default COM Security tab.

Launch Permissions can be set for individual applications. Examine a few applications, and you will learn that most simply use the default, but there are exceptions. If you open the properties for Automatic Updates, as shown in Figure 4-35, you can see that the launch permissions are customized. They are restricted to the SYSTEM and Administrators, while the default permissions are INTERACTIVE, SYSTEM, and Administrators.

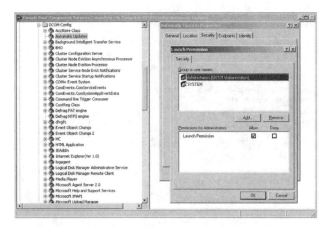

Figure 4-35   Automatic Updates is assigned custom launch permissions.

Setting launch permissions is a good way to restrict software use. You can set launch permissions on any Component Services application and allow only certain users to run them. For example, the default for Media Player is the default settings: Administrator, SYSTEM, and INTERAC-TIVE. If you want to restrict startup (launch permissions), use (access permissions), or configuration (configuration), you can make those adjustments here.

WARNING: Modifying Settings
Before you jump in and modify settings, you need to understand the impact of your actions. If you don't know what an application is doing, don't change its settings. If you do know, consider where you might want to restrict the application's use. If you feel no need to manage Media Player so closely, well then, how about NetMeeting? Should NetMeeting sessions be run from a server? Any desktop? By anyone? You can easily make locking down Component Services applications a part of a comprehensive security policy strategy. Just make sure it does not become part of a strategy that makes systems unusable.

Limiting Application Privilege with Library Applications

There are two types of COM+ applications: applications and libraries. Libraries are hosted by another process, which means they run under the host security rather than their own user's identity. Their privilege is only that assigned to the host. Library applications may participate in authentication by default, but they can be configured not to use authentication by disabling it. (This is not a good idea.) A COM+ application can be deliberately limited by developing it as a library application. It can only access the resources that its client, the host process, can access. When calls are made outside of the application, or access to resources such as files depends on a security descriptor, they appear to be the client. If you are developing an application that performs sensitive work, and you want to limit its use to only those with permissions to do that work, then make it a library application.

Assigning Users to Roles

Roles are user categories defined within an application by the developer. Like Authorization Manager-enabled applications, COM+ applications may define roles that dictate what a user can do when running the application. The roles enforce an access control policy specific to the application and are built into the application by the developers. Administrators assign Windows users and groups to application roles. An example of COM+ application roles can be viewed in the Component Services console. Open the console and expand My Computer, COM+ Applications, System Application, and then Roles. Expand each role and the `Users` container underneath it. The results are illustrated in Figure 4-36.

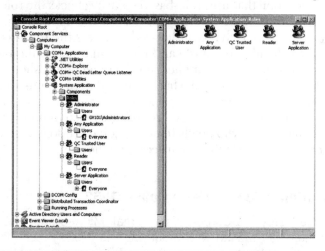

Figure 4-36   The System Application has roles defined, and in many cases, Windows groups are assigned.

Each role also has a description that explains what the user who is assigned that role can do. For the System application, the roles, descriptions, and user groups are defined in Table 4-4.

Table 4-4   System Application Roles

Role	Description	Default Users
Administrator	Can configure this COM+ application on this system.	Local Administrators
Any Application	Identities under which any application on this system may run.	Everyone
QC Trusted User	Trusted to transmit messages for queued components on behalf of other users.	No users are assigned to this role
Reader	Examine configuration of items and view performance information on running applications.	Everyone
Server Application	Identities under which COM+ Server applications run on this system.	Everyone

An application that uses role-based security checks the role membership of a user every time he uses any part of the application. If he doesn't belong to the role that is authorized to access the resource or make the call, the call fails. You must carefully assign users to the roles that match their real-world roles. Application documentation should clearly state what each role means and what rights and permissions within the application it has. Administrators need to know which users' business needs map to the defined role. A breakdown in communications here can mean that a user who needs to do her job can't do it or that some unauthorized individual might gain access he shouldn't.

Can Application Role Confusion Cause DoS?

At the Advanced Services Corporation, a small Midwestern consulting firm, Donna Advertius was tasked with modifying the PBX system. This system had just been upgraded to Windows Server 2003 and used Microsoft SQL Server for its database of users, messages properties, rules, and restrictions. An advertised benefit of the system is the ability to record incoming calls and mail them to Microsoft Exchange so that mailbox owners can listen to their voice messages from their PCs. The company decided that this feature would be especially helpful to traveling consultants because they could check their voice mail at the same time they checked their email. The feature would also give all users more flexible access to messages. Another advantage would be that immediate callbacks could be made without entering a phone number.

Documentation was sparse, but Donna had studied the PBX systems and was very comfortable with Windows Server 2003, Exchange, and SQL Server. It looked like all she needed to do was set up SQL Mail and make a few other minor changes. Setting up SQL Mail is not difficult, but it requires a number of steps, one of which is to set up an account for the service to use and to create a profile for the account. SQL Mail then uses that account to send messages to any user account. A few quick adjustments, and SQL Mail was working.

Next, one line in the PBX documentation indicated changing the service account for the PBX system to the same account used for SQL Mail. Do you get the picture now? The PBX system would record the message and use SQL Mail to deliver it to the user's mailbox. Donna easily changed the account, and the PBX service started right back up. Good, she thought as she looked at the clock. A quick test of the system, and I'll be home by midnight.

To test the system, she decided to call her own number from the phone in the server room and then visit her PC to listen to the message. She couldn't make the call. There was no dial tone. Nothing. She checked at least a dozen phones—nada, no dial tone. She'd killed the phones. Was it some new problem with Windows Server 2003? Was the documentation missing steps? Had she done something wrong?

Then it hit her. COM+ roles? She fired up the Component Services console, and sure enough, the PBX application was listed there. A role called Administrator was present, but only the SYSTEM was assigned. She checked Launch Permissions and found that they, too were limited to SYSTEM. Because the initial PBX setting assigned the Local System as its service account, the system had worked fine. When she changed the account, PBX no longer had permission to access its own components. End of phone service. Changing the Administrator role assignment and giving Launch Permissions to the new service account was all that was needed to get the phones running again.

Even if you do not want to configure COM+ application security or don't have applications that have built-in roles for you to administer, you should manage roles on the System Application. These roles determine who can install COM+ applications and who can administer COM+ applications and the COM+ application environment. By default, the local Administrators group is a role member. While only members of the Administrators group can administer COM+ security, you may want to restrict administration further. To do so, follow these steps:

1. Open the Component Services Console (`Start`, `Programs`, `Administrative Tools`).
2. Expand the `System Application` node and then expand the `Roles` icon.
3. Expand the `Role` node.
4. Right-click the `Users` folder under the role, select `New`, and then click `User`.
5. Enter the username in the `Select Users or Groups` windows or use the `Advanced` button and then the `Find now` button to select a user or group from a list of users and groups on this computer.
6. Restart the computer for the changes to take effect.

Setting Software Restriction Policies for a COM+ Application

A Software Restriction Policy can be set directly in COM+ Application properties on a Windows Server 2003 server. By default, the system-level Software Restriction Policy security level is set the same for all server applications because they all run in the same file, dllhost.exe. If you need to change the policy for specific COM+ applications, you do so by setting Software Restriction Policies directly in the properties of a COM+ application. Software Restriction Policies set here take precedence over system-wide policy settings.

To set COM+ application Software Restriction Policy, do this:

1. Open `Administrative Tools`, `Component Services Tool`.
2. Right-click the COM+ application you want to manage.
3. Select the `Security` tab.
4. Select the `Apply software restriction policy` check box under `Software Restriction Policy` to enable setting the security level, as shown in Figure 4-37. (If the check box is clear, the system-wide Software Restriction Policy is in effect.)

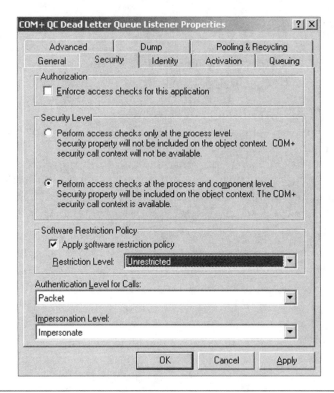

Figure 4-37   Software Restriction Policy for a COM+ application can be set in its property pages.

5. Set the restriction level, either `Disallowed` (the application can load untrusted and trusted components but cannot use the full privileges of the user) or `Unrestricted` (the application has unrestricted access to the user's privileges; only components with an `Unrestricted` trust level can be loaded into it).

Summary

The methods that can be used to restrict application execution are many, but for restriction to be granular, security must be built into the application in the form of roles. To be effective and easy to administer, roles should map to actual user job functions.

Even if sophisticated application security is in place, it is wise to remember that the first level of defense may be file, folder, and registry key ACLs. ACLs can prevent someone from running an application at all. If that is your purpose, even if you have more sophisticated tools to configure security, you would be wise to set file ACLs, too. The next chapter will discuss ACLs on files, folder, and registry keys.

CHAPTER 5

Controlling Access to Data

Controlling access to data is the reason for information security. Let's not forget that. The reason for protecting servers or the network is to protect the data that resides on them. The best approach to controlling access to data is to use defense in depth. This can be accomplished by using perimeter controls such as firewalls, by monitoring the internal network using intrusion detection, by insisting on the use of VPNs and other types of encrypted data transport, and by properly managing authentication and the rest of the principles and practices that are explained elsewhere in this book. Ultimately, however, when all is done, if these other systems fail, it's the controls that are closest to the data that protect them, becoming their last bastion of defense.

Two kinds of data access controls exist—technical and cultural. Technical data controls are the permissions set on files, folders, shares, web folders, registry keys, and other objects. You should know them well; apply, maintain, and audit them. Cultural controls are the security orientation of the IT administrators, software developers, and data owners. This not only means they support, they are eager for the necessary technical controls to be properly in place, but also that they have an understanding of data security that allows them to evaluate new technologies with an eye to preventing users from getting around the technical controls used with older technologies. This chapter will provide information primarily to assist you with technical controls, first by reviewing the traditional technical controls for file systems and registry data, and then by examining new and improved data management technologies in Windows Server 2003 with an eye to securely implementing them.

Controlling Access to Files and Folders Using NTFS Permissions

You do not have to use the Windows NTFS file system, but you should. If you do, different permissions can be applied to every file and folder. This is not usually necessary or practical. Instead, if data files are organized in folders according to data sensitivity and by ownership, permissions can be set at the folder level and applied carte blanche to all subfolders and files. If there is a need to modify permission settings within this hierarchy, it can easily be done. The hierarchical nature of the file system allows file permissions set on a top-level folder to be inherited by the files and folders below it. Permission inheritance reduces the burden on the administrator.

NTFS was introduced with Windows NT and modified for Windows 2000. Windows 2000 and Windows Server 2003 use a new model of inheritance, which changes the way permissions are applied and evaluated. Chapter 3, "Authorization—Limiting System Access and Controlling User Behavior," introduced the basics of object permissions and inheritance. This chapter will provide the details.

New in Windows Server 2003 are more secure volume root permissions, more secure default share permissions, and a change in the location of security descriptors.

File and Folder Permissions

Configuring file permissions for files and folders is easy; determining the appropriate permissions you should set is not. Two problems exist: understanding the large number of permissions that can be set, and deciding which Windows groups should have which permissions. The latter must be determined in concert with the data owners. Administrators should not be deciding who should have access to specific folders, documents, and databases. Each department should inform IT of its needs. However, once an administrator understands the requirements, she can implement them within the framework of the permissions available. File and folder permissions are composed of generic permission sets, as shown in Figure 5-1 and defined in Table 5-1. Each generic permission is actually a permission set. Several special permissions are included in the permission set. Each special permission can be assigned individually. Figure 5-2 displays the special permissions that make up Full Control. These permissions are defined in Table 5-2. A permission can be set to either `Allow` or `Deny`. Some permissions are only used for files, and others are only used on folders (as indicated in the table).

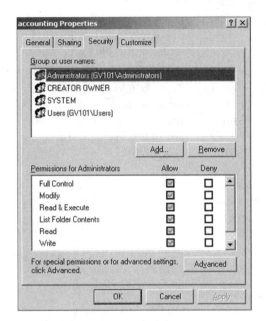
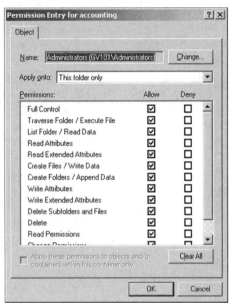

Figure 5-1 Generic permissions sets.

Figure 5-2 Special permissions that make up Full Control.

Table 5-1   Generic File/Folder Permissions

Permission	Description	Composed of Special Permissions
Full Control	All permissions	All permissions
Modify	Change data	Cannot delete subfolders and files (can delete the files in this folder or this file). Can change permissions, take ownership
File: Read & Execute Folder: List Folder Contents	Read files, execute programs and scripts, see folder contents. Both permission sets are visible at the folder level, but the `List Folder` permission set is only inherited by subfolders, not files. You will never see the `List Folder Contents` permission applied to files.	Traverse folder/execute files, list folder and read data, read attributes and extended attributes, read permissions, synchronize
Read	Read files	List folder/read data, read attributes and extended attributes, read permissions, synchronize
Write	Write files, add files to folder	Create files and write data, create folders, append data, Write attributes and extended attributes, read permissions

Table 5-2   Special File/Folder Permissions

Permissions	Description	Folder/File
Traverse Folder/ Execute File	If the Bypass traverse checking user right is not granted, this permission can be granted to allow programmatic traversal of a directory tree to get to files and folders.	Setting Traverse Folder permission on a folder does not set the Execute File permission on the files in that folder.

Permissions	Description	Folder/File
List Folder/ Read Data	List Folder will allow or deny viewing of filenames and subfolder names within the folder. It only affects the contents of the folder on which it is granted, not the folder itself. (The folder the permission is applied to may not be viewable. Read Data will grant or deny reading of file content.)	List Folder only applies to folders. Read Data only applies to files.
Read Attributes	Allows or denies viewing of attributes on a file or folder. Attributes are things such as read-only and hidden.	Applies to both.
Read Extended Attributes	Allows or denies viewing of attributes. Extended attributes are defined by programs and may vary.	Applies to both.
Create Files/ Write Data	Create Files allows or denies adding files to the folder. Write Data allows or denies changes to the file or overwriting of contents.	Create Files only applies to folders. Write Data only applies to files.
Create Folders/ Append Data	Create Folders allows or denies creating folders within the folder to which it is applied. Append Data allows or denies adding data to the end of the file. (It does not allow changing, deleting, or overwriting existing data.)	Create Folders only applies to folders. Append Data only applies to files.
Write Attributes	Allows or denies making changes to attributes of a file or folder.	Applies to properties of both files and folders.
Write Extended Attributes	Allows or denies changing the extended attributes of a file or folder.	Applies to both the extended properties of files and folders.
Delete Subfolders and Files	Allows or denies deleting subfolders and files.	Applies as stated.

Table 5-2   Special File/Folder Permissions Continues

Permissions	Description	Folder/File
Delete	Allows or denies deleting a file or folder.	Applies to both.
Read Permissions	Allows or denies reading permissions.	Applies to both files and folders.
Change Permissions	Allows or denies changing permissions.	Applies both to files and folders.
Take Ownership	Allows or denies taking ownership of a file or folder.	Applies to both files and folders.
Synchronize	Allows or denies threads (executable code running on a system) the ability to wait on the handle of the file or folder and synchronize with another thread that may signal it. Think of the handle of a file or folder as the connection point to it. If multiple threads in a program need access to the same file or folder, they must wait their turn and synchronize access to the object between them.	Applies to both files and folders.

WARNING: Full Control Implies Delete Permission

If the Full Control permission is granted on a folder to a user or group, then that group may delete files within the folder, even if the user or group is not provided explicit access to the file or folder. This is also true if permissions are explicitly set on the file to deny that user or group access to the file. This property is called Child File Delete and was originally implemented to give the Windows NT Posix subsystem compliance with Posix 1.1. Posix is a Unix standard. At one time, compliance with the Posix standard was necessary to sell computers to branches of the federal government. The permission Child File Delete is part of the Posix standard.

Default Permissions

By default, Windows Server 2003 applies stronger access controls than Windows 2000. During installation, Windows 2000 applies granular permission sets to its system files. However, the group Everyone is granted Full Control at the root of the system drive. One concern at the time of its release was that changing permissions on the root drive during an upgrade might interfere with currently installed applications. Weak root file system permissions, however, weaken the security of the entire computer. When new applications are installed, they inherit the same weak permissions.

Windows Server 2003 applies stronger root file system permissions. The installation process sets access control lists on the root of the system volume that are more secure.

- **Administrators and SYSTEM**—Full Control
- **CREATOR OWNER**—Full Control on subfolders and files
- **Users**—Create folders, append data on folders and subfolders
- **Users**—Create files and subfolders only

However, the default permission set should be reviewed, and stronger permissions should be applied in many cases.

First, for some servers, it may be best to limit administrative access. An Exchange server or database server may be a good candidate for this treatment. To restrict administrative access, create a custom Windows group and add administrators who are authorized to administer the specific server. Grant this custom group Full Control and remove the local Administrators group.

The CREATOR OWNER group represents the account that created the file or folder. Any permissions granted to this group are assigned to the file or folder creator. If applications create folders and files, these permissions will be granted to the account that provides the security context for the application. That account may be an account assigned to the service or a user running the program. The CREATOR OWNER permission is often used to ensure that the appropriate permissions are applied. For example, when an application creates a file, the permissions applied to the file might be less than Full Control, thereby denying the person running the application ownership of the file. This is important because only the owner of a file can change its permissions to provide himself more access; therefore, if as the creator of the file, the user is not given ownership, he will be restricted to the access assigned. (Administrators and those assigned the user right Take Ownership can always take ownership and assign themselves any permissions on the file, but ordinary users do not have this right by default.) The specific requirements of applications and security policies of the organization may be different from those granted by the default permissions. Therefore, adjusting the default CREATOR OWNER permissions may be necessary. Default user permissions may also grant excessive permission on the files and folders they are authorized to create and should be reviewed to determine if they are appropriate. To determine the permission sets required for users, determine if users should be able to create files and folders on the server and determine where this may be necessary. It's not typically a requirement for the root of the drive. In many cases, a preferred arrangement is to provide users no access at the root and assign custom permissions to server folders where user access is required.

In all cases, permission inheritance should be reviewed. Unless a subfolder is marked to prevent inheritance, subfolders will inherit the permissions set on the root.

Watch Out for Special Permissions

The CREATOR OWNER assignment at the root demonstrates an issue with the way that NTFS permissions are reported. When the CREATOR OWNER group is highlighted in the Security page of the root properties, as shown in Figure 5-3, it looks as if the group has no permissions assigned. However, when the Advanced button is used and the group permissions are opened in the editor, as shown in Figure 5-4, the special permissions are revealed. This combination of special permissions does not map to a task set and therefore is not displayed in the Security page. Take care to review special permissions on all groups and users assigned on the Security page.

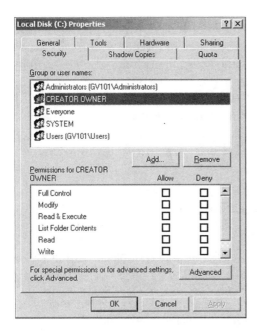 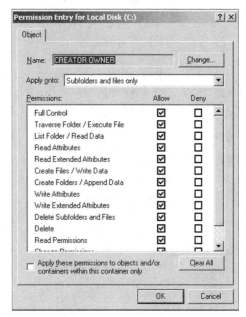

Figure 5-3   CREATOR OWNER does not appear to have permissions applied.

Figure 5-4   Check for special permissions by editing the CREATOR OWNER assignment from the Advanced page.

Instead of granting the Everyone group Full Control, creating a new file share grants the Everyone group Full Control. In addition to strengthening default access to shares, Windows Server 2003 does not include the anonymous SID in the Everyone group. Therefore, even if an anonymous connection can be made to the server, the anonymous user has no default permissions via the shares.

Permission Interpretation

Permission interpretation explains how permissions are evaluated. In its simplest form, the permissions that a user or group has on a file or folder are the combination of the permissions assigned. Realistically, however, the ability of a user to do something with a file or folder depends on a number of factors. Basically, the user requests some form of access, and the operating system walks the access control list (ACL) assigned to the file or folder looking for a match. Both the user's account SID and his group membership SIDs are reviewed. If access is explicitly denied, then the processing stops, and access is denied. If access is not explicitly granted, then it is denied. This is the same algorithm used to determine access since Windows NT. However, there is one difference between the old algorithm and Windows 2000/Server 2003: Inheritance may break the old NT rule that any Deny would automatically override any Allows and stop processing of the ACLs. To understand this difference, you must learn more about the NTFS disk structure and the location of ACLs.

WARNING: Deny Does Not Always Override Allow
A different inheritance mode for NTFS means that old rules about access control permission may not be valid. This is true because of a change in ACL location and therefore in the manner in which permissions are evaluated. It is possible that a Deny permission may not be interpreted before the required Allow permission is processed. This is because permissions applied directly on the object are applied first, and the inherited permissions are not considered if the directly applied permissions grant the required access. More information is in the section "Permission Inheritance," later in this chapter.

NTFS Disk Structure

Knowledge of file system architecture is useful should you need to forensically examine a disk, but more importantly, it can help you understand much about how NTFS works and the relationship between DACLs and performance. (For the basics of object security-object permissions, access tokens, groups, permission assignment, ACEs, and DACLs, refer to Chapter 3.) A significant change in the NTFS file structure was made for Windows 2000, and it was tweaked for performance in Windows Server 2003. This architectural change can affect security because administrators may still be approaching NTFS without understanding the change. Worse, trainers and experienced Windows administrators may communicate misinformation and perpetuate the problem. The change in the file structure itself is not a plus or a minus security-wise, unless you are forensically examining a disk, but it is important to understand. The primary change involves the location of the security descriptors.

Windows NT, Windows Server 2003, and Windows 2000 NTFS file volumes use a small database, the Master File Table (MFT), to assist in the location of files. MFT includes file and directory records that store and index filenames and other attributes, such as reparse points (mounts points for additional disks), link tracking information (to help in the location of files when locations are moved), and security descriptors. This is different than it was in Windows NT 4.0, where security descriptors (the attributes of files and folders that contain access control lists) were stored as attributes of the file objects they protected. Instead, a pointer in the file's attributes points back to the location in the MFT where the file's security descriptor can be found. Within the MFT, each file and folder has a record. The MFT metadata includes the $Secure record, which contains security descriptors for all MFT records. This does not mean that the MFT is bloated with double the data of earlier versions of NTFS. Instead, it only contains one copy of each unique security descriptor, which, of course, means that instead of one security descriptor for each file and folder on the entire disk, only a few security descriptors are stored. This arrangement also means that if a file has a large security descriptor (if many groups or users are given specific Allows or Denies), the security descriptor will not be fragmented and won't cause excessive disk activity when the file is accessed.

Permission Inheritance

The easiest way to think about permission inheritance is to construct a logical model that aligns with the file, folder, and subfolder hierarchal model of the file system. While security descriptors are actually stored in the MFT, they are applied to physical files and folders, so it's okay to speak of them as if they actually were properties of the files and folders, instead of talking about pointers to records. In the file system model, the root of the volume is divided into multiple volume-level folders, each of which can be divided up into subfolders, and on and on. Files can be located at the root and within every folder. The identification of a specific file is presented in a path that starts at the root and then may be followed by any number of subfolders until the file itself is named. In the NTFS file system, not only can each file and folder have files directly assigned permissions, but through permission inheritance, permissions assigned to a folder in the hierarchy can also be applied to every subfolder and file in the path. Inheritance can also be blocked or limited. If a new file is added to a folder, by default, it inherits its security descriptor from the parent folder. The security descriptor may include a combination of inherited and directly applied permissions.

Results of Inherited and Directly Applied Permissions

On any specific file, a combination of both directly applied and inherited permissions may be assigned. Effective permissions are the resultant set of these permissions—the actual result of interpreting them. To determine what the effective permissions will be, use the following formula:

1. List the Deny permissions that are explicitly applied to the file.
2. List the Allow permissions that are explicitly applied to the file.
3. List the Deny permissions that are inherited.
4. List the Allow permissions that are inherited.
5. Review the requested access against each permission set in the order expressed above. Ask the following questions:
   If the request is denied by an explicitly applied permission, then the access is denied, and processing stops.
   If it is not denied, is it explicitly allowed by the set of explicitly applied permissions? If so, then it is allowed, and processing stops.
   Is it denied explicitly by inherited permissions? Then access is denied, and processing stops.
   Is it explicitly allowed by inherited permissions? Then access is granted, and processing stops.
   Have all permissions been evaluated and access is not allowed? Then Access is denied and processing stops.

Windows Server 2003 also provides a report mechanism to evaluate permission combinations. To determine the effective permissions:

1. Open the `Properties` page of the file or folder.
2. Click the `Advanced` button.
3. Select the `Effective Permissions` page.
4. Click the `Select` button.
5. Enter the user or group name desired, or use the object picker to select the user or group.
6. Click `OK` and review the `Effective permissions`, as shown in Figure 5-5.

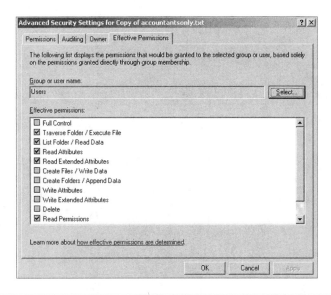

Figure 5-5   The effective permissions are those actually available for a user or group on the selected object.

Impact of Copying and Moving NTFS Files and Folders

Copying and moving files or folders may change the permissions applied to them. The resulting permission set applied to either object is dependent on on the following:

- The change is from and to folders on the same volume or to different volumes.
- The object is copied or moved.
- The object is marked to prevent inheritance.
- Permissions on parent folders or the root are modified.
- The inheritance mode of the objects is overridden.

The examples in this section can be reproduced on any Windows Server 2003 computer using the NTFS file system on which there are at least two volumes. The instructions listed were used to produce the results shown. Before proceeding, three top-level folders—test1, test2, and test3—were created on drive C:\. Each folder inherits permissions from the root, as shown in Figure 5-6. In addition, two new Windows groups— the Accountants group and the Sales group—were created.

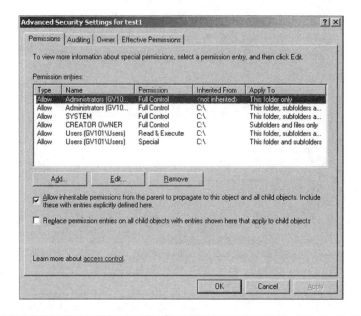

Figure 5-6 New top-level folders inherit permissions from the root.

To prepare folders for testing, make the following changes:

1. Open the security property page for the test2 folder.
2. Click on the `Advanced` button and uncheck the `Allow Inheritable Permissions from the Parent to Propagate` check box.
3. When prompted, copy all permissions and click `OK`. At this point, all three folders still have the same permission sets, but the test2 folder's permissions are directly applied, as shown in Figure 5-7.
4. Change the permission set of test2 by granting the Accountants group the Modify permission, and remove the Users group, as shown in Figure 5-8.
5. Change to the second volume and change its root permissions to `Everyone Full Control`, as shown in Figure 5-9.

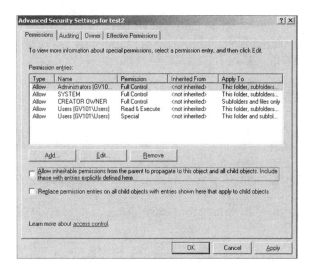

Figure 5-7 Blocking inheritance will prevent changes made to the parent folder from propagating to this folder.

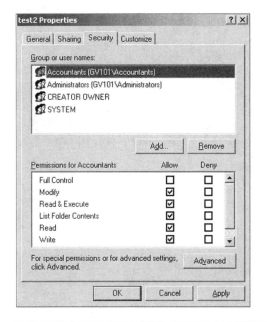 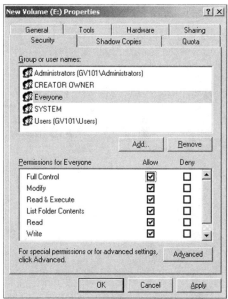

Figure 5-8 Change permissions on the folder.

Figure 5-9 The second volume is set to different permissions to show inheritance issues in later examples.

Moving Files from Folder to Folder on the Same Volume

When existing files and folders are moved to a new location on the same volume, they do not immediately lose their current permissions.

1. Create a file in the test2 folder called accountantsonly.txt.
2. Create a copy of the accountantsonly.txt file and save it in the test2 folder.
3. Create a copy of the copy of the accountantsonly.txt file and save it in the test2 folder.
4. Change the permissions on accountantsonly.txt to prevent inheritance.
5. Move both accountantsonly.txt and its copy of accountantsonly. txt to the test1 folder.
6. The test1 folder inherits its permissions from the root of C:\. When new files are added, they will inherit these permissions. However, moved files do not immediately inherit their new folder's permissions. View the copy of the accountantsonly.txt file permissions, as shown in Figure 5-10. The permissions will show that they have retained the permissions that were set earlier. This is also true of the accountantsonly.txt file, as shown in Figure 5-11. (Note that the permissions here are not inherited as they are in Figure 5-10 because of step 4.)

 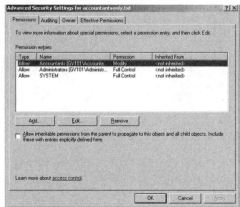

Figure 5-10   Permissions are retained when a file is first moved from one folder to the next.

Figure 5-11   When inheritance is blocked, permissions remain the same when a file is moved.

7. Change the permissions on the test1 folder to provide the Modify permission to the Sales group.
8. View the permissions on each file. The copy of the accountantsonly.txt file will have been modified via inheritance to provide access to the Sales group and to remove access from the Accountants group, as shown in Figure 5-12. This is because files moved from one folder on a drive to another will inherit the permissions of the new folder if and when the permission set is modified. This is not true of the accountantsonly.txt file because inheritance was blocked, so the permission set remains the same.

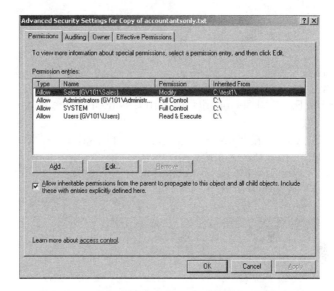

Figure 5-12 When permissions on the parent object are changed, the moved file will inherit its permissions unless inheritance is blocked.

Copying Files from Folder to Folder on the Same Volume

1. Create a text file in the test3 folder called forall.txt.
2. Open the forall.txt security properties page and note the permission inheritance, as shown in Figure 5-13.

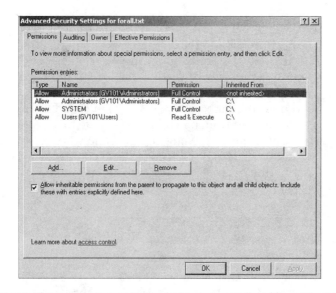

Figure 5-13   The Forall.txt file inherits its permissions from the folder it is created in.

3. Copy the forall.txt file to the test1 folder.
4. Open the security properties page of the forall.txt file and note that the file has inherited new permissions from the test1 folder, as shown in Figure 5-14.

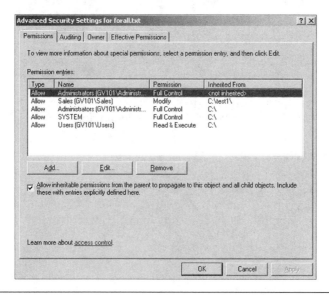

Figure 5-14   Files copied from folder to folder inherit the permissions of the new folder.

Moving Files from One Volume to Another

When files are moved between folders on the same volume, they retain their permissions until the parent permissions are changed. However, when moved between volumes, moved files inherit the permissions set in the new volume.

1. Move the copy of accountantsonly.txt from C:\test1 to the second volume.
2. Open the security properties page and note that permissions are now inherited immediately from the new volume, as shown in Figure 5-15.

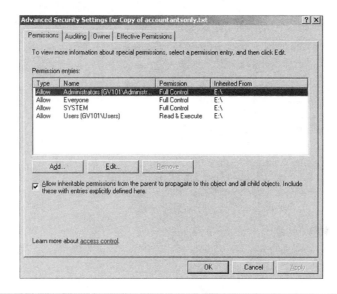

Figure 5-15   Files moved between volumes immediately inherit the permissions from the new volume.

Overriding Blocked Inheritance

If copied or moved files have inheritance blocked, the files will not inherit permissions from the new folder. However, blocked inheritance can be overridden.

1. Open the advanced security page of the test1 folder.
2. Check the box `Replace permission entries on all child objects with entries shown here that apply to all objects`, as shown in Figure 5-16.

3. Open the advanced security property page of the accountantsonly.txt file, as shown in Figure 5-17. You should recall that this file had inheritance blocking turn on. Note that the permissions have now been inherited from the folder, and the inheritance blocking is turned off.

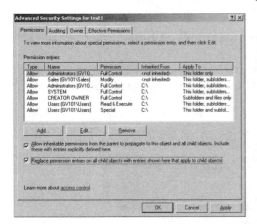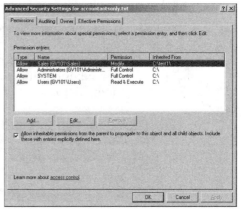

Figure 5-16   Inheritance blocking can be overridden.

Figure 5-17   When inheritance blocking is overridden, permissions will be inherited, and inheritance blocking will be turned off.

Copying DACLs with Xcopy

If the xcopy command and its /O switch are used for copying, existing permissions are retained, and permissions are inherited from the new location.

1. Open a command prompt.
2. Enter the command:

```
xcopy /O C:\test1 E:\test1
```

3. When prompted, enter a D to indicate that the test1 name represents a folder name.
4. Open the advanced security property page, as shown in Figure 5-18, and note that the Sales group still retains its permission and is not inherited. Other permissions are inherited from E:\.

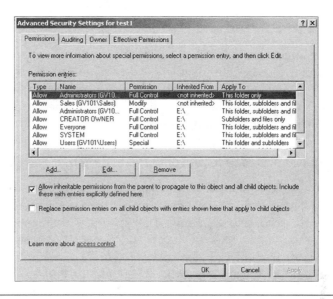

Figure 5-18   Xcopy can be used to copy ACLs.

Permission Summary

Be sure to determine if moving and copying files will have the correct effect on file access. As demonstrated previously, permissions may change. Prevent unexpected improper access control settings by keeping in mind that the permissions that are applied to moved or copied files and folders may change depending on these factors:

- Where they were created
- Whether they were moved or copied to a new location
- Whether xcopy or Windows Explorer was used
- Whether the new location was on the same volume or a different one
- Whether they had their own security descriptor or an inherited one
- Whether inheritance was blocked
- What the inheritance settings were on the folder moved or copied to

NTFS Attributes and Performance Versus Security

Using a more complex file system and adding security may impact performance. The benefits of granular security must be weighed against any performance losses. Before making any configuration choices intended to improve performance, the new features and the security implications of making changes should be evaluated.

NTFS Performance Improvement—Location of File Descriptors

Each file and directory contains a number of attributes. The file property $Standard_Information contains the regular file attributes, such as Read-Only, Hidden, System, Archive, Timestamps, and a pointer to the security descriptor in the $Secure record in the MFT. Locating the security descriptor in the MFT does aid file system performance and to some degree refute the argument that we should not add security information because it will hinder performance. (When discussing file system security, Windows NT 4.0 users often heard the argument that many large ACLs would reduce performance because the ACLs might become fragmented, or because when ACLs are changed in Windows NT 4.0, all subfolders and files would inherit the new ACL. Because the assignment of ACLs is now handled using pointers to the new ACL, and because all ACLs exist only in the MFT, the old argument is no longer valid.)

The file system can quickly figure out whether a new security descriptor is unique and must be stored, or whether it already exists and just needs to be pointed to. To do so, the file system stores a hash of each security descriptor in the MFT. When a new ACL is created on a file or folder, the new security descriptor is hashed by the system and then compared to those that already exist in the MFT. If no match is found, then the security descriptor must be stored; if a match is found, then it does not need to be stored. As you may already know, many hash algorithms exist for which it is statistically infeasible that two different pieces of data can produce the same result when hashed. This is why a match with an existing hash means no new security descriptor needs to be stored.

Timestamp Performance Issues

Another potential performance issue concerns timestamps. Timestamps stored in file attributes indicate record creation, attribute modification, and data or index modification in addition to the time of last access. Updating timestamps does require disk activity. On a large disk with a large number of files that are frequently accessed, this could be significant enough that reducing the timestamp activity might provide some small gain in performance. However, be wary of advice that calls for eliminating the "update to last access" timestamp. The last access timestamp, of course, indicates when a file was last changed and can be useful forensics information, as a simple indication of possible tampering, or as proof that a file has not been affected by an attempted attack.

Administrators may eliminate last access update timestamps in an attempt to improve performance, but they should not. Accurate timestamps are necessary to obtain accurate audit and forensic information and to comply with policies that require it. You can determine if last access update has been modified by inspecting the REG_DWORD value NtfsDisableLastAccessUpdate at HKEY_LOCAL_MACHINE\SYSTEM\ Current Control Set\Control\filesystem. Protect this value from change by using registry permissions, and turn on auditing to capture any change that might be performed by administrators.

Controlling Access to Shares

Shares are connection points that provide access to data stored on Windows computers. Shares can be created at the root of a drive or on any folder or subfolder on the drive. Once a connection is established to the share, access may be provided to the contents of the drive that exist within the underlying folders, files, and subfolders. The ability to connect to the share is managed by access controls set on the share; access to data is managed by permissions set on folders and files in combination with the share permissions. While shares are created to provide authorized access, they must be protected to prevent unauthorized access and to manage authorized access.

The default permission, Everyone Read, as shown in Figure 5-19 and described in Table 5-3, may not be appropriate. It may be necessary to lock it down further by applying specific permissions to the share for unique Windows groups, or it may be necessary to modify the Everyone permission.

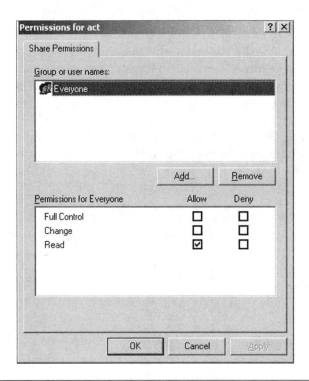

Figure 5-19   Default share permissions may not be correct for all situations.

Manage access control of shares according to the following:

■ Shares should not be set at the root of drives or volumes.
■ Permissions should be set on shares to prevent unauthorized access and manage authorized access to the computer.
■ Permissions should be set on the underlying shared folder or drive to prevent unauthorized access and manage authorized access to the data.

NOTE: Historical Hysteria

Prior to Windows NT, access to Windows shares was limited by placing a password on the share. Knowledge of the password was the only barrier to connecting to the computer and accessing data. The FAT file systems used on these early Windows computers could not be permissioned; therefore the simple connection to the share provided carte blanche access to all of the data. Many of these early systems are still in use, and many of them have open shares. Open shares are shares with no passwords at all. All NT-based systems, when the NTFS file system is properly used, can provide solid security for files and folders and the ability to use this same user-based approach to shares.

Develop a strategy for share management of Windows Server 2003 networks by considering the available share permissions, the File and Printer sharing mode, default shares, simple file sharing for Windows XP, and the impact of combining share and folder permissions.

Share Permissions

Table 5-3   Share Permissions

Permission	Description
Full Control	All access is granted or denied.
Change	Grants or denies the ability to read, write, and delete files; list folders and files.
Read	Only grants or denies read and list permissions.

File and Printer Sharing Mode

The default installation of Windows Server 2003 automatically enables File and Printer Sharing. Unless the server will be a domain controller, print server, or file server, this capability should either be disabled immediately after installation, or where possible, a custom installation script should ensure that File and Printer Sharing is *not* enabled during installation.

To disable File and Printer Sharing after installation:

1. Open the Control Panel and double-click `Network Connections`.
2. Click the `Properties` button.
3. Click to deselect the `File and Printer Sharing for Microsoft Networks` check box, as shown in Figure 5-20.
4. Click OK.

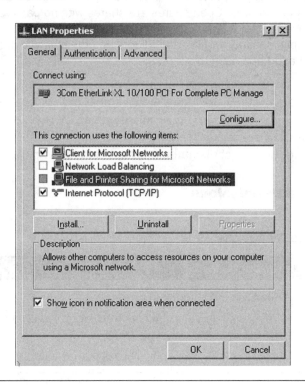

Figure 5-20   Disable File and Printer Sharing.

Default Shares

Default shares are created during the installation of Windows Server 2003 systems and may also be created when server applications are installed. If File and Printer sharing is left enabled, access to the server via these shares is enabled by default. Access to these shares may be restricted to members of the local Administrators group, and the shares are not browsable—that is, they cannot be viewed when using Windows network browsing tools. Nevertheless, the share names are well known. Access to these shares should be curtailed by disabling the shares unless there is a reason for their existence on the specific computer. Determine the need for each share based on the security policy, risk picture, and access needs for computer roles. Weigh the risk of the shares' presence against their benefit; for example, many default shares are used for many remote administration tasks, are required on domain controllers, and are necessary when scanning for patching requirements with tools such as Microsoft Baseline Security Analyzer. The shares on the computer can be viewed by opening the Computer Management console, expanding the `Shared Folders` container, and then selecting `Shares`, as shown in Figure 5-21. Table 5-4 lists and describes the default shares.

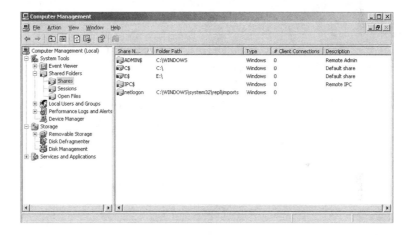

Figure 5-21   Default shares can be viewed in the Computer Management, Shared Folders, Shares container.

Table 5-4 Default Windows Server 2003 Shares

Share Name	Location	Description	When to Enable/Disable
ADMIN$		The system folder. Used during remote administration of the computer.	Disable if using other methods for remote administration or if remote administration is not required.
IPC$		Interprocess Communication. Supports Remote Procedure Call (RPC) connections between Windows computers. The Named pipes necessary for many communications between programs are shared here. This share cannot be disabled.	Cannot be disabled. Is required for normal communications.
Sysvol	Windows\ Sysvol\Sysvol	This share should only be present on domain controllers. This share is required for Active Directory to function, for logon, and for the distribution of Group Policies and logon scripts.	Should not be present on non-domain controllers. Must be present on domain controllers.
Netlogon	windows\sysvol\ Sysvol\scripts	This share is the authentication share and is the classic systems policies and downlevel logon scripts location.	Do not disable.
Print$	windows\ system32\spool\ drivers	Drivers for each printer installed on the server can be downloaded from this share.	Do not disable on print servers.

Share Name	Location	Description	When to Enable/Disable
FxsSrvCp$	Documents and Settings\All Users\ Application Data\Microsoft Windows NT\ MsFax\Common Coverpages	Enabled when the fax service is installed and is the location of fax cover pages.	
RemInstall		If the Remote Installation Service (RIS) is installed on the server, this share gives PXE (Preboot Execution Environment) clients access to installation files.	Remove if the server will not be used as an RIS server.
Driveletter$ (C$, D$, etc)		Each local root partition and volume is shared but hidden from view and only accessible to members of the local Administrators group.	Disable.

Simple File and Printer Sharing: A New Model for Windows XP

This book is about securing Windows Server 2003. However, Windows Server 2003 security may be impacted by the security status of clients on its network. Therefore, to manage security, the security policies of Windows XP clients must also be considered. The file sharing models available for XP Professional may surprise uninformed administrators. Standalone XP desktops do not have network sharing enabled by default; instead, they use the Simple File Sharing model. It is the only option on Windows XP Home, but it may be modified on Windows XP Professional standalone systems. If the Windows XP Professional computer is joined to a domain, the model is changed to network shares.

To determine or modify file sharing on Windows XP Professional, open the Windows Explorer, Tools, Folder Options, View tab to display the Simple File Sharing check box. Alternatively, examine the registry value ForceGuest at

    HKEY-LOCAL_MACHINE\SYSTEM\CurrentControlSet\Control\Lsa\

When `ForceGuest` is set to 1 (the `Simple File Sharing` check box is checked), Simple File Sharing is used, and when it is set to 0 (the box is unchecked), the normal Windows NT model is used. When Simple File Sharing is set the following applies:

- All access to the file share is through the Guest account. Every user who connects will only receive the permissions granted to the Guest account. Because the Guest account is disabled by default, there should be no accidental access to a shared folder.
- The `MyDocuments` folder can be made completely private if NTFS is the file system. A "private" setting means NTFS permissions for each user's `MyDocuments` folder are set to the user and SYSTEM Full Control. Another alternative is Private with access by local Administrators, which adds the local Administrators group. The `All Users Documents` folder is shared, giving all users access.
- Shares can be made available on the network by using the `Sharing` tab in folder properties and selecting `Share this folder on the network`. Checking or unchecking the `Allow users to change my files` option manages access to the share. If the setting is checked, permissions are set to `Everyone Change`, and if unchecked, permissions are set to `Everyone Read`.

Creating Shares

When a share is needed, it must be created using appropriate permissions. Both share permissions and underlying folder permissions should be carefully determined and applied. Share permissions are set to manage access to the computers. However, previous versions of Windows NT-based systems set the default share permission to `Everyone Full Control`, and this is the way most administrators left it. In doing so, they missed a valuable ally in controlling access. Windows Server 2003 shares are created with the default access permission `Everyone Read` to prevent accidental privileged access to the computer. A default access permission of `Everyone Read` can have the following impact:

- Prevent accidental full access to data on the networked server. While access can be curtailed by setting permissions on underlying folders and files, if these permissions are not set correctly, unexpected access might be available.
- Require administrators to think through the permission sets on shared folders. In the past, many administrators left the Full Control permission in place and controlled access to folders via NTFS permissions.
- Create unnecessary troubleshooting efforts as administrators unfamiliar with the new permission settings attempt to determine why authorized users cannot manipulate data.

While many administrators will change the setting back to `Everyone Full Control` and only manage access via the underlying folder permissions, this is not a good practice. They do so to avoid the confusion that is sometimes caused by attempting to understand how share and folder permissions combine to restrict access to data. However, they miss an important tool for defense: if an intruder cannot gain access to the computer, the intruder cannot directly attack specific files and other resources. If there is no barrier to his access, the intruder's job is easier.

To create a share, follow these steps:

1. Right-click the folder in Windows Explorer and select `Sharing and Security` or `Properties`, as shown in Figure 5-22.
2. If necessary, select the `Sharing` tab.
3. Click the `Share this folder` radio button. This shares the folder with the share name equivalent of the folder name and the default permissions of `Everyone Read`.
4. Click the `Permissions` button to set the correct share permissions for the share.
5. Click to change the share name. A share name cannot be longer than 255 characters.
6. Click the radio button `Allow this number of users` and set the number in the adjacent text box to limit the number of simultaneous users who can connect to this share.
7. Click `OK`.

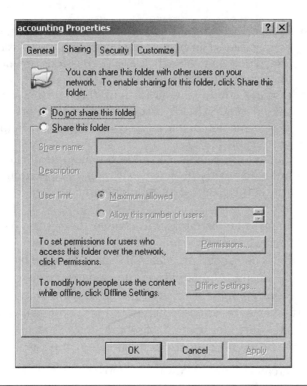

Figure 5-22 The Sharing property page is configured to create a share.

Alternative methods for creating shares are as follows:

- A share can be created on a remote computer using the Computer Management console's `Shared Folders`, `Shares` container.
- Shares can also be created at the command line.

The `net share` command is used to create shares at the command line. For example, to grant `Everyone Read` on a new share named "test," use the following command line:

```
Net share F:\test /grant:Everyone,Read
```

Impact of Combining Share and Folder/File Permissions

The combination of share and underlying folder permissions controls access to data. In every case, the most restrictive access will be allowed. For example, because the default share permission is `Read`, even if NTFS permissions on the folder are `Full Control`, the only network access allowed to the data will be Read. (Console-based access is not affected by share permissions.)

Determining actual access by examining share and folder access permissions can become difficult, though, when many permissions are set. However, the correct interpretation can always be determined by using the following process for each group or user:

- Determine the permission granted on the share.
- Determine the permission granted on the folder.
- Select, from the two, the most restrictive permission, and that will be the access granted.

Table 5-5 describes permissions on a sample folder and its share.

Table 5-5   Folder and Share Permissions for the Folder Test

Folder Permissions	Share Permissions
John—Change, Read and Execute, List Folder contents, Read, Write	John—Full Control
Accountants—Full Control	Accountants—Change
Users—Read	Users—Read

A quick scan of the table shows that the most restrictive permission for John is Read. This permission is granted to him directly, and via his membership in the Users group. However, relying on this evaluation to determine John's access to the data in the test folder is incorrect. John actually has Read and Execute, List Folder Contents, and Read and Write permissions. This is because access is determined by looking at the share and folder permission sets separately to determine what access each would grant and then selecting the most restrictive of the two access options. If only the share permissions are considered, John has Full Control. If only the folder permissions are considered, John has Change, Read and Execute, List Folder Contents, and Read and Write. Of the two options, the folder permission set is more restrictive and thus is the access that John is granted.

Remote Administration of Shares

Remote administration of share permissions via Windows Explorer is not a good idea. When remote permissions are examined, only the permissions set on the folder is visible, not the permissions set for the share. Changing the folder permissions may or may not have the desired effect because changing folder permissions does not change share permissions, and users may not be given the correct access. Furthermore, when you change permissions this way, you remove the inherited permissions from the folder and by extension its subfolders. Manage shared folder permissions from the console. (Remotely changing the permissions of a subfolder of a shared folder will not affect inherited permissions.)

Best Practices for File and Printer Sharing

File and Printer Sharing is on by default; when should it be disabled or enabled, and how should shares be protected?

- File and Printer Sharing is required on a domain controller. If you are going to use the server as a domain controller, do not turn off File and Printer Sharing.
- File and Printer Sharing is not required on a server unless the following applies:
  - The server will be a file server.
  - A remote management or vulnerability scanning tool requires it.
- Turn off File and Printer Sharing if you do not need it.
- If remote management tools are used, a server that contains sensitive information or performs a critical service may be too important to risk leaving File and Printer Sharing enabled. You can monitor, manage, and scan this server at the console or use management tools that do not require File and Print services.
- Bastion servers (servers with one network interface on an untrusted network, such as the Internet, and one network interface on a trusted network) should not have File and Print Services on the untrusted network interface.
- Remove, disable, or replace shares that are not required.
- Do not use Windows Explorer to delete default installation shares because they will reshared when the server service is stopped and then restarted. Instead, configure the `AutoShareServer` value at `HKEY_LOCAL_MACHINE\SYSTEM\CurrentControlSet\Services\ LanmanServer\Parameters`. To permanently delete a default

share, delete its value or set the value to 0 to remove the share, or 1 to replace shares, and then stop and restart the server service. This registry key has no effect on the IPC$ share.

■ Shares for CD-ROM, CD-R/RWS, DVD-ROM, and DVD-RAM drives are not created by default; however, if you change system-assigned drive letters for them, they are shared. Configure security options to prevent network sharing of these devices when an administrator is logged on, and remove shares created when drive letters are changed.

Controlling Access to Web Folders Using WebDAV

Web-based Distributing Authoring and Versioning (WebDAV) is an extension to the HTTP/1.1 standard, which allows clients to remotely publish, lock, and manage resources on the web. Before you discount this technique as just another way to update websites, and thus an area of concern only for those responsible for website security, think again.

■ WebDAV can be used to transfer data to and from a web folder for which the user is given permissions. The data does not have to be HTML files or web-executable scripts and programs. It can be Word files, text files, or any kind of file.
■ WebDAV folders allow properly permissioned users to copy and move files around in the WebDAV directory.
■ If permissioned, users can retrieve and modify file properties.
■ Multiple users can read a file concurrently, but only one user can modify a file at a time. (Files can be locked and unlocked.)
■ Web folders can easily be created on any IIS server. The permissions assigned to these folders determine who can transfer data files to them.

Since these are the very things that server message block (SMB) shares allow users to do on a remote server, WebDAV should loom as large on your security horizon as SMB-based shares. (And perhaps it should be considered as a valid substitute for SMB-based shares, if properly secured.) Table 5-6 presents the similarities and differences between WebDAV publishing and SMB-based sharing.

Table 5-6 WebDAV Versus SMB Shares

Item	WebDAV	SMB Shares
Service	Requires IIS.	Requires File and Printer Sharing enabled, Server service.
Who can access data and what they can do	Depends on permission assigned.	Depends on permissions assigned.
Default permissions	`Read`.	`Everyone Read`.
Effect of underlying NTFS permissions	Most restrictive wins.	Most restrictive wins.
Created	A virtual directory must be created on a website.	A folder on the file server must be shared.
Authentication	Anonymous and Windows Integrated available on website by default.	Windows authentication required.
Authentication	Available at folder level settings.	Available at computer and domain level.
Clients	Windows 2000 and Windows XP; Internet Explorer 5.0 and 6.0; Microsoft Office 2000, 2003, and Office XP.	All Windows and DOS clients with networking.
Connection	Windows XP and 2000: Add directory to list of network places or command line. Internet Explorer 5.0 and 6.0. Open target directory as web folder.	Map drives, browse to drives, `net share` command.
Drag and drop?	Drag and drop file publishing.	Drag and drop file copies.
Command line	Set up connection using `net use` and UNC-formatted location. Uses WebDAV redirector.	Set up connection using `net use` and UNC-formatted location. Uses SMB.

WebDAV is not new to Windows Server 2003, but in Windows Server 2003, implementation changes mean that from Windows XP or Windows Server 2003, a user can use simple UNC-based connections to copy files to WebDAV folders and use browser-based publication. For example, connecting to a WebDAV folder is now similar to connecting to a share. If the name of a WebDAV folder is HR Feedback and it resides on the server IAM, a user can connect using the net use command. Windows will also look for the virtual directory HR Feedback using HTTP and make a new network connection:

```
net use \\iam\HR Feedback
net use * http://IAM/HR Feedback
```

WebDAV cannot be used by default to provide access to data on Windows Server 2003 because IIS is not installed by default. Even if IIS is installed, WebDAV is not enabled by default. To use WebDAV, IIS must be installed, and WebDAV must be enabled. However, once enabled, clients can connect to and use WebDAV folders across a firewall if port 80 is open to the server. Unlike SMB ports, there is no special WebDAV port, so you cannot provide access to a website and block access to WebDAV shared data by setting firewall ports. Since port 80 is often open to allow access to a web server, and WebDAV uses HTTP, clients can connect to and publish and manipulate files on servers where connections to SMB shares are blocked. This is important to remember. For years, the security community has advised against allowing access to SMB shares over the Internet (and has not been successful in convincing companies and individuals to do so). Now, if WebDAV publishing is enabled, and access to the website is allowed, a connection is possible via the Internet right through the firewall. It is for this reason that you must develop a policy concerning when WebDAV is allowed, if it is allowed on Internet-accessible web servers, and how permissions and web server authentication will be configured to ensure the least risk of intrusion.

WebDAV permissions are not meant to replace NTFS permissions; they are meant to be used with NTFS permissions. Like share permission, WebDAV permissions combine with underlying NTFS permissions, and the most restrictive permission is the one that will be used. However, unlike share permissions, WebDAV permissions affect every user. You cannot give Read permission to one group of users and not to another. However, you can use the underlying NTFS permissions to implicitly or explicitly deny groups of users that you don't wish to read the files. Table 5-7 lists and describes the WebDAV permissions.

Table 5-7   WebDAV Permissions Are Virtual Directory Permissions

Permissions	Description
Read	View directory and file content and properties.
Write	Change directory and file content and properties. Modify files, change properties, publish files to folder.
Directory Browsing (called Browse in the wizard)	View a list of the contents.
Script Source Access	If enabled, users can read source code for scripts. If disabled, they cannot.
Execute: None, Scripts Only: Scripts and Executables	None—no scripts or executables can be run. Scripts Only—run only scripts on the server. Scripts and Executables—both scripts and executables can be run. (Only one execute permission can be assigned.)

Enabling `Script Source Access` is a bad idea because users can read and possibly modify scripts. (If `Script Source Access` is enabled and either `Write` or `Read` is also assigned, users can access source files. If `Write` is assigned, then users can modify scripts.) It is always a good practice to place scripts and executable files in a separate folder on a website, and then set appropriate permissions. For example, set `Execute` permission in a folder that contains scripts and executable that users should be allowed to run, set `Read` permissions on folders used to make stored files available for reading, and set `Write` permission on folders used for file publishing. Never set both `Execute` and `Write` permissions on the same folder, because a malicious user could then publish a script to the folder and run it. Scripts may also contain sensitive information such as passwords and therefore should not be readable by all users.

Appropriate file and WebDav combinations are as follows:

- `Read`, `Write`, **and** `Directory Browsing` **enabled**—Clients can see a list of resources, modify them, publish their own resources, and manipulate files.
- `Write` **enabled and** `Read` **and** `Directory Browsing` **disabled**—Clients can publish information but cannot list or read anything published.

- `Read` **and** `Write` **enabled and** `Directory Browsing` **disabled—** Clients can open and read the files they know the names of, and publish files to the folder, but they cannot list the contents of the folder.

The `Write` access permission does not provide clients with the ability to modify script-mapped files. Script-mapped files are Active Server Pages (ASP) and others. To modify these files, both the `Write` and `Script` source access must be assigned.

To create a publishing directory, enable WebDAV, create a directory to share and assign NTFS permissions, create a virtual directory on IIS, and configure virtual directory permissions.

Enable WebDAV

When IIS is installed, WebDAV is not enabled. To enable WebDAV, do the following:

1. Open the Internet Information Services (IIS) Manager and note that WebDAV is not enabled, as shown in Figure 5-23.

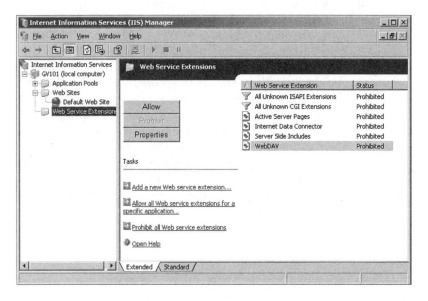

Figure 5-23   WebDAV is not enabled by default.

2. Select the task `Allow all Web service extensions for a specific application` and then select WebDAV from the drop-down box.
3. Click OK to enable WebDAV.

Create a Folder to Share and Set NTFS Permissions

Create a file system folder where files to be shared will be placed. Set appropriate NTFS permissions on the folder. For example, if the folder will be a repository where accountants may store and modify files, NTFS permissions should give the Accountants group `Modify` permission. `Full Control` would not be required.

Create a Virtual Directory

The next step is to create a virtual directory on the web server that points to the created folder:

1. Open the Internet Information Services (IIS) Manager.
2. Right-click on the website and select `New, Virtual Directory`, and then click `Next`.
3. Enter an alias (name for the WebDAV folder) for the directory.
4. Use the `Browse` button to browse to and select the folder created earlier, and then click `Next`.
5. Assign virtual directory permissions, as shown in Figure 5-24. In this example, `Read` (read contents of a file) and `Write` (access and change source of script and publish files) were selected. (If scripts or Common Gateway Interface files must be executed, the `Read` and `Execute` permissions need to be applied. In this case, the stated purpose is to store and access files. It is always a poor practice to allow `Write` and `Execute` permissions on web folders because a malicious script might be written to the folder and then executed.)
6. Click `Next` and then click `Finish`.

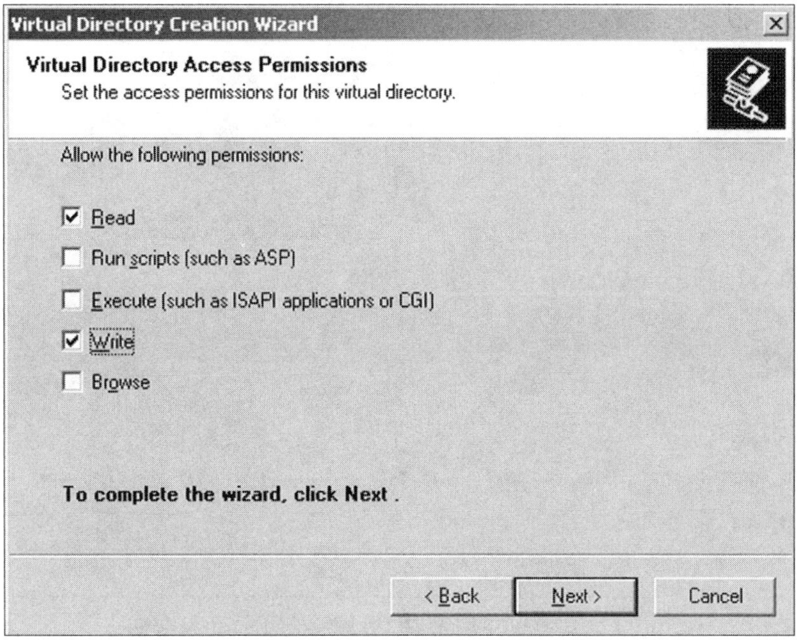

Figure 5-24   Assign virtual directory permissions.

Configure Virtual Directory Security

The wizard does not allow completion of security configuration. Immediately after creating the virtual directory and before allowing client access, care should be taken to apply further security:

1. Right-click on the new virtual directory and select `Properties`.
2. On the `Virtual Directory` page, as shown in Figure 5-25, note that indexing and log visits are selected by default. Confirm that permission settings here match what is required on the site. If searching is required, make sure that the indexing service is running.
3. Select the `Directory Security` page, and then click the `Edit` button to edit `Authentication and access control`.
4. Select to disable the `Enable Anonymous Access` feature. Ensure that `Integrated Windows` authentication is checked, as shown in Figure 5-26, or that the appropriate authentication mechanism for your organization is selected.

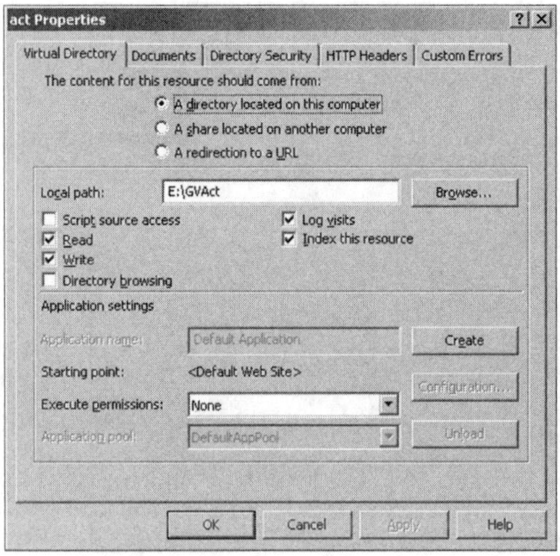

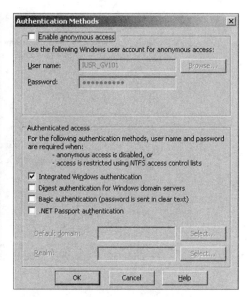

Figure 5-25   Confirm permission settings on the virtual directory.

Figure 5-26   Disable anonymous access to WebDAV folders.

Client Side Configuration

Once WebDAV has been configured, enable and start the Web Client service on the client to take full advantage of the benefits. The Web Client service is disabled by default.

WebDAV may already be in use in your organization. To make sure it doesn't become part of the data misuse in your organization, follow these best practices:

- Ensure WebDAV directories reside on NTFS-formatted volumes.
- Assign NTFS permissions on files and folders in the WebDAV directory.
- Use web folder permissions.
- Insist on Windows Authentication on intranet.
- Use but protect basic authentication on the Internet with SSL.

Controlling Access to Registry Keys

Registry keys are permissioned by default and should not be modified without a thorough understanding of the impact of the modification. Registry keys are also added by applications and via configuration settings. Changing permissions on these keys may prevent applications from running.

Default Registry Permissions

Figure 5-27 displays registry permissions, and they are listed and described in Table 5-8. Alhough registry permission names are different from file permissions, they are similar in use. Two main permissions, `Full Control` and `Read`, are composed of special permissions. Special permissions can be explicitly assigned.

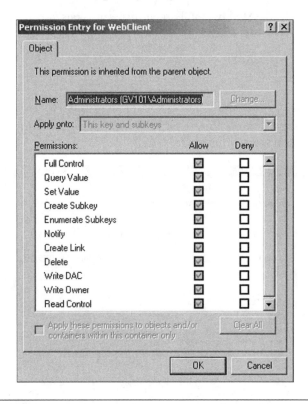

Figure 5-27   Registry permissions work similarly to file permissions but consist of a different permission set.

Table 5-8   Registry Permissions

Permission	Description
Full Control	Combination of all permissions
Read Query	Includes enumerate, notify, read control
Query Value	Read value of a key
Set Value	Create, delete a set registry value
Create Subkey	Add a key
Enumerate Subkeys	List subkeys
Notify	If present, can request change notifications for a registry key or its subkeys. This is useful, for example, in auditing.
Create Link	Used by the system to create links between registry paths
Delete	Delete key
Write DAC	Modify DACL, security permissions
Write Owner	Rights write, set value, create subkey
Read Control	Read permissions

Registry key permissions inheritance is similar to that described in the file system and can be blocked to protect permissions on sensitive subkeys, as shown in Figure 5-28.

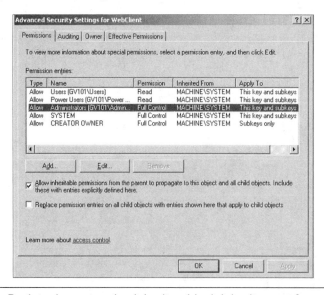

Figure 5-28   Registry keys can also inherit or block inheritance of permissions.

Applying Registry Permissions

Registry permissions, like object permissions for files and folders, may be applied directly using the object picker within the Registry Editor, by application through security templates, and by using Group Policy,

The regedt32.exe program is not part of Windows XP or Windows Server 2003. However, the features that differentiate it from regedit.exe, such as the ability to set security permissions, set audit permissions, and assign ownership of a key, have been added to regedit. An additional feature of regedit in Windows Server 2003 is the Favorites feature. As you work with registry keys, you can put your frequently used keys on the Favorites menu in regedit. Clicking the menu entry opens the stored subkey record.

To modify registry key permissions, follow these steps:

1. Select the key.
2. From the Edit menu, select Permissions, and then click Add.
3. Use the Locations box of the Select Users, Computers or Groups dialog box to select the computer or domain of the users and groups to give permission to.
4. Enter the group name and click Check Users to verify, or click the Advanced button and then the Find Now button to obtain a list of the users and groups. Then select the user or group to give permissions to.
5. In the Permissions dialog box, assign the type of access to the selected user or group, or click the Advanced button, select the User, and click the Edit button to select special permissions.

Changing ownership of a registry key is a two-part process: First, an administrator or other user with ownership permission must assign ownership to a new user, and then the designated user must take ownership. The exception to this rule is that users with the Take Ownership permission may change ownership to their own account. To change ownership of a registry key, do the following:

1. Select the key to change ownership for.
2. Select Permissions from the Edit menu.
3. Select Advanced, and then select the Owner tab.
4. Select Change Owner to select the new owner.

The new owner completes the owner change process by using `Take Ownership` of the key to complete the process. This two-part process serves a distinct security role. It separates the process of giving owner-ship permission from the process of taking ownership. This is important because it prevents a malicious person with the Take Ownership right from taking ownership, giving themselves permissions, changing, view-ing, or deleting data, and then giving ownership back to the original owner in an attempt to avoid detection or to avoid being held account-able for his act. Because the duties are separated, the attacker retains ownership of the object and cannot deny that he had the opportunity to use this capability to obtain information or to do some task that he is not authorized to do.

Practical Deployment Issues

Setting object permissions using the object picker is not the only way to secure objects. A sound understanding of object permissions and inheri-tance is critical; however, there are a number of processes that also affect data security and tools that can be used to further secure data. Object per-missions cannot always be locked down to the requirements defined by data owners, and the operating system cannot be hardened as well as could be. These processes and tools are issues having to do with the following:

- Legacy applications
- Data streams
- Recovery and fault tolerance
- Native tools for permission application
- Clustering
- Distributed File System (DFS)
- Data security options in Group Policy and security templates
- Event log access security

Legacy Application Permission Issues

Each new Windows version has made improvements in security and sta-bility. However, these changes have often meant application compatibil-ity issues. Applications designed to run on less secure versions of Windows may not be able to run on newer versions without significantly weakening security settings. Unfortunately, these issues are most frequently resolved by giving users administrative rights on their own desktop systems. This is not a good solution to the problem, though. It does work, however, because many of the compatibility issues have to do with file system and registry permissions. Older versions of Windows had little or no restrictions on file access. Newer versions of the operating system often give users little or no permissions to sensitive folders, files, and registry keys. The Administrators group, however, is given full access. By giving users Administrative group membership, the applications then work as expected. An alternative approach would be to determine exactly which files and folders the applications require access to and to provide users access to those files. This would allow the applications to run but would not provide users with elevated privileges on their systems. Many attacks attempted by viruses and worms will not work if the user running the infected file does not have administrative privileges. If applications disregard the permission requirements of newer operating system versions, and administrators cannot or do not want to create workarounds and thus provide users with administrative privileges, this weakens security.

To determine exact permission requirements, other options are as follows:

- Replacing older applications with applications that are built to conform to the new operating system.
- Using the pre-Windows 2000 compatible access group. This group can be used to provide backward compatibility access to domain resources for computers running Windows NT 4.0 or earlier that must be part of a Windows Server 2003 domain. For example, a Windows NT 4.0-based RRAS server that is a member of a Windows Server 2003-based domain must be able to access the remote access credentials of domain accounts. Adding the Everyone group to the pre-Windows compatible access group permits the RAS caller to be authenticated by the Windows NT 4.0 server.
- Determining the required permissions and replacing default permissions with these permissions.

Legacy Application Permission Example

Permissions on system files, folders, and registry keys are based on the needs of the operating system. Where users only need `Read`, they are only granted `Read` permissions, not `Change`. Administrators have broader permissions and use them to install programs that must change data in protected areas of the system and its registry. Unfortunately, applications are often written without careful regard to default permissions. Instead of only requesting `Read` access, they often request `Change` or `Full Control`. Often, the application does not need this permission; it was just easier for the developer to write it this way. It is also possible that the application does need elevated permissions at a location now protected from such activity. And sometimes an application places its own information in an area of the file system or registry where it does not need to be when it should have defined its own folder or key. When these applications are installed, they may work just fine for administrators but not for users. To compensate, the organization may believe it must give users `Administrator` rights on their systems.

Examples of applications that have caused problems in the past are RealPlayer Version 7 and Acrobat Reader 4.0. In both cases, the applications attempt to write to registry keys that by default only grant `Read` permission to ordinary users. RealPlayer attempts to write to the `HKEY_CLASSES_ROOT\Software\RealNetworks` key, while Acrobat Reader attempts to write to the `HKEY_CLASSES_ROOT\\AcroExch.Document` and the `HKEY_CLASSES_ROOT\CLSID\{B801CA65-A1FC-11D0-85AD-444553540000}` keys. Fortunately, the problem can be fixed by giving the Users group the "Set Value" permission on the keys. Administrative group membership is not required.

These permissions should not be changed on servers, but these applications should not be run on servers either.

To determine which file, folder, or registry key permissions must be changed to allow legacy or poorly designed applications to run, two free tools can be downloaded from sysinternals.com: Filemon and Regmon. Running these tools while running the suspect application will provide a list of files and registry keys accessed. If users are denied access to any of these objects, or if the access granted them does not provide the application the access it needs, this is probably why the application doesn't work. Another way to determine problems with object access is to set system access control lists (SACLs) and record an audit of access failure. After compiling the list of objects where access is denied, grant users the access required instead of granting them administrative rights on the computer.

Providing users with elevated access permissions to some files or registry keys is a far more secure option than giving users administrative privileges.

Alternative Data Streams

Data streams are locations assigned to files created in the NTFS file system. NTFS allows multiple data streams for each file. The first data stream is visible in Windows Explorer and is accessed by using the filename. Additional file streams can be created under the same filename but are not visible in Explorer. These alternative data streams (ADSs) are used for many things, including accommodation of dual-forked Macintosh files (which can be stored on Windows NT-based systems when Services for Macintosh (SFM) is installed), the summary information property tab of a text file as displayed in Figure 5-29, and the web sharing property page of IIS folders. More information can be found in the Microsoft document "Multiple Data Streams" at http://www.microsoft.com/resources/documentation/Windows/XP/all/reskit/en-us/Default.asp?url=/resources/documentation/Windows/XP/all/reskit/en-us/prkc_fil_xurt.asp.

Although ADSs perform useful functions, they are hard to detect without specialized non-native software and may be difficult to remove. Furthermore, an ADSs could pack a malicious payload. A proof-of-concept virus, the W32.stream virus, developed in 2000, attached itself to a harmless file as an ADSs.

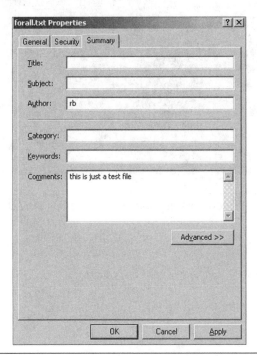

Figure 5-29   The Summary page information in a text file is stored in a data stream.

Creating and Manipulating ADS

Alternative data files can easily be created at the command prompt. An ADSs can be created using the following commands:

1. From a command prompt, enter the command below to create the file test.txt:

```
Echo "this is a text file" >C:\test.txt
```

2. Create an ADSs for this file:

```
Echo "stuff in a data stream" >
    C:test.txt:mydatastream.txt
```

The ADS is not displayed in Explorer or by using the `dir` command, as shown in Figure 5-30.

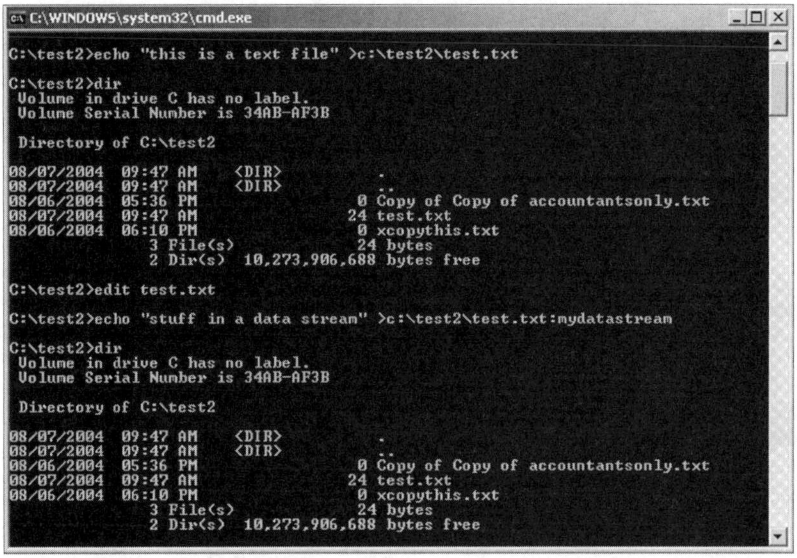

Figure 5-30   Listing the contents of a folder will not show the ADSs.

To read the ADSs, use Notepad with the following command:

```
Notepad file.txt:mydatastream.txt
```

The file contents will be displayed in Notepad, as shown in Figure 5-31.

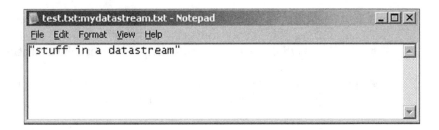

Figure 5-31   The content of an altered datastream can be read in Notepad.

Reading a single data stream when you know it's there is not hard, but how do you discover the data streams that you don't know about? Data streams used by legitimate Windows systems are of little interest, but rogue data streams that contain malicious or undesirable data might be stored on a computer's hard drive. ADSs have been found on computer disks that contain pornographic material. At the least, unauthorized data streams use disk resources. If you don't know if any are present, how can you determine if any of them hide malicious code or data that should not be on the computer? This is one of several security issues engendered by ADSs. Issue include these:

- Few administrators or security officers understand them; therefore, few administrators or security officers look for them. Data streams that harbor malicious code might be saved as the data stream of an innocent file. Two known viruses, Dumaru.y and W2K.Stream, take advantage of ADSs.
- Some anti-virus products may not scan data streams.
- Products that wipe disks (that replace data on the disk with zeros to ensure that no one can obtain the data that was once resident on the disk) may not replace the content of ADSs.

Tools That Make Detection Easier

There are third-party tools that check for ADSs. A few of the available tools are as follows:

- LADS (list alternative data streams) scan through directories and find ADS files. Available from http://www.heysoft.de/nt/ep-lads. htm.

- Streams is freeware available from Sysinternals (http://www.sysinternals.com/ntw2k/source/misc.shtml#streams).
- Crucial ADS is available from http://www.crucialsecurity.com/downloads.html.
- TDS-3 commercial can scan specific directories. A demo copy is available for download at http://tds.diamondcs.com.au/.

Deleting ADSs is difficult. To delete an ADS, you must either delete the file it is linked to, or delete the folder it resides in. You can also copy the file to a FAT file system (data streams cannot be preserved) and then copy the file back to the NTFS location. You cannot delete ADSs attached to the root directory. If the ADS is large, you can, however, create small ADSs and use them to overwrite the ADSs attached to the root.

Executable files can be attached as ADSs. Running them requires use of the `start` command.

At one time, anti-virus programs and disk-wiping programs had problems processing ADSs, but today most products are ADS-aware.

Setting Permissions Using Security Templates

File, folder, and registry permissions can be set in Security Templates and then applied to a single system or imported into a Group Policy. Permission settings can also be made directly in the GPO. The default security template, defltsv.inf, is used during Windows Server 2003 installation to set system, volume root, and registry permissions. If and when the server is dcpromoed (made into a domain controller), defltdc.inf is used to apply additional domain controller-specific permission sets. If you have additional security permissions for files, folders, and registry keys that are placed on every server, you can create your own default templates, save them using these names, and use them during your installs instead of using the ones provided on the installation CD-ROM. (You can find a copy of these templates in the <system root>\inf folder). Security templates can also be used to set permissions, test that permissions have not been altered, and reapply permissions as necessary.

More information on the use of security templates is provided in Chapter 11, "Securing Infrastructure Roles."

WARNING: Beware of Using Group Policy to Set Permissions
The Security Setting portion of Group Policy is refreshed every 16 hours, even if nothing has changed. If a large number of permissions is changed via Group Policy, this can become a performance issue, as can replication of large GPOs.

Recovery and Fault Tolerance

Several services that impact data security are as follows:

- The Windows File Protection (WFP) service protects the integrity of system files by preventing their replacement. WFP can help protect against accidental deletion or replacement and can prevent malicious replacement of system files.
- The System File Checker application can be used to check the status of system files on a specific computer.
- Volume Shadow Copy allows end users to recover previous versions of their files. This helps reduce help desk efforts required to recover files from backup when the user accidentally deletes them.

These items will be discussed, along with other recovery and fault-tolerant services and practices, in Chapter 16, "Maintenance Strategies and Administrative Practices."

Clustering

Clustering technology in Windows Server 2003 consists of two distinct technologies:

- Network load-balancing balances the network load between multiple (up to 32) identical computers. NLB is available on Windows Server 2003 Standard Edition and Web Edition. An example of such a cluster would be a group of ISA Server firewalls or a group of IIS web servers.
- Server clusters provide up to 8-way failover for network resources. Server clusters are available on Windows Server 2003 Enterprise and Datacenter Editions. This may be used to provide redundancy and fault tolerance for databases and other large collections of files.

Clusters present a challenging data security issue. They are often used to ensure data availability, which is usually considered to be part of security. However, they can cause a security issue. Permission sets must be kept consistent across multiple computers in the cluster. The following are best practices for permissions on clusters:

- Configure file share access by using permissions on the `Parameter` tab in Cluster Administrator, not the local computer file system share security. If permissions are changed using Windows Explorer instead, permission settings are lost when the resource is taken offline.
- Do not give permissions to local groups and user accounts, with the exception of the local Administrators group. All other local groups and user accounts only have meaning on the local system, not on other nodes in the cluster. In the case of node failure, any permission set for local groups or users is meaningless; it will have no impact on the other node.
- Set auditing for files and folders based on local user and group accounts using Windows Explorer. Audit events are by nature recorded only on the computer where they occur. If, however, you want to monitor usage by auditing, you will have to set consistent audit settings on resources of all nodes in the cluster.
- Protect the folder on the quorum disk that stores the quorum log. This log stores all the changes to the cluster state and configuration changes that cannot be committed to other nodes.

Because clustering hardware can be more proprietary than the average server, it is important to pay close attention to the manufacturer's recommendations. You'll find that many of the security issues pertaining to clusters will be unique to that manufacturer.

DFS

To the ordinary computer user, file location on the network is a mystery. In fact, many users do not even recognize that the files they access every day are not stored on their local disks. If users are allowed to make their own connections to file shares to access network resources, it may be a daunting task for them. Even administrators, who must set up drive mappings for users, can have difficulty locating just the right mapping when there are many and the organization of shares is volatile or nonexistent. Browsing, the de facto way of locating resources, does not work well in large distributed environments. The distributed file system (Dfs) was created to alleviate this situation. Dfs enables an organized architecture to be created. Once connected to the appropriate Dfs root, the user can expand the root to reveal resources named for their content. Just as resource location is unimportant to users, resource location is not important to Dfs, and multiple locations for the same resource can be listed. The selection of which specific resource to visit is made by the system, and if a server that maintains a copy of the resource is not available, another may be.

Dfs network resources do not have to be located on Windows systems. Dfs can be configured to point to targets on Novell servers and Unix systems in addition to Windows systems.

This great network resource management system does introduce new security issues. First, Dfs adds no additional security. Security must be configured at the network resource location. Second, although data can be in diverse locations, when planning the location of network file resources, consider how they will be secured. It is not a good idea, for example, to place network resources where no file permissions can be applied, or where the ability to set file permissions may weaken access controls. Finally, if multiple copies of the same data exist, care must be taken to ensure that the security permissions are consistently kept.

Effective Security Options and User Rights Management

In addition to explicit permissions on file, share, and registry objects, the Security Options and user rights portions of Group Policy affect data security. The following elements should be considered when creating a secure data access architecture.

Restriction on Anonymous Access

Chapter 2, "Authentication: Proof of Identity," described the need for controlling anonymous access. If anonymous access is granted to shares, the permissions created for shares will only restrict authorized users.

Do Not Make Anonymous Members of the Everyone Group

Some anonymous access may be required. For example, users must be able to connect to domain controllers to authenticate. Nonetheless, take care to restrict anonymous access to data. In addition to preventing direct application of permissions for the Anonymous group, the Anonymous group should not be added back into the Everyone group. The Everyone group is granted broad access to files, folders, and registry keys.

The Bypass Traverse Checking User Right

This user right allows the user to programmatically access files he has permission to access, even if he does not have access permission to the parent folders.

More information on this right can be found in the section "User Rights " in Chapter 3.

Format and Eject Removable Media

The Security Option `Devices: Allowed to format and eject remov-able media` controls permission to format removable disks and remove them. Although most removable disks, such as USB and Firewire-based drives, can simply be unplugged, there is some danger that data will be damaged. Managing the ability to format may be more important because accidental or malicious formatting of these drives could be a problem.

Restricting Remote Access to CD-ROMs and Floppies

If a user is logged on, the Security Option `Devices: Restrict CD-ROM Access to Locally Logged on User` prevents remote access to the CD-ROM. However, if no user is logged on locally, this setting will not prevent remote access to the CD-ROM drive.

- `Devices: Restrict floppy Access to Locally Logged on User`—If a user is logged on, this setting prevents remote access to the floppy. However, if no user is logged on locally, this setting will not prevent remote access to the floppy drive.
- `Network Access: Remotely Accessible Registry Paths`—Allows controlled access to registry paths.
- `Network Access: Remotely Accessible Registry Paths and Subpaths`—Allows controlled access to registry paths and their subpaths.
- `Network Access: Shares that can be accessed anonymously`—Only these shares allow anonymous access if other anonymous restrictions are set.
- `Shutdown: Clear Virtual Memory Pagefile`—On shutdown, clears the pagefile. Any type of data may be paged to the pagefile while the system is running. The pagefile is protected while the system is operational; however, when the system is shut down, it is just an ordinary file and might be accessed from a boot to another OS. To ensure that sensitive data cannot be accessed in this manner, use this setting.

Controlling Access to Event Logs

The operating system, services, and some applications automatically record information in the Windows event logs. Additional events are recorded when applications are configured to do so. These events may include useful information for troubleshooting, warnings that something needs attention, alerts of potential attacks, and historical documentation that may be necessary to compose an audit trail for criminal prosecution.

Processes within applications can be coded to post records, to read records, and to archive or clear the event logs. To perform these actions, the application must be running in the security context of an account with the privileges to do so, either because an individual with those privileges runs the application, or because the service account used to run the application is given those privileges. For example, Microsoft Exchange Server posts records to the logs under the authority of its services accounts. Logon audit records are posed by the SYSTEM account. On the other hand, only an administrator can use the Event Viewer application to delete the content of an event log.

By default, each log has its own permission settings. Default permissions on Windows Server 2003 event logs are displayed in Table 5-9.

Table 5-9 Permission on the Event Logs

Log	Local System	Local Administrators, Domain Admins	Ordinary Users
Application Log	Full access	Read, Write, and Clear.	Read and Write
System log	Full access	Local administrators have Read, Write and Clear permissions. Domain Administrators have Read and Clear.	Read
Security	Full access	Administrators by default are assigned the Managing Auditing and Security Log user right (the SE_SECURITY_NAME privilege), which gives them Read and Clear permissions.	Users can be assigned the Managing Auditing and Security Log user right.

Prior to Windows Server 2003, event log access could be granted to members of the Guest account by modifying the registry key RestrictGuestAccess at HKEY_LOCAL_MACHINE\SYSTEM\CurrentControl Set\Services\EventLog\Application. In Windows Server 2003, RestrictGuestAccess is ignored, and two new registry values can be used to determine access: one for access to the Application log and the other for the System log. Both values are part of subkeys of the EventLog key above. To manage access to the Application log, use the CustomSD key under the EventLog\Application key; to manage access to the System log, use the CustomSD key under the EventLog\System key. Acceptable values are as follows:

- 0x0001—Permission to read the log file.
- 0x0002—Permission to write to the log file.
- 0x0004—Permission to clear the log file.

These permissions have no value for the security log file. Regardless, only the Local Security Authority has write permission for the security log files. Likewise, if a user has the SE_Security privilege, he can read and clear the security log regardless of how CustomSD keys are configured.

WARNING: Do Not Weaken Security on the Security Event Log
Access to the security log is limited to prevent tampering with audit records. Rather than broadening access to this log, consider restricting it to a subset of administrators. The integrity of the records in this log is critical to proving an audit trail of activity on the system. This may be important for discovering security breaches and holding accountable system users and attackers.

Summary

Many things contribute to data security. Of prime importance, though, are file, folder, and registry permissions. These form the foundation upon which other defenses can rely. Should all else fail, these need to be strong. This chapter explained these permissions and how they can work with other items to protect data. It also introduced interesting developments such as WebDAV, which can change the way data is remotely accessed and thus the way it must be secured. Protection for data in flight will be covered in later chapters, and the use of the Encrypting File System to encrypt data files will be introduced in the next chapter.

CHAPTER 6

EFS Basics

September 16, 2001—the Hyatt Regency Hotel, Irvine, California. Qualcomm founder and self-made billionaire Irwin Jacobs turned from speaking with journalists and realized his laptop was missing. Just minutes before, he'd been using it to give a presentation to the Society of American Business Editors. On the laptop were company financial statements, secret data, email, and, of course, his contact list and pictures of his grandchildren. It was the first widely publicized laptop theft, and it was the first one to bring to everyone's attention the fact that laptop theft might not just be about pawning a piece of expensive hardware. There has been much speculation that the theft was not routine but instead was a case of corporate espionage.

Jacobs's security? He relied on a BIOS password. None of the data on his computer was encrypted. As you know, a BIOS password is a good physical deterrent, especially on stationary computers. It is not, however, an effective security device for laptops. BIOS passwords can be circumvented by simply removing the hard drive, an especially simple task on a laptop. Had Jacobs encrypted his data and kept the keys separate from the laptop while in public places, he could have at least worried a little less about what thieves might be doing with his data.

It's ironic that he certainly could have afforded the highest level of data encryption protection for his data but had none. But it's even more interesting because Windows 2000, which introduced the Encrypting File System (EFS), had been available for seven months. Data encryption would have been possible for him at no extra charge. Today, you can incorporate strong data encryption in your enterprise security design by using EFS, but you must understand EFS to avoid pitfalls and ensure data security, integrity, and recovery. This chapter will help you do so.

What Is the Encrypting File System?

EFS is a component of the NTFS file system that can be used to encrypt data files. Ordinary users of Windows systems can encrypt and decrypt their data files if the following conditions are met:

- The operating system is Windows 2000, Windows XP Professional, or Windows Server 2003.
- The file system is NTFS.
- Data files are not placed in the root or %systemroot% folders. (These areas cannot be encrypted).
- Files are not marked with the System attribute. (System files cannot be encrypted.)
- EFS has not been disabled.

It is not necessary for the computer to be joined in a domain, to implement certificate services, or to institute administrative management of certificates and files. However, the security of the system will be enhanced if you do these things. In fact, without such management, it is possible for data loss to occur.

Have You Implemented EFS?

At a series of Microsoft security summits for IT pros, I asked the question, "How many of you have implemented EFS?" Very few hands were raised. I told them they were liars because EFS is implemented by default. Any user can encrypt files without the benefit of administrative implementation, instruction, or management.

Therein lies a very large problem: Without training, ordinary users can live with a false sense of security, and IT pros can find themselves with data recovery problems and privacy issues.

- If users do not realize access to their password allows transparent access to their encrypted files, they may use weak passwords, write their passwords down in plain view, or share passwords with coworkers and friends.
- If users don't understand the necessity of backing up their private key, they may lose access to encrypted files if their profile becomes corrupt or if their system is rebuilt.

■ If IT pros ignore EFS while their users adopt it, IT pros may be left with critical but unrecoverable company data, find that unauthorized administrators have accidental access to sensitive data, and end up spending troubleshooting, training, maintenance, and implementation time needed for other projects fighting EFS issues.

Without doubt, important data has been lost and needless hours spent all for the want of a sound EFS policy. I cannot emphasize strongly enough that your policy toward EFS should be to disable it until you can implement a sound, practical, and recoverable EFS strategy. This chapter will provide you with the basics; Chapter 12, "PKI Basics," and Chapter 13, "Implementing a Secure PKI," provide information that can be used to develop such practices.

Implementation Differences Between Windows Versions

Many of the differences between Windows Server 2003 and Windows 2000 were first implemented in Windows XP Professional, which added the following:

■ Ability to work with offline files
■ Ability to back up keys directly from the command line and from the `File Details` property page
■ Stronger encryption algorithms
■ Multiple user access to encrypted files
■ Ability to use WebDAV to store encrypted files on the server

Also new but dependent on the implementation of Windows Server 2003 Certification Authority is the ability to centrally archive the user's private encryption key. This capability provides efficient recovery management, something that has been missing and is desperately needed. The new process, known as *key archival*, means that instead of recovering the file, the encryption key is recovered. Not only is this a sounder practice than relying on a file recovery agent, but also the key recovery agent, unlike the file recovery agent, does not automatically have the ability to read the file. The key recovery agent is able to retrieve the private key and return it instead of a decrypted file to the owner.

WARNING: Key Recovery Agents Have Powerful Abilities
It is true that the key recovery agent cannot automatically open another user's encrypted file. However, because key recovery agent can recover the private key, key recovery agents have the ability to import that key into their profile and decrypt any file that the user has encrypted using the public key paired with that private key. Strict policies and monitoring of key recovery processes should be in place to guard against this possibility. One helpful policy is to require that after the key is recovered and used to recover encrypted files, the user must request a new EFS certificate. The new keys received should be used to encrypt the data files.

Managing EFS in a mixed client and server environment will be considerably easier if you are aware of the differences between the three implementations in the three different versions of Windows. All three have in common the requirements for NTFS and provide transparent encryption and decryption. All three use the same basic algorithms for the process. Table 6-1 provides a list of the areas where the operating systems' EFS implementations differ. For completeness, information on differences in Certificate Authority capabilities is included, even though it is not discussed until Chapter 12.

Table 6-1   EFS Differences

Feature	Windows 2000	Windows XP	Windows Server 2003
Can share encrypted files	No	Yes	Yes
Recovery Agent necessary for encryption	Yes	No	No
Local administrator on standalone is recovery agent	Yes	No	No
Default file encryption algorithm	DESX	DESX, after service pack 1 AES	AES
File Encryption algorithm choices	DESX	DESX, 3DES, AES	DESX, 3DES, AES

Feature	Windows 2000	Windows XP	Windows Server 2003
Public key encryption algorithms	RSA	RSA	RSA
Data Recovery	File recovery	File recovery, Key recovery if Certificate Authority for domain configured	File Recovery, key recovery if Certificate Authority for domain configured
How to determine encryptor and recovery agent for file	Esfinfo—a resource kit utility	See file Advanced properties	See file Advanced properties

Basic Operations

Nothing has to be done to implement EFS. It's already available to any user who can select a check box. Unless EFS is disabled or a policy is implemented that denies the user this right, the user determines which of his files will be encrypted. Most users will be oblivious to the impact of doing so, other than it appears as if others cannot view their files. While users only see the result (their files appear to be impenetrable to others), IT needs to provide a structure that will ensure that files are private when they need to be and can be recovered if the user is unable to do so. The first step in developing sound administrative practices and polices for EFS is to understand EFS basic operations.

While there are no operating system restrictions on encryption of application or data files, system files cannot be encrypted. The reason is that the file system must be available before files can be decrypted, and some files are needed to boot the OS that therefore would be encrypted and unavailable.

Encrypting and Decrypting

Individual files can be encrypted one by one, or a folder can be marked for encryption, in which case every file placed in the folder is encrypted. Users may decrypt an encrypted file by modifying the file's encryption property using Windows Explorer, by using the cipher command, or by opening the file in the application used to create it. When the file's encryption property is used, users must re-encrypt the file. However, when an application is used to decrypt the file, the file is re-encrypted when the file is saved.

If a folder is marked for encryption, often called encrypting the folder, files placed or saved in the folder will be encrypted. When the user who encrypted it accesses the file, it is automatically decrypted. For example, if the user saves a Word document in the encrypted folder, the document is encrypted. When the user opens the document, it is automatically decrypted. To the user, it appears as if nothing has happened; encryption and decryption are transparent to the user.

Encryption transparency has several advantages. First, the user is not required to understand how to encrypt or decrypt files and doesn't have to do anything to accomplish it. Instead, she just does her work. Second, when a file is first saved in plain text and then later encrypted, a temporary file is made. Since the plaintext copy of the file is marked for deletion, it might be possible for someone to forensically examine the drive and recover the data. However, when a file is first stored in an encrypted folder, no plaintext copy of the file is stored.

WARNING: Deleted Plaintext Copy May Still Be Present

When ordinary files are deleted, they are not really removed from the drive. Instead, they are simply "marked for deletion" and gradually overwritten as new data is added to the drive. Forensic applications and techniques exist that can gather these "remnants," or "data shreds." To prevent data remanence (the existence of leftover shreds) from exposing sensitive data, organizations often use special utilities to overwrite data multiple times, use magnets to degauss drives before they are reused, and destroy drives rather than resell them or give them away.

To prevent encrypted file data remanence from becoming a problem, always encrypt folders, not files. However, if plaintext shreds of sensitive data may exist on a drive, or you want to be sure that there aren't any, the cipher.exe tool can be used to overwrite data marked for deletion.

Using File and Folder Properties to Encrypt and Decrypt Files

When the folder property is set to encrypt files, files are automatically encrypted when placed in the folder. However, individual files can be encrypted or decrypted by using the Advanced file properties page of the file. To encrypt a file, follow these steps:

1. In Windows Explorer, right-click the file and select `Properties`.
2. Click the `Advanced` button on the `General` page.
3. Select `Encrypt contents to secure data` and click `OK` twice.
4. In the Encryption Warning dialog box, as shown in Figure 6-1, do one of the following:
   To just encrypt the file, select `Encrypt the   le only`,
   OR
   To encrypt the folder and all files in it, select `Encrypt the   le and the parent folder`.

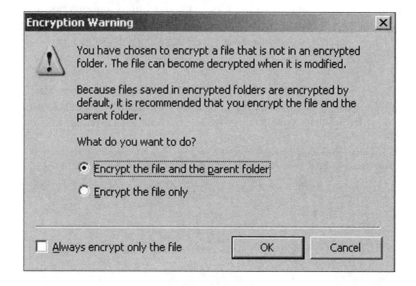

Figure 6-1   The warning box informs users that they can encrypt all files.

5. If you select `Always encrypt only the   le`, the warning will not appear the next time you encrypt the file.
6. Click `OK`.

To decrypt a file:

1. In Windows Explorer, right-click the file and select `Properties`.
2. Click the `Advanced` button on the `General` page.

3. Select `Encrypt contents to secure data` to remove the check mark.
4. Click `OK` twice.

To encrypt a folder (to create a folder that will automatically encrypt files placed in it):

1. In Windows Explorer, right-click the folder and select `Properties`.
2. Click the `Advanced` button on the `General` page.
3. Select `Encrypt to secure contents` and click `OK` twice.
4. If subfolders are present, configure whether subfolders should be changed. In the Confirm Attribute Changes popup, as shown in Figure 6-2, do one of the following:
   Select `Apply changes to this folder only` to only encrypt files in this folder,

OR

   Select `Apply changes to this folder, subfolders and les` to encrypt the files in the folder and its subfolders and files.
5. Click `OK`.

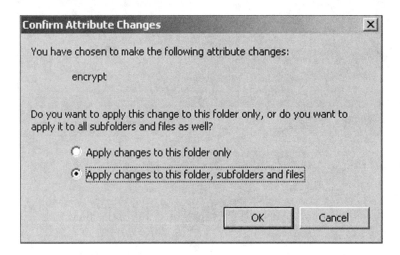

Figure 6-2   Encrypt all files in this folder and all files in all subfolders of this folder.

To decrypt a folder, follow these steps:

1. Right-click on the folder in Windows Explorer and select `Properties`.
2. Click the `Advanced` button.
3. Select the `Select to encrypt to secure contents` box to remove the check mark.
4. Click OK twice.
5. In the Confirm Attribute Changes popup, as shown in Figure 6-3, do one of the following:

   Select `Apply changes to this folder` only to remove the encryption property but not decrypt the files,

   OR

   Select `Apply changes to this folder, subfolders and les` to decrypt all the files.
6. Click OK.

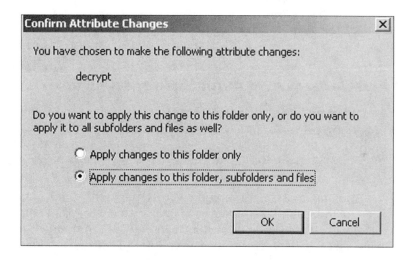

Figure 6-3   Decrypt all the files in the folder and subfolders.

Using the Cipher Command to Encrypt and Decrypt Files

Cipher.exe is a utility that can be used at the command line to manipulate EFS encrypted files. It is particularly useful if you have large numbers of files to encrypt or decrypt, as in recovery operations. The syntax for cipher is provided in the "Tools" section later in this chapter.

To encrypt the reports folder and all subfolders, enter the following command:

```
cipher /e /s:reports
```

To encrypt a single file—in this case the `JanuarySales.doc` in the `Midwest\Sales` folder—enter the following:

```
cipher/e /a C:\Midwest\Sales\JanuarySales.doc
```

To decrypt the `JanuarySales.doc` file, enter this:

```
cipher /d /a C:\Midwest\Sales\JanuarySales.doc
```

Archive/Backup of Certificates and Keys

An understanding of EFS architecture and how it works is not necessary to perform backup of its keys. Users should be trained, however, to back up both an EFS certificate and its associated private key. If this backup or archival of certificate and private key is not done, users will eventually lose critical or sensitive data. It's just a matter of time.

Administrators, information security personnel, and policymakers need to understand the process and develop a strategy and policy so that data loss will not occur. That information will be presented in the sections "EFS Architecture" and "Avoiding Data Loss—Planning for Recovery," later in this chapter.

Meanwhile, if EFS is not disabled, certificates and keys must be backed up, and the backup must be secured. Backup should be periodically repeated to ensure that a good copy is available in case it is needed to recover encrypted files.

Users and IT pros should be aware that the archived certificate and private key can be imported into the certificate store of any user, not just the original user. This is a good thing because the original user account may also have been deleted or destroyed in whatever circumstances damaged or destroyed their keys. However, it can mean that if the archived certificate and key become available to an unauthorized individual, that person might be able to use the keys to decrypt files to which he or she should not have access. To prevent this from happening, a complex password should be used to protect the file, and the media should be stored in a safe place. The password will be needed to use the backup. Because this password may be infrequently used, it may also need to be stored in a safe location, separate from the media. Storing the password on the hard drive or in documents kept with the computer or with the media is not acceptable.

During the archival process, the private key must be selected for backup. Instruct users to do so because the certificate alone will not be sufficient to recover encrypted files. When prompted, users should not remove the private key from the computer. Removing the private key will make it impossible for existing encrypted files to be decrypted.

Getting users to follow this procedure may be difficult, and some explanation of how EFS keys can be damaged or destroyed may help encourage the practice. Any operation that can damage data can damage keys. Keys are part of the user's profile. Keys might be accidentally deleted, for example, if an administrator deletes the user's profile. (Profile deletion is a common practice when profile problems occur. Because a new profile is created when the user logs on, the new profile may solve the problem. Unfortunately, it may also create a new one—loss of access to encrypted files.) Another way keys are destroyed is when a drive crashes or when the operating system is reinstalled. In some cases the keys remain, but since they are not associated with any current user, they cannot be used to decrypt the files.

To archive certificate and private keys, you can use the Certificates snap-in, the file system `Backup Keys` button, or the `cipher` command.

Use the Certificates Snap-In to Archive Keys

1. Add the Certificates snap-in to an MMC console.
2. Expand the `Certi cates` container and select the `Certi cates`, `Personal`, `Certi cates` folder, as shown in Figure 6-4.
3. Right-click the EFS certificate in the details pane and click `All tasks, Export`.
4. Click `Next` at the wizard Welcome screen.
5. To archive the private key to ensure later recovery, select `Yes, export the private key` and click `Next`. (The default, as shown in Figure 6-5, is not to export the key. The certificate, without the key, is worthless for recovery.)

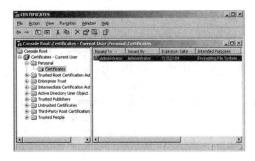 

Figure 6-4   Be sure to verify that the certificate you are archiving is current.

Figure 6-5   Always remember to add the private key to the export when backing up keys for archival purposes.

6. Note, as shown in Figure 6-6, that strong protection is selected. This will ensure that access to the private key is protected by a password. Click Next.

7. Enter a complex password and confirm it, as shown in Figure 6-7. Then click Next.

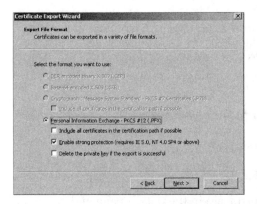 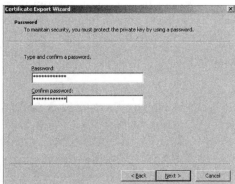

Figure 6-6   Do not delete the private key—without it, you cannot decrypt files.

Figure 6-7   The password will be required to import the key. Do not forget it!

8. Browse to or enter a location to store the file. Add a filename and then click Next.

9. Review the settings, and then click Finish. You should see a popup telling you the export was successful.

When the private key is exported, the .PFX file format is used. This format is based on the PKCS#12 standard, a standard for storing or transporting private keys, certificates, and other miscellaneous secrets.

Use the Cipher Command to Archive Keys

Enter the following `cipher` command to back up the EFS keys to the EFS folder on the A:\ drive and save them in the `RBkeys` file.

```
Cipher /x:A:\efs\RBkeys
```

Use the Backup Keys Button

1. Right-click on a file that has been encrypted and select `Properties`.
2. Click the `Advanced` button.
3. Click the `Details` button.
4. Select the username in the `Users who can transparently access this` le box.
5. On the `Advanced` page, click the `Backup Keys` button, as shown in Figure 6-8.

Figure 6-8   The certificate owner's name must be selected before you can back up their keys.

6. This starts the Export wizard. Follow the procedure as described in the previous instructions for using the Certificates console, starting with step 4.

Import Certificate and Keys

If keys are archived, they can be used if the originals are destroyed or if it is necessary to decrypt files encrypted by someone who has left the company. To do so, import the keys into the profile of an account. This account does not have to be the one that originally was used to create the keys.

1. Create or open a Certificates console for the logged on user.
2. Right-click the `Certi cates - Current User, Personal, Certi cate` container and select `All tasks, Import`. Then click `Next`.
3. Browse to the certificate file and select it or enter the path and filename of the certificate file. Then click `Next`. If the `Browse` button is used, change the `File Type` box to all files to see the certificate file.
4. Enter the password for this certificate file.
5. Select `Mark this key as exportable`, as shown in Figure 6-9, and then click `Next`. This will allow backup of the key at a later time. If this selection is not made, the newly imported keys cannot be archived.
6. Check that the keys will be stored in the `Personal` store, as shown in Figure 6-10, and click `Next`.
7. Review the settings and click `Finish`. Click `OK` in the popup indicating successful import.

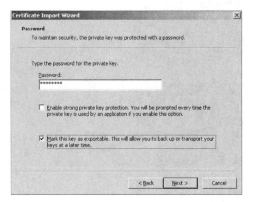 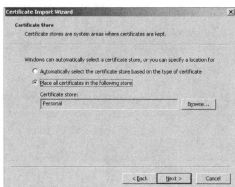

Figure 6-9   Don't forget to prepare for future key backups.

Figure 6-10   Keys should be stored in the Personal store.

Remove the Private Key

When traveling with encrypted data on a Windows XP or Windows Server 2003 laptop, a sound practice is to remove the private key and carry it separately from the laptop or data storage device. If the laptop is lost or stolen, even if the password for the account used to encrypt the data is known, the encrypted data cannot be decrypted without the private key. The laptop owner can decrypt files by importing the private key. A Windows 2000 laptop computer that is a domain member also can have this protection if a domain account was used to encrypt the files. When local user accounts are used to encrypt data on a Windows 2000 computer, a recovery agent may also be able to decrypt data. (Windows XP and Windows Server 2003 standalone computers do not automatically create a recovery agent.) If recovery agent credentials can be compromised, an attacker might use them to decrypt encrypted files. The recovery agent private key should also be removed to mitigate the impact of such an attack. To delete the private keys for each account that may have keys stored on the computer, export the keys, including the private key, but select the choice `Delete the private key if the export is successful` during step 6 in the earlier "Archive/Backup of Certificates and Keys" section of this chapter (refer to Figure 6-6).

Recover Files

Windows XP and Windows Server 2003 computers do not automatically create a recovery agent for EFS files. However, Windows 2000 computers do. In a Windows Server 2003 domain, the first domain administrator to log on after dcpromo will become the recovery agent. Windows XP and Windows Server 2003 computers joined in either a Windows Server 2003 or Windows 2000 domain will use the recovery agent keys to make their own protected copy of the file encryption key. This means that the recovery agent can recover the encrypted files—in fact, the recovery agent can transparently view any encrypted files that use the recovery agent's certificate to protect a copy of the file encryption key. It also means that anyone who can log on using the recovery agent account can read the encrypted files. The recovery agent account should be protected with a strong password and should not be used for day-to-day activities. While the files can be recovered (decrypted) by opening them, proper procedures dictate that they should be recovered by using the `cipher` command. This way, the recovery agent recovering the files will not see the data during the recovery process. It also means that many files can be decrypted at the same time. To recover encrypted files using the recovery agent, follow these steps:

1. If necessary, back up the encrypted files and move the backup to an isolated location. (Backed up encrypted files remain encrypted.)
2. If necessary, restore the files from backup to an NTFS partition on a computer dedicated to file recovery. (Restored encrypted files remain encrypted.)
3. Use the recovery agent account to log on from the console of the computer where the files have been placed.
4. Enter the `cipher` command, as shown here. The `encrypted-fileslocation` is the folder where the encrypted files are located.
   ```
   cipher /d /s:encryptedfileslocation
   ```
5. Return files in a secure fashion to the authorized user who should immediately encrypt them.

Obtaining Encryption Keys

If EFS has not been disabled, a user will obtain his EFS keys when he first encrypts a file. If the computer is joined in an Active Directory domain, the operating system will first look for the existence of a Certification Authority (CA) by searching the Active Directory. (If the Active Directory cannot be located, the request will fail.) If a CA is present, the operating system will request a certificate from the CA. If no CA is present, a self-signed certificate will be created for the user. A self-signed certificate is one that has not been issued by a CA. On Windows XP Professional, Windows 2000, and Windows Server 2003, the operating system automatically creates these certificates. This operation is transparent to the user.

However, the user can request a new certificate either using the Certificates snap-in or the `cipher` command. Before a new certificate is requested, the old certificate should be archived. Until an encrypted file is decrypted and then encrypted again, the new certificate will not be used, so its associated private key cannot be used to decrypt the file. To use the Certificates snap-in, do the following:

1. Open the Certificates snap-in for the current user.
2. Right-click on the `Certi cates, Current User, Personal` container and select `All tasks`. Then select `Request new certi cate`.

3. If the Active Directory cannot be located, the request will fail.
4. If the Active Directory is located and a CA is not present, the request will fail, as shown in Figure 6-11.

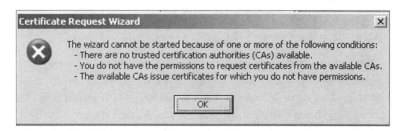

Figure 6-11 In a domain, a new EFS certificate can only be obtained if none is present, or if a CA is present to issue the new certificate.

5. If a CA is present, a list of available certificate types will be presented, as shown in Figure 6-12. Select the EFS Certificate and click OK.

The cipher command cipher /k can also be used.

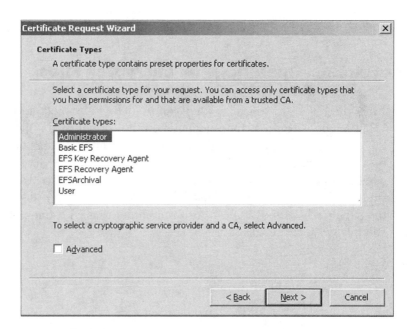

Figure 6-12 Available certificate types for the logged on user will be displayed in the Certificate Request Wizard.

Old EFS keys should be archived, including the private key, but not destroyed. All files encrypted using the old keys need to be decrypted using the old key and then encrypted using the new one. The best way to do so is to use `cipher /u`.

Adding a Recovery Agent

The default recovery agent in the domain is the first administrator account to log on to the domain after the domain is created. Nothing specific has to be done for this to occur. If this certificate and key are archived, the certificate and key can be added back to the recovery policy if this is ever necessary. Additional recovery agents for the domain can be created if a CA is available. A CA is necessary to create the new recovery agent certificate.

On a Windows Server 2003 standalone system, no recovery agent is created. By default, there is no recovery policy for the standalone system. This is a rather large difference between Windows 2000 and Windows Server 2003. Windows XP also operates like Server 2003; there is no default recovery agent for a standalone computer. When the computer is joined to the domain, it will obtain and use the domain recovery policy and recovery agent if EFS has not been disabled.

Effect of Normal Operations on Encrypted Files

Encrypted files are still files. They can be deleted, copied, and moved. What happens to them then depends on the format of the file system, the encryption properties of the parent folder, and whether or not the user performing the option has the ability to decrypt the file. To know what to expect, remember that only NTFS on Windows 2000 and above supports file encryption and that file decryption may be transparent to the person who can decrypt it. Also remember that EFS-encrypted files still follow NTFS permissions.

Enabling Silent Decryption for Remote Storage

By default, encrypted files cannot be stored to a remote location that has not been properly set up to store them. A user can, of course, decrypt the file and store a plaintext copy at the remote location. There are also `xcopy` (`/G`) and `copy` (`/d`) switches that allow the process. When these switches are used to copy encrypted files, if the user is able to normally decrypt the file, the files are decrypted and stored remotely in plain text. Alternatively, a registry value may be modified to allow the file to be silently decrypted and saved to a remote location. The value is only used when storage is performed using `copy` or `xcopy` at the command line or when invoked programmatically. While this process changes the default behavior of EFS-encrypted files, it may be necessary in certain circumstances; for example, when EFS is used to locally encrypt files, IPSec encrypts data in flight, and some other server-based process protects the files at their remote location. The DWORD value, `CopyFileAllowDecryptedRemoteDestination`, is located at `HKEY_LOCAL_MACHINE\Software\Policies\Microsoft\Windows System\`. Giving this DWORD a value of 1 enables this activity.

Normal results for moving and copying EFS-encrypted files are as follows:

- If the encrypted file is copied or moved where EFS is not supported (FAT, FAT32, or NTFS on Windows NT 4.0 and below), and the user copying the file has permission to write to the new location and to decrypt the file, the file will be silently decrypted and saved to the new location; otherwise, an error will occur.
- If the encrypted file is copied or moved to another location on the same computer and EFS is supported, the file will retain its encryption.
- If the plaintext file is copied or moved to a folder on the same machine that is marked for encryption, the file will be encrypted, and the encryption key will be protected using the current user's key.
- If the encrypted file is copied or moved to another computer, the user has the ability to decrypt the file, and the computer and user accounts are trusted in the Active Directory for delegation (this is not so by default), then the file is silently decrypted, copied across the network in plain text, and encrypted on the remote computer. The user's encryption credentials must be available on the remote computer.

- The error message will always be `Access Denied`.
- If the computer is either Windows XP Professional or Windows Server 2003 and the user encrypted the file and is now copying it to a location where it will be decrypted and stored in plain text because the location does not support encryption, the user will be warned and allowed to cancel the operation. If the operation is not cancelled, the file will be decrypted and stored in plain text.
- If the user has `Delete` permission for the file and chooses to delete it, he can do so whether or not he has the ability to decrypt the file.
- Systems files are protected from encryption as are locations in the %SYSTEMROOT%\... path. If a user attempts to copy an encrypted file to this path, she will receive the `Access Denied` error message.
- When encrypted files are backed up using Ntbackup or another EFS-aware backup program, they retain their encryption. When they are restored, they are still encrypted.
- The `xcopy` and `copy` commands can be used to copy encrypted files. When the `/D` switch is used, the file may be decrypted if required and stored in plain text.

WARNING: Copied and Shared EFS Files May Not Retain Approved User Information

If multiple users can decrypt the file, as is the case when encrypted files are shared, it may not always be possible to save this information when the file is copied. A new API, developed when EFS was developed, must be called. Office XP will do this, and all EFS sharing information for the file is retained. Other versions of Office and other products may remove the additional user information. You will have to consult the manufacturer of the program to determine what will happen when its product is used.

For more information on using file encryption on remote systems, see the section "Remote Storage," later in this chapter.

EFS Architecture

To troubleshoot EFS, or to be able to design proper EFS recovery and EFS policy for the organization, you must understand how EFS works.

EFS is a component of the NTFS file system of Windows 2000 and above. Thus, its operations are mostly transparent to the user and to the application that needs to open and close the files. If the user has the ability to encrypt and decrypt the files, when the file is opened, it is decrypted, and when it is saved, it is encrypted. The setup of shared EFS files is not transparent.

File System Operations

Several operating system components both in user space and in the kernel participate in the operation of the EFS. These components are listed and described in Table 6-2.

Table 6-2   Components of EFS

Component	Description
Local Security Authority (LSA)	Responsible for a number of EFS operations and provides the interfaces for other EFS components such as feclient and efsadue. LSA creates the file encryption key (FEK) and then encrypts it using the public key of the user and separately with the public key of the recovery agent if one is present. LSA also checks to see if the file can be encrypted. During decryption, LSA checks for changes in user encryption and recovery agent encryption keys. LSA exports interfaces for use via RPC with feclient and LPC with ksecdd.
Feclient	Receives Win32 API calls and calls the EFS remote procedure call (RPC) or local procedure call (LPC) interfaces in the LSA. Feclient determines where the file resides (locally or on some remote server) and calls the LSA of the appropriate server.
Efsadu	Provides the EFS user interface (the Advanced sub-dialog of file Properties and the Details button).
The shell	Displays the filenames in Windows Explorer in green.
Winlogon	Creates the domain controller default recovery policy when a domain administrator logs on for the first time to a domain controller. On a domain member computer, Winlogon calls the security configuration engine to process EFS recovery policy from the domain.

Table 6-2 Components of EFS Continued

Component	Description
NTFS driver	Contains most of the EFS code in the kernel and responds to requests from the LSA to encrypt or decrypt. The NTFS driver passes the encrypted FEK to ksecdd for passing to LSA for decryption. NTFS then decrypts the data. NTFS functions also include reading and writing encrypted file functions in raw mode so that NTBACKUP can be used to back up and restore encrypted files.
The WebDAV redirector	Used to handle encrypted files in WebDAV folders.
Ksecdd	Used to communicate NTFS LPC calls to LSA.

When a request to encrypt an existing file is received by the file system, the following steps occur:

1. The NTFS driver passes the request to feclient.
2. Feclient determines if the file will be located locally or on a remote server and then passes the request to either the local or remote Local Security Authority (LSA).
3. LSA verifies the following:
   - The file may be encrypted.
   - There is enough disk space to do so.
4. LSA then generates the file encryption key (FEK).
5. The LSA encrypts a copy of the FEK using the user's public key.
6. If a recovery policy is in effect, the FEK is also encrypted with the recovery agent's public key.
7. The EFS metadata is created. This consists of the EFS information such as version and encryption algorithm and the Data Decryption Fields (DDF) and Data Recovery Fields (DRF). Each DDF is the FEK encrypted with the public key of a user who is authorized to encrypt the file. Each DRF is the FEK encrypted with the public key of a recovery agent.
8. A temporary file is created in the current directory.
9. Each data stream in the file is copied into the temporary files in the directory for backup, and the original file is emptied.

10. EFS reads the streams from the temporary files, encrypts the file using the FEK passed to the kernel by the LSA, and writes encrypted data into the original file.

11. When all the data is written back into the file, EFS verifies that it is encrypted and then deletes the temporary file.

NOTE: Role of the User's Master Key in EFS

The user's certificate and private key are stored in the user's profile and protected by the user's master key. The master key is based on the user's password. When the master key is not in use, it is encrypted and stored in the user's profile. Knowledge of the user's password at the time the master key was encrypted is necessary to decrypt the master key. This is why a normal password change instituted by the user will not affect EFS-encrypted files, but a password reset done by an administrator will. It is also why even though encryption keys can be found on the disk, EFS-encrypted files cannot be decrypted without knowledge of the user's password at the time of the encryption. Without the password, the master key cannot be decrypted, and the encryption keys cannot be used.

Encrypting, Decrypting, and Recovery Algorithms

EFS uses two types of encryption: symmetric (single key) and asymmetric or public key encryption. Files are encrypted using symmetric algorithms, which are very fast. The symmetric key is protected with public key encryption.

Symmetric key encryption uses the same key both to encrypt and decrypt. This is similar to using a physical key to lock the door to a house. The security of the data, or of the house, depends on keeping tabs on the symmetric key. The house key should not be left in the lock, and it should not be stored nearby and easily found. Likewise, the symmetric key used in encryption must be protected. It is typically stored separately from the data. When it is necessary to decrypt the data, the symmetric key (or a copy of it) must be produced and used. For two parties to share encrypted data, the symmetric key must be securely provided to both parties and therefore cannot merely accompany the encrypted data. The problem of key distribution can be difficult to solve.

Asymmetric key encryption, also known as public key/private key encryption, can be used to solve the key distribution problem. Asymmetric key encryption uses an associated key pair approach. If one of the keys is used to encrypt, only the other associated key can be used to decrypt. Therefore, one key can be made public (the public key) and widely available as long as the other (the private key) is kept private. Public key encryption is used for key distribution in many email encryption schemes. In the typical email encryption scheme, a symmetric key is used to encrypt the message, and the recipient's public key is used to encrypt the symmetric key. The protected symmetric key can therefore be sent with the encrypted email. The recipient can use his private key to decrypt the encrypted symmetric key, and the symmetric key can be used to decrypt the message.

EFS uses a similar approach. An asymmetric key pair is used to protect the file encryption key. In EFS, each user who is allowed to encrypt files is provided a public key/private key pair to do so. The public key is placed in a certificate and bound to the user account. The private key is stored separately. A symmetric key, the FEK, is used to encrypt the file, and the user's public key is used to encrypt the file encryption key. The public key cannot be used to decrypt the FEK. Instead, the associated private key must be used.

NOTE: Why Are Both Algorithms Used?

Both email and EFS schemes might have been developed to only use public key encryption. Instead of first using a symmetric key to encrypt the data, the public key could be used. The observed result would be the same—only the holder of the private key would be able to decrypt the data. However, asymmetric key encryption is very slow. The difference might not be noticed when small amounts of data are encrypted, but it would be very noticeable if larger amounts of data were encrypted.

If multiple users are authorized to encrypt the file, or there is a designated File Recovery Agent, the FEK is also separately encrypted with these public keys. All encrypted copies of the FEK are stored in the files properties. Decryption and recovery work the algorithm in reverse. First, the appropriate private key is used to decrypt the encrypted FEK, and then the FEK is used to decrypt the file.

File Encryption

The file encryption process is illustrated in Figure 6-13 and described in the following steps.

1. A file marked for encryption is saved, or a file is saved to a folder marked for encryption.
2. A random encryption key (the FEK) is generated and used to encrypt the file. A different key is used for each file encrypted.

File Encryption

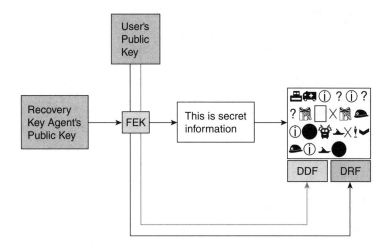

Figure 6-13   The file encryption key is protected by encryption using the user's public key.

3. The public key of the user is used to encrypt the FEK and stored in the file's Data Decryption Field (DDF).
4. If other users are authorized to share the encrypted file, their public keys are used to encrypt the FEK, and the result is stored in the file properties.
5. If a recovery agent exists, his public key is used to encrypt the FEK, and the results are stored in the Data Recovery Field (DRF) of the file properties.
6. If additional recovery agents exist, their public keys are used to encrypt the FEK and are stored with the file properties.

File Decryption

File decryption is illustrated in Figure 6-14 and described in the following steps.

1. A user attempts to open a file or to use `cipher` or the file system to decrypt the file.
2. If her public key is one that encrypted the FEK, then the associated private key related to her public keys used to encrypt the FEK is used to decrypt the FEK.
3. The FEK is used to decrypt the file.

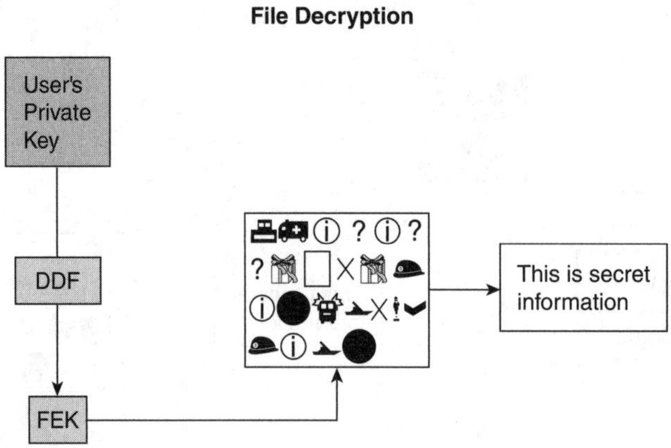

File Decryption

File Decryption

Figure 6-14   The encrypted file encryption key can be decrypted using the associated private key.

File Recovery

File recovery is also illustrated in Figure 6-14.

1. A recovery agent attempts to open a file or to decrypt the file using `cipher` or the file properties.
2. If her public key is one that encrypted the FEK, then the associated private key related to her public keys used to encrypt the FEK is used to decrypt the FEK.
3. The FEK is used to decrypt the file.

Encryption Types and Strength

The symmetric and asymmetric algorithms used for EFS are industry standards. A Windows Server 2003 computer may be configured to use DESX, 3DES, or AES symmetric encryption algorithms. RC4 is used for asymmetric encryption. Earlier versions of the operating system may not be able to use all of the encryption algorithms. Windows 2000 uses DESX. XP Professional pre-service pack 1 uses DESX by default, but it can be modified to use 3DES. Post-service pack 1, Windows XP Professional defaults to AES but can be modified to use DESX or 3DES. This can mean problems if users attempt to move encrypted files to different OS-based machines and decrypt the files. Caution should be used to select the algorithm that will work in your environment and prevent potential damage by setting all versions of the OS that are capable of doing EFS to use the same encryption algorithm. Instructions for configuring the symmetric key algorithm using the registry are located in the section "Changing Encryption Algorithm," later in this chapter.

Another way to manage the file encryption strength for EFS is to modify the Security Option `System cryptography: Use FIPS compliant algorithms for encryption, hashing and signing`. This setting manages the encryption strength for all operations, including the use of SHA-1 for hashing, 3DES for Transport Layer Security (TLS) traffic and EFS, and RSA for TLS public key exchange.

NOTE: FIPS

The Federal Information Processing Standard (FIPS) 140-1 is required by the U.S. government certification of cryptographic software.

On Windows Server 2003, the default encryption key strength can also be modified. To do so, you must add the value `RSAKeyLength` to the EFS registry key and set it to a value between 1024 and 16384. The entered value will be rounded to the next multiple of 8. While the Microsoft Base Provider Cryptographic Service Provider (CSP) is used for encryption, if the key strength is greater than 1024, the Microsoft Enhanced Provider CSP will be used.

Avoiding Data Loss—Planning for Recovery

Before EFS is used, a recovery plan should be developed and put into place. Unfortunately, EFS is enabled by default, and few organizations create and implement an effective EFS policy before users are logged on to the system. Users can easily encrypt and decrypt files without realizing that they should be archiving keys. Using EFS to encrypt and decrypt files is easy. On the other hand, while recovery is not difficult, it requires thought and potentially substantial action. Private keys must be archived and protected.

Recovery Plans for Standalone Systems and Domains Without CAs

It will be difficult to institute a plan for EFS file recovery based on end users' archival of EFS keys. Most users don't back up their data and aren't expected to do so. Data is often stored by policy on network servers and backed up by using automated programs and dedicated staff. When standalone systems are used to encrypt files with EFS, there is no centralized mechanism for archiving keys. (In a domain environment, other options exist.)

Unless EFS is restricted to a few users, it will be impossible to create a workable and sustainable EFS key archival plan.

Classic EFS, as implemented in Windows 2000, attempts to solve this problem by requiring the presence of a recovery agent before encryption can occur. On the standalone machine, this recovery agent is the local administrator. In the Windows 2000 domain, it's the first administrator who signed on after the first DC in the domain was depromoed. The recovery agent public key is used to encrypt every FEK; the recovery agent's private key can be used to recover all EFS-encrypted files. In a perfect world, there is no need for archived end-user encryption keys. The recovery agent can be used to recover EFS-encrypted files for which the original end user's keys are damaged or lost. For extra insurance, a recovery plan need only include the archival of the recovery agent keys. However, where all computers are standalone, archival of these keys presents the same problem that archiving end-user keys does: There is a unique recovery agent for each stand alone system. Furthermore, many of the reasons that can cause end-user keys to become damaged and lost can also impact recovery keys, so the archival of these keys is important. Windows XP and Windows Server 2003 standalone systems do not automatically create a recovery agent, and the existence of recovery agent keys is not necessary for encryption. In all cases, the recovery plan depends on the scrupulous archival and maintenance of asymmetric keys.

NOTE: Public Key Policy Resides at the Domain Level
Public key policy is configured at the domain level—that is, recovery agents are created by default in the PKI policy of the domain. A forest-wide public key policy on recovery can be technically controlled by implementing PKI and controlling the assignment of recovery certificates.

Another problem with this plan is that on the standalone computer, the recovery keys are present on the local hard drive. That means that a Windows 2000 laptop has not only user keys but also recovery keys traveling right along with it. If the laptop is stolen, there are two chances to subvert the process and decrypt the files. If the password to either the user's account or the local administrator's account can be cracked, the thief has access to the file. The legitimate administrator also has free and easy access to encrypted files, either as recovery agent or by changing the password of the user account and logging on as the user.

Windows XP Professional and Windows Server 2003 attempt to correct this issue by removing the requirement for a recovery agent. This means that XP Professional in a domain will use a recovery agent if one is present, but a standalone Windows XP system does not have a recovery agent. Another change in Windows XP Professional and Server 2003 is that on a standalone machine, if an administrator resets the user's password, the association with the public key set is lost. Even though the administrator can now log on as the user, he cannot decrypt the files. (Should this accidentally occur, if the user has a password reset disk, she can use it to reset the password to the original one and thus can decrypt her files.) Ordinary password changes made by the logged on user do not cause a problem with EFS-encrypted files. In a domain, of course, the user's password may be reset with no ill effect.

The fact that there is no recovery agent in a standalone system means there is no fall back if the user's keys are destroyed or if the user forgets his password and doesn't have a password reset disk. The EFS-encrypted files cannot be decrypted. To ensure a recovery strategy, each user's EFS keys must be archived.

Recovery Policy and Disabling EFS

In Group Policy, the Encrypting File System policy can be used to disable EFS or to manage the recovery agent certificates. This policy is located in local or domain-based Group Policy in the `Windows Settings`, `Security Settings`, `Public Key Polices` container. The recovery agent certificate(s), if present, can be viewed in the policy, as shown in Figure 6-15. The certificate information shows the account assigned as the recovery agent. On a standalone Windows Server 2003 and Windows XP Professional computer, by default, there is no Encrypting File System policy recovery agent, as shown in Figure 6-16. However, the property page of the policy can be used to disable or re-enable the use of EFS on the system.

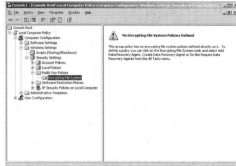

Figure 6-15 In a domain, the EFS policy displays the recovery agent certificate(s).

Figure 6-16 On a standalone system, the EFS policy remains empty unless a recovery agent is added.

Six operations can modify the domain EFS recovery policy:

- Delete the policy for the domain—thus allowing possible EFS policies for OUs.
- Delete the policy and create an empty policy—thus preventing OU-level policies but not preventing EFS file encryption on local machines.
- Delete certificates and private keys for recovery agents, creating a "no recovery policy"—This policy would allow users of Windows XP Professional and Windows Server 2003 systems the ability to encrypt files, but since no recovery agent certificate is available, its keys cannot be used for recovery.
- Add additional recovery agents by implementing certificate services, creating additional recovery agents, and then adding their certificates to the policy—Doing so is not difficult but is not trivial since proper planning and design is necessary to ensure security. Both operations are covered in Chapter 12.
- In a Windows Server 2003 domain, implement certificate services and add key archival.
- Disable EFS for each computer by modifying the registry of each standalone computer or by configuring the local Group Policy.

Delete the EFS Policy and Create an Empty Policy

1. Click `Start`, `Administrative Tools`, `Domain Security Policy`.
2. Expand `Security Settings`, `Public Key Policies` and select `Encrypting File System`.

3. If a recovery agent certificate(s) is present, back up the certificates and private keys and store them in a safe place. Be sure to remove the private keys from the system. They may be needed to recover encrypted files or to implement a new recovery policy at a future date.
4. Delete the certificates. (This is a "no recovery policy.")
5. Right-click `Encrypting File System` and select `Delete Policy`.
6. After deleting the policy, right-click the `Encrypting File System` and select `Create empty Policy`.

Disable EFS

Different techniques can be used to disable EFS. Some of them are dependent on the operating system.

- To disable EFS for Windows 2000, delete the recovery agent certificate from the Local Security policy of a standalone system or from the domain public key policy of the domain GPO.
- To disable EFS for a Windows XP Professional standalone system, right-click on the `Local Security Policy`, `Public Key Policy`, `Encrypting File System` and uncheck the box `Allow users to encrypt les using Encrypting File System (EFS)`, as shown in Figure 6-17. This sets the registry key shown in the next bullet.

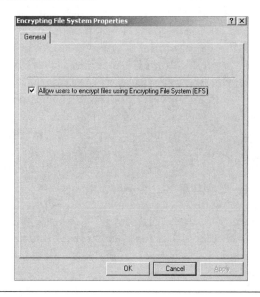

Figure 6-17 Clearing this box will disable EFS.

- To disable EFS for a Windows Server 2003 standalone system, edit the registry value `EfsCon guration`. (You may need to add the value.) The value 0x01 will disable EFS, while resetting it to 0 will enable EFS. The value is located at `HKEY_LOCAL_MACHINE\ SOFTWARE\Microsoft\WindowsNT\CurrentVersion\EFS\`

  If the system is joined in a domain, use Group Policy. The registry value is modified when the Property page of the `Computer Con- guration`, `Windows Settings`, `Security Settings`, `Public Key Policies`, `Encrypting File System` folder is changed.

- To disable EFS for Windows XP Professional and Windows Server 2003 systems joined in a Windows 2000 domain, you must either edit each machine's Local Security Policy or registry keys, or add the information to a security template and import the template into a GPO for the domain to automatically accomplish this.
- To disable EFS for Windows XP and Windows Server 2003 clients in a Windows Server 2003 domain, you can change the Public Key policy of the domain GPO by right-clicking on the Encrypting File System policy and selecting `Properties`, and then clearing the check box for `Allow users to encrypt  les`.

Tools for Recovering the Unrecoverable

For several years, there has been little help for users of EFS who failed to archive keys and develop and implement a reasonable recovery policy. Today, though, several products offer possible file recovery. These solutions, however, rely on the existence of the keys in the file system and knowledge of the user's password, or the ability to crack the user's password. Since many otherwise hopeless scenarios can provide this information, these products have met with some success. For example, if the operating system is reinstalled, it is possible that the original user's profile is still on the disk, even though it is impossible to reassociate the profile with any new account or gain access to old accounts. If the user still knows the password used with the now-defunct account, recovery may be possible using one of these tools. In addition, if forensic tools can be used to access data on the disk, even if the loss is the result of a hard disk crash, recovery may still be possible. Solving this problem resolves many of the legitimate "Help, I encrypted my files and now I can't access them" issues.

The tools are not going to be useful if the password is not known and cannot be deduced.

The following products may be useful in recovery of EFS-encrypted files.

- **Encase**—A forensic program available from Guidance Software (www.guidancesoftware.com) has an EFS module available.
- **Advanced EFS Data Recovery**—A commercial utility available for purchase from Elcomsoft (http://www.elcomsoft.com/aefsdr.html).
- **EFS Key**—A utility available from http://www.lostpassword.com/efs.htm.
- **reccerts.exe**—A Microsoft Product Support Services (PSS) tool (www.microsoft.com/support).

Best Practices for Recovery

When authorized individuals cannot decrypt critical, sensitive files, it can mean disaster. A sound recovery policy needs to be designed, implemented, and maintained. Following are several best practices to incorporate:

- Ensure that recovery agent keys are frequently backed up.
- Don't forget to back up the associated private key when using the export program to do so.
- Ensure that multiple recovery agents or alternative keys exist that can be used to recover files. Using certificate services is one way to accomplish this. Another is to share critical encrypted files with additional user accounts. This will provide a higher likelihood that keys will exist on different systems that can recover files if the owner's keys are damaged or destroyed. Be aware, however, that having multiple user accounts that can decrypt files poses other risks. See the section "Sharing Encrypted Files" later in this chapter for more information.
- Have a policy in place for file recovery. The policy should require safe transport of encrypted files to an isolated recovery station, the use of a dedicated recovery agent certificate and private key that is not imported to the recovery station until needed for recovery, the use of cipher to decrypt the files, and safe transport back to the owner of the files and immediate encryption.

Are you confused as to what keys need to be present to ensure recovery? Trust me: If you aren't, it's only a matter of time before some well-meaning person confuses you by handing out the wrong information. Keep this in mind. The private keys are only needed for decryption. If recovery agent private keys are archived, their presence on the drive is not necessary. The recovery agent public key *does* need to be present, though. Without it, the FEK of the encrypted file cannot be protected for recovery. Likewise, if the user's private key is not present, encryption can occur, but the user will not be able to decrypt the file. If he saves a file in Word and then tries to open it, he will be unsuccessful. Don't let anyone tell you that you can remove the user's certificate and still encrypt the files. The public key, which is necessary for encryption, is on the certificate. Delete the certificate, and there can be no encryption. The private key, which is only necessary for decryption, is not part of the certificate.

Special Operations and Issues

In addition to the basic EFS operations, there are additional operations that can extend its usefulness, protect the encrypted files, and make the EFS environment easier to work with. These operations are as follows:

- Changing encryption algorithm
- Placing Encrypt and Decrypt on the Windows Explorer menu
- Backing up encrypted files
- Working with offline files
- Sharing encrypted files
- Protecting password reset
- Coloring encrypted file and folder names in Windows Explorer
- Using third-party EFS certificates

Changing Encryption Algorithm

The default encryption algorithm for EFS is different depending on the OS. If you require them to be the same, or if you must change them for some other reason, you can do so by following these steps:

1. Decrypt all files before making this change. This is important, as you will not be able to decrypt the files afterward.

2. Add the DWORD value `AlgorithmID` to the registry key
   `HKEY_LOCAL_MACHINE\SOFTWARE\Microsoft\WindowsNT\`
   `CurrentVersion\EFS`
3. Set the value for the algorithm you want:
   - 3DES for Windows XP, Windows Server 2003: 0x6603
   - DESX for all versions of Windows 2000 and above: 0x6604
   - AES for Windows XP and above: 06610
4. Close the Registry Editor.
5. Restart Windows.

Placing Encrypt/Decrypt on the Windows Explorer Menu

If you want, you can put the ability to select file/folder encryption/decryption on the Windows Explorer menu. You must create the DWORD value `EncryptionContextMenu` at the following location and set it to 1:

`HKEY_LOCAL_MACHINE\SOFTWARE\Microsoft\Windows\CurrentVersion`
`\Explorer\Advanced`

Backing Up Encrypted Files

The account used to back up or restore the encrypted files does not require special access and should not be given any. If the user has the right to back up a file, then he can back up the file if it is encrypted. Normal backup using NTBACKUP will back up encrypted files. When the files are restored to an NTFS partition, they are still encrypted and can only be decrypted by someone who has the private key associated with one of the public keys used to encrypt the FEK. If you attempt to restore a backed up encrypted file to a FAT volume, you will receive an error. Again, do not provide the user restoring the files any special access. Do not share the encrypted file with him. If you do, he will be able to decrypt the files.

Working with Offline Files

Offline files is a Windows 2000 and above IntelliMirror management technology that allows users to store a local copy of files they access on a network share. When the client computer is disconnected from the network, the files are still available for the user to work with. In Windows

2000, these offline files cannot be encrypted. Windows Server 2003 introduces the ability to encrypt the offline files on Windows XP Professional and Windows Server 2003 systems. This feature is only available if the server-side files are accessed through a standard Windows share, the server message block (SMB) share. The Web Distributed and Versioning WebDAV protocol, which presents a different way of storing EFS encrypted files on a server, cannot be used. For more information on server-side storage of EFS-encrypted files, see the section "Remote Storage" later in this chapter.

Because all offline files are stored in a common local database on the client machine, when offline files are encrypted, the entire database is encrypted using a local computer EFS certificate. Individual files or folders cannot be selected or deselected for encryption.

To encrypt offline files:

1. Open Windows Explorer.
2. Select the `Tools` menu, `Folder Options`, and select the `Of ine Files` tab, as shown in Figure 6-18.

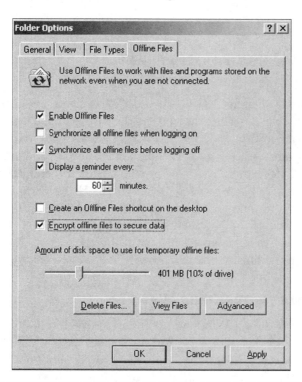

Figure 6-18 Use the Offline Files tab to configure encryption for offline files.

3. Select `Enable Of ine Files` and `Encrypt of ine  les` to secure data.
4. Click `OK`.

Sharing Encrypted Files

Windows XP introduced the ability to share encrypted files. Once a file is encrypted, the encryptor of a file can provide access for other users by adding their EFS certificate to the file properties of the file. This is an interesting feature because it both adds security risk and provides some additional mitigation for file recovery issues. When you provide another user the ability to encrypt and decrypt files, he also has the ability to give other users this right. Thus, a sensitive file can quickly become exposed to many people. Each new encryptor can also add others to the list and can remove them. It is possible that one of these individuals may remove the original owner of the file's certificate and thus his ability to work with the file!

For each file that requires sharing, the process must be repeated. Each added user means that another new encryption key (the FEK) is created and encrypted by the new user's public key and stored with the file.

The estimated limit to the number of users who can be provided access to the same encrypted file via adding their certificate is 800. This is not due to some hard-coded stop but rather because there is only 256K of room in the file header for EFS metadata.

There is currently no way to centrally manage who can encrypt or decrypt a specific encrypted file or to provide a printed list of who has the ability on what files. You can, of course, list the approved users by displaying file properties, and the Resource Kit utility efsinfo can be used to enumerate the certificates that have been used to encrypt a file.

Only someone with the ability to encrypt and decrypt a file can share this ability with others. To share the file follow these steps:

1. Right-click on the file in Windows Explorer and select `Properties`.
2. Click the `Advanced` button.
3. Click the `Details` button.
4. Click the `Add` button.

5. When PKI is integrated with Active Directory, the EFS certificates of all users are stored in the Active Directory and can be added by clicking the `Find User` button and using the object picker to select the usernames to add to the file. If a user does not have a certificate, the username will not be added to the `Select User` property page. (In a standalone environment, the user certificate may have to be added to the certificate stores of the computer before this option can be used.)

6. When users have been added to the `Select User` page, as shown in Figure 6-19, select a user certificate and click `OK` to give users the right to access the file. On a standalone system, each certificate must be manually added to the user's certificates store. If the certificate is part of a trusted chain (signed by a CA), the certificate itself is added to your "Other People" certificate store. If the certificate is self-signed, it is stored in the "Trusted People" certificate store. If the user has a local private key on the computer, his certificate is added to the "Trusted People Store" in addition to the "Other People" store.

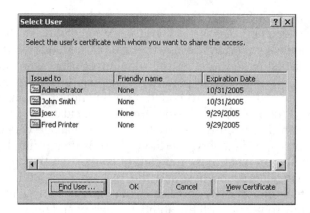

Figure 6-19   The available EFS certificates in the domain are displayed.

7. The EFS private key is used to decrypt the FEK, and a copy of the FEK is made. The current user's public key encrypts the FEK and stores it in the file properties. The new user's public key (the public key on the certificate selected) is used to encrypt the copy of the FEK, and then it is added to the file properties. The certificate information is added to the properties, as shown in Figure 6-20.

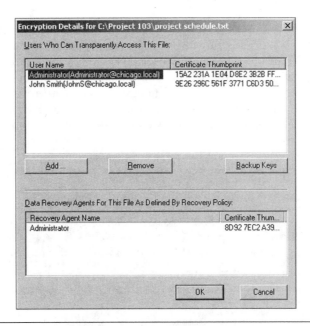

Figure 6-20 A list of certificates that have encrypted the FEK is displayed.

8. Click OK twice to close the file properties.

If the computer is not joined to a domain, you can still share encrypted files. You simply must be able to provide a copy of the user's certificate when sharing the file. To do so, ask the user to export a copy of their certificate (without the private key) to a file and provide you with the file. During the sharing process, you can browse to the location of the file and import it.

Password Reset

To prevent a rogue administrator from logging on to a standalone computer, changing the user password, and then logging on as the user to view his encrypted files, Windows XP and Windows Server 2003 disassociate the user's certificate and keys from the user account if the password is reset by the local administrator. (If the user uses the change password utility, this will not happen.) If the administrator resets the user's password and logs on as the user, she will not be able to decrypt the user's files. However, neither will the user. To return this ability to the legitimate user, the user can use her password reset disk made before the incident to return her password to the original. Then she can decrypt the files.

Because users do forget their passwords, and the passwords thus need to be administratively reset, make sure users of standalone systems make themselves password reset disks and store them in a safe place. The password reset function cannot distinguish between a rogue administrator's play for power and a necessary password reset due to the user forgetting his password. It does, however, warn both types of administrators what will occur if the password is reset with the message shown in Figure 6-21.

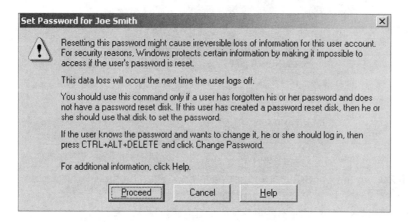

Figure 6-21   An attempt to reset the password results in a warning that the user may not be able to access files.

Coloring Encrypted Files and Folder Names in Windows Explorer

Encrypted files and folders are shown in green in Windows Server 2003 automatically. To turn on this feature for Windows XP clients or to turn it off for Windows Server 2003, follow these steps:

1. Select the Folder Options, View tab in Windows Explorer.
2. Check or uncheck the box for Show encrypted or compressed NTFS les in color, as shown in Figure 6-22.

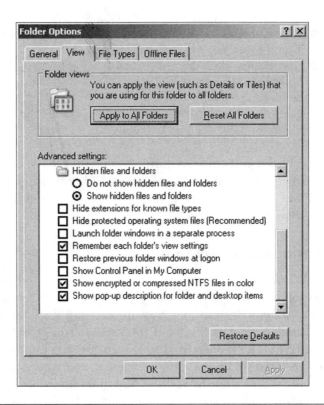

Figure 6-22   You can modify the color of encrypted folders and files in Windows Explorer.

3. To apply the setting to all folders on the computer, select the `Apply to All Folders` button and choose `Yes` when prompted.

Use of Third-Party EFS Certificates

Third-party EFS certificates can be used with EFS. They must, however, meet stringent requirements. This list is an example of the items that must be checked before considering the use of third-party certificates. You should also test certificates and third-party certificate services such as enrollment to ensure compatibility.

- Two Key Usage extensions are required: Key Encipherment and Data Encipherment.

- The Enhanced Key Usage extension must contain the EFS identifier number 1.3.6.1.4.1.311.10.3.4.
- Certificates that do not contain a Certificate Revocation List Distribution Point (CDP) will not be validated (so they cannot be used).
- File Recovery Certificates must include the File Recovery identifier 1.3.6.1.4.1.311.10.3.4.1.

To read more on the use of third-party certificates, see the Knowledge Base Article "Third Party Certification Authority Support for Encrypting File System" at http://support.microsoft.com/default.aspx?scid =kb%3Ben-us%3B273856.

EFS and System Restore

On a Windows XP Professional system, the System Restore function allows the return of system state to some previously recorded status. By default, System Restore monitors all disks but does not monitor redirected folders or data excluded from monitoring. System Restore has little effect on EFS-encrypted files, with two exceptions. First, if a system is restored to a point before a file was encrypted, then the file will not be encrypted after the restore. Also, if multiple users are enabled on the monitored file, after performing System Restore, you may find that only the original encryptor of the file can decrypt it.

Discovering and Viewing the Certificate

The certificates used for encrypting the FEK, including the recovery agent certificate, can be viewed from the File Properties, Advanced, Details page. To see them, click the `View certi cate` button. This can be a useful troubleshooting technique. When multiple recovery agents are or have been used, it may be difficult to recover a file until the recovery agent certificate can be viewed to determine which recovery agent's certificate was used. Once this is known, it can be used to decrypt the file. This information is available by viewing the certificate or by using the efsinfo.exe utility.

Remote Storage

In many organizations, policy states that no data files can be stored on local systems. To store encrypted files on file servers, the servers must be configured and care must be taken to protect the data during transport. There are two ways to remotely store EFS-encrypted files on a Windows Server 2003 server: SMB file shares and WebDAV folders. WebDAV is Distributed Authoring and Versioning, part of the HTTP 1.1 standard. It provides the ability to store files in a web folder using the HTTP PUT command. A new redirector implements WebDAV in Windows XP and Server 2003. Sharing of files can be enabled in this manner on the local intranet and across the Internet. Firewalls that allow HTTP access to internal web servers will pose no barrier to this process. Both SMB and WebDAV storage of EFS-encrypted files offer their own challenges and issues. Three main issues stand out.

First, if SMB file shares are used, files are decrypted before being transported across the network and then are re-encrypted on the file server. To protect the files during transport, they must be encrypted by some alternative method, sent across the network, and then decrypted. IPSec can provide this function. WebDAV storage works differently. When an encrypted file is stored to a WebDAV-enabled folder, the file crosses the network encrypted and is saved in the remote folder still encrypted. When retrieved, it is not decrypted until it reaches the local machine. If the file is created on the remote server, a temporary file is used on the local host, and the file is encrypted and then transported to the remote server.

Second, however, are the issues related to preparing the server for storing encrypted files. When SMB is used, the computer and user account must be trusted for delegation in Active Directory. When computers are trusted for delegation, they can act as if they were the user, obtaining the authority to use his privileges and obtaining access to resources that he is authorized to use. This may not be an acceptable risk. WebDAV storage does not require the remote server to be trusted for delegation because files are not encrypted or decrypted on the server. However, WebDAV does require IIS to be installed, which requires additional security awareness and policy to ensure that this does not open new risks.

Third, WebDAV folders are Internet-accessible via HTTP wherever HTTP access is provided. Unlike SMB, which can be safely blocked at the firewall because there is no legitimate usage necessary for external users, WebDAV access cannot be blocked where web servers must be accessed. However, you can control access by ensuring sound permission sets and by restricting access to internal WebDAV folders where possible to local users only. That is, if port 80 HTTP access must be available from the Internet to internal web servers, the access should be explicitly contained to those servers. WebDAV folders for EFS files should be located on servers that are not Internet-accessible.

SMB Shares

Before SMB shares can be used for storing encrypted files, they must be prepared. The computer must be trusted for delegation in the Active Directory, and the user's keys must be present on the file server. The easiest and most preferred way to do the latter is to use roaming profiles. However, if a roaming profile is not available, the server can create a new local profile for the user. Because the local host creates an EFS key, the new local profile on the server would contain a different set of keys than the profile on the client. Therefore, attempting to store EFS-encrypted files on a remote file server without using roaming profiles is not a good idea because two different sets of keys must now be managed. To trust the computer for delegation, follow these steps:

1. Open `Active Directory Users and Computers`.
2. Expand the `Computers` container, or the OU where the computer account resides, right-click the computer account in the detail pane, and then select `Properties`.
3. Select the `Delegation` page.
4. Click to select `Trust this computer for delegation to any service (Kerberos only)`, as shown in Figure 6-23. There are other options for delegation, as displayed on the page. These options are discussed in Chapter 10, "Securing Active Directory."
5. Click `OK`.

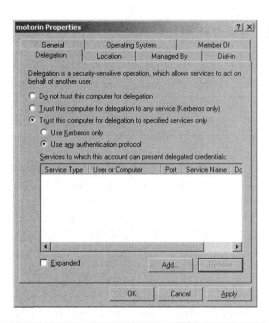

Figure 6-23   You must trust the computer for delegation before you can store encrypted files there.

NOTE: Caching Key Handles for Performance
By default, Windows Server 2003 when trusted for delegation and used for storage of EFS encrypted files will cache up to 15 user key handles. (Handles are pointers to the location of the keys; caching handles improves performance.) This number can be changed (the range is from 5 to 30) by modifying the DWORD value `UserCacheSize` located at `HKEY_LOCAL_MACHINE\SOFTWARE\Microsoft\Windows NT\Current Version\EFS\UserCacheSize`.

WebDAV

WebDAV can be set up easily but does require configuration. Files and folders will not appear as encrypted to any user locally logged on to the server. It's important not to locally encrypt files on the server and not to administer the files locally. Use WebDAV to do so. You can, however, use NTBACKUP to back up the encrypted files. WebDAV must be enabled on the IIS computer and then configured using web permissions. Use NTFS file permissions to further enhance security. For more information on configuring WebDAV, refer to Chapter 5, "Controlling Access to Data."

Sound Enterprise Strategies

A number of best practices when using Encrypted File System should be incorporated into your overall public key strategy, regardless of the size of your enterprise. Best practices for the use of certificate services and EFS will be provided in Chapter 12.

Here are general best practices:

- **Clear pagefile at shut down**—Sensitive information such as passwords and plaintext copies of data in encrypted files may remain in the pagefile. To ensure that an offline attacker cannot recover this information, clear the pagefile at shutdown.
- **Encrypt temporary folders**—Many applications, including Microsoft Word, use temporary files to store changes to documents. If the temporary files used while modifying encrypted files are not themselves encrypted, there is a risk that they might be used to discover sensitive information.
- **Use certificates issued by CAs**—It is not possible to successfully manage recovery of EFS-encrypted files without using a domain-based policy that incorporates PKI.
- **Use more than one Data Recovery Agent per domain**—This allows backup in the event that recovery agent keys are damaged or lost. It also allows segmentation of encryption domains. That is, the person who is authorized to recover data belonging to the Production department can be a different person from the one authorized to recover data belonging to the Accounting department.
- **Store the private keys of the DRAs on a disk, not on a production machine**—Private keys stored offline can be protected from a network-based attack.
- **Use a Central Recovery workstation**—Isolating data under recovery can prevent data leaks during the process.

Best practices for mobile users include the following:

- **Provide physical protection**—If a laptop is lost or stolen, it eventually may be possible for an attacker to read the content of encrypted files.
- **Join the computers to the domain**—Centralized management and recovery is possible in a domain environment, and there is less risk.

- **Remove private keys from the machine and keep them separate, importing them when necessary to decrypt data**—Although extreme, this policy will help protect data files if mobile systems are lost or stolen.
- **Encrypt the** My Documents **folder.**
- **Encrypt the temporary folders.**
- **Always create new files in an encrypted folder**—Don't create in plain text and then encrypt.
- **Use offline folder encryption if offline folders are used**.
- **Use Syskey in Mode 2 or Mode 3 (password on boot floppy or manual password entry required)**—Using Syskey in this manner prevents the computer from being booted unless the boot floppy is inserted into the floppy drive or the password is entered at the console during boot.

For an excellent overview of EFS in Windows XP and Server 2003, see the "Encrypting File System in Windows XP and Windows Server 2003" white paper at http://www.microsoft.com/technet/prodtechnol/winxp-pro/deploy/cryptfs.mspx.

Tools

Tools available for working with EFS-encrypted files include cipher and esfinfo.

Cipher

The following statement is the syntax of the command. Table 6-2 explains the switches.

```
cipher [{/e | /d}] [/s:foldername] [/a] [/i] [/f] [/q] [/h]
[/k] [/u[/n]] [{pathname[...]] | /r:pathnamenoextension |
/w:pathname | /x[:pathname] pathnamenoextension}]
```

Table 6-2 Cipher Switches

Switch	Description
/e	Encrypts folders. Cipher cannot encrypt files that are marked as read-only, or those that are marked as system files.
/d	Decrypts folders.
/s:foldername	Operates on this folder and all its subfolders. Multiple folders can be specified using wildcard characters.
/a	Operates on files and directories.
/i	Continues even if errors occur; for example, if cipher has a problem decrypting a specific file in the specified folder, it will continue decrypting the rest of the files. By default, an error halts its operation, and this switch overrides that behavior.
/f	Forces encryption or decryption of all objects. By default, cipher would skip those files that have already been encrypted or decrypted.
/q	Provides minimal reporting.
/h	Displays files with hidden or system attributes. (These files are not encrypted or decrypted by default.)
/k	Obtains a new file encryption key for the user running cipher. (All other operations are ignored.)
/u	If the user's file encryption keys or the keys of the recovery agent have been changed, updates all encrypted files (can only be used with the /n switch).
/n	Used with the /u switch, will not update keys. Instead, it will find all of the encrypted files on local drives. (It can only be used with the /n switch.)
/r:pathname noextension	A new recovery agent certificate and private key are generated and then written to the files specified in pathnamenoextension (cipher ignores all other options).
/w:pathname	Removes data remnants on unused portions of a volume. (All other options are ignored.) Use this switch if files have been encrypted after being written to the disk.

Switch	Description
/x:pathname pathnameno extension	Will find and identify certificates and private keys used by EFS for the logged on user and back them up to a file. When pathname is given, only the certificate used to encrypt the files at that location is backed up. If pathname is not given, the user's current EFS certificate and keys is backed up. Keys are written to a filename specified by pathnameoextension and are given the extension .pfx. (All other options are ignored.)
/?	Displays help.

Example uses of the cipher command are as follows:

- To back up certificates and keys to a file called efskeys:
  ```
  cipher/x c:\efskeys
  ```
- To encrypt the reports folder and all subfolders:
  ```
  cipher /e /s:reports
  ```
- To encrypt a single file, in this case the JanuarySales.doc in the Midwest\Sales folder:
  ```
  cipher/e /a Midwest\Sales\JanuarySales.doc
  ```
- To determine which files in the JanuarySales folder are encrypted:
  ```
  cipher monthlyreports\may\*
  ```
- To remove data remnants in the D volume:
  ```
  cipher /w
  ```

Cipher /w does not lock the drive. Other programs can still operate and thus may prevent cipher from erasing portions of the drive. For this reason, stop these programs and do not use the drive until cipher has completed this task. Cipher /w can take a long time to complete. Do not use cipher /w unless it is necessary.

Esfinfo

Efsinfo.exe is a command-line tool available in the Windows Server 2003 Support Tools and the Windows XP Professional and Windows 2000 Resource Kits. It can be used to display the encrypted files in a folder and list the certificates used to encrypt a file. You can also download esfinfo from http://www.microsoft.com/windows2000/techinfo/reskit/tools/default.asp.

Troubleshooting

Many of the issues with EFS-encrypted files boil down to one: Encryption keys must be archived. Without a valid private key from a key pair used to encrypt the FEK, file decryption is impossible. If a recovery agent exists, then its keys may be used to recover the files, but the existence of the recovery agent keys cannot be assumed.

Other issues with encrypting files include issues that result from not understanding how EFS works (in which case system files cannot be encrypted, and password resets in Windows XP Professional and above prevent the user from decrypting files he has encrypted) or things such as `access denied` errors during anti-virus scans (the anti-virus product can only check the files that are encrypted by the logged on user) or changes in encryption strength. (If a file is encrypted on XP Professional Service Pack 1, AES is used; you cannot decrypt it on a Windows 2000 system.) Additional reasons for problems include the following:

- A profile is overwritten and the user's encryption keys are no longer available.
- Sysprep is used on a production machine and EFS is re-enabled or keys are changed so they can no longer be used to decrypt encrypted files.
- Autoexec.bat gets encrypted, and because it is needed before log on, the log on process hangs.
- A dual-boot machine is used, so the user loses access to encrypted files when logged on to a different OS than the one used during encryption.
- Encrypting temporary folders of some applications can result in the application not starting.
- Mandatory profiles cannot store encryption keys; access to encrypted files is lost when the user logs off and logs back on again.

Summary

The Encrypting File System is a valuable addition to data security, whether implemented in a domain or on a single standalone machine. A sound recovery policy is needed, however, because encryption keys can become damaged, accidentally deleted, or destroyed. Best practices dictate that the implementation of CA-produced encryption keys will make the system easier to manage.

PART III

Securing Domain Services

CHAPTER 7

Active Directory's Role in Domain Security

"Sixty-five percent of attacks exploit misconfigured systems, and only 30% exploit known vulnerabilities where there's a patch out. Only 5% exploit things we didn't know where there was a problem. Address the 65% and check that things are configured right, and you've just eliminated two-thirds of your problem. Focus on patch management and forcing software vendors to write better software, and you've got the other 30% taken care of. Then, later on, worry about the 5% of evil geniuses who are attacking us with zero-day attacks."

Gartner Vice President John Pescatore in an interview with Search Windows2000.com's Michael S. Mimoso, June 9, 2003, http://searchsecurity. techtarget.com/qna/0,289202,sid14_gci905234,00.html

For many, the preceding conclusion is just common sense. Configure your system correctly, and you have probably eliminated 65% of its vulnerabilities. Therein lies the rub. How do you correctly configure each machine in your network? First, there is the enormity of the situation. Imagine configuring and securing thousands of desktop systems, hundreds of server, and dozens of domain controllers in an enterprise network from an easy-to-understand, granularly configurable, and ultimately manageable console. Then add to that picture the capability to back up and restore security configurations, easily document settings, and reproduce your entire enterprise security configuration in a test environment or migrate settings from one domain to another. Take it a step further and include the opportunity to understand the impact of changes, determine the current security status of a single machine without sitting at its console, and troubleshoot security policy when things aren't right.

Is this too much to ask? No, it's mandatory for security maintenance. Although it is a large task, you can obtain this control over Windows systems today with native Windows Server 2003 tools.

NOTE: Use Best Practices Tempered by Security Policy

This book can show you how to use native tools to configure and secure systems. It can even provide you with some best practices. Ultimately, however, you must understand your systems and make the best choices based on their intended use and the established security policy of your organization. This chapter concentrates on how to use Active Directory and Group Policy to configure and secure systems, but it does not tell you what settings to use. Additional chapters in this book provide information on the use of specific security settings and alternative ways to implement security. The following chapters are specifically related to using Active Directory to secure Windows Server 2003:

- The impact of trust relationships on security—Chapter 8, "Trust"
- Troubleshooting Group Policy Implementation—Chapter 9, "Troubleshooting Group Policy"
- Securing Active Directory—Chapter 10, "Securing Active Directory"

In this chapter, you'll learn how to use many of these tools successfully based on a sound understanding of the role that Active Directory can play in security, and how to map your written IT security policy to Group Policy settings.

Active Directory and Security

An in-depth knowledge of Active Directory (AD) is critical for security. The fundamental reasons are the following:

- First, AD is the seat of all information about users and computers. It contains the security policy and provides information on network structure and the details of many critical enterprise applications. It is absolutely imperative that this knowledge be protected both from unauthorized viewing and from unauthorized alteration.
- Second, because security configuration and maintenance are built-in features, proper design and implementation of Active Directory will support the maximum use of Group Policy.

- Third, if correctly designed, appropriate and secure delegation of authority can be used to support sound administrative practices.

Obtaining the necessary foundation knowledge requires immersion in documentation, hands-on experience in test deployments, and where possible, supervised experience in existing Active Directory environments. This chapter merely reviews basic concepts. If you are new to the Active Directory concepts covered in this chapter or want to broaden your knowledge of Windows Server 2003, you can obtain supplementary knowledge from the following sources:

- Product documentation available online at http://www.microsoft.com/windows/default.mspx
- White papers and other technical information available from www.microsoft.com/technet
- Bill Boswells, *Inside Windows Server 2003*, Addison Wesley, 2003

Group Policy, the ultimate tool for managing computers and users in a domain and the seat of the initially established security for the domain, is a powerful tool when used to set security settings for all domain member computers and users. Group Policy was introduced in Windows 2000, and significant additions and improvements are available in Windows Server 2003. In order to understand, configure, and troubleshoot security by using Group Policy, you must first look at Active Directory from a security perspective.

Active Directory: Organization, Structure, and Function

Active Directory provides a hierarchical directory for Windows 2000 and Windows Server 2003 domains. Objects in the directory, computers, users, shares, printers, and so on can be defined, managed, and secured using native tools. There are several security-specific characteristics:

- Active Directory's hierarchical structure, flexible domain architecture, and replication and Group Policy functions allow granular configuration of security settings and automatic maintenance across large numbers of computers and users at far less administrative cost than would be possible without it.

- Because its structure separates sites and domains and provides for the segmentation of domains into Organizational Units (OUs), administrative authority can be delegated.
- Active Directory's reliance on DNS provides additional opportunities for security infrastructure and new potential vulnerabilities.
- Kerberos-style transitive trust relations exist between domains within a forest, and access to resources within one domain can be granted to users from another domain.
- Tight coupling of domain infrastructure within the forest enables potential breaches of domain boundaries by rogue administrators. The domain is not a rigid security boundary.

Trust relationship and critical security boundary issues will be covered in the next chapter.

Successful Active Directory designs and implementations are the result of applying key concepts and knowledge of the needs and requirements of the organization. Active Directory key concepts are as follows:

- The hierarchical structure of Active Directory and its schema
- Active Directory Replication
- Group Policy structure and function
- Delegation of Authority
- Reliance on DNS

Hierarchical Structure

The Active Directory security boundary, or forest, is composed of one or more trees. Each tree represents a contiguous DNS namespace. For example, an Active Directory forest might be composed of two trees: the chicago.local tree and the sanfrancisco.local tree. The trees are joined during the creation of the second namespace. Within each tree, any number of domains can be added. Each domain will incorporate the name of its parent domain. Figure 7-1 shows a representative forest with several subdomains.

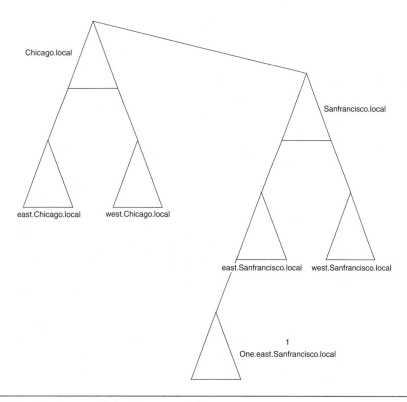

Figure 7-1   Each tree of the forest maintains its own namespace.

Each domain represents a logical division of the network and is represented by a security policy boundary. A security policy boundary is a part of the network that is bound by a common security policy. A security policy boundary differs from a security boundary because a trusted administrator in one security policy boundary might be able to breach another security policy boundary. The security of each domain relies on the cooperation and trustworthiness of its administrators and that of the other domain administrators in the forest.

The domain security policy is unique for each domain. A security policy defined in one domain has no bearing on the security policy of another domain, with one exception. Forest-wide permissions are granted by default to members of the Enterprise Admins and Schema Admins group. The privileges and rights that these group members hold define the forest-wide security policy. For example, a member of the Enterprise Admins group can modify security settings in any domain in the forest.

Domains can be further divided into logical units called OUs. Each OU can have a unique security policy. However, each OU is affected by the security policy of the domain. OUs can be subdivided into a hierarchical structure of child OUs.

NOTE: Security Policy Boundary

The term "security policy boundary" is not a Microsoft term. It is used in this book to define an area where a security policy applies. Security policy boundaries are defined in Active Directory by the forest, site, domain, and OU. It is a useful way to explain the difference between a security boundary, such as a forest (which also is a security policy boundary), and an area like a domain, where security policy can be uniquely applied and administered but that is not a security boundary. However, a security policy boundary is not a security boundary. The security policy implemented within the boundary may be the result of the application of a GPO, other configuration tools may have been used, and it may even consist of administrative policy that cannot enforce or is not enforced by technical controls. It also may consist of rights and privileges granted inherently, not configured. You should not equate a security policy boundary with a security boundary or with GPOs. It may be that you can implement the entire security policy by applying a GPO to a security policy boundary, but this is not necessarily the case.

Domains and OUs are logical boundaries in the forest. Sites represent physical boundaries. Sites roughly correspond to physical network locations. There may or may not be an exact one-to-one correspondence because sites are administratively defined, and there is nothing to prevent administrators from leaving all physical locations in one Active Directory site or dividing one physical location into multiple sites. Sites are defined by recording the physical subnets within their boundaries. A site may consist of only computers joined in a single domain or may include domain controllers or client machines from multiple domains. Figure 7-2 illustrates this fact. In the illustration, the downtown site includes Chicago.local DCs and a SanFrancisco.local DC. The burbs site just contains a Chicago.local DC. Sites are not designed to be security boundaries; however, a unique security policy can be defined for a site.

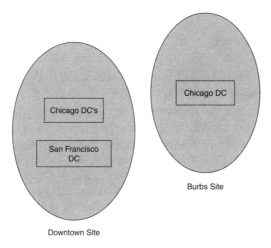

Downtown Site

Burbs Site

Chicago DC's

San Francisco DC

Chicago DC

Figure 7-2   Sites can be composed of computers from multiple domains.

The information that describes Active Directory objects (sites, domains, OUs, user and computer accounts, information on printers, shares, applications and system services, and so on) is stored in the Active Directory database. The structure of these objects and the attributes that described them (and the permissions that can be applied to them) are defined in templates called classes. Each object class and its attributes are defined in the Active Directory schema.

The hierarchical structure of AD lends itself to delegation of authority and merged security policy. Administrative authority is by default structured to match the hierarchy and can be further delegated. Forest-wide administration and domain-wide administration are natively ascribed to Enterprise Admins and Domain Admins Windows groups, respectively. Custom Windows groups can be created, and control over subcontainers in the forest can be delegated to these groups. Security policies defined at higher levels in the forest can be merged with security policies applied at lower levels, although there are rules that constrain and precisely define the impact of multiple policies on objects such as users and computers. Security policy is applied by defining GPOs and linking them to appropriate containers.

Replication

Two types of replication are used in a Windows Server 2003 forest: Active Directory replication and file replication. Active Directory replication ensures that changes made to the database on one domain controller are transferred to all other appropriate domain controllers in the forest. Replication between domains located in the same site occurs automatically—it is managed by the Knowledge Consistency Checker (KCC). The default implementation of Active Directory creates one site. However, additional sites may be added, and when they are, a site link, which manages replication between sites, is created. The creation of sites modifies replication patterns and both inter- and intrasite replication patterns, and schedules can be manually configured. File replication is managed by the File Replication Service and is used by default to replicate files necessary for forest functioning. It can also be manually configured and used to replicate other files.

Domain controllers (DC) contain a copy of AD. Each domain controller in the domain contains both AD information that is forest-wide, such as the schema and configuration data, and domain-specific data, such as user and computer accounts. For example, if new domain-specific information, such as a new user account, is added at a specific DC, the information will be shared with all DCs in the domain via replication. On the other hand, changes to the schema, such as new classes added during the installation of Microsoft Exchange Server, will be replicated to every DC in the forest.

Windows Server 2003 DCs also may contain an Active Directory Application partition. The application partitions make it possible to restrict application-specific data to only those DCs where it is desired. An example of an application partition might consist of the specification of which DCs would contain DNS data when DNS is integrated with Active Directory. In Windows 2000, AD-integrated DNS data is replicated to all domain controllers. However, with Windows Server 2003, you can specify which DCs will have a copy of the DNS data. The use of application partitions can improve replication performance because less data must be replicated to every DC.

Most replication in Active Directory is multimaster—that is, it can be created on any DC and is then replicated between all DCs in the domain; if it is not domain-specific, it is replicated among all domains in the forest. However, there are some exceptions to this rule. Two are especially important to a discussion of security: Global Catalog replication and the role of the PDC Emulator.

The Global Catalog server (GC) is a designated DC whose Active Directory database contains an additional partition. This partition hosts a record of all objects in the forest but does not include all of the attributes of all of these objects. The GC is important to forest-wide functioning because it provides enough information so that objects can be easily located within the forest, or so that objects that refer to objects in different domains have a centralized storage place. For example, when

Universal groups (which can contain users from any domain in the forest) are assigned resource permissions, it must be possible during logon to discover any Universal group memberships that a user might have. It must be possible, for example, to search for a specific user account membership in Universal groups to assign them access to resources in other domains.

The GC role is not the only unique role that may be assigned to a DC. Five Flexible Single Master Operations (FSMOs) manage specific functions within the AD, and these roles are assigned to DCs. Another name for FSMOs often used in Microsoft documentation is Operations Masters. FSMOs and their roles are defined in Table 7-1.

Table 7-1   FSMOs

FSMO	Location	Role
Schema Master	1 for the entire forest; in the forest root domain	Updates and modifies the schema
Domain Naming Master	1 for the entire forest; in the forest root domain	Adds or removes domains to AD
Relative ID Master	1 in each domain	Allocates relative ID (the unique portion of the SID) to domain controllers
PDC Emulator	1 in each domain	Acts like a Windows NT PDC for those domains with NT BDCs still in use. It is the seat of time synchronization and the default location for newly created GPOs. Password changes are also replicated to the PDC Emulator first so that a failed password attempt can be retried at the PDC.
Infrastructure Master	1 in each domain	Updates object references via the global catalog and replicates them to other DCs in the domain

Group Policy

Group Policy is an administrative tool that can be used to manage domain user and member computer accounts. A wide range of items can be managed, including the following:

- Installing software on domain member computers
- Applying startup and shutdown scripts
- Applying security settings
- Applying configuration settings as defined in administrative templates
- Maintaining Internet Explorer settings
- Restricting Remote Installation Services
- Restricting which software can run
- Providing for folder redirection

Group Policy Configuration and Inheritance

Configuring Group Policy consists of creating a Group Policy Object (GPO) and defining the settings for each of the items listed in the previous section. Two main divisions of the GPO exist: one that is applied to computers and one that is applied to users. Several default GPOs exist, including a local GPO for each Windows XP, Windows 2000, or Windows Server 2003 computer, and if a forest is established, a unique default domain GPO and unique default domain controller GPO for each domain in the forest.

A GPO can be linked to a site, domain, or OU object in the Active Directory. Windows 2000 documentation often refers to these containers by naming them in the order in which they are applied: local, site, domain, OU, and child OU. Instead of repeating the entire list of possible objects to which a GPO can be linked, or using the initials SDOU, Windows Server 2003 documentation refers to each of these containers as a Scope of Management (SOM). When a GPO is linked to an SOM, the policies within the GPO are applied to any user, group, or computer account that resides in the SOM. For example, if Mary's account is in the Accounting OU and Fred's is in the Users container of the domain, then a GPO linked to the Accounting OU will impact Mary's account but not Fred's. A GPO can be linked to many SOMs, and many GPOs can be linked to a single SOM.

NOTE: The User and Computer Containers Are Not SOMs
User and Computer containers in Active Directory are not SOMs; therefore, a GPO cannot be linked to them. User accounts in the User container are affected by site and domain GPOs, as are computer accounts in the Computer container. The Domain Controllers container is, however, a SOM (it's an OU). The default domain controller's GPO is linked to this container, and additional GPOs also can be linked there.

Because multiple GPOs exist by default, and more can be created, Group Policy rules define how settings are applied and what occurs when a conflict between settings in a GPO exists. Five main concepts apply.

First, the computer portions of a GPO are applied during boot, and the user portion of a GPO is applied during the user's logon process. This means that some parts of policy remain constant no matter which user logs on to a computer, and other parts are uniquely applied depending on the logged on user. During computer boot and logon or user logon, the relevant GPO GUIDs are collected from Active Directory. The policies are then downloaded from their location on a DC sysvol share. If a policy is changed, and the user or computer is still logged on, the process of applying these changes is begun approximately within five minutes on DCs and within 90 minutes on member computers. The security settings portion of AD is applied every 16 hours regardless of whether changes have been made to this section. However, how quickly a new Group Policy or changes to Group Policy are applied is a function of other higher priority activity occurring on the DC, replication processes, the refresh process, and what part of the GPO the policy changes reside in. The latency of GPO application needs to be considered when updating security policy. Knowing the replication latency for a specific network will help you understand normal delays in policy application. Remember that two types of replication, AD and FRS, impact GPOs. Active Directory replication and FRS must both be working correctly for security policy to be applied and maintained.

Second, when a GPO is created or modified in a Windows 2000 domain, the information is written by default to the domain controller that is the PDC Emulator. If and only if this DC is not available, an authorized administrator may select another DC. One feature that is new to Windows Server 2003 is that the default DC location for the creation of GPOs can be selected by an administrator who has the `Create and Manage GPO` right.

GPO information is written to two different places—some to Active Directory and some to the `%windir%\SYSVOL` folder—as shown in Figure 7-3. Each GPO is given a unique GUID, or globally unique ID number, and this number is used to coordinate the parts of the GPOs. The information in Active Directory is replicated through the normal Active Directory Replication process. However, the information in the SYSVOL share is replicated to the `%windir%\SYSVOL\sysvol` folder (shared as SYSVOL) on each domain controller using the File Replication Service (FRS). Each policy is placed in this share within a folder named by the domain name. Any scripts are placed in the `%windir%\SYSVOL\sysvol\scripts` folder (the netlogon share) under that domain.

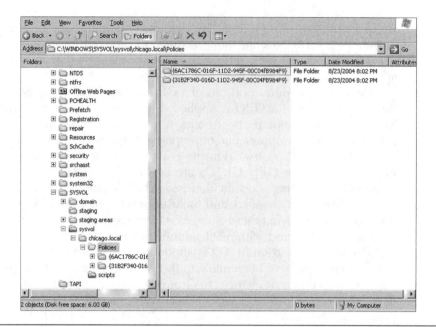

Figure 7-3   Scripts and the system policy part of the GPO are first written to the `SYSVOL\domain` directory and then replicated using FRS to `SYSVOL\sysvol\domainname`.

Policy Replication Latency

Many domain operations can impact how long it takes to apply changes to Group Policy.

If the domain controller or the client computers are busy processing higher-priority tasks, the time it takes to apply changes to Group Policy will be extended.

Before a changed policy can be applied, it must replicate to the domain controller at which the user will log on. By default, the change is written to the Active Directory on the PDC-Emulator.

The Security Settings container of the GPO is refreshed every 16 hours, whether or not changes are made to security settings. This means that changes made at the local level to security settings will not be returned to the correct state for some time. Evidence of security settings refresh is published to the Application log of all domain member computers that are powered on and connected to the network for more than 16 hours. Event number 1704, displayed in Figure 7-4, will appear every 16 hours.

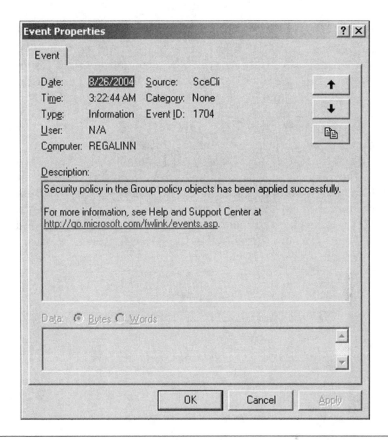

Figure 7-4   After the security settings are applied, an information message will be
logged to the Application log.

Third, a GPO will apply to all computer or user accounts that exist within
the SOM to which the GPO is applied unless special options are set.
Because some SOMs contain other SOMs (domains contain OUs, for
example), multiple GPOs may be applied to computer and user
accounts. You can determine which GPOs are applied to a specific
account by applying the SDOU rule mentioned in the "Group Policy
Configuration and Inheritance" section previously. First the local policy
is applied, followed by the site policy, the domain policies, and then the
OU policies. If, for example, Fred's user account is in the Accounting
OU, which is a child OU, of the Finance OU in the Chicago domain, his
account will have any local GPO, any site GPO, the default domain

GPO, and any GPOs linked to the Accounting OU. Figure 7-5 illustrates this example. In the figure, Fred's user and computer account are located in the Accounting OU. The Accounting OU is a sub-OU of the Finance OU, and both are located in the Chicago.local domain. The Chicago.local domain has servers, users, and computers in the Downtown site and the Burbs site. Fred is affected by every GPO linked to SOMs within the hierarchy of the OU structure and the local GPO on the computer he logs on from. If Fred, who has an account in the Accounting OU of the Chicago.local domain and is sitting at a computer in the Burbs site, logs on, he will be affected by settings in the Local GPO of his computer and in any GPOs linked to the Burbs site, the default Domain Security Policy of the Chicago.local domain, and any GPOs linked to the Finance and Accounting OUs. If user and computer accounts exist in different OUs, the GPOs for those OUs are applied.

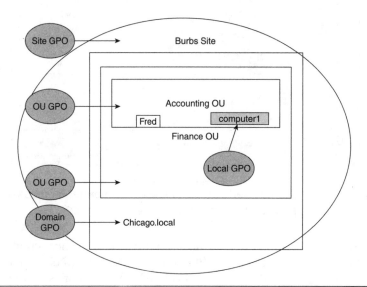

Figure 7-5   The security policy applied to a user or computer account is dependent on the location of the account.

Fourth, while all of the relevant GPOs are applied and in essence merged, if a conflict exists, the last setting applied wins. Examples of policy conflicts are further discussed in Chapter 9.

Finally, in reality, many factors can affect the process of inheritance. Table 7-2 lists these issues.

Table 7-2   Exceptions to GPO Application

Exception	Result
Broken GPO links	If links are not working, then the GPO will not be applied.
Multiple GPOs linked to a SOM	If multiple GPOs are linked to the same SOM, then Link Order determines how they are applied.
Block Inheritance	If the Block Inheritance property is set, then a parent GPO may not be applied.
Enforcement	If the Enforcement (formerly No Override) property is set, then regardless of the settings in later processed GPOs, the Enforced GPO will win.
Loop Back	If Loop Back is used, then the user settings in the local computer's GPO will replace or be merged with those applied via the user's account location.
Link Enabled	If the GPO is not Link Enabled, the GPO will not be processed.
Conflict Resolution	If multiple GPOs attempt to set the same settings, then assuming Block Inheritance, Enforcement, or Loop Back is not set, the last GPO that modifies the setting wins.

Delegation of Administrative Authority

In versions of Windows prior to Windows 2000, administrative authority is defined for selected built-in groups (administrators, domain admins, server operators, account operators,) and accounts (Administrator, Guest). A custom group or new user account can be given some administrative authority by granting predefined user rights such as `Add workstations to domain`, or `backup files and directories to a group or user account`. In a Windows 2000 or Windows Server 2003 domain, an extremely granular level of administrative authority can be granted by modifying access control lists (ACLs) on Active Directory Objects. To simplify the process, the Delegation of Control Wizard can be used. Instructions on using this wizard to develop administrative roles in Windows Server 2003 can be found in the section "Delegation of Administration—Using the Delegation of Control Wizard."

Reliance on DNS

Active Directory forests are defined by DNS namespaces. Without access to a properly configured and active DNS server, Active Directory cannot function. Member computers cannot connect to the domain controllers, users cannot log on, and security policy cannot be applied. These functions can only occur if users and computers can locate the following services on the network.

- **_ldap**—Necessary to use ldap to query AD.
- **_Kerberos**—Necessary for Kerberos authentication.
- **_gc**—The Global Catalog servers, necessary for lookup of forest-wide data including membership in Universal Groups (caching of Universal group membership is an option in Windows Server 2003 domains. If enabled, access to a global catalog server is not necessary at every logon.)

These services are advertised in DNS as Service locator (SRV) resource records, and an example is shown in Figure 7-6. Multiple servers that offer TCP/IP-based services can advertise the same service, and a single DNS request can locate them. Each SRV record in DNS includes the following:

- DNS domain name
- Service (many services are defined in RFC 1700)
- Protocol (typically TCP or UDP)
- Priority, which sets a preference among multiple servers offering the same service
- Weight, which can be used with preference to provide load balancing (several servers with the same priority can be weighted so that one is chosen more or less frequently than the others)
- Port number (service port on target host)
- Host offering this service target or DNS host name, which provides the service

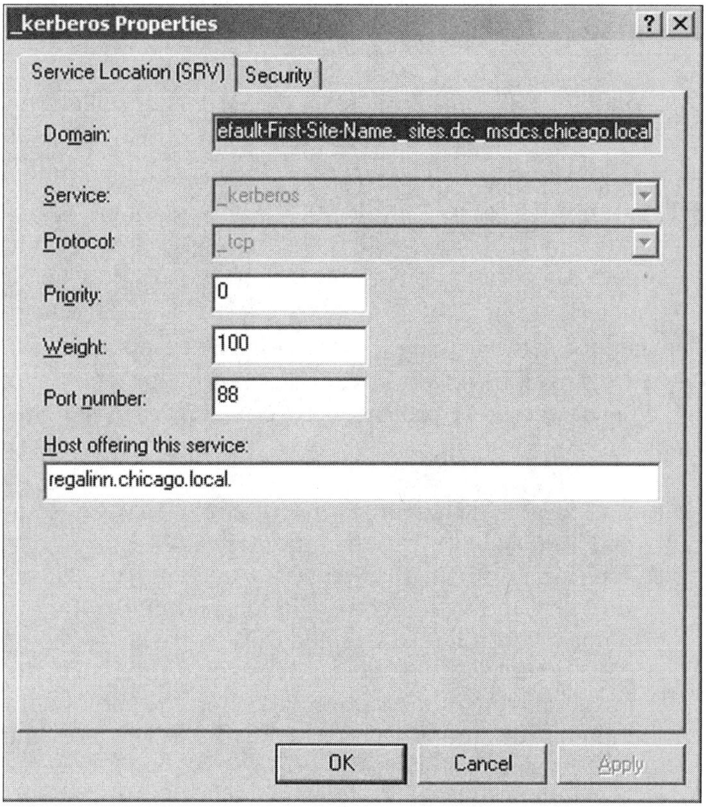

Figure 7-6 SRV records help clients access domain services.

During logon, computer and user accounts query DNS for appropriate services, obtain the DNS name of the hosts offering them, select a host, and query DNS for the IP address of the host. The authentication process continues, and once authenticated, the current security policies or GPOs are downloaded and applied to the computer or user.

When DNS is not functioning due to misconfiguration or as the result of an attack, users may have trouble locating network resources, and security policy is not applied.

Active Directory Installation: Changes During dcpromo

The Windows NT domain model assigned each installed server a single, unchangeable role. Servers could only be a primary domain controller, backup domain controller, or server. To change a computer's role, reinstallation was necessary. This is not true for Windows 2000 or Windows Server 2003. Any Windows 2000 or Windows Server 2003 server can be promoted to become a domain controller, and any domain controller can be demoted and become a simple server. This change to server role is managed using the dcpromo command. The exception to this rule is the Windows Server 2003 web server edition, which cannot be promoted.

When a server is promoted to domain controller, many changes occur:

- The local SAM becomes inaccessible. All groups and computer and user accounts reside in the Active Directory.
- The local administrator account becomes the account used for recovery and will become the local administrator account if the domain controller is demoted using the dcpromo command.
- New groups and user accounts are made available; they are either created by the process or replicated from another domain. A complete list of groups is described in Table 7-3 and Table 7-4, and a list of users is shown in Table 7-5.
- New administrative tools are present (Table 7-6), and the ability to manage items such as local users and groups is removed.
- The SYSVOL and sysvol folders and sysvol and netlogon shares are created.
- The sample AD database or template, ntds.dit, is copied from the %windir%\system32 folder to the %windir%\NTDS folder. Ntds.dit contains the basic active directory structure and includes the default policies for domain controllers and the domain.
- If the option to install DNS is selected, DNS is installed.
- The domain controller attempts to register itself with the DNS server that is authoritative for the domain. If DNS is created on the domain controller, it will become authoritative for the domain. In addition to an A, or host record, the SRV records are created for _ldap, _Kerberos, and _gc.
- Additional services are enabled and started, including FRS, the distributed file system (DFS), and the Kerberos Key Distribution Service (KDS).

- The defltdc.inf (default domain controller) security template is applied. (Security templates hold security settings; when applied to a computer, the security settings in the template become the local Group Policy settings for the computer.)
- If this is not the first domain controller in the domain, Active Directory data and Group Policy files and folders are replicated from another domain controller.
- If this is not the first domain controller in the domain, the Domain Security Policy and Domain Controller Security Policy, in addition to any additional GPOs linked to the domain or Domain Controller OU, are applied.
- In the first domain controller in the domain, the Default Domain Policy (GPO) is created and linked to the root of the domain, and the Default Domain Controller Policy (GPO) is created and linked to the Domain Controller's OU.

Table 7-3   Groups Established During dcpromo in the Built-In Container

Group	Privileges
Account Operators	Create, modify, and delete groups and user and computer accounts in the User and Computer containers of the domain and for Organizational Units except the Domain Controller's OU. Account operators cannot add or remove members from the Domain Admins or Administrators group or modify existing accounts that are members in these groups. Account Operators' default user rights are log on locally and shut the computer down.
Administrators	Complete control of all domain controllers in the domain. The Domain Admins and Enterprise Admins groups are members of this group.
Backup Operators	Back up and restore files on all domain controllers in the domain. Default user rights are log on locally and shut the computer down.
Guests	Domain Guests are member, of this group by default, as is the Guest account.

Table 7-3   Groups Established During dcpromo in the Built-In Container Continued

Group	Privileges
Incoming Forest Trust Builders	This group is only created in the root forest domain. Members have the right to create a one-way incoming forest trust. If two forests—forest one and forest two—have the root forest domains, Domain A and Domain B respectively, members in this group in Domain A can create a one-way incoming trust with Domain B. This means that users in Domain A can be given resource access rights in Domain B. There are no default users in this group. More information on trusts is in Chapter 8.
Network Configuration Operators	Make changes to TCP/IP settings.
Performance Monitor Users	Have the ability to remotely monitor the computer.
Performance Log Users	Have remote access to schedule logging of performance counters on the computer.
Pre-Windows 2000 Compatible Users	Read access on all users and groups in the domain. Provided for backward capability with Windows NT. The identity Everyone is a member of this group. Only add members to this group if you have Windows NT 4.0 member servers or BDCs in the domain.
Print Operators	Administer domain printers.
Remote Desktop Users	Right to log on remotely.
Replicator	Supports file replication.
Server Operators	Log on interactively, create and delete shared resources, start and stop some services, back up and restore files, format disks, shut down the computer.
Users	Interactive and authenticated users groups and domain users are members of this group. Any user created in the domain becomes a member of this group.
Terminal Server License Servers	Can manage licenses for terminal services.
Windows Authorization Access Group	Access to the computed tokenGroupGlobalAndUniversal attribute on User Objects (membership=Enterprise Domain Controllers).

Table 7-4   Groups Created During dcpromo in the Users Container

Group	Privilege
Cert Publishers	Publish certificates for users and computers.
DNS Administrators	Created if DNS is installed. Can administer the DNS server.
DNSUpdate Proxy	Created if DNS is installed. Can update DNS records for other computers, such as DHCP servers.
Domain Admins	Full control of the domain member of administrators groups in all computers joined in the domain.
Domain Computers	All workstations and servers joined in the domain.
Domain Controllers	All domain controllers in the domain.
Domain Guests	All domain guests.
Domain Users	All domain users.
Enterprise Admins	This group only exists in the root domain of the forest. Full control of all domains in the forests. This group is a member of all domain administrator groups on all domain controllers in the domain.
Group Policy Creator Owners	Create and modify Group Policy in the domain. The Administrator account is a member of this group by default.
HelpServicesGroup	Used by the Help and Support Center. The Support_388945a0 account is a member. This account is used for remote assistance logon. When a remote assistance invitation is used to provide remote assistance, a password must be entered. This password is assigned to the Support_388945a0 account during the creation of the remote assistance invitation. The helper uses this account to log on to the user's desktop computer to provide remote assistance. This group may be used to contain accounts created by third-party products used in managing the computer. For example, owners of Dell computers may find a support account added here.
RAS and IAS Servers	Permitted access to user remote access properties.
Schema Admins	This group is only created in the root forest domain and can modify Active Directory Schema. The Administrator account is the default member of this group.
TelnetClients	Access to Telnet server on this system.

Table 7-5   User Accounts Established During dcpromo

User	Description
Administrator	All powerful root account.
Guest	Access to domain resources (disabled by default).
Support_388945a0	This group allows signed scripts to interact with the Help and Support Service. It can be used so that ordinary users can run signed scripts from links in the Help and Support Service. The scripts are programmed to use this account instead of the user's account to perform administrative functions on the computer. This account is used by the Remote Assistance program.

Table 7-6   New Administrative Tools for Domain Controllers

Tool	Description
Active Directory Domains and Trusts	Manage domains and trusts.
Active Directory Users and Computers	Manage users and computers, links to tools to manage Group Policy.
Active Directory Sites and Services	Manage sites and services.
DNS	Manage DNS (if DNS is installed during dcpromo).
Domain Controller Security Policy	Manage default domain controller security settings portion of GPO.
Domain Security Policy	Manage security settings portion of default Domain GPO.

Managing Computers and Users Using Active Directory

Unmanaged users and computers put the organization at risk. Managed users can be provided just the privileges and permissions required to do their jobs and prevented from inadvertently compromising security. Managed computers can be hardened against attack and provide platforms on which the integrity of data can be guaranteed to a reasonable degree. In addition, managed users and computers require less manpower to maintain and secure. Active Directory is designed to provide a sound management base, and tools are available to automate the process.

Users and computer accounts are created and placed within a specific Active Directory container and can be managed via Group Policy, Windows Management Instrumentation, direct configuration, and other administrative tools. Much of the direct configuration operations can be scripted and coupled with Group Policy processing to provide a largely automated environment. In addition, the administration of management processes for specific collections of users and computers can be delegated.

The simple act of adding an account places it in an environment that already has some management in place. Default GPOs provide minimum management and security for new accounts. The first step in providing a customized, managed environment is to understand the default configuration specifics and the available tools and account properties. Understanding the direct configuration tools will aid you in developing and using scripted tools.

The Impact of Default GPOs

When a new domain is created, two default GPOs are established that set the initial security policy via the Domain Security Policy and the policy for DCs in the domain via the Domain Controller Security Policy. These policies affect the security settings of every new computer and user account. As additional domain and OU GPOs are created and linked to SOMs, their settings can modify some of the default security provided by the default GPOs. Other changes must be made by directly configuring the default GPOs; some settings, made at the domain and domain controller level, cannot be overridden by OU-linked GPOs.

The Account Policy portion of the Domain Security Policy sets the Account policy (Kerberos, Password, and Account Lockout Policies) for the domain. If a new GPO is created and linked to an OU, and that GPO has its own Account Policy configured, it will have no impact on domain users when they use domain accounts to log on. (OU Policies of this type will impact local user accounts on the computers whose accounts reside in the OU. If a local account is used to log on to the computer, then the OU policy will be in effect.) Figure 7-7 displays the default domain policy Account Policy and the details of the Password Policy portion.

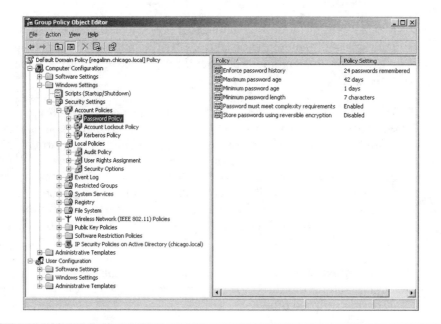

Figure 7-7 The default domain account policy sets the account policy for all users in the domain.

The Domain Controller Policy only affects the domain controllers whose accounts reside in the Domain Controller OU. This policy sets the Audit Policy and Security Options for all domain controllers. In addition, the User Rights Portion of the Domain Controllers GPO affects all domain user and computer accounts and groups. If User rights are set in another GPO linked in any other SOM, they will only affect local user, computer, and group accounts. The practical end result is that a domain user can obtain domain-based users rights and may also obtain additional rights on the computer at which he is interactively logged on. In addition, the following Group Policy components contain settings used to manage computers and users:

- **Security Options**—Allow the setting of multiple registry entries by using a GUI. Many of them affect users and groups.
- **Restricted Groups**—Allow management of group membership by policy. Adding groups to the `Restricted Groups` container turns the control of membership over to the Restricted Groups policy. If users are added to the group account in Active Directory but not in its representation in Restricted groups, the account will be removed upon the next policy refresh. Likewise, if a user is

added to a restricted group within the security settings of the GPO, the account, if not present in the Active Directory group, will be added.

■ **Registry and File System Permissions**—Provide a way to deny or allow users, groups, and computers to access these resources.

■ **System Services**—Provide the ability to disable or set startup function of services and control over who can modify these settings. Permissions determine which users and groups can enable, disable, start, stop, or set the startup function of services. The presence of an enabled or disabled service may impact what a user can do. For example, the Domain Users group may have permission to remotely access the network, but if the Remote Access service is stopped or disabled, they will not be able to do so.

■ **Public Key Policies**—Indicate whether or not certificates will be issued and whether they can be used for certain purposes.

■ **Software Restriction Policies**—Indicate who can run or not run specific software.

■ **IP Security Policies**—IPSec policies implemented in Group Policy manage communications with and between computers affected by the Group Policy.

■ **Wireless Network Policies**—Manage wireless network policy for affected computers.

■ **Administrative Templates**—Provide hundreds of configuration parameters affecting many operating system functions, programs, and software as well as the user interface.

Creating and Configuring Users, Groups, and Computers in Active Directory Domains

When user and computer accounts are created, their rights and privileges on the network are determined by their account location within the OU structure, by default domain security policy, by their account properties, and by the access they are granted either directly or by membership in Windows groups. Some default groups exist, and custom groups can be created to simplify management of and access to resources and the management of privileges through the domain. Within the forest, groups can also be used to grant access to resources in one domain to users whose accounts reside in another domain. Access can be granted directly to user or computer accounts; however, this is not recommended because it is too difficult to manage and audit. Assigning rights and privileges to groups simplifies the management of resources. Using domain-based groups and accounts eliminates the need for users to maintain user accounts in multiple computers and domains. In a single domain, forest rights and privileges on computers joined in the domain are assigned to domain users and computers via membership in domain groups.

Using Groups to Manage Access and Rights

On a single standalone Windows NT and above computer, local computer user groups are assigned rights and privileges on that computer. Group member accounts placed in the groups receive those rights and privileges. In a domain, one additional step may be practiced—creating domain-wide groups. Domain user and computer accounts are placed in the domain group. Some domain groups are used to grant domain privileges to users. Others are used to give users privileges and rights on computers joined in the domain by adding domain groups to local groups on the member computer. In a Windows 2000 or Windows Server 2003 domain, computer accounts can also be added to domain computer groups. The rights and privileges of the domain computer groups are assigned to group member computers.

Local user accounts and local groups exist in the SAM of the local computer and can be used only to grant access to resources or rights on that computer. It is not possible to place a local user account in a domain group and thus give local computer users access to domain resources or privileges. The concept that some accounts and groups can only contain certain types of accounts and can only exist in certain circumstances is called group scope.

Active Directory domain group management concepts are defined in the following. Some of these concepts have no impact in a single domain forest and will be discussed further after the concept of trust has been explained in Chapter 8.

- **Group Types**—These include Security, groups that can be granted access to objects by adding their SIDs to the discretionary access control list, and Distribution, groups used solely for creating email lists at this time. Distribution groups cannot be used to grant access to objects.
- **Forest functional mode**—A classification that can be set when the types of domain controllers in the domain move from mixed to Windows 2000 and above to Windows Server 2003. Each mode provides specific benefits, additional functionality, and options.

- **Group Scope**—Rules that define where groups can be created and where they can be used. Group scope changes with functional mode. In a single domain forest, group scope consists of the following:
  Global groups and Domain local groups can be created only on domain controllers.
  Local machine groups can be created only on Windows NT and above computers.
  Global groups can be nested either in local groups on domain member computers or in Domain local groups.
  Global groups and Domain local groups can be granted privileges and rights on domain controllers.
  Global groups, local groups, and Domain local groups can be nested in Domain local groups and Groups that are local to a specific computer.
  Local groups can be created only on a single computer.
  Local user accounts can be added only to local groups.
- **Impact of Global Catalog Server (GC) on group**—Information on membership in Universal groups, which can only be created in Windows 2000 or Windows Server 2003 functional-mode domains, must be available at logon. This can mean logon issues for those logging on remotely across the WAN. A GC and DC must be located and used during the logon process or a DC must be available and group caching must be enabled. (When group caching is enabled, the membership of Universal groups is cached on the local domain controller.)
- **SID History/SID Filtering**—SIDs are unique user identification numbers. If a user account is moved from one domain to another, that user's SID changes, and thus that user's ability to access resources changes. Maintaining SID History is a way to ensure access to objects based on SIDs.

Basic Account and Group Management Operations

The basic operations for account and group management remain similar to that done on a standalone computer. The advantages in a domain and in a forest are single sign-on (only one account and password needs to be known) and the capability to manage resources and privileges across multiple computers.

In the domain, User and Computer accounts can be created from the Active Directory Users and Computers (ADUC) console or via scripts. Domain user accounts have a larger variety of configuration properties than local user accounts do. During or after account creation, they can be added to groups.

Creating and Configuring Users and Groups

User accounts can be created initially by simply adding an account name and password, but there are many attributes that can be configured. If additional Active Directory-aware services such as Exchange Server are added to the domain, additional attributes are added, too.

Create a User Account Using ADUC

1. Right-click on the container where the account will reside, choose New, then select User. (Containers may be User, Built-in, or specific OU.)
2. Enter the first name, initials, and last name. The concatenation of these three fields becomes the full name, otherwise known as the *display name*, and it must be unique within the domain and no more than 64 characters long. (The display name can also be changed to any string of alphanumeric and unique characters.)
3. Enter a User logon name, as shown in Figure 7-8, and click Next. This name is used by the user to log on to the domain and must be unique throughout the domain. It can be up to 256 characters, but a pre-Windows 2000 logon name will be truncated to the first 20 characters of the logon name. Logon names can include spaces, periods, underscores, and all other special characters, except for the following: ° / \ [ ] : | = , + = ? < >. Logon names are not case-sensitive.
4. Enter a password for the user and confirm the password by entering it again.
5. Check property boxes as desired and click Next. It is a good policy to leave the User must change password at next logon box checked. This forces the user to create their own unique password during their first logon. The password initially created for the account is known to someone other than the user and therefore might be used to compromise the account. Many organizations also check the Account is disabled box when creating accounts sometime prior to users joining the company. The box must be unchecked before the account can be used, and thus there is no risk that accounts created for employees

who never actually log on might be used by unauthorized individuals. The property boxes available are as follows:

```
User must change password at next logon (only default
checked box)
User cannot change password
Password never expires
Account is disabled
```

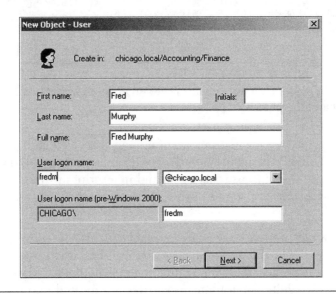

Figure 7-8 A pre-Windows 2000 logon name is created for the user account.

NOTE: Default Password Policy
The default password policy for Windows Server 2003 is different than it
was in Windows 2000. In Windows Server 2003, the password complexity
requirement is enabled by default. Passwords must be composed of three
of the following: uppercase and lowercase letters, numbers, and non-
alphanumeric characters.

6. Review object information and click `Finish`. If the password
   does not meet the password policy requirements, a warning will
   appear, as shown in Figure 7-9. If it does, to complete the new
   account creation, click `OK` and enter a password that meets the
   requirements before you can complete the account creation.

The setting of a default password policy for a new domain is new with Windows Server 2003. If the default policy does not meet the required security policy, it should be changed.

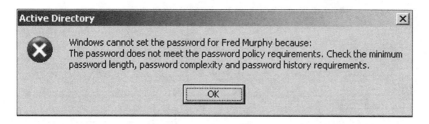

Figure 7-9 The system will not let you create an account whose password does not meet the password policy.

User, computer, and group accounts can also be created using the `dsadd` command. When large numbers of user accounts need to be created, it is more useful to use this command in a script or to use utilities developed specifically for this purpose than to use the GUI.

Configure a User Account

Multiple property pages are available for use in configuring the user account. On the General page, basic information about the account including office, telephone number, email address, and web page can be added. Additional account properties are located on other pages. The most important account information is located on the Account property page, as shown in Figure 7-10. This information can be modified to increase security in several ways.

To restrict logon hours, click the `Logon Hours` button. Setting a schedule here, as shown in Figure 7-11, controls the hours of the week the user may log on. Restricting logon hours prevents the user or someone with their account credentials from using domain resources when they are not authorized to do so. This can reduce the number of potential attacks because an attack during normal business hours might be more easily noticed, and if fewer accounts have access, there are fewer opportunities for misuse of domain user credentials. If users are not authorized for remote access, restricting access to normal business hours prevents individuals who have evening or night access, such as cleaning crews, from using employee's credentials for system access. Any attempt to use the restricted account outside of the hours authorized for use will fail, and if auditing is configured, the attempt will be logged.

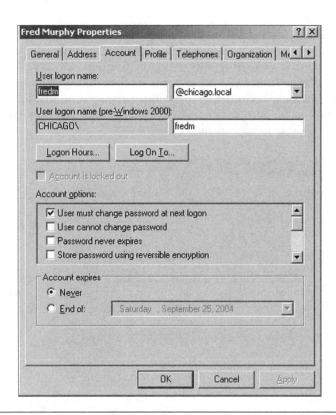

Figure 7-10   The default Account property page of the user account.

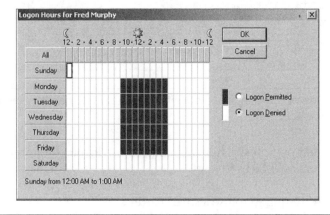

Figure 7-11   Setting logon hours can deter unauthorized access.

To restrict users to specific computers, click the Log On To button. Figure 7-12 displays the Logon Workstations dialog box. When users are limited to the use of specific computers, the possibility that they will gain access to resources in other areas or that their credentials will be used for attacks is reduced. It may also prevent unauthorized access from intruders because they must know where the account can be used and must be able to access that computer.

Figure 7-12   Restricting users to a specific workstation(s) can reduce the attack surface.

In addition to restricting logon hours and logon computers, domain user accounts can be as follows:

- Required to use a smart card
- Trusted to delegation
- Prevented from being delegated
- Required to use DES encryption types
- Prevented from requiring Kerberos pre-authentication

Create a Group and Add Members

Groups should be used to assign access to resources and operating system rights. Users can obtain these privileges by becoming group members. To create a group, follow these steps:

1. Open Active Directory Users and Computers.
2. Right-click on any SOM, select New, and then select Group.
3. Enter a Group name. (A pre-Windows 2000 group name is created.)
4. Select the Group scope (Domain local or Global).
5. Select the Group type, as shown in Figure 7-13, and then click Next.

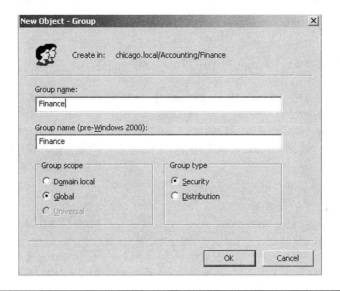

Figure 7-13   Create a new group.

User and computer accounts are added to groups by adding the account to the user or computer Member Of property page or by adding the user or computer account to the group's Member page. Membership is restricted by using group scoping rules.

Adding and Managing Computers

Computers can be joined to the domain to centralize computer management and centralize control over computer-based resources. Member computers can be remotely managed using domain administration tools such as the Computer Management console and can be controlled via Group Policy.

Making a computer a domain member is a two-step process. First, the computer account is created in the AD, and then the computer is joined to the domain. The joining process includes the creation of a password and the establishment of a secure channel. By default, the new computer account is created in the `Domain Computers` container. This container is not an OU, and a GPO cannot be linked to it. Because its location is within the domain container, computers in this container will, however, receive the Default Domain GPO. Move computer accounts to OUs to do the following:

- Delegate authority for their management to another user or group
- Delegate some part of their management to another user or group
- Configure and apply a unique security policy to these computers by creating or linking a GPO to the OU that they reside within

Creating and Configuring Computer Accounts

Computer accounts can be created when a computer is joined to a domain. The computer account can also be prestaged or created directly in the Active Directory without actually joining a computer to the domain. The account can then be used when a computer is joined to the domain. The advantage of prestaging is that the SOM for the computer account can be preselected, and the user account with the privilege to create the account can be designated. To prestage a computer account, follow these steps:

1. Right-click the SOM where the computer account will reside, and then click `New` followed by `Computer`.
2. Enter a computer name. The pre-Windows 2000 computer account name is created, as shown in Figure 7-14.
3. If desired, click the `Change` button to change the name of the user or group that can join the computer to the domain.

4. If desired, select `Assign this computer account as a pre-Windows 2000 computer`.

5. If desired, and if creating an account for a Windows NT 4.0 backup domain controller, select `Assign this computer account as a backup domain controller`.

6. Click `Next`.

7. If the computer will be a managed computer, select `This is a managed computer` and enter the computer's GUID, as shown in Figure 7-15.

8. Click `Next`; review the new object and click `Finish`.

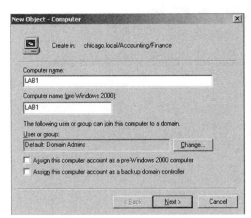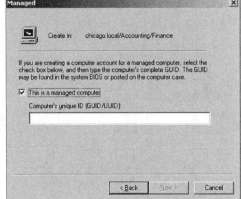

Figure 7-14   Pre-Windows 2000 names and characteristics can be configured while creating the computer account.

Figure 7-15   Enter the computer's GUID to make it a managed computer.

NOTE: GUID Discovery

The computer GUID is a unique number (sometimes referred to as a Universally Unique ID, or UUID) assigned by the computer manufacturer. It may be provided on a label on or inside the computer case. It may also be discovered by using WMI to obtain it from the computer BIOS. Another way is to use a sniffer and identify the DHCP discover packet sent by the computer when it attempts to obtain an IP address. This packet will include the computer GUID.

Management via the Computer Management Console

After a computer is joined to the domain, the Computer Management console can be used to remotely manage it. Security items such as Local Users, Groups, Shares, Services, and Event Logs can be accessed via this tool, as can drives and volumes. The Computer Management console is accessible via Active Directory Users and Computers. To open it, right-click the computer account and select Manage from the menu. The Computer Management console for the remote computer will be opened, as shown in Figure 7-16.

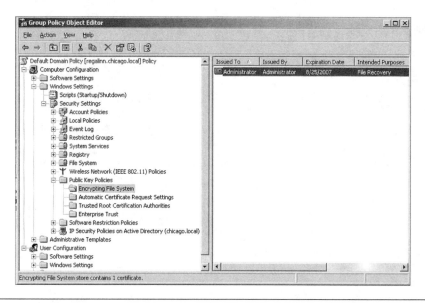

Figure 7-16 Remote access to a domain member computer is possible from the computer's account in Active Directory Computers and Users.

Management and Control via Group Policy

New computer accounts are created by default in the Domain Computers container. This container is not an OU, and a GPO cannot be linked to it. Assigning a GPO to a select group of computers within the domain requires moving the location for their computer account creation to a specific OU and then linking the computer-specific GPO to the OU. Any number of OUs can be created and computer accounts moved to them. It is also possible in a Windows Server 2003 functional level domain to redirect default computer account creation to a specific OU.

To do so, an attribute of the PDC emulator must be modified. The primary advantage to doing this is that when computer accounts are created, they are immediately placed in an OU, and the GPO linked to the container will be applied to the computer. This means that current security configuration and any additional Group Policy directives will be applied to the computer more quickly. If the default container for computer account creation is not changed, only the domain GPOs are applied to new domain member computers. During all computer joining processes, whether initiated from the computer using the System applet or using command-line utilities such as `net user`, `net computer`, `net group`, or `netdom`, there is no opportunity to specify an OU.

If the functional level of the domain is Windows Server 2003, two tools, redircmp.exe and redirusr.exe, can be used to change the default container for new computer and user accounts, respectively. Both utilities are native Windows Server 2003 utilities. The command syntax is as follows:

```
Redircmp OU=container_distinguished_name and Redirusr
OU=container_distinguished_name
```

The `container_distinguished_name` represents the distinguished name of the OU desired. For example, the following statement will assign the BaseComp OU in the Chicago.local domain to be the default location where computer accounts created in the chicago.local domain will be created.

```
Redircmp ou=BaseComp,dc=chicago,dc=local
```

The BaseComp OU must exist before the command is run. As an added precaution, you must rename the default `Computers` and `Users` containers. You can do so by using ldp.exe.

To learn more about these utilities, read the "Redirecting the Users and Computer Containers in Windows Server 2003 Domains" knowledge base article 324949 at http://support.microsoft.com/default.aspx?scid=kb;en-us;324949.

Delegation of Administration—Using the Delegation of Control Wizard

The Delegation of Control Wizard can be used to assign administrative authority to non-administrative groups over collections of users and groups. This control empowers the non-administrative group members to perform their required administrative duties without giving them full Domain Admin privileges. The scope of their authority is limited by granting control over a specific subcontainer (site, domain, OU) within Active Directory and by granting them only specific rights over objects in that container. The Help Desk group, for example, can be given `reset password` rights for several OUs of user accounts without giving them `reset password` rights for accounts that are members of domain or local computer administrative groups.

The process is simple because a wizard is provided; however, it may be difficult to obtain exactly the results required. Delegation is accomplished by assigning groups permissions on Active Directory objects. It may be difficult to determine which objects to grant which permissions to because there are almost infinite combinations of objects and permissions that can be assigned, and it is difficult to determine exactly which of the ACLs to select to grant a specific privilege.

Distributed administrative authority is not a good idea if you do not have clear goals in mind and if some required information is difficult to ascertain. There are, however, some well-defined tasks, such as complete control over user accounts in a target OU or password reset, that can and should be delegated. Additional, less well-known tasks can be delegated after research and testing.

If the role the user needs to fill can be defined, and the ACLs on Active Directory objects that need to be set are well defined, the Delegation of Control Wizard can be used to perform the delegation. A small selection of common roles and tasks is defined by the wizard, and it also allows selection from the available ACLs on a selected container. The following step-by-step procedures detail how to use the wizard to assign administrative roles and privileges. Two procedures are provided. First, the ability to easily select predefined tasks is listed. Then an example of a common use of delegation of authority—the creation of a Help Desk role—is detailed.

TIP: How To Expose More Permissions

Not all permissions that can be assigned to objects are exposed via the wizard or through the ACL editor. A special file in the `%windir%\System32` folder, the dssec.dat file, contains a list of these permissions. The items are marked with the number 7. The file can be edited by changing the 7 to a 0, and the permission will be displayed in the wizard. However, this is not necessary in most cases and should only be done if a unique need to allow or deny a specific permission is required.

Granting Standard Tasks

1. Right-click on the SOM object in one of the Active Directory administrative tools and select `Delegate Control` from the context menu. Then click `Next`.

2. Click `Add` and use the Select Users, Computers, or Groups dialog box to add the user or group who will be given the delegated authority; then click `Next`, as shown in Figure 7-17.

3. Select the `Tasks to Delegate`, as shown in Figure 7-18, and then click `Next`. Tasks that can be delegated are listed in Table 7-7.

4. Review the wizard results and click `Finish`.

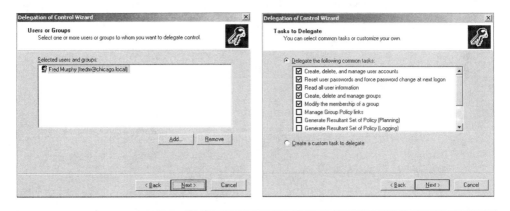

Figure 7-17   Add the users and groups who will have this authority.

Figure 7-18   Select tasks to delegate.

Table 7-7   Standard Tasks

Task	Possible Delegation Target
Create, delete, and manage user accounts	OU Administrator
Reset user passwords and force password change at next logon	Help Desk
Read all user information	Audit
Create, delete, and manage groups	OU Administrator

Table 7-7   Standard Tasks Continued

Task	Possible Delegation Target
Modify the membership of a group	OU Administrator, Group Administrator
Manage Group Policy Links	OU Administrator
Generate Resultant Set of Policy (Planning)	OU Administrator, Group Policy Designer
Generate Resultant Set of Policy (Logging)	Group Policy Designer, OU Administrator
Create, delete, and manage inetOrgPerson accounts	OU Administrator
Reset inetOrgPerson passwords and force password change at next logon	Help Desk
Read all inetOrgPerson information	Audit

Developing the Help Desk Role

When the task that must be delegated is not preconfigured, custom tasks can be created for any role. The role of help desk operator requires a unique assortment of privileges and rights that are defined by an organization's policy. Within the organization, specific groups of computers and users may be managed and assisted by placing their accounts in OUs and then delegating administrative rights over objects in these OUs to a custom Windows group. To create the role, follow these steps:

- Create the custom user group for Help Desk.
- Determine which objects, such as users and computers, the Help Desk group should control.
- Determine which permissions on these objects should be granted.
- Use the Delegation of Control Wizard to assign these permissions to the Help Desk group.
- Add Help Desk employee user accounts to the Help Desk group.

The following instructions provide an example of how to assign a common Help Desk task. To complete the Help Desk role, assign all of the permissions required by your organization.

1. Right-click on the OU in Active Directory Users and Computers and select Delegate Control from the context menu.
2. Click Next on the Wizard Welcome page.
3. Click Add and use the Select Users, Computers, or Groups dialog box to add the Help Desk group; then click Next.
4. Select the Create a custom task to delegate button and then click Next.
5. Select Only the following objects in the folder and then select User objects, as shown in Figure 7-19. (If you want to give the group granular control over multiple objects, you must use the wizard multiple times because each object has unique and general properties.) Then click Next.
6. On the Permissions Page under Show these permissions, select Property-specific.
7. Select specific permissions from the permission window; as shown in Figure 7-20, the Reset Password permission has been selected.

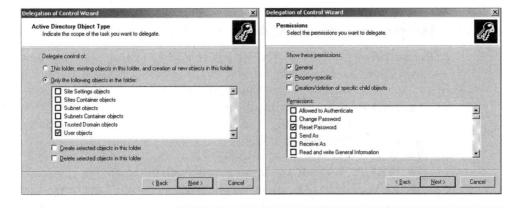

Figure 7-19 Custom delegation of tasks requires that you select the objects you will delegate some control over.

Figure 7-20 The Reset Password task is one that can be easily delegated.

Understanding Active Directory ACLs

When the Delegation of Control wizard is used to assign tasks to users and groups, it does so by assigning ACLs to objects in the Active Directory. The permissions can also be assigned directly. Just as access control lists on files, folders, printers, and registry keys must be understood before you can appropriately apply them, you should understand Active Directory permissions, or rights, before attempting to apply them. Unfortunately, it's not an easy task. Object permissions are different from file or registry permissions, and each object within the Active Directory also has its own set of permissions based on the unique properties or attributes of the object. There are so many unique permissions that it would be nearly impossible to list all of them, and it would be impossible for mere mortals to remember what each one of them means by itself, let alone what they might mean if granted on a specific object or if used in combination with other permissions.

However, it is possible to define the types of permissions that it is possible to set and in that way at least obtain an introduction into the miasma that is object rights in Active Directory. To do so, first examine standard and extended rights as they can be programmatically defined, and then match these rights with the specific permissions displayed through the Delegation of Control Wizard and through the ACL editor.

Standard and Extended Rights

Standard rights are those generic rights that can be applied to every object. These include the following:

- **DELETE**—Delete the object.
- **READ_CONTROL**—Read data from the security descriptor, but not the SACL.
- **WRITE_DAC**—Modify the DACL.
- **WRITE_OWNER**—Assume ownership of the object.
- **SYNCHRONIZE**—Use the object for synchronization. A thread can wait until the object is in the signaled state.
- **ACCESS_SYSTEM_SECURITY**—Read or set the SACL.
- **GENERIC_READ**—Read permissions and all properties on the object, and list the object name if the parent container is listed. Alternatively if this object is a container, list its contents.
- **GENERIC_WRITE**—Read permissions, write properties, and perform validated writes to the object.
- **GENERIC_EXECUTE**—Read permissions and list contents of a container object.
- **GENERIC_ALL**—Create or delete children, delete subtree, read and write properties, examine children and the object, add and remove object from the directory, and read or write an extended right.

- **DS_CREATE_CHILD**—Create children. The ACE Object-Type member can contain a GUID, which IDs the type of child object that can be created. If there is no GUID in the Object-Type, all child object types can be created.
- **DS_DELETE_CHILD**—Delete children of the object. The ACE ObjectType member can contain a GUID, which identifies the type of child object that can be deleted. If there is no GUID in the ObjectType, all child object types can be deleted.
- **ACTRL_DS_LIST**—The right to list children of this object. For more information about this right, see Controlling Object Visibility.
- **DS_SELF**—Perform an operation controlled by validated write access right. The ACE member ObjectType can contain a GUID identifying the validated write. If noGUID is in the ObjectType, all validated write operations possible for this object can be performed.
- **DS_READ_PROP**—Read the object properties. A property set or property can be defined by a GUID in the ObjectType member of the ACE. If no GUID is present, all object properties can be read.
- **ADS_RIGHT_DS_WRITE_PROP**—Write object properties. A property set or property can be defined by a GUID in the ObjectType member of the ACE. If no GUID is present, all object properties can be written.
- **DS_DELETE_TREE**—Delete all children of this object. (Permissions on the children do not matter; that is, a user with this right can delete a child object even if the child object denies deletion.)
- **DS_LIST_OBJECT**—List this object. Without this right or the ACTRL_DS_LIST right, the object is hidden from the user. However, this right is ignored if the dsHeuristics property is not set or set so that its third character is "0."
- **DS_CONTROL_ACCESS**—Perform an operation that is controlled by an extended access right. The ObjectType member of the ACE may contain a GUID that identifies the extended right. If it does not, all of the extended right operations that are associated with the object can be performed.

Extended rights are those rights that are specific to only some objects within the Active Directory. This list is very long; however, Table 7-8 defines a few of the extended rights specific to Windows Server 2003.

Table 7-8   Extended Rights Examples

Rights Object(s)	Objects to Which Right Applies	Explanation
Allowed to authenticate	inetOrgPerson	inetOrgPerson is an alternative user object that is required for compatibility with other directory structures and applications developed to use those structures.
Allowed to authenticate	User or group	This is a new permission that is explained in more detail in Chapter 9.
Create inbound forest trust	User or group	The ability to create an inbound-only trust between forests.
Enable per user reversibly encrypted password	User or computer	Allows the user to enable or disable the Reversible Encrypted Password setting for a user or computer account.
Generate RSoP logging	OU or Domain	Grants the right to generate resultant set of policy logging of the specific domain or OU.
Generate RSoP Planning	OU or Domain	Grants the right to generate resultant set of policy planning on the specific domain or OU.
Migrate SID-History	User or group	Migrate SID-history without administrator privileges.
Refresh Group Cache	Domain	In Windows Server 2003, it is possible to cache group membership for universal groups. This means that a remote branch office need not have access to a GC. Instead, universal group membership is cached local on a domain controller. To update the cache on demand, this privilege is necessary.

Rights Object(s)	Objects to Which Right Applies	Explanation
Controlling Object Visibility	AD container	In normal operation, you can hide the contents of an Active Directory container by denying the ACTRL_DS_LIST right. The user who is denied this right can see the container but cannot list or bind to any of the objects within the container. You can allow the user to see selected objects in the container while hiding others by putting the Active Directory into list object mode. Doing so will substantially decrease performance because a larger number of access check calls must be made to determine if an object should be visible.

Matching Rights to Delegation of Control Selections

When the Delegation of Control Wizard is used to build a custom task to delegate, there are three decisions to make. First, you must decide which group of users to delegate the task to. Second, you must decide whether the task will give the right to manage all of the objects in the container or only certain objects within the contain. Finally, you must decide which permissions, or rights, to delegate.

The Permissions page of the wizard, as shown in Figure 7-21, is used. Permissions are divided into three types: General, Property-specific or Creation/deletion of specific child objects. A detailed list of permissions is then available in the Permissions box on the page depending on this choice. For example, if only the General box is checked, the generic permission, Read, can be selected. However, this permission is actually composed of many standard object rights. If the Property-specific box is checked, the ability to read specific object attributes is exposed. Instead of granting the generic right to Read, you may grant only the right to read specific object attributes. The available permissions displayed in the wizard depend on the choices made about objects and permission types.

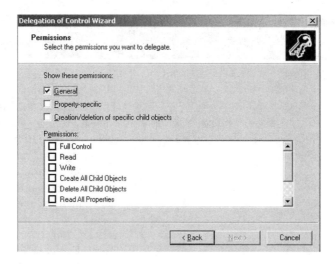

Figure 7-21   The choice of permission type determines which standard rights are available for assignment.

Generic Permissions

Generic permissions include categories such as Full Control, Read, Create All Child Objects, and so forth. Each category is composed of specific permissions, and choosing the generic permission gives access to those included permissions. For example, if the generic category is chosen, two related "read" permissions are exposed: Read and Read All Properties. Read is the GENERIC_READ permission and is composed of READ_CONTROL, DS_READ_PROP, ACTRL_DS_LIST, and DS_LIST_OBJECT. Read All Properties is the reduced set: DS_READ_PROP and DS_LIST_OBJECT.

Property-Specific Permissions

Property-specific permissions expose the properties of the general categories. For example, the read and write permissions that are specific to the type of objects in the selected container will be displayed. If the wizard is run at the OU level, this results in a long list of read and write permissions, including Read street, Read cn, Read adminDisplayName, Read Managedby, and so forth. If another container such as the domain or site container is chosen, a different list may be available. In addition, if Active Directory-aware applications are installed, and they have modified the Active Directory schema, then additional permissions will be available. Instead of granting Read permission on a user object, you might grant Read permission on specific user object properties.

If the choice of objects is narrow, then in addition to generic rights, extended rights are exposed in the property-specific permissions area, and they can also be assigned using the Delegation of Control Wizard. An example of a useful extended right is `Reset password`. This extended right was examined in the "Developing the Help Desk Role" section earlier in this chapter.

NOTE: Permission Management via ACLs

Granular permissions can be easily selected in the GUI. How are they managed in the ACLs? The `DS_READ_PROP` right is a standard right applicable to AD objects. This right includes an ObjectType member. ObjectType is used to identify which property the `DS_READ_PROP` right applies to. To designate a specific property, a unique GUID is entered in ObjectType. When no GUID is present, the `DS_READ_PROP` right applies to all object properties—they can all be read. When individual property permissions are selected in the wizard, their GUIDs are included in the ObjectType member of the Access Control Entry (ACE) of the ACL. When the object is accessed, only those properties will be available for reading.

Creation/Deletion of Specific Child Objects

Generic `write` and `child object creation and deletion` rights are exposed by selecting `General`. Specific `write` and `child object creation and deletion` permissions are exposed from the `Property-specific` and `Creation/deletion of specific child objects` selections, respectively.

Removing Rights Granted by the Wizard

Each object within the OU has its own set of permissions. They can be set quite easily by using the Delegation of Control Wizard. However, there is no "reverse" wizard. To remove permissions granted with the wizard, you must edit the object properties directly.

To delete permissions granted by the Delegation of Control Wizard or to assign or modify them directly, the ACL Object Editor or the new dsrevoke utility is used. To use the Object Editor, open the Security property page of the OU on which the wizard was run. In the ACL editor, delegated permissions are often "special permissions." Click the `Advanced` button as shown in Figure 7-22. On the Advanced security page, select a user or group and click `Edit` to see the special permission applied to this group. Figure 7-23 displays the `Reset Password` permission as assigned in the Help Desk role section. To remove the delegation, remove the permission.

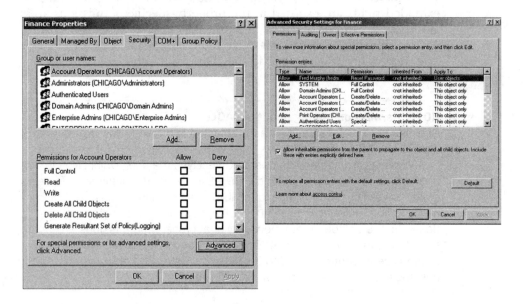

Figure 7-22   To remove delegated permissions, use the Security property page.

Figure 7-23   Clicking the Edit button on the Advanced security property page for a specific user reveals the specific properties selected.

Dsrevoke.exe is a new tool that can be downloaded from the Microsoft site and used to view all of the Active Directory permissions assigned to a user or group. It can also be used to revoke these permissions. This tool provides a service that was missing from Windows 2000 and Window Server 2003. To use the tool to display all permissions for a user or group on an OU, use the following command:

```
Dsrevoke /report domainname\usergroupname
```

To use dsrevoke to remove these permissions, use the following command line:

```
Dsrevoke /revoke domainname\username
```

Dsrevoke can be downloaded from http://www.microsoft.com/downloads/details.aspx?familyid=77744807-c403-4bda-b0e4-c2093b8d6383&displaylang=en.

NOTE: Best Practices for Delegation
Download "Best Practices for Delegating Active Directory Administration"
(http://www.microsoft.com/downloads/details.aspx?FamilyID=631747a3
-79e1-48fa-9730-dae7c0a1d6d3&displaylang=en). It provides comprehensive instructions on setting up and using delegation.

Group Policy Tools

Group Policy Editor (GPE) is the native Windows tool for managing
Group Policy. The GPE snap-in can be added to an MMC console and is
opened when a GPO is created or modified from the Group Policy property pages of a container in Active Directory Users and Computers. The
GPE is easy to use and provides basic utility. However, it does not provide many features that are essential for managing Group Policy. You
cannot tell, for example, the impact of a combination of multiple GPOs
on a specific workstation, server, or user. You cannot copy the GPO or
export it and use it in another domain. You cannot even print the policy.
To examine the settings in the policy, you must browse through the policy, opening many subcontainers to determine if anything in them is set.

A new tool, the Group Policy Management Console (GPMC), fills in
these holes. The tool, which can be downloaded by licensed owners of
Windows Server 2003, can be used to manage Group Policy in a Windows 2000 domain. GPMC can only be run on a Windows XP Professional or Windows Server 2003 computer. While it is not necessary to
obtain the tool to create and use GPOs, without the tool, it is much more
difficult to manage Group Policy.

NOTE: GPMC for Windows 2000 Domains
Although you can manage a Windows 2000 domain with GPMC, some fea-
tures of GPMC are only available with Windows Server 2003 and Windows
XP clients.

After GPMC is installed on a DC, attempting to create or edit a GPO
using the Group Policy property page of an object will not work. Instead,
doing so will provide a link, as shown in Figure 7-24, to GPMC, instead
of access to the GPE. When GPMC is used to manage Group Policy and
Edit is selected from a context menu, the Group Policy Editor is loaded.

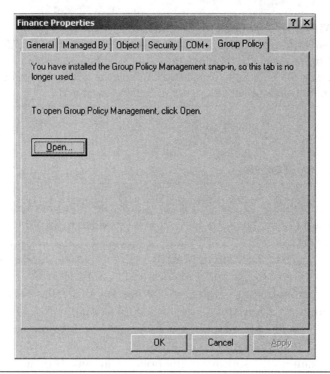

Figure 7-24 The GPMC replaces the Group Policy Page. You can still invoke the
Group Policy Editor from the GPC, but options that affect policy
implementation are configured using GPMC.

Group Policy Editor

If you have installed GPMC, you will still use GPE to edit a GPO. However, if you installed GPMC, some features of GPE will be managed in
the GPMC interface. Prior to installation of GPMC, GPE can be used to
do the following:

■ Create a GPO and edit its features
■ Manage a GPO inheritance
■ Filter a GPO application

After GPMC is installed, only GPO editing is done using the GPE.

Creating, Linking, and Editing GPOs

To create a GPO, you will edit a blank template until it contains the desired settings. For the settings to be applied, the GPO must be linked to a SOM. GPO creation and linking are two separate actions. It is possible to have a GPO that is not linked to SOM, and it is possible to link a GPO to many SOMs. Prior to the installation of GPMC, a new GPO is created using the property pages of a SOM and is linked automatically to that SOM. When GPMC is used, a GPO *may* be created and linked to a SOM using one operation or two.

To create a new GPO, follow these steps:

1. Select the Group Policy tab, as shown in Figure 7-25.
2. Click New.
3. Enter a name for the new GPO and click OK.
4. To edit the GPO, select the new policy and click Edit.
5. Edit the policy by selecting a container and navigating to the specific option. Then open the item from the details pane, as shown in Figure 7-26.
6. When the edit is complete, close the GPO by closing the policy windows.

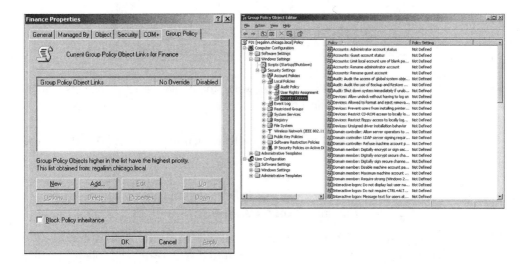

Figure 7-25   New GPOs are created using the New button.

Figure 7-26   The entire policy is listed for viewing or editing.

An existing policy can be edited by opening it from the Group Policy property page of the SOM, or it can be loaded in an MMC console and edited. To edit a GPO in a console, follow these steps:

1. Open the console by using the `Add/Remove Snapins` choice from the `File` menu of an empty console and selecting `Group Policy Object Editor`.
2. On the Welcome page of the wizard, use the `Browse` button to locate the policy to edit, as shown in Figure 7-27, and then click `OK`.

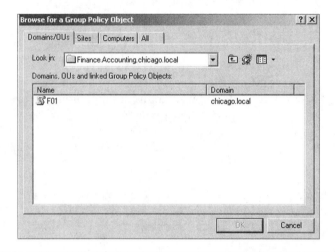

Figure 7-27   Select the policy to edit by browsing the Active Directory objects where the policy can be linked.

3. Click `Close`; then click `OK` to return to the console and edit the policy.

Controlling GPO Inheritance Using GPE

The Active Directory structure is hierarchical, and GPOs are processed according to where they are linked in that structure. The following rules of inheritance apply:

- GPOs can be linked to sites, domains, and parent and child OUs.
- GPOs are inherited by users and computers whose accounts reside either directly in a container or in a child container of these objects.

- All of the security settings from all GPOs are applied cumulatively, unless there is a conflict.
- A conflict is resolved by allowing the last setting to overwrite all previous settings. For example, if the DNS Server service is disabled in a GPO linked to the domain but is set to start automatically in a GPO linked to the OU within which a server account is located, the server, if DNS has been installed, will be able to start the DNS service successfully. A server whose account may be elsewhere in the domain (where no other GPO makes a change) will not be able to start the DNS service, even if the service is installed.

Modifying this standard behavior is sometimes necessary. GPOs in Windows 2000 and Windows Server 2003 domains can be marked to block the inheritance of other GPOs to prevent a GPO from overriding settings and allow machine settings to be reapplied over individual settings. Best practices require that these techniques are applied sparingly. Many problems with Group Policy processing are discovered not to be problems at all. Instead, they are traced back to the unwise, unauthorized, or simply "set and forget" usage of these properties.

Block Inheritance

The Block Inheritance property is used to prevent inheritance of a GPO. The configuration and management of computer and user accounts may be so critical that it is necessary to block potential changes from a GPO linked to an object above. For example, to manage users and computers in an OU, a GPO may be created and configured to apply security and other configuration settings appropriate for these accounts. Settings configured in the GPO linked to the OU will automatically override any settings configured in GPOs linked at the domain or site level. However, if some settings are not configured at the OU level and are configured at the domain or site level, the settings will be inherited by the OU. There are hundreds of settings, and it is possible for an inherited setting to aversely impact users and computers. To prevent this from happening, two things can be done. First, all non-policy configured settings can be set so that they match the default settings for users and computers in the OU. Second, the `Block Inheritance` setting can be selected, which will block inherited settings.

To set block inheritance, follow these steps:

1. Select the `Group Policy` property page from the SOM's property pages.
2. Select the `Block Policy inheritance` check box, as shown in Figure 7-28.

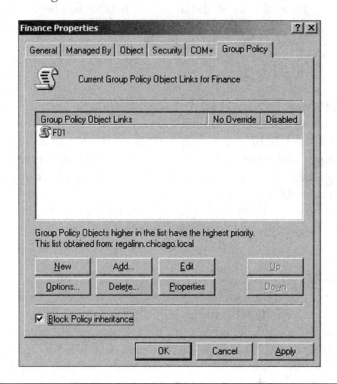

Figure 7-28 Block Inheritance can be set to prevent the application of a GPO from a parent object.

3. Click OK.

No Override

The No Override or, as it is called in GPMC, Enforcement property ensures that a `Block Inheritance` setting has no effect. In an environment where the responsibility for GPOs is delegated, it is possible that the administrator of an OU might inadvertently or maliciously use Block Inheritance and therefore thwart the organization's security policy. The security policy specified in a domain or parent OU is blocked when

`Block Inheritance` is set. It is also possible that some policy settings in a GPO are so critical that it is desirable to ensure that no present or future GPO will override them. In either case, setting the No Override/Enforcement property of a GPO will ensure that the GPO settings of a parent object are inherited. If Enforcement is set on an inherited GPO, and `Block Inheritance` is set on a local GPO, then Enforcement will win.

To set No Override, follow these steps:

1. Open the Group Policy property page of the SOM.
2. Double-click on the policy in the `Enforce` column of the GPO.
3. Click `Close`.

Loopback

The loopback property is used to reapply the user portion of the GPO applied to the computer account after all GPOs have been applied. This option may be required when it is desirable that a specific security policy is applied, no matter which user logs on to the computer. This is a good policy for kiosks or other public computers where both employees and non-employees may log on. Ordinarily, when a user logs on, he inherits user settings from each GPO that is applicable to his account. His environment will be configured exactly the same way, no matter which workstation he uses, as long as policy can be obtained and as long as the computer supports the settings in the policy. This user-based consistency is desirable in most circumstances. However, there may be a situation in which it is preferred that every user is treated the same or a situation where it would be undesirable if the elevated privileges of administrators or other privileged users was applied. Instead, it must be ensured that no matter who the user is, he has limited access and privileges on the specific system or network. Situations where this is important are those where a specific computer(s) is used for a unique purpose. Examples of kiosks are computers in a mall used for gift selection, a workstation on a plant floor used for product location, a lobby kiosk that provides public information, an Internet browsing station at a conference, a computer in a learning lab, and so on. You can imagine, for example, what might happen if an unprotected public system was used by a domain admin, who then left it without logging off. If the next user is able to access the system before the logon times out, this user may now have administrative privileges on the network. He certainly has them on the current computer. To ensure that this type of vulnerability does not occur, use loopback processing.

Unintended Consequences

During a recent consultation, the network administrator of a school complained that his Group Policy computer lockdown efforts were not being applied to workstations in the student labs. He reported that students had still been able to access and change operating system features and change registry settings that should have been blocked by Group Policy.

Using GPMC, I quickly established that the Group Policy should have worked as he expected. We visited the lab, and I logged on using a student account and was unable to make any of the changes he said the students could. I suspected that either students had administrator account credentials or perhaps an administrator had visited the lab and not logged off. The school did not have auditing enabled for workstations in the lab.

As we were returning to his office where I intended to propose loopback and auditing, the administrator was paged. He then proceeded to log on to a lab computer and use it to complete a request. His pager went off again, and he started to leave the lab without logging off. I called his attention to it, logged him off, and followed. Later I was able to explain loopback and my opinion on doing administrative work from a student lab (you shouldn't). It turned out that lab supervisors had administrative privileges and did use student computers. In the hectic atmosphere of the lab, they often forgot to log off, or they logged on and allowed students to use their account to install software. The student access problem was solved with a change in procedures, which now specify that student computer lab computers must be remotely administered, and the implementation of a loopback policy.

Loopback processing has two modes: merge and replace. In practical application, however, few loopback situations require the merge mode. In the merge mode, the user's settings are kept, but the computer policy user settings are applied. Since they are applied last, if there is any conflict, the computer policy settings will win; however, any configuration not set by the loopback policy will remain. Replace mode ensures that none of the user's settings is available.

To set loopback replace mode, follow these steps:

1. Open the GPO for editing.
2. Navigate to Computer, Administrative Templates, System, Group Policy, and double-click to open the User Group Policy Loopback Processing Mode in the details pane.
3. Select Enabled.
4. Use the drop-down box to select Replace, as shown in Figure 7-29.

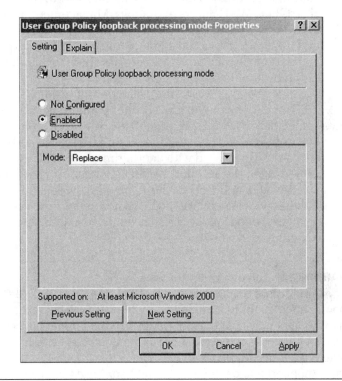

Figure 7-29   Loopback is configured by using GPO Administrative Templates.

5. Click OK; then click Close.

Filtering by Groups

The Security property page of a GPO defines which groups receive the policy. Those groups given the Read permission and the Apply Group Policy permission will be assigned the policy. By default, the Authenticated Users group is assigned these permissions. This means that the

GPO will be read and applied to all accounts that exist in the SOM where the policy is linked. It is possible, however, to manipulate the application of a GPO by adding specific groups to the security page and either giving them the `Allow` or `Deny Apply Group Policy` permission. Best practices recommend that if you need to filter by groups, you should add all groups that should receive the policy and remove the Authenticated Users group. By default, a group that is not given this permission will not receive the policy.

Windows Server 2003 introduces another way to modify the application of a GPO: WMI filters. Windows Management Instrumentation (WMI) is a way to manage Windows computers. WMI filters on GPOs are used to limit the application of the GPO to computer or user accounts that meet specific characteristics. Rather than filtering a GPO application by membership in a group, a dynamic group can be created. The dynamic group consists of a collection of accounts with a specific characteristic. For example, a WMI filter could select all computers that have a specific network card, or all users who work for a specific manager, and apply a GPO only to those computers or users. If a computer's network card was replaced with another model, or the user was assigned to a new manager, the accounts would no longer be a part of the dynamic group and would not receive the policy. Likewise, if a new computer received the specific network card, or a new employee was transferred to the manager's department, the accounts would become part of the dynamic group and would receive the policy.

WARNING: Watch out for WMI Errors
If an error occurs during the use of a WMI filter on a GPO, GPO processing may be affected. If the error is known, the GPO will be applied, although the WMI filter may not be used. However, if the error is unknown, the GPO may not be processed at all. More information can be found in the Knowledge Base article 814613 at http://support.microsoft.com/default.aspx?scid=kb;en-us;814613.

A Practical Use for WMI

Even though some environments do not use DHCP, disabling the DHCP client service is not recommended because the DHCP client service may also be used to automatically update DNS records. When the DHCP client service is disabled, DNS updating must be done manually. In a locked down environment, however, policy may require the disabling of all non-essential services. In one such environment, the decision was made to disable the DHCP client service and take the responsibility for manually updating any changes to the statically assigned DNS records. Everything worked just fine, until some new network cards were installed. Machines with these cards installed ceased to function on the network. They could not communicate with other computers. Re-enabling and starting the DHCP client service had no effect. After a reboot, however, they returned to full function. Because the computers were joined to a Windows Server 2003 domain, a WMI filter was created to ensure that computers with the offending network card receive a policy that enables the DHCP client service, while other computers do not. Because the filter works on a machine characteristic, there was no need to create a special OU of these machines, and when a computer received a change in network card, it was automatically detected, and the computer received the right policy.

Resultant Set of Policy

One of the problems with Group Policy in Windows 2000 is that it can be difficult to determine the actual results of a Group Policy implementation. It's difficult to keep straight the impact of multiple policies and the options that can impact inheritance. There is no native Windows 2000 tool to help do this. A Windows 2000 resource kit tool, gpresults, can be used to determine the outcome for a single user logged on to a specific workstation. In effect, it reads the policy applied. You must, however, log on as that user at that machine to use the tool. Afterward, you must analyze the text-based report and examine other information to determine the results. If you want a picture of policy at another machine or the effect of policy on the current machine but for a different user, the process must be repeated.

A second problem with Windows 2000 Group Policy is its inability to help in the design of a Group Policy architecture. Policies have to be created and assigned to real computers and users to confirm the results.

Using a new tool in Windows Server 2003 domains solves both of these problems. This tool is Resultant Set of Policy (RSoP). The tool can poll existing policies by using logging mode or planned policies by using planning mode and display the results. When logging mode is used, the effect of GPOs on a specific computer and user are evaluated by connecting to the computer. When planning mode is used, any combination of user and computer account location can be selected to test the effect of the GPOs that are linked to the location and the combinations of policies applied. Planning mode allows the determination of the "what if" effect of GPOs. Because no actual computer is accessed, planning mode can be used even before a computer is joined to a domain. All GPOs, including site, domain, and OU policies—may be reviewed, depending on the mode. (Local and site policy, for example, cannot be evaluated for a computer that does not yet exist because no local policy is established and there is no way to tell what site the computer might ultimately be located in.) RSoP uses the Common Information Management Object Model (CIMOM) database (the CIM-compliant object repository) through Windows Management Instrumentation.

RSoP queries are created using the Resultant Set of Policy Wizard, which is accessible as a snap-in loaded into an MMC, by right-clicking a site, domain, or OU object, and from the Group Policy Management Console. (Once GMPC is installed, the wizards supplied with GPMC are always used.) If the created query is saved, it can be accessed again to refresh or modify the query.

To create an RSoP planning mode query, follow these steps:

1. Open Active Directory Users and Computers.
2. Right-click the SOM, select `All Tasks`, and then select `Resultant Set of Policy (Planning Mode)` from the context menu. The `User and Computer Selection` page is populated with the SOM, as shown in Figure 7-30.

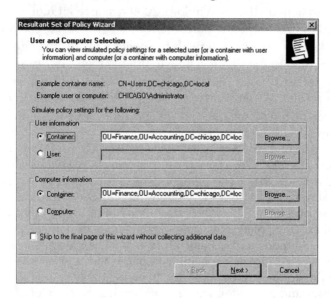

Figure 7-30   Confirm that the correct user and computer container, user, or computer account is selected.

3. Accept the selected container for user and computer accounts, and click Next.
4. If desired, select simulations of slow network connection or loopback processing.
5. Select the site and click Next.
6. Add or remove security groups to simulate user membership and click Next.
7. Select whether or not to assume that the user meets criteria for specific WMI filters and click Next.
8. Select whether or not to assume that the computer meets criteria for specific WMI filters and click Next.
9. Review selections.
10. Select a domain controller on which to process the simulation; then click Next.
11. Some time may elapse. Click Finish when the process is complete.
12. The Resultant Set of Policy is displayed in an MMC, as shown in Figure 7-31, and can be browsed to view the results.

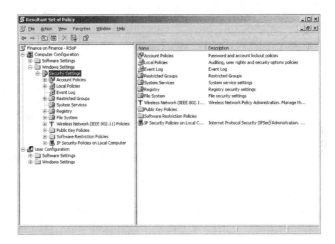

Figure 7-31   The RSoP Wizard displays results in an MMC, which can be saved for viewing and analysis and to be used to refresh or change the query.

RSoP planning and logging can be generated from an MMC to which the Resultant Set of Policy snap-in is added.

To do RSoP logging:

1. Add the snap-in to a console.
2. Select Generate RSoP Data from the Action menu.

3. On the welcome page of the wizard, select `Next`.
4. From the mode selection page, select `Logging mode`, as shown in Figure 7-32, and click `Next`.
5. Select the computer to generate data for. The computer must exist and be reachable.
6. Select whether to display computer and user settings or just user settings and click `Next`.
7. Select the user to display, as shown in Figure 7-33, or select not to display user results (display computer policy settings only) and click `Next`.
8. Review your selection and click `Next`. Click `Finish` when complete.

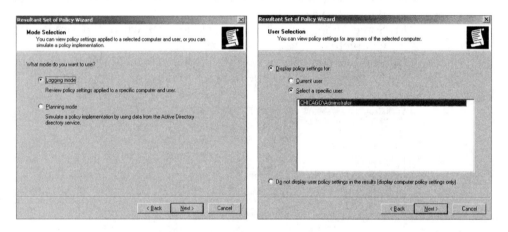

Figure 7-32   The RSoP snap-in can be used to generate planning or logging RSoP data.

Figure 7-33   Select the user for which to display the policy.

Group Policy Management Console

GPMC provides the answers for many Group Policy management issues and concerns, empowers the Group Policy administrator, and has the potential for eliminating the need for third-party products and for reducing staff requirements. GPMC provides all of the following:

- An easy-to-use GUI, making Group Policy easier to use

- Backup, restore, and copying of GPOs
- HTML reporting of only the GPO settings that are actually configured
- HTML reporting of Resultant Set of Policy (RSoP) data
- Simplified management of Group Policy security
- Import and export of GPOs and WMI filters
- Copy and paste of GPOs and WMI filters
- Scripting of policy tasks exposed within the tool (it does not include the ability to script settings within a GPO)
- The ability to administer Windows 2000 GPOs

GPMC can be used to manage Group Policy for multiple domains and multiple forests and is an effective Group Policy troubleshooting tool. These capabilities will be described and illustrated in Chapters 8 and 10, respectively. This chapter will look at using GPMC in a single Windows Server 2003 domain.

Installing and Configuring GPMC

GPMC is not a native Windows Server 2003 utility. It was released after Windows Server 2003 shipped, but it is available as a free download. The console can be downloaded from http://www.microsoft.com/downloads/details.aspx?FamilyId=F39E9D60-7E41-4947-82F5-3330F37ADFEB&displaylang=en.

While GPMC can be used to manage Windows 2000, Windows XP Professional, and Windows Server 2003 computers, it must be installed on a Windows XP Professional or Windows Server 2003 computer. If Windows XP is used, it must have the following:

- Service Pack 1
- The Microsoft .NET Framework
- The post SP1 hotfix (QFE 326469), which updates gpedit.dll to version 5.12600.1186, which is required by GPMC

To install GPMC, follow these steps:

1. Double-click the gpmc.msi package and then click Next.
2. Read and accept the End User License Agreement (EULA). Note that the license specifies that you must have a valid license for Windows Server 2003 to run the utility. Click Next.

3. If installing on Windows XP, if the gpedit.dll has not been updated, you will be prompted to install post SP1 hotfix 326469. The hotfix is delivered with the download and can be installed at this time.

4. Click Close to complete the installation.

To open the GPMC console, you can do one of the following:

- Click Start, click Run, type GPMC.msc, and click OK.
- Use the Group Policy Management shortcut from Administrative Tools.
- Open GPMC from the property pages of sites, domains, and OUs.
- Create a custom GPMC console by adding the Group Policy Management snap-in to an MMC.

First Looks

When first loaded, the GPMC console, as shown in Figure 7-34, displays the forest in which the account used to run the utility exists. Additional forests can be loaded and managed if the account has authority to manage Group Policy within those forests. Each forest will have three or four containers: Domains, Sites, Group Policy Modeling, and Group Policy Results. (The Group Policy Modeling node will not be present in a pure Windows 2000 forest.)

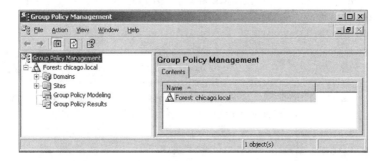

Figure 7-34   GPMC is a tool that provides superb management of Group Policy.

The Domains and Sites containers have subnodes. Each domain in the forest is represented below the domain node, while each site is represented below the site node. Group Policy Modeling and Group Policy Results work like the RSoP logging and planning modes, respectively.

Expanding a domain container displays a policy-based view of Active Directory and lists additional Group Policy elements. All GPOs that are linked to the domain can be reviewed from the Group Policy Objects container, or by expanding the Domains or OU containers. WMI filters are also listed.

The Group Policy Objects container holds the GPOs, whereas the SOMs (Domains, OU, Sites) contain only the links from that SOM to the GPOs. GPOs can be linked to more than one SOM. This fact is graphically displayed. The detail pane of a selected SOM displays three tabs, as shown in Figure 7-35. In the figure, below each SOM, links are displayed as a shortcut, while in the Group Policy Objects container, they are shown as little scrolls without the shortcut arrow. This graphical illustration shows that the GPO exists separately from any container (SOM). This distinction is true in Windows 2000 and in Windows Server 2003, but in Windows 2000, the GUI does not aid in its understanding and instead gives the false impression that a GPO does not exist separately from a container. It's also important to understand that GPO-related operations, such as backup and copy, must be performed from the GPO, not from the link.

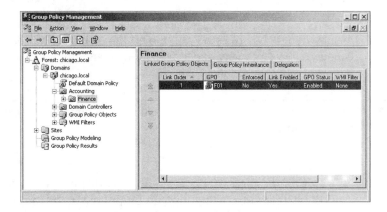

Figure 7-35   Each SOM is defined by several property pages.

In addition to the Linked Group Policy Objects tab, the Group Policy Inheritance tab, as shown in Figure 7-36, displays a list of GPOs that are inherited from parent containers by the SOM in the order of their application (precedence). The list does not include any Site policies. Read the list from the bottom up to see the order in which the policies are applied. In the figure, the default domain policy is applied, and then the F01 policy. Settings in the F01 policy will have precedence over most settings in the default domain policy. (Exceptions are the domain Account policy and User rights on the domain policies, as outlined earlier.)

The `Delegation` tab, as shown in Figure 7-37, details the delegated administrative permissions on the SOM. The drop-down list is used to view the Link GPOs, perform group policy modeling analysis, and read group policy results data permissions. Note that both inherited and explicit permissions are listed. To view delegated permissions at the GPO level, you must examine the property pages of the GPO.

GPO-specific properties can be examined by double-clicking on the GPO. `Scope`, `Details`, `Settings`, and `Delegation` tabs are available.

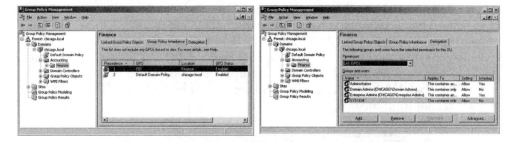

Figure 7-36   All inherited GPOs are listed with the exception of Site policies because these may vary depending on the computer and user account and what site they are in.

Figure 7-37   Delegated permissions are listed. You must change the drop-down list to view different permissions.

- `Scope` is detailed in Figure 7-38 and displays what SOMs the GPO is linked to; which users, computers, and groups the GPO will apply to; and which WMI filter the GPO is linked to.
- The `Details` tab of a GPO provides information relative to the GPO, including whether or not the user or computer portions of the GPO are enabled.
- The `Settings` tab displays only the settings configured for this GPO.
- The `Delegation` tab lists the explicit permissions on this GPO and will include the users, computers, and groups to which the GPO will apply.

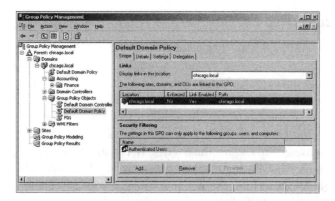

Figure 7-38 The Scope pane is used to determine where the GPO is linked.

GPMC Options

Several options are available to customize how GPMC works. The following options can be selected from the View, Options menu of the GPMC.

- **Options**—Customizes the location of columns for some tables.
- **Reporting**—Sets the location of .adm files used for reporting. The default search path for .adm files is the system folder and then the sysvol folder of the GPO. You can, however, override this option to provide a custom location.
- **General**—Enables or disables several options:
  - Enable or disable trust detection—By default, a two-way trust with a forest is required to add the forest to GPMC. You can remove this distinction, allow connection, and work with a one-way forest-trust, or use the Stored User Names and Passwords feature for Windows XP and Windows Server 2003 to enable access to untrusted forests.
  - Enable or disable confirmation of GPO or GPO link distinction.
  - Display domain controller name beside domain name.

Basic Operations

Creating, editing, testing, protecting, reporting, backup/restore, and copy/paste are all basic Group Policy management processes available via GPMC. Other operations, such as setting the DC to use for Group Policy, can also be managed from the console.

Setting the DC to Use for Group Policy Development

By default, GPMC, like its predecessor the Group Policy Editor, will default to using the primary domain controller emulator DC in the domain to access Group Policy information. It is possible to use another DC as the location for storage of the GPO, but arbitrary DC selection is not a good idea. A policy should be established that selects and maintains a specific DC as the GPO location for all GPOs that can be created by the same group of administrators. If Group Policy management is delegated and distributed, such as on an OU-by-OU basis, then selection of a single DC is of less importance. The reason for limiting the DCs is that the use of multiple DCs can cause issues due to replication. If two different administrators are editing the same GPO, but on different DCs, what will be the result? It is possible that the GPOs will become out of synch, or that policy written by one administrator will be overwritten by another. The end result is that policy may be different than intended. Good reasons for using multiple DCs are as follows:

- The administrator in charge of Group Policy for a specific domain, OU, or site is not physically present in the location where the default or preselected GPO management DC resides. In this case, a WAN connection would be required for him to modify GPOs. To avoid this, a local DC can be selected for his use. Administrators at other physical locations should not select different DCs if they also are privileged to modify Group Policy for that domain.
- If the majority of the users and computers affected by the policy are in a location different from the default DC used for GPO management, a DC at their location as the configuration point for modification of GPOs that affect them may be a good choice. If it is, replication latency will be less of a factor for these users. Because policy is available locally, users will be more likely to quickly receive policy changes. This can be especially important if the changes are to security settings.

■ Management of Group Policy is delegated and distributed. In this case, all domain-linked GPOs are created and managed on a single DC, but GPOs linked to a specific OU may be created on different DCs. Again, the arbitrary selection of a new DC for each OU would be pointless. However, there may be reasons, such as the two preceding examples, that would make this desirable. It may also be used when it is desirable to limit administrative access to specific domain controllers; in this case, ensuring that administrative authority does not extend to other DCs can be accomplished by allowing the management of GPOs on a DC. However, you should be cautious in deploying this solution because any administrative function that can modify replicated data on a single DC will in essence modify all other DCs due to replication. In addition, if not done carefully, restricting access to specific DCs can cause issues for users in normal day-to-day operations.

To select the domain controller to use:

1. Open GPMC, right-click the domain, and select `Change Domain Controller` from the context menu.

OR

Right-click the site to set the domain controller to be used for site policies.

2. In the Change Domain Controller dialog box, as shown in Figure 7-39, select from the following choices:

■ `The domain controller with the Operations Master token for the PDC emulator`—The default.

■ `Any available domain controller`—The first domain controller that responds to GPMC will be used.

■ `Any available domain controller running Windows Server 2003 or later`—This is important if you want to do Group Policy modeling.

■ `This domain controller`—Select a specific DC from the provided list. If selecting a domain controller to be used for a site GPO, you can also select which domain the DC should be from.

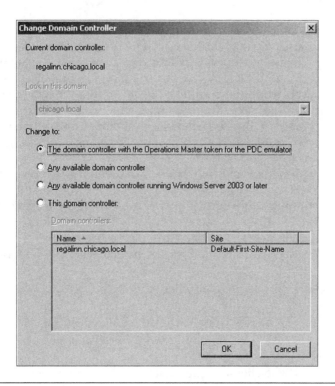

Figure 7-39 A DC can be specified for use to modify a GPO.

NOTE: Site GPO Storage
Because a site can contain domain controllers from many domains, which DC will be used to store a site GPO? By default, the PDC emulator in the domain of the administrator who created it is used. With GPMC, you can select the domain controller to be used for this purpose.

Creating a GPO Using GPMC

A GPO can be created using GPMC in several ways. Once the GPO is created, the Group Policy Object Editor is used to define the settings for that GPO. The GPE tool is the same tool used in Windows 2000 and in Windows Server 2003 prior to installing GPMC.

The choices for creating a GPO using GPMC are as follows:

- Right-click on any domain or OU and choose Create and Link a GPO here from the context menu. This operation creates the GPO and links it to the domain or OU selected.
- Use a script.
- Right-click the Group Policy Objects node in any domain and click New. A new, unlinked GPO is created.

To edit the settings in any GPO, right-click the GPO and select Edit.

Scoping GPOs

Determining and assigning the computer and user accounts that will be impacted by a GPO is called *scoping the GPO*. To scope a GPO, follow these steps:

- Link the GPO to a domain, site, or OU by doing one of the following:
  - Create a GPO by right-clicking on a SOM and choosing Create and Link a GPO here.
  - Link an existing GPO to a SOM by right-clicking the site, domain, or OU node and choosing Link an existing GPO here. (This is like choosing the Add button in the Group Policy user interface prior to installing GPMC.)
  - Drag a GPO from the Group Policy Object node to an OU in the same domain.
- Use security filtering on the GPO. Prior to GPMC, this required using the ACL editor to set the Read and Apply Group Policy permissions for specific users and groups. With GPMC, the user or group is added to the Scope tab for the GPO or GPO link. This automatically sets the Read Group Policy permission. However, should you want to deny these permissions, you must use the ACL editor.
- Use a WMI filter on the GPO. WMI filters dynamically determine the scope of GPOs based on attributes. The scope of a GPO consists of the users and computers it will be applied to. WMI client-side support is only available for Windows XP Professional and Windows Server 2003. (Windows 2000 will ignore WMI filters.) The filter is always evaluated on the client computer. This means that each client computer will examine the WMI filter to see if it applies. Be sparing with the application of WMI filters because they can mean extended processing time.

GPMC Reporting

Documenting a GPO without GPMC is a tedious manual chore. GPMC provides extensive HTML reporting. Reports can be viewed and printed. Representative reports are as follows:

- Settings in GPO—Click the `Settings` tab of the GPO or GPO link pane to produce a report like the one shown in Figure 7-40.

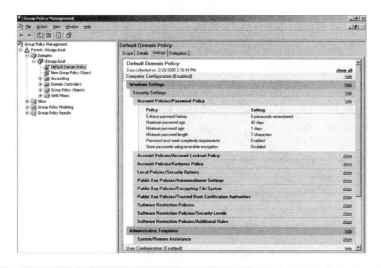

Figure 7-40   Use the show all link to see all settings in the GPO, or only view selected areas. Only those settings that are configured will display.

- Group Policy Modeling (RSoP planning)
- Group Policy Results (RSoP logging)

When RSoP logging is performed, some settings may not be displayed. Microsoft lists the following items:

- IE Maintenance section; does not include the details of Content Ratings
- IE Settings in Preference mode
- Some cookie settings
- Customized Java settings in Zones and Privacy
- Some details for Wireless and IPSec settings

To save a report, right-click on the SOM and select `Save Report` (or select `Save Report` from the `Action` menu), name the report, and then save it as an XML or HTML file. The report can then be printed after opening the file.

Reports, as shown in Figure 7-41, are automatically displayed in a condensed fashion and only show areas where settings are established. This simplifies their viewing. To examine the settings, you need only expand the appropriate category. To expand all of the settings, you can use the `show all` option at the top of the report. In the Administrative templates portion of the report, additional meaning, the "Explain" information, can be viewed by clicking the setting name, as shown in Figure 7-42.

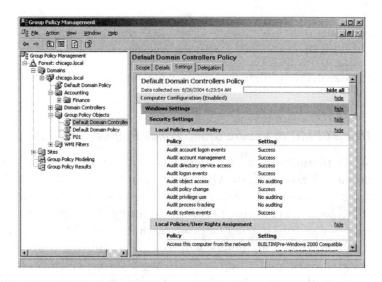

Figure 7-41   A full report of the GPO settings can be produced by clicking the Settings tab.

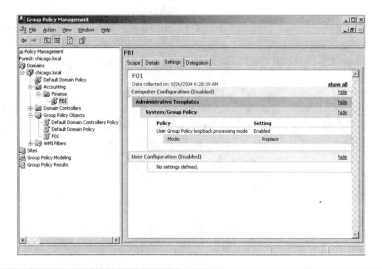

Figure 7-42   Administrative Template settings can display the "Explain" information.

Using GPMC to Ensure Group Policy Permission Consistency

When permissions are modified on a GPO using GPE or GPMC, they are modified on both the GPO information in AD and in sysvol. Permissions can also be set outside of these interfaces, so it is possible for them to become out of synch. Permissions settings in both areas must be the same, or policies will not be properly processed. GPMC checks permission consistency in Windows Server 2003 domains when the GPO is selected. If there is a problem, a dialog box warning appears that, if the user is authorized, allows the user to click OK and fix the sysvol permissions to be the same as those in Active Directory.

Windows 2000 domain GPOs can be checked for this issue by looking at the Default Domain Policy and the Default Domain Controllers Policy from the GPMC. There actually is a bug in Windows 2000 with respect to this issue. The ACLs on the sysvol portion of the GPO are set to allow inheritance, but they should not be. Because of this, the permissions can easily be out of synch with the permissions set in the Active Directory. To correct the error, examine the GPOs in GPMC and when prompted to click OK to make the permissions match, do so. The permissions will be synched with the ACLs on the Active Directory portion of the GPO, and the allow inheritance feature will be removed.

Backup and Restore

When Backup is selected from the context menu, a copy of the GPO is made to the file system. Backup also serves as the export function for the GPO. A GPO backup can be used with either the restore or import function. The backup includes each of the following:

- The GPO GUID and domain name
- The GPO settings
- WMI filter links (not the filter itself)
- Permissions settings on the GPO
- An XML report of the GPO settings

Backup does not include items that are not stored outside the GPO. (Only items that are stored in sysvol or AD portions of the GPO are backed up.) The following items, which many think are part of the GPO, are not stored with the GPO and thus are not backed up:

- WMI filters. (These can be backed up separately using GPMC.)
- IPSec Policies. (Export to a file from the IP Security Policy snap-in.)
- Links from the SOM to the GPO.

WARNING: Backups Create New Security Issues
Being able to back up a GPO allows the restoration of an Active Directory Group Policy environment. However, anyone who can access the backup, copied, or exported GPOs has a large amount of information about the security configuration of the enterprise. This is not information that should be exposed. Only authorized administrators, security teams, and auditors should have access to this information. The location and the DACLs set on the files are critical. GPO backups should be treated as carefully, if not more carefully than, other backups. On- and off-site storage locations are important. In addition to providing an attacker with security information, a backup might be used in an attack. Older, incorrect GPOs might be restored in place of the correct versions, thus weakening security. Ensure that access to these files is limited and that access to all GPMC operations is limited to those trusted individuals who are authorized to perform them.

Restore takes a backup and puts it back in the domain just the way it was when it was backed up. The GUID of the original GPO is used, as is the domain information. You cannot use a backup and restore to move a GPO to another domain. The restore replaces the GOP setting, the ACLs on the GPO, and the WMI filter links.

To back up a GPO, follow these steps:

1. Right-click on the GPO in GPMC and select `Backup` from the context menu.
2. Provide a file system location, name of file, and description, and then click `Back Up`, as shown in Figure 7-43.
3. Click `OK`.

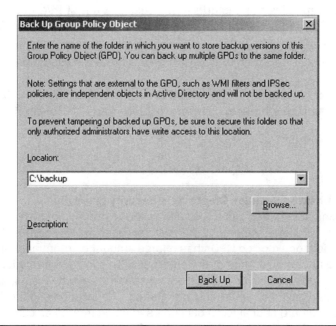

Figure 7-43   GPOs may be saved to the file system. Make sure this is done to a secure location—not somewhere where unauthorized individuals can access the file.

To back up all GPOs, follow these steps:

1. Right-click on the `Group Policy Objects` node and select `Backup All` from the context menu.
2. Provide a file system location and description.
3. Click `Back Up`; then click `OK`.

Rapid Adoption Is Not the Best Policy

Shortly after the introduction of the GPMC, many companies downloaded the tool and immediately put it to use without thoroughly understanding it. Sound familiar? Like any new tool, you should always use GPMC first in a test environment, read all the documentation, and note any inconsistencies, warnings, and unique issues. If White Star Electronics had done so, it might not have spent hours troubleshooting GPO restore issues.

White Star Electronics invested heavily in the use of Group Policy to manage many of the 1,000-plus desktops in its Windows domains. Without a way to back up and restore GPOs, the company was often put in the position of re-creating a GPO for purposes of extending its usefulness to another OU, and occasionally restoring an accidentally deleted GPO. GPMC was seen as a life-saver. Soon after implementing GMPC, a new administrator deleted a GPO. After the restore, the company began having a seemingly arbitrary problem with the Software Installation component of the restored GPO. Some users found that previously installed applications disappeared from their desktop. After some research, the company found that the problem was that a restored Software Installation component received a new GUID. To the OS, it looked like a new policy. In the White Star Electronics implementation, some software installation policies had been set to remove the application if the computer account fell out of scope. Because a new GUID was assigned, the computer account was not in the scope of the "new" policy.

If White Star Electronics had read the GPMC documentation, it would have learned this, and a workaround involving reanimating the tombstone of the deleted object (thus the original GUID could have been reused). The company also found that restore attempts to reanimate the tombstone cannot succeed if the domain controller is not a Windows Server 2003 domain controller. (While it may be necessary to programmatically reanimate some objects, KB article 840001, http://support.microsoft.com/default.aspx?scid=kb;en-us;840001, describes how to reanimate deleted user objects.)

To restore a GPO that still exists, it is necessary to have the edit settings, delete, and modify security permissions; however, to restore a GPO that has been deleted, the `Create GPO` right is required. If software installation portions of GPO are populated, it is possible that there may be some problems with the restored GPO due to the population of the new GPO with a new GUID (see Chapter 9). To restore a GPO that has been deleted, use the `Manage Backups dialog box` as described in the next section, "Managing Backups."

A GPO that is backed up prior to a domain rename cannot be restored. Make sure you do a new backup of GPOs immediately after a domain rename.

To restore a GPO that still exists, follow these steps:

1. Right-click on the GPO in the `Group Policy Objects` container and select `Restore from Backup` from the context menu.
2. In the `Restore Group Policy Object Wizard Welcome` page, click `Next`.
3. Enter or browse to the GPO location and click `Next`.
4. Select the backup and then click `Next`.
5. Review the settings and click `Finish`.
6. Click `OK`.

Sample scripts that perform basic functions are provided with GPMC. To back up, use the provided script BackupGPO.wsf or BackupAllGPOs.wsf. To restore a GPO(s), use the example scripts RestoreGPO.wsf or Restore-AllGPO.wsf. Information about GPO backups can be found by using the QueryBackuplocation.wsf script.

Managing Backups

Information on backups, and the ability to delete, organize (sort), restore, and view backup settings, is located in the Manage Backups dialog box.

To access the Manage Backups page:

1. Right-click on the `Domains` container and select `Manage Backups` from the context menu.

OR

   Right-click on the `Group Policy Objects` container and select `Manage Backups` from the context menu.
2. Enter or use the `Browse` button to locate and select the file location of the backups and click `OK`.

Import

A backed up GPO can be imported to an existing GPO. Import can be used to restore a GPO or to completely replace the existing settings in a GPO with the settings in the backup GPO. Import can be used to move

GPO settings from one domain to another, even if the new domain is in another forest, and even if there is no trust relationship between the original and destination domain.

To import a GPO, right-click the GPO under the `Group Policy Objects` node and follow the wizard.

Copy

The GPO copy process uses an existing GPO to obtain settings, which it then transfers to a new GPO in a new domain. (If the copy function is used in the same domain, it will link the GPO to the new SOM instead of producing a new GPO.) Copying a GPO is like copying a file to a new location. In the file copy process, the original file still exists, and a new file is created. In the GPO copy process, the copied GPO still exits unmodified, and a new GPO with the same settings is created at the new location. No intermediate step, such as placing a backup of the GPO in the file system, is performed. To copy a GPO, creation rights in the destination domain and read access to the source GPO are required. Trust is required between the source and destination domains.

Practical Copy and Migrate Scenarios

As wonderful as the ability to back up and restore GPOs or duplicate a GPO in a new OU within the domain is, even more powerful is the ability to migrate policy to a new domain and forest. In addition, you can reproduce exactly the entire GPO structure in a test environment or rebuild your current structure in the event of cataclysmic disaster. Both of these scenarios will be discussed in Chapter 8.

Delegating Group Policy

Group Policy changes can either increase or decrease the security level of every computer in the forest. Therefore, creation of GPOs and their management is by default restricted to the Group Policy Creator Owners group. Members of this group can create and manage Group Policy. However, the ability to delegate some of the workload of Group Policy is an intrinsic part of proper Group Policy Management. Like many administrative privileges, Group Policy management can be assigned in a granular fashion. Authority can be given at a specific domain or OU level, and authority does not have to be carte blanche. The privileges of creating, editing, linking, and performing modeling or results analysis in addition to creating or editing WMI filters GPOs can be granted or denied separately. You can design a Group Policy delegation strategy that includes security to meets your needs.

Using GPMC to Obtain RSoP

Using GPMC to produce RSoP is also easier than doing so with the RSoP tool. GPMC can be used to obtain planning and logging data.

GPMC can be used by a user with `read` privileges to produce a report on the settings in the GPO. Prior to GPMC, a report could only be viewed by examining the GPO in the Group Policy Editor; however, this required `read` and `write` permissions. Auditors do not need `write` permissions and in fact eschew them. With `write` permissions, an auditor could modify the very information she is charged with providing an analysis of, which would be a conflict of interest and a violation of the separation of duties security principle.

GPO Delegation

The Group Policy Objects `Delegation` tab displays all users and groups that can create GPOs in the domain. Three privileges can be granted at the SOM level:

- **Linking**—Use the `Delegation` tab of the SOM.
- **Group Policy Modeling (available only to domain admins by default)**—In a Windows Server 2003 schema forest, this can be delegated from GPMC using the `Delegation` tab of a domain or OU. The privilege is called "Perform Group Policy Modeling Analyses" and can be found on the `Permissions` drop-down box of the `Delegation` tab on the SOM.
- **Group Policy Results**—A permission normally only granted to members of the local Administrators group or the local administrator of the target computer. The permission is also referred to as the `Generate Resultant Set of Policy (Logging)` permission.

To delegate creation of WMI filters, use the `Delegation` tab of the WMI Filters pane. WMI filters are stored in the domain's system container in AD, so permissions applied to this container can also delegate the same rights. Two possible permissions are available: `Creator Owner` (can create new WMI filters, but has no access to WMI filters created by others—by default, members of Group Policy Creator Owners), and Full Control (by default, domain admins and enterprise admins—can create own and full control on all WMI filters in the domain). You can also apply permissions to a specific WMI filter, either Edit or Full Control. All users have, by default, read permission to all WMI filters. This is necessary to allow Group Policy processing on the client and cannot be removed.

To manage delegation for a GPO, use the `Delegation` tab of the GPO, as shown in Figure 7-44, or permissions directly on the GPO. These privileges are more granular and include the following:

- **Read**—Read the GPO
- **Edit settings**—Read, write, create child objects, delete child objects
- **Edit, delete, and modify security**—Read, write and create child objects, delete child objects, delete, modify permissions and modify owner (apply group policy right is not set)
- **Read as used in security filtering**—Displayed but cannot be set from GPMC
- **Custom**—Displayed but cannot be set from GPMC; combinations of rights such as deny

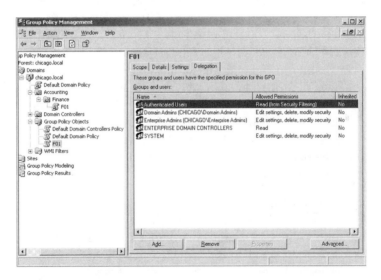

Figure 7-44   For each GPO, specific rights can be delegated.

Deny can be set using GPMC, but you must use the `Advanced` tab.

GPO Planning and Analysis Modeling

Implementation of an extensive Group Policy design is a daunting task. The more computers and users that must be managed, and the more diverse the roles are that they play, the harder it is to keep track of the hundreds of settings and multiple GPOs that are implemented. It is also difficult to design a GPO strategy for a large enterprise. Windows Server 2003 introduced the MMC snap-in RSoP, which can be used in both logging and planning mode.

GPMC provides an interface to this process. Group Policy Modeling can be used to plan and design a GPO hierarchy and see what the results will be. Group Policy Results allow the administrator to examine the current GPO structure and determine what its impact is on a specific user or computer. In a Windows 2000 forest, no Group Policy Modeling node exists.

Modeling a Group Policy Hierarchy

GPMC provides the ability to simulate policy deployment. No GPOs are actually applied, but the results of applying the GPOs can be determined. Known as Resultant Set of Policy (RSoP) Planning Mode in Windows Server 2003, Group Policy Modeling, as it's called in GPMC, requires a domain controller that is running Windows Server 2003 in the forest, but it can simulate a resultant set of policy for any Windows 2000, Windows XP Professional, or Windows Server 2003 computer in the forest. A special service, Resultant Set of Policy Provider, runs on the Windows Server 2003 computer and must be enabled for the process to work. In Figure 7-45, Group Policy Modeling is selected, and you can see in the details pane queries that have already been performed.

To do Group Policy modeling, you must create GPOs. You can provide a test forest (best practice), provide a test domain, or do modeling by creating empty OUs. In each case, you do not populate the OUs or domain with real user or real computer accounts. It is enough to use dummy accounts. In a large environment, you can do much modeling on a single test domain controller in its own test forest.

To model Group Policy, follow these steps:

1. Right-click the Group Policy Modeling container and select Group Policy Modeling from the context menu. (You can also open the wizard directly from a SOM, and the wizard will prepopulate the User and Computer Selection page of the wizard.)
2. On the Group Policy Modeling Wizard welcome page, click Next.

3. Select a domain controller to process the simulation.
4. Enter or browse to the container to be used for user information.
5. Enter or browse to the container to be used for computer information, and then click Next.
6. Continue the wizard as listed in the RSoP section.
7. The report is displayed in the details pane.

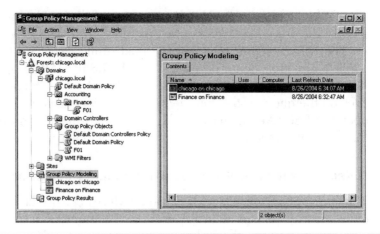

Figure 7-45 Previous queries are displayed and can be accessed from the Group Policy Modeling node.

The report summary tab displays information that impacts the results, including these:

- A list of GPOs that will be applied
- Security group members affected
- WMI filters that are applied
- The settings configured during modeling

The Settings tab displays the settings that will be applied, and the Query tab displays the parameters used to create the query. The results of the query are available for later review, or the query can be re-run after changes in the GPOs have been made. You must delete any queries that are no longer needed.

To save a copy of the report to the file system, follow these steps:

1. Right-click on the query in the details pane and select Save from the context menu.
2. Enter or browse to a location and enter a filename; then click Save.

The GPMC tool provides HTML reporting of the results but does not provide the precedence information provided by the RSoP MMC snap-in. The HTML report tells you the final result—what setting will be applied. The precedence information in the RSoP MMC snap-in shows where all settings are coming from. The Advanced View option (right-click on the query in the console pane and select Advanced View) will open the RSoP MMC snap-in and provide information on every GPO that attempts to set the setting and what it would have set the setting to.

Determining the Results of Group Policy Implementation

The Group Policy Results node of the GPMC can be used to analyze the exact security configuration for users and computers in a production environment. The analysis, the resultant set of policy logging mode, is useful for confirmation of expected results, troubleshooting issues of policy application, and auditing security implementation against official policy for compliance. The data is especially important because it is not simulated on the DC but rather calculated at the target computer. However, the client must be running Windows XP or Windows Server 2003. GPMC cannot be used to get Group Policy Results data for a Windows 2000 computer. Using the logging tool is similar to using the RSoP console and the Group Policy Modeling tool in the GPMC.

Difference in Managing Windows 2000 GPOs

GPMC may be used to manage four different Windows 2000 scenarios:

- A Windows 2000 domain
- A Windows 2000 domain in a forest that has been upgraded to the Windows Server 2003 schema but that has no Windows Server 2003 domain controllers

- A Windows 2000 functional domain with at least one Windows Server 2003 domain controller
- A Windows Server 2003 functional domain

The following list summarizes areas where GPMC management of GPOs is different for Windows 2000 GPOs:

- The Group Policy Modeling node is not shown, and modeling cannot be done unless the Windows Server 2003 schema for Active Directory is available to the Windows 2000 DC. It is also necessary to have at least one Windows Server 2003 domain controller to perform group modeling.
- Group Policy Results can only be obtained for Windows XP or Windows Server 2003 or above computers. To use Group Policy Results, the forest must have had the Windows Server 2003 schema applied.
- Delegating Group Policy Modeling or Group Policy Results requires the Windows Server 2003 Active Directory schema.
- To use WMI filters, the Windows Server 2003 domain configuration (ADPrep/Domain Prep) must have been run.

Best Practices for Group Policy

The following best practices should be used for Group Policy:

- Use block inheritance, no override, and loopback sparingly. Their use makes the results of GPO application difficult to predict.
- Limit the number of GPOs applied to user and computer accounts. The more policies that are applied, the harder it is to determine what will happen, and the longer policy application may take.
- Do not use GPOs to do extensive file system and registry ACL assignment. Security settings in a GPO are applied every 16 hours. If these permissions are extensive, in a large enterprise, they can increase replication latency and possibly have a significant impact on DC performance.
- Use implicit deny where possible instead of explicit deny. When permissions are specifically granted, access is denied. Access can also be denied using Deny permission; this is known as an explicit deny.

- When planning the hierarchical application of security settings, be most restrictive with the first GPO applied, and then relax security where necessary to allow approved operations only by accounts within the container to which a GPO is linked.

TIP: Disable Nodes in GPOs

One other thing—disable the user node in GPOs that modify computer settings and vice versa. When naming GPOs, use descriptive names so that you can look at a GPO and know what it does without having to do extensive digging and searching. "FolderRedirectMyDocs" is more descriptive than "UserNodeModificationLambda."

Summary

Active Directory plays an enormous role in the security of each domain. It is within the object settings and properties of objects that the security parameters for the use of all aspects of the domain are controlled. Group policies, delegation of authority, direct permission setting, and object configuration define the domain and provide permissions on the use of its facilities. The Group Policy Management Console, extensions and improvements to Group Policy, and delegation of authority improve the ability of the IT professional to manage and secure both the domain and Active Directory.

CHAPTER 8

Trust

The concept of trust is an ancient one. On a personal level, it evokes relationships in which we give another person access to secrets, use of our belongings, even the very safety of our family and ourselves. The meaning of trust is often extended to nation-states when they write treaties or businesses when they form partnerships. Each agrees to some sort of goal sharing, perhaps resources and knowledge. The use of the term "trust" in describing relationships between computers and collections of computers on a network is sound, as long as we understand exactly what various kinds of "trust" mean.

In a Windows NT 4.0 and Windows 2000 network, trust relationships enable powerful interactivity between domains. Users in one domain can be given access to resources in another. It is no longer necessary to provide each user unique accounts in each domain. Consequently, users do not have to remember multiple account names and passwords just to access the resources they need to do their jobs. User identity can also be maintained across domain boundaries. No one needs to wonder if domain1\joe is the same individual as domain2\joe. Administration can also be shared. Users can obtain administrative privileges across domain boundaries. In a Windows Server 2003 network, these concepts are still applicable; however, additional benefits are available, and access across domain boundaries can be more tightly controlled.

- A new type of trust, the forest trust, extends the trust concept. A forest trust can provide complete Kerberos-style trust between all domains in two forests.
- A new type of control, selective authentication, empowers administrators of a forest trust to more closely restrict access of users from the trusted forest to only some of the domains within their forest.
- The control offered by selective authentication empowers administrators of an external trust to limit the access of a trusted domain's users to only some of the servers in their own domain.

The purpose of a trust is not to remove all boundaries between forests. The purpose of a trust is to allow some activity across forest boundaries to permit activity that might not otherwise occur due to forest boundaries. (For example, providing users in one forest access to resources such as files in another forest is a typical reason for a trust.) This chapter will do the following:

- Define and explore the many types of trust in a Windows Server 2003 network and explain the ways in which they may best be used.
- Explore the new issues trust relationships bring or benefit from, such as group scope, choosing the direction of trust, penetrating security boundaries, SID-history transitivity, and forest functional level.
- Explain trust relationships in the single forest.
- Discuss forest functional level.
- Explain cross-forest trust relationships.
- Discuss Group Policy Issues and the use of Group Policy Management Tools in multidomain and multiforest management.

New Trust Features in Windows Server 2003

Windows Server 2003 offers the following trust-related features:

- A new trust wizard. Both sides of the trust can be created in one operation. You must have credentials from both parties in the proposed trust relationship.
- Incoming Forest Trust builders. A new group that can create inbound forest trusts. There are no members in this group by default.
- Trust over firewalls is possible using a reduced number of ports.
- Users can now use the User Principal Name (UPD) format (user@usersdomain.com) for authentication even when logging on from another forest.
- Trusts enable the use of Microsoft Identity Integration Server services to synchronize data such as global address and public folders, directory objects, PKI certificates, and Certificate Revocation Lists (CRLs).

Trust Types

Intra-forest trusts describe trust relationships that exist between computers in the same forest. Inter-forest trusts describe trust relationships that exist between domains in two different forests. Appropriate management of authentication and resources is dependent on knowledge of trust types. Three types of intra-forest trusts exist automatically because of computer memberships in domains:

- Two-way, transitive Kerberos-style trust between all domains in the forest. These trusts are established when a Windows 2000 or Windows Server 2003 domain is added to the forest.
- Trust between all domain controllers in a domain. These trusts are established when a Windows 2000 or Windows Server 2003 computer is promoted to DC in a domain. A unique primary domain controller (PDC)/backup domain controller (BDC) is established when a Windows NT 4.0 server is installed as a BDC. Only one PDC can exist in a Windows NT 4.0 domain.
- Trust between a member computer and a Windows DC. This trust relationship is formed by joining a Windows Server 2003, Windows 2000, Windows XP, or Windows NT 4.0 computer to a Windows Server 2003, Windows 2000, or Windows NT 4.0 domain.

These trust relationships are formed automatically when some activity is completed. A fourth kind of intra-forest trust, the shortcut trust, can be created between two domains in the same forest and is explained in the section "Shortcut Trusts." A trust console or special command can be used to manually create intra-forest trust relationships. To complete the trust, an administrative account in each forest and a special unique trust password are necessary. A unique trust password is created and used to establish each new trust. Inter-forest trust types are as follows:

- Kerberos two-way, transitive trusts between domains in a Windows 2000 or Windows Server 2003 forest
- Windows NT 4.0 one-way, non-transitive trusts
- External trusts between a domain in one forest and a Windows Server 2003, Windows 2000, or Windows NT 4.0 domain
- External trusts with non-Windows Kerberos realms
- Trusts between two Windows Server 2003 forests—the forest trust

Inter-Domain Kerberos Trusts

The Kerberos trust relationship formed between domains in the same forest is transitive and two-way. Transitive trust means trust relationships exist between all domains in the forest. Figure 8-1 shows a simple example. In the figure, Domain A trusts Domain B, and Domain B trusts Domain C. This implies that Domain A trusts Domain C. Two-way trust means that because Domain A trusts Domain B, Domain B trusts Domain A. To get the same result with Windows NT 4.0 domains, multiple trust relationships would need to be created individually. In fact, if n represents the number of domains that need this complete transitive two-way trust, n^2-1 trust relationships will have to be created.

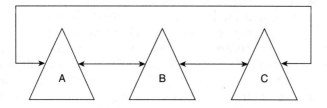

Figure 8-1   Windows Server 2003 trusts between domains in the forest are transitive.

Furthermore, in Windows 2000 and Windows Server 2003 domains, these Kerberos trust relationships are automatically created when a new DC is created. It is not necessary to create trust relationships between domains in the forest. During `dcpromo`, a new domain controller establishes a new domain in an existing forest, joins an existing domain, or creates a new domain and a new forest. When a Windows 2000 or Windows Server 2003 server is promoted to become a domain controller, the following trust relationships may be established:

- If it does not become part of an existing forest, then a single-domain new forest is created; no trust relationship with other domains is established.
- If it joins an existing forest and a new domain is created, trust is Kerberos-style transitive trust between the new domain and every other domain in the forest.
- If it is with an existing forest, it may become another domain controller in an existing forest; it becomes part of the trust relationships already established for that domain.

Shortcut Trusts

Shortcut trusts are one-way trusts that can be administratively created between two domains in the same forest. Because all domains in the forest already trust every other domain in the forest, the shortcut trust needs only to be created when it might expedite some authorization processing. In Chapter 3, "Authorization: Limiting System Access and Controlling User Behavior," the process of obtaining authorization to access resources in a domain other than the domain in which a user's account exists was described. Figure 8-2 illustrates the process. In the figure, solid lines indicate that all domains are in the same forest. Also DNS-style names are not included for simplicity; instead, the domains are simply numbered. John, who has an account in domain 8, has been given permission to access files in domain 12. The arrows show the trust path his request for a session ticket must follow. In a large forest, this process can delay his access, or even prevent it, if a domain controller for one of the domains on the trust path cannot be located.

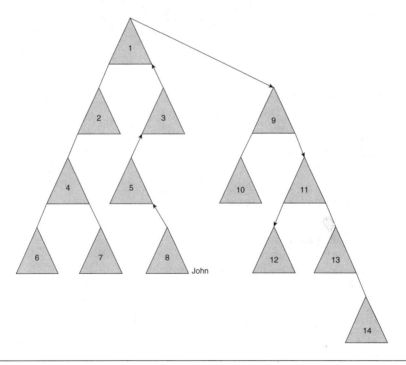

Figure 8-2   The forest trust path.

If there is a need for frequent access between specific domains in a forest, a shortcut trust can be created between the two domains. In Figure 8-3, a shortcut trust has been created between domains 8 and 12. In the figure, the solid arrow indicates the direction of the trust. When John needs to access the files in domain 12, the authorization process is simplified. Instead of many domains, only one other domain, domain 12, needs to be contacted.

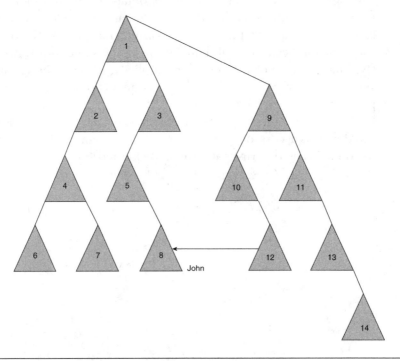

Figure 8-3   The shortcut trust authentication path.

Shortcut trusts are one-way and are not transitive. By one-way, we mean trust only extends in one direction. In Figure 8-3, John can access resources in domain 12. However, no user in domain 12 can access resources in John's domain, domain 8. To provide a full trust relationship, a second one-way trust would need to be created going in the opposite direction. The direction of the trust determines the type of access provided and is discussed in the section "Benefits of Forest Trust" later in this chapter.

Windows NT 4.0 Trusts

Trusts formed with Windows NT 4.0 domains are nontransitive and one-way. Although the concept of forest is foreign to a discussion of Windows NT 4.0, you can think of the Windows NT 4.0 domain as if it is logically a single domain forest—a forest to which no other domains can be added. If trust is necessary between two Windows NT 4.0 domains, or between a Windows NT 4.0 domain and a Windows 2000 or Windows Server 2003 domain, then the trust relationship between them must be created as one-way. A second trust in the opposite direction can be created between the two domains to simulate a two-way trust. Figure 8-4 illustrates a one-way trust between a Windows Server 2003 domain and a Windows NT 4.0 domain. Note the trust direction (solid arrows) the trust path is in the opposite direction. Trust arrows point from the trusting domain to the trusted domain. A popular mnemonic device for Microsoft trainers is the expression "The arrowHEAD points at the trustED."

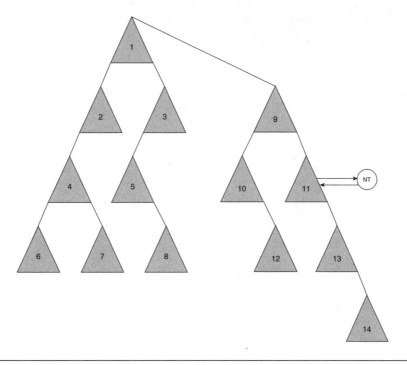

Figure 8-4   Simulating a two-way trust with two one-way trusts.

External Trusts with Windows 2000 or Windows Server 2003 Domains

When a trust relationship is desired with Windows domains in another forest, an external trust relationship may be created. It is important to understand that this trust relationship only exists between the external domain (a single domain in another forest) and the single domain within the local forest. There is no trust relationship between the external domain and the other domains in the local Windows Server 2003 or Windows 2000 forest, nor is there a relationship between the local domain and any other domains in the external forest. Like the shortcut trust and the Windows NT 4.0 trust, the external trust is nontransitive and one-way. A second one-way trust in the other direction may be created between the two domains. Figure 8-5 illustrates an external trust. Note that in these figures, domains are symbolically identified by using numbers and letters instead of the domain DNS names. In the real world, each domain must be named correctly. One forest has its domains numbered; in the other, letters of the alphabet are used. Domain 3 has a trust relationship with Domain B. Users in Domain 3 can be granted access to Domain B. For them to be given access to other domains, new external trust relationships must be created.

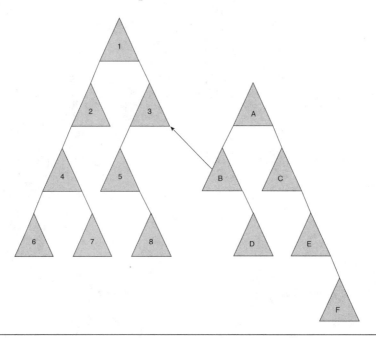

Figure 8-5 The external trust.

Trusts with Non-Windows Kerberos Realms

Windows 2000 and Windows Server 2003 use Kerberos as their primary form of authentication. It is also possible to create a trust relationship with a Kerberos V realm. A realm is logically similar to a Windows domain. Kerberos software is available for many other types of operating systems. A Kerberos realm is often implemented in Unix, and it is this type of Kerberos system for which utilities and instructions are available if the benefits of Kerberos and cross-realm trust are desired.

Creating trust relationships with Unix-based Kerberos realms is described in "Step-by-Step Guide to Kerberos (krb5 1.0) Interoperability" at http://www.microsoft.com/technet/treeview/default.asp?url=/tech net/prodtechnol/windows2000serv/howto/kerbstep.asp. Instructions for creating a realm trust between Windows Server 2003 and a non-Windows realm are found at http://www.microsoft.com/technet/treeview/default.asp?url=/technet/prodtechnol/windowsserver2003/proddocs/entserver/domadmin_createRealmTrust.asp.

A realm trust can be one- or two-way and transitive or nontransitive, depending on how it is implemented and what the capabilities of the realm are.

Forest Trusts

A forest trust is a trust relationship in which every domain in each forest trusts every domain in every other forest. This is new to Windows Server 2003. It is not possible to have a forest trust between two Windows 2000 domains. Two one-way trusts can be created between each domain in each of the forests to provide access across all boundaries; however, this requires the creation of multiple trusts, which will always be NTLM-style trusts. Windows Server 2003 forest trusts are the result of creating a single trust relationship between two forests. These trusts are Kerberos-style, transitive two-way trusts—that is, trust exists between every domain in each forest.

Trust Relationships

The trust relationship between domains in Windows forests provides many benefits. It also creates new headaches. On the one hand, single sign-on across multiple domains makes administration of resources easier; on the other, the tight coupling between domains makes it easier for an administrator of one domain to mount an elevated privilege attack against another domain in the forest. To take advantage of the benefits and minimize the problems, you must understand the following:

- The benefits of trust
- Forest functional level
- Group scope
- Function of the Global Catalog

Benefits of Forest Trust

Trust relationships with the forest offer many benefits to users and administrators. Three major benefits are as follows:

- Single sign-on
- Ease of resource sharing
- Forest-wide administration

Single Sign-On

No matter how many domains exist in the forest, every user needs only a single account to access any resources that she is authorized to access. A user needs to log on only one time, and wherever resources are, she needs only that account, and she doesn't need to provide credentials at any time to access the resources she is authorized to access throughout the forest. This concept extends to local logon access to desktop computer systems, no matter to which domain they are officially joined. If a user has physical access to the machine and has not otherwise been restricted, the user can log on to her assigned domain. There is no need to provide a workstation that is joined in the user's domain.

For performance, and to reduce logon over the WAN, a domain controller from different domains may be added to each site. How many DCs to add and which domain should be represented at each site will depend on the number of users who may travel to sites other than their home sites, in addition to network connectivity speeds and issues.

Single sign-on is a benefit; however, there is another side to consider. Where single sign-on does not exist, users must manage multiple accounts. Each account is necessary to provide them access to some resource. Although this is annoying and makes it more likely that passwords will be forgotten or written down where they may be observed, there is a benefit. If a user's password is cracked or discovered, an attacker only has access to the resources that can be accessed by the use of that password. All other resources remain safe. Where single sign-on is available, the account, once compromised, provides the attacker with access to every resource the user is authorized for.

While the default partitioning that exists via multiple accounts and passwords is useful, a far better system can be used to mitigate the effect of single sign-on. You can partition access to privileges and resources into normal and sensitive and assign the user additional accounts where necessary. For example, system and network administrators have extraordinary access to system- and network-wide resources and extensive privileges. These individuals also do ordinary things such as read email, compose reports, browse the Internet, and even play games. They should not do these mundane things while logged on as administrators. Instead, provide these users with two accounts: one with their full administrative privileges, and the other for less sensitive activities. To avoid the excess activity necessary to log off and on, these users can use the Secondary Logon service. While logged on as an ordinary user, they can run administrative programs under the authority of their administrative account. The Secondary Logon service is better known as Run as.

Using Runas to Mitigate the Impact of Single Sign-On

The run as command is available from the command prompt, but many programs can be run under a different identity using the Run as command from the context menu, as shown in Figure 8-6. To obtain a context menu that includes the Run as command, hold down the Shift key while right-clicking the program on the menu.

Figure 8-6   Running local security policy under an alternative identity.

A dialog box, as shown in Figure 8-7, will prompt you to enter the alternative ID and password.

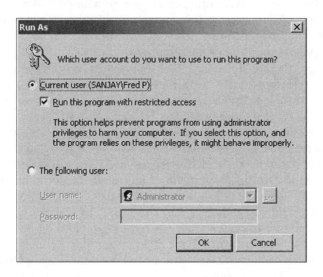

Figure 8-7   When prompted, enter the user ID and password.

Creating Shortcuts That Use Run as

Alternatively, if you create a shortcut for the program, you can use the shortcut property pages to invoke the `Run as` command. When the shortcut is clicked, you will be prompted to enter a different account and its password. To create and use such a shortcut, follow these steps:

1. Create a shortcut by holding down the Alt key and dragging a file from Windows Explorer to the desktop.
2. Right-click the shortcut and select `Properties`.
3. On the shortcut page, click the `Advanced` button.
4. Check the `Run with different credentials` box, as shown in Figure 8-8, and click `OK`.
5. Click `OK` to close the shortcut.
6. To run the program, click on the shortcut.
7. Select the button `The following user`, as shown in Figure 8-7, and enter the domain name\username and password for that account. Then click `OK`.

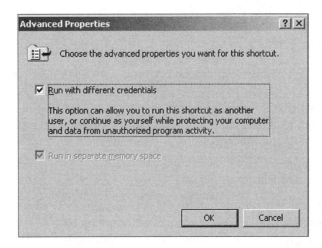

Figure 8-8 Preparing a shortcut that uses Run as.

Using Run as from the command prompt is equally simple. You must provide the user domain or computer name, account, and the name of the program. After entering the command, you will be prompted to enter the account password.

User credentials follow this format:

```
/user:computername\account name
/user:accountname@computername
/user:domainname\accountname
/user:accountname@domainname
```

Program commands follow this format:

```
"mmc %windir%\system32\snapinname.msc" "programname
parameters"
```

Examples:

To open the Monday.txt file in Notepad using the Companion domain and the Jsmith account, enter the following:

```
Runas /user:Jsmith@Companion "notepad Monday.txt"
```

To open Active Directory Users and Computers as Administrator, enter the following:

```
Runas /user:Companion\Administrator "mmc %windir%\system32\dsa.msc"
```

Some programs and administrative tasks cannot be run using the Run as command. For example, upgrading the operating system and configuring system parameters is not supported.

Resource Sharing

Many of the reasons for trusts include the ease of assigning resource access across domains. Because each domain has its own list of users and its own bevy of computers and resources such as database servers, file servers, print servers, and the like, a way to grant access to users from one domain to resources in another domain is useful.

Within the forest, this capability exists across all domains. Figure 8-9 illustrates this concept. Users in domain 1 can be given access to resources in domain 2, domain 3, domain 4, and in fact any domain in the forest. Conversely, all other users from any of these domains can be given access to any resources in any of the other domains. The double arrows extending back and forth between all domains symbolize this trust. The users do not gain access to these resources by default, but domain administrators within these domains can grant them that access. The ability to provide this access is determined by the permissions on the object, by membership in domain and forest administrative groups, and possibly by delegation of administrative authority. The arrangement of access is usually granted via inclusion in groups that have actually been assigned the access or privilege. The types of accounts that can be group members and where different types of groups can be granted access are covered later in the "Group Scope" section.

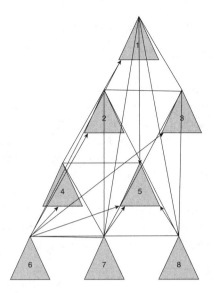

Figure 8-9   Determining trust relationships within the forest.

Forest-Wide Administration

Most domain-centric access and privilege is managed and controlled by domain administrative groups. However, forest-wide groups also exist. In addition to enterprise admins and schema admins, several computer groups exist. Cross-domain or forest-wide administration plays a role in preventing Windows 2000 and Windows Server 2003 domains from being security boundaries. Forest-wide administration and the unintended issue of unauthorized access by domain administrators into another domain are discussed in the section "Piercing Security Boundaries—The Ultimate Forest Design Issue."

Forest-wide administration, however, is important when centralized control is desired, or when it is necessary to regain control over resources.

Forest and Domain Functional Level

Functional level is a Windows Server 2003 concept that extends the Windows 2000 native and mixed mode domain concept. A Windows 2000 domain is by default in mixed mode and cannot be changed to native mode if it includes Windows NT 4.0 BDCs. If the domain contains only Windows 2000 domain controllers, it can be changed to native mode and cannot be changed back to mixed mode. The key concept to remember is that mixed mode means it is possible to have Windows NT 4.0 BDCs. Windows NT 4.0 member workstations and servers may be part of a Windows 2000 native mode forest. Windows Server 2003 domains have more choices for domain controller membership; therefore, some definition other than mixed and native mode is necessary. Windows Server 2003 changes the name "mode" to functional level.

NOTE: Why Bother to Change Mode or Functional Level?
Windows 2000 and Windows Server 2003 domains will continue to operate just fine if left in the default mode or functional level. Why change it? Mode- and functional-level changes make sense because they offer additional functionality.

Windows Server 2003 forests can contain Windows 2000 domains. In addition, Windows Server 2003 domains can contain Windows NT 4.0, Windows 2000, and Windows Server 2003 domain controllers. However, some advanced features of Windows Server 2003 require a domain to consist of only Windows Server 2003 domains. Other features require the entire forest to be Windows NT 4.0 and Windows 2000 domain controller-free. (Windows 2000 and Windows NT 4.0 member servers may exist in these domains.) The absence or presence of Windows Server 2003 purity is referred to as *forest functional level*.

New and wonderful functionality is available when Windows Server 2003 domains can be raised to an advanced functional level. However, you should note that even before this occurs, many Windows Server 2003 advantages are available. For example, Universal Group Caching, replica from media, No GC full synchronization, application partitions, DNS in an application partition, administrative tool improvement, reset Restore Mode Password online, reduce storage requirements, and object quotas do not require Windows Server 2003 functional level.

Functional Levels

Each domain or forest functional level has specific qualifications that must be met before it can be assigned, and each level delivers different advantages. Domain levels are assigned domain-by-domain. Domain levels and the types of domain controllers they support are as follows:

- **Windows 2000 Mixed**—Windows NT 4.0, Windows 2000, and Windows Server 2003 domain controllers.
- **Windows 2000 Native**—Windows 2000 and Windows Server 2003 DCs only.
- **Windows Server 2003 Interim**—Windows NT 4.0 and Windows Server 2003 DCs only.
- **Windows Server 2003**—Windows Server 2003 DCs only.

Forest functional levels map to the entire forest and are as follows:

- **Windows 2000**—Windows NT 4.0, Windows 2000, and Windows Server 2003 DCs.
- **Windows Server 2003 Interim**—Windows NT 4.0 and Windows Server 2003 DCs only.
- **Windows Server 2003**—Windows Server 2003 DCs only.

NOTE: A Reminder
Operating system requirements for domain or forest functional level apply only to domain controllers. No matter the domain or forest functional level, the operating system of member servers and workstations is unimportant to functional level.

Functionality

Many of the new functions available at a higher functional level offer increased security functionality. Table 8-1 lists domain features and identifies the domain functional level necessary. Table 8-2 lists forest-wide features and the forest functionality required.

Table 8-1   Domain Functional Level Necessary for New Functionality

Function	Domain Functional Level Necessary
Install from media.	Windows NT 4.0, Windows 2000, Windows Server 2003
Global catalog not required for logon.	Windows NT 4.0, Windows 2000, Windows Server 2003
Application directory partitions.	Windows Server 2003
Domain controller rename.	Windows Server 2003
Update logon timestamp. (Find all users who have not logged on in a specific timeframe across all DCs in a domain.)	Windows Server 2003
User password on InetOrgPerson object can be set using the user Password attribute.	Windows Server 2003
Universal groups.	For distribution groups—Windows 2000 mixed; for both security and distribution groups—Windows 2000 native, Windows Server 2003
Group nesting.	For distribution groups and for nesting global groups in local groups—Windows 2000 mixed; For full group nesting—Windows 2000 native and Windows Server 2003
Converting groups.	Conversion between security groups and distribution group—Windows 2000 native and Windows Server 2003
SID history.	Migration of security principals from one domain to another—Windows 2000 Native and Windows Server 2003

Table 8-2   Forest Functional Level Necessary for New Functionality

Function	Forest Functional Level Necessary
Install from media. (A new DC can be promoted using a CD-ROM copy of AD instead of waiting for network-based replication.)	Windows 2000, Windows Interim, Windows Server 2003

Function	Forest Functional Level Necessary
Universal group membership caching.	Windows 2000, Windows Interim, Windows Server 2003
Application Directory partitions.	Windows 2003, Windows Interim, Windows Server 2003
Global catalog replication improvements.	If both replication partners are Windows Server 2003—Windows 2000; and Windows Server 2003
Defunct schema objects. (Schema classes and attributes can be deactivated.)	Windows Server 2003
Forest trusts. (Kerberos-style trusts between all domains in two forests.)	Windows Server 2003
Linked value replication. (Individual group members can be replicated across the network, instead of the entire group.)	Windows Server 2003
Domain rename.	Windows Server 2003
Improved Active Directory replication algorithms.	Windows Server 2003
Dynamic auxiliary classes (dynamically link class to objects and not just to entire classes of objects).	Windows Server 2003
Convert InetOrgPerson objectClass to user.	Windows Server 2003
New dynamic groups (basic and query) to support authorization models.	Windows Server 2003

Raising Functional Level

Administrators can manually change domain and forest functional levels when the operating system conditions are met. Windows will not make the change automatically. Once a level has been changed, you cannot return the domain or the forest to a previous level. By default, when a Windows Server 2003 domain controller is deployed, it operates at the lowest functional level: Windows 2000 mixed. If there are no Windows NT 4.0 or Windows 2000 DCs, and there will never be a need to add them, the functional levels can be changed to Windows Server 2003. If a Windows NT 4.0 DC is upgraded to Windows Server 2003, then the Windows Server 2003 Interim can be set for the domain and the forest.

Before attempting to change domain or forest functional level, you should review your current domains and document the operating system of all domain controllers in each domain. You should also review the additional functionality that you will achieve and determine how important that functionality is to your organization. Remember: There is no need to immediately change a functional level just because the current domain controller operating system will enable it. You cannot reduce the functional level of your domain or forest should you want to do so in the future.

Raising Domain Functional Level

When the first Windows Server 2003 domain controller is introduced into a Windows 2000 or Windows NT 4.0 domain, the domain functional level is automatically set at Windows 2000 mixed. In a mixed domain with both Windows NT 4.0 and Windows Server 2003 domain controllers, the domain functional level can be changed to Windows Server 2003 Interim level. If all domain controllers in the domain are Windows 2000 or Windows Server 2003, the domain functionality can be changed to Windows 2000 native. When all domain controllers are Windows Server 2003, the domain functional level can be changed to Windows Server 2003. To change domain functional level, you must be a member of the Domain Administrators group.

Changing domain or forest functional level is irreversible. Once the level is raised, you cannot go back. Note that an attempt to raise the forest level while Windows NT 4.0 DCs are present will not be blocked; however, replication to all Windows NT 4.0 domain controllers will stop. Best practices include identification of the functional level of all DCs prior to changing the level. You should also ensure that replication is occurring properly throughout the forest (use Repadmin and Replmon to verify) and make a system state backup of at least two DCs from each domain in the forest.

Strategies for Raising Forest Functional Level

You can approach the raising of forest functional level in different ways. Possibilities are as follows:

- Raise domains to Windows 2000 native level one at a time; then raise forest to Windows Server 2003. (When the forest is raised to Windows Server 2003 level, Windows 2000 native level domains will be automatically moved to Windows Server 2003 level.)
- Increase domains to Windows Server 2003 level one at a time; then increase the forest level to Windows Server 2003.

Either strategy will work, and each has advantages and disadvantages. In the first example, you avoid revisiting each domain because the movement to Windows Server 2003 domain level is automatic. In the second option, however, you may be able to reap some benefits by having a domain at Windows Server 2003 level, even though the entire forest is not. Review Tables 8-1 and 8-2 for some ideas as to what those benefits are.

The main advantages to Windows Server 2003 functional level are Schema redefine, cross-forest trusts, and more replication improvements.

Raising the Functional Level to Windows Server 2003 Interim

Raising the functional level to Windows Server 2003 Interim improves replication and allows groups to contain more than 5,000 members per group. You can raise the functional level during an upgrade of the Windows NT 4.0 PDC to be the first DC in a Windows Server 2003 forest. You can also configure the forest functional level prior to the upgrade or afterward by using an LDAP tool.

NOTE: Other Methods for Changing Domain Functional Level
You can also use ldp.exe and adsiedit.msc to view and raise the domain and forest functional level. To learn how, see Knowledge Base article 322692 "HOW TO: Raise Domain and Forest Functional Levels in Windows Server 2003" at http://support.microsoft.com/default.aspx?scid=kb; en-us;322692.

Raising the Domain Level to Windows 2000 Native or Windows Server 2003

You cannot have Windows NT 4.0 DCs in either of these domain functional levels. Before raising the domain functional level, you should make sure you have no Windows NT 4.0 DCs in the domain. In a large domain, especially one with a remote site, this may not be an easy chore. To determine if any Windows NT 4.0 domain controllers exist in a domain, you can use an LDAP query.

1. Log on as a member of the domain Admins group to a Windows Server 2003 DC.
2. Open `Active Directory Users and Computers`.
3. Right-click the domain object and click `Find`.
4. In the `Find` drop-down box, select `Custom Search`; then click the `Advanced` tab.

5. Enter the following LDAP query, as shown in Figure 8-10:

```
(&(objectClass=computer)(operatingSystemVersion=4*)
(userAccountControl:1.2.840.113.556.1.4.803:=8192))
```

6. Click `Find Now` to produce a list of Windows NT 4.0 domain controllers in the domain or to find that none exist, as shown in Figure 8-10.

Figure 8-10   Querying for the existence of NT 4.0 BDCs.

If no NT 4.0 domain controllers are located, then it is okay to proceed with raising the domain functional level.

To raise the domain functional level to Windows Server 2000 or Windows Server 2003, follow these steps:

1. Log on as a member of the domain administrators group to the PDC emulator.

2. Open `Start`, `Administrative Tools`, `Active Directory Domains and Trust`. You can also use the `Active Directory Users and Computers` console and right-click on the domain then select `Raise Domain Functional Level` from the context menu.

3. Right-click the domain for which you want to raise functionality and select `Raise Domain Functional Level` from the context menu.

4. In the `Select an available domain functional level` box, select either Windows 2000 native or Windows Server 2003, as shown in Figure 8-11, and then click `Raise`. If a Windows Server 2003 level is chosen, and any Windows Server 2000 domains exist, the raising will be blocked; otherwise, the change takes place at the PDC emulator and then is replicated to all domain controllers in the domain. If you need a specific forest level to use some feature, be sure to wait until replication has occurred.

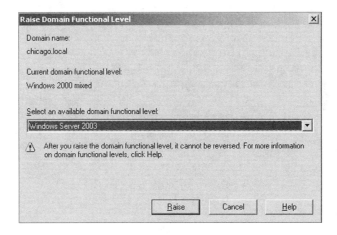

Figure 8-11 Selecting a domain functional level.

5. Click OK in the warning box, as shown in Figure 8-12.
6. Click OK in the confirmation box, as shown in Figure 8-13.

Figure 8-12 Accept the warning. **Figure 8-13** Acknowledging the completion.

Raising Forest Functional Level

Raising the forest functional level is also a matter of ensuring that conditions are met for forest member domains, and then following a simple procedure. Once the forest level has been changed, it cannot be returned to its previous status. To change the forest functional level, follow these steps:

1. Log on to the PDC emulator of the forest root domain as a member of the Enterprise Admins group. The change takes place on the Schema FSMO and then is replicated. If this operations master is not available, the functional level cannot be raised.
2. Open `Start`, `Administrative Tools`, `Active Directory Domains and Trusts`.
3. Right-click on `Active Directory Domains and Trusts` and select `Raise Forest Functional Level`.
4. In the `Select an available forest functional level`, click Windows Server 2003 and then click `Raise Forest Functional Level`, as shown in Figure 8-14.

Figure 8-14   Select the forest functional level.

5. Click OK on the warning, as shown in Figure 8-15.
6. If there is a problem, and the functional level cannot be raised, you can click Save As in the Raise Forest Functional level dialog box, and a log will be saved that includes a list of all DCs that must be upgraded before you can raise the functional level. If there are no problems, click OK in the confirmation box, as shown in Figure 8-16.

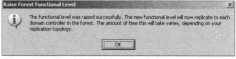

Figure 8-15   Accepting the warning.   **Figure 8-16**   Acknowledging completion.

Group Scope

Changing the forest functional level to Windows 2000 or Windows Server 2003 adds the Universal group type and changes the meaning of group scope. Group scope defines which groups and users can be a group member and where groups can be used to grant rights and access to resources. Group scopes are defined in Table 8-3.

Table 8-3 Group Scope

Scope	Definitions
Local	The group only exists on a single server and can only be granted access to local server resources.
Universal	The group exists in the forest and can be granted access anywhere in the forest and in trusted domains in other forests.
Global	The group exists in a domain and can be granted access to resources in other domains in the forest and in trusted domains in other forests.
Domain Local	The group exists in the domain and can only be granted access to resources in the domain.

The meaning of group scope changes with the functional level. Table 8-4 provides examples.

Table 8-4 Group Scope

Functional Level	Universal	Global	Domain Local
Windows 2000 native or Server 2003	Membership: Accounts, global groups, and Universal groups from any trusted domain. Group Nesting: Groups can be added to other groups and assigned permission in any domain. Group	Membership: Accounts and global groups from the same domain. Group nesting: Groups can be added to other groups and assigned permisions	Membership: Accounts, global groups, and Universal groups from any domain as well as domain local groups from the same domain. Group Nesting: Groups can be added

Table 8-4   Group Scope Continued

Functional Level	Universal	Global	Domain Local
	conversion: can be converted to domain local scope. Can be converted to global scope as long as no Universal groups are group members.	in any domain. Group conversion: Can be converted to Universal scope as be converted long as no other groups with global scope are a member.	to other domain local groups and assigned permission only in their own domain. Group conversion: Can to universal scope as long as it does not have as a member a group with domain local scope.
Windows 2000 mixed	Universal groups cannot be created.	Can include accounts from the same domain. No group nesting or conversion.	Accounts and global groups from the same domain. No group conversion.

Group Types

Two types of groups exist: security groups and distribution groups. Security groups are groups that can be granted access to objects by adding their SID to the discretional access control list (DACL). Distribution groups are used solely for creating email lists for use by Exchange Server but could be utilized by other server applications. Distribution groups cannot be used as security groups. However, security groups can also be used as email lists. Best practices indicate that distribution groups should only be created if a security group that matches its requirements does not exist.

Enterprise Groups

Two groups that have extended administrative rights throughout the forest are Enterprise Admins and Schema Admins. These groups are created in the forest root domain. In a Windows Server 2000 Mixed Functional Level domain, these groups are Global Groups. By default, the Administrator account of the root forest domain is a member of both of these groups. Because these groups have administrative roles throughout the entire forest, their membership should be carefully considered. The Enterprise Admins group, by default, is given membership in the Domain Admins group of every domain and thus has far-reaching administrative privileges. Membership in Schema Admins is necessary to modify the schema. Because changing the schema should not be undertaken unless absolutely necessary and typically must be reviewed extensively before application, best practices indicate that the membership of the Schema Admins group should be empty. If a Schema Admin is necessary, an administrative account can be temporarily added.

Global Catalog Function

Domain-specific object information is replicated among all domain controllers in a domain. Only some of the characteristics of a domain object are replicated to other domains. This information is only stored on domain controllers that have been designated as Global Catalog servers (GCs). Global Catalog servers maintain a partial replica of domain information from every domain in the forest. Where multiple global catalog servers are present in a domain, the information is maintained on all GCs. The GC provides the following functionality:

- Enables user searches across all domains in the forest, such as using the Start, Search, Other Search Options, Find People or Printers functionality.
- Supplies Universal Group membership information in multiple domain environments. This information is necessary during logon in Windows 2000 native and Windows Server 2003 domains.
- Provides user principal name authentication. If Jeff Smith, a user in the east.newyork.nomoore.com domain, logs on from a workstation in the west.newyork.nomoore.com domain using the UPN Jsmith@east.newyork.nomoore.com, the DCs in the west.newyork.nomoore.com domain will not be able to find the account and will contact the GC to complete the process.
- Validates object references. A cross-domain object reference is a reference from an object in one domain to an object in another. If, for example, a reference to an OU in the west.newyork.nomoore.com domain is made by some activity on the east.newyork.nomoore.com domain, it can be checked to see if such an OU exists.

The GC data is not unique; it represents partial information from each domain. The information is stored in the GC because specific attributes are identified in the object class in the Active Directory Schema. Some attributes are marked by default, and a member of the Schema Admins group can add additional attributes by modifying the Schema properties of the attribute.

WARNING: Modify Schema Attributes with Caution
This feature should be used with caution. If the forest functional level is not Windows Server 2003, modifying an attribute will cause the entire global catalog attribute set (not just the new attributes you have selected) to replicate, which can cause a temporary performance issue.

In addition to providing forest-wide information, the GC plays a unique role in relationship to Universal Groups and User logon. During logon, the Local Security Authority must create a security token. This token includes the security identifiers (SIDs) of the user and groups she is a member of. The token is used when the user attempts to access resources. Starting with Windows 2000, a new type of group, the Universal group, can be used to grant permissions through the forest and can contain as members users and groups from the forest. Membership in Universal groups must also be included in the security token. However, because the membership information may include users and groups from all over the forest, instead of visiting each domain in the forest, the logon process obtains the information from the GC. To do so, the DC authenticating the user connects to the GC. In a single domain forest, all DCs contain the same information, and there is no need to access the GC. If the functional level of the Windows Server 2003 domain is Windows 2000 mixed, no Universal groups can be created, and there is no reason to contact the GC. However, in a multidomain, Windows 2000 native mode, or Windows Server 2003 forest, if the GC is not accessible, the account is not the built-in Administrator account, and cached credentials are not available, the user will be denied logon. Universal group enumeration is also necessary for computer accounts and occurs during computer startup.

The problem of GC access across the WAN is often resolved in Windows 2000 domains by adding a DC and GC in every physical location. Likewise, to improve performance, additional GCs can be created. However, in both cases, adding GCs increases the replication traffic.

Configure Additional GCs

By default, the first domain controller in a Windows Server 2003 domain is automatically made a GC. If additional GCs are necessary, they can be created. To do so, follow these steps:

1. Log on as a member of Domain Admins to the DC that will be made a GC.
2. Click `Start`, `Administrative Tools`, `Active Directory Sites and Services`.
3. Double-click `Sites` and then double-click the site name where the domain resides.
4. Double-click `Servers` and click the domain controller to be made into a GC.
5. Right-click `NTDS settings` and select `Properties`.
6. Select the `global catalog` check box on the `General` page, as shown in Figure 8-17.
7. Restart the domain controller.

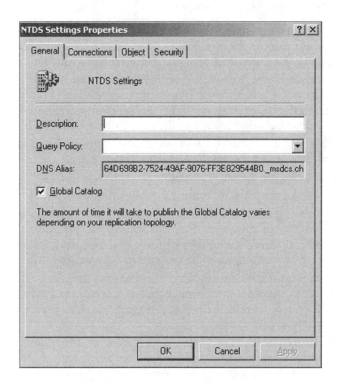

Figure 8-17   Adding an additional Global Catalog server.

Use Global Catalog Caching

Because the global catalog is used to enumerate membership in Universal groups during user logon, it is often good practice to include a GC in each site. This way, it is not necessary to use a WAN connection to authenticate a user. In many cases, a local DC from the user's domain is already present at the site and can also be used for this purpose. (If no DC is present, users are already using the WAN connection for authentication.) However, adding the GC role to a local DC increases replication traffic across the WAN and could necessitate a hardware upgrade. This may not be acceptable if replication is already heavy or if the connection speed is slow.

Some GC Communications Cannot Use Universal Group Caching
Universal Group Caching will not help if applications are querying the GC for information on port 3268. These queries will still need to access a GC directly. If a site requires this type of GC communications, placing a GC in the site is still the best solution.

Windows Server 2003 solves this dilemma by providing the option to locally cache Universal group membership on the DC. Once membership information is cached, user logon does not require a WAN connection to a GC or the existence of a local GC. The Universal group membership information will be periodically refreshed (by default every 8 hours). Caching refresh is limited to 500 Universal group memberships at one time. After Universal group membership caching is enabled, users should experience faster logon times.

Enabling Universal Group Membership Caching

Universal group membership caching must be enabled at all DCs in the site:

1. Log on as a member of the Domain Admins group in the forest room domain or as a member of Enterprise Admins.
2. Open the Start, Administrative Tools, Active Directory Sites and Services console.
3. Click the site where you want to enable Universal group membership caching.
4. In the details pane, select NTDS Site Settings and click Properties.
5. Select Enable Universal Group Membership Caching, as shown in Figure 8-18.

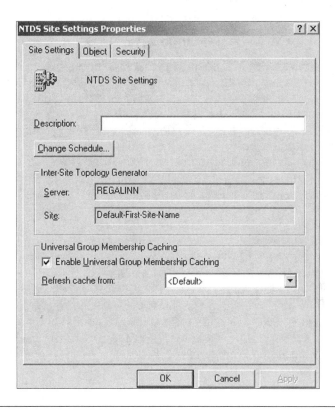

Figure 8-18 Enable Universal Group Membership Caching.

6. In Refresh cache from, click a site for this site to use to refresh its cache or accept the default to use the nearest site with a GC.

External Trust Creation Procedures

Trust creation is automatic when a new domain controller is added to a domain or when a new domain is added to a forest. Other trust relationships must be created manually. Cross-forest trusts are examined later in the "Forest Trust" section.

The Importance of Time Synchronization

Sometimes it pays to be in a business for a long time. Recently, I was called in to resolve trust issues in a Windows Server 2003/NT 4.0 environment. Like many customers, my client could not afford to upgrade all Windows NT 4.0 domains at one time and required some trust relationships between Windows NT 4.0 domains and Windows Server 2003 domains. In most cases, this had not been an issue. Trust relationships were created, users were authorized to access resources, and so on. However, one stubborn Windows NT 4.0 domain refused to enter into a trust relationship with its Windows Server 2003 companion. Networking and name resolution issues had been eliminated, but still the trust could not be created.

I was able to solve the problem in minutes by checking the time on the Windows NT 4.0 PDC. The time was one hour different from that of the Windows Server 2003 DC. You might either think that this was an obvious solution, or if you know Windows NT 4.0, you know that it does not synchronize time, and time is not a large issue. However, Windows NT 4.0 does have some time issues. For a Windows NT 4.0 BDC to install, and for Windows NT 4.0 trusts to successfully be created, the time difference between the two systems must be within 30 minutes.

Windows Server 2003 trust creation is straightforward and non-problematic. However, some new terms are introduced in the trust creation process. In a Windows NT-style one-way trust, the concept of "trusting" and "trusted" is used to define which domain's user accounts can be given access to the other domains. These same concepts describe the relationship between a Windows 2000 or Windows Server 2003 domain and an externally trusted domain. Although both domains may have resources, to define the one-way trust, we often identify one domain as the domain with the resources and the other as the one with the accounts. The trust then consists of a trusted domain (the one with the accounts) and a trusting domain (the one with the resources).

However, much trust relationship documentation and the trust wizard for Windows Server 2003 defines trust relationships by using the words "incoming" and "outgoing." If a trust relationship is incoming, this indicates that the users in the internal, or local, domain can be granted access to resources and privileges in the external or specified domain. Think of the incoming trust as bringing the promise of resource access and privileges into the domain. If a trust relationship is outgoing, users from the other domain can be granted access and privileges in the local domain. Think of outgoing trust as people who are outgoing—they tend to trust outsiders.

The trusting domain can assign privileges and access to its resources to accounts that exist in the trusted domain. Figure 8-19 illustrates this concept and compares Windows NT 4.0 and Windows 2000/Server 2003 naming conventions. In the figure, which shows just the trust-related domains from Figure 8-5, the user Peter in the trusted domain 3 is granted access to resources in the trusting domain B. Domain 3 is the trusted domain (Windows NT 4.0 naming convention) and has an incoming trust relationship (Windows Server 2003) with domain B. Domain B is the trusting domain (Windows NT 4.0 naming convention) and has an outgoing trust relationship (Windows Server 2003 naming convention) with domain 3.

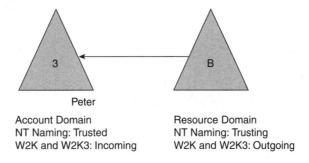

Figure 8-19   Trusting and trusted domains.

Windows Server 2003 also makes it possible to limit authentication for users from trusted domains. During trust creation, the administrator can choose to restrict authentication. This means that until servers are approved for authentication, access cannot be assigned to their resources for accounts that exist in the trusted domain. An administrator of the servers in the trusting domain must configure them to allow authentication. Until servers are configured, access to resources on any servers in the trusting domain by trusted accounts in the trusted domain is not possible.

External Trust Creation

To create an external trust, follow these steps:

1. Log on as a domain administrator and open the `Start`, `Administrative Tools`, `Active Directory Domains and Trusts` console.
2. Right-click the domain and select `Properties` from the context menu.

3. Click the `Trusts` tab and then click `New Trust`.
4. On the Welcome page, click `Next`.
5. Enter the DNS or NetBIOS name of the domain to create a trust with and click `Next`. If the other domain cannot be located and identified, Windows provides an opportunity to create a realm trust. (A realm trust is a trust created between a Windows domain and a non-windows Kerberos realm.)
6. On the `Trust` page, click `External trust`, as shown in Figure 8-20, and then click `Next`.

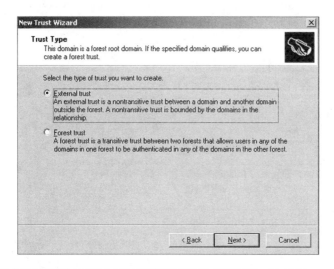

Figure 8-20   Selecting an external trust type.

7. Select the `Direction of Trust`, as shown in Figure 8-21. In this example, a one-way outgoing trust is selected. A two-way trust will mean users in both domains can access resources in either domain. A one-way trust will either be incoming or outgoing.
8. Select the `Sides of Trust`, as shown in Figure 8-22, and then click `OK`. In this example, `Both this domain and the specified domain` is selected. Note the terminology. "This domain" is the local domain—the domain from which the trust is being configured. The "specified" domain is the domain with which the trust is being created. Configuration of both sides of the trust will be done at the same time. (Credentials in both domains are necessary to do so.) If only one side of the trust is completed, an authorized administrator of the other domain must complete the trust.

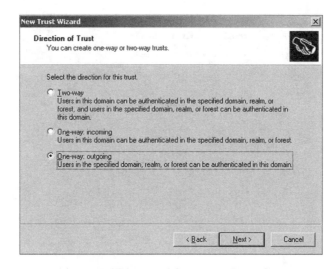

Figure 8-21 Selecting the direction of trust.

9. Enter a username and password for an account in the specified domain with authority to create a trust. (This step is not necessary if only one side of the trust is created at a time.)
10. Select the `scope of authentication`, either domain-wide or selective, as shown in Figure 8-23, and click `Next`.

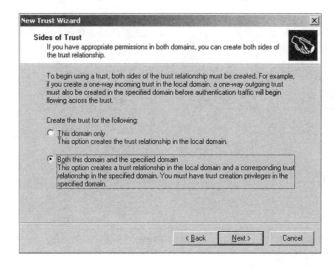

Figure 8-22 Selecting which sides of the trust will be created.

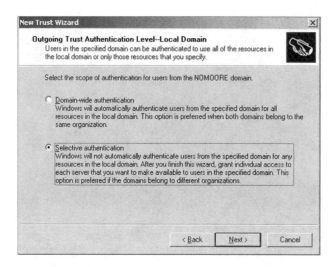

Figure 8-23   Selecting scope of authentication.

11. Note the summary and then click Next.
12. Note the trust completion message and click Next, as shown in Figure 8-24.
13. Click Yes, confirm the outgoing trust box, as in Figure 8-25, and confirm the trust by clicking OK. (Do not attempt to confirm the trust if only one side of the trust is being created.)

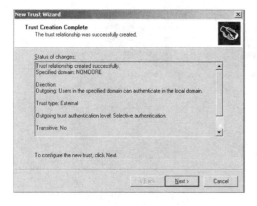

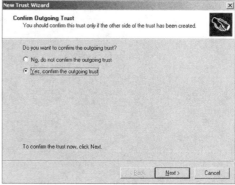

Figure 8-24   Noting completion.   **Figure 8-25**   Confirming the trust.

14. Click OK in the SID Filtering warning page. (SID Filtering is defined in the later section "SID Filtering—Catching SID Spoofs.")

15. In the Trusts property page, as shown in Figure 8-26, note that the domain now shows up in the proper category.

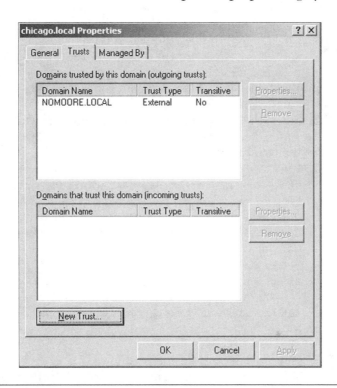

Figure 8-26 Reviewing trust properties.

External Trust Creation with a Windows NT 4.0 Domain

Creating a trust relationship with a Windows NT 4.0 domain is different from creating an external trust with a Windows 2003 or Windows 2000 domain because the Windows NT 4.0 domain only understands its own type of trust relationships. A Windows NT 4.0 trust can only be created by creating one side of the trust in Windows Server 2003 and one side of the trust from the Windows NT 4.0 PDC.

The first step is to determine the direction of trust. Does the Windows Server 2003 domain trust Windows NT 4.0, or does the Windows NT 4.0 trust Windows Server 2003? Are two trusts to be created, one in each direction? For simplicity, the following example uses an outgoing trust in which the Windows Server 2003 domain trusts the Windows NT 4.0 domain.

1. Log on to Windows Server 2003 as a domain administrator and click `Start`, `Administrative Tools`, `Active Directory Domains and Trusts`.
2. Right-click the desired domain and select `Properties` from the context menu.
3. Select the `Trusts` tab, `New Trust`, followed by `Next`.
4. Enter the NetBIOS name of the Windows NT 4.0 domain and then click `Next`.
5. Click `One-way: outgoing Users in the specified domain, realm or forest can be authenticated in this domain` for the `Direction of Trust Window`, and then click `Next`. Outgoing means that the Windows Server 2003 domain trusts the external domain. The users and groups in the Windows NT 4.0 external domain can be assigned access to resources in the Windows Server 2003 domain.
6. Select the scope of authentication for users from the Windows NT 4.0 domain and then click `Next`. Two choices exist: `Allow authentication for all resources in the local domain`, or `Allow authentication only for selected resources in the local domain`.
7. Enter a password for the trust in the `Initial Password` box, as shown in Figure 8-27. This password will be used when creating the NT 4.0 side of the trust. After trust creation, Active Directory updates the trust password periodically.

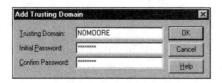

Figure 8-27   Provide a password for the trust creation.

8. Confirm the trust password by entering it again in the `Confirm Password` box and then click `Next`.

9. Review the settings and then click Next. A confirmation message should appear.
10. Click Next and then click Yes. Click Finish followed by OK. A warning will inform you that the trust will not be created until the other side is configured.
11. Log on to the Windows NT 4.0 PDC as a domain administrator and open the Start, Programs, Administrative Tools, User Manager for Domains applet.
12. From the Policies menu, select Trust Relationships.
13. Click the Add button in the Trusting domains box.
14. In the Add Trusting Domains dialog box Trusting Domain box, enter the Windows Server 2003 NetBIOS domain name.
15. In the Initial password box, enter the password used in step 8. Click OK. Then when the Windows Server 2003 domain name appears in the Trusting Domains list, as shown in Figure 8-28, click Add.

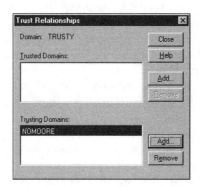

Figure 8-28 The trusting domain name is added to the Trusting Domains box.

To create a trust in which Windows NT 4.0 trusts Windows Server 2003 follow these steps:

1. Log on to the Windows NT 4.0 PDC as a domain administrator and open the Start, Programs, Administrative Tools, User Manager for Domains applet.
2. From the Policies menu, select Trust Relationships.
3. Click the Add button in the Trusted Domains box.
4. In the Domain box, enter the Windows Server 2003 NetBIOS domain name.
5. Enter a password for the trust, as shown in Figure 8-29, and click OK. Note that no confirmation password is entered.

Figure 8-29 Enter the domain name and add a password for the trust.

6. Read the message noting that the trust cannot be verified and click OK.
7. Click Close.
8. Log on to the Windows Server 2003 domain as an administrator and click Start, Administrative Tools, Active Directory Domains and Trusts.
9. Right-click the desired domain and select Properties from the context menu.
10. Select the Trusts tab; then click New Trust, followed by Next.
11. Enter the NetBIOS name of the Windows NT 4.0 domain and click Next.
12. Click One-way: incoming Users in this domain can be authenticated in the specified domain, realm or forest. Then click Next.
13. Enter the password used in step 5 in the Trust password box.
14. Enter the password again in the Confirm trust password box and click Next.
15. Review settings; then click Next.
16. Read the message, as shown in Figure 8-30. Then click Next and click OK.
17. The domain is represented in the Trust property pages, as shown in Figure 8-31.

WARNING: Seeing Is Not Believing
If a trust relationship is defined in the trust property pages, it does not mean that the trust is currently working. Validate that trusts are working by using the Trust property pages of Windows Server 2003 or the netdom utility.

Figure 8-30 The trust cannot be created until it's confirmed from the Windows Server 2003 domain.

Figure 8-31 Configured trusts are shown in the Trust property pages.

A two-way trust can be created between Windows Server 2003 domain and a Windows NT 4.0 domain. To create a two-way trust, follow these steps:

1. Log on as a member of the Domain Admins group to the Windows Server 2003 domain controller.
2. Open the Active Directory Domains and Trusts console and right-click the domain; then click Properties.
3. Click the Trusts tab, New Trust, followed by Next.
4. Enter the NetBIOS name of the Windows NT domain for the trust and then click Next.
5. Select Two-way Users in this domain can be authenticated in the specified domain, realm or forest, and users in the specified domain, realm or forest can be authenticated in this domain. Then click Next.
6. Select the scope of authentication, and then click Next.
7. Enter a password for the trust. Then enter it again in the Confirm trust password box and click Next.
8. Review settings; then click Next.
9. Review the message, click Next, click Yes to confirm the outgoing trust, click Yes to confirm the incoming trust, and then click Next.
10. Enter the user name and password of an account with administrative privileges for the specified domain and then click Next.

11. The trust will fail because the NT domain does not support trust password verification. A Windows 2000 or a Windows Server 2003 domain does. Click OK in the warning message box that indicates that the trust must be completed at the other domain.
12. Click Finish and then OK.
13. Log on to the Windows NT 4.0 PDC as a domain administrator and open User Manager for Domains.
14. Select Trust Relationships on the Policies menu.
15. Click the Add button on the Trusted Domains box.
16. In the Domain box, enter the Windows Server 2003 NetBIOS domain name.
17. In the Password box, enter the password for the trust from step 7 and click OK.
18. Click the Add button on the Trusting Domains box.
19. Enter the Windows Server 2003 NetBIOS name.
20. Enter the password used in step 7; then click Close.

TIP: Trust Creation Problems

Trust creation may fail. Typically, you will see some indication while creating the trust. For example, networking problems or name resolution problems may prevent the connection with the other domain. In this case, a warning will appear. You must resolve these issues before you can proceed.

One common error is the lack of name resolution. Each domain must be able to locate the other. If DNS is not correctly configured, this can be a problem. Lmhost files may be used to assist with name resolution, especially if Windows NT 4.0 domains are not listed in DNS. If you are unfamiliar with creating and using lmhosts files, see Knowledge Base articles 181171 (http://support.microsoft.com/default.aspx?scid=kb;en-us;181171) and 102725 (http://support.microsoft.com/default.aspx?scid=kb;en-us;102725).

Forest Trust

When an external trust is created between a Windows Server 2003 domain and another Windows Server 2003 domain in another forest, the trust relationship can be one-way or two-way, incoming or outgoing.

Selective authentication can be used to limit the domains in the trusting forest that will participate in the trust. However, the trust relationship only exists between the two domains and is not a Kerberos-style trust. Authentication across the trust relationship will be NTLM. If you require trust between all domain controllers in each of two forests, you must create a forest trust. If you do so, the trust can be one-way or two-way and will be a Kerberos transitive trust. The following requirements must be met before the trust can be created:

- Both forests must be Windows Server 2003 forests.
- All DCs must be running Windows Server 2003.
- Both forests must be at Windows Server 2003 level functionality. (The trust is created between the root forest domains of each forest.)
- The DNS infrastructure must be configured correctly.

Transitivity exists between forests in a forest trust but does not extend to other forest trust relationships. Transitivity between forests means that the trust relationship extends to every domain in both forests. That is, if Forest A is trusted by Forest B, and Forest B is trusted by Forest C, there is no trust relationship between Forest A and Forest C. Users in Forest A may be granted access to resources in Forest B, and users in Forest B may be granted resource access in Forest A, but users in Forest A cannot be given access to resources in Forest C.

SID filtering is enabled automatically across a forest trust, thus helping to prevent elevation of privilege attacks.

Incoming and Outgoing Forest Trusts

Trust relationships between Windows Server 2003 forests are also defined using the incoming and outgoing convention. If a forest has an incoming forest trust, this indicates that the users in the internal or local forest can be granted access to resources and privileges in the external or specified forest. This is roughly equivalent to saying that the local forest is trusted and the specified forest is trusting. When a forest has an outgoing forest trust, it means that users in the specified forest can be granted access to resources and privileges in the local forest. This is roughly equivalent to saying that the local forest is trusting and the specified forest is trusted. Figure 8-32 displays these relationships. In the figure, the domain 1 forest has incoming and outgoing forest trusts with the domain

B forest. John and Peter, who have accounts in domains 3 and 8, respectively, can be given permission to access resources in any domain in the domain A forest. Likewise, Francine, with an account in domain E, can be given access to any domain in the domain 1 forest.

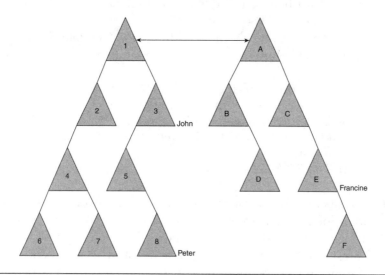

Figure 8-32   Incoming and outgoing forest trusts.

The words "can be given access" mean just that. After the completion of a trust, no user in either forest, just like no user in an external trust, has privileges or permissions in the other forest, with the possible exception of authentication and access granted to the group Everyone. Windows Server 2003 trusts can also limit that possibility. Previously, the right to authenticate in the trusting domain was a default. This allowed users from the trusted domain to sit down at a workstation in the trusting domain and authenticate to their own domain. It allowed them to cross the security boundary. In Windows Server 2003, selective authentication, if specified, allows the boundary between external domains to remain intact unless authentication is specifically granted domain-by-domain (forest trust) or server-by-server (external trust). More information about selective authentication can be found in the earlier "External Trust Creation Procedures" section.

Reasons for creating forest trusts are as follows:

■ An organization with multiple forests establishes trust between the two forests to provide resource access and authentication between all domains in the forests.

- Two separate organizations may want to create a forest trust to provide access to selected resources. Although external trusts can be used instead, the number of domains involved and thus the number of trusts is extensive. Creating a forest trust reduces the number of trusts to create and manage.
- An organization with multiple forests establishes a granular level of transitive trust between its forests. While the goal may be full-transitive trust between all domains in both forests, specific domains are excluded from that transitivity.

Cross-Forest Authentication and Authorization

The process of obtaining ticket granting tickets (TGTs) during authentication and service tickets to enable resource access in a single forest was described in Chapter 2, "Authentication: Proof of Identity." When a forest trust exists and requests that resource access lie outside the forest, a special additional action is necessary. Figure 8-33 illustrates the process. In the figure, Peter, whose workstation and user account is in domain 8, wants to access a resource in domain F on its server 1 across a forest trust between the domain 1 forest and the domain A forest. The following steps match the numbers in the figure.

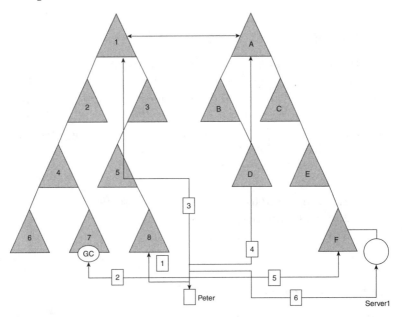

Figure 8-33   Obtaining tickets across a forest trust.

1. Peter's workstation contacts a local DC in its domain, domain 8, with a request for a TGT for access to server 8 in the F domain.
2. The DC queries its domain GC for a location, in this case on server 7. The GC recognizes that the Service Principal Name (SPN) of the request is not in its forest and returns the request to the workstation, telling it to send its request to the root domain of its forest, domain 1. The GC includes a "routing hint" or location of the forest root domain. The SPN is either a DNS name of a host, a DNS name of a domain, or the distinguished name of a service connection point object.
3. The workstation passes its request to a DC in its forest root domain, domain 1. The forest root domain of the workstation's forest (domain 1) provides a TGT to the forest root domain, domain A, of the other forest.
4. The workstation sends its request to the forest root domain, domain A. The forest root domain returns the location of and TGT for the DC for server 8, domain F.
5. The workstation requests a service ticket from the domain.
6. The workstation sends its request to a DC in domain F and receives a TGT for server 8.
7. The workstation sends its request for access and its TGT to server 1.

Creating a Forest Trust

By default, only a member of the Enterprise Admins group or a member of the forest root domain Domain Admins group can create a two-way forest trust. Members of the Incoming Forest Trust Builders group can create one-way incoming forest trusts. The right to create a forest trust can be delegated. To create the forest trust from one location, you must also have like credentials for the other forest.

Forest trust creation consists of three steps:

1. Prepare the forest for forest trust creation.
2. Create the trust.
3. Configure resource assignment.

Prepare the Forest

Two steps are necessary: providing name resolution via DNS and changing functional level to or verifying that functional level is Windows

Server 2003. A third step, removing external trusts between the forests, may be necessary.

If name resolution is not working, the trust relationship will fail. There are several alternatives for ensuring name resolution between forests. Only one of them needs to be done.

- Make one root DNS server authoritative for both forest DNS namespaces. (The root zone contains delegation for each of the DNS namespaces and updated root hints of all DNS servers with the root DNS server.) Zone delegation can be verified using `nslookup`.
- If both forest root DNS servers are running Server 2003, configure conditional forwarders in each namespace to route queries for names in the other namespace.
- Configure secondary zones in each DNS namespace to route queries for names in the other namespace.

If both forests are not at Windows Server 2003 functional level, the trust will fail.

If an external trust exists between domains in the two forests, the forest trust cannot be completed. Before starting the New Trust Wizard, remove any external trusts that may prevent it from completing. (External trusts with domains in forests other than the two forests between which a forest trust will be completed are okay.)

Create the Trust

To create a forest trust follow these steps:

1. Log on as a member of Domain Admins in the forest root domain or as a member of Enterprise Admins and click `Start`, `Administrative Tool`, `Active Directory Domains and Trusts`. This domain is now identified as the "local" domain in the screenshots and documentation.
2. Right-click the domain node for the forest root domain and select `Properties` from the context menu.
3. Select the `Trust` tab, click `New Trust`, and then click `Next`.
4. Enter the DNS name or NetBIOS name of the other forest. This forest is identified as the "specified" domain in the screenshots and documentation.
5. Select `Forest Trust` and then click `Next`.
6. On the `Direction of Trust` page, select the `Trust` direction, as shown in Figure 8-34, and click `Next`. For this example, a two-way trust is selected.

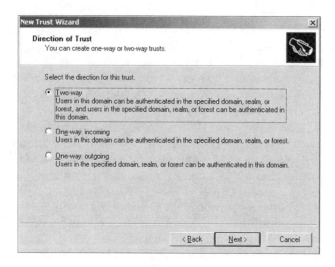

Figure 8-34   Selecting direction of trust.

7. Select the `Incoming Trust Authentication Level`, as shown in Figure 8-35, and then click `Next`.

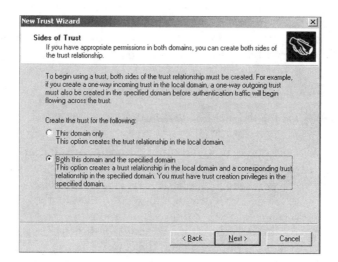

Figure 8-35   Selecting outgoing trust authentication level.

8. Select the `Outgoing Trust Authentication Level` and click `Next`.

9. Note the summary information and then click `Next`.

10. Select `Yes, confirm the outgoing trust` and then click `Next`.

11. Enter the user name and password from the other forest authorized to create a trust relationship and click OK.
12. Select Yes, confirm the incoming trust and then click Next.
13. Review Trust status and then click Next.
14. In the Trust properties page, note that the specified domain name is listed in the trusted (outgoing trusts) and trusting (incoming) trust boxes, as shown in Figure 8-36.

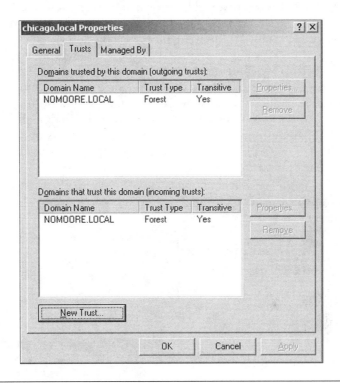

Figure 8-36   Confirming trust.

Grant Permissions to Resources in Trusting Forests

Granting access to resources across forests is similar to granting access across domains. The trust must be in place, and if selective authentication is chosen, the Allowed to Authenticate permission must be granted to the groups of users that should have this permission. If users are granted access to resources before the Allowed to Authenticate permission is granted to them, the users will still not be able to access the resources.

To grant the `Allowed to Authenticate` permission, add the group to the security property page of the domain controller and then select the `Allowed to Authentication` permission, as shown in Figure 8-37. The property page of the domain controller can be accessed from the Domain Controller OU. To grant the permissions, use the `Security` tab of the resource and then the object picker to select the group. When you open the object picker, be sure to select the location. In the `Locations` box, the trusted forest will be shown at the same level as the entire local directory, as shown in Figure 8-38. You must select it and click `OK` to be able to search for groups to include. On computers that are not Windows XP SP2 or Windows Server 2003, you cannot browse user and group names to select and then assign access. Instead, you must enter User Principal Names (UPN, or user@domainname format) or Windows NT 4.0-style names (domainname\username). In addition, users wanting to use workstations in the trusting forest to log on to domains in the trusted forest (where their accounts are) must use the UPN or Windows NT 4.0 format. They will not be able to select the domain names from a drop-down list in the logon screen.

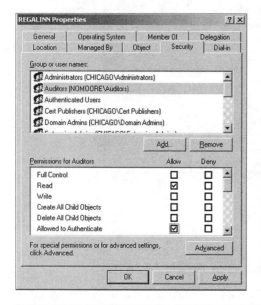

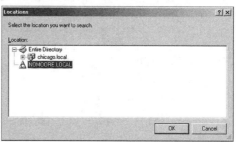

Figure 8-37   Grant user groups permission to authenticate to domains in the trusting forest.

Figure 8-38   Selecting the location of groups across a forest trust.

Cross-forest trusts include new challenges. Before you attempt to grant access to users from another forest, you should ensure that the time between the forests is synchronized. This might be done via a designated timeserver in the organization or via a public timeserver. If time is not synched, you cannot read the list of user and group accounts in the domain in the other forest.

Protecting Forests in a Cross-Forest Trust from an Elevation of Privileges Attack

Unless selective authentication is chosen during trust creation, it is possible for users to authenticate to their home domain across forest boundaries, and it may be possible for them to access resources in the trusting forest without having an account in any domain in that forest and before resources have been explicitly configured to allow their access. This is because the group Everyone is assigned access to some resources and because anonymous access may be available on one or more computers in the trusting forest. In other words, the security boundary of a forest is pierced when a forest trust relationship is created and the possibility of successful elevation of privilege attacks is increased. Three mechanisms exist that can help mitigate this effect:

■ Other than anonymous access and resources available to the group Everyone, users from the trusted forest can log on from a workstation in the trusting forest but do not automatically obtain elevated privileges to access resources inaccessible via anonymous access or to the group Everyone. The rights and permissions needed by the user must be granted explicitly. Careful planning and administration of group membership and the granting and denial of rights and permissions will prevent unauthorized access or exercise of rights.

■ SID filtering is automatically enabled between forests in a forest trust. User and group SIDs include information that identifies which domain their account resides within. When SID filtering is turned on, a user from one forest cannot include SIDs from another forest in his authorization information, thereby fraudulently obtaining access to a resource in another forest. SID filtering evaluates all of the SIDs in a user's authorization information and drops SIDs presented by the member of another forest that don't come from her forest. The user's access token will therefore not contain these SIDs.

- Selective authentication can be used. If it is, then the `Allowed to Authenticate` permission must be granted before users who have accounts in the trusted domain can do anything or obtain access in the trusting domain. Selective authentication and the `Allowed to Authenticate` permission are only available in the Windows Server 2003 domain. More information is available in the section "Piercing Security Boundaries—The Ultimate Forest Design Issue" and in the document "Planning and Implementing Federated Forests in Windows Server 2003," available at http://www. microsoft.com/technet/treeview/default.asp?url=/technet/prodte chnol/windowsserver2003/maintain/security/fedffin2.asp.

Group Policy in Forest and Multiforest Scenarios

Group Policy is primarily a domain-centric process. That is, Group Policy Objects (GPOs) are created to control users and computers that have accounts in specific domains. The GPOs are linked to the domain or the domain's OUs. The exception to this is the Site GPO, a rare beast that can impact users in multiple domains depending on the location of domain users and computer accounts and where they log on. However, site policies only affect computers and users whose accounts reside in that site. The site GPO is limited to a single forest. There is no Group Policy mechanism for managing users forest-wide, and there is no mechanism for implementing a single GPO that can impact multiple forests.

However, it is still necessary to manage Group Policy across multiple domains in a forest to ensure consistency of policy. It may also be useful to be able to manage Group Policy across forest boundaries. The tedious practice of inspection, reviewing, querying, using, and understanding Group Policies in the forest can be alleviated by using the Group Policy Management Console (GPMC).

Using GPMC in a Multidomain Forest and with Multiple Forests

GPMC was introduced in Chapter 8, and its functionality was described for use by a single domain. In a multidomain forest, you can use these same functions to view GPOs for a domain, and you can use GPO planning and logging mode for each domain in the forest. Remember: There is no such thing as a GPO that is created at the forest level. If you understand and have practiced with GPMC in a single domain, you have most of the knowledge needed to use it in a multiple-domain forest or with multiple forests. However, there is one major issue with using GPMC in this environment. When GPMC is used to copy a GPO from one domain to another, you must be aware of domain-specific information and make adjustments accordingly.

Most of the information in a GPO is not domain-specific, and copying this part of the GPO to another domain does not cause a problem. Other information, such as user and Group SIDs, is domain-specific, and URLs may be, too. Leaving these items as they are in the original GPO may interfere with proper functioning of the new GPO at its new location. For example, if a group of user rights is assigned to domain A's groups, and the GPO is copied for use in domain B, what will it mean? Users from domain A will have access to domain B rights—is this what you wanted? Users from domain B will not have the rights they expected. Even the SIDs of built-in domain groups will vary from one domain to another.

Because this domain-specific information cannot be changed automatically, GPMC provides a tool called migration tables to assist you in using a copy of a GPO in another domain. Before making the copy, you prepare a migration table. The table is used during the copy to translate or replace one domain's domain-specific information with the appropriate information from the other domain.

Working with multiple forests in GPMC is similar to working with one forest. Each forest has its own root. Adding a forest to GPMC is a simple process:

1. Right-click the GPMC root and select Add Forest.
2. Enter the name of a domain in the other forest, as shown in Figure 8-39, and click OK.
3. The forest is added to the GPMC console.

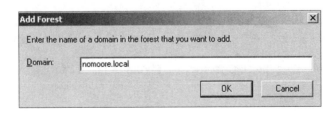

Figure 8-39 Adding a forest.

Using Migration Tables

User- and group-related information varies among domains in a forest and between forests. When a GPO is copied between two forests, the GPO may not function, or may not function as designed. To ensure that the GPO does its job, use migration tables to map users and groups from one domain to another.

To create the migration table, follow these steps:

1. Decide which GPO will be copied and where it will be copied.
2. Right-click the GPO container in GPMC and select Open migration Table Editor.
3. Select Populate from GPO from the Tools menu.
4. Select the forest and domain.
5. Select the source GPO and check During scan, include security principals from the DACL on the GPO, as shown in Figure 8-40, and then click OK.
6. The table is populated with any users, groups, or URLs specific to the GPO. Enter the correct security principal or URL that will be used by the destination domain in the name column for each entry, as shown in Figure 8-41.

Figure 8-40 Selecting the GPO to copy.   **Figure 8-41** Creating the migration table.

7. Save the file and close the Migration Table Editor.

To copy a GPO from a domain in one forest to a domain in another trusted forest follow these steps:

1. Right-click the GPO in Group Policy Objects and select Copy.
2. Right-click Group Policy Objects in the destination domain and select Paste.
3. On the welcome page of the Cross-Domain Copying Wizard, click Next.
4. Select Preserve or migrate the permissions from the original GPOs, as shown in Figure 8-42, and then click Next.
5. The wizard scans the GPO to determine if items need to be migrated, as shown in Figure 8-43. When it is done, click Next.

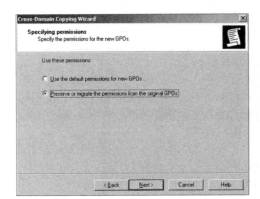
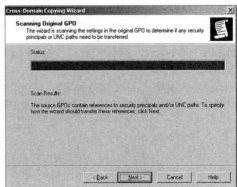

Figure 8-42   Specify whether permissions should migrate.

Figure 8-43   Scanning the GPO.

6. Select Using this migration table to map them to new values in the new GPOs and enter or browse to the location of the migration table made earlier, as shown in Figure 8-44. Then click Next.
7. Click Finish and then click OK.

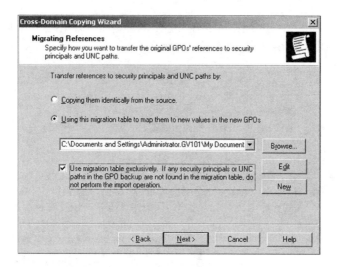

Figure 8-44 Selecting the migration table to be used.

After the GPO has been copied to its new domain, it must be linked to the domain or OU before it will have any effect on users or computers. To link the GPO to a domain or OU:

1. Right-click the OU or domain and select `Link existing GPO`.
2. Select the new GPO and click `OK`.

Finally, check the GPO to ensure that names were migrated. For comparison, Figure 8-45 shows the details of the copied GPO, while Figure 8-46 shows the GPO implementation in the new domain. As you can see, the appropriate domain and group names were changed.

Figure 8-45 Viewing the copied GPO.   **Figure 8-46** Comparing the new result.

TIP: Selective Authentication and GPMC
If selective authentication is required, GPMC cannot add another forest until the Administrator using GPMC has been given access in the other domain.

Piercing Security Boundaries—The Ultimate Forest Design Issue

Trusting someone has its risks. There is always the chance that the person will dishonor that trust and do you harm. This is also true of trust relationships between Windows domains and forests. Whenever you pierce a security boundary, you open another avenue of attack. Should an attacker obtain access to one domain, he may be able to more easily penetrate the defenses of the other. You will need to plan for this eventuality. You should also realize that your own trusted administrators might use the new conditions to fraudulently obtain privileges in the trusting domain or forest.

Windows NT 4.0 domains are security boundaries. Administrators in each Windows NT 4.0 domain have no rights in each other's domain. Windows 2000 and Windows Server 2003 domains are not security boundaries. Enterprise admins and schema admins have authority that can impact every domain in the forest. In addition, because of the tight coupling of domains, a rogue administrator could programmatically insert the SIDs of another domain's administrators in her authorization data and thus elevate her privileges in the other domain. A defense against this possibility is to evaluate current and potential administrators for their trustworthiness and to audit every administrator's activities. Alternatively, multiple forests can be used because the forest is a security boundary. The possibility of an attack by rogue admins is not the only reason for multiple forests. Multiple forests also provide administrative autonomy, which may be necessary due to a lack of trust within an organization or different requirements for domain-wide structure (such as password policy or schema). Multiple forests may also be deployed where politics or law requires proof of complete separation of assets.

The possibility of successful elevation of privilege attacks also arises when external trusts and forest trusts are created. Administrators in trusted domains could obtain unauthorized administrative privileges in another domain. To combat this possibility, two additional strategies,

SID filtering and selection authentication, can be implemented. It is important to develop a security plan for this action before creating the external or forest trust.

TIP: Resources on Security Boundaries and Forest Design

Three excellent references on security boundaries and forest design issues are "Planning and Implementing Federated Forests in Windows Server 2003" (it even obtains a list of appropriate firewall ports to open for different scenarios involving Windows trusts), available at www.Microsoft.com/technet/prodtechnol/windowsserver2003/maintain/security/fedffin2.asp; "Multiple Forest Considerations," available at www.Microsoft.com/technet/prodtechnol/windowsserver2003/plan/mtfstwp.asp; and "Design Considerations for Delegation of Administration in Active Directory," available at www.Microsoft.com/technet/prodtechnol/ad/windows2000/plan/addeladm.asp.

These countermeasures, if used improperly or misunderstood, may hamper legitimate administrative access. Plans for managing any such issues should be established so that restricted access does not eventually result in the removal of the countermeasures. Keep in mind that although evaluating risk and imposing a security solution is a management decision, your job is to provide the technical advice to make this possible.

SID Filtering—Catching SID Spoofs

Authorization for access to objects or to use rights on a system is granted to users, computers, and groups. The operating system determines access by comparing lists of approved SIDs against a list of SIDs belonging to the requesting user or computer. The security of the system, therefore, is based on the assumption that the list of SIDs and privileges assigned to an object or right is correct, and that a user's or computer's lists of authorized SIDs is also correct. Careful administration of objects and rights makes the system more trustworthy.

However, an escalation of privilege attack is possible if an attacker is authorized for some access to the system and is able to programmatically spoof or insert additional unauthorized SIDs into his authorization material. If the attacker knows the SIDs of privileged accounts and uses them, then his ability to manage the system or access its resources is only limited by those rights and privileges granted to the SID he uses. Within a Windows Server 2003 or Windows 2000 forest, there is no defense against this type of attack except the selection and monitoring of trustworthy administrators.

When a trust is established within an external domain or with another forest, these same types of attacks are possible. However, SID filtering can be used to defend against this type of attack. When SID filtering is enabled and a user crosses the trust boundary from the trusted domain into the trusting domain, his authorization list is stripped of any SIDs that belong to the trusting domain. It's as if an authorization firewall exists between the external and local domain or between the forests of the forest trust. SID filtering is turned on by default between forests in a forest trust, and it is recommended for external trusts.

SID filtering does not prevent assignment and use of privileges across domains; the list of these SIDs is added to the user's access token when the user first connects to the resource computer. The only SIDs stripped from her authorization material are those SIDs that are in her authorization material when she authenticates to the trusting domain but before she connects to the resource computer.

SID filtering is not always appropriate. It can negate the use of SID history. When a user from an external domain is migrated to the local domain, SID history is used to maintain her access to resources in the external domain. SID history maintains the list of SIDs assigned to the user in the external domain. These SIDs become part of her authorization material and hence her access token when she is connected to resources. SID filtering will remove the SIDs in SID history from the user's authorization material.

SID filtering can be turned on and off by a member of the Domain Admins group in the trusting domain by using the Windows Server 2003 support tool `netdom`. `Netdom` is added to the server when you run the suptools.msi file in the `Support Tools` folder of the Windows Server 2003 installation CD-ROM.

To enable SID filtering, use the following command:

```
Netdom filtersidstrusteddomain
```

To disable SID filtering, use this command:

```
Netdom filtersidsnotrusteddomain
```

NOTE: Catch 22?
SID filtering is used in an attempt to prevent escalation of privilege attacks across domain trusts. But SID filtering can be disabled by a member of the Domain Admins group of the trusting domain. A determined attacker with privileges in the trusted domain might convince or coerce a member of the Domain Admins group in the trusting domain to do so. So why apply SID Filtering in the first place? While this scenario could occur, without SID filtering, no manipulation of an administrator or complicity is necessary. Whenever two people must cooperate to do something untoward, it's less likely for it to happen and much easier to find out about. Making it necessary that two or more people must collaborate is using the separation of duties security principle. However, you should not rely on the prohibiting effect of such action, and you should audit administrative actions.

Selective Authentication—The Trust Firewall

In an external or forest trust scenario, users must be authorized to access resources or exercise privileges in the trusting domain. However, when users authenticate to the domain, the Authenticated User's SID is added to their authorization material. Because many privileges of access and rights are granted to holders of this SID, users may have more access than you desire. You cannot change the membership of the Authenticated Users group; however, with Windows Server 2003, as discussed in the section "Creating a Forest Trust," you can limit their ability to authenticate to a specified domain or server.

If a user cannot authenticate, she has no access via the Authenticated Users group and cannot utilize authorized access specifically granted by administrators. For example, during the completion of the forest trust described in the "Creating a Forest Trust" section, selective authentication was turned on. An administrator in the nomoore.com domain can use the object picker to grant the noless.com\Accountants group access to resources in his domain. However, until the noless.com\Accountants group is explicitly given the permission `Allowed to Authenticate`, it cannot access those resources.

If the noless.com\accountants group is given that permission, then when a member of that group authenticates to the nomoore.com domain, their access token is given the "Other Organization SID."

If selective authentication is used, then you must assign the `Allowed to Authenticate` right to every group that needs it. This could be a large administrative chore if not carefully planned, or if the need to address authentication is dynamic—that is, if frequent changes to access must be undertaken.

Best Practices for Trusts

Creating trusts enables the use of resources across domains and forests. Use the following best practices when considering the creation of trust relationships:

- Create shortcut trusts when long trust paths must be frequently used to access resources in other domains within the forest.
- Create trusts with external domains only when there is a need to access resources between forests.
- Create one-way trust relationships if that will fulfill the requirement. Do not make every trust a two-way trust.
- Create a forest trust only if many domain trust relationships between domains in the different forests are necessary. If only a few trust relationships are necessary, it may be better to create separate external trusts.
- Use selective authentication to limit access to resources in a domain across a trust. If the reason for the trust is to provide access to only a few of the resources in the specified domain, require selective authentication and provide the ability to authenticate to those groups from the other domain on only those resource servers required.
- Use selective authentication to limit access to domains in a forest trust.
- Depending on the need for resource access, use external trusts with or without selective authentication, or use forests trusts with or without selective authentication. Trusts without selective authentication offer the most access, while forest trusts with selective authentication offer the least.
- Use SID filtering with external and forest trusts. (SID filtering is enabled in Windows Server 2003 trusts by default.)

Summary

Trust between computer systems, domains, and forests parallel that which we see in our own lives. When trust is enabled, we empower people and organizations to do better work. However, we also empower those who would for whatever reason cause harm. At first blush, it seems that we need to stop the widespread access that trust entails. However, the answer is not to withdraw behind the boundaries of the past but instead to expand or increase in number better controlled, trusted access. Alhough there is no risk-free way to share resources, we must use the defenses we have. Limit the trusts to only those that are necessary, within the trust limit the access to those systems that need to be shared, and on those systems have tight control over the data that is exposed. This chapter has covered in broad strokes the ways that you can implement and limit trust between domains and forests with Windows Server 2003, but it is only your diligence and expertise that will ensure the best solution for your organization.

CHAPTER 9

Troubleshooting Group Policy

Good news! I love being the bearer of good news! The Group Policy Management Console (GPMC) provides infrastructure and processes that will enable you to effectively troubleshoot many Group Policy problems. But GPMC does not answer all your troubleshooting issues. The problem is that Group Policy relies on more than Group Policy. Proper Group Policy processing relies on all of these:

- **User and computer account placement**—Is the account within the hierarchy of the object that the Group Policy Object (GPO) is linked to?
- **Link status**—Is the GPO linked and enabled?
- **DNS**—Is DNS working appropriately?
- **The health of Active Directory**—Is replication timely and occurring appropriately?
- **The health of the file replication service (FRS)**—Is file replication occurring appropriately and in a timely fashion?
- **The client**—Is the client authenticating to the domain or using cached credentials?
- **The proper design of the GPO**—Are the right choices being made in its implementation?
- **GPO inheritance**—Which policies does the client receive last? Are any policies enforced or blocked? Is loopback processing used?

Because so many factors contribute to whether a GPO does what it is designed to do, it's important to have a strategy for determining what might be wrong. Like most troubleshooting strategies, the first step is to create a decision tree that reduces the number of things that have to be done to resolve the problem. Figure 9-1 illustrates the GPO troubleshooting decision. Table 9-1 lists where to find information necessary to perform troubleshooting.

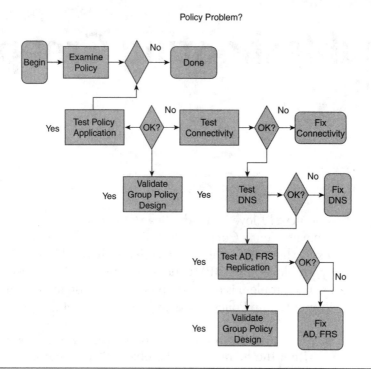

Figure 9-1 The GPO troubleshooting tree.

Table 9-1 Group Policy Troubleshooting Decision Tree

Test#	Test	Chapter Section or Other Resource
1	Is it a Group Policy problem?	See the following paragraph:
2	Has the GPO been applied?	Chapter 7, "Group Policy"; Chapter 9, "Determining If the Policy Has Been Applied"
3	Is GPO application correct?	Troubleshooting Group Policy Application Issues
4	No: Are clients using cached credentials?	Troubleshooting Networking Problems
5	No: Is the network running properly?	Troubleshooting Networking Problems

Test#	Test	Chapter Section or Other Resource
6	No: Is Active Directory or FRS replication operating correctly?	Troubleshooting Active Directory and FRS Replication
7	Yes: Are settings configured correctly?	Troubleshooting GPOs

The first step is to determine if the reported problem is a Group Policy problem or the way things are supposed to be. For example, the help desk may report that it cannot connect to some computers to remotely assist those users with computer problems. However, the help desk can remotely assist other users, and the computers in question can be pinged by the help desk operators. Is this a Group Policy problem? Or is it the way things are supposed to be? Are there computers that should not be remotely connected to? Before classifying the problem as a Group Policy problem, make sure that you know what the security policy is. Don't troubleshoot and change a GPO without first understanding your organization's security policy.

After determining that there is a problem, you still must determine if it is a Group Policy problem. That is, is a Group Policy not having the desired effect, or are other issues thought to be a Group Policy issue? If a Group Policy has been implemented and is not working as expected, then troubleshooting Group Policy is the next step. However, a number of security-related activities may not be due to Group Policy issues. Local configuration such as file permissions, a local IPSec policy, or personal firewall may be blocking access to a specific computer. Networking problems may also play a role. The instructions in this chapter only relate to Group Policy problems and presume that a specific GPO has been identified. An inspection of the Group Policies applied to a specific computer or user can be used to determine whether the problem is a result of a Group Policy Object's application. If that is the case, return to the first question: Is this the way things are supposed to be? If not, removing the offending setting or GPO (or removing the user or computer account from its application either by changing the OU location of the account or by using security filtering) can solve the problem.

Determining if the GPO has been applied is a critical step because the answer may determine whether to test networking issues or GPO configuration next. If the GPO hasn't been applied, then a number of issues may be preventing it—from networking issues to replication or a poor Group Policy design or implementation. If the GPO is being applied but is not doing what was expected, then the problem is either in GPO design or application. By asking questions and looking for answers in an organized way, the problem may be resolved in a more efficient manner. Approaching troubleshooting in the order listed is one way to do so.

However, there are no hard and fast rules, and even information about the experience and knowledge level of the individuals who maintain the network and Active Directory and configure the GPOs can play a role. For example, if network problems are rampant in your organization, then networking may be the reason that a GPO is not applied. If the Active Directory is not working as it should, then that is usually the cause, and if administrators do not understand Group Policy, then its configuration is probably the issue. This means that you may be able to more clearly predict the most likely cause of the problem for your environment. If everything in your environment runs equally well (or is equally messed up), I would suggest that you verify network issues first, simply because this is generally easier and because network issues can cause problems with replication and with Group Policy.

TIP: Install Resource Kit Tools and Support Tools

Many important troubleshooting and monitoring tools for Group Policy are provided in the Support Tools group on the Windows Server 2003 installation CD. Other tools are available in the Windows Server 2003 Resource Kit available for free download from `http://www.microsoft.com/downloads/ details.aspx?FamilyID=9d467a69-57ff-4ae7-96ee-b18c4790cffd& DisplayLang=en`. Install the tools, read their help files, and become comfortable with their use before you need them. Get a copy of the Windows Server 2003 Resource Kit.

That said, dcdiag.exe, a support tool, runs a number of tests that require a properly functioning DNS server with correct DC records to return a pass. If you run dsdiag and get a pass on these tests, you can eliminate connectivity and DNS issues. You may also eliminate Active Directory replication and File Replication Service (FRS) issues. Errors returned by dsdiag may not explicitly point to the cause of the Group Policy problem, but because it can eliminate many problems and identify general areas for further research, it's a good baseline tool. Run it periodically, before you have a problem, as a general monitor of Group Policy health.

Determining If the Policy Has Been Applied

Determining if the policy in question has been applied up front can save you hours of troubleshooting. After all, if a DNS problem prevents the policy from being applied at all, then there is no sense in analyzing policy hierarchy or the details of GPO configuration. Likewise, if everything's copasetic in the network, you'll need to evaluate the GPOs in question. Finally, a visual inspection of a complex Group Policy configuration and hierarchy can still leave you unsure of whether a specific GPO will be applied to a specific account. The answer is to determine if the policy has been applied. If the policy has been applied, you may still have to do some visual inspection to determine its effect. If the policy has not been applied, your quest to determine this may show the reason why. For example, a GPMC Group Policy Results scan may show why a GPO is not applied to a specific account.

To determine if a Group Policy has been applied, use GPMC. If GPMC is not available or cannot be used, the Resultant Set of Policy MMC snap-in can be used on Windows Server 2003 and Windows XP, and the GPResults Windows 2000 Resource Kit Tool can be used on Windows 2000.

Use GPMC

The easiest way to determine if a policy has been applied to a user or computer is to use the Group Policy Management Console (GPMC) to create a Resultant Set of Policy report using the Group Policy Results Wizard for the specific user or computer. In the report, select the Summary tab; then use the show statement next to Group Policy Objects to reveal the Group Policy Objects Applied and Group Policy Object Denied sections of the report, as shown in Figure 9-2. These sections list the GPOs applied or denied. If the GPO does not appear in either of these sections, then determine why by reviewing the "Troubleshooting Networking Problems" and "Troubleshooting Active Directory and FRS Replication" related problems sections of this chapter. If the GPO does appear in one of the lists, review the "Troubleshooting Group Policy Object Design" section of this chapter.

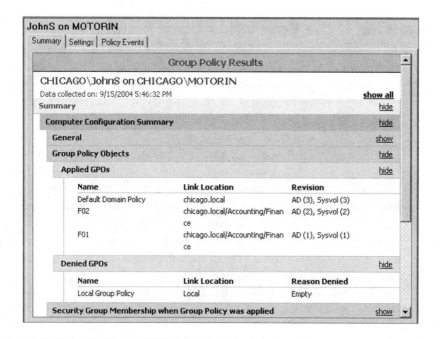

Figure 9-2   Determining GPO application.

To create a Group Policy Results report, follow these steps:

1. Click the `Start`, `Administrative Tools`, `Group Policy Management` console.
2. Right-click on the `Group Policy Results` node and select the `Group Policy Results Wizard`.
3. Click `Next` on the Welcome page.
4. On the Computer Selection page, as shown in Figure 9-3, click to select `Another computer`. Then enter or browse to the other computer name and click `Next`.
5. Select the user, as shown in Figure 9-4, and then click `Next`. Only those users who have logged in and for whom you have permission to view Group Policy will be displayed.

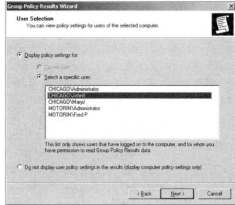

Figure 9-3   Selecting the computer.

Figure 9-4   Selecting the user.

> **6.** Review the summary of your selections and click Next. Then click Finish. The Report will be displayed in the GPMC, as shown in Figure 9-5.

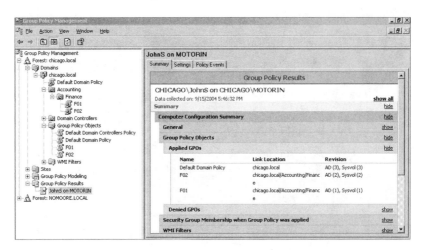

Figure 9-5   Obtaining the report.

If the GPOs that should be applied are being applied, you might be able to find the problem right away by looking for the use of a double negative. This happens when a setting starts with the word "disable." If you disable it, you have effectively enabled the setting. It's easy to misunderstand how a setting works when it starts with a negative word, and you should always scan the applied GPO settings in the report to see if any double negatives are the cause of your problem. Figure 9-6 shows an example of a setting that might be misapplied because it begins with the word "disable." The setting, `Disable machine account password changes`, can be used to prevent the automatic password change for computer accounts. By default, computer account passwords are periodically changed. If a computer is offline for a significant amount of time, its account password can be out-of-synch with that known to the Active Directory. To avoid this situation, this Group Policy setting is available. However, many administrators will disable the setting. They think they have stopped the automatic password change, but instead, they have just explicitly enabled it. They should have set this Group Policy setting to "enable."

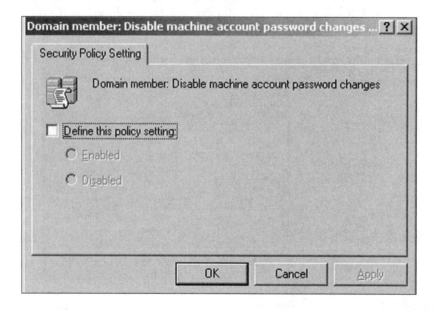

Figure 9-6   Disable this setting, and you have enabled computer password changes.

Use Resultant Set of Policy

The Resultant Set of Policy Wizard is available as an MMC snap-in for both Windows Server 2003 and Windows XP. To run the wizard on Windows XP, follow these steps:

1. Open a blank MMC.
2. From the `File` menu, select `Add/Remove Snap-in`.
3. Click the `Add` button. Then scroll the `Add Standalone Snap-in` windows and select `Resultant Set of Policy`. Click `Add`, and click `Next` twice.
4. Select `This computer` or use the `Browse` button to select another computer.
5. If only user policy settings are desired, check the box `Do not display policy settings for the selected computer in the results (display user policy settings only)`.
6. Click `Next`.
7. Select `Current user`, or select `Another user` and then select one of the listed users.
8. If only computer settings are desired, check the box `Do not display user policy settings in the results (display computer policy settings only)`.
9. Click `Next`, and review the summary. Then click `Next`, followed by `Finish`.
10. Click `Close`. and then click `OK`.
11. To view the results, expand the report in the console.

To run the wizard on Windows Server 2003, do the following:

1. Open a blank MMC.
2. From the `File` menu, select `Add/Remove Snap-in`.
3. Click the `Add` button. Scroll the `Add Standalone Snap-in` windows and select `Resultant Set of Policy`; then click `Add`.
4. Click `Close`, followed by `OK`.
5. Right-click the `Resultant Set of Policy` node in the console and then select `Generate RSoP Data`.
6. Click `Next`, select `Logging mode`, and then click `Next`.
7. Select `This computer`, or select `Another computer` and `Browse` to locate the computer.
8. If only user policy settings are desired, check the box `Do not display policy settings for the selected computer in the results (display user policy settings only.)`.
9. Click `Next`.

10. Select Current user, or select Another user and then select one of the listed users.
11. If only computer settings are desired, check the box Do not display user policy settings in the results (display computer policy settings only).
12. Click Next, review the summary, and then click Next.
13. When the processing is complete, click Finish.
14. To view the results, expand the report in the console.
15. Browse to an area the GPO should have applied results in and view details in the details pane. The source GPO is displayed in the Source GPO column. If the GPO in question is listed, then it has been applied. If it is not, and the item in question is definitely in the GPO, then the GPO has not been applied.

WARNING: Don't Limit Testing to One Item
If a single item that you believe should be applied by the GPO is not listed, do not assume that the GPO has not been applied. The problem could be with your assumption. The GPO could be configured incorrectly so that this one item is not showing up in the report. Check other items before assuming that the entire GPO has not been applied. Better still, install GPMC and use it whenever possible because it does indicate directly whether a GPO has been applied.

Use GPResult

GPResult is a native Windows Server 2003 command-line tool and a Windows 2000 Resource Kit tool that can be downloaded from the Microsoft site (http://www.microsoft.com/windows2000/techinfo/reskit/tools/existing/gpresult-o.asp). The Windows 2000 version of GPResult must be run while locally logged on to the computer as the user to test. The following information can be obtained:

- Computer-specific information such as OS and group memberships.
- User-specific settings such as group membership and security privileges.
- A list of GPOs and their details.

- The last time policy was applied and from which domain controller the policy was downloaded. If this varies by user or computer, the information will be reported.
- IP security settings.
- Downloaded scripts.
- Folder redirection settings.
- Applied registry settings.

The Windows Server 2003 version of GPResult can be run against a remote computer. Table 9-2 lists the command syntax.

Table 9-2 GPResult Syntax

Switch	Purpose
/S	Specify the remote system to connect to.
/U	Specify the user context under which the command should execute. Use the domain\user format.
/P	The password for the user context.
/SCOPE	Specify whether user or computer policy information should be listed. The only valid values are USER or COMPUTER.
/USER	Specify the user to display the RSoP data for. Use the domain\user format.
/V	Display verbose information. Use this switch to obtain the security settings applied.
/Z	Displays super-verbose settings. This setting may help when settings are applied from more than one location.

Issuing the command GPResults without switches will provide minimal information for the currently logged on user on the local machine. The GPOs applied are listed, but not the settings applied. Use the /V switch to see the list of settings each GPO applies. The following command runs GPResult on the local computer and provides verbose results for the logged on user. The results will be logged to the GPResult1.txt file.

```
Gpresults /V > GPResult1.txt
```

The following listing is the first bit of the nine-page report generated:

```
Microsoft (R) Windows (R) Operating System Group Policy Result
tool v2.0
Copyright (C) Microsoft Corp. 1981-2001


Created On 9/12/2004 at 2:58:39 PM



RSOP data for CHICAGO\Administrator on REGALINN : Logging Mode
--------------------------------------------------------------
-


OS Type:                      Microsoft(R) Windows(R) Server
2003, Enterprise Edition
OS Configuration:             Primary Domain Controller
OS Version:                   5.2.3790
Terminal Server Mode:         Remote Administration
Site Name:                    Default-First-Site-Name
Roaming Profile:
Local Profile:                C:\Documents and
Settings\Administrator
Connected over a slow link?: No



COMPUTER SETTINGS
------------------
    CN=REGALINN,OU=Domain Controllers,DC=chicago,DC=local
    Last time Group Policy was applied: 9/12/2004 at 2:57:35
PM
    Group Policy was applied from:     regalinn.chicago.local
    Group Policy slow link threshold:  500 kbps
    Domain Name:                       CHICAGO
    Domain Type:                       Windows 2000

    Applied Group Policy Objects
    ----------------------------
        Default Domain Controllers Policy
        Default Domain Policy
```

Determine If the Group Policy Design Is Correctly Implemented

If the GPO is not applied, there may be a number of reasons why this is true. A number of Group Policy-related issues may prevent the policy from being applied. Often these reasons can be viewed by looking on the Summary tab or the Group Policy Results report created in GPMC under the computer configuration summary or user configuration summary. The possible reasons include:

- **Security filtering**—GPOs are linked to sites, domains, and OUs. By default, the GPO will be applied to the accounts that exist within these containers. However, the permissions page of the GPO can be used to limit which accounts get the GPO. By default, the Authenticated Users group is given the Apply to permissions. This means that the GPO will be applied to every Authenticated User account in the container to which the GPO is linked. To filter GPOs, instead of using this generic Authenticated Users group, specific groups can be designated as those who can apply the policy. Any groups, and thus users, not explicitly given permission will be denied. Of course, explicit denial can also be configured. If you determine that a specific user or computer, or a group of users or computers, is not getting the policy applied while all others are, the usual answer is security filtering. Determine who should get the policy and then check the permissions page of the GPO or the Scope page of GPMC to determine if it is set up correctly. To display the Scope page, select the GPO in the GPMC console, as shown in Figure 9-7. In the figure, note that the security filter is configured to apply the GPO to users who are members of the CHICAGO\Finance group. If a user account is in the OU hierarchy for this GPO and is a member in the Finance group, the policy will be applied. The policy will not be applied to other user accounts that reside in the OU hierarchy.
- **Disabled GPO Link**—A disabled GPO will not be applied. Look at the Links section of the Scope page of the GPMC report for the specific GPO, as shown in Figure 9-8. If you find that a valid GPO is marked as disabled, you can correct this by enabling it; however, the wise solution would be to attempt to determine why the GPO is disabled. The reason for disablement might be that some severe, unwanted effect occurs when the policy is applied. Rather than enabling the GPO, the problematic effect of the GPO should be determined and corrected first.

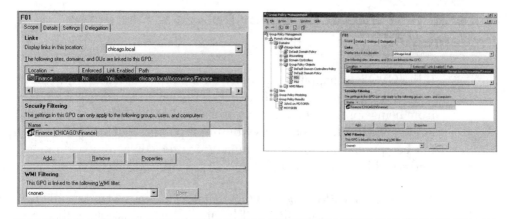

Figure 9-7   Checking security filtering.

Figure 9-8   Checking for Link enabled.

- **Inaccessible GPO**—This can occur if a link to a GPO exists, but the GPO cannot be found or cannot be accessed. This might be due to insufficient permissions on the GPO or on folders in the path to the GPO template. In this case, the Component section of the Group Policy Results summary tab of the GPO report indicates "failure" for Group Policy Infrastructure. Figure 9-9 shows the location of the Group Policy Infrastructure status. In the figure, no problems are reported. Other reasons may be network connectivity, replication, DNS, or AD processing.

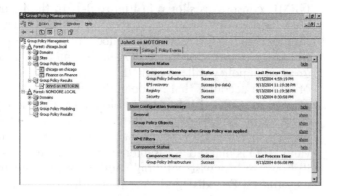

Figure 9-9   Checking Group Policy Infrastructure status.

- **Empty GPO**—A GPO without settings can be configured and linked but will not be processed.
- **WMI filter**—A WMI filter restricts GPO processing to computers and users who meet specific qualities as defined in the filter. If the filter is not correctly designed, or if something is wrong in its processing, then a policy may not be applied.

Even if the GPO is applied, the specific setting that is desired may not be. Look in the policy to see if the setting is listed. Look also at the results of one of the tools listed previously. If the setting is not listed in a results set but is in the GPO, then a change to the policy hasn't reached the client, the change is not supported by the operating system, or the change has been overridden by inheritance or the application of special Group Policy settings. The following possibilities should be checked:

- **Group Policy refresh**—By default, the client checks for changes to its GPOs every 90 minutes and will refresh if a change has occurred. Security settings are refreshed periodically, whether or not changes have occurred. Some portions of a GPO will not be applied until a user logs on, and others such as Software Restriction policies require a reboot. If a change occurs to Folder Redirection, Roaming Profiles settings, or Software Installation settings while the user is logged on, it will not take affect until the user logs off and then logs back on again. The use of asynchronous processing can also have an impact. You can check the last time of policy refresh by checking the summary table of the Group Policy Results report under Computer Configuration Summary and User Configuration Summary. Use the `secedit /refreshpolicy` command on Windows 2000 systems or the `gpupdate` command on Windows Server 2003 and Windows XP Professional systems to force an update and reexamine the results.
- **Replication problems**—If either AD or FRS replication is not occurring correctly, changes to the policy will not be available. See sections on troubleshooting these systems later in this chapter.
- **Replication latency**—Normal AD and FRS replication is not instantaneous. The process by which changes replicate and all domain controllers obtain them is called *replication convergence*. The time it takes for complete replication is the *replication latency*. Replication latency will vary depending on bandwidth, number of sites, and amount of replication traffic. If the normal

latency of replication of the organization is known, it can be determined whether that is the problem. Consider also that it's not just policies and their associated files that must be replicated but also changes to group membership or domain membership for users and computers. If, for example, a GPO is linked to the Accountants OU, and Jeff Smith's account has just been added to that OU, the user portion of the GPO will not apply until knowledge of his account in that OU has replicated to the domain controller at which his authentication takes place. Likewise, if security groups filter the GPO, and membership in the group has recently changed, the GPO may not be applied to the new members of the group.

■ **Default behavior**—The determination of which GPO will win when multiple policies are applied can usually be ascribed to inheritance rules. The last policy applied wins. However, some settings, such as those in the password policy, can only be set in a specific location. Only the final settings will appear in the Group Policy Results Report in the "Winning GPO column," as shown in Figure 9-10.

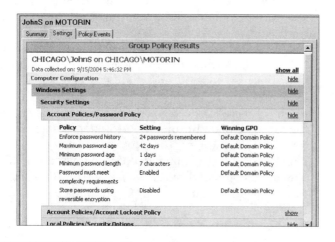

Figure 9-10   Viewing the winning settings.

- **Operating system support**—Several hundred new Group Policy settings are available in Windows Server 2003, and many of these are not supported by Windows 2000. If the setting is not supported, it cannot be applied. To determine if a setting is supported by the client operating system, download and examine the Excel file "Groups Policy Settings Reference for Windows Server 2003" from http://microsoft.com/downloads/details.aspx?FamilyID=7821c32f-da15-438d-8e48-45915cd2bc14&DisplayLang=en.

- **Service pack issue**—Service Pack 2 for Windows XP includes a large number of new XP-related Group Policy settings. The settings are included in a new system.adm file. When a Windows XP SP2 computer is used to edit GPOs, the new adm file is added to the GPO. Each GPO that will be used to manage Windows XP computers must be updated. To use these settings for XP in a Windows Server 2003 domain, the system.adm file must be copied from the `systemroot\inf\` folder on the Windows XP computer, renamed, and added to the `systemroot\inf` folder on the Windows 2000 domain controller. The old system.adm file should then be removed from the Group Policy Object that is linked to the OU within which the XP computer accounts reside. The new .adm file can then be linked and used to apply the new XP settings. If the new .adm file is not added, then the new settings will not show up in the GPO.

- **GPO inheritance**—Remember the rules of Group Policy inheritance. When multiple policies are applied, the last one applied wins, unless blocking or overriding has been configured. Blocking and overriding inheritance exceptions can also prevent a GPO from being applied at all. A detailed explanation of how Group Policy inheritance works was included in Chapter 7, "Active Directory's Role in Domain Security." Figure 9-11 displays the `Group Policy Inheritance` tab of the Chicago\Finance\Accounting OU. The top GPO (listed as 1 in the figure) is the "winning" GPO, but all GPOs may contribute to the policy setting. A results report for a specific computer or user in this OU will display the exact settings that are applied.

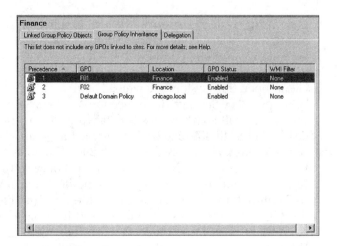

Figure 9-11 Viewing GPO inheritance.

- **Loopback processing**—Loopback processing applies the User sections of a computer GPO after all other GPOs have been applied. Normally, the User sections of a GPO in the location where the user account lies will be the last GPO applied, and thus will "win." If loopback processing is used, the local computer policy is reapplied after all other normal processing. When loopback processing is in place, all normal processing rules are followed, but because the final settings that are applied are from the local computer, settings that differ may be lost. If a GPO in the accounting OU, for example, enables access to the Run button and exposes Control Panel applet access, but the local computer GPO disables them, users of this computer who have accounts in the Accounting OU will not be able to use Control Panel applets or the Run button. On a computer without loopback configured, users would be able to use control panel applets or the run button. While loopback seeks to solve the problem presented by computer labs, kiosks, and other generally publicly exposed computer systems, remember that loopback will only impact users whose accounts are in Windows 2000 or Windows Server 2003 domains. If a trust exists with a Windows NT 4.0 domain, and a Windows NT 4.0 domain user is allowed to access the computer, no loopback will occur. To check for loopback processing, directly check the Group Policy loopback settings in the administrative templates section of all GPOs that affect the computer, as shown in Figure 9-12, view the Settings page of the GPO in GPMC, or check the User Group Policy loopback processing mode setting from the Settings tab in the GPMC Results report, as shown in Figure 9-13. The setting is recorded in Computer Configuration, Administrative Templates, System, Group Policy. For more information, refer to Chapter 7.

- **Client-side extension**—After a GPO is downloaded, client-side extensions perform some of the processing. Examples of client-side extensions are Folder Redirection, Registry, and script processing. If the extension is missing or corrupt, processing will be incomplete.

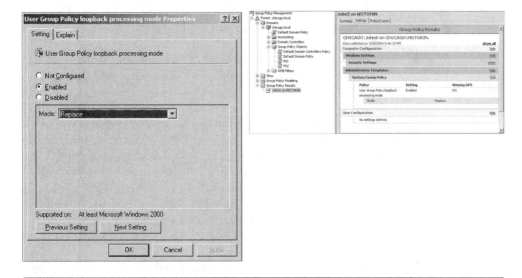

Figure 9-12   Loopback is configured in Administrative Templates.

Figure 9-13   Loopback settings can be discovered easily in a Group Policy Results report.

- **Asynchronous processing**—Group Policy processing can be synchronous or asynchronous. That is, either GPO processing is completed before a user may use the computer (synchronous), or it is not. In asynchronous processing, policies are applied as a background task during and after startup and logon. If asynchronous processing is used, a user may be able to do something that, once GPO processing is complete, he will not be able to do. By default, startup and logon processing for Windows 2000 and Windows Server 2003 is synchronous. The user will have to wait to log on until Group Policy application is complete. If the client is Windows XP, asynchronous processing during startup and logon is automatic. This means to the user, startup appears to be faster. There is another side effect to asynchronous possessing. When asynchronous processing is used, and changes are made in items such as `Folder Redirection`, `Roaming Profiles`, `Script Processing`, and `Software Installation`, the changes may not be available until the user logs off and logs on again. If the behavior is not desired, then processing should be changed. To do so, use the GPO settings `Computer Configuration`, `Administrative Templates`, `System`, `Logon Always Wait for the Network at Computer Startup and Logon`. Group Policy Refresh is asynchronous for Windows 2000, Windows XP Professional, and Windows Server 2003.

- **Slow network links**—Some parts of Group Policy processing can be restricted when the computer is connected via a slow link. Application installation, for example, will not occur over a slow link by default, while the application of administrative templates will. A slow link is defined as 500 kilobits per second or less. You can modify the specifics of slow link connections and Group Policy in the `Administrative Templates`, `System`, `Group Policy` section.

- **GPO editing issues**—If a GPO is edited at two different DCs, the last change wins. This means that the current GPO might not reflect the desired settings. To help counter this issue, it is always wise to make GPO changes at the same DC and to have designated administrators responsible for specific GPOs or GPOs on specific OUs.

- **True policies versus preferences**—Administrative templates include both true policies and preferences. Preferences can be deployed using Group Policy but cannot be enforced as well and are not removed even when the GPO that first set them is removed. Many preferences do not take affect when set, but only after the next startup or logon. Preferences are hidden by default in the Group Policy Editor. If preferences are used, users may see their behavior as unpredictable and wrong, even though the processing of these settings, which are made directly in the registry, is working as designed. To view preferences, in the Group Policy Editor, select an Administrative Templates node, and on the `View` menu, click `Filtering`. Then clear the `Only show policy settings that can be fully managed` check box.

- **Script processing**—Startup, logon, and logoff scripts can be applied using a GPO. However, the scripts merely update the registry with a script location so that normal user initialization processing knows where to look. The CSE reports success when this is accomplished, not after the script has run. The script CSE has no way of reporting errors in scripts and thus can't report that a script failed due to an error. Another possible problem is that the script processing can time out. A setting for `Maximum wait time` for Group Policy Scripts can be adjusted if this is the case. To find script-processing errors, look in the Application Event log for errors with a source of UserInit.

- **Software installation**—Network connectivity issues can prevent software installation. Other problems include misspelled or non-existent shares or paths within the share, and insufficient permissions on the share. Software installation can also be used to remove software should conditions change and the user or computer be removed from the scope of the policy. This condition should be checked for. When Windows Installer packages are used for software installation, the policy can be configured to install even if the user does not have administrative privileges. If it is not used, this can be a cause of software installation failure. Windows Installer package problems can also be the cause if they are corrupt. Use the Software Installation Diagnostics tool (addiag.exe) to find the details of applications installed via AD for the current user.

- **Folder redirection**—Only the `My Documents`, `Application Data`, `Desktop`, and `Start Menu` folders can be redirected. Problems can occur if the share and file system permissions are incorrect. The user must have ownership privileges on the redirected folder. Allow the system to create the folder, and permissions will be set correctly. The minimum permissions that are necessary are listed in Table 9-3.

Table 9-3   Minimum Folder Redirection Permissions

Group or User	Folder Redirection Root	Share	Each User Folder
Creator/Owner	Full Control, Subfolders and Files Only	N/A	N/A
All users who need to store data here	List Folder/Read data, create folders/append data—This folder only	Full Control	N/A
Local System	Full Control, this Folder, Subfolders and Files	N/A	Full Control
%username%	N/A	N/A	Full Control, Owner of Folder

NOTE: Troubleshooting Resource
A good source for additional troubleshooting information is the article
"Troubleshooting Group Policy in Windows Server 2003" at http://
microsoft.com/downloads/details.aspx?FamilyId=B24BF2D5-0D7A-4FC5-
A14D-E91D211C21B2&displaylang=en.

Troubleshooting Networking Problems

Three specific network questions must be asked:

- Does basic connectivity exist?
- Is DNS working?
- Can the client and the user authenticate to the domain? (If the computer and user cannot authenticate to the domain, then the policy will not be downloaded.)

It's probably most efficient to troubleshoot network problems by starting with the last issue first. If the client and user can authenticate to the domain, then basic networking and DNS are working. If the client or the user cannot authenticate to the domain, it may seem logical to test DNS. However, there are many DNS issues that can prevent logon and Group Policy operations. Before launching extensive DNS tests, perform basic connectivity tests. If these are not working, they need to be corrected first. If they work, then begin investigating DNS. Finally, don't ignore the rest of the world. It may be that some other recently conducted test has established that DNS is working correctly, or a user may provide helpful information. While many users are not network-literate, they may say something that provides enough information to indicate a more specific problem.

Troubleshoot Authentication

Another class of network-related problems occurs when the user is currently logged on to the domain. This can happen when cached credentials are used or when the user uses a local computer user account to log on. Cached credentials may be used when a DC cannot be located or when a VPN connection or some other remote connection is used.

When cached credentials are used, the last GPO policy stored locally on that computer will be applied. This may not be the current policy. If cached credentials usage is the result of LAN issues, troubleshoot and fix the LAN issues. If the user uses a VPN to connect to the network and does so after logging on to the computer, the latest GPOs will not be downloaded because the user is already authenticated. The VPN problem, however, can be rectified if the user will use the logon with the option to connect to a remote network from the initial logon—a choice presented when using Ctrl+Alt+Del.

To determine if cached credentials are being used, check the computer System log for event ID 5719, which states `No Windows domain controller is available for` `domain_name.` `The following error occurred: There are currently no logon servers available to service the logon required.` In some cases, a warning may also appear when the user logs on.

Troubleshoot Basic Network Connectivity

Basic TCP/IP troubleshooting and connectivity is covered extensively in networking tutorials and texts, and simple steps are listed in Knowledge Base articles. If the troubleshooting techniques for DNS return data, basic network connectivity can be assumed. Proper network configuration, however, may be an issue and is discussed within this chapter where relevant. Still, it's useful to remember that some estimate that 80% of all networking issues are a loose or disconnected cable. Before assuming a more complicated problem, check connections via observation of link lights on network ports, look for unplugged or damaged cables, and attempt to `ping` or `pathping` known routers, DCs, and other computers on the network. `Pathping` is a command available with Windows 2000, Windows XP, and Windows Server 2003. While the `ping` command can determine if packets are reaching the desired destination, `pathping` performs a trace route and additional tests. `Pathping` can identify the path to the destination and record packet loss and delays possibly due to network congestion.

In addition to basic network connectivity, the following items are necessary to support Group Policy infrastructure:

- TCP/IP must be running on all member and domain controller computers.
- ICMP is used to detect a slow link when the client first connects to the domain controller. If a firewall sits between the client and the domain controller, be aware that the firewall must allow ICMP if the connection is not tunneled.

- For slow detection to work, a feature that will avoid attempts at downloading GPOs, firewalls, and routers must support the use of a 2048-byte packet because the slow link detection packet is of this length. Group Policy settings determine what happens when a slow link is detected.
- Multihomed computers must have the high priority set for the network card that connects the client to the network from which GPOs are obtained.

Troubleshoot DNS

Many authentication issues and problems with replication and Active Directory can be traced back to problems with DNS. DNS must be working for these processes to work. This is why testing DNS before testing replication is a good choice. If DNS is broken, fix it, and many of these problems will go away. There are several ways to verify DNS configuration and functioning, including:

- Check client computer configuration.
- Use DNSLint.exe.
- Use DCDiag.exe.
- Use Portqry.exe.
- Examine Event Viewer events.
- Examine DNS records and make manual tests.

Most of these tools are provided in the `support tools` folder of the installation CD-ROM but are not installed by default. You can install them by inserting the installation CD-ROM and double-clicking on the support.msi file in the Support folder on the CD-ROM. DNSLint must be obtained via download from the Microsoft site.

Use caution when installing support tools. These tools can provide an attacker with much information and power over servers and your domains should he obtain the proper privileges to run them and find them loaded on the compromised server. While these tools are readily available for free download, an attacker would have to obtain them, install them, and then load them on the server (hopefully you've made that hard to do). While an attacker who has obtained the appropriate privileges will not have difficulty finding the tools and installing or using them, every extra step you burden the attacker with is one more reason that many of them will move on to easier targets. It may also provide you with the time to discover that you are under attack so that you can respond. Leaving excess tools lying about on every server is not a good security practice.

Check Client Computer Configuration

The most obvious problem is often the most frequently overlooked. Never assume that the client computer is correctly configured. A quick manual inspection of network properties may alert you to a necessary change. Use the `ipconfig /all` command or open the computer's network configuration, as shown in Figure 9-14.

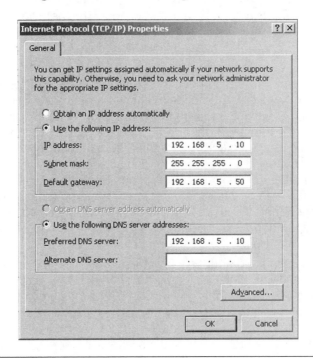

Figure 9-14   Always check to make sure the client computer knows the location of the correct DNS server.

Always Check the Obvious

In addition to not assuming that simple configuration is correct, never assume that others who should be knowledgeable really understand how DNS works and the interrelationship between DNS and Active Directory. As an adjunct teacher at a community college, I taught a class on designing security for a Windows network to seniors in a networking program. I had never met or worked with the students or the other instructors. The students in this class were about to graduate from the program. They had at least two years of training on Microsoft technologies, and many of them had on-the-job experience administering networks. After the introductory lecture, I divided them into four groups of six and assigned each group the task of implementing a six-computer single domain Windows 2000 network consisting of two domain controllers, two servers, and two clients. This network was for use in their assignments throughout the semester to implement their security designs.

Only one group was able to complete the assignment. The three other groups could not implement a second domain controller. They had failed to realize that the server they were attempting to configure as the second domain controller needed to be configured with the address of the DNS server authoritative for the domain. Instead, they configured this server to look to itself for DNS. Basic knowledge of DNS and adding domain controllers to a domain would have ordinarily been taught in a basic class about Active Directory or network infrastructure and may have been. However, the students didn't learn it, hadn't a clue on what to do to correct the problem, and did not even appear to understand the issue when told about it. As soon as they changed the DNS configuration for the server, they were able to successfully add the second domain controller.

Were the students stupid or their instructors inept? That is not the point, and you should not dwell on it. Instead, you should see this as just another example of the assumption that the person configuring a computer will know how to do so and will do so correctly every time. Experienced IT professionals, and students often make mistakes. What we should learn from this example is that in troubleshooting issues with DNS, or any other technology for that matter, you cannot assume that the problem is a difficult one. It may be that some simple error is the cause. I'm sure many of you can recall a time in which you spent time troubleshooting a networking problem, only to discover that the network cable was unplugged. Always check the simple things, like cable connections and TCP/IP configuration.

Using DNSLint

The DNSLint tool can be used to determine if problems exist with DNS. DNSLint is a Windows Server 2003 support tool, but it can also be used with Windows 2000 DNS. (DNSLint can be downloaded by following the link in the Knowledge Base Artile 321045 "Description of the DNSLint Utility," http://support.microsoft.com/default.aspx?scid=kb; en-us;321045#kb1.) DNSLint can also report on issues with AD Replication.

DNSLint produces an HTML report or a text file that lists problems with DNS, such as:

- **Lame delegation**—Lame delegation is the situation in which a DNS server delegates authority over a subdomain to another DNS server, but the server that the subdomain is delegated to cannot be reached or is not configured to be authoritative for that domain. It's analogous to the requirement that you obtain a badge from the security office, but when you get to the security office, it cannot issue that type of badge. If lame delegation exists within your environment, client systems will seek an authoritative DNS server for their domain but will never find one. Therefore, the client will not be able to locate a domain controller to authenticate to. Access to resources will be more difficult, if not impossible, and changes to security policy (GPOs) cannot be downloaded.
- **Missing CNAME or host (glue or A) records for domain controllers**—Clients search for a domain controller in their site by finding the GUID for the domain, resolving the associated CNAME, and then obtaining an IP address from the associated glue record. The glue record is the DNS record that ties, or glues, the computer or host name with the IP address that is assigned to it. The CNAME record is a record that identifies a device but does not provide an IP address. It may provide another associated name for the host, in this case the GUID. If either the CNAME or glue record is missing, the client may not locate a DC to authenticate to.
- **Improperly configured TCP/IP**—It is possible that the DNS location configured is not authoritative for the client's domain. In this case, the primary or alternative DNS server identified in the TCP/IP configuration of the computer is the wrong DNS server. When the computer boots, it cannot find the DNS server

authoritative for its domain. If it cannot find this DNS server, it cannot determine the location of a DC in its domain. Without a DC, the computer and user cannot authenticate to the domain or download the latest security policy.

■ **Missing Server Locator (SRV) records**—_ldap, _kerberos, _gc, and _msdts SRV records must be available for domains and global catalog servers. If these SRV records are missing, authentication cannot occur.

If these problems exist, then clients cannot access domain controllers, and replication between domain controllers may also be affected. The impact of these problems depends on the number of domain controllers and the number of problems there are. DNSLint does not just identify these problems, but many times it will also offer a possible solution. Using DNSLint to produce a report is simple. In the following sections, techniques for obtaining help with DNS are explained. Help using DNSLint to discover Active Directory replication problems is in the later section "Active Directory Replication Problems."

Basic DNS Configuration Check

Obtaining useful information is quite simple. To produce a report, use the following command at the command line:

```
Dnslint /d domain-name
```

This command will check for lame delegation and related DNS problems. The `domain-name` stands for the name of the domain to be checked. The `/s` switch is used to specify the IP address; otherwise, DNSLint will use the Internet to do an Internic Whois. This command will attempt to find all DNS servers that are authoritative for the domain and test all of them. If your DNS domain is not registered, use the `/s` switch.

Entering the following command produced the report displayed in Figure 9-15:

```
Dnslint /d tailspintoys.com
```

Figure 9-15   Viewing a DNSLint report.

In the figure, an Internic Whois generates a list of servers that are authoritative for the domain and some warning messages. The domains do not seem to have domain records on the servers, or that information may not be available.

To test the DNS server established for the local Chicago.local domain, the /s switch can be used, followed by the IP address of the local DNS server. Using the /s switch prevents DNSLint from doing an Internic whois. The following command is used and produces the report shown in Figure 9-16:

```
Dnslint /d Chicago.local /s 192.168.5.10
```

DNSLint Report

System Date: Thu Sep 16 09:12:11 2004

Command run:

dnslint /d chicago.local /s 192.168.5.10

Domain name tested:

chicago.local

The following 2 DNS servers were identified as authoritative for the domain:

DNS server: User Specified DNS Server
IP Address: 192.168.5.10
UDP port 53 responding to queries: YES
TCP port 53 responding to queries: Not tested
Answering authoritatively for domain: Unknown

Figure 9-16   Using DNSLint against a specific DNS server.

In both cases, the information that DNSLint attempts to report is as follows:

- Is each DNS server responding?
- What is the SOA data for zone?
- Are there additional authoritative DNS servers?
- What are the Host (A) records for name?
- What are the Mail Exchange (MX) and glue records for name?
- Are all records the same on every authoritative DNS server? (If not, intermittent name resolution problems may result.)
- Is a summary of errors and warnings, including Non-authoritative, missing glue records, and unresponsive servers shown?

Additional Switches and Special Considerations

The DNSLint switch `/ql:inputfile_path` will allow you to verify user-defined sets of DNS records on multiple DNS servers. You identify the DNS servers in a text file and use the command `dsnlint /ql:inputfile_path`, where `inputfile_path` specifies the path and filename of a text file that lists the IP addresses of the DNS servers you want to test.

Additional switches are as follows:

- `/v`—Reports additional information about the process while the report is begin generated.
- `/t`—Enables the production of a text file in addition to an HTML report.
- `/r`—Is used to specify the path of the report file.
- `/no_open`—Prevents the default file, dnslint.htm, from opening.
- `/c SMTP`—Checks for SMTP server records and tests connections for Pop, SMTP, and NNTP.
- `/test_tcp`—Checks if DNS responds on TCP port 53.

How does DNSLint work? By default, DNSLint uses a Whois command to check with the Internic to find the name of the authoritative DNS server for the domain and to obtain this DNS server's IP address. Next, it uses `nslookup` to query the returned IP address for a name and an MX record name server and attempts to discover other authoritative DNS servers for the domain. DNSLint queries these servers and compares records on all authoritative servers. The records should reflect the correct information, and all of them should be the same. If the information is incorrect, DNSLint will report it, and then it needs to be corrected. That step, however, DNSLint cannot do for you.

Use DCDIAG and NetDiag to Find DNS Problems

DCDiag is a multipurpose domain controller troubleshooting tool. Net-Diag is used to troubleshoot client domain/DNS issues. Simply issuing the dcdiag.exe command on a domain controller will perform most of its diagnostic tests. Because they test DC-specific functions, many of which rely on proper DNS functioning, a pass on these tests can mean that there are no DNS issues. To run a specific test, enter the following:

```
Dcdiag /test:testname
```

Some DCDiag tests that are helpful in troubleshooting DNS include:

- ForestDNSZones and DomainDNSzones, two tests that check for proper domain records.
- Connectivity checks for basic network connectivity.

Figure 9-17 is a screen capture of part of a DCDiag report. DCDiag provides extensive information. If desired, you can redirect the results to a text file to make it easier to study.

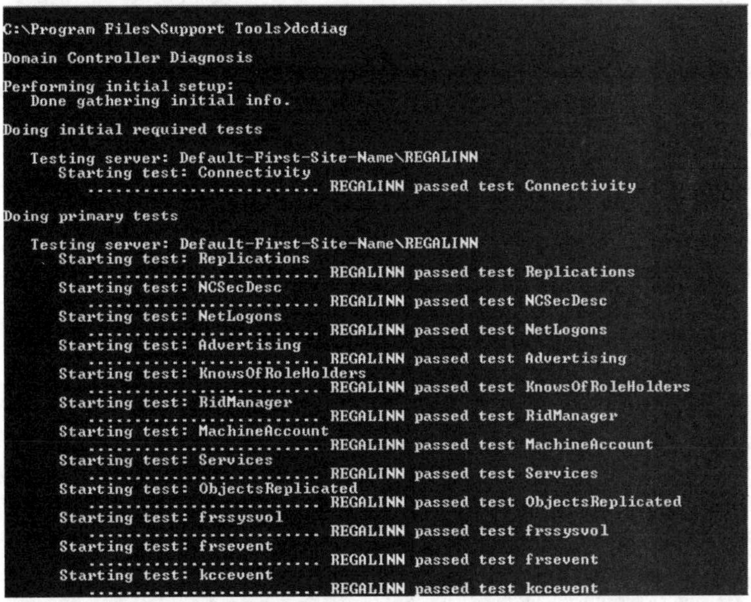

Figure 9-17 Using DCDiag to find DNS problems.

The Knowledge Base article 265706, "DCDiag and NetDiag in Windows 2000 Facilitate Domain Join and DC Creation" (http://support. microsoft.com/default.aspx?scid=kb%3ben-us%3b265706) provides more in-depth information on DCDiag and NetDiag.

NetDiag is similar to DCDiag, but because it tests client-to-DC/DNS connectivity, it has fewer tests. Run NetDiag from the client. To see if a client can access a domain controller in its domain, use the following command:

```
NetDiag /d:domainname
```

To use NetDiag with specific tests, use the following command:

```
NetDiag /test:testname
```

An example test command and its results are displayed in Figure 9-18.

```
NetDiag /l /test:dsgetdc
```

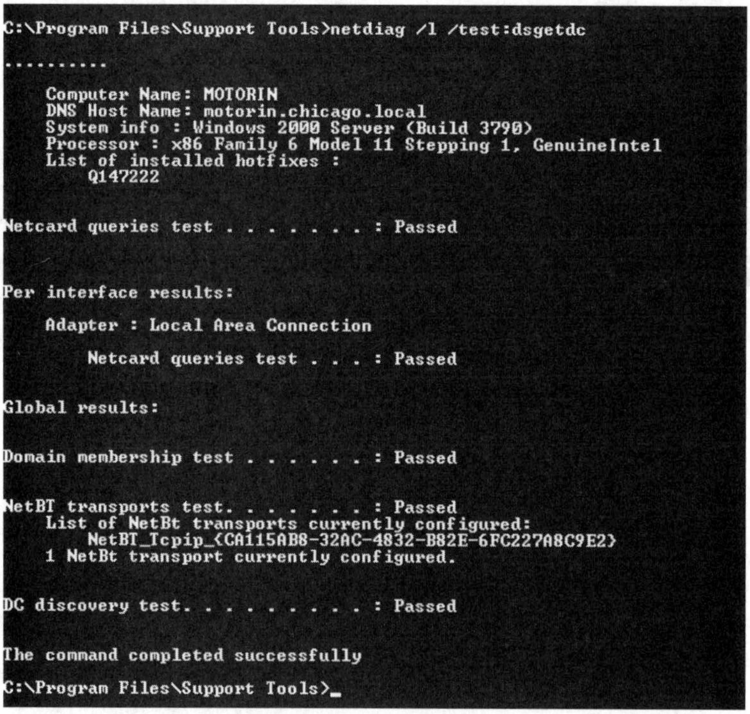

Figure 9-18   A NetDiag test.

The /1 switch outputs data to the NetDiag log file. The dsgetdc test tests the network card, computer domain membership, and access to the DC. Useful tests for testing connectivity to domain controllers include the following:

- **DcList**—The domain controller list test
- **DNS**—DNS tests
- **DsGetDC**—The domain controller discovery test
- **Kerberos**—The Kerberos test

Use Portqry

Portqry.exe is a simple tool that can be used to determine if specific ports are listening on specific computers. To verify that DNS is listening on the DC1, enter the following command, as shown in Figure 9-19:

```
Portqry -n regalinn.chicago.local -p udp -e 53
```

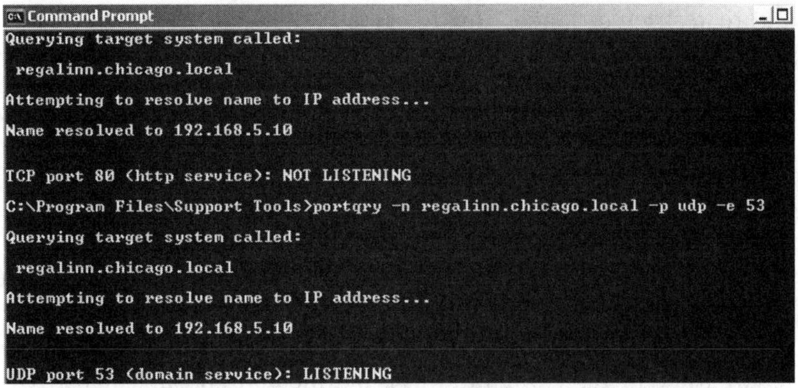

Figure 9-19 Testing DNS ports.

Manually Examine DNS Records Looking for Problems

Although it is a potentially more difficult and less desirable way to troubleshoot DNS problems, you can examine the DNS records manually. There are common problems that occur, and the experienced DNS administrator can spot them quickly without the use of diagnostic tools.

Use nslookup to Test DNS

Nslookup is used by DNSLint, but it may be used on its own to look for DNS issues. Nslookup can be used to locate DNS servers, check for specific records, and test name resolution. Two modes are possible. In interactive mode, if nslookup is entered without parameters, it can be used to examine many parameters. In noninteractive mode, nslookup with specific parameters can be used to find specific data and move on.

Entering nslookup at a command prompt will produce the name and IP address of the default name server (the one identified in the network TCP/IP configuration for the local computer). If entering the command does not produce this information, this is the first sign of a problem. After a successful return, a caret ">" prompt allows entry of other requests. A good check is to use the `ls` command to list specific types of records on the server. Use the `/t` switch to limit the record type. Entering `ls -t a Chicago.local` will list the host records for the Chicago.local domain. If the command does not return the expected results, further examination should be done to determine and then fix the problem.

If the servers that can obtain a zone transfer from the DNS server are restricted, make sure to issue the `ls` command from one of the servers identified as allowed to request and receive a zone transfer. `Ls` works by doing a zone transfer. Allowing zone transfer by only a limited number of servers is a sound security practice. Information about the records in your DNS server should be restricted.

Examine Event Viewer Records

Check the DNS event log for DNS errors. Any DNS error can mean potential trouble for Group Policy because the error may mean interference with the logon process. Some of the errors that should be resolved are listed in Table 9-4, but this is not meant to be an exhaustive list. Two warnings are also frequently seen. Warning 2630 will be recorded when there are multiple namespaces as the result of a multihomed DNS server for which the DNS server has not been correctly configured. An interface on which DNS should listen must be established in the DNS properties. Warning 414 indicates that there is no DNS domain name for the host. This often is registered when a server is being dcpromoed and DNS is being installed at the same time. If the DNS name is not preconfigured before the dcpromo, the warning is recorded, but later the DNS name is configured and recorded for the host automatically. If this is the reason for the warning, then it can safely be ignored.

Table 9-4   Event Errors

Error	Meaning
6524	Zone transfer failure
4011	Failure to update _ldap record in DNS
5781	Failure of DNS registration
1056	DHCP on a domain controller

Troubleshooting Active Directory and FRS Replication

A GPO will not be downloaded to the client if the client cannot authenticate to the domain. When this occurs, the cached policy is applied. Any changes made since the policy was cached will not be applied. A number of Active Directory and related GPO issues, such as problems with trust relationships or Active Directory Replication, Domain Controller/Active Directory Configuration, and even the File Replication System (FRS) can either prevent GPOs from downloading or hinder proper processing for appropriate computer and user accounts.

Trust Relationship Problems

Although it is not advised, GPOs can be linked across domains if a trust relationship exists between the domains. By default, all domains in the forest have a trust relationship, and additional external and forest trusts can be configured. If a GPO is linked across a trust, and the trust fails, the GPO cannot be processed. A list of denied GPOs can be found in the GPMC Resultant Set of Policy report, and if a GPO cannot be processed due to a failed trust, it will appear there. You can also use NTtest.exe or view Active Directory Domains and Trusts to verify the trust relationship and to repair it if this is necessary. However, best practices recommend that a copy of the GPO be placed in the domain and used for the link, rather than linking GPOs across domains.

TIP: Best Practices for GPO Links
A GPO should never be linked across domains. Instead, place a copy of the GPO in the domain and link to the copy.

Active Directory Replication Problems

In addition to name resolution, DNS stores Active Directory-related records that must be accessible and that must resolve to domain controller computers for authentication and replication to occur. AD replication is necessary for Group Policy information to reach all domain controllers. When there are problems with replication, many users and computers will not have the most current versions of the GPOs they must process. Problems with DNS can impact replication.

Before replication can occur, a domain controller must find its replication partners. Replication partners are those domain controllers assigned to replicate with each other. Assignment can be automatic or can be assigned manually. Each domain controller knows the names of its replication partners and uses DNS to find the DC IP address. However, this is not simple DNS name resolution. Instead the following steps take place:

1. Each DC registers a number of DNS records when netlogon starts. (The specific records are listed in knowledge base article 178169.) These records can be confirmed by examining the text file C:\Windows\System32\Config\netlogon.dns.
2. The DC finds the GUID in the Active Directory for the domain controller it seeks. (Each DC in the forest has its own unique GUID, and a listing of these GUIDs can be found at the following location: CN=NTDS Settings, CN=Sites, CN=Configuration, DC=domain_name, DC=domain_name_extension.)
3. The DC sends a recursive query to DNS, looking for a CNAME record. CNAME records for DCs are of the format *guid.*_msdcs.forest root. Figure 9-20 shows the GUID for regalinn in the Chicago.local forest.
4. If the query is successful, the DNS server returns the name of the related domain controller in the form dcname.root_of_forest, the fully qualified domain name (FQDN) for the DC. The alias for DC1 is DC1.chicago.local.
5. The DC sends a recursive query to DNS for a Host (A) record that matches the alias. DNS returns the IP address mapped to the alias.
6. The DNS server responds with the IP address for the replication partner.
7. The DC can connect to its replication partner and replicate.

If anything is missing, such as the GUID CNAME, its alias, or the correct IP address for the server, replication cannot occur.

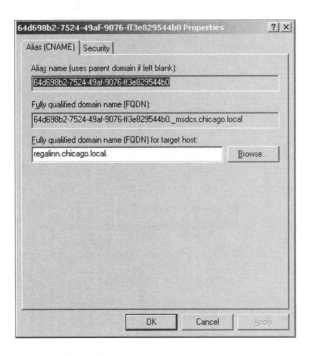

Figure 9-20   Locating GUIDs for DCs in DNS.

Use DNSLint to Test Replication

DNSLint simulates this process and reports back on any issues and successes. The DNSLint /ad switch uses LDAP to connect to the root forest of AD and gets the GUIDs for all DCs in the forest. Then it queries DNS to resolve the CNAME and obtain the alias and then the IP addresses of the DCs. This information reveals if the proper SRV records are registered on the correct DNS server, and therefore if all replication partners are listed and accessible in DNS. Because DNSLint must authenticate to AD to find the GUID information, it may also find netlogon problems and report them. DNSLint also looks for zone delegation and queries additional DNS servers. Use the command dnslint /ad IP_address_of_the_forest_root /s IP address of the DNS server. Local host can be used with the /s switch if the command is issued at the DNS server. The following command was used at the DNS server authoritative for the _msdcs.chicago.com zone (the forest root _msdcs zone) and produced the report in Figure 9-21. Figure 9-22 shows the CNAME and glue records for DCs with GUIDs in the _msdc.root_of_forest_zone.

```
dnslint /ad  /s localhost
```

DNSLint Report

System Date: Thu Sep 16 10:40:53 2004

Command run:

dnslint /ad /s localhost

Root of Active Directory Forest:

chicago.local

Active Directory Forest Replication GUIDs Found:

DC: REGALINN
GUID: 64d698b2-7524-49af-9076-ff3e829544b0

DC: MOTORIN
GUID: e52950e4-bde3-4f88-8ccc-52306c57b79c

Figure 9-21   Finding GUIDs with DNSLint.

TIP: More information on DNSLint can be found in the Knowledge Base articles 321045, "Description of the dnslint Utility," http://support. microsoft.com/support/misc/kblookup.asp?id=Q321045, and 321046, "How to Use dnslint to Troubleshoot Active Directory Replication," http://support.microsoft.com/support/misc/kblookup.asp?id=Q321046.

Results from querying the locally configured DNS server(s):

Alias (CNAME) and glue (A) records for forest GUIDs from server:
CNAME: 64d698b2-7524-49af-9076-ff3e829544b0._msdcs.chicago.local
Alias: regalinn.chicago.local
Glue: 192.168.5.10

CNAME: e52950e4-bde3-4f88-8ccc-52306c57b79c._msdcs.chicago.local
Alias: motorin.chicago.local
Glue: 192.168.5.199

Total number of CNAME records found by local system: 2

Total number of CNAME records local system could not find: 0

Total number of glue (A) records local system could not find: 0

Figure 9-22   DNSLint report shows CNAME and glue record for those DCs with GUIDs in the _msdc.root_of_forest zone.

If domain controllers cannot find replication partners, the problem may be missing records in the DNS server that is authoritative for the domain. DNSLint can determine if all DNS servers that are supposed to be authoritative for the root of the forest have the correct records to allow synchronization. DNSLint will indicate which records are missing so that you can correct the situation. DNSLint can also test a specific domain controller to see if it can resolve the necessary DNS records and will report those that cannot be resolved.

To verify DNS records used in Active Directory replication, use `dnslint /ad:ip_address /s DNS_ip_address` where `ip_address` is the IP address of a domain controller in the forest and `DNS_ip_address` is the IP address of the DNS server authoritative for the zone where Active Directory replication records are located. By default, this zone will be the _msdcs zone in the AD forest root. The zone may be delegated, and if so, it may be somewhere else. You must enter the IP address for the correct DNS server. (If you are running the test from the DNS server, you can use localhost instead of an IP address, but you cannot use the server or domain name.) More information on DNSLint is in the earlier "Troubleshoot DNS" section.

Because DNSLint contacts the DC at the IP address after /ad and uses an LDAP query to get all the GUIDs in the Active Directory forest, the user running DNSLint must have proper permissions to access the information. If he does not, the command will issue an error and terminate. If the command is successful, DNSLint contacts the DNS server identified by the /s switch to obtain the CNAMEs for each GUID, and then the glue or A record for each CNAME. If the IP address is not the address of a server authoritative for the _msdcs.root_domain, then the CNAME records may not be found. If other DNS servers that are authoritative for the root of the forest can be found, DNSLint will look for CNAME records there, too. Finally, DNSLint produces its report, which details what it finds and the records that should be available that are not found. This report can be used to identify necessary corrections that must be made to DNS.

Use replmon.exe to Check Replication

Replmon.exe, the Replication Monitor, is a GUI tool that can be used to find information about replication and replication partners. To use the program, follow these steps:

1. Open replmon.exe by double-clicking on the command in the file system.

2. Right-click the monitored servers node and select Add monitored server. Then click Next.
3. Enter the server name to monitor and click Next; then click
   Finish.
4. The server information is displayed in the GUI, as is information
   about recent replication event success or failure.
5. Expand the server and select the DC node; then select its replication partner to see specific results, as shown in Figure 9-23.

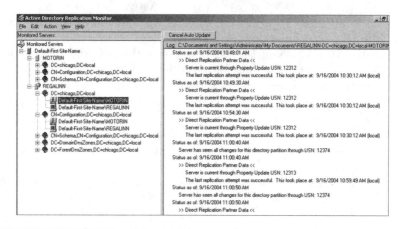

Figure 9-23   Using replmon to seek replication information.

6. From the View menu, select Options and select Show Transitive Replication Partners and Extended Data. If desired,
   use the Options page to set up notifications, log locations, and so
   forth (see Figure 9-24). Notifications can be emailed.
7. Click OK to return to the replmon main window.
8. Select the DC container in the console and select the Action
   menu, replication partner, Check Current USN, and Unrepli-
   cated objects command. A popup, as shown in Figure 9-25,
   should confirm replication when the replication partner is up to
   date.
9. Click OK to return to the replmon main window.

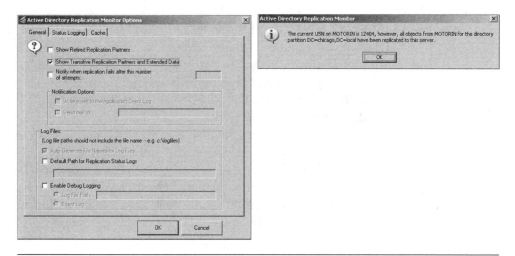

Figure 9-24   Setting replmon options.

Figure 9-25   A popup confirms replication.

Use Repadmin.exe to Check Replication Links Between Replication Partners

Repadmin is a command-line tool that can be used to check replication links and replication latency, summarize information about replication, and report information on replication exchanges. The following commands are displayed in Figures 9-26 and 9-27, respectively.

```
Repadmin /showreps regalinn.chicago.local
```

```
Repadmin /replsummary regalinn.chicago.local
```

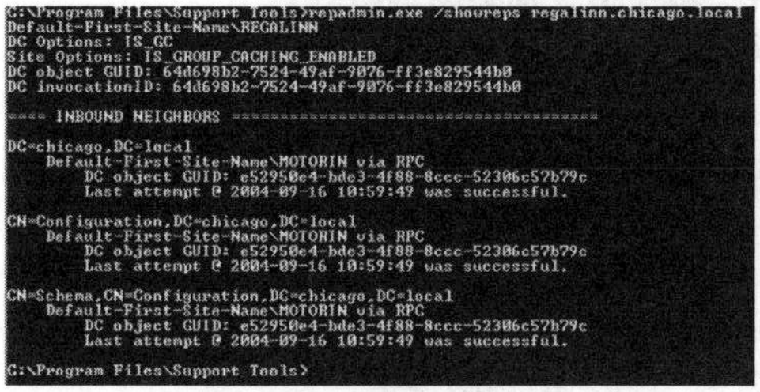

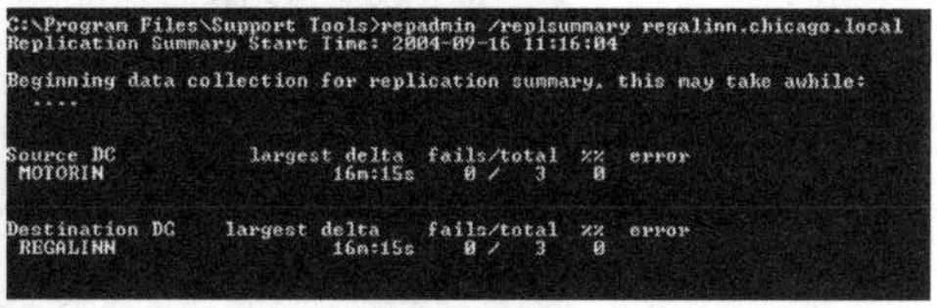

Figure 9-26   Testing for replication success.

Figure 9-27   Displaying replication statistics.

Active Directory and Domain Controller Configuration and Health Problems

If the Active Directory is not working well, and if domain controllers are not correctly configured, many problems can occur. One of these problems can be with Group Policy. Periodic checkups are in order.

Use DCDIAG to Check Health of DC

A healthy domain controller is one that is properly registered in DNS, is replicating with its replication partners, and is authenticating clients. To verify domain controller health, the dcdiag /replication test can be used. This command tests DNS registration, checks replication permissions, and reports any replication errors that exist between domain controllers.

```
Dcdiag /test:replications
```

Other tests and commands can be used to find information specific to a single domain controller or to examine the replication topology of the domain. To test a specific domain controller, use the following:

```
Dcdiag /s:regalinn
```

This command is shown in Figure 9-28. It tests connectivity and then performs replication-related tests and other domain controller tests.

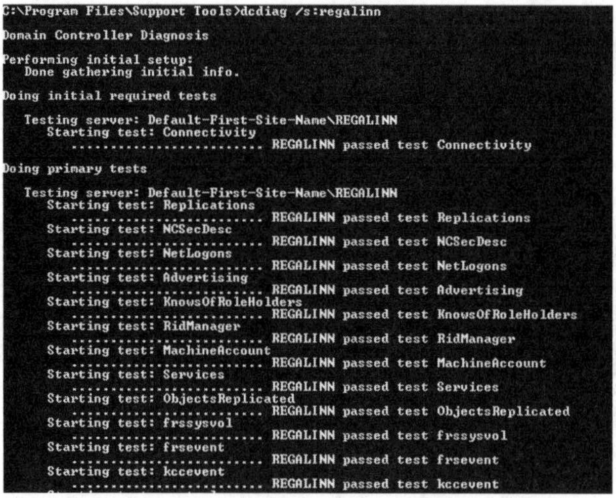

Figure 9-28   Testing replication using DCDiag.

Use GPOtool to Check Template and Policy Version Synchronization

If the GPO policy gets updated but the templates and other files have not yet replicated, GPO processing will not give the correct results. Each Group Policy container and each Group Policy template is assigned a version number, which is incremented when the GPO is changed. Use GPOtool to check for version synchronization and to determine if policies are valid. It will also display the details of GPOs that have replicated. GPOtool is a Windows Server 2003 resource kit tool. GPOtool can do the following:

- Check GPO consistency.
- Check GPO object replication.
- Display information about a GPO, such as functionality, version, and extension GUIDs.
- Search GPOs based on friendly name or GUID. Partial match is supported.
- Use specific domain controllers or all domain controllers.
- Check policies in remote domains.
- Provide more information if run in verbose mode.

Run gpotool.exe at the command line to see a summary report on policy consistency and replication. Each GPO is tested, and either errors will be listed, or a "Policy OK" statement will be generated, as shown in Figure 9-29. More details will be shown if running `gpotool.exe /verbose`.

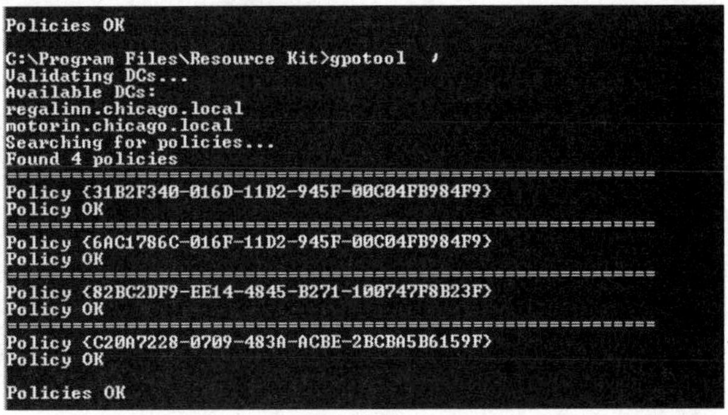

Figure 9-29 Checking policy consistency.

Use LDP.exe to Check DC LDAP Ports

The LDP.exe support tool can be used to find out if a domain controller is responding to LDAP queries ports 389 and 3268.

1. Open the ldp.exe GUI and select `Connect` from the `Connection` menu.
2. Enter the name of the domain controller to connect to and click `OK`.

The default port used will be the 389 port and will produce results as shown in Figure 9-30. Port 3268, used with SSL, can be tested if a certificate is available for use by the DC. The results show that the DC is listening on LDAP ports, and they provide some additional useful information.

Use Portqry to Troubleshoot AD Connectivity

Portqry can be used to check the status of TCP/IP and UDP ports on a remote computer. Use it to test the status of Active Directory-specific ports. If these ports are not listening, replication and other functions will not be possible. In addition to simply reporting if a port is listening, portqry obtains additional information. Testing the RPC endmapper port, 135, for example, lists the ports used by RPC for specific services. When the LDAP port, 389, is queried, a range of useful information is reported, as shown in Figure 9-31.

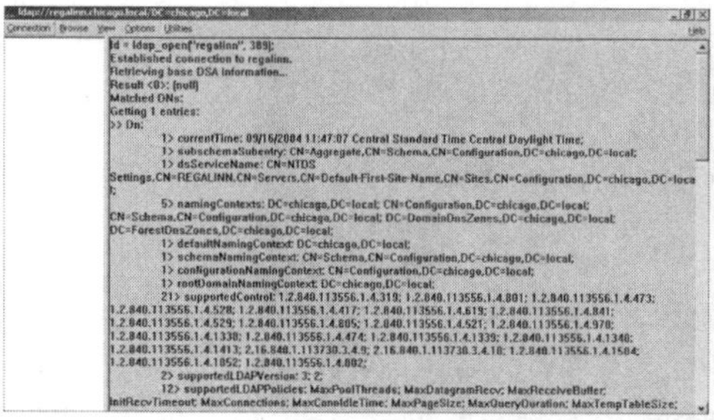

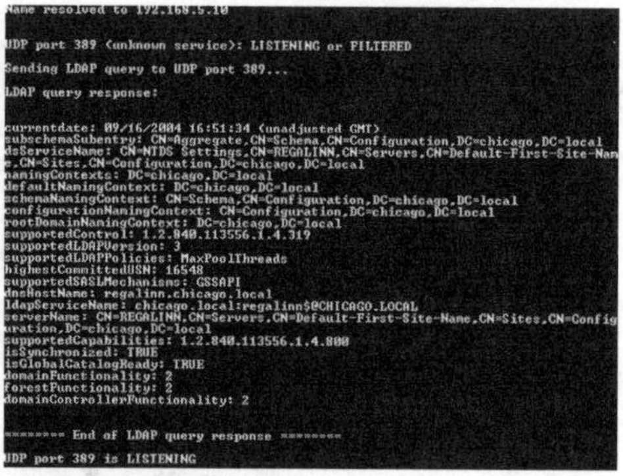

Figure 9-30   Displaying replication statistics.

Figure 9-31   Use portqry to test LDAP connectivity and learn about the domain.

More information on using portqry can be found in Knowledge Base article 816103, http://support.microsoft.com/default.aspx?scid=kb; en-us;816103.

Portqry reports the status of a port in one of three ways:

- **Listening**—Portqry received a response from the port.
- **Not Listening**—Portqry received an ICMP "Destination Unreachable—Port Unreachable" from the UDP port or a TCP acknowledgement packet with the Rest flag set.
- **Filtered**—Portqry did not receive a response from the port and doesn't know if the port is listening or not.

To verify connectivity with AD, use portqry to verify ports for LDAP, DNS, RPC, and AD. To verify LDAP connectivity for the DC, use the following command:

```
Portqry -n nameofDC -p udp -e 389
```

This command will cause portqry to first send an unformatted datagram to UDP port 389 on the domain controller. Because LDAP only responds to a formatted request, no response is returned, so portqry reports that the port is listening or filtered. Next, portqry sends a properly formatted LDAP query. If a response is received, the port is reported as listening, and the response is printed to the screen. If no response is received, the port is listed as filtered. The port should be listening on a domain controller, so a "filtered" report indicates a problem.

Use GPOTool.exe, Event Viewer, and GPMC to Check for Missing or Corrupted Files

Group Policy information is contained in numerous files. If these files are missing or corrupted, Group Policy processing is affected. A number of tools, including GPOTool.exe, GPMC, Event Viewer, and manual inspection, may be used to spot problems with files. You can use GPOTool.exe to check for the presence and integrity of these files in the SYSVOL share and its subfolders on DCs. These include files in the template and registry.pol.

GPMC will report file access problem events in the `Policy Events` tab in the Group Policy Results report. You can also view the events listed here in the Application log events in the DCs Event Viewer. Setting up verbose logging for UserEnv and for specific client-side extensions (CSEs) will also provide information.

Verbose Logging

Verbose logging enables the collection of more detailed event messages. Log files are created for the core client engine (userenv) and all CSEs except the scripts processing CSE. You can also enable verbose logging for other Group Policy processing issues and tools you use.

You'll find CSE-related logs in the following locations:

- Group Policy Core and registry CSE (userenv.log) in the `%windir%\debug\usermode`
- Security CSE (Winlogon.log) at `%windir%\security\logs\winlogon.log`
- Folder Redirection CSE (fdeploy.log) at `%windir%\debut\usermode`
- Software Installation CSE (appmgmt.log) at `%windir%\debut\usermode`
- Windows issues (MSI*.log) at %windir%\temp\

Turning on verbose logging for CSEs requires registry changes as noted in Table 9-5.

Table 9-5   Turn on Verbose Logging

CSE	Add This Key	Registry Location
Group Policy Core	UserENvDebugLevel = REG_DWORD ox10002	HKEY_LOCAL_MACHINE\Software\Microsoft\Windows NT\Current Version\Winlogon
Security	ExtensionDebugLevel = REG_DWORD ox2	HKEY_LOCAL_MACHINE\Software\Microsoft\Windows NT\Current Version\Winlogon\GpExtensions\{827d318e-6eac-11d2-a4ea-00c04f79f83a}\
Folder Redirection	FdeployDebugLevel— REG_DWORD 0x0f	HKEY_LOCAL_MACHINE\Software\Microsoft\Windows NT\Current Version\Diagnostics
Software Installation	Appmgmtdebuglevel=d	HKEY_LOCAL_MACHINE\Software\Microsoft\Windows NT\Current Version\Diagnostics
Windows Installer	Logging = voicewarmup Debug = 00000003	HKEY_LOCAL_MACHINE\Software\Policies\Microsoft\Windows\Installer

To set up verbose logging for GPMC and GPO Editor errors, use Table 9-6.

Table 9-6 Verbose Logging for GPMC and GPO Editor

Type of Entries	Add this key	Registry Location

GPMC error logging	gpmgmttracelevel=1	`HKEY_LOCAL_MACHINE\`
		`Software\Microsoft\Windows NT\`
		`Current Version`

GPMC error and verbose logging	Gpmgmttracelvel=2	`HKEY_LOCAL_MACHINE\`
		`Software\Microsoft\Windows NT\`
		`Current Version\Diagnostics`

GPMC ouput to log file only	Gpmpmtlogfileonly=1	`HKEY_LOCAL_MACHINE\`
		`Software\Microsoft\Windows NT\`
		`Current Version\Diagnostics`

GPO Editor core entries	GPEditDEbugLevel = REG_DWORD 0x10002	`HKEY_LOCAL_MACHINE\`
		`Software\Microsoft\Windows NT\`
		`Current Version\Winlogon`

GPO Editor CSE specific	GPTextDebugLevel = REG_DWORD 0x1002	`HKEY_LOCAL_MACHINE\`
		`Software\Microsoft\Windows NT\`
		`Current Version\Winlogon`

The entries generated are placed in `%temp%gpmgmt.log` for all GPMC errors, `%windir%\debug\usermode\gpedit.log` for all GPO Editor core entries, and `%windir%\debug\usermode\gptext.log` for all GPO Editor CSE-specific entries.

Check for client files, and if necessary, replace corrupted or missing files from the installation CD. (Use System File Checker (SFC.exe) to scan all files to verify versions.) Client files are found in the `%windir%\system32` folder and are as follows:

- Userenv.dll
- Dskquota.dll
- Fdeploy.dll
- Gptext.dll
- Appmgmts.dll
- Scecli.dll

Examine the File Replication and Directory Service Event Log

FRS errors will have the source NTFRS.

Before replication occurs, problems that prevent it may be reported in the directory services log. The error messages 1925 as shown in Figures 9-32 and 9-33 appeared when DC2 was first dcpromoed. The error message confirms the DNS lookup failure.

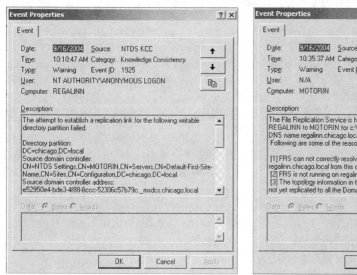 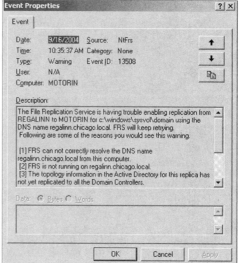

Figure 9-32   Displaying a replication failure.

Figure 9-33   Revealing the error due to DNS lookup.

Once replication has occurred, the directory service log will report replication errors. Replication errors have the source KCC. Typical errors, which may impact Group Policy, are as follows:

- 1311: The replication configuration information in the Active Directory Sites and Services does not accurately reflect the physical topology of the network—This can be as simple as one of the domain controllers being offline, as complex as configuration problems with bridgehead servers and site link configuration, or as annoying as problems with the WAN links.

■ 1265: DNS Lookup Failure or RPC server is unavailable—This error is also produced, along with `Target account name is incorrect`, when the problem exists and repadmin is run. The errors all mean DNS problems, typically that the GUID-based domain name of the source replication partner cannot be resolved. Use `dcdiag /test:connectivity` to verify CNAME and A records. If records are missing, it may be possible to fix the situation. Four steps toward resolution are as follow:

  1. Stop and start the net logon service on the DC and then run ipconfig /registerdns.
  2. Check TCP/IP configured DNS server and alternate DNS server addresses for correctness. (Running `dcdia /fix` will sometimes fix misconfigured DNS records.)
  3. Check dynamic zones, and set them if not found. Use the command `dynamic zones dcdiag /test:registerdns/ dnsdomnain`.
  4. Ping the GUID-based name of the DC where replication is failing if this is resolved, and then the next replication cycle should occur.

■ 1265: Access Denied or the repadmin command returns the same—The domain controller failed to authenticate against its replication partner. This can happen when the DC is offline for a long time. When this occurs, its password is not synchronized with its computer account password in the Active Directory of its replication partner. To correct, do this:

  1. Stop the Key Distribution Center (KDC) service.
  2. Purge the ticket cache. (Tickets are stored in a cache in memory while the current user is logged on the domain.) The Klist.exe command-line tool can be used to delete tickets.
  3. Reset the domain controller password on the PDC emulator master using the Support tool `netdom /resetpwd`.
  4. Synchronize the domain directory partitions of the replication partner with PDC emulator.
  5. Manually force replication between replication partner and PDC emulator master.
  6. Start the Kerberos Distribution Center on the local domain controller. Use the command `net start KDC`.

Generic AD Troubleshooting Steps

In addition to the specific tools and commands, there are items that should be checked manually to eliminate them as possible causes of replication failure. Check each of these:

- CPU utilization at each DC to make sure it's not overloaded
- The time on the DC and on the client
- Event log records on each DC
- For the existence of the SYSVOL share on every domain controller

Check File Replication

The .adm templates, scripts, and other files that are used for Group Policy processing are not part of Active Directory. Instead, they are stored in the SYSVOL share and its subfolders and are replicated via the File Replication Service (FRS). (The Group Policy container is an Active Directory container that stores GPO properties.) If FRS is not functioning properly, then the information needed to apply the policy may be missing or out of date. The files are automatically replicated to all domain controllers by default according to a schedule and cannot be forced.

GPO File Components and Locations

Each GPO's file-based components are located in their own subfolder of the System Volume folder (Sysvol) \Policies subfolder. The GUID of the GPO becomes the folder name. Each GPO fills a Group Policy template that includes security settings, Administrative Templates-based policy settings, applications for software installation, and script files. Each Group Policy folder contains the gpt.ini file at its root. This file stores information on which client-side extension contains user or computer data, whether user or computer portions are disabled, and the version number of the GPO editor extension that created the GPO. The collection of files and subfolders and their contents is the Group Policy template.

NOTE: Local GPO

Don't confuse the GPO folders with the local GPO folder and files. Each computer also stores a local GPO, which contains security policy only. It is stored in `%systemroot%\system32\grouppolicy`.

Each GPO folder contains multiple subfolders, including these:

- `User`—A registry.pol file, it contains the registry setting for users. It may also include Applications advertisement files (.aas files) if applications are indicated for installation via Group Policy.
- `Documents and Settings`—fdeploy.ini, which is status information about folder redirection options.
- `Microsoft /remoteinstall`—The OSCfilter.ini file, which contains user options for operating system installation through the Remote Installation Service (RIS).
- `Microsoft \IEAK`—Setting for Internet Explorer maintenance snap-in.
- `Scripts`—All Group Policy-based scripts.
- `Machine`—registry.pol for computer (registry settings for the computer).
- `Scripts startup`
- `Scripts shutdown`
- `Applications`
- `Microsoft\windows  NT\secedit`—The Gpttmpl.ini file, the default security configuration settings for a Windows 2000 domain controller.
- `Adm`—All the .adm files for this GPO.

The .adm files are refreshed when service packs are installed. If the correct .adm files are not installed, or if they vary between domain controllers, the results of Group Policy can change. While .adm files are replicated, problems with replication will prevent this. In addition, .adm files are overwritten by .adm files of a later date, which also can cause problems. Suppose, for example, that .adm files are updated to provide up-to-date configuration for Windows XP computers after the installation of Windows XP Service Pack 2. Then suppose that a service pack for Windows Server 2003 is added. The new Windows Server 2003 service pack .adm files will have a later date than the Windows XP .adm files and will therefore replace them. This can cause problems.

Check the File Replication Service Event Log

The File Replication Service Event Log will record errors and information about the function of FRS. The DNS issues at the promotion of DC2 also produce an FRS error, 13508, as shown in Figure 9-34.

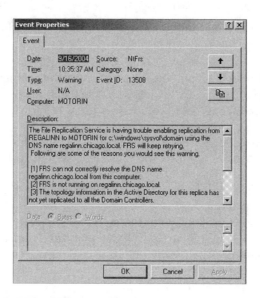

Figure 9-34   Displaying a FRS error message.

The sonar.exe help file provides a table of all FRS messages and their meanings in addition to a list of some helpful troubleshooting tips. Table 9-7 is adapted from this information and my own experiences and provides several common event warnings and errors and how to respond to them.

Table 9-7   Responding to FRS Error Messages

Event ID	Meaning	How to Respond
13508	This error may commonly appear after a new domain controller is added to the domain. If it is not followed by event 13509, it represents connectivity problems between replication partners.	Suspect DNS, network connectivity, or perhaps a stopped FRS service on the replication partner.
13511	The FRS database is out of space.	Add space or move the database to another partition. KB article 221093 provides instruction on how to do so.

Event ID	Meaning	How to Respond
13526	A domain controller is unreachable. FRS polls AD for FRS configuration information and to resolve the SID of its FRS replication partner. If FRS cannot bind to its replication partner, it will produce this error.	Restart FRS on the computer that is logging this error.
13548	There is greater than a 30-minute time difference between two replication partners.	Check time on the replication partner. Check time zone correctness.
13557	A duplicate connection object exists between replication partners.	Remove one of the connection objects.
13567	More than 15 times per hour, an application opens a file for changing, but nothing is actually changed.	Troubleshoot excessive disk/CPU usage looking for an application that is generating this activity.
13568	NTFS journal wrap. NTFS keeps a high-level description of changes to its files and directories, and FRS uses this to track changes that it needs to replicate. The journal is given a fixed size and periodically removes old records. During times of high activity, such as authoritative restore, or if FRS is not running, processing may fall behind, and the information FRS needs may be gone from the file.	This error means the information needs to be rebuilt. If a larger size for the journal is required, the size can be adjusted. For more information, see KB article 221111.

Use Sonar.exe to Check FRS Functioning

Sonar.exe is a Microsoft Resource Kit tool that can be used to check FRS functioning. Sonar is a file replication service status viewer that can be used to monitor FRS statistics and the health of the SYSVOL share by providing information on traffic levels, backlogs, and free space. Download sonar from http://www.microsoft.com/downloads/details.aspx? FamilyID=158cb0fb-fe09-477c-8148-25ae02cf15d8&DisplayLang=en.

To use sonar, run the program by double-clicking on the executable in the file system. Sonar begins monitoring FRS in the domain, as shown in Figure 9-35. The tool queries AD and displays the last information it received. You can limit the columns shown by using the `Columns` drop-down box, change the collection timeframe, and produce a log of all statistics.

Use the `Filters` box drop-down to produce a number of reports, such as:

- Backlogged member
- Current involved in join
- DC not sharing sysvol
- FRS in error condition
- Low disk space
- Sharing violation
- Staging area problems
- Worst backlogged members

Use the `Columns` box to determine the display:

- All columns
- Backlog
- Error conditions
- Replication status
- Resource usage
- Settings
- Sources of change
- Topology

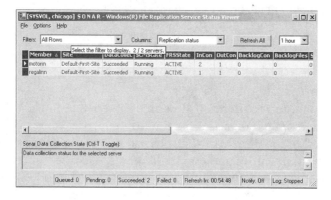

Figure 9-35   Using Sonar to check FRS.

Troubleshooting Group Policy Object Design

If network connectivity, DNS, Active Directory replication, and FRS are not the problem, then the problem must be in Group Policy design or implementation. This can mean that either a well thought-out and correct design was not implemented correctly, or the design was flawed to begin with. Finding the root cause can help prevent similar problems in the future. If the designer does not understand Group Policy, he will continue to present flawed designs that will not work even if they are implemented exactly as written. If the implementer makes a mistake and does not learn where the error is, then she will continue to repeat the error.

The section "Determining If the Policy Has Been Applied" examined reasons why a Group Policy implementation may mean that a GPO is not applied or, if it was applied, why specific security settings might not be applied. If these issues are not the problem, the only remaining possibility is that the correct setting for the desired result is not selected. This might be due to a misunderstanding about what specific settings do, or about the container to which the GPO containing them must be linked.

An example of the first problem might result from reading one of the many setting statements that are confusing and getting it wrong. For example, the Security Option `Domain member: Disable machine account password changes if Enabled` will prevent computers from updating their machine account. If the setting is `Disabled`, the account password will change periodically. It would be very easy to think that if you want to prevent machine passwords from changing, this setting should be `Disabled`, when what you want to do is to `Enable` it. In other words, the use of two negative words (Disabled and Disabled) produces a positive—machine accounts are changed. If the setting had read instead `Domain Member: Change machine passwords periodically`, then making the right choice would be easier.

An example of the second problem results when an attempt is made to apply a different password policy for a user in a specific OU. Password policy can be set only in the Domain GPO. Password policy settings made in GPOs linked to specific OUs are disregarded when users log on using their domain account. (If they use a local machine account to log on to a specific machine, the password policy dictated by an OU-level GPO will be effective.)

Determining where Group Policy settings are misinterpreted and thus misapplied can be an exhausting task. The problem can be alleviated by taking the time to understand what settings mean what and where they can be effectively applied before attempting to use them. Far too often, administrators simply read the settings and guess at their meanings. A good source for learning the ins and outs of Group Policy settings is the white paper "Threats and Countermeasures: Security Settings in Windows Server 2003 and Windows XP" at http://www. microsoft.com/downloads/details.aspx?FamilyID=1b6acf93-147a-4481-9346-f93a4081eea8&DisplayLang=en. New settings introduced for Windows XP in SP2 are listed in the Excel file PolicySettings.xls available from http://www.microsoft.com/downloads/ details.aspx? FamilyID=7821c32f-da15-438d-8e48-45915cd2bc14&displaylang=en.

Monitor GPO Health

Troubleshooting problems with Group Policy is a necessary art. Problems will occur, and you will need to resolve them. However, you may be able to head off Group Policy issues by monitoring GPO health. If you find problems before they are reported via user complaints, or before the lack of security enforcement results in a successful attack, all the better. To monitor GPO health, you should monitor each of these:

- DNS
- Network connectivity
- DC health
- Replication
- GPO-specific issues

The first four items are discussed in earlier sections. You can monitor many GPO-specific issues by using the GPMonitor.exe tool and by using the reporting features of GPMC. GPMonitor.exe is a resource kit tool that creates reports when policy settings are refreshed. Policy stability and replication can be checked. To get started, run GPMonitor.exe on each DC to extract the .msi file, the help file, and the gpmonitor.adm template. The gpmon service monitors refreshes and updates info to a centralized share; the share location is set through the gpmonitor.adm template.

Run the msi file on every domain controller (you can distribute the files through Group Policy) to install the gpmon service and start it. The service does not listen on the network.

To add the new gpmonitor.adm template and configure gpmonitor, follow these steps:

1. Open the domain controller policy in the GPO editor.
2. Right-click the administrative templates folder in the Computer configuration node and select Add/remove templates.
3. Click the Add button, browse to the gpmonitor.adm file, and click Open.

To configure the policy do the following:

1. Select the Group Policy Monitor node of administrative templates.
2. Open the Group Policy Monitor item and select Enabled.
3. Enter a UNC path for the share as shown in Figure 9-36 on which the results will be collected, and click OK.

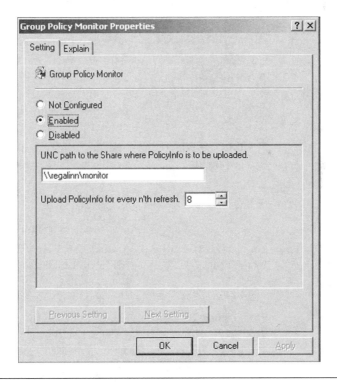

Figure 9-36   Setting the collection share.

The reports and the information they provide are listed in Table 9-8. More information on GPMC scripts can be found in the `%Programfiles%\gpmc\scripts\gpmc.chm` file on a computer where GPMC has been installed.

Table 9-8   Monitor GPO Health via GPMC Reports

Report Title	Report Script	GPO Health Function
List all GPOs in a Domain	ListAllGPOs.wsf	Are all those GPOs that are supposed to exist there? Are rogue GPOs evident?
List Disabled GPOs	FindDisabledGOPs.wsf	Why are they disabled? Are they supposed to be? Are some enabled that should be disabled? Check disabled GPOs against a maintenance list.
List GPO Information	DumpGPOInfo.wsf	A list of information about the GPO is produced.
List GPOs at a Backup Location	QueryBackupLocation.wsf	Backup locations are checked to see if all GPOs are backed up and if the backups are where they are supposed to be.
List GPOs by Policy Extension	FindGPOsByPolicy Extension.wsf	Specific policy extensions may be the purview of specific people or may be critical to some operations. Being able to list the location of these GPOs is a quick check on their availability as it should be.
List GPOs by Security Group	FindGPOsBySecurity Group.wsf	A quick check on which GPOs belong to which security groups. Policy application permissions are checked for correctness.
List GPOs Orphaned in SYSVOL	FindOrphanGPOsin SYSVOL.wsf	Looks for GPOs that have files but for which Active Directory records no longer exist.
List GPOs with Duplicate Names	FindDuplicateNamesd GPOs.wsf	Lists any GPOs that do not have unique names.
List GPOs Without Security Filtering	FindGPOsWithNo SecurityFiltering.wsf	Lists GPOs that are not applied to a security group.

Report Title	Report Script	GPO Health Function
List SOM Information	DumpSOMINfo.wsf	What SOMs exist—sites, domains, OUs? Is one not accessible?
List SOMs with Links to GPOs in External Domains	FindSOMsWith ExternalGPOLinks.wsf	If there are external links to GPOs in other domains, this can be a problem and should be avoided.
List Unlinked GPOs in a Domain	FindUnlinkedGPOs. wsf	It is possible to create a GPO without linking it to any container; likewise, it is possible to remove all links from a GPO. Should the GPOs found be without links, or is this an error?
Print the SOM Policy	ListSOMPOlicyTree.wsf	

The Group Policy Monitor tool, GPMonitor.exe, can be used to collect information during every Group Policy refresh and send it to a central location. It consists of a gpmonitor service that runs on the client and collects the data, and the viewer that can be used to look at the data. This tool is part of the Microsoft Windows Server 2003 Deployment Resource Kit (Microsoft Press, 2003).

Summary

Troubleshooting Group Policy is an easier task in Windows Server 2003 because of the Group Policy Management console, but Group Policy problems may be the result of problems with networking, DNS, Active Directory, or Active Directory or FRS replication. To troubleshoot Group Policy problems, you must be able to troubleshoot these items, too. While there is no one way to go about this, running DCDiag can eliminate some possible problems when tests are returned with a pass. Its error messages may point to an area for further testing. Doing the troubleshooting job well requires experience and knowledge. Take the time to learn how to use troubleshooting tools before they are needed.

CHAPTER 10

Securing Active Directory

If an attacker can obtain unfettered access to Active Directory (AD), he gains absolute control over every computer, resource, and user account in the forest. Even limited privileged access can provide a wealth of information useful in future attacks. Active Directory is not only the seat for critical information in your network, but it is also the repository for major security controls and information such as password policy, security configurations, and audit policy. To ensure security for a Windows Server 2003 or Windows 2000 Active Directory network, you must secure the Active Directory. The steps that you take to do so will also support and improve the security status of other Windows systems and the data that they manage. To secure Active Directory, the following practices must be applied:

- Physically secure domain controllers
- Establish security configuration and administrative boundaries
- Establish secure administration practices
- Secure application and user access to domain controllers
- Use secure Active Directory installation and deployment practices
- Deploy secure DNS
- Establish and use security maintenance practices
- Monitor and audit directory access
- Implement response to detected attack

Several of these practices are detailed in other chapters, specifically, securing DNS (see Chapter 11, "Securing Infrastructure Roles") and monitoring, auditing, and responding to attacks (see Chapter 19, "Monitoring and Assessment"). This chapter addresses physical security, secure installation, and deployment and administration practices for AD.

When following these practices, consider the typical locations where DCs are found: corporate headquarters and regional data centers, branch office locations and perimeter networks, or extranets. There are many differences between these deployment scenarios, and therefore, although some aspects of their management and security remain the same, the uniqueness of the setting may mean your approach may have to be modified. The differences include the following:

- **Corporate locations and regional datacenters**—These have centralized IT operations housed in secured facilities, high bandwidth, established places to build and configure systems, written policies and procedures, dedicated IT staff, and monitoring and auditing facilities.
- **Branch offices**—These may have slow and even intermittent connectivity. Domain controllers are not segmented from client networks, nor can they always be isolated from running additional services, including print and file services. There typically is no dedicated secure facility to house the DC and other servers. No dedicated IT staff exists, and it is difficult to restrict administration to IT. Physical access is also more difficult to restrict. It is harder to detect problems and attacks, and remotely manage these systems. Each branch office presents its own unique situation, and it is difficult to uniformly establish good physical or other controls.
- **Extranets**—These typically have high bandwidth and secured facilities. The location provides facilities for testing and central IT staff. An outward-facing DC provides authentication and access to customers and partners. Internet exposure is a given but is usually highly protected by firewalls and other network devices. If administration is provided externally to the extranet, it is usually established via a VPN.

Physically Secure Domain Controllers

A copy of the domain's Active Directory resides on each domain controller, and therefore, the physical security of computers used as domain controllers should be planned and maintained. Although it's easy to insist that all domain controllers exist within the corporate data center, this is not possible in all organizations. Therefore, it's important to consider the possible different locations for domain controllers and establish physical security guidelines for each. For many deployments, domain controllers will be located at the main offices of an organization or at its large regional offices where there are established data centers. However, there are other situations where domain controllers may reside at branch offices or offices where establishing a formal data center would be cost prohibitive. All these locations can apply physical security, and guidelines for each are outlined in the following section. First, however, common security guidelines can be met at any location.

Physical Security for All Domain Controllers

Physical security is the first line of domain controller defense. Physical security includes physical barriers to DC access, securing network infrastructure, providing support and control mechanisms, establishing procedural controls, ensuring a location safe from possible hazardous threats, such as water leakage, excessive heat, and power fluctuation, and securing administrative access and physical security for backups.

Physical Barriers

Physical barriers should secure all domain controller access. All DCs must be kept behind locked doors, and there must be standard policies and procedures that dictate who and how these locked enclosures can be entered and DCs accessed. The locked enclosures used for DCs may range from locked racks within a corporate data center, which is itself protected by locked doors, to locked rooms and cabinets in remote branch office locations. In any situation, there is a way to provide this type of conditional access. Even an authorized administrator is required to pass through these barriers.

The devices that lock these barriers should, wherever possible, be card key locks or cipher locks. Cipher locks are protected by some cryptographic mechanism, such as a biometric lock or token lock. The use of cipher locks can improve security because they typically require some form of authentication beyond just the physical possession of a card or key.

In addition to locks on entry to the data center, DCs should be further protected by locks on each DC or on doors for racks that house the DC. These additional locks ensure that two levels of physical entry exist. Typically, within the data center or locked area, additional equipment is also protected. Servers, cable plants, routers, switches, and other devices may also be present. Although it is important to physically secure these devices, the level of security required by domain controllers is higher, so additional physical security should be maintained.

In addition to locks and other physical barriers, consider deploying monitoring devices, such as CCTV.

This model supports a multi-tiered administrative model. For more information on this model, see the section "Establish Security Configuration." In this model, some administrators are given a higher level of privilege than others. Therefore, not all administrators require physical access to DCs. Having a separate lock for DCs ensures that fewer employees, including administrators, have actual physical access to them.

Is Security by Obscurity Worthwhile?

During an internal audit of a large organization's NT network, I examined physical security for domain controllers. All domain controllers were located within the data center. All servers in the data center were identified by a six-digit number that indicated their position as row number followed by rack number and then rack position. No servers were labeled as to use or classification. In short, to locate a specific server, a directory was consulted, and then the server was located by its number.

When queried about providing additional locks for the DCs, the response was that providing obvious symbols of the importance of a server would attract attention to the server and make it the object of a console-based or physical attack. In short, by treating all servers the same, IT management felt that an attack by an employee or contractor made from within the data center would be less likely to succeed because the attacker would not know which systems were most worthy of attack.

This is a false assumption. A data center is not a public place. Sure, if it were penetrated either by force or via social engineering, extra locks on systems would draw attention to them. But the people who are authorized to be in the data center can, by observation or via access to the data center "directory," discover the critical systems.

Unless they have been trained to do so, no one will notice that an unauthorized employee is fooling with a sensitive system. By physically obscuring the identity of these servers, they've only become as ordinary as the rest of the machines when viewed as a whole. An attacker could easily discover which computers are worth spending time to break into. Putting extra locks on sensitive machines that are already protected is a good thing. It provides extra protection in two ways: First, it makes it physically harder for an attacker to breach security, and second, it makes it more obvious that an unauthorized person is working on it.

On the other hand, identification on the network should not be obvious. For example, domain controllers should not be named DC1, DC2, DC3, and so on. When a network includes thousands of computers, giving computers names that mean something attracts undue attention without providing any benefit.

Secure Network Infrastructure

Additional physical network security should be applied to the network infrastructure. If cabling, routers, switches, and other devices are not located in the same locked area with DCs, these items should be provided their own secure location. This location should not be shared with items such as telephony cabling to which outside contractors or consultants require access. For example, a typical configuration is to locate branch office patch panels and network devices in the same wiring closet with telephone switching equipment and cabling provided and serviced by local telephone contractors. Even within larger organizations, these telephony closets may be located throughout the plant to ease configuration and maintenance. If these locations are serviced by non-IT personnel, they should not include network infrastructure devices and cabling plant equipment. Sharing access with other equipment may seem a valid way to provide security. After all, the locked location may have been present when the location was computerized or upgraded. However, though physically secured from casual access, these locations are highly available to outsiders—either authorized telephony contractors or people who may pretend to be them. Because phones are not considered to be sensitive equipment, less attention is paid to them.

Do not allow direct access to DCs from the Internet. Although authentication from DCs may be necessary to provide access to internal sites, access to DCs should be via processes designed and implemented for secure access, such as VPNs, SSL, and RADIUS. Differentiation should be made between employee authentication needs, such as providing employee access to company email or intranet sites via the Internet and the authentication requirements for public or partner access. In the later case, you may want to establish a separate forest. If the forest used for public or partner access is compromised, access to the organization's internal forest is still protected. Public or partner access forest DCs should also be physically secured.

Support and Control Mechanisms

In addition to locks, physical security for DCs includes the physical security of DC support and control mechanisms. All domain controllers should be supported by a UPS system for power management and power supply backup. A steady source of power will ensure healthy domain controller operation. The security of Active Directory relies on the healthy operation of all domain controllers. When DCs are unavailable because of lack of power or unclean power, security in the network is reduced. By keeping the UPS systems with the DC in a locked area, the operation of the DC, and thus the security of Active Directory, is enhanced. Removing power to a DC can cause data corruption and may, if done deliberately, be one form of a Denial of Service attack. Be sure to calculate power backup needs. UPS systems are not meant for long-term power supply. Generators may be required where critical operations must remain operational even under extreme conditions.

Physical Security Procedural Controls

Specific processes and procedures for any physical access to DCs should be implemented and maintained. This includes items such as logging physical access and requiring documentation on changes to DC location, configuration, backup, and restore. It should also include a requirement for the signature of an authorized administrator before archived backup media is brought back on site or returned from onsite secured storage to the physical domain controller location. The reason for this requirement is that a backup could be accidentally or maliciously restored. Controlling backup media and logging its return from storage will not always prevent its misuse; however, it will help, and it will provide an audit trail (a record of who did what) that might be used if an abuse occurs.

Secure Backup Tapes

Backup procedures should be established and maintained, and the physical management of backup media should be controlled. Procedures to follow include limiting who can check out or in backup media, requiring a secure backup media location on site and off site, and not having backup media physically present unless a backup or restore is being performed. Consider encryption and/or password protection of backup tapes. Another sound practice is to require management authority and signature before backup media is returned on site from offsite storage.

Secure Administrative Access

Secure any remote administrative access. Although a discussion of security for remote access often revolves around logical security structures, such as software-based authentication and authorization, the physical devices and cabling used to provide remote access should also be secured. For example, in a data center, a management network might be established, which is physically separate from the network that provides access to services. This network can be a separate physical network segment that is isolated from clients. At a branch office, an out-of-band management device, such as a dialup modem, can provide remote management that can be physically secured and kept isolated from common access.

Additional security is possible if smart cards or other hardware devices for authentication are required for console access to domain controllers. In addition, the privilege to log on locally to the DC can be restricted to only those administrators authorized to manage and maintain DCs. Require these administrators to use smart cards or other devices when logging on.

Beware Remodeled Offices

Several years ago, as a network administrator for a consulting firm, I often was the first person to arrive at the office in the morning. Like many small companies, we rented office space in a suburban area. One morning, I was in a particular hurry, and traffic had been particularly heavy. An extra room had been rented, and the day before, all servers and the resident domain controller along with the firewall and other equipment had been moved to this more secure location. Everything was OK when I left the night before, but that day, I needed to verify operations and ensure new access and maintenance procedures were in place before anyone else arrived.

I entered the building and quickly headed down the hall. I turned the corner and fell flat on my back. Water seeped into my clothing from soaked carpeting. All I could think of was the safety of the servers, so I got up and carefully and quickly went to the new server room. When I unlocked the server room and opened the door, more water gushed out into the hall. Inside, water was spurting from the opposite wall.

A quick call to building maintenance got the water supply turned off and prevented more water in the room. The day was spent cleaning up the mess. Fortunately, because I arrived early, and because no equipment was directly within range of the leakage, damage was contained to the floor covering and wall. The cause of the leakage was a concealed water pipe. Our new server room had originally been a large maintenance closet, complete with a sink. When it was remodeled, the pipes had not been removed or properly sealed, and thus caused the accident.

It's always a sound practice to examine building blueprints and infrastructure history before creating data centers and server rooms.

Protect from Accidents

DCs should also be protected from building physical plant operations and conditions that might threaten DC operation. DCs should not be near items such as boilers, air conditioner and heating plants, power stations, or storage areas for chemicals, flammables, or hazardous wastes. A problem with the operation of such areas could cause extensive damage to nearby IT operations. Because these areas pose a risk to any organization's ability to function, ensure that DCs and indeed data centers or IT locations are not directly adjacent to, above, or below them.

Protect from Sabotage

Data centers, and thus DCs, should not be located in a place where it might be easy to sabotage them via explosives or other another physical activity or accident. For example, if a data center is located on a ground floor next to a poorly secured external area, a truck could be filled with explosives and parked nearby.

Physical Security for Data Center Locations

Corporate data center locations typically house all servers, administrative workstations, cabling plants, and other network infrastructure devices for the main corporation location. Thus, physical security can be applied more easily, and the location can even be designed with this in mind. All domain controllers at this location should be placed within the data center. In addition, if external forests are deployed to manage border networks, such as extranets and other Internet accessible operations, the domain controllers that support these operations should also be housed in the data center.

Where appropriate and possible, larger, separate geographical locations should also have data center operations.

Extreme physical security measures are often possible, practical, and provided by corporate network data centers. A long history of securing sensitive digital-processing systems is often present, and the model is well known and understood. In addition to the physical securing operations described previously, important considerations for data centers include

- Locating the data center at the center of the building and away from the location of hazardous materials or operations, such as power plants and chemicals storage.

- Providing tiered entry to data center operations. An outer area may be opened to Help Desk or monitoring staff and equipment. A middle area may contain administrative offices and monitoring stations, while a third, inner area contains servers and other hardware and cabling. Additional, separate locked racks are provided for DCs, and a separate "vault" may exist for other specialized servers, such as certification authorities and for securing backup media. Physical access to each area is managed by locks, and administrative procedures require that only authorized personnel have physical access.
- Providing sprinkler systems for offices (and fire suppression systems in data centers) and other emergency systems, such as emergency power shutoff switches.
- Establishing detailed business continuity plans that specify secure movement of operations to alternative secure physical sites in the event that some disaster prevents the use of the data center for IT operations. The physical security both for the transfer of operations and for securing operations at the other location is specified and tested.

Correctly Label All Physical Controls

In London in 2001, a large data center housing a huge server farm in support of a very large web site was shut down because of inadequate labeling. The informational and e-commerce sites supported by the data center were inaccessible because a data center employee flipped the emergency power shutoff switch.

This particular data center did not provide automatic egress. A card key was required for exiting and entering the facility. One night, a single employee found himself trapped in the data center without his card key. He could not leave the center and was unable to enter locked offices to gain access to a phone. Spotting the large "In case of emergency, pull switch" sign over the power shutoff switch near the door, he wrongly assumed that it would open the door or alert security guards of a problem in the data center. He pulled the switch.

Needless to say, he did attract the attention of security guards, who hastened to investigate when monitors viewing the inside of the data center went dark.

Physical Security for Branch Offices and Small Offices

Branch offices and small offices do not typically provide sophisticated data centers to house servers and DCs. Instead, a locked room may be provided. If this is impossible, a locked cabinet can provide some security. The purpose of a locked location is to provide a strong physical boundary between the DCs and ordinary office operations. This allows access to be restricted. In addition to the problem of providing adequate basic physical separation, branch offices potentially suffer from the lack of dedicated IT personnel. Instead of trained and supervised operators, administrators, and so on, branch offices may have to rely on staff that has other duties and has had very little technical training.

In addition to providing a physical barrier, other steps can be taken to enhance the physical security of DCs in branch offices. These actions can also be taken in data centers, but they may prove impractical when large numbers of systems must be managed, and they may be less necessary because of the higher level of basic physical security that can be provided. Branch offices and other less protected locations can

■ Protect systems from booting into alternative operating systems (OSs) by disabling or removing floppy disk drives and CD-ROMs and the ability to use other devices, such as USB connections or network boot. The exception to this rule is when the DC is protected by using a floppy/syskey operation. It is important to protect systems from booting into alternative operations systems because if a system can be booted into an alternative OS, access to sensitive data is not protected by Windows Server 2003. An attacker could obtain password databases for offline cracking, copy other sensitive files, and damage or delete data.

■ Protect systems from booting into alternative operating systems by setting the [timeout] in the boot.ini file to 0. Typically, the timeout setting provides time for the selection of an alternative OS if one is present on the system. Setting boot.ini to 0 removes that option. (No alternative OS should be loaded onto the system in the first place, especially on a domain controller.)

■ Protect systems from booting into an alternative operating system by not creating dual-boot systems.

■ Disable remote boot and installation. Although automated installation is a sound security practice, once a domain controller is deployed, it should not be exposed to accidental or malicious installation. It should not be possible to overwrite an existing installation or make the system dual-boot. In some cases, remote boot, if properly protected, may be a sound choice. An organization may require remote maintenance of servers and DCs, and available maintenance procedures for Windows Server 2003 can provide secure remote maintenance. More information on remote maintenance is in Chapter 18, "Auditing."

- Use a BIOS password. This can prevent the unauthorized boot of a DC. However, if a BIOS password is implemented, someone must be present to enter the BIOS password when the system reboots or the system will remain offline. If the system is located at a branch office, this may represent an unacceptable situation. Branch offices do not typically have dedicated staff present or available at all hours. Also note that BIOS passwords on most systems can be bypassed using maintenance techniques provided by the hardware manufacturer.

- Use additional security offered by syskey password or floppy disk choices. Syskey adds a layer of protection to the AD password database and other security data. It can be further secured by changing its operation to use either an entered password at boot or the insertion of a floppy disk on which a system-generated password exists. When this syskey functionality is used, be sure to physically secure the floppy disk and provide a secure copy off site (perhaps in a bank safety-deposit box), or if the password method is used, secure a copy of the password off site. Like the entry of a BIOS password, when these methods are implemented, someone must be present if the domain controller must be restarted. Another downside to using syskey is that the DC cannot be restarted if the password or floppy disk is lost. Also note that using syskey is not an effective protection from password-cracking applications. Attack code exists that can crack passwords in an offline copy of a syskey-protected password database or extract the password hashes from an online syskey-protected password database. Once extracted, the password hashes can be fed to password-cracking software. Syskey alone cannot be the only defense for a domain controller. However, when coupled with physical security and sound administrative practices, syskey can help can resist attacks.

- Secure backup media and store off site. The off site storage should not be in unsafe places, such as the trunk of an employee's car. Instead, a useful offsite location for branch office backups may be a bank safety-deposit box or a registered company that specializes in secure offsite media storage.

■ Audit backup and storage practices. A higher level of attention to backup procedures is often necessary at branch locations. In the data center, backup often becomes part of a carefully maintained list of procedures, and checklists and supervision often ensures this process is followed. However, at branch offices and other sites that lack dedicated staff, it is often neglected.

■ Restrict network access to DCs. Although it may not be possible to secure DCs on a secured network segment, it is possible to limit external access. No Internet access to DCs or indeed to the branch office network should be allowed. Internet access by branch office employees should be filtered and appropriately restricted and not performed from the DC.

■ Secure routers, switches, firewalls, proxy servers, and other devices. These items should be in the locked area with the DC or, at the least, in a locked room or closet where access from outsiders is not permitted and access by local employees is restricted.

■ Use strong passwords for access to DCs, routers, and other devices that provide administrative interfaces. Many network appliances provide default external administrative access. This should be blocked, and default passwords should be changed. Passwords should be different for each administrative account and should not be the same for any two devices.

■ Use a dialup modem for remote management services. This out-of-band management can isolate external administrative access because a specific phone line can be dedicated to the interface, knowledge of the phone number can be limited, and settings can require dial-back to a limited list of numbers. User ID can be required for call back. Remote access using built-in remote access services can be tuned to use only secure authentication services.

■ Secure additional services that are added to branch office DCs. Branch offices may require the DC to host additional services such as file and print services. Consider headless operations. When the DC has no monitor, keyboard, or mouse, only remote access can be used to administer the system. This prevents local staff from inadvertently making changes or deleting items. Although it will not prevent a determined attacker, it does make things a bit harder for him. Headless operations have their own challenges, and access to the out-of-band access equipment (such as a modem) must be provided. Headless operation may be acceptable for some sites and unmanageable for others. Although it may be argued that local users shouldn't have the authority to log on to the DC and that a headless server provides no additional advantage, remember that all local users have domain accounts. A small slip in administration or a successful escalation of privilege attack might add them to a group that can log on to the server. The headless server provides defense in depth.

■ Consider the problem presented for remote management by the need to perform a secure remote restart. This cannot be done via terminal services if the system is not operational because Windows must be running in order to use terminal services. Possibilities include a smart UPS, remote access hardware that is integrated into the server, such as the Compaq RILO or Dell Drac II boards, or video switches that connect to the keyboard and mouse as well as the display and provide services, which are similar to terminal services. Remote management can be also be effective at corporate data centers and is often provided by RS 232 or Ethernet connectivity and managed as a separate management network that is isolated from clients.

To use syskey, follow these steps:

1. From a command prompt on the domain controller, enter `Syskey`.

2. In the popup, note that `Encryption Enabled` is selected, as shown in Figure 10-1, and click `Update`. Syskey is enabled by default on Windows 2000 and Windows Server 2003.

Figure 10-1   Starting the syskey utility.

3. On the `Startup Key` dialog box, as shown in Figure 10-2, either select `Password Startup` or, in the `System Generated Password` box, select `Store Startup Key on Floppy Disk`.

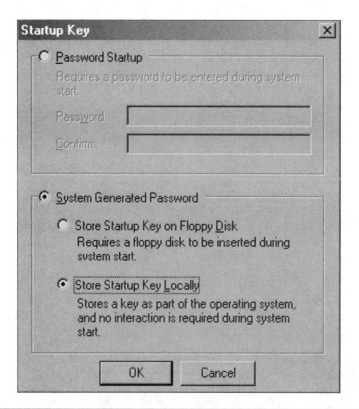

Figure 10-2   Configuring syskey.

4. If `Password Startup` is selected, enter a password, confirm it, and then click OK. Be sure to record the password and store it in a safe place, apart from the floppy disk. Without the password, you cannot start the server.

5. If `Store Startup Key on Floppy Disk` is chosen, insert a floppy disk and click OK. Make copies of this disk and secure all copies. This disk must be used when the system is rebooted.

As an alternative to requiring local management to manage and support the use of syskey, it is possible to use products, such as Compaq's Remote Insight Lights-Out (RILO) or Dell Remote Access Card III, to transfer the sysprep floppy disk image to a remote DC, start the DC, and then delete the remote image. Both of these cards enable additional remote management.

Physical Security for Extranets and Perimeter Networks

The authentication and management infrastructure that is provided by Active Directory can be an essential ingredient for applications that live in perimeter networks and extranets. However, these networks may be best and more securely served by creating a separate forest in the perimeter network. Because no connectivity with or replication to DCs in the corporate internal forest is necessary, if a perimeter network is breached, it cannot be used to directly compromise the internal forest.

Perimeter DCs, however, should be secured within the data center, along with web servers, database servers, and other devices that make up the perimeter network. Place the perimeter network on its own segment and use firewalls and/or packet-filtering routers to protect it from Internet access and to protect the internal network.

Best Practices for DC Physical Security

Consider the following best practices for physically securing DCs:

- Place DCs in locked rooms.
- Use locking racks or hardware locks on servers.
- Require smart cards or biometric or other two-factor authentication for local logon to DCs.
- Reduce the number of administrators that can physically access DCs and locally log on to manage them from the console.
- Provide adequate power and other physical requirements for DCs.
- Consider boot controls such as a BIOS password and syskey for branch office DCs.
- Consider headless operation for branch offices.
- When access to the corporate network is required for external employees, use VPNs and SSL.
- Protect DCs from physical threats such as natural disasters and maintenance accidents.
- Remove remote access tools with the exception of terminal services by administrators or other approved and secured remote administration tools.

Establish Security Configuration

In addition to physical security, DCs must also be secured by configuring DC security settings and by establishing administrative boundaries. Proper configuration supports administrative boundaries, which can ensure better security configuration.

Best practices require the establishment of a DC security configuration baseline that can be applied to all domain controllers. Modifications to this baseline can be constructed where necessary. Security baselining is a good practice to establish for all server roles; Chapter 11 gives more information on using security baselines to establish security for systems throughout the forest.

Administrative boundaries are created by ensuring that administrators are limited to a role-specific scope. Examples of this are using default groups to assign privileges, creating custom groups for this purpose, and using delegation of authority.

DC Security Baseline Configuration

A DC security baseline is the sum of all DC, Active Directory, and DC-based security configuration. Each organization should establish the written policy, document, set using technical controls, and maintain a baseline. Establishing a security configuration baseline for domain controllers consists of accepting or modifying the following:

- Default Domain GPO Account Policy settings
- Default Domain Controller GPO User Rights policy and Auditing Policy settings
- Server-related security settings in the default Domain Controller GPO or in additional GPOs linked to the Domain Controller OU
- Domain security settings such as Public Key Policy, IPSec Security Policy, and Software Restriction Policies in either or both default GPOs
- Additional security settings, such as permissions on files, folders, registry keys, and printers

A good way to document and provide a tool for quickly setting, resetting, or auditing the base security of DCs is to use security templates. Security templates are collections of security settings that can be either applied to a one computer at a time or imported into a Group Policy and, therefore, applied automatically to many computers. Although not all security settings are exposed in the templates, many are. Additional settings can be added. Default security settings for domain controllers are preconfigured in the default Domain Controller Security Policy, and default security settings for the domain are pre-configured in the default Domain Security Policy and the default Domain Controller security policy. The settings can be adjusted in the default policies. However, you can use security templates as an alternative method of adapting default settings to those more appropriate for your organization. The "Windows Server 2003 Security Guide" provides and describes a baseline template for DCs that hardens DC security. Organizations can use this template, modify it to fit their circumstances, or create their own. Once a security baseline template is constructed, the template is applied by importing it into a GPO that is linked to the Domain Controller OU. You can find more information on the recommendations made in the following by obtaining the guide that comes with preconfigured security templates. The guide includes a baseline template for DCs, servers, and many other server role-specific templates. Download the guide and the templates at `http://www.microsoft.com/downloads/details.aspx?familyid=8a2` `643c1-0685-4d89-b655-521ea6c7b4db&displaylang=en`.

Using the template provided with the guide is a good way to get started, but you should establish your specific requirements and adjust the template for your own use. The guide also provides a realistic approach to security by listing settings for legacy clients, enterprise clients, and high-security situations.

Security Template/Domain Policy Configuration

Sections within the Security Template correspond to areas of the DC that should be secured. These same areas are also represented in the Security Settings portion of a Group Policy Object. Two types of security settings, the Account Policy and the Local Policy, are not typically set in security templates. Instead, they are configured directly in the Default Domain Policy and the Default Domain Controller Policy, respectively. Each following section represents some portion of the total security policy that protects Active Directory. Recommendations for their configuration are provided, but the best settings for each organization will have to be determined by that organization.

Domain Account Policy

A strong domain account policy is critical to the protection of AD. Weak passwords and account controls can allow unauthorized access to network resources and to the domain controller. Weak passwords could also allow an attacker to modify Active Directory schema, change data in the Active Directory, and modify permission on Active Directory objects. (Modifying permissions on Active directory objects is also a subtle way to take control of other parts of the network because changes in these permissions is ordinarily difficult to detect. Permissions on active directory objects, for example, can provide administrative control to Exchange Servers, Certification Authorities, certificate templates, and so on.) Administrative accounts cannot be protected if the account policy is not hardened. The account policy consists of Password Policy, Account Lockout Policy, and Kerberos Policy.

Password Policy

A strong password policy cannot be entirely enforced by technical means. While one of the potential password policy settings is Passwords Must Meet Complexity Requirements, this setting requires only that users create passwords composed of three of four things: uppercase and lowercase letters, numbers, and symbols. It does not allow additional specifications. A strong password policy incorporates the complexity requirements enforced by this setting and other practices that help make them more crack-resistant.

Best Practices for Password Policy

Increasing the complexity of passwords provides better protection from known password crackers. A strong password policy should require the following:

- Passwords should not incorporate dictionary words, account names, real names, or company names, and of course, passwords should be unique.

- Passwords should consist of uppercase and lowercase letters, symbols, and numbers.

- Passwords should incorporate the use of a symbol and number(s) in the second to seventh position. When users are asked to make complex passwords, they often do so by putting numbers at the end. Because this practice is well known, modern password crackers search there first, so incorporating numbers elsewhere means cracking the password will take longer.

- Password history should be kept. A password history stores a user's previously used passwords and prevents reuse.
- Minimum password length should be as long as possible, given the tradeoff that longer passwords are more frequently written down. Remember that increasing the length of the password to greater than 8 characters makes it harder to crack with current cracking tools. A password over 14 characters is almost impossible to crack in a reasonable amount of time.
- Some accounts should be required to have longer passwords, such as administrative accounts, key recovery or key archival accounts, member of the Schema Admins and Enterprise Admins groups, and so on.
- Password aging should be configured to require regular password changes and to prevent immediate password changes. When a password can be immediately changed, some users will do so, even multiple times until they exceed the history limit and thus can reuse a comfortable, familiar password. Combine a 45- to 60-day maximum password age requirement and a long password for the best results.

Requirements must be part of the written password policy and must be enforced through user education and auditing. Some of them can be enforced through the Windows password policy. Each Windows Server 2003 domain has a default password policy, as shown in Figure 10-3. This policy is located in the default domain policy. This policy can be modified, and each domain in the forest can have a separate password policy, but for each domain, all users with domain accounts are subject to the same policy. Thus, the tailspintoys.com domain might have a password policy that specifies a password minimum length of 12 characters, while its child domain, newyork.tailspintoys.com, can have a password policy that specifies a minimum length of 8 characters. However, all users with an account in the domain must have a minimum password length of 12 characters. To modify the policy, do the following:

1. If using GPMC, navigate to the default domain policy, right-click it, and select Edit.
2. If you have not installed GPMC, open Active Directory Users and Computers, right-click the domain container, select Properties, select the Group Policy tab, and click the Edit button.
3. Select the Windows Settings\Security settings\Account Policies\ Password policy.
4. In the detail pane, double-click the setting to change it.

5. From the Setting Con guration page, ensure that De ne this policy setting is checked and either change the number or select the disabled/enabled box, as shown in Figure 10-4.

6. Click OK.

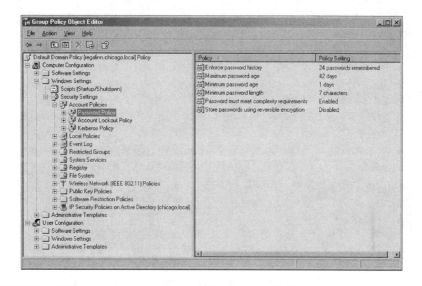

Figure 10-3 Viewing the default domain password policy.

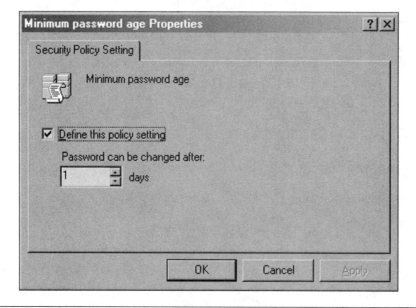

Figure 10-4 Setting password age.

The password policy for the domain affects all domain accounts, but a password policy created for a server or workstation will control passwords created for its own local accounts. To create a password policy that affects all domain accounts, modify the default domain GPO. To create a password policy that affects the local accounts of specific computers, create a GPO and link it to the OU where these computer accounts reside. If a user has both a domain account in the domain and a local account on his workstation, when he logs on using his domain account, the domain password policy will be in effect; when he logs on using his local account, the policy effective for that local computer account will be in effect.

The minimum recommendations for Windows Server 2003 domain password policy are set as the defaults. Table 10-1 lists defaults and recommendations for improving security.

Table 10-1 Password Policy Defaults and Recommendations

Setting	Information	Default	High Security
Minimum password length	The password must be at least this number of characters long.	8	12
Enforce password history	This number of passwords will be remembered.	24	24
Maximum password age	Number of days before the password must be changed.	42	42
Minimum password age	Number of days until the password may be changed.	1	2
Password must meet complexity requirements	Use 3 of these 4 upper- and lowercase characters, numbers, and symbols.	Enable	Enable
Store passwords using reverse encryption for all users in a domain	When selected, passwords are not hashed before being stored. Some applications require this less secure format. It is not recommended that this setting be enabled.	Disable	Disable

Account Lockout Policy

The account lockout policy is not set by default. As shown in Figure 10-5, it can be set to lock out accounts for which a number of incorrect password attempts have been entered.

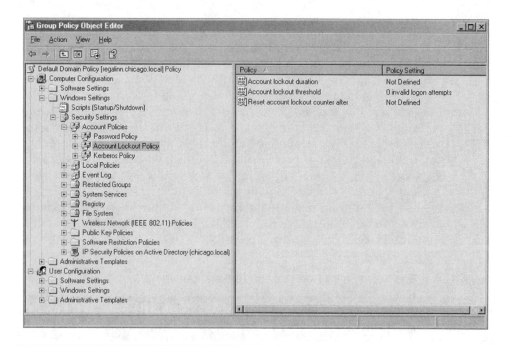

Figure 10-5   The account lockout policy can lock out accounts after a number of incorrect passwords are entered.

Account Lockout settings are

- **Account Lockout Duration**—Indicates the amount of time before a locked out account is automatically reset. A value of 0 means that an administrator or account that has been given that privilege must manually reset it.
- **Account Lockout Threshold**—Indicates how many password errors can be made before the account is locked out.
- **Reset Account Lockout Counter After**—Indicates how many minutes to wait before resetting the counter to 0. For example, if 3 is the threshold and 2 wrong attempts have been entered, and the user stops, the counter is reset to 0 after the number of minutes entered for `Reset Account Lockout Counter After`.

When an online guessing or brute-force attack is launched against the account database, the account lockout feature can prevent all but the very lucky attacker from succeeding. However, should an attack be launched against the entire database, it could lock out so many users that, although no password is compromised, a denial of service attack is successful. Another problem can occur if the accounts do not reset fast enough: remote users might accidentally lock themselves out, and because they are unable to reach the help desk, might not be able to obtain critical access.

Although opinions vary, a reasonable approach is to set account lockout threshold high, for example, 25 attempts. In this way, accidental lockouts cannot occur, and the chance for compromise is slim. The account lockout reset function should also be used. Also, if systems are being monitored, and a large-scale attack is occurring, it will be obvious, and it may be possible to block any access from that source before the DoS causes undue harm.

Best Practices for Account Lockout Policy

No monitoring system is foolproof, and it may be that you will not set a lockout policy to avoid the chance of a DoS. The decision to set or not set an account lockout policy may also be based on determining which is more important. In a large organization where such a DoS would prevent operations that are critical to the business, you may determine that account lockout will not be set. However, where ultimate security (rather than operations) is the driver, account lockout will be set. In this case, the possible harm done by unauthorized access due to a remote cracking attack on accounts may be worse than a loss of operations caused by to a DoS. To summarize:

- Set an account lockout policy to prevent remote account cracking attacks from succeeding.
- Do not set an account lockout policy if operations are more important than blocking remote cracking attacks using lockout.
- If an account lockout policy is set, set the number of incorrect attempts required before lockout to a high number.
- Do not require administrator reset of locked accounts except in high-security situations.

Kerberos Policy

The Kerberos Policy settings should remain as set by default, as shown in Figure 10-6.

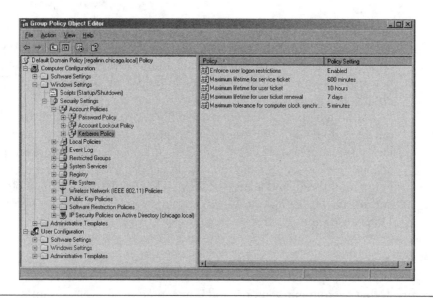

Figure 10-6   Keep Kerberos settings at their defaults.

Two settings are often changed because administrators are seeking better performance. However, these settings should not be changed:

- **Enforce User Logon Restrictions**—Enabled by default, this setting ensures that the user rights policy is checked before users are granted service ticket. The user rights policy includes items such as the right to log on from the network, which may affect whether a ticket is granted or not. When this setting is disabled, the check is not made, and it may be possible for a user who is not authorized to authenticate to a server to do so.

- **Time   Maximum   Tolerance   For   Computer   Clock Synchronization**—This setting is set by default to 5 minutes, and it defines the amount of time difference between the time-stamp on client authentication requests and the time on the DC. If the time difference is greater than this value, the request is denied. When this setting is increased, there is more time for a possible replay attack. An example of a replay attack would be the case where a user Kerberos TGT is captured and repurposed in an attempt to obtain a session ticket for some resource. Such an attack would be difficult, but given enough time, anything is possible. However, with the default tolerance intact, it is likely that the timestamp on the credentials would be much older than the time on the KDC computer, and therefore, the replay attack would be unsuccessful.

Local Policy

The Local Policy section of Group Policy consists of Audit Policy, User Rights Assignment, and Security Options. Audit Policy, including the ability to monitor the use of Active Directory objects, is discussed in Chapters 19.

User Rights

User Rights for users in the domain should be defined in the default Domain Controllers Policy, as shown in Figure 10-7. (User Rights for local users on specific servers should be defined in a GPO linked to the OU in which the computer account resides.)

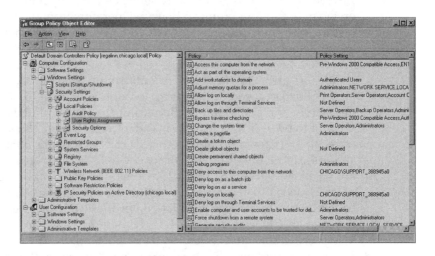

Figure 10-7   User Rights for domain users are configured in the default Domain Controllers policy for the domain.

User rights in Windows Server 2003 are less extensive than in previous version of the Windows operating system but can still be hardened. Consider the following suggestions for user right management as part of your security plan for AD:

- The Allow Log On Locally right is necessary for interactive logon at the DC console. This right is given by default to the groups Administrators, Backup Operators, Account Operators, and Server Operators. Account Operators manage domain accounts but do not need to do so by logging on to a DC console.

Instead, they should be using administrative tools from a workstation. Remove the group Account Operators from this right.

- The `Shut Down The System` right is necessary to shut down the DC using operating system commands. This right is given by default to the groups Administrators, Backup Operators, Print Operators, and Server Operators. Print Operators and Account Operators do not need this right. Remove the groups Account Operators and Print Operators from this right. Backup Operators should not need this right, and you may find you can remove that group.

- The `Backup Operators` group has the right to back up and restore files and directories. If followed, the security principles of least privilege and of separation of duties would separate these rights. Instead of giving this group both rights, create a separate "recovery operators" group; remove Backup Operators from the right to restore files and folders, and add the new recovery operators group to that right.

- The `Deny Access To This Computer From The Network` right should be given to the local Administrator account, the Support_388945a0 account, the guest account, and all NON operating system service accounts. Requiring the local Administrator account to be used locally prevents attacks that rely on the knowledge of the known administrator SID. The support_388945a0 account can be programmed for use by help services and should not be allowed access to a DC. If a domain account is assigned as a service account on some server in the domain, that account may have elevated privileges, and its compromise might be used to leverage an attack against the DC. If these accounts are denied logon access, that attack vector will be mitigated.

- For similar reasons, the `Support_-388945a0` account and the `Guest` account should be denied the ability to log on as batch job to prevent these accounts from being used to execute a virus, Trojan, or worm.

- The `Deny Log on Through Terminal Services` right should be given to the built-in administrator account and the NON-operating systems account for the reasons given previously.

Careful consideration of the way groups are used in your organization may suggest other uses of User Rights to provide protection for domain controllers, and hence Active Directory. Be sure to test these changes before using them on production domain controllers.

TIP: USE AD SECURITY SETTINGS TO BENEFIT OTHER SYSTEMS

Active Directory is not the only beneficiary of hardening user rights. Other computers and operations can benefit as well. For example, the user right Logon To This System From the Network can be modified on servers and other computers to which you want to restrict access. To secure file servers that store sensitive documents, change this right to only include those groups that should have access to the documents. There is no need to allow every employee access to the servers. Although file permissions allow you to control access to the files, preventing unauthorized users from even authenticating to the file server provides another layer of protection.

Security Options

Security Options make registry changes that affect security. Several of these options can be used to secure DCs. In addition to the registry changes made by Security Options that are visible in the GUI, other registry entries can be made that will tighten security. These registry entries can be applied in numerous ways, one of them being by adding them to a security template and then importing the template into a GPO.

Table 10-2 lists and discusses the recommendations for Security Options settings that differ from the default. Security Options, such as auditing related policies, that are discussed in other chapters are not included in Table 10-2.

Table 10-2 Security Options for DCs

Policy	Recommendation	Information
Accounts: Guest Account Status	Disabled	The guest account can provide access for those without credentials and should be disabled.

Table 10-2 Security Options for DCs Continued

Policy	Recommendation	Information
Devices: Allowed to Format and Eject Removable Media	Define and grant to administrators	Preventing unauthorized individuals from obtaining data by removing drives is always a good idea. However, realize that most drives can be physically removed; do not rely on the operating system to eject them. Setting this option only prevents the operating system's utility from working. This is a somewhat helpful deterrent because when drives are removed without stopping, or ejecting using this utility, the data on them may be corrupted.
Devices: Prevent Users from Installing Printer Drivers	Enable	Enabling this option restricts this right to server operators and administrators. Users won't be able to install printers. Although installing printer drivers may seem harmless, a malicious person might disguise attack code in a printer driver, and simple disk space attacks can be mounted that cause a DoS attack by filling up the printer spool and hence the disk by submitting large print jobs.
Devices: Restrict CD-ROM Access to Locally Logged on Users	Enabled	If enabled, when an administrator is logged on at the console of the DC, only administrators can access CD-ROM media in the computer drive. When administrators are installing software and service packs, no one should be able to interfere or copy data from the CD-ROM. If no one is logged on, this restriction is not enforced. (Administrators should be counseled to remove CD-ROMs.)

Policy	Recommendation	Information
Devices: Restrict Floppy Access to Locally Logged on User	Enabled	See the previous paragraph on restricting CD-ROM access.
Devices: Unsigned Driver Installation Behavior	Do not allow installation	Ensure unsigned, possibly unsafe drivers are not loaded on DCs. If a driver that must be used on the DC is not signed, temporarily change the policy to allow a warning, install the driver, and then return the policy to Do not allow installation.
Domain Controller: Allow Server Operators to Schedule Tasks	Disabled	Disable to restrict task scheduling to administrators. Scheduling tasks on a domain controller should be restricted. This option applies only to domain controllers.
Domain Controller: LDAP Server Signing Requirement	Require signing	Protect LDAP traffic between Active Directory and administrator workstations by using LDAP packet signing. LDAP packet signing does not encrypt; instead, it digitally signs the packets. If an attacker were to alter the packet and put it back on the network, the digital signature would be incorrect, and the receiving DC recognizes this and drops the packet.
Interactive Logon: Do Not Display Last User Name	Enabled	Protect the names of authorized administrator accounts. Enable this setting, and the account name of the last user logged on won't be displayed to the next person who happens to come along. Keeping administrator account names secret ensures that an attacker must work harder to obtain access.

Table 10-2 Security Options for DCs Continued

Policy	Recommendation	Information
Interactive Logon: Message Text for Users Attempting to Logon	Provide a message that warns users that only authorized administrators have the right to logon interactively	A legal notice announces that attempting to gain access is wrong. Although it will not prevent an attacker from compromising a system, it may help in their prosecution. Cases have been thrown out of court because the computer splash screen or notice message said "welcome," and an attacker said she thought that meant she was welcome to attempt access. Obtain approval from your legal department for the wording of this message.
Interactive Logon: Message Title for Users Attempting to Logon	Provide a title for the warning	See previous paragraph on using message text.
Interactive Logon: Number of previous logons to cache (in case domain controller is not available)	0	When set to 0, no logon credentials are cached. Each time an administrator needs access, his logon credentials will be checked against the domain database. When this option allows cached logons, a rogue administrator whose administrative status may have been revoked might be able to gain access to a domain controller based on a cached logon.
Interactive Logon: Prompt user to change password before expiration	14 days	Advance notification allows users to prepare and figure out a password to be used. When users are given this time, there is a better chance that stronger passwords will be used, and that passwords will not be written down or written down in insecure places.

Policy	Recommendation	Information
Interactive logon: Require Domain Controller Authentication to Unlock Workstation	Enabled	The locking function prevents unauthorized access (only the account that locked the computer or an administrator can unlock the system). By default, cached credentials are used; that is, the user's account is not authenticated with the DC. This means that no password changes, account status, or group membership is checked. It would be possible to disable the administrator's account and not keep him from returning and unlocking the account. If the setting Interactive Logon: Number of Previous Logons to Cache is set to 0, this is not possible. However, if it cannot be set to 0, this setting should be enabled.
Interactive Logon: Smart Card Removal Behavior	Force Logoff	This setting has no effect if smart cards are not enabled. However, if they are, when a smart card is removed, the user will be logged off. If administrators are required to use smart cards, this policy ensures that as long as the administrator removes her smart card, the administrator's console session will not be left open.

Table 10-2 Security Options for DCs Continued

Policy	Recommendation	Information
Network Access: Allow Anonymous SID/NAME Translation	Disabled if legacy systems do not need it	If enabled, because the administrator SID is well known, it could be used to find the name of the administrator account and then use this to initiate a password-guessing attack. Some legacy systems (NT 4.0 RAS, Windows 2000 RAS in Windows NT 4.0 domains, web applications using basic authentication with anonymous access disabled) need this ability, so you may not be able to implement in all domains.
Network Security: Force Logoff when Logon Hours Expire	Enabled	Forcibly disconnects SMB sessions after logon hours expire. Logon hours are set per user account in the user account properties pages. If logon hours are set, this setting prevents users from leaving a system logged on and connected after hours. When sessions are left unattended, an unauthorized user can gain access. These sessions are especially vulnerable to abuse during hours when few people are around.
Network Security: LDAP Client Signing	Required—unless legacy clients are used	When LDAP signing is required by domain controllers, workstations must be able to do so, or there will be failure in authentication, group policy, and logon scripts. If legacy clients are used, LDAP signing cannot be required. This setting is also necessary in the domain controller policy because domain controllers must also communicate with each other.

If you are familiar with previous versions of Windows, you may recognize Security Options as items previously set directly in the registry. In fact, when Security Options are enabled and Group Policy applied, equivalent registry settings are made. Using Security Options prevents the problems that direct registry editing can cause, such as adding the wrong settings (hence security is not strengthened) or the destruction of some critical part of the registry (hence possibly damaging operating system or other component operation). In addition to preconfigured Security Options, however, other hardening techniques can be implemented directly through registry entries. These changes can be automated by making them part of a security template and automatically applying them instead of requiring a direct registry edit. An example of such an entry is disabling 8.3 names. The NTFS file system automatically creates old 8.3 names from long file names. 8.3 names can therefore be used to support legacy applications. However, they may provide attackers access from systems that do not understand longer file names or allow hard-coded attacks that use 8.3 names to succeed. You should not be running applications on the DC that need the 8.3 name. Because many malicious scripts, including viruses, are 16-bit applications and are written with 8.3 names coded in, preventing 8.3 name generations may block some of these scripts from running. To disable 8.3 name generation, set the value of the following REG_DWORD value to 1:

```
Hklm\system\currentcontrolset\control\ le system\
NtfsDisable8dot3NameCreation
```

Event Log Settings

Event log settings for the three logs identified in Group Policy (security, application, system) as displayed in Figure 10-8 should be adjusted to support the amount of security auditing enabled. By default, these settings are not defined. Recommended settings for the domain controller event logs are as follows:

- **Log file size**—128 MB
- **Prevent local guest group from accessing application, security or systems log (3 policies)**—Enabled
- **Retain *eventlog* log** (where *eventlog* is the name of a log)—Can remain not defined because the retention method is set to overwrite events as needed
- **Retention method for logs (3 policies)**—Overwrite events as needed

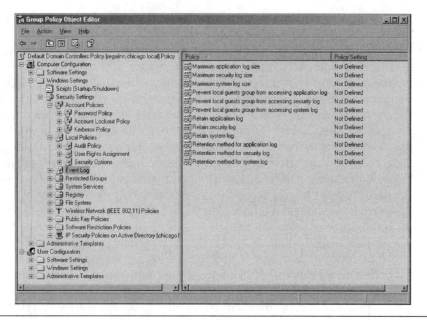

Figure 10-8 The security log settings on a DC should be increased to manage the large volume of audit records that will be produced.

In addition to the event log files available on all Windows Server 2003 computers, several other event logs are present on domain controllers:

- Directory Service
- DNS Server
- File Replication Service

Settings for these event logs must be set by opening their property pages, as shown in Figure 10-9, or must be scripted. Property pages are available by opening the Event Viewer, right-clicking the event log, and selecting `Properties`.

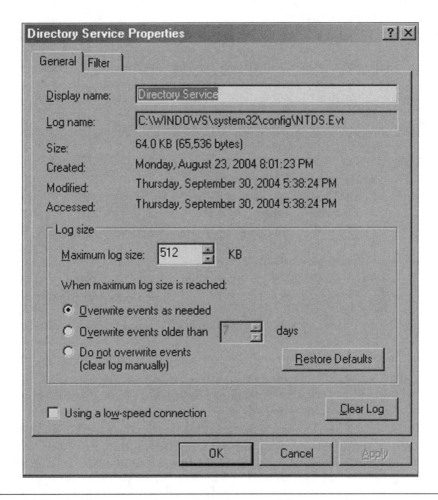

Figure 10-9   Configure event log settings from event log property pages.

System Services

Windows Server 2003 disables many services by default and doesn't start others. However, ensure that disabled services remain disabled unless needed, and you may want to disable other services. A full discussion of services in a baseline template for servers and workstations in a domain is included in Chapter 11. You need to add additional services to this baseline in order for domain controllers to function.

The following services are disabled in sample Microsoft baseline security templates for servers, but they need to be enabled for domain controllers. (A baseline template for domain controllers is also available from Microsoft.) You may need to enable other services, depending on the other functions a specific DC is used for. For example, if DNS is installed on a domain controller, the DNS server service needs to be enabled. The following additional services are necessary for domain controllers to function:

- **Distributed File System**—Required for the Active Directory SYSVOL share.
- **File Replication Service**—Needed for File Replication of SYSVOL.
- **Kerberos Key Distribution Center**—Enables logon using Kerberos protocol.
- **Intersite Messaging**—Used for mail-based replication between sites.
- **Remote Procedure Call (RPC) Locator**—Used for management of RPC name service database. RPC is used during replication.

In addition to controlling whether services are disabled or enabled, services settings determine whether a service is interactively started or stopped and whether it is started or not during boot. These settings can be configured interactively through the Services administrative tool, or set in the Services section of a GPO. The Services section of a GPO can be used to control who has the authority to stop, start, and otherwise change services configuration. To prevent unauthorized management of services, follow these steps:

1. Open the GPO in the GPO editor and select the System Services node.
2. In the details pane, right-click the service and select Properties.
3. Check De ne this policy setting and click the Edit Security button.
4. Note that the default setting only allows Administrators and the system to change settings. Use the object editor to select a group that represents a subset of Administrators who are authorized to manage services. For example, you may want to allow only the EnterpriseAdmins group Full Control over the DNS Server service. The DnsAdmins group already has, by default, the right to stop, start, pause, and continue the service, as shown in Figure 10-10.

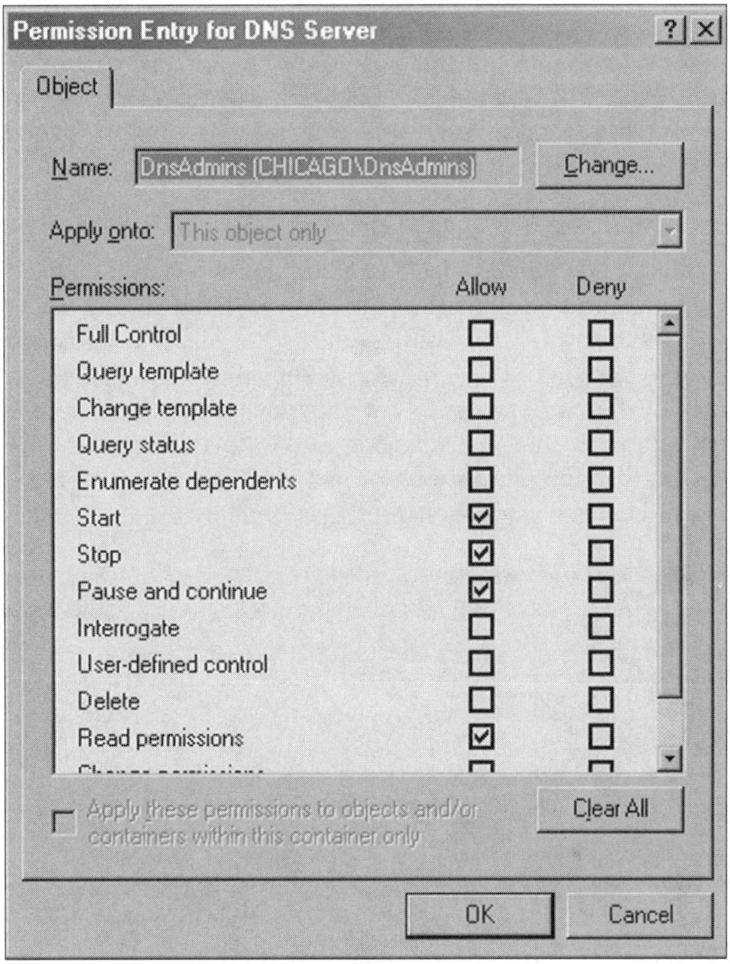

Figure 10-10   Control who can manage services by setting permissions on the service object in the GPO.

Registry and File System

The Registry and File System section of a GPO can be used to provide systematic refresh of critical security permission on registry keys, files, and folders. However, even if there are no changes, security settings are periodically refreshed. If a significant number of permissions are part of the GPO, the amount of information replicated can impact the efficiency of replication and even prevent it from occurring. The constant, large download to domain member computers can significantly impact network efficiency. Best practices now recommend that this element be used cautiously in a GPO and rarely, if ever, in a large Active Directory forest. However, the use of a security template and the Security Configuration and Analysis tool to set security on the entire systems path is a sound concept. A template is used during server installation and during dcpromo to initially set file and folder security. These default templates should be modified, if necessary, with any specific changes required by your organization. After installation, browse the Setup Security template to see the security that was set during installation. Looking at the File System portion of this template, as shown in Figure 10-11, gives you an idea of the large number of permissions. This template could also be used to reset these permissions to the defaults. However, you should realize that any permission set on a file or folder not listed here would not be changed when the template is applied.

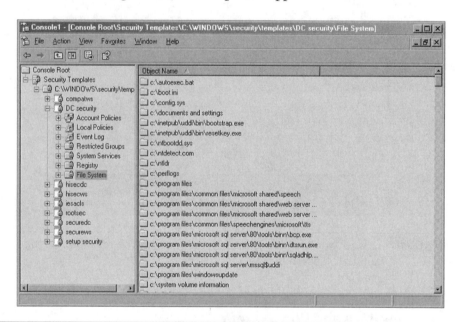

Figure 10-11   Security templates are used to set file system permissions.

Be extremely careful when modifying permissions on system folders, files, and registry keys. There are many reasons for the settings as they stand, and it is possible that changing these settings will break some critical function. Be especially careful in implementing without first reviewing recommendations found in articles and on web sites because they may have been developed for very specific circumstances. Look for evidence of testing in environments similar to yours, and prepare to do significant testing of your own. Any change to system file and folder permissions or registry permissions, especially on a domain controller, can cause problems that are not immediately evident and may not be immediately diagnosed as a file or registry key permission problem.

TIP: TEMPLATE REGISTRY SETTINGS ARE ONLY FOR PERMISSIONS

The Registry section is just for setting permissions on keys. You cannot change registry settings at that location. To make changes to registry settings using GPOs or security templates, you must either use the predefined security options from the Security Options section of the GPO or template, or add registry settings to the Registry Keys section of a security template, as shown in Figure 10-12. A modified security template can be imported into a GPO.

Figure 10-12   A registry setting added to the Registry Values section of a security template will be applied to any computer the security template is applied to.

Additional Security Configuration

In addition to the security configuration that can be done in GPOs and security templates, other items should be addressed:

- **Group membership**—Membership in groups that have administrative privileges should be carefully considered and monitored. Examples of groups to pay particular attention to are Enterprise Admins and Schema Admins. Enterprise Admins can administer every domain in the forest and have additional forest-wide administration privileges not given to Domain Admins. Membership in Enterprise Admins should be restricted. Schema Admins can modify the Active Directory schema, a privilege that should not be given out lightly; in fact, best practices recommend that this group be empty until the need to modify the schema and the approval to do so is obtained.
- **Active Directory object permissions**—Active Directory objects are also permissioned. Permissions on these objects also provide the holder with possible privileges, such as resetting account passwords for other users, full control including the development of GPOs, and so on. Active Directory object permissions should not be changed without a firm understanding of what the change does.
- **Secure configuration of server services implemented on DCs**, such as DNS, Certification Authority, DHCP, WINS, and so on.
- **Direct registry modification**—The registry can be directly modified.
- **Direct change of file and registry permissions**—Permissions can be changed directly on files, folders, and registry keys.

Establish Secure Administration Practices

Security configuration is useless without secure administration practices. An untrustworthy administrator can remove security, or worse, go around security settings and polices. There are two ways to reduce the risk of administrative abuse; both should be used:

- Understand that administrators are people and resolve personnel issues.
- Apply the security principles of least privilege and separation of duties to secure the administrative role.

Personnel Issues

Just because someone has network or systems administration skills is no guarantee that they know or have the best interests of the company at heart, that they share the company's ethical beliefs, or that they will not change their practices over time. In addition to forest-wide administrative groups such as Enterprise Admins and Schema Admins, each member of any Domain Admins group has potential access to every domain in the forest. Members of the local Administrators group hold the keys to sensitive server operation and data, and delegation of authority can provide ordinary users with elevated privileges. Therefore, all administrators, whether they have that official title or not, must be trusted individuals, and their activity must be audited. The degree of trust required is directly related to the administrative duties they will perform. A background check should be required for every new administrative hire and repeated periodically thereafter. Administrative access should also be audited, and not solely by administrators. Every person who will have elevated privileges on the network should have the following characteristics:

- Understands the security policy
- Applies the security policy to themselves
- Is willing to enforce the security policy
- Is a team player

Although most employees will not be involved in security policy enforcement, they should have the other three characteristics.

Securing the Administrative Role

In addition to hiring and monitoring trustworthy administrators who support and will implement and enforce your security policy, many technical and operational controls can be implemented. You can take steps to secure the administrative role. Two security principles will help you to structure administration in your network:

- **Least privilege**—This principle says that, in every case, you should only give people the privileges they need to do their job. For administration, that means not giving everyone membership in every administrative group, as well as creating specific administrative groups and providing these groups with only the administrative rights they require. When delegating permissions in Active

Directory OUs, it means not delegating full control over an OU when only user and group administration or some other smaller task is necessary and approved.

■ **Separation of duties**—This principle defines the parts of a job that should be done by different people to prevent one person from having the ability to cause harm. An earlier example, the separation of backup and restore rights, fulfills this principle.

Apply these principles to administrative duties to secure the administrative role. Several operations and functions that are native to Windows Server 2003 can be used to do so. Most of these processes, such as the use of groups and delegation of authority, are described in Chapter 7, "Active Directory's Role in Domain Security." Others, like SID filtering, are defined in Chapter 8, "Trust." An understanding of the concepts of isolation and autonomy and how to split administrative duties into service and data administrators will give you better control over the scope of any administrators privileges.

Best Practices Administrative Role

Best practices for securing the administrative role are as follows:

- Limit the number of administrators.
- Limit the duties of administrators.
- Assign trustworthy personnel.
- If forest trusts are in place, do not assign administrators from other forests administrative privileges to this forest.
- Require smart cards for administrative logon—If smart cards can be implemented forest-wide for all users, this is great, but this is not always immediately possible. The user account option `Smart card is required for interactive logon` in the account Property pages can be used to require smart cards for administrators.
- Share logon for sensitive administrative accounts—This can be a good practice if it also requires that each user only knows part of the password and both are required to be present during the administrative task.
- Secure administrator workstations.
- Restricting the use of administrator account logons to administrative workstations—Log on to is a property of each user account that restricts that account's logon to specific computers by name.

- Use IPSec between administrator workstations and domain controllers.
- Don't delegate security-sensitive operations such as installation of a CA, modifying the schema, managing operations master roles, managing site topology, installation and removal of active directory, software installation on domain controllers, managing outbound trusts, managing replication, and modifying domain controller and domain security policies.
- Restrict access to Group Policy to trusted administrators.
- Restrict data administrators.
- Hide domain administrator—rename the Administrator account, and prepare a decoy account with the name Administrator. Audit logon attempts.
- Create a controlled subtree to manage service administrator accounts in Active Directory. Use an OU and add all service administrator accounts and the accounts of their workstations. Ensure management by another service administrator through ACLs. Block inheritance of other Group Policies to this OU to prevent changes made by non-service administrators. Set the ACLs to give Enterprise Admins, Domain Admins, and Administrators groups full control on this object, and for all child objects, allow `Pre-Windows 2000 Compatible Access all Read` rights for User objects only. Move the service administrator groups to this OU. (You cannot move the Built-in Administrators group. This group is protected by a special default security descriptor that is applied during the installation of Active Directory.) Enable auditing of this OU.
- Periodically check status of restore mode admin password—This password is required in order to do an Active Directory restore and should be a strong password that is not widely known. It should not be the same password as the Administrator account. To change the password, you have to start the DC in Directory Services Restore mode, change the password, and then start the DC again in Active Directory mode.
- Enable auditing of the %WINDIR%\system32\config folder—the only valid use is a virus scan or system backup. Other access should be investigated.
- Set administrative boundaries—See the section "Delegation of Administration—Using the Delegation of Control Wizard," in Chapter 7.

- Set security boundaries—Domains are boundaries for administration and policies, but are not security boundaries. The forest is the security boundary. See the upcoming section, "Autonomy and Isolation."

- Maintain physical security—Keep DCs secured against physical access by not moving them from proscribed secure locations and not admitting unauthorized individuals to data centers and secured locations. Physical security of network infrastructure should also be maintained.

- Secure backup media.

- Use SID filtering on externally trusted domains or forests—In normal practice, this does not cause a problem. However, if users from trusted domains or forests are migrated to the trust partner, their SID history will include the SIDs from their former domain. This allows them to continue to access resources in that domain. Unfortunately, if SID history can be modified, these users could then elevate their privileges across a trust. Modifying SID history would be difficult and would require administrative credentials on a trusted domain and the technical ability to modify low-level OS functions and data structures. Nevertheless, it is a risk.

- Do not use administrative accounts for mundane tasks—every administrator should have two accounts: one used for mundane tasks and the other for administration. The administrator should log on using the mundane account and use the runas facility when needing to perform administrative tasks.

- Remove all members of the Schema Admins group. No membership in this group is needed unless the Schema needs modification. Schema modifications should not be made arbitrarily. Instead, planning and thought is required. To prevent inadvertent schema changes, remove membership in this group and carefully control its membership. This can be enforced by using the Restricted Groups setting in the default GPO for Domain Controllers.

Service and Data Administrators

It is a mistake to make all administrators equal. The best approach is to narrowly define administrative practices—like users, administrators should only be given the ability to do what they need to do. There are many different administrative roles that can be configured, but two broad categories exist: service administrators and data administrators.

Service administrators control Active Directory configuration and policy and have physical access to the domain controller and forest infrastructure. They can add DCs and new domains and have the ability to attack the entire forest. Service administrators are members of the Domain Admins, Enterprise Admins, or Schema Admins groups.

Data administrators play a role similar to NT domain admins. They support ordinary users and computers, add and remove users and groups, and modify group policy settings. They may also be administrators over single computers or computer roles such as file servers, database servers, and so on. Data administrators should not be given the right to manage administrator accounts. Data administrators are members of groups created to manage specific OUs or may be members of the local Administrators group on specific servers.

Skillful use of existing Windows groups, User rights, and delegation of authority can split administrative roles into service and data administrators. This not only fulfills the principle of least privileges but also enforces separation of duties to some extent. You can limit data administrators to the data administrator role. However, because of the nature of the service administrators group membership, and the inherit ability of an administrator to take ownership of any object, you cannot prevent service administrators from performing data administrative roles. You can, for example, delegate the user and group creation rights for a specific OU to a group designed to manage that data. Members of that group will only have the right to manage and create users and groups within that OU, and not within the domain. However, the domain administrator will have the ability to manage users and groups in the OU and will have to be limited by written policy, not by technical controls.

Autonomy and Isolation

In designing a secure Active Directory infrastructure, consider the need for autonomy and isolation. Autonomy means that areas of independent management are required. This ability can be gained by creating a single forest with multiple domains, and to some extent by creating OUs within the domain. Administrators of domains and OUs have the ability to manage the objects (users, groups, computers, etc.) that exist within their domain or OU. However, another administrator, one with authority over all domains, such as the Enterprise Admin, or over all OUs, such as the Domain Admin, can also manage those objects. A Schema Admin can modify the schema and impact all domains. Isolation, on the other hand, requires a complete security boundary. The Active Directory domain is not such a security boundary. In addition to forest-wide administrative groups, it may be possible for a member of the Domain Admins group to fraudulently obtain administrative access to other domains within the forest. Isolation is not possible within a forest. It can be accomplished by creating multiple forests. Only in separate forests can the interference or access to AD service or data by other administrators be prevented.

The article "Design Considerations for the Delegation of Administration in Active Directory" details the concept of isolation and autonomy. Read it at http://www.microsoft.com/technet/treeview/ default.asp?url=/ technet/prodtechnol/ad/windows2000/plan/addeladm.asp. Then, read Windows Server 2003–specific documentation in the Windows Server 2003 Deployment Kit.

To decide which approach is best for an organization, the needs of the organization should be established. Because the forest is the security boundary, separate forest should be used where

- An extranet will be established.
- There is a legal requirement to provide isolation.
- There is a lack of trust between divisions or other structures of the organization.

Secure Application and User Access to Domain Controllers

At a minimum, all users need the ability to remotely access the domain controller to authenticate. They do not require carte blanche access to all drives, files, and utilities on the DC or the ability to log on locally to the DC. Likewise, applications that run as services should not have unwarranted privilege to access resources on DCs. You can prevent unnecessary access by

- Managing user rights
- Managing membership in privileged groups
- Managing share permissions
- Managing file, folder, and registry permissions
- Using domain controllers only as domain controllers and not installing additional services on them
- Ensuring that the group Pre-Windows Compatibility Access has no members

The group Pre-Windows Compatibility is used to provide backward compatibility with legacy applications. These applications require elevated privileges and access to files, folders, and registry keys that go beyond what is assigned to the Domain Users group. It is populated by

the group Everyone if the option to set `Permissions Compatible with Pre-Windows 2000 Server Operating Systems` is selected during `dcpromo`. It may have been selected by accident or may have been necessary at the time the domain was created, but it may no longer be necessary. You may be able to safely remove any members of this group and improve
security on DCs, but first check to see if it is necessary . An example of applications that need this is using Routing and Remote Access Services on Windows NT 4.0 computers.

Deploying Secure Domain Controllers

One of the best ways to ensure secure domain controllers is to install them securely configured to start and to deploy them in a secure manner. The DC is secured before it is placed into production. Many of these security steps can be incorporated into an automated installation process.

Best Practices for DC Deployment

Five distinct sets of steps must be completed to bring up a DC securely:

- Practice secure preparation steps
- Use a secure installation procedure
- Secure the server post installation, but prior to `dcpromo`
- Use a secure `dcpromo` process and secure the server during `dcpromo`
- Secure the server post `dcpromo`

Preparation

Before a domain controller is established on the network, prepare for its installation. Some steps are done before the first DC in the forest is established and then maintained, while others need to be prepared before each new DC is installed. Prior to installing the first domain controller, do the following:

- **Secure DNS**—Active Directory depends on DNS. Securing DNS is paramount. Steps for securing DNS are detailed in Chapter 11.

- **Secure the Network Infrastructure.** Although the DC itself should be hardened, it should always be operated in a secure environment. Routers, network segments, and switches should all be secure. An excellent source of information on network infrastructure security can be found in *Hardening Network Infrastructure* by Wes Noonan (McGraw-Hill Osborne Media, 2004).

- **Prepare a secure physical location**—Specifics may vary from a locked cabinet in a small branch office to a data center. The objective is to secure from theft, restrict access, and prevent the addition of rogue applications, drivers, services, or configuration.

- **Secure the computer itself**—Hardening the server hardware includes removing or securing removable drives, establishing a boot policy, and removing access to unnecessary ports, such as unused USB or serial ports.

- **Prepare the server post installation but prior to** `dcpromo`.

- **Establish policy and procedures for domain controller installation**—Prior to establishing the first DC of the production network, policy and procedures should be written. If those responsible for writing policies and procedures are unfamiliar with Active Directory, a test network should be provided along with proper education and training.

Policies and Procedures for Domain Controller Installation

Policies and procedures for domain controller installation should include the following:

- Specifying who has the authority to install the DC.
- Specifying that if the server can't be physically secured from console access during installation, it should not be left unattended.
- Specifying where domain controller installation can be done, such as doing as much as possible outside the production network.
- Providing automated processes for as many phases of installation as possible.
- Developing a procedure for secure installation of DCs at remote locations. Some organizations install the DC and then ship them. Specify a secure shipping method to prevent theft of the DC during shipping.
- Specifying that only service administrators do DC installations.

Here are the sound steps to include in policies and procedures:

- Provide multiple physical drives so that Active Directory components can be on separate drives, and the AD database can be separate from the Windows Server 2003 operating system. Taking these actions improves performance and availability and protects AD from potential directory traversal attacks and disk-filling DoS attacks. In a directory traversal attack, an attacker gains access to one directory on a disk, then uses tools and commands in an attempt to access other folders. Thus, access to a mundane folder with no sensitive items might be leveraged into access to more sensitive ones, such as AD. By placing components on different physical disks, you can thwart these attacks.
- Create or modify security templates that meet the DC security baseline—potential settings were described previously, and potential preconfigured secure DC baselines can be downloaded from Microsoft.
- Prepare a separate build network for installations if network install is your choice. Otherwise, prepare custom bootable CD-ROMs with changes made.
- Modify default security settings by modifying default security templates used by server install and `dcpromo`. Make sure these modified templates are available to the system during install by modifying the defaults and ensuring that they are located on the installation media where the system expects to find them during install.

Server Installation

Before a server becomes a DC, the Windows operating system must be installed. The following steps will provide a more secure base on which to create a DC:

1. Do a base minimal install. Do not install IIS, indexing services, or any extra services. Do not install additional administrative tools, such as support tools or resource kit tools. (When these tools are available, they may prove useful to an attacker.) Do not connect the server to the production network during or after installation to avoid the risk that it may be compromised or infected by a virus, Trojan, or worm. Do not connect the server to the Internet for the same reason.

2. Apply all service packs and updates according the latest security bulletins. Even if this DC will receive updates automatically from SUS or other patching services on your network, it should be placed on the network as secure and up-to-date as it can be. Discovering update needs and getting a system updated, even automatically, can take time, during which the system might be compromised. (If you must put the server on the network to complete updates, enable the built-in firewall. Remember to disable the firewall before dcpromo.)

3. Check root volume permissions. These should be set via security templates during installation, but check them anyways and adjust as required by your security policy.

After Server Installation But Before dcpromo

After the server is installed, scan for viruses and create a reserve file.

Virus scanning should always be done before dcpromo to ensure that the server is virus-free. Then, the virus scanner should be turned off.

Create a reserve file to enable recovery in the case of disk space attacks. A reserve file is a file created on the same drive as the ntds.dit (the AD directory) file. The reserve file does not contain useful data; it just takes up room on the disk. If these attacks include adding objects to the Active Directory, even though the administrator deletes the unneeded objects, it will take a while before their tombstones are gone, thus the size of the AD is not reduced. This is only one type of disk space attack. A disk space attack can fill up the disk and cripple AD, but it won't overwrite the reserve file. The administrator can recover AD by removing the reserve file and thus giving AD room to operate while the unneeded objects' tombstones are still present.

TIP: Don't Let Virus Scanners Scan SYSVOL

After dcpromo, virus scanners should be modified to prevent the scanning of SYSVOL and other folders that are replicated by the file-replication service. Many anti-virus products modify file settings when scanning files. This modification on folders that are replicated can trigger replication. A large amount of file replication can severely affect the performance on the network.

During dcpromo

The dcpromo process promotes an ordinary server and makes it a DC. Here are the guidelines to follow for dcpromo:

- Disable pre-Windows 2000 compatibility. Pre-Windows 2000 compatibility needs to be enabled if legacy applications that require anonymous access to AD are present, such as RRAS or RAS on NT 4.0 or SQL Server 6.0 applications. It also provides access to many files, folders, Active Directory objects, and registry keys to members of the group. For example, it provides read permission on the domain root and on all user, computer, and group objects when enabled. The group Everyone is added to the Pre-Windows 2000 Compatibility group. In Windows Server 2003, this does not include the anonymous SID; it does, however, provide access to every authenticated user and the Guest account. This access is far too broad.
- Place database and SYSVOL on same physical drive but separate from the system volume. The system volume is a common place where large print jobs are spoofed, thus filling up the folder. If AD is on the same drive, it may be crippled because the drive may be filled by other activity, and AD will not have room enough to operate. (If the DC will not be a print server, disable the print service.)
- Improve performance by placing log files and the paging file on their own dedicated physical drive(s)—not the system drive.

After Installation

After the DC is installed, additional steps should be taken:

- Configure virus protection to skip virus checking on any drives that are or will be configured for the File-Replication Service. (Otherwise, every replication will trigger excessive virus checking.) Turn virus checking back on.
- Prepare for secure replication and other communications.
- Move the domain controller into a secured place in the data center.

Best Practices for Branch Office Builds and Rebuilds

Installing a DC at a branch office can be a challenge. If, however, you must build or rebuild a DC at a branch office, the following guidelines will make the process more secure:

- Do not leave unattended.
- Use automated method.
- Locate in a lockable room.
- Restrict access during install.
- Provide for restricted access after install.
- Do not let computers remain connected to the network or Internet during installation and configuration of server.
- Avoid `dcpromo` replication over the WAN by using the `dcpromo /adv` command. You need to bring with you a backup copy of Active Directory and use that during installation. During the installation process, select "`from these restored backup les`" instead of "`over the network from a domain controller`". `dcpromo` will be able to use the provided files to get up and running. Once completed, normal replication over the WAN will bring the DC up to the current Active Directory status.

Automate Domain Controller Installation

Where possible, automate domain controller installation. This has more benefits than just speeding up the task and removing some of its labor. When procedures are automated, they are done the same exact way every time. When procedures are done manually, mistakes and omissions can happen. It's also true that because installations can take a while, systems may be left open with administrator privileges for some time before anyone returns to start the next stage of the process. Automated installation, when done correctly and tested, will complete the process without any gaps. Several possibilities for configuring automated installation exist. Remote Installation Services (RIS), sysprep, and third-party products all do a good job. The basic process consists of preparing the automated installation media or process, starting the installation, and moving the DC into production. To prepare and utilize an automated install, follow these steps:

1. Create a clean server install. Modify server default templates as previously discussed.

2. Configure security (apply templates and other configuration).
3. Prepare an answer file so that questions that normally would require user input will be entered automatically.
4. Prepare an answer file for `dcpromo` and use the `dcpromo.exe /answer:answerfilename` command to run `dcpromo`. This command should be run when the server first restarts so as to reduce the potential for introduction of unauthorized files. To make this happen, place this command under the registry key:

```
Hklm\software\microsoft\windows\currentversion\runonc
e
```

Or, if using `Sysprep`, modify the `[GuiRunOnce]` section of the `sysprep.inf` answer file before running sysprep. The setting should look like this:

```
[GuiRunOnce]
Command0 = "dcpromo /answer:ans le.txt"
```

5. Prepare so that the latest service packs and updates are installed automatically as well.
6. Create the image using sysprep, RIS, or third-party tools.
7. Deploy image to target computer.
8. Configure computer-specific settings.
9. If this is the first DC in the domain, and security settings were not defined during install or `dcpromo` or if more are required, define users and administrative rights in domain. Create user groups, give rights, create OUs, and so on. Add any additional GPO and link to domain container and OUs.
10. Ship or move to place in production. If it is necessary to ship, use a trusted shipping method—one that requires signatures.

Secure Replication

Active Directory changes are replicated between all domain controllers in a domain and between the Global catalog servers in each domain in the forest. By default, all replication is encrypted and authenticated. Securing replication is part securing the domain controllers, part adding security to the data transfer, and part improving the security of the networks over which it may pass. Govern the private network with sound network security practices, and this will do much to ensure the security of AD replicated data. When replication data must pass over untrusted networks, additional steps should be taken. Possibilities are using SMTP as a replication protocol and using IPSec or a VPN.

SMTP-Based Replication

Normal Active Directory replication uses RPC over TCP/IP. SMTP can be also be used for replication but requires certificates and can be used only to replicate schema, configuration, and application directory partitions. SMTP cannot be used to replicate domain directory partitions. Hence, if a DC for a domain resides in one site, it may be possible to use only SMTP replication, but where DCs of a domain are spread across multiple sites, RPC over TCP/IP must also be used. Using SMTP can improve security because RPC ports do not need to be opened on firewalls and because using SMTP requires certificate-based authentication.

Using IPSec or a VPN

An extra layer of security can be achieved by using an IPSec Policy for domain replication or, where data must traverse networks such as the Internet, a VPN connection between the two sites should be established and used for replication.

Summary

Securing Active Directory is a multidisciplinary task. The primary objective, an Active Directory infrastructure that is protected against attack and accidental misuse, can be accomplished by securing network infrastructure, securing Administrative practices, installing and maintaining secure domain controllers, providing physical security, and securing data during replication.

CHAPTER 11

Securing Infrastructure Roles

The first computers were all-purpose megaliths. They were used for every approved computing purpose within an organization. "Approved" is the operative word here. It was sometimes difficult to get new applications approved, and once approved, a new application could take years to develop and implement. As computing needs grew, specialized systems were adopted: a payroll system, financials, inventory control. Many of these systems were installed outside of the official data center. Computers as functional units, as role-fulfilling parts of the greater computational whole became the norm. Today, some organizations still attempt to use one computer for all things; these organizations are large and should perhaps know better, or they are very small with smaller budgets and few requirements. Most organizations, however, have many computers and, if asked, can easily sort them into roles such as desktops, databases, domain controllers, messaging, firewalls, DNS servers, WINS servers, DHCP servers, and many others. All these computers, though they play different roles, have many common elements. Chapters 7 through 10 examine the role of the Windows Server 2003 domain controller and how to use Group Policy to secure all systems joined to the domain. They do not, however, provide the specifics of how to maximize the use of this process to address the multiple computer and user roles on the network. Likewise, in Chapter 3, the use of Local Security Policy to manage users and secure individual desktop computers and servers is detailed, but a way to quickly apply and enforce recommended security settings or to automate the process of dealing with multiple Windows systems that are not joined in a domain is not discussed. This chapter addresses these issues: the details of what to put into and how to best use Group Policy and automating the application of security on standalone computers. The following topics and techniques are discussed:

- The development of security templates to address the general needs of servers on the network.
- The use of incremental templates to further relax or tighten settings for specific infrastructure roles.
- The details of how these templates can be used with Group Policy in a domain setting.
- How to use Security Configuration and Analysis outside of the domain to secure these servers in an automated fashion.
- Security specifics that cannot be incorporated into security templates.

Although this chapter describes these techniques as a way to harden infrastructure servers, these same techniques can be used to secure other server roles, to manage specific collections of users, and to secure workstations.

These infrastructure roles are discussed:

1. Domain Name Services (DNS)
2. Windows Internet Naming Service (WINS)
3. Dynamic Host Control Protocol (DHCP)

Security Templates

Security templates are a collection of security settings in a format that can be applied to Windows computers to configure security. In Windows Server 2003 and Windows 2000, security templates exist as text files, but they are more easily understood and modified when displayed, as shown in Figure 11-1, in their own Security Templates Microsoft Management Console (MMC). A security template has many uses such as the following:

- Used to test the effect of security settings on a single computer
- Imported into a Group Policy Object (GPO) and therefore used to secure servers, workstations, and users across an entire domain, or for a smaller portion of a domain
- Imported into GPOs in multiple domains in order to provide consistent security to every domain in the forest

- Applied directly to a single computer that is or is not a member of a domain
- Applied via a script to multiple computers
- Periodically reapplied to these computers via scripts or tasks
- Used to audit security compliance

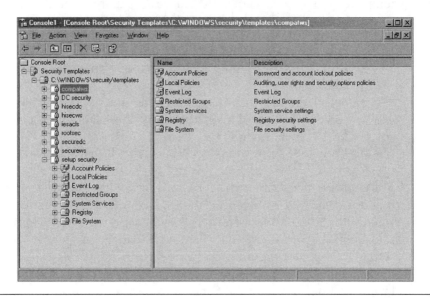

Figure 11-1 Viewing Security Templates and settings.

Security templates do not provide the ability to configure all the security settings that may be necessary to secure a computer. Templates should be supplemented with the use of other Group Policy features, such as Public Key Policies, IPSec Policies and Administrative Templates, the use of role-specific management tools, and direct registry settings where necessary. The section, "Using Incremental Templates and other Techniques to Provide Security for Infrastructure Servers," describes other security settings and additional security templates for computers with infrastructure roles. Each computer role and each server application provides unique security challenges, and you should study and apply appropriate security using any role- or application-specific tools they provide.

Developing a security template is not difficult, but it does require intimate knowledge of Windows services and security settings. To make the job easier, Microsoft provides sample security templates as part of the operating system install, and special baseline and incremental templates are available for download. To inspect the provided security templates and provide a utility to manage any additional templates, build a security template console by doing the following:

1. Open a new MMC console.
2. From the `File` menu, choose `Add/Remove Snap-in`.
3. Click `Add`.
4. Select the Security `Templates` snap-in, click `Add`, click `Close`, and then click `OK`. The basic Security Templates are added to the MMC, as shown in Figure 11-1.
5. From the `le` menu, select `Save`, name the console, and click `OK`.

Microsoft provides three types of templates: default templates that are used to set security during installation and `dcpromo`, basic templates provided with the operating system that can be used to modify security, and role templates provided with security white papers for specific operating systems. Table 11-1 describes the basic security templates available with the operating system. Role-specific templates are discussed in the following section, "How to Use Security Templates to Secure Computers by Role."

Table 11-1   Default Security Templates

Template	Purpose
Compatws	Provides relaxed file and registry permissions to support legacy applications
DC Security	A baseline for domain controller security
Hisecdc	Highest security template for DCs
Hisecws	Highest security for workstations and servers
Iesacls	Sets registry permissions and values for IE
Rootsec	Root permissions for os partion
Securedc	Higher security for DCs
Securews	Higher security for workstations and servers
Setup security	The settings applied to the specific computer during installation

How to Use Security Templates to Secure Computers by Role

The first step in using security templates to secure computers by roles is to design a template that applies the baseline security for all servers on the network. The objective of the baseline template is to tighten every aspect of computer security. It follows the principle of reducing the attack surface. This principle increases security by relying on the simple fact that the less a server is doing, the fewer potential vulnerabilities or attack surfaces will be available. After the baseline security template is applied to a server, the server will still run, but it may not be able to perform the services for a specific network role.

NOTE: See Microsoft Documents for More on Securing Computers by Role

Microsoft's "Windows 2000 Security Operations Guide" introduced the concept of using baseline and incremental templates to secure Windows servers. You can download a copy of this guide and the templates from `http://www.microsoft.com/downloads/details.aspx?FamilyID=f0b7b4ee-201a-4b40-a0d2-cdd9775aeff8&displaylang=en`.

The second step resolves this problem by creating incremental templates that include the changes necessary to support specific roles. These templates may, for example, enable services that are required by a specific server role. A DNS incremental template, for example, enables and sets to automatic start at boot the DNS Server service, a service that is disabled in the baseline template.

Baseline and incremental templates are designed to be assigned in a hierarchical fashion. First, the baseline template is applied and then the appropriate incremental template. When multiple templates are applied to the same computer, settings are merged unless a conflict occurs. When a conflict exists, the most recent setting wins. This is why the baseline template can disable a service and the incremental template can enable the same service. A conflict exists, but because the incremental template is applied after the baseline template, its configuration for the specific service will win. Hierarchical assignment can be done either manually by applying the templates consecutively to each server, or automatically by importing the templates into Group Policy Objects. When Group Policy is used, a baseline template is applied at a top-level OU created for servers, and the incremental templates are applied to child OUs created for each server role. For example, a DNS incremental template is applied to an OU that contains the computer accounts for all DNS servers, and a file server incremental template is applied to an OU that contains all the computer accounts for file servers. Because of the way Group Policy works, the baseline template will be applied to all servers, and the incremental DNS template will only be applied to the DNS servers, and so on.

Although the basic templates provide examples that may be used to provide tighter security, none of them are baseline templates. Microsoft provides sample baseline templates, along with incremental templates. These templates can be downloaded with companion documents that detail the security settings they provide and discuss other sound security practices. The templates have been tested in many production networks. The documents and templates are available by download:

- The "Windows Server 2003 Security Guide" provides templates and instructions for securing Windows Server 2003 (`http://www.microsoft.com/downloads/details.aspx?displaylang=en&familyid=8a2643c1-0685-4d89-b655-521ea6c7b4db`).
- The "Windows XP Security Guide" provides instructions and templates that can be used to secure Windows XP (`http://www.microsoft.com/downloads/details.aspx?displaylang=en&familyid=2d3e25bc-f434-4cc6-a5a7-09a8a229f118`).
- The "Threats and Countermeasures: Security Settings in Windows Server 2003 and Windows XP" details every security setting (`http://www.microsoft.com/downloads/details.aspx?displaylang=en&familyid=1b6acf93-147a-4481-9346-f93a4081eea8`).
- The "Windows 2000 Security Operations Guide" provides similar information and templates for Windows 2000 (`http://www.microsoft.com/downloads/details.aspx?displaylang=en&familyid =f0b7b4ee-201a-4b40-a0d2-cdd9775aeff8`).

NOTE: THE TRUE IMPACT OF SECURITY TEMPLATES

The templates and methodology of the "Windows 2000 Security Operations Guide" have been tested several times in "hacking" contests. One such contest was at the Microsoft Certified Professional Magazine Security Summit in July 2002. The Windows challenge consisted of an entire network hardened using the templates from the "Windows 2000 Security Operations Guide." The challenge network was put on the Internet for 48 hours and was subject to thousands of online attacks—but none of them broke through the defenses.

Building security templates for computer roles is not just a matter of picking and clicking within the template or using carte blanche templates provided by Microsoft or others. Each setting in the template must be set to fulfill the security policy of your network. The provided templates and documentation, however, provide an excellent starting point, ideas for discussion, and a system that has been tested and that works.

The approach described in the documents and discussed in this chapter is to separate computers by the roles they play on the network, apply a baseline template to all computers, and then apply incremental templates to each computer according to its role. Infrastructure servers, for example, may need to run DNS, DHCP, or other services, while domain controllers and ordinary file servers do not. File and print servers should not run these services, but they do need to run the print spooling service and have file sharing enabled. Finally, other tools and recommendations for security that cannot be implemented via the security templates will also need to be implemented. Instructions for infrastructure roles are documented.

Each role that a Windows computer plays within your network may entail many different security configurations. Although not all security can be configured through templates, it is important to use templates wherever you can because you can more efficiently configure, apply, and maintain a large number of security settings. The simple discussions within this chapter should not be your only source for determining the security necessary for these computers. However, this chapter provides you with a framework on which to build appropriate security for a specific network.

Creating and Manipulating Templates

Security templates are text files and can be created from scratch. However, while much of the syntax that must be followed is straightforward, in some areas (such as permissions), it is difficult to correctly enter the information when working within a text file. Instead, a better way to get started is to copy a template that is close to what you need and then adjust it. To copy the template, first create a Security Templates console as described in the section, "Security Templates," then perform the following instructions. Using this method ensures the resulting file syntax will be correct. A good practice is to create a secure folder to store custom templates in and use it for your development work. In the following examples, it's assumed that a "custom templates" folder has been created, but the folder can have any name.

To create the new template, first add the path to the new folder, and then copy the template:

1. Open the `Security Templates` console.
2. Right-click the `Security Templates` node and select `New Template Search Path`.
3. Browse to the custom templates folder and click `OK`. The path appears in the console.
4. Browse to the security template you want to copy, right-click it, and then select `Save As`.
5. Browse to the location to store the new template and enter the new template name. Always name the template with a new name so that you will be able to distinguish it from the original template.
6. Click `Save`.
7. Expand the new path in the `Security Templates` console to see the new template, as shown in Figure 11-2.

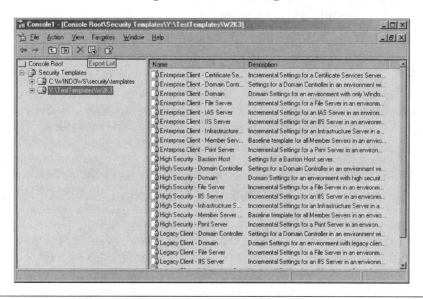

Figure 11-2 Viewing the default new path and template.

After a copy of the template is made, revise it as necessary. To modify a template, follow these steps:

1. Expand the template sections until the section you want to modify is available.

2. Select the template section. In the detail pane, double-click the item to modify.

3. Modify the setting as needed in the item's Property pages. The settings and techniques available will vary depending on the setting. Many settings first require you to check De ne This Policy setting in the template before changing any specific settings using Add buttons, text boxes, drop-down lists, and radio buttons.

4. Save the template.

Templates should be modified by using the GUI whenever possible; however, there are three reasons to make changes directly to the template file:

- Comments should always be added to templates that have been modified. Doing so provides documentation on how the template was changed and where important elements lie within it.
- Unnecessary information should be removed. A template may be created for a simple purpose, such as setting permissions on a few registry keys and/or files. Removing the extraneous information, such as information on settings that are "not defined," can make it easier to work with the template and understand what it's doing. An example of such a template is the iesacls template, as shown in Figure 11-3. The only settings in this template are for the registry keys displayed. All other sections will be noted as "Not Defined."
- Additional registry keys can be added. Registry changes not represented in the GUI of the template can be added to the template by adding them to the template file. Any registry change added to the template file will be made when the template is applied.

The addition of comments and the removal of extraneous information can be done by simple editing. New registry changes, however, must be added to the proper section. To do so:

1. Use Explorer to browse to the template location.

2. Double-click the template to open it in Notepad.

3. Examine the [Registry values] section, as shown in Figure 11-4. This is where you can edit or add registry values that will then be applied at the same time as the template.

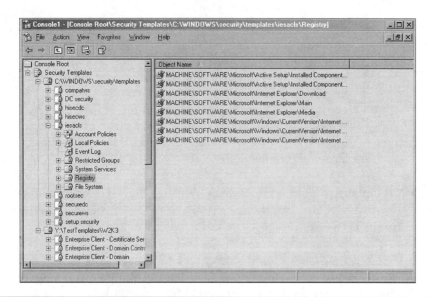

Figure 11-3   Examining a simple template.

```
hisecws.inf - Notepad
File Edit Format View Help
AuditSystemEvents = 3
AuditObjectAccess = 3
AuditPrivilegeUse = 3
AuditPolicyChange = 3
AuditAccountManage = 3
AuditProcessTracking = 0
;AuditDSAccess=0
AuditAccountLogon=3
AuditLogonEvents = 3

;-----------------------------------------------------------------
;Registry Values
;-----------------------------------------------------------------
[Registry Values]
; Registry value name in full path = Type, Value
;  REG_SZ                       ( 1 )
;  REG_EXPAND_SZ                ( 2 )   // with environment variables to expand
;  REG_BINARY                   ( 3 )
;  REG_DWORD                    ( 4 )
;  REG_MULTI_SZ                 ( 7 )

MACHINE\System\CurrentControlSet\Control\Lsa\AuditBaseObjects=4,0
MACHINE\System\CurrentControlSet\Control\Lsa\CrashOnAuditFail=4,0
MACHINE\System\CurrentControlSet\Control\Lsa\DisableDomainCreds=4,1
MACHINE\System\CurrentControlSet\Control\Lsa\EveryoneIncludesAnonymous=4,0
;Leave model alone
```

Figure 11-4   You can add registry settings to the INF file, and they will be applied
when the template is applied.

Create Baseline Templates to Secure All Servers

The first step in the process is to create a baseline template to secure all servers. A good place to start is to examine the security templates provided by Microsoft for this purpose.

Microsoft Sample Baseline Templates

The "Windows Server 2003 Security Guide" provides two baseline templates, one for server and one for domain controllers, for each of three categories:

- **Legacy clients**—The domain may have a wide range of Windows clients and servers, including Windows 98, Windows NT 4.0, Windows 2000, Windows XP Professional, and Windows Server 2003.
- **Enterprise clients**—Only Windows 2000, Windows XP, and Windows Server 2003 may exist in the domain.
- **High security**—Only Windows 2000, Windows XP, and Windows Server 2003 may exist in the domain, and the template applies tighter security than the enterprise client templates does.

In addition, templates are defined for infrastructure servers, file servers, IIS Servers, Print servers, bastion hosts, IAS servers, and Certification Authorities. The templates provide solid security guidance; you should also look for additional generic baseline checklists. Here are some good sources:

- www.Microsoft.com/technet/security/tools/w2ksvrcl.asp
- The National Security Agency web site, www.NSA.gov
- The Center for Internet Security, www.cisecurity.org
- SANS Organization, www.sans.org

WARNING: The Meaning of Baseline Can Be Different

Some security baseline providers also provide preconfigured security templates that match their recommendations. However, those templates are not designed to work in the hierarchical design presented in this chapter. The meaning of "baseline" may also be different because it may mean "minimum security baseline" instead of the strict maximum-security baselines developed by the Microsoft strategies and described in the following sections.

Hardening Servers Can Cause Production Problems

Avoid recovery costs and consulting bills; if you are deploying or using AD, read and understand AD documentation as well as security guides and recommended practices. Central to the concept of hardening tasks and the guides is to create security based on computer roles. It is easy to be overzealous. I once received a call asking for help in determining why hardening servers had caused failures in building DCs. The person said that he had simply followed security checklists. A common security recommendation, one you can find on many checklists, is to disable File and Print Sharing for Microsoft Networks. Doing so prevents successful attacks that seek to take advantage of this service. Before promoting servers to DCs, the administrator had hardened servers according to one such checklist. However, file sharing is required by AD. If a server is secured by disabling File and Print Sharing, dcpromo fails.

The Microsoft baseline template for servers is not designed to be used for domain controllers. Some of the services disabled in the server template are required, additional file, folders, and registry keys need protection, and areas that may have been locked down, such as TCP/IP properties, need to be relaxed. The baselineDC.inf template is designed to accommodate what it can of these settings. The specifics of security for domain controllers are discussed in Chapter 10, "Securing Active Directory."

One specific change in the domain controller template enables the DNS service. It is not necessary to install DNS on a DC. However, if separate infrastructure servers do not run DNS for the Windows domains, the logical place is on the domain controller. Also, when dcpromo is used to create the first domain controller in the domain, if you do not have DNS services available, you may want to choose the option to create the DNS server during dcpromo. If you do so, dcpromo installs DNS and populates the DNS server with the records needed for smooth function. If DNS is not installed on a DC, disable DNS in your domain controller baseline template.

Review Sample Templates and Adjust for Your Environment

Not all baseline security settings can or should be in baseline templates. Others may need to be adjusted to meet your security policy. When evaluating the baseline templates, and when attempting to configure security for computers, keep this in mind.

Specifically, consider what should reside elsewhere and what must be configured elsewhere. Even when your analysis of templates is complete, your work on a baseline security for servers is not:

- Configuring an alternative name for the administrator account should not be done in a template that will be applied to all servers in the domain. Instead, each server should have a unique replacement name.
- The password policy for the domain is configured in the default domain GPO, not in the baseline templates. A password policy for local accounts on member computers, however, can be configured in a template designed for the OU where these computer accounts reside.
- File, folder, and registry permissions should not be set within baseline templates because a large number of settings can interfere with the efficiency of replication.
- Security settings are not entirely located in templates. Some settings, such as Public Key Policy and IPSec policies, are part of GPOs but not security templates. Other settings are applied directly, such as in the Property pages of services.

Templates are divided into sections. Review each section and make sure you understand it, why the settings have been set the way they are, and how you might need to change them to meet your policy and needs.

Account Policies

Account Policies are Password Policies, Account Lockout Policies, and Kerberos Polices. Kerberos Polices are used only in the default domain GPO. Likewise, password policies, such as those shown in Table 11-2, are not configured in the baseline template because the password policy for the domain must be configured in the default domain GPO, and password policies for the local accounts of member servers should be configured in the GPO of the OU where they reside. The table presents and defines the parts of a security template. In addition, Microsoft recommendations in its security guide for different settings dependent on the security models are provided in the center column. If no difference is provided, N/A is listed.

Table 11-2   Server Baseline Account Policy

Account Policy Part	Differences in Templates	Explanation
Password policy history	N/A	Remembering password history prevents users from reusing passwords. If a password cracker is run, but the password is changed before it can be cracked, this is a good thing. If users can't easily repeat passwords, this ensures the uselessness of the cracked password.
Password policy minimum age	N/A	Making users wait between password resets prevents them from cycling through an entire password history list in order to use their original password again.
Password policy maximum age	N/A	Frequent password changes reduce the risk of password-cracking and guessing attacks.
Password policy minimum length	8 characters when legacy clients must be supported. 12 characters for high security.	Longer passwords are better, but harder to remember. When passwords are hard to remember, it's more likely they will be written down where they might be discovered.
Passwords must meet complexity requirements		Complexity requirements require users to create passwords that include three of four options: upper- and lowercase letters, numbers, and special characters.
Account Lockout duration	30 minutes versus 15 minutes for high security.	The number of minutes a locked out account will remain locked out.

Account Policy Part	Differences in Templates	Explanation
Account lockout threshold	50 invalid attempts versus 10 invalid attempts for high security	The number of incorrect attempts before an account will be locked out. Set this higher than you might think because many users can easily make mistakes. Use caution here because remote users cannot easily contact staff to reset their account.
Account lockout reset	After 30 minutes versus after 15 minutes	The number of minutes that can elapse before the threshold is reset.

User Rights

User rights for the domain are set in the default domain controller GPO; however, user rights are also defined in server baseline templates and/or in templates for use with specific server roles. Table 11-3 defines user rights in the baseline template.

Table 11-3 Server Baseline Template User Rights

Right	Difference in Templates	Comment
Access this computer from the Network	Defined for high security and then limited to Administrators and Authenticated Users.	This right is required to access servers using SMB, CIFS, HTTP, COM+,and NetBIOS. On some servers, or for some OUs, further restriction might be required. For example, you might want to restrict access to a server that holds financial databases or research data.
Act as part of the Operating System	Defined for high security: Revoke all security groups and accounts.	This right is not required by any user account and is not, by default, assigned to any. By revoking all groups, this right is explicitly denied in the high-security environment.

Table 11-3 Server Baseline Template User Rights Continued

Right	Difference in Templates	Comment
Add workstations to the domain	Limited to Administrator in the high-security template.	This right by default is given to every user. Restrict in high-security environments by using the Administrators group. Alternatively, create a special group and assign the group this right. This right can also be granted by providing users the Create Computer Objects permission for an OU.
Adjust memory quotas for a process	Limited to Administrators and the network service and local service accounts.	This right allows the holder to change the amount of memory that is available for a process. It could be used to prevent a process from getting enough memory or to give some process excessive access to memory, thus denying critical processes the ability to function correctly.
Allow log on locally	Limited to Administrators, Backup Operators, and Power Users for all templates.	By default, this right is given on servers to the Users group. There is no reason that users should be able to log on locally to every server. (I'd even argue for removing the group Power Users. If non-administrative, non-backup operators need this type of access to the server, a special group should be created for them, and the generic group should not be used.)
Allow log on through terminal services	Limited to administrators and remote desktop users in the x template, and limited to administrators in the high-security template.	This right allows the use of terminal services. Most servers are not terminal servers and are not used to provide application access for users. Therefore, this logon right should be restricted to administrators. (The template advocates access by remote desktop users; do you really want ordinary users to control a server?)

Right	Difference in Templates	Comment
Change the system time	Limited to administrators in high security.	This right allows the holder to change the system time. This should be restricted because Kerberos relies on correct system time to operate and security logs should have the correct time so that they give the correct picture of when events happen.
Debug programs	Revoke all groups and all accounts for high security.	This right allows a user to attach a debugger to a process. It provides access to sensitive and critical operation system components and should not be available on a sensitive production system. Known attacks exploit this right to elevate the privileges of the user.
Deny Access to this computer from the network	ANONYMOUS LOGON, built-in Administrator, Guests, Support_388945a0, all non-operating system service accounts, all templates.	This right should not be defined in the template as these accounts' SIDs vary by domain and must be added manually.
Deny logon as a batch job	Guests, Support_388945a0, Guest, all templates.	This right should not be defined in the templates as these accounts' SIDs vary by domain and must be added manually.
Deny log on through Terminal Services	Built-in Administrator, Guests, Support_388945a0, all NON-operating system service accounts.	Do not define in the template as these accounts' SIDs vary by domain and must be added manually.
Enable computer and user accounts to be trusted for delegation	Revoke all security groups and accounts in high security template.	This right provides users with the ability to change the Trusted for Delegation setting on a user or computer object. Misuse could result in the unauthorized impersonation of users by other users on the network.

Table 11-3   Server Baseline Template User Rights Continued

Right	Difference in Templates	Comment
Force shutdown from a remote system	Administrators only in high-security template.	This right gives a user the ability to remotely shut down a server. There is no reason that an ordinary user should be able to do this, and giving them this right enables a DoS attack.
Generate Security Audits	Network service and local service only in high-security template.	This right provides the ability to generate audit records and record them to the security log. It is an often-misunderstood right and often given to groups because administrators think it is the right to start the recording of audit records. It is not. This right should properly belong only to the service account.
Impersonate a client after authentication	Local service and network service.	This right allows applications running on behalf of a user to impersonate the user—to act using the user's rights and privileges. Requiring this right prevents RPC based attacks where a client might connect to an RPC service and then the service acts as the user to do unauthorized actions. Watch for application compatibility issues and resolve by creating a group, giving the group this privilege, and adding the account to the group. Do NOT resolve by adding accounts to the local administrators group.
Log on as a batch job	Revoke all groups and accounts in the high-security template.	This right allows a user to log on using a facility such as the task scheduler service.

Right	Difference in Templates	Comment
Profile single process	Revoke all groups and accounts in high-security template.	This right determines who can use performance-monitoring tools to monitor non-system processes. Using these tools, an attacker might see which services are running on the system.
Profile system performance	Administrators.	This right determines who can use performance-monitoring tools to monitor system processes. Using these tools, an attacker might see which services are running on the system.
Restore files and folders	Limit to administrators in the high-security template.	This right gives users the ability to bypass file, directory, and registry permission to restore backed-up data. The right could be abused to restore old data over current data.
Shut down the system	Limit to administrators in the high-security template.	This right allows the holder to shut down the operating system. Shutting down the system provides an opportunity to perform several different attacks; most user groups do not need this privilege on servers.
Synchronize directory service data	Revoke all security groups and accounts in the high-security template.	This right allows a process to read all objects and properties in the directory, regardless of DACLs. It is required in order to use LDAP directory synchronization.

Security Options

Security Options are a collection of security features. Table 11-4 provides only a listing of Security Options that are changed in the templates. It also does not include settings that are covered elsewhere, such as settings specific to domain controllers.

Table 11-4   Security Options

Template Area	Legacy Clients/Enterprise Clients /High Security	Comments
Devices: Restrict CD-ROM access to locally logged on user only	Not defined/Not defined/Enabled for High Security	Prevents network access to CD-ROM when an account is logged on locally.
Devices: Restrict floppy access to locally logged on user only	Not defined/Not defined/Enabled for High Security	Prevents network access to floppy drive when user is logged on locally.
Interactive Logon: Message text for users attempting to log on	Message specific for organization/ Message specific for organization/ Message specific for organization	Provides notice that unauthorized use is prohibited. Necessary to prove that attacks are not welcome.
Interactive Logon: Message Title for users attempting to log on	A title for the logon message/A title for the logon message/A title for the logon message	Provides notice that unauthorized use is prohibited. Necessary to prove that attacks are not welcome.
Interactive Logon: Number of previous logons to cache (in case domain controller is not available)	1/0/0	When set to 0, prevents caching of logon credentials on the client. Be aware that local logon to the server will not be possible when caching is set to zero and a domain controller is not available. (If a similar policy might be designed for workstations, do not apply this policy to laptop computers.)

Template Area	Legacy Clients/Enterprise Clients /High Security	Comments
Interactive Logon: Require domain controller authentication to unlock workstation	Enabled/Enabled/Enabled	Prevents the use of cached credentials to unlock a system. The use of cached credentials means that current account settings are not checked. An account could be disabled, and the user or administrator still would be able to get back on the system.
Interactive logon: Smart card removal behavior	Not defined/Lock workstation/ Lock workstations	Locks the workstation when a smart card is removed (only applicable if smart cards are implemented). This provides a failsafe if users are trained to remove cards when leaving their machines. If cards are also used for ID, and ID is necessary in the building, this works well.
Network access: Do not allow anonymous enumeration of SAM accounts and shares.	Enabled/Enabled/Enabled	Prevents anonymous access to share and account information. Anonymous access to this information is required by legacy services.
Network access: Do not allow storage of credentials or .NET passports for network authentication	Enabled/Enabled/Enabled	Prevents credential storing. Storing of user names and passwords on a production server is not necessary for its function and leaves the system open to attack by any user who finds a system open or by anyone who compromises this account. Stored passwords therefore would elevate the attacker's privileges on other systems.

Table 11-4   Security Options Continued

Template Area	Legacy Clients/Enterprise Clients /High Security	Comments
Shutdown: Allow system to shut down without having to log on	Disabled/Disabled/Disabled	Provides the ability to shut down a system from the CTRL+ ALT+DEL screen. Shutting down a system can enable specific attacks against password databases and files as well as make the server unavailable to legitimate users. This option does not prevent someone from just pulling the plug but will prevent normal shutdown.
Shutdown: Clear virtual memory pagefile	Disabled/Disabled/Enabled	Empties contents of paging file when the system is shut down. Many important and sensitive bits of information may be periodically paged to the pagefile. If the system is rebooted into another operating system, this information might be retrieved. Clearing at shutdown prevents this from occurring. However, doing so extends the time it takes to shut down.
System cryptography: Force strong key protection for user keys stored the computer	User is prompted when the key is first used/User is prompted when the key is first used/User must enter a password each time they use a key	Prevents an attacker who has compromised the user account from using cryptographic keys because a different password must be entered.

Template Area	Legacy Clients/Enterprise Clients /High Security	Comments
System Objects: Default owner for objects created by members of the Administrators group	Object creator/ Object creator/ Object creator	Restricts ownership to the creator instead of granting Full Control to all Administrators.
System Settings: Optional Subsystems	None/None/None	Prevents the use of the POSIX subsystem. The default is POSIX. By setting this to None, attacks that use programs that must run in the POSIX subsystem will not run.

In addition to those security settings visible in the security template GUI interface, the Microsoft templates provide additional security settings. These settings are defined in the template text file. You can also add settings to the text file. If a security setting is implemented by modifying the registry, it can be added to a security template file and will be applied when the template is applied. Settings must be added to the [registry values] section of the template. The settings listed in Table 11-5 (and are defined following the table) are present in the Microsoft Enterprise Client and High-Security baseline templates. Most of these settings harden TCP/IP against network attacks. By applying these settings, the template helps mitigate certain types of network attacks, especially DoS attacks. These settings are recommended for any computer that may be Internet-facing. All settings in the table fall below the `HKEY_LOCAL_MACHINE\CurrentControlSet\path`.

TIP: Adding Custom Security Options

This technique, adding a registry setting to the [Registry Values] section of a template file, can be used with any registry setting. Instructions for doing, so are in the article, "How to Add Custom Registry Settings to Security Configuration Editor," which helps you understand how to perform this task. You can find it at `http://support.microsoft.com/?kbid=214752`.

Following the table is a list of all settings added to the templates and an explanation of each.

Table 11-5 Additional Security Settings Added to the Enterprise Client and High-Security Baseline Templates

Path	Setting	Value
\Services\Tcpip\Parameters\	TCPMaxPortsExhausted	5
\Services\Tcpip\Parameters\	TcpMaxDataRetransmissions	3
\Services\Tcpip\Parameters\	TcpMaxConnectResponseRetransmissions	2
\Services Tcpip\Parameters\	SynAttackProtect	1
\Services \Tcpip\Parameters\	PerformRouterDiscovery	0
\Services \Tcpip\Parameters\	KeepAliveTime	300000
\Services \Tcpip\Parameters\	EnablePMTUDiscovery	0
\Services \Tcpip\Parameters\	EnableICMPRedirect	0
\Services \Tcpip\Parameters\	EnableDeadGWDetect=	0
\Services \Tcpip\Parameters\	DisableIPSourceRouting	2
\Services \Netbt\Parameters\	NoNameReleaseOnDemand	1
\Services \Eventlog\Security\	WarningLevel	90
\Services \AFD\Parameters\	MinimumDynamicBacklog	20
\Services \AFD\Parameters\	MaximumDynamicBacklog	20000
\Services \AFD\Parameters\	EnableDynamicBacklog	1
\Services \AFD\Parameters\	DynamicBacklogGrowthDelta	10
\Control\Session Manager\	SafeDllSearchMode	1
\Control\FileSystem\	NtfsDisable8dot3NameCreation	1

The following TCP/IP settings are added to the templates:

- **TCPMaxPortsExhausted**—This number is a total of how many dropped connect requests before the SYN-ATTACK protection is operated. A SYN-ATTACK works because connections are opened and not used, eventually exhausting the number of connections that the server can have. Open and unused connections will eventually be closed, but in many cases, not before a DoS has occurred. This setting allows the administrator to control when the SynAttackProtect parameter is triggered.

- **TcpMaxDataRetransmissions**—When data is sent and not acknowledged, it is resent. An attacker could take advantage of this by not responding, thus keeping the server busy resending packets. Set at three, the number of transmissions is reduced, hopefully enough to reduce the impact of an attack.

- **TcpMaxConnectResponseRetransmissions**—If a connection request is not acknowledged, TCP attempts the connection again. In a SYN flood attack, the attacker continues to send a stream of connection requests, or SYN packets, but does not respond.

- **SynAttackProtect**—When set, connection requests time out more quickly, thus mitigating the effect of a DoS attack.

- **PerformRouterDiscovery**—This setting allows a DHCP client to receive routes from the server via the ICMP router discovery protocol. An attacker could spoof these messages and cause the computer to use routes that do not exist, are not correct, or that redirect packets to the attacker.

- **KeepAliveTime**—TCP attempts to verify if a connection is intact by sending a "keepalive" packet, which is then acknowledged by the remotely connected machine if it is still connected. Establishing many connections could cause a DoS condition. By making this setting low, such as five minutes, inactive sessions are discovered sooner.

- **EnablePMTUDiscovery**—This setting causes a system to attempt to find the largest possible packet size over the path to another host. If necessary, the packets to be sent are fragmented. Without this setting, an attacker might attempt to force the MTU to a small value and overwork the stack by forcing the fragmentation of many packets.

- **EnableICMPRedirect**—Set to disabled to prevent ICMP overriding Open Shortest Path First (OSPF) router-generated routes. Otherwise, the ICMP override could prevent traffic from going where it should because the timeout on this action is 10 minutes.

- **EnableDeadGWDetect**—Set to disabled. When enabled, an alternative gateway may be used if many connections are having problems. An attacker might force the use of an alternative gateway of his choosing—that is, redirecting traffic in a manner that suits his purpose.

- **DisableIPSourceRouting**—IP source routing allows the sender to determine the route a packet will take through the network. An attacker could obscure the route his attack has taken.
- **NoNameReleaseOnDemand**—When set, Windows ignores Windows name release request unless they come from WINS servers. (An attacker could pose as a legitimate system by using its name. Dupliciate names are not allowed on the network, so the attacker may try to get the legitimate computer to release its name.)
- **AFD**—There are four AFD settings (MinimumDynamicBacklog, MaximumDynamicBacklog, EnableDynamicBacklog, and DynamicBacklogGrowthDelta). Afd.sys handles connection attempts to services such as FTP and web servers. These modifications help afd.sys handle large numbers of connections by creating a dynamic backlog.

The following entries, which are not related to TCP/IP hardening, are also added to the template:

- **Disable8dot3NameCreation**—Prevents 16-bit scripts and others that rely on 8.3-style names from running, preventing the automatic creation of 8.3 names. The REG_DWORD value is set to 1 for HKLM\System|currentControlSet\Contol\FileSystem\NtfsDisable8dot3Name Creation.
- **NoDriveTypeAutoRun**—Disables autorun so that a possible introduction of a virus or Trojan from inserting a CD-ROM does not happen. If the value is set to 0xFF at HKLM\Software\Microsoft\WIndows\CurrentVersion\Policies\Explorer\NoDriveTypeAutoRun, AutoRun is disabled for all drive types (removable, CD-ROM, hard drive, etc.).
- **ScreenSaverGracePeriod**—Reduces the time between when a screen saver is activated and when it locks the system. If the password feature of the screen saver is enabled, the string value is set to 0 for the registry entry HKLM\Software\Microsoft\Windows\CurrentVersion\Winlogon\ScreenSaverGracePeriod.
- **WarningLevel**—Warns when the security log is near capacity. (To use this setting, the security log must be set to not overwrite events.) To set the percentage of log fullness at which to warn the administrator, the number 90 is set for the value at HKLM\system\currentControlSet\Services\EventLog\Security\Warninglevel.

- **SafeDllSearchMode**—Enables a safe DLL search order. DLLs should be searched for first in the system path, and then in the current working folder. This means a regular system file will be used, and an attack that places a malicious DLL with the same name will not be run. The value is set to 1 at `HKLM\system\Current ControlSet\Control\Session Manager\SafeDllSearchMode`.

Services

Although Windows Server 2003 does not install some services and disables others by default, there are many Windows services present and running after a default system install. The presence of additional software on any service can represent a vulnerability. Vulnerabilities may exist because of the potential use of the service or because of some as-yet undiscovered vulnerability in the code of the service. Templates can be used to improve security by setting the startup mode of unnecessary services to "disabled." The problem, of course, is which services are unnecessary? Caution must be used when disabling services, as some application or other service running on a server may need them.

NOTE: Startup Modes

The startup mode of each service is configurable and can be either manual (must be started by a program, command, or by manual access to the services console), automatic (started at boot), or disabled (cannot be started). When evaluating the risk presented by services, remember that it is not necessary to use the GUI to start services set to manual.

The baseline server security template enables the services listed in Table 11-6. All other services should be marked as disabled in the console, even if they are not installed. This can prevent or cripple rogue installations of a service. In developing a baseline template for a specific network, you may decide to disable additional services as well. For example, if the Automatic Updates service or the Volume Shadow Copy Service will not be used on the majority of servers, disable these services. The baseline template should disable as many services as possible, and then incremental templates should be used to enable services that may be required by specific computer roles.

Table 11-6 Services that should be enabled in the baseline template

Enabled Services	Manual	Auto
Automatic Updates		X
COM+ Event System	X	
Computer Browser		X
Cryptographic Services		X
DHCP Client		X
DNS Client		X
Event Log		X
IPSec Policy Agent	X	
Logical Disk Manager	X	
Logical Disk Manager Administrator	X	
MS Software Shadow Copy Provider	X	
Net Logon		
Network Connections	X	
Network Location Awareness		X
NTLM Security Support Provider		
Performance Logs and Alerts	X	
Plug and Play		X
Protected Storage		X
Remote Administration Service	X	
Remote Procedure Call (RPC)		X
Remote Registry Service		X
Security Accounts Manager		X
Server		X
System Event Notification		X
TCP/IP NetBIOS Helper Service		X
Terminal Services		X
Volume Shadow Copy	X	
Windows Installer		X
Windows Management Instrumentation		X

Enabled Services	Manual	Auto
Windows Management Instrumentation Driver Extensions	X	
Windows Time		X
WMI Performance Adapter	X	
Workstation		X

Using Incremental Templates and Other Techniques to Provide Security for Infrastructure Servers

The baseline template locks down servers. It is applied to all servers. To secure infrastructure servers (DNS, DHCP, WINS servers), two types of security configuration must be done. First, incremental templates are required in order to enable services that infrastructure servers require and that are disabled in the baseline template. Second, specific security configuration in and outside of the security templates is necessary. All these settings become part of an infrastructures baseline security, even though not all of them can be applied using a baseline security template.

Using Incremental Templates

Some changes should be made for all infrastructure servers, and others are specific to the type of infrastructure server. An incremental template for infrastructure servers is part of the Windows Server 2003 Security Guide, but it only sets the status of infrastructure services from disabled to automatic. This template does not configure Auditing, User rights, Security Options, or Event Log Settings because these settings are configured in the baseline policy, and no formal recommendations exist for change.

However, you may want to modify the template for your specific environment. The incremental infrastructure template sets the DNS server, DHCP server, and WINS services to automatic. For example, if you do not use WINS servers, the WINS service should not be set to automatic.

Another approach would be to use separate incremental templates for each class of infrastructure server: one for DNS, one for WINS, and one for DHCP. Each template would include settings that fit the specific server type. However, note that most changes specific to infrastructure servers either cannot be made in the templates or should not be shared across multiple machines.

Techniques for All Infrastructure Servers

Here are changes that need to be made for all infrastructure servers:

- Secure service accounts
- Protect well-known accounts
- Block ports using IPSec filters

Secure Service Accounts

Wherever possible, don't run services using domain accounts. When services use domain accounts and the server is compromised, the domain account password can be obtained from the Local Security Authority (LSA) Secrets database. (This area is protected from normal access, but tools such as Bindviews lsadump2 can be used to obtain its contents.) If a domain account password is obtained, it might be used to attack other computers in the domain. Instead of using a domain-level account, use the built-in network service or local service account. If a domain account must be used, configure the logon rights for specific computers to deny it the ability to access any servers it does not need access to.

TIP: Prevent the Use of LSADUMP2

LSADUMP2 is a tool available from `http://www.bindview.com/Support/ RAZOR/Utilities/Windows/lsadump2_readme.cfm`. This tool can be used to examine the contents of the LSA Secrets database. The Debug privilege is required to successfully use this tool. By default, only administrators have this right. You can protect servers from attack via LSADUMP2 by removing the Administrators group from the Debug Programs user right. However, the application of some Microsoft patches requires that the person updating the computer has the Debug Programs user right.

Block Ports Using IPSec Filters

IPSec filters can block ports on infrastructure servers. IPSec filters can be used to allow only those connections that are desirable based on IP address and/or port number or to block specific connections. For example, an IPSec policy could be implemented in a GPO on an OU that blocks the use of telnet services on all servers within the OU. Alternatively, all ports except DNS ports might be blocked on a standalone DNS server. Policies can be created with multiple filters to allow and block ports as required. Information on writing IPSec policies is in Chapter 15, "Protecting Data in Flight." Command-line scripts for producing policies for infrastructure servers can be downloaded with the "Windows Server 2003 Security Guide."

The following list includes recommendations for implementing a protection policy for DHCP servers. The list could be adapted for use with other infrastructure services:

- Blocking all traffic to all TCP ports on the DHCP server. (The DHCP service uses UDP ports 67 and 68.)
- Allowing all traffic to port 3389 on the DHCP server to allow management using terminal services. Blocking all ports prevents management tools that use RCP ports such as the DHCP administration console. Leaving port 3389 open allows management via terminal services.
- Adding a filter to allow any traffic from the DHCP server to a Microsoft Operations Manager (MOM) server if one is used.
- Adding additional filters as required to support additional applications on the servers or additional management products.

Protect Well-Known Accounts

Attempts are often made to use two well-known accounts, the Guest account and the Administrator account, to attack Windows systems. The Administrator account should be renamed. The Guest account should be disabled and renamed. Although the Guest account is a typical low-privilege account, it can be used to find information that may assist an attacker with another attack.

To protect the built-in Administrator account, perform these tasks:

- Rename the account—many scripts hard-code the user account Administrator, so if the account does not exist under that name, the script will fail. Newer scripts use the well-known SID for the administrator account instead of the name Administrator, so changing the Administrator account name does not protect against those scripts. However, changing the name is still a valid opportunity to prevent some scripts from running and to prevent casual snooping.
- Require and use different replacement names on each server.
- Require and use different Administrator passwords on each server.
- Change the account descriptions!
- Record changes and store in a safe location.
- Use the Security Option `Accounts: Administrator account status` to disable the Administrator account. (The account is still usable in Safe Mode.) Disabling the Administrator account should not be done until an alternative is determined, such as

using a domain level account or creating another local account and giving it membership in the Administrators group.

■ Create an ordinary user account and give it membership in the Administrators group to use it for administration.

Neither the Guest account nor the Administrator account is renamed in the baseline or infrastructure templates. This is done to encourage the use of different account names for different servers. If the same name is used, the attacker's job is easier.

Techniques Specific to Infrastructure Role

In addition to general infrastructure role hardening, each infrastructure role, DNS, DHCP, and WINS, must also be hardened.

Secure DNS Servers

DNS is a primary attack target because DNS servers contain sensitive information that can be used to attack the network and because a successful denial of service attack can prevent computers from accessing resources. The types of attacks that are usually attempted are

■ **Footprinting**—Learning about your network computers and the services they offer
■ **Denial of Service**—Preventing access to DNS information
■ **Redirection**—Redirecting DNS enquiries to rogue servers
■ **Data modification**—Changing information that therefore may result in clients using rogue services instead of legitimate ones

To rebuff or mitigate the impact of these attacks, the Windows Server 2003 DNS server is preconfigured with several security features. In addition, other actions can be taken to protect DNS. Several recommendations for securing DNS have to do with the design of your DNS infrastructure, others have to do with DNS server configuration, and still others rely on changes made at the client level.

The infrastructure should be designed to provide a secure base for DNS. Several items should be considered. Here are the recommendations:

■ Host a separate internal DNS infrastructure to manage name resolution for internal computers. Use a different DNS server and zone to manage name resolution information that must be provided externally, such as addresses for email servers, web servers, and the like. This allows you to host your internal DNS servers inside the firewall and prevent access to them from external sources. It also prevents exposure of internal addressing information to external sources.

■ Set the internal DNS servers to use forwarders to forward requests for external name resolution to the external DNS infrastructure. Figure 11-5 shows the DNS server property page (in the DNS console, right-click the server and select `Properties`, and then select the `Forwarders` tab) where forwarders are configured.

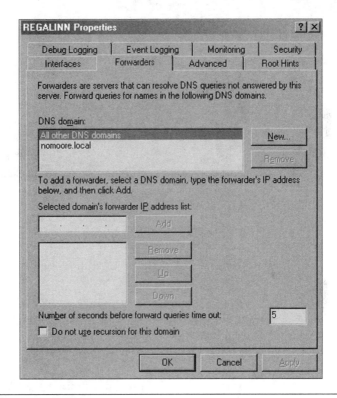

Figure 11-5   Setting forwarders.

■ Configure routers and firewalls to allow only external traffic to the internal DNS server but to allow traffic to and from the external DNS server.

■ Use Active Directory integrated zones. This provides the ability to use secure dynamic updates and to secure zones using DACLs set in the Active Directory. By setting permission in AD, permissions are set uniformly. The type of zone is configured on the property page for the zone. (In the DNS console, right-click the zone, select `Properties`, and then click the `Change` button next to Type). Figure 11-6 shows the location on the General page; Figure 11-7 shows the `Change` button.

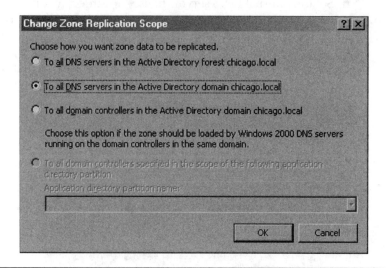

Figure 11-6   Setting the zone type to AD integrated.

Secure DNS Clients

DNS clients can be configured with the IP address of the DNS server, or if they obtain their IP address from a DNS server, they can obtain the DNS server address from DHCP as well. Specifying static DNS server addresses and alternative addresses directly in the client configuration is preferred. Although it is more convenient to allow the client to download this information from the DHCP server, if a rogue DHCP server is on the network, or if the DHCP server is compromised, the client may receive an incorrect DNS server address. You can also limit the clients that can use the DNS server by configuring clients with the DNS server's IP address and by configuring the DNS server to only listen on that address.

Secure DNS Zones

To secure zones, secure the Registry DNS entries, configure secure dynamic updates, and restrict zone transfer. To secure Registry DNS entries, modify the DACLs on the registry keys. Registry entries for DNS are at

```
HKEY_LOCAL_MACHINE\System\CurrentControlSet\Services\DNS\
```

Configure Secure Dynamic Updates

Configure secure dynamic updates, as shown in Figure 11-7. Using secure dynamic updates prevents a rogue computer from changing zone information. To update a record, a computer must be authenticated by and joined to the Active Directory domain where the DNS server resides. Further restrictions are placed by the ACLs configured on the zones. Although pre-Windows 2000 clients cannot update their own DNS records, DHCP can be configured to do so for them.

When DNS zone information is stored in Active Directory, setting the DACLs in the DNS administration console has the same affect as changing ACLs on the Active Directory objects. If different administrators manage DNS than those that manage Active Directory, care should be taken to ensure that ACLs are consistently set.

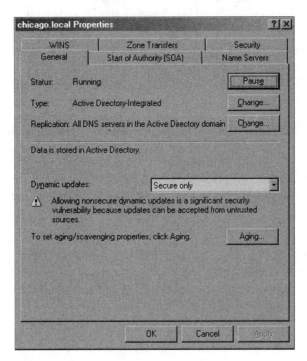

Figure 11-7   Configure secure dynamic update.

Restrict Zone Transfers

Zone transfers allow the coordination and sharing of zone information across multiple DNS servers. This provides redundancy and backup. However, should zone transfer to an unauthorized DNS server take place, it might make available information that could be used to mount an attack on your network. This technique, obtaining DNS information, is called footprinting. If DNS is Active Directory-integrated, zone transfers are not used. Instead, zone information is stored in and replicated as part of the Active Directory database. However, in a standalone DNS server, by default, zone transfers only occur between the DNS servers listed in the name server (NS) resource records of a zone. To further secure zone transfers, change this setting to only exchange zone information with specific IP addresses. Should a resource record be compromised and an IP address of a name server be changed, the IP address will still be correct in the configuration, and an unauthorized zone transfer will not occur. Take care to ensure that authorized changes to the IP address of a name server are also made in the zone configuration.

To restrict zone transfers to specific IP addresses perform these steps:

1. Log on as a member of the local Administrators group or the DNSAdmins group. (If the server is a domain member, the Domain Admins group is a member.)
2. Open the DNS console.
3. Right-click a DNS zone, and then click `Properties`.
4. On the `Zone Transfers` tab, select the `Allow Zone Transfers` check box, as shown in Figure 11-8.
5. Click `Only` to the following servers.
6. Add the specific IP address of one or more DNS servers.
7. Click `OK` to close the property pages.

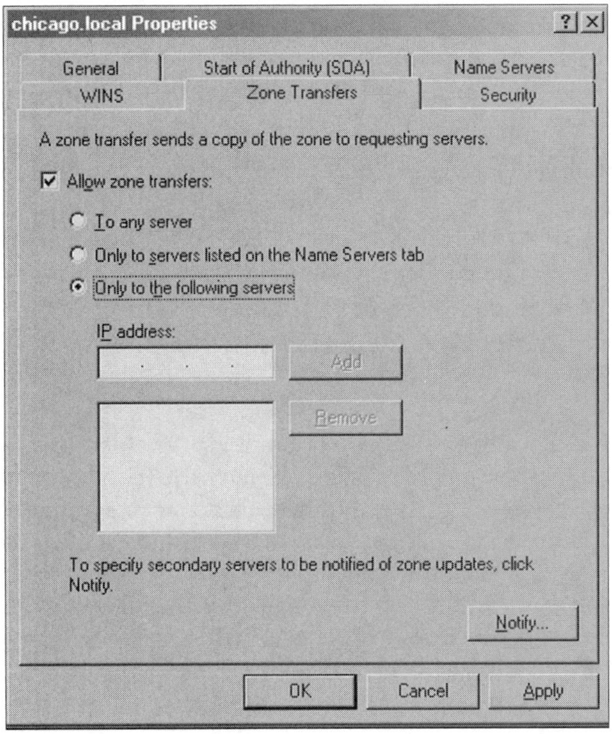

Figure 11-8   Restricting zone transers.

Alternatively, the `dnscmd` command can be used at the command prompt or in a script. The command must specify the name of the DNS server, the name of the zone, and the IP address. To allow a zone transfer, the command takes the form:

```
Dnscmd dnserver_name zone_name /SecureList
Secondary_IP_address
```

Consider carefully before delegating zone authority. Management of part of the DNS information for the organization can be delegated by allowing zone delegation to another DNS server that is managed by different individuals. Whenever control over sensitive information or objects is changed, the implications should be weighed against the convenience.

Back up zone information so that it can be recovered if necessary. Zone information includes information on which server is authoritative for each zone and which domain controllers house application partitions for DNS zone information when DNS is integrated with Active Directory.

Monitor and Adjust Security Settings in DNS Configuration

By default, the `Secure Cache Against Pollution` setting is enabled. This helps to prevent incorrect IP addresses received in response to a query from being cached. When the cache is secured against pollution, only IP addresses received from the DNS server authoritative for their domain are stored. Additional DNS settings that can be configured for security are

- **Disable recursion**—Recursion is enabled by default so that the DNS server can provide recursive queries for its clients. If a DNS server will not be required to do so, recursion can be disabled. (DNS servers use iterative queries to communicate with each other.) An attacker might flood a DNS server with recursive queries and therefore successfully deny service to legitimate clients. Recursion is necessary if DNS servers use forwarders.
- **Root hints**—If an internal root exists in your DNS infrastructure, configure the root hints on other DNSs to point to this root rather than Internet root servers. This prevents internal information from going to the Internet.

Secure DHCP

DHCP servers should be protected because an interruption in their service can mean the inability of clients to obtain an address. Two areas to be concerned about are preventing or mitigating a denial of service attack and being able to monitor the access and use of the DHCP server and its service. In addition to applying the baseline and infrastructure template, the DHCP server should be configured to

- Turn on extended DHCP logging. By default, events are logged on startup and shutdown.
- Secure log access.
- Configure DHCP servers in pairs to provide redundancy and partial protection from a denial of service attack.

Turn On Logging

To enable extended DHCP logging perform these steps:

1. Log on to the DHCP server.
2. Open the DHCP console.
3. Right-click the DHCP server and select `Properties`.
4. On the `General` tab of the `Properties` dialog box, click `Enable DHCP Audit Logging`.
5. Click OK to close the Properties pages.

The DHCP server creates a log file at %windir%\system32\DHCP. This log contains detailed information about the activities of clients and does include both Media access control (MAC) and IP addresses. This information may help in finding the source of an attack or problem. Although not foolproof (MAC and IP addresses can be spoofed), the information is invaluable in managing DHCP.

Secure Log Access

Limit access to this log by changing the DHCP folder access control list (ACL). By default, Administrators have Full Control, and Server Operators and Authenticated Users have read access. Remove the groups Server Operators and Authenticated Users so that only Administrators have access to the logs.

Frequently archive the log because it can grow quite large. By default, the system will stop logging when there is less than 20 MB of free disk space left. This setting can be changed.

Configure DHCP Servers in Pairs

To configure the IP address scope of the DHCP pair, use the 80/20 rule. Split the address range that must be serviced by giving one DHCP server 80 percent of the addresses and 20 percent to the other. Remember, the idea is to ensure that if one server is under attack, there is still a DHCP server service on the network.

Create IPSec Policies

Blocking all access except that needed to provide management and functionality of the DHCP server can provide additional security. The following IPSec filters should be created:

- A filter to allow access from the DHCP server to all domain controllers from any port to any port.

- A filter to allow any traffic from ANY address, UPD port 68 to the DHCP server on port UDP 67 (DHCP service).
- A filter to block all inbound traffic.

Secure WINS

To secure the WINS server, create IPSec policies that limit the type of traffic the WINS server will respond to. Blocking all access except what's needed to provide management and functionality of the WINS server can provide additional security. The following IPSec filters should be created:

- A filter to allow access from the WINS server to all domain controllers from any port
- A filter to allow access from ANY computer on ANY port to port 1512 TCP (WINS Resolution server) on the WINS server
- A filter to allow access from ANY computer on ANY port to port 1512 UDP (WINS Resolution server) on the WINS server
- A filter to allow access from ANY computer on ANY port (WINS client or server) to port 42 TCP (WINS Replication Partner) on the WINS server
- A filter to allow access from ANY computer on ANY port (WINS client or server) to port 42 UDP (WINS Replication Partner) on the WINS server
- A filter to block all inbound traffic

Extend the Concept to Other Roles

A number of other computer roles exist in the network that can be secured in the same fashion. An incremental template can be created for each unique server role. An example of such a role is the File and Print Server role.

The File Server template disables the DFS and File Replication Services and enables File and Print Sharing. The Print Server template enables the Print Spooler service and sets it to automatic. If these services are used in your organization, do not disable them.

It may be tempting to combine the functions of file and print; however, you should consider that a combination file and print server may be subject to a disk space DoS. In this type of attack, the disk is filled by sending a large number of print jobs to the server. Likewise, a busy file server might eventually leave little space for print spooling. If the disk can be filled, the server may become unavailable to other clients. You must judge whether the risk of such an attack is high enough to warrant splitting these roles if you do not already.

File servers must open ports that are generally considered to be problematic. Many known attacks use these ports, and they cannot be blocked or the servers will become useless. However, IPSec blocking policies can still be used to protect the server from attacks using other ports. If all inbound traffic is blocked, the following traffic should be allowed:

- Destination ports 445 TCP and 445 UPD for CIFS
- Destination ports 137 TCP and 137 UDP for NetBIOS
- Destination ports 138 UDP and 139 TCP for NetBIOS
- Destination port 3389 for terminal services (if used for administration)
- Any local source ports for traffic to the domain controllers

Apply Security Templates

Security templates have no effect upon the operating system unless they are applied. This can be done by using Group Policy, by using Security Configuration and Analysis, or by using the `secedit` command.

WARNING: On the Other Hand...

If a security template is incorrectly configured and then applied, it can make a computer inoperable. If it is imported into a Group Policy Object, it can make many machines inoperable.

Use an Active Directory Design to Secure Computer Roles

An appropriate Active Directory design to fulfill your needs is beyond the scope of this book. However, the following Active Directory design supports the security architecture defined by server roles. It allows the majority of security settings appropriate for securing various servers to be applied periodically and efficiently across multiple servers. It utilizes the templates provided with the "Windows Server 2003 Security Guide" and allows for its extension via the creation of additional templates.

Active Directory planning information, including design tips and best practices, is presented in the Windows Server 2003 Development Kit. This set can be purchased or searched online. Specifically, Active Directory design is addressed in the "Designing and Deploying Active Directory and Security Services" book at http://www.microsoft.com/downloads/details.aspx?displaylang=en&fami lyid=6cde6ee7-5df1-4394-92ed-2147c3a9ebbe.

In this design, two top-level OUs are created; one for servers and one for workstations. Underneath these OUs, sub-OUs are created, one for each computer role. This allows the development of unique security designs for each role and their implementation, as much as possible, through GPOs linked to the appropriate OU. Figure 11-9 displays the design. In the figure, two top-level OUs are labeled WorkstationOU and ServerOU. The workstationOU has a sub-OU for Windows 2000 Professional and one for Windows XP.

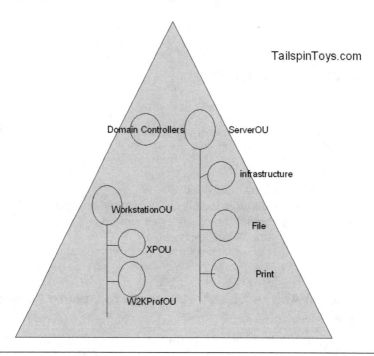

Figure 11-9 Designing OUs for Role Management.

The computer accounts for each type of workstation and server can then be added to the appropriate OUs. Each OU as well as the domain must have an appropriate GPO created and linked to its container. A security template can be designed for and then imported into the appropriate

OU. Templates created by Microsoft or third parties can be used, or custom templates can be created. Be sure an appropriate template is available for each OU.

Table 11-7 is a hypothetical design that lists each OU, template type, and a number of unique templates that might be created if these specific roles exist. Each template is given a name, but those that begin with an asterisk (*) are not provided by Microsoft. You can create templates with any name you choose.

Table 11-7 Security Templates/OU matching

Active Directory Location	Computer Role	Template Name
ServerOU	Server	High Security—Member Server Baseline.inf
WorkstationOU	Workstation	*High Security—Workstation.inf
W2KProfOU	Windows 2000 Professional	*W2kprof.inf
XPOU	Windows XP Professional	*XP.inf
Infrastructure	DHCP, DNS	High Security Infrastructure Server.inf
File Server	File server	High Security File Server.inf
Print Server	Print server	High Security Print Server.inf
Domain Controllers	Domain controller	High Security Domain Controller.inf

To apply this design, the templates must be created, and then they must be imported into the Group Policy Object that is linked to the appropriate OU. Before taking this action, be sure to back up the GPO. To import the settings, perform these steps:

1. Open the `Active Directory Users and Computers` console.
2. Right-click the OU and select `Properties`.
3. Select the `Group Policy` tab.
4. Select the GPO that the security template will be imported into, and click the `Edit` button.

5. Expand the GPO and right-click `Windows Settings`, `Security Settings`, then select `Import Settings`.
6. Select, or browse to and select, the appropriate template file and click `OK`.

Alternatively, if GPMC has been installed, right-click the GPO in the GPO section of the GPMC and then select `Import Settings`, as shown in Figure 11-10. In either case, the Import Settings Wizard will run and allow you to select and apply the desired security template. When GPMC is used, you are prompted to back up the GPO before importing the settings.

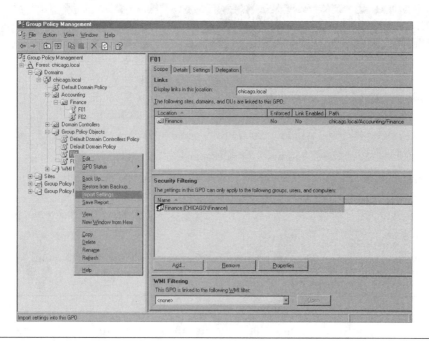

Figure 11-10   Importing a security template into a GPO.

Using the Security Configuration and Analysis Tool

Security Configuration and Analysis is a MMC snap-in tool that can be used to apply security templates to a single computer or to compare a specific security template to the computer's current settings. A command-line version of the tool, `secedit`, is also available. This tool fits both in the standalone and Active Directory approach to security configuration.

In an Active Directory Environment, the tool can be used in a test lab to configure systems and test new templates. Instead of applying a new template to many machines at once, with potentially harmful results, the template can be tested on a single machine. It can also be used in the production environment to test the security status of specific computers.

Where no Active Directory environment exists, or where some computers are not joined to the domain, Security Configuration and Analysis can be used to apply standard security settings to a single computer in an automated fashion. The `secedit` command-line tool can be used in a script to apply settings on a single computer or potentially many computers. Both tools can be used to audit current security settings against an approved template.

The best way to apply security templates to domain member computers is to use Group Policy and Active Directory. If you correctly configure the GPOs, settings will be applied, and security settings will be refreshed at regular intervals. However, Windows 2000, Windows XP Professional, or Windows Server 2003 computers that are not members of a domain can still benefit from the use of security templates and the baselining process. The Security Configuration and Analysis console or its command-line version, `secedit`, can be used to apply the templates. The following procedures tell you how.

Using Multiple Templates with Security Configuration and Analysis

A great way to apply security using Group Policy is to incorporate a design using multiple policies, each of which may utilize a different template. The use of a baseline hardening template and an incremental role-specific template is one such design. The same sort of security design can be planned for standalone computers; however, you must pay attention to the order of template application. Applying multiple templates using Security Configuration and Analysis may seem simple, but it can become complicated. Three factors play a role: the current security status of the machine, the order of template application, and whether or not the database is cleared before a new template is applied. When the tool is first run, it creates a database whose settings are based on your selection of a preconfigured security template. Alternatively, you can select and use a previously created database. If an old database is cleared when the new template is added, only the settings in the new template are applied. However, if the old template settings were previously applied to the machine, clearing the template from the database does not remove these settings. If the database is not cleared, adding an additional template means the following:

- If the new template setting is not defined and the old template setting is defined, the setting remains the way it is in the old template.
- If a setting in the new template is defined and the setting is not defined in the old template, the setting changes to the setting in the new template.
- If a setting is defined in both the old template and the new template, the new template setting is applied.

Apply the Template

The process for applying a template is simple. In the following example, a custom adaptation of the Enterprise Client Member Server Baseline template is applied. The template is named baselineB.inf. A good practice is to create a rollback template, which can be used in case the template causes a problem. In the following example, the command line used to create the rollback template baselineBrollback.inf is given and the syntax is explained in Table 11-8. You do not have to create a rollback template; however, doing so provides you with a quick way to reverse the settings made by applying the template.

Use secedit to Apply Security Templates

secedit is a command-line version of the Security Configuration and Analysis snap-in. It also provides the ability to create rollback templates, which, when applied, reverse settings established by another template. Basic `secedit` commands are defined in Table 11-8.

Table 11-8   secedit Syntax

Setting	Description
Analyze	Compares settings in a database template to those set on the machine. This setting can be used to audit security settings.
Con gure	Applies security settings from a template.
Import	Imports a template into a database. This command can be used with the con gure or analyze command.
Export	Exports a template from a database. Apply two or more templates to the same computer, and then use this command to export the combined settings into a new template.
Validate	Validates syntax of a template.

Setting	Description
Generate rollback	Makes a reverse template, that is, a template that removes most of the settings applied with a template. (File and registry permissions settings made in a template cannot be rolled back.)
Db	Specifies the name of the database file to create or to use.
Cfg	Specifies the name of the template to use.
Overwrite	Overwrites any existing template in the file with another. If this switch is not used, and a template has been added to the database, the combined settings in both templates will be applied.
Log	Specifies a log file to record errors. If no log file is specified, the system uses WINDOWS\Security\Logs\Scesrv.log.
Quiet	Specifies that no data should appear on the screen, and no comments on progress should be provided to the user.
Areas	Applies only the settings as listed in a specific area of the template. Other settings are ignored.
Merged policy	Merges and exports domain and local policy.
RBK	Specifies the name of the security template to be created.

To configure the machine using the XYZ template, use the following command:

```
secedit /con gure /db xyz.sdb /cfg xyz.inf /log xyz.log
```

To create a rollback template for the XYZ template, use the following command:

```
secedit /generaterollback /cfg xyz.inf /rbk xyzrollback.inf
/log xyzrollback.log
```

1. Create the rollback template baselineBrollback.inf by using secedit:
   ```
   secedit /genereaterollback /cfg baselineB.inf /rbk
   baselineBrollback.inf /log baselineBrollback.log
   ```
2. Add the Security Configuration and Analysis snap-in to an MMC, as shown in Figure 11-11.

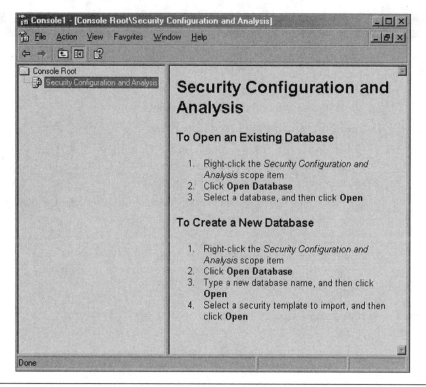

Figure 11-11   The Security Configuration and Analysis snap-in must be added to an MMC.

3. Right-click the Security Configuration and Analysis container in the console and select Open database. (You do not have a database yet; creating one is the first step.)
4. In the File Name box, enter the name for the new database and click Open.
5. The Import Template box is opened to the default security template path, as shown in Figure 11-12. Select a template, or browse to a new location and select a template.
6. Right-click Security Con guration and Analysis and select Con gure Computer.
7. Click OK when asked to confirm the location of the error log.
8. Wait for the configuration to complete and close the console.

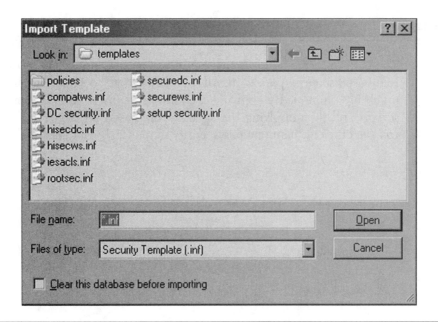

Figure 11-12   To create the database, you must import a template. From the Import template box, browse to the location for your template, select it, and click Open.

Test Before Applying

A small business consultant in my community, we'll call him John, called me on a Thursday night. John's customer is a branch office of a large multi-national organization. Users at the branch office were not able to access resources on file servers. John had determined that the users were not able to connect to the file servers to retrieve files, but they could do so locally. John had administrative privileges in the domain.

I asked John to use GPMC to look at the GPOs that had been applied to the file server. Sure enough, one of the GPOs had removed all groups except the Administrators group from the user right `Access This Computer From The Network`. John called the company's support group, and the GPO was changed. Later, he found out what had happened.

It seems that a new administrator imported a new custom template to a new GPO and then linked the GPO to the OU for file servers. After John's call, the GPO was unlinked from the OU, and things returned to normal. If the new administrator had tested the template by applying it to a test server, the problem could have been avoided. Furthermore, if he had created a rollback template, he could have immediately rolled back the settings to those prior to the application of his new template.

Summary

The path to securing infrastructure servers is an exercise in exploring a role-based security paradigm. All servers are not the same, but all have much in common. By applying a common security baseline across all servers and then applying the specific role-based security for a server role, an efficient, maintainable security status can be obtained.

PART IV

Public Key Infrastructure

CHAPTER 12

PKI Basics

Implementing a public key infrastructure (PKI) to support IPSec, EFS, VPNs, smart cards, SSL server and client authentication, and wireless networks is not difficult. Implementing it correctly is. This is true because the process for installing the basic PKI components is simple and requires little obvious preparation. Because PKI can quickly become the security backbone for your organization's network, implementation should be preceded by careful thought, the creation of a PKI security policy, and thorough implementation planning to assure that the policy is followed. The first step is a clear understanding of what PKI is and how it works. This chapter defines the components of PKI, explains how they work, and details the specifics of Windows Server 2003 PKI. The design and implementation of a simple, secure PKI is detailed in Chapter 13, "Implementing a Secure PKI."

Introduction to PKI

A public key infrastructure (PKI) is the sum total of the components (certificates, certification authority, registration authority, and Certificate Revocation List) and processes (key management, certificate enrollment, certificate revocation, etc.) that are necessary to implement the use of public key cryptographic processes. Although some uses of public key cryptography can be integrated into a process without a PKI in place, public key cryptography is easier to manage when the structure and processes provided by a PKI is present. An example of public key encryption outside of PKI and the problems that result is detailed later in this chapter in the section "Self-signed Certificates."

Public Key Cryptographic Processes

Two major uses of public key cryptography are encryption and signing. Unlike *symmetric key cryptography*, which uses a single key to encrypt and decrypt, *public key cryptography* uses an associated key pair: a public key and a private key. In public key cryptography, one key is used to encrypt and the other to decrypt. Because there are two keys, the public key can be made available to anyone, and the private key can and should be kept secret.

Encryption

Figure 12-1 illustrates the public key encryption process.

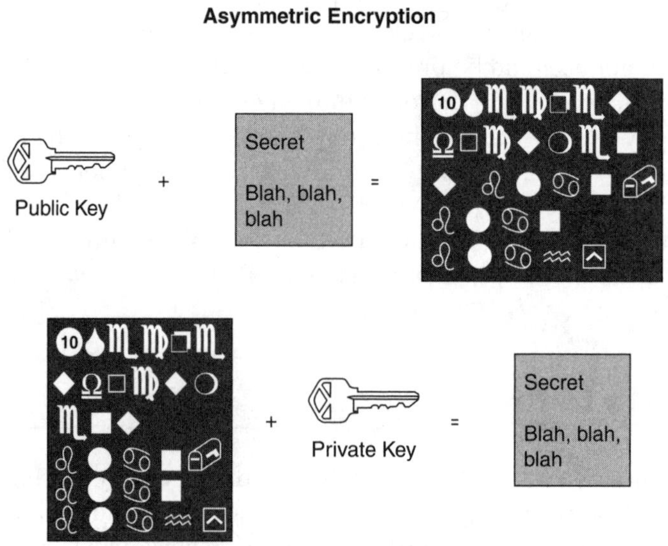

Asymmetric Encryption

Figure 12-1   Two keys are used in public key encryption: one encrypts and the other decrypts.

Two common uses for public key encryption are email and the Encrypting File System (EFS). In both cases, symmetric and public key cryptography is used. The reason for this is the slow speed of public key encryption. (More information on EFS can be found in Chapter 6, "EFS Basics.") The following process is used to send encrypted emails:

1. A symmetric key is generated and used to encrypt the message.
2. The public key of the recipient is used to encrypt the symmetric key.

3. The encrypted message and the encrypted symmetric key are sent.
4. Upon receipt, the recipient's private key decrypts the symmetric key.
5. The symmetric key decrypts the message.

NOTE: Incorrect Definitions Abound
It is common to find descriptions of secure email and other uses of public key encryptions that do not mention the use of a symmetric key. Instead, they just describe the process as if the public key encrypts the entire message or file, and the private key is then used to decrypt it. This is incorrect.

Digital Signing

Digital signing is the process of using cryptography to ensure the authenticity of some electronic data, such as a software application. Digital signing of email is also used to provide non-repudiation. *Non-repudiation* provides non-deniability; if an email is digitally signed by the sender, the sender cannot claim that the email was not sent by him. A *digital signature*, which is the result of digital signing, can also aid in determining the integrity of the message. Of course, the private key used for the digital signature must be protected. If someone can obtain the key, they could sign an email as the individual.

To create a digital signature, public key cryptography is used in a slightly different way than it is for encryption. The following process is used to sign an email:

1. A message digest of the message is created.
   Applying a cryptographic hash algorithm to the message creates a *message digest*. The hash algorithms produce a small, unique abstract of the message. The message digest itself cannot be decrypted, but if the same algorithm is used against the same message, the message digests will match, and a hash of a different message will not produce the same message digest.
2. The sender's private key encrypts the message digest.
3. The plain text message and the encrypted message digest are sent to the recipient.

4. Upon receipt, the public key of the sender decrypts the encrypted message digest. (The message digest itself is not decrypted.)

5. The recipient creates a message digest of the message and compares this message digest to the one sent with the message. If the two message digests match, this proves the message was sent by the sender because only the sender holds the private key, and his public key decrypted the encrypted message digest. If the two message digests match, the message has not changed.

Public Key Cryptography Pros and Cons

Symmetric key cryptography is faster and less complex but cannot solve some problems that public key cryptography can. When symmetric key cryptography is used, the security of the message depends on knowledge of the key. Because the key must be distributed to both parties, this creates a problem. How can the key be securely communicated to both parties? Symmetric keys may also create a management problem. Imagine that email messages between 100 users must be secured, and only the sender and recipient of a given message can be allowed to read it. This means that a large number of keys must be generated, shared between users, and both stored and managed. Public key cryptography can solve these problems. Because the private key can be kept secret and never transported, it is easier to protect it. On the other hand, all the associated public keys can be stored in a public database and made available to everyone. Knowledge of public keys is acceptable.

Public key cryptography appears to be a sound solution for these issues. Then why is it not used more? The following issues may have kept this technology from widespread use:

- **Speed**—Public key encryption is slow. Compared to symmetric key encryption, asymmetric key encryption is very slow. Even with the enormous improvement in processing speed today compared to when the technique was first developed, encrypting large messages is not practical. In most uses of public key encryption today, a combination of public key (asymmetric) and private key (symmetric) encryption is used.

- **Identity**—If a large number of keys are stored in a public database, how can we be sure that a stored key actually belongs to whom the database says it belongs to? Some way of representing the relationship between the public key and its owner must be present. Implementations of public key technology today use a data structure called a certificate for this purpose.
- **Private key storage**—Public keys can be stored in a database because the public key cannot decrypt what it has encrypted. The secrecy of the message relies on the secrecy of the private key. The private key must be protected and kept from public access.
- **Portability**—A certificate and its associated private key are typically installed on a single computer. Although it may be possible to export the certificate and key and import them into another computer, the process may be complicated for typical users, and its practice may mean a reduction in security. Someone other than the assigned owner might obtain access to the keys.
- **Key safety**—Public keys can be copied, distributed, managed, and protected from loss and destruction in a central location under the control of knowledgeable people using well-developed processes. The safety and storage of private keys relies on the technical controls provided by the operating system, and, when these technical controls must be enforced by the owner, on the whims of their owner in applying them. Private keys can become corrupt and lost. In some implementations, this means only that new keys must be issued, and the only loss is the current message, which can be resent. The loss may be substantial depending on the nature of the message, but the process is recoverable. However, in other uses, such as file encryption, loss of a private key can mean the loss of critical data. Key backup and key archival databases are possible solutions for this problem.
- **Key distribution**—Obtaining a public key so that a message can be encrypted and sent to another person may or may not be a problem. If the public key database belongs to an organization, it may be easy to provide access for all employees. This does present a problem for others from outside the organization, though. How can they obtain public keys when they want to use them to communicate with the organization's employees?
- **Enrollment**—In order to put the public key in a database, an enrollment process must take place. If only a few sophisticated users must follow some process in order to do so, this is not a problem. But enrolling thousands of individuals by this method is a major impediment to the adoption of the technology.

All these problems can be managed by the use of a public key infrastructure. Then, the problem becomes complexity and cost. The technology can seem complex and obscure, necessitating teams of consultants to make it work. In addition, the cost of the products has been high in the past, but this is no longer true. Both Windows 2000 and Windows Server 2003 include certificate services with the base operating system, which can be used to create a PKI.

PKI Components

A public key infrastructure may be implemented in different ways. The model used by Windows Server 2003 is the certification authority (CA) hierarchy model. In this model, a root CA serves as the parent of additional CAs. This type of PKI consists of the following components:

- **Practice Policy Statement**—Provides the rules by which the CA is managed.
- **Certificates**—The data structure used to bind a public key to an identity.
- **Keys**—Encryption keys.
- **Certification Authority (CA)**—The computer that issues certificates.
- **Registration Authority (RA)**—The computer that provides enrollment services. In many PKI implementations, the CA and RA function are performed at one computer.
- **Certification Revocation List (CRL)**—A list of revoked certificates.
- **Certificate Trust List (CTL)**—A list that identifies CAs approved to issue certificates for a web site.

Practice Policy Statement

The Practice Policy Statement is a document that details exactly how the PKI will be managed. Some of its information may be expressed in a file and used to enforce adherence to the policy. The statement may identify the following:

- How enrollment is approved
- The revocation process and the reasons for revocation
- The location of the CRL

- The publication schedule for the CRL
- The location where a copy of the CA certificate may be downloaded
- Who may administer the CA
- How administrative duties are split
- The CA hierarchy
- The types of certificates that are issued and whom they can be issued to

The Practice Policy Statement is a result of planning, development, and approval of management. Subjects that should be addressed in the planning stage include those listed previously, as well as the following:

- The solutions and goals of using this technology, including the projected cost and return on investment (ROI)
- Requirements of applications that will use PKI
- Service-level requirements
- The use of CRLs, delta CRLS, and possibly the Online Certificate Status Protocol (OCSP), a protocol in which an enquiry on the status (expired, unknown, or current) may be made in lieu of checking revocation against a CRL

Some of the CA practice policy can be implemented through the use of a capolicy.inf file. You must create the file and name it capolicy.inf. It should be added to the computer to be used as the CA before certificate services are installed. Both the Authority Information Access (AIA), the location where a copy of the root CA certificate can be downloaded, and the CRL Distribution Point (CDP), the location where the CRL can be downloaded, should be empty in the root CA because they are not needed on the root CA certificates. If the root CA is kept offline, which is recommended as a best practice, any attempt to locate the certificate or the CRL will fail. Leaving the AIA and CDP empty prevents such false attempts. The locations can be kept empty by designating them as empty in the capolicy.inf file. The locations should be added to the CA configuration files after its installation, and then they will be included in each certificate the CA issues. The capolicy.inf file can contain the following:

- The location from where the CA certificate can be downloaded.
- The location where the CRL and, if implemented, delta CRLs can be downloaded.

■ A constraint on the number of subordinate levels by adding a maximum path length in the basic constraints extension of a CA certificate and defining the constraint and path length in the capolicy.inf file. A path length of zero means that the CA can only issue end-entity certificates (smart card, EFS, etc., as opposed to CA certificates).

Use A Hardware Security Module

A hardware security module (HSM) is a dedicated hardware device that can store CA keys. The device is managed separately from the operating system. Protection is provided via multi-layered hardware and software tokens and may additionally

■ Provide load balancing and failover if multiple HSMs are linked together in a daisy chain.

■ Secure management of private keys.

■ Provide cryptographic acceleration. The host server does not have to perform processor-intensive cryptographic calculations.

■ Provide hardware-based protection of private keys.

■ Provide hardware-based cryptographic operations, including random number generation, key generation, digital signatures, and key archival and recovery.

HSMs are available from multiple sources.

Certificates

A *certificate* is a data structure that binds the public key to an identity. A *data structure* is a programming construct that represents a collection of different types. The x.509 certificate standard is an international standard that defines parts of a certificate. If the certificate meets this standard, it may be used in applications written to the standard. You can view the certificate information by clicking its `Details` tab when viewing the certificate. When one of the fields is selected, any additional contents will be displayed. Figure 12-2 displays the `Details` tab. The information that may be viewable on the details pane is:

- **Basic Constraints**—Identifies subject type and path length constraints. More information on constraints is listed in the section "Cross-Certification and Qualified Subordination."
- **CRL Distribution Points**—Indicates the location where the CRL may be downloaded.
- **Issuer**—The name of the CA that issued the certificate.
- **Key Usage**—Indicates what the certificate may be used for.
- **Netscape Cert Type**—Lists the certification usage information in the Netscape browser format.
- **Public Key**—A copy of the public key from the public/private key pair.
- **Serial Number**—A serial number assigned to the certificate.
- **Signature algorithm**—Indicates the algorithm used to create the thumbprint.
- **Subject Alternative Name**—The RFC 822 name format for the subject name.
- **Subject Name**—The name of the identity the certificate was issued to, such as the user's Active Directory identity.
- **Thumbprint**—A hexadecimal string that contains the SHA-1 hash of the certificate.
- **Valid From**—The beginning date that the certificate is valid.
- **Valid To**—The date at which the certificate is no longer valid.
- **Version**—The version number of the certificate. x.509 certificates have been through three versions.
- **Identity of the owner of the certificate**.

NOTE: The Public Key is Included with the Certificate, But Not the Private Key

Note that the public key is included with the certificate. The private key is never part of the certificate. Although it is a common misconception that both keys are part of the certificate, you can use your common sense to see why this could not be so—if the private key were part of the certificate, it wouldn't be private. It would be available to anyone that could retrieve the certificate.

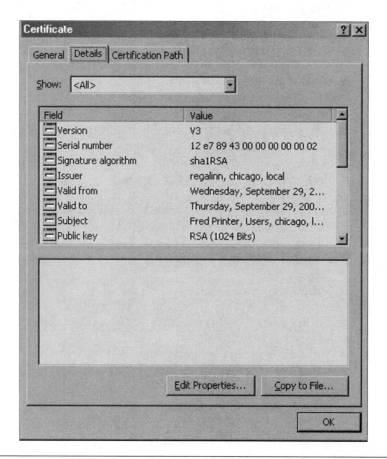

Figure 12-2 Examine the Details page to learn about the certificate.

Certificates can be saved to a file for storage, backup, and transfers. Different file formats are used for different purposes. When standard file formats are used, applications can be written that can import the certificates for use. Common file formats are

- **Cryptographic Message Syntax Standard (PKCS #7)**—Enables the transfer of the certificate and all the certificates in its certification path. Uses the .p7b extension.
- **Personal Information Exchange (PKCS #12)**—The certificate and its private key are stored in the same file. This format is often used for archiving the private key. Uses the .pfx extension.

- **Distinguished Encoding Rules (DER) Encoded Binary x.509**—A platform-independent method for encoding objects for transfer. Most applications use DER because a portion of the certificate must be DER-encoded in order to be signed. Uses the .cer extension.
- **Base64 Encoded x.509**—Uses an encoding method for Secure/Multipurpose Internet Mail Extensions (S/MIME). Uses the .cer extension.

Keys

A key pair is required for public key cryptography. The public key is provided as part of the certificate. Each certificate maps to an identity. Each certificate holds one and only one public key, and there must be an associated private key for each public key. Although a single certificate can only hold one key, many certificates can be bound to a single identity; therefore, any identity may have multiple key pairs. For any encryption done with a public key, only the associated private key can decrypt it. Though an identity (user or computer) can have multiple public key pairs, only one private key can be used to decrypt something encrypted by a specific public key.

How Strong Are Public Encryption Keys?

We often hear that encryption is only as good as the key, and that in general, the larger the key, the stronger the encryption. We know this intuitively. If a key is composed of only two digits, for example, we can surmise that it would be a lot easier to guess that key than if it were 50 digits long. Only a few possible combinations of digits exist for a two-digit key, while many exist for the 50-digit key. The possible combinations that can make up a key of a specific length and type are called its *keyspace*. The larger the key length, the larger the keyspace and the harder it is to guess any given key. Numerous attacks have been developed in an attempt to deduce a key. Brute-force attacks attempt every possible combination. When passwords or other alphabetical keys may be used, dictionary attacks use a dictionary of words encrypted via the same algorithm in an attempt to find a match. If the algorithm is weak, it may be possible to use some flaw in the algorithm to more quickly discover the key. Even well-known modern encryption algorithms with no apparent flaws are constantly tested with new mathematical attacks in an attempt to find a method to break them. The strongest algorithms resist these attacks or require a very long time frame in order for any key to be cracked. As the speed and processing power of computing systems increase, it may be that algorithms that cryptographers projected would take a long time to break may be broken in a few days or even hours. This has already happened. The Data Encryption Standard (DES) algorithm was once projected to take thousands of years to crack and at much expense. It now can be cracked with minimal equipment investment (several years ago, less than $30,000) and in a few days.

The strength of any encryption algorithm is partially based on the size of the key, partially on the strength of the algorithm used, and partially on the power and availability of computing devices that can be used to break it. Public key algorithms are very strong; there are no commercial or readily available applications for cracking their code. However, keys produced via the public key algorithms used today have been cracked in contests. This means that you should carefully evaluate the need for large keys for your CAs and keep tuned to advances in technologies and contest results to determine when you should change the key size in the future. For information about such cryptographic contests, visit `http://www.rsasecurity.com/rsalabs/challenges/index.html`.

When reading the results of successful challenges, note the length of time and resources taken to decrypt the message, and remember that this represents the decryption of one key. If the algorithm is implemented and configured to change keys, the process used to solve the puzzle for one key would have to be repeated for each key used.

Certification Authority

The *certification authority* (CA) is the server application that both issues the certificates and manages the certificate database. The name may also represent a public entity that offers certificates for sale to third parties, but that is not the meaning used in this chapter. The CA also manages revocation. The CA does not issue keys. Instead, the device used by the entity to which they will be bound generates the keys. The public key is then transferred to the CA where it is added to the certificate that will be issued. The private key remains on the device that generates it.

The CA also has a certificate. The keys for this certificate are generated on the CA computer. The root CA issues its own certificate and issues CA certificates for subordinate CAs. The CA's private key is used to digitally sign the certificates it issues. Digital signatures are effective proofs of certificate origination. Copies of the signed CA certificate are publicly available so that the digital signature may be verified.

Registration Authority

In some PKI implementations, a second server application, the Registration Authority (RA), shares some of the CA duties. The RA and the CA are implemented on separate servers. The RA handles certificate enrollment. In this arrangement, the RA receives the enrollment request, verifies the identity of the requestor, and passes the public key and credentials to the CA. The CA issues the certificate and passes it back to the RA that passes it back to the requestor. By separating the contact with the requestor from the CA, an additional layer of protection can be provided. One example of this protection is that network access to the CA can be restricted to the RA. If no RA is used, every computer and user must be provided access to the CA so they can request certificates. Restricting access to the CA can provide protection from attack.

Certification Revocation List

Certificates are issued with a designated expiration date. Even so, you may need to prevent some certificates from being used before they expire. They may have been compromised, an employee may have left the company, or the certificate may need to be replaced by one with different characteristics. The revoked certificates are placed on a Certificate Revocation List (CRL), and the list is published. Applications can then check the CRL to see if the keys used in a transaction are still good.

TIP: Which Key?
Although the certificate is revoked, the private key must be made useless. The private key cannot be destroyed or accessed by the CA because it does not reside in the CA database. The key is made useless when its associated public key, which is part of the certificate, can no longer be used. For example, if a client were to use their private key to encrypt authentication information, the public key would need to be available to decrypt the data and thus prove the identity of the client. If the certificate is on the CRL, and the application checks this list, the client will not be authenticated.

Certificate Trust List (CTL)

A certificate trust list is a list of CAs whose issued certificates will be accepted by a web site. The list is signed by a trusted entity. If a certificate is received and a CA included in the list did not issue the certificate, the certificate is rejected.

PKI Interoperability

When PKI components are implemented according to standards, interoperability may be the result. For example, SSL certificates issued by many different vendor CAs are used to provide SSL-secured transactions on the Internet. You can purchase an SSL certificate issued by a non-Microsoft CA, install it in your IIS web server, and it will work. It may not be possible to do this for other applications. Standards do not specify how the standard should be implemented, and often, the standards provide alternatives or optional items that an implementer may use. Each implementation may therefore vary, and full interoperability between them may not be possible. One of the areas where problems may occur is in the use of the Certificate extension.

If certificates are constructed to the specification, it may be possible for certificates produced by one PKI to be used in another. Yet certificates produced to the specification by one PKI may not be 100 percent compatible with the applications developed to be used with certificates produced to the specification from another PKI. The is because there are alternative fields or extensions within the certificate specification. If an application is expecting a specific extension, and it is not found, the certificate cannot be used. Alternatively, if an extension is present in a certificate, and an application does not understand it, the certificate may be invalidated. An example of issues with interoperability is EFS and IPSec certificates. Third-party EFS certificates can be used, but they must meet Microsoft specifications. Third-party IPSec certificates can be used, but if they do not make CRL checking available, you may need to turn off CRL checking or IPSec authentication will fail.

CRL Location Is Important

A few years ago, VeriSign, a public Certification Authority, issued two Microsoft software signing certificates to someone who did not work for Microsoft. Because Microsoft software signing certificates are used to validate software produced and distributed by Microsoft, the implications of such a breach in trust could have been very damaging. To correct the problem, VeriSign revoked the certificates. However, the VeriSign certificates did not include the location of the VeriSign CRL. Applications written to use the certificate and to check the CRL could not have done so because there would have been no way to locate the CRL. To prevent the use of these certificates, Microsoft created a patch for Internet Explorer that would reject the specific certificates.

PKI Architecture in Windows Server 2003

The certificate services provided by Windows Server 2003 are the fourth implementation of certificate services in Windows. Certificate services in Windows are implemented in

- NT 4.0 via the option pack.
- Microsoft Exchange prior to Exchange 2000 via implementation of the Key Management Service (KMS). (Microsoft Exchange 2000 uses KMS and Windows 2000 certificate services.)
- Windows 2000.
- Windows Server 2003.

Each implementation has offered increasing flexibility and security. New in Windows Server 2003 is

- An RA via implementation of the certificate enrollment pages on a separate web server
- The ability to customize templates
- The ability to archive private keys
- Development of trust between two or more CA hierarchies using cross-certification and qualified subordination

PKI is implemented in Windows Server 2003 via the following components:

- Certificate store
- Certificate templates
- Certificates, both self-signed and issued by a CA
- Practice policy and practice policy files
- CAs
- CA hierarchy

Certificate Store

Even if no PKI is established, each Windows computer has several certificate stores. Certificate store types are described in Table 12-1.

Table 12-1 Certificate Stores

Store	Use
Personal	Certificates associated with private keys held by a user or computer.
Trusted Root Certification Authority	Implicitly trusted CAs. All the Third-Party Root CA stores and root certificates from your organization and from Microsoft.
Disallowed Certificates	Explicitly disallowed certificates. May be the result of a Software Restriction policy or the result of clicking Do Not Trust This Certificate if the choice is presented in the web browser.
Third-Party Root Certification Authorities	Trusted root CA certificates from organizations other than yours and Microsoft.
Intermediate Certification Authorities	Certificates issued to subordinate CAs.
Trusted People	Certificates belonging to explicitly trusted people. Usually from some application, such as Microsoft Outlook.
Other People	Certificates issued to implicitly trusted people. Possibly cached certificates used by EFS when EFS encrypted files are shared.
Certificate Enrollment Requests	Pending or rejected certificate requests.

The certificate store can be examined by doing one of the following:

- Clicking the Certificates button from the Content Property page of IE.
- Opening the Certificates snap-in in an MMC console.

Examine Certificates Stores Using Internet Explorer

The certificates stores can be viewed from the Internet Explorer Prop-erties, Content pages. To examine the stores and look at certificates in one of them, follow these steps:

1. Right-click IE or select Tools, Internet Options from the menu if IE is already open.
2. Select the Content page, and then click the Certificates button.
3. Select the Trusted Root Certification Authorities tab, as shown in Figure 12-3.

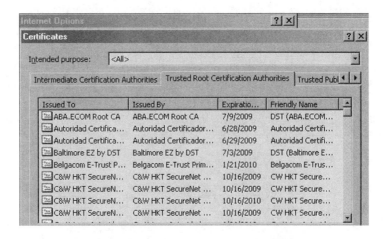

Figure 12-3 The Trusted Root Certification Authorities page lists the root CAs trusted by this computer.

Examine Certificates Stores in the Certificates Console

The advantage of creating the Certificates console is that a user may manage personal certificates, and an administrator may manage com-puter certificates. The console can be saved and easily opened to man-age certificates at a later time. To create the console follow these steps:

1. Use the Start, Run option and enter mmc to open a Microsoft Management Console.
2. From the File menu of the console, select Add/Remove Snap-ins.

3. Click the Add button.
4. Select the Certificates snap-in, and then click Add.
5. Select My User Account, and then click Finish.
6. Click Close to return to the Add/Remove Snap-ins page.
7. Click OK to return to the console.
8. In the console, expand the Certificates - Current User path.
9. Select the Trusted Root Certification Authorities, Certificates container to display a list of trusted root certificates, as shown in Figure 12-4.

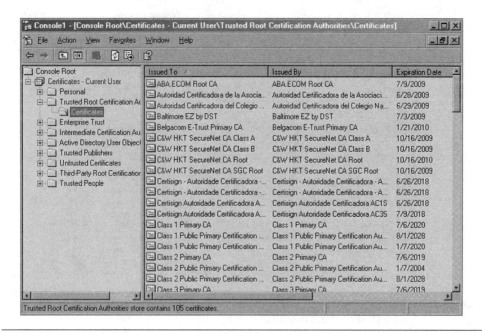

Figure 12-4   Trusted Root Certification Authorities can be displayed in the Certificates console.

Certificate Templates

Windows 2000 introduced certificate templates to make certificate enrollment and usage more flexible. Also, setting permissions on the templates can restrict certificate usage. A user without the Enroll permission on a template cannot obtain a certificate of its type.

Windows Server 2003 introduces version 2 (V2) templates. V2 templates can be customized to provide additional flexibility. V2 customizable templates are only available if the CA is integrated with Active

Directory and is Windows Server 2003 Enterprise Edition. When the CA is integrated with Active Directory, the combination of the V1 or V2 template definition and the information available in Active Directory makes enrollment quick and easy because the requestor is not required to enter much information. If the CA is not integrated with Active Directory, the enrollee must add more information during enrollment. For more information on CA types, see the section "Certification Authorities."

To examine certificate templates, open the Certificate Templates snap-in in an MMC console, as shown in Figure 12-5.

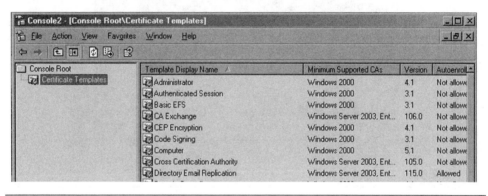

Figure 12-5   Viewing Certificate Templates.

Restricting Certificate Enrollment

Certificate enrollment can be restricted in the following ways:

- **Changing permissions on the certificate templates**—Changing permissions on the certificate template can restrict certificate enrollment. The Enroll permission, as shown in Figure 12-6, is necessary to successfully obtain a certificate. By creating special Windows groups and giving only these groups the Enroll permission on a certificate template, enrollment is restricted to members of the groups. Permissions can be set on templates in the Certificate Template Console by right-clicking the template and selecting `Properties` and then `Security`.

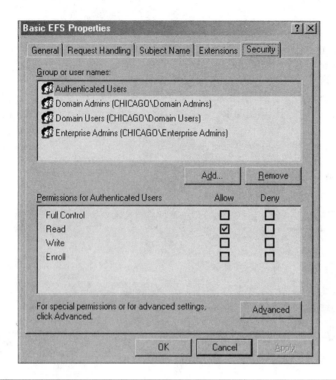

Figure 12-6 Set permissions on certificate templates to restrict the enrollment process to approved identities.

- **Setting the CA enrollment policy to require approval**—The Public Key Policy of the default domain policy specifies the CA enrollment policy for CAs integrated with Active Directory. The policy is listed as the Autoenrollment Setting Properties and is shown in Figure 12-7. By default, CAs that are integrated with Active Directory are set to automatically issue certificates required by authenticated identities. This means that a user with an account in Active Directory can request and be issued any certificate for which he has the enrollment permission on the template. The default can be changed in Windows Server 2003. If you do this, every certificate request must be approved. This process may prove unwieldy.
- **Using custom templates and requiring some certificates to be manually approved**—Others can be automatically enrolled, as shown in Figure 12-8.

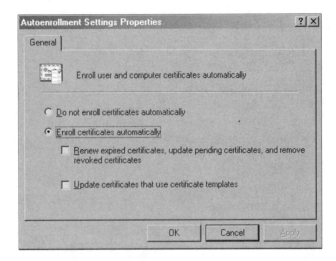

Figure 12-7   The enrollment policy of a CA can either automatically issue all certificates or require approval before issuing any certificate.

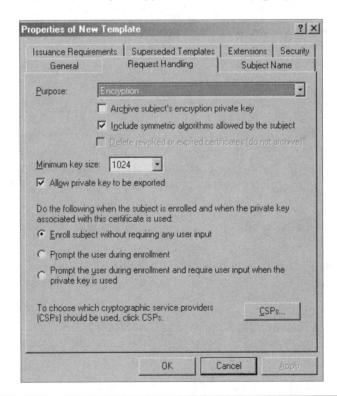

Figure 12-8   Custom certificate templates provide the option to restrict enrollment by requiring approval for the issuance of a specific template type.

Standard Template Types

CAs integrated with Active Directory provide the types of templates described in Table 12-2. In this table, those identified as V1 templates are available on all versions of Windows Server 2003 and on Windows 2000 CAs. V2 templates are only available on Windows Server 2003 Enterprise Edition Enterprise CAs. V1 certificate template types on a Windows Server 2003 Enterprise Edition Enterprise CA are V2 versions and can be customized.

Table 12-2   Standard Template Types

Template Type	Version	Description
Administrator	1	Identifies the user as an administrator
Authenticated Session	1	Client authentication
Basic EFS	1	EFS file encryption
CEP Encryption	1	Acts as a registration authority
Code signing	1	Sign code
Computer	1	Authentication, IPSec
Domain controller	1	Client and server identification as a domain controller
EFS Recovery Agent	1	Can be used to recover EFS encrypted files
Enrollment Agent	1	Can enroll another user
Enrollment Agent (computer)	1	Requests certificates for the computer
Exchange Enrollment Agent (Offline Request)	1	Request email certificates for users
Exchange Signature Only	1	Digital signature only
Exchange User	1	Secure email, client authentication
IPSEC	1	Computer certificate for IPSec authentication
IPSEC (offline request)	1	Device certificates for IPSec
Root Certification Authority	1	The root CA certificate
Router (offline request)	1	Authentication for a router

Template Type	Version	Description
Smartcard Logon	1	Client authentication certificate for a smart card
Smartcard User	1	Client authentication and email certificate for smart card
Subordinate CA	1	Subordination CA
Trust List Signing	1	Used to sign CTL
User	1	Authentication, secure email, EFS
User Signature only	1	Digital signature only
WebServer	1	Server authentication
CA Exchange	2	CA encryption
Cross-Certification Authority	2	Qualified subordination
Directory Email Replication	2	Directory replication
Domain Controller Authentication	2	Client and server authentication
Key recovery agent	2	Recovers archived private keys from the CA database
RAS & IAS Server	2	Can be an RAS and IAS server
Workstation Authentication	2	Authentication

Custom Templates

When certificate services are installed on a Windows Server 2003 Enterprise Edition server, the certificate templates can be modified. Saving a copy of a standard template to a new file and then making changes produces a customized template. Custom template choices include items such as key archival and enrollment approval. More information on custom templates and how to implement them is provided in Chapter 13. Figure 12-9 displays the General page of a new custom template file.

Self-Signed Certificates

In Chapter 6, the use of self-signed certificates and their problems were outlined for the Encrypting File System. Self-signed certificates are used in other places as well. The root CA, the first CA in a hierarchy, creates and signs its own certificate. This use of a self-signed certificate is necessary. (The root of trust must start somewhere.) Another use of a self-signed certificate is the production by Small Business Server 2003 of a self-signed SSL certificate for use by the IIS server that is part of its configuration. Small Business Server 2003 IIS can also utilize an SSL certificate produced by a CA, either public or private. A primary use for the self-signed certificate is to protect Outlook Web Access. Although the use of privately produced SSL certificates is not advised for public web sites, especially commercial web sites, the use of privately produced SSL certificates makes good sense when the usage is for employees only. This is the case here: The users of SSL will all be employees of the small business.

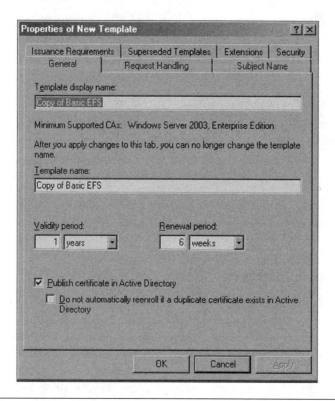

Figure 12-9   Customize templates by making changes to a copy of the custom template.

In any case where self-signed certificates are used by Windows OSs, no key management is provided. To ensure the availability of the keys, and therefore the ability to recover the root CA, keys should be backed up and secured in a safe place.

Best Practices for Certificates and Certificate Templates

- Restrict usage of certificates by setting permissions on certificate templates.
- For each CA, allow only the certificate issuance of those certificates the CA is allowed to issue. Remove all others.
- Document which certificate types are allowed at each CA and audit certificate issuance.
- Document custom template definitions.

Practice Policy and Practice Policy Files

The practice policy is the most important part of the CA implementation. One of the major issues with any PKI is that if it's not correctly planned, deployed, managed, and protected, it provides a false sense of security. When the CA is not protected, it may be easy to compromise. When certificate enrollment is not carefully controlled, the wrong individuals may obtain valid certificates and use them for unauthorized purposes. If the CA certificate and private key are not archived, it may be impossible to recover the CA after a disaster. If private keys are not protected, sensitive information may be exposed. If the CA activity and administration is not audited, mistakes and improper activity may never be uncovered and thus cannot be rectified. In short, a poorly designed, poorly implemented, and unprotected PKI is worse than no PKI at all. This is true no matter whose implementation of PKI is used. For many PKIs, a large barrier of cost and implementation knowledge currently tends to inhibit casual and possibly improper implementation. Cost and complexity may serve to assist in the development of a strong PKI model because many of these PKI products also require a large amount of consulting services to successfully implement them. If consulting services provide sound advice, and the product provides the tools necessary, a strong, properly implemented PKI can be the result.

TIP: Use Face-to-Face Registration
The most secure form of enrollment is to insist on face-to-face authentication at a RA and to store user certificates on hardware token. However, doing so is cost-prohibitive. In a large organization, doing so may also be impractical because of the large number of people, locations, and the mobility of many of the people.

There is no similar barrier to PKI in Windows Server 2003. PKI can easily be installed and comes as part of the operating system. To install a Windows Server 2003 CA that is integrated with Active Directory, you must be a domain admin. To install a CA that is not integrated with AD, you only need to be a member of the local administrators group on that server. There is no requirement for understanding PKI. The GUI interface makes it possible to install and use certificate services in Windows Server 2003 with little to no use of the extensive help files. Therefore, the security of the PKI and the processes it controls through certificate issuance is directly related to the quality of the PKI design and its implementation and management. This information should be part of the practice policy. Management should prepare this document with input from those qualified to assess the technical, legal, and security implications of the choices.

The technical decisions made in the CA practice policy must then be implemented in the configuration and management of the CA. Many elements of the policy can be configured in the interface. These items are as follows:

- The *security policy* is a high-level document created by corporate IT management, security management, or some combination of the two. Its purpose is to define the use of security services and the security posture of the organization, as well as to establish the rules that must be followed to ensure the security of the organization's assets. An organization's security policy is usually composed of specific, individual security policies that pertain to different areas. For example, security policy that creates the security infrastructure for PKI might include answers to questions such as which application will use certificates, how they will use certificates, and whether role separation will be enforced.
- The *certificate policy* is a set of rules that details the certificate purposes that are provided by the CA and how usage, enrollment, and issuance will occur. The *policy authority* is a group of members of the organization from many areas who are selected to define the policy. Because the policy should be inline with the security policy, those who develop the security policy are typically also part of the policy authority. The policy defines
    - Purpose of the certificate, such as EFS, IPSec, or authentication.

- Legal issues. For example, if the CA is compromised or used for a purpose outside its defined scope, are there liability issues?
- Minimum length of the public and private key pairs.
- Requirements for enrollment and renewal.
- User authentication for certificate enrollment.
- Private key management requirements, such as hardware-based storage.
- Whether or not the private key can be exported.
- Responsibilities of the users, such as what they should do if the private key is lost or compromised.
- The *certificate practice statement* (CPS) defines the CA policy. It is a statement about the way the CA issues certificates. Legal staff, especially those who worked on the certificate policy, IT staff, and those that administer IT infrastructure should define the CPS. Some of the elements in the CPS can be implemented in an .inf file. Although it is not always necessary to implement an .inf file, the file may be necessary in some circumstances. One use of such a file is the management of the location for the CRL publication and the location of an accessible copy of the CA certificate. The capolicy.inf file is used for this purpose for the Windows CA. The CPS should include
  - CA name, server name, and DNS address
  - Certificate policies
  - Certificate types
  - Policies, procedures, and process for certificate issuance, renewal, and recovery
  - Policies for CRLs, including CDP and publication schedule
  - Crypto algorithms, CSPs, and the key length of the CA certificate
  - Security for the CA
  - Certificate lifetime for each certificate issued by the CA
  - CA certificate renewal process

Certification Authorities

Four types of certification authorities can be installed as part of a Windows Server 2003 PKI:

- **Enterprise Root Certification Authority**—The first server in a CA hierarchy and also one that is integrated with Active Directory. The root issues its own self-signed certificate.
- **Enterprise Subordinate Certification Authority**—A server that is given its authority by a root CA. The root CA can either be enterprise or standalone. The keys are generated at the subordinate CA, but a CA above it in its hierarchy issues the subordinate CA certificate.
- **Standalone Root Certificate Authority**—The first server in a CA hierarchy and one that is not integrated with Active Directory. The standalone root can be a parent to both enterprise and subordinate CAs.
- **Standalone Subordinate Certification Authority**—A server that is given its authority by a root CA.

CA Hierarchy

Windows Server 2003 CAs can be implemented as part of a CA hierarchy. The top-most CA in a hierarchy is a root CA. In theory, any number of layers of CAs can be implemented, each with its own complement of CAs. In practice, a three-layer CA hierarchy appears to be the best application of the model. In the three-layer hierarchy, only the bottom or third layer issues end-use certificates, such as those for smart cards, IPSec, EFS, and so on. The top layer is the root CA, and the middle layer is composed of intermediary CAs. Technically, every CA can issue any type of certificate that its administrator has assigned. Best practices recommend that intermediary CAs and root CAs issue only CA certificates. Such a hierarchy is illustrated in Figure 12-10.

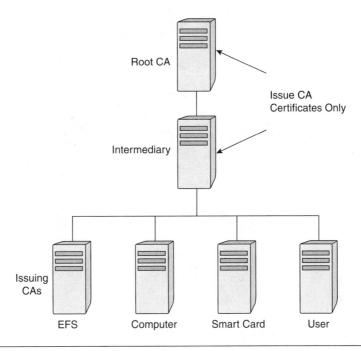

Root CA

Issue CA
Certificates Only

Intermediary

Issuing
CAs

EFS   Computer   Smart Card   User

Figure 12-10   The three-layer CA hierarchy model.

TIP: Constrain Certificate Types

When multiple CAs are cross-certified, the issuance of certificate types
can be limited by applying constraints. For more information, see the section "Cross-Certification and Qualified Subordination."

The depth in layers and the use of each CA in the hierarchy is dictated
by the purpose for which they will be used. The intermediary layer is
typically used to divide the management and distribution of CA processing to different geographic or organizational purposes. For example, as
shown in Figure 12-11, an international organization might create a hierarchy with an intermediary CA at each of its major locations. In this case,
Tailspin Toys has three major locations (Paris, Sydney, and New York),
each with its own intermediary CA. By placing intermediary CAs at geographical points, the CA management can be localized, and redundancy
is provided. It is also possible that fewer WAN enrollment and CRL
requests may be needed, but there is no way to restrict enrollment and
CRL download requests to the nearest CA. The use of an organizational
model, as shown in Figure 12-12, may be due to the use of a distributed
management model.

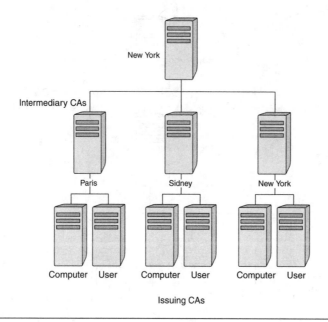

Figure 12-11   Use a geographical model where management is decentralized by geography.

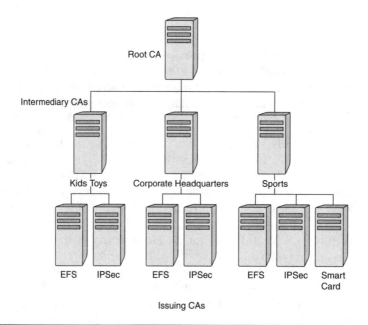

Figure 12-12   Use an organizational model where management is decentralized by organizational function.

An additional mechanism used in a CA hierarchy is to use CA hierarchy level for certificate-specific CAs. This allows management by function. For example, as shown in Figure 12-13, each CA issues one type of certificate. One issues smart card certificates, another issues EFS certificates, and a third issues all others. In this figure, these CAs are in the second level of the hierarchy. It is common to find a CA hierarchy that combines geographical and organizational CA hierarchy models and the functional model, as shown in Figure 12-13.

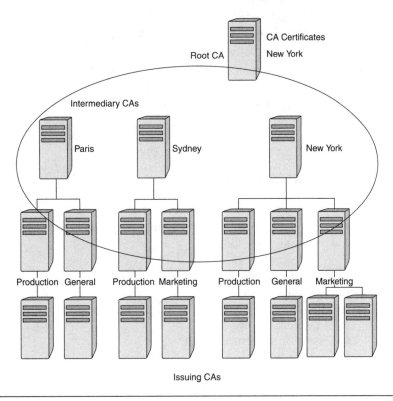

Figure 12-13   Combine geographical and functional models.

Best Practices for CA Hierarchies

- Keep the CA root offline and provide it with extra protection.
- Provide hardware-based storage for the CA keys.
- Use at least a two-tier model with an offline, standalone root CA and an Enterprise subordinate CA.
- The root CA should issue only CA certificates. (Other CAs in the hierarchy will issue end-use certificates.)
- If a three-tier model is used, the intermediary CAs should issue only CA certificates.
- The final CA layer, the issuing CAs should not issue CA certificates. It should be restricted to end-use certificates.
- Provide redundancy for all subordinate CAs.
- Provide backup of the root CA keys and practice its recovery.

Certificate Revocation List (CRL)

Certificates are revoked at the CA where they were issued. When a certificate is revoked, a reason for its revocation is selected. Possible reasons for revocation are as follows:

- KeyCompromise
- CACompromise
- AffiliationChanged
- Superceded
- Cessationofoperations (ca)
- CertificateHold
- RemovefromCRL
- Unspecified

Only the certificates revoked for the CertificateHold reason can be removed; in other words, certificates revoked using this purpose can be made valid again. (The certificate is removed from hold status. It is still listed in the CRL but is given the RemovefromCRL status.) After certificates are revoked, they are added to the CA's Certificate Revocation List (CRL), which is made available to users of the certificates. The Windows Server CRL is published according to a schedule configured at the CA and published to locations set within the CA CRL Distribution Point

(CDP). Figure 12-14 shows the Extension Property page of the CA where CDP locations are recorded. The CRL publishing schedule is configured in the Revoked Certificates Properties, as shown in Figure 12-15.

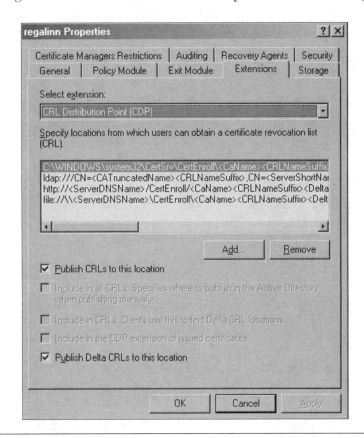

Figure 12-14   The CDP specifies where the CRL will be published.

Applications must be written and may sometimes need to be configured to work with CRLs. For example, computer certificates are used with IPSec for authentication. Certificate revocation checking is on by default, and a revoked certificate cannot be used. The process of certificate revocation checking can be turned off in order to implement the use of third-party certificates that may not provide the location of a CRL. If these third-party certificates are used and CRL checking is not turned off, the IPSec authentication will fail.

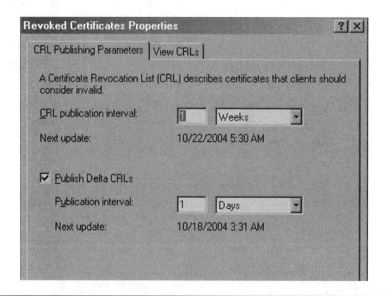

Revoked Certificates Properties   ?│×│

CRL Publishing Parameters │ View CRLs │

A Certificate Revocation List (CRL) describes certificates that clients should consider invalid.

CRL publication interval: 1   Weeks   ▾

Next update: 10/22/2004 5:30 AM

☑ Publish Delta CRLs

Publication interval: 1   Days   ▾

Next update: 10/18/2004 3:31 AM

Figure 12-15   Configure the CRL publication schedule.

Best Practices for CRLs

- A root CA certificate should have an empty CDP because the certificate issuer defines a CDP, and the root CA certificate is the root CA.

- An offline CA should still publish a CRL.

- A CRL should be available from more than one location for redundancy.

- Add to the CRL time so that it will be valid for the amount of time it takes for CA recovery.

- Plan alternative methods if, for some reason, scheduled publications do not occur.

- If CRL distribution is via the AD, take its replication schedule into account.

Delta CRLs

Several problems may be created because of the latency introduced by Active Directory and CRL processing. If a CRL must be retrieved from the Active Directory, the list must replicate from the domain controller on which it is originally published to all DCs in the domain. This may require that the time between the publishing of CRLs be set longer than desired. It also means that the availability of new CRLs will vary with the replication latency of Active Directory. In addition, if a client has a copy of a valid CRL in its cache, it will not download another CRL until the one it has is about to expire. This may mean that a revoked certificate is not invalidated but is accepted when it should not be. This means that even a manually published CRL that does not require AD replication to be available will not be used until the current CRL expires.

Delta CRLs can make newly revoked certificates available between CRL downloads. Windows Server 2003 CAs can be configured to issue delta CRLs. A delta CRL does not include revoked certificates previously published to the CRL. Instead, a delta CRL includes only those certificates revoked since the CRL was published. Only Windows XP and Windows Server 2003 clients can use delta CRLs. The use of delta CRLs will not interfere with the normal processing of CRLs in other OSs. These OSs will download the regular CRL and, when it is about to expire, will download the next CRL. The use of delta CRLs is configured in the Properties pages of the Revoked Certificates folder, as shown previously in Figure 12-15.

NOTE: OCSP Support
Support for Online Certificate Status Protocol (OCSP) is not provided by default but can be added by installing a revocation provider in CryptoAPI or by using a third-party OCSP responder that can communicate with the CA.

CA Roles

Another new feature of Windows Server 2003 CAs is the use and enforcement of role separation. The role separation model follows the separation of privileges security principle, which states that, wherever possible, critical and sensitive functions should be split so that no one individual has the power to steal or damage assets or otherwise cause harm to the organization. This principle has been implemented in manual processing for a long time. In accounting, for example, the accounts payable clerk may approve or even issue checks to vendors but cannot issue purchase orders. Purchasing clerks issue POs but have no authority to issue checks or approve them. In a completely manual system, this separation of duties is defined not only by policy and job description but also by management of the business forms used. Both purchase orders and checks are carefully controlled and restricted to use by the appropriate groups.

Business Forms Administration and Role Separation

Many years ago, one of my first management positions was as administrator of the business forms management department. One of the first management projects I supervised was an inventory of "critical" business forms. Critical forms were defined as those that could cause the movement or distribution of assets. Although everyone agreed that checks and purchase orders were critical and should be protected, management wondered if other forms should also be given special attention. A total of 23 forms were identified. Some critical forms were properly managed; others were not. For example, for a vendor invoice for parts to be paid, a valid purchase order, packing slip (indicating delivery), and warehouse supervisor signature were necessary. In reality, data entry entered the invoice as approved for payment (after which the next print run printed the check) based on the attachment of a small accounts payable form to the invoice. Accounts payable clerks filled out this form based on the existence of the required forms and approval, but anyone could obtain a copy of the form. The form was printed in the company print shop and stored in the basement with other printed forms, scotch tape, and envelopes. A rogue employee or even a visiting vendor representative easily could have obtained a form, attached it to an invoice, and slipped it in an interoffice mail. The bill would have been paid.

This is an excellent example of how people and procedures can circumvent technical controls. The process that enabled it was not intentionally created; it just happened because no one initially realized the results of the change from manual to automated processing. Take care that your implementation of role separation is supported by sound policies and procedures and is audited.

By default, Windows Server 2003 CAs can be administered by members of the local administrators group. If the CA is installed on a member server, members of the Domain Admins and Enterprise Admins groups may also be able to administer the CA. Most CA administration should be removed from the responsibilities of the operating system administrator and split by function. This allows for separation of duties and, in addition to following sound security principles, follows the standard specified by Common Criteria. Common Criteria is an international standard that seeks to define security standards by which security products can be evaluated. If a product is evaluated against the standard, purchasers can avoid extended testing of their own. They must only find a Protection profile (a specific definition for a specific purpose) and then select from among the products that have been evaluated against the standard. Windows 2000, for example, was evaluated and received EAL4 certification in October 2002.

NOTE: Common Criteria
For more information on Common Criteria, read the article "Windows 2000 and Common Criteria" at `http://mcpmag.com/backissues/columns/article. asp?EditorialsID=521`, and visit the Common Criteria web site at `www.commoncriteria.org`.

The Common Criteria PKI roles are defined in Table 12-3, along with the equivalent Windows Server 2003 roles.

Table 12-3   Common Criteria PKI Roles

Common Criteria Role	Windows Server 2003 Role	Tasks
Administrator	Implemented by developing the CA Administrator role. This new role can be implemented by giving a custom Windows group the Manage CA permission on the CA.	Administer the CA.
Operator	Implemented by default as any member of local Administrators group.	Backup and Recovery, including backup of CA private key.
Officer	Implemented by developing the Certificate Manager role. This new role, can be implemented by giving a custom Windows group the Manage Certificates permission on the CA.	Manage certificates.

Table 12-3   Common Criteria PKI Roles Continued

Common Criteria Role	Windows Server 2003 Role	Tasks
Auditor	Implemented by developing the Auditor role. Although not specifically defined in CA documentation, this new role can be implemented by giving a custom Windows group the user right Manage auditing and security log.	View and maintain audit logs.

The two new roles, CA Administrator and Certificate Manager, are implemented by giving two custom Windows groups Issue and Manage Certificates or Manage CA permissions on the CA object and then adding members to the group. The Administrators group has both of these permissions by default, as shown in Figure 12-16. Common Criteria also recommends—and requires, depending on evaluation level—the ability to enforce role separation. That is, if a user is given the ability to perform the duties of two roles, technical controls prevent them from doing the duties assigned to either. For example, if you were to enforce role separation in Windows Server 2003 by implementing the groups CA Administrator and Certificate Manager and giving them the appropriate permissions, if you were to place the user John Doe in both groups, John would not be able to perform either function.

In addition to administration roles, three other unique certificate services roles exist:

- **Certificate holder or enrollee**—Has the Read and Enroll permissions on a certificate template. They have the right to request, be issued, and use the certificates issued to them using templates that they have Enroll permission on. (If they do not have Enroll permission on a template, they cannot be issued the template. If the certificate must be manually approved, they might not be issued the certificate.)
- **Enrollment agent**—Can obtain certificates on behalf of another user. The user must have Read and Enroll permission on the template. An example of an enrollment agent is the smart card.
- **Recovery agent**—Has the ability to recover EFS encrypted files.

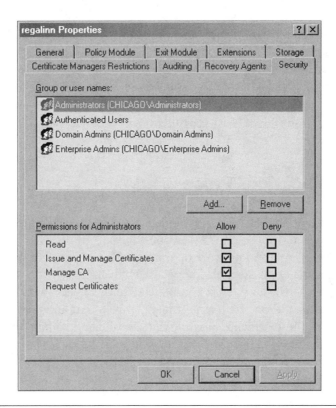

Figure 12-16   CA permissions.

Another benefit of implementing role separation is that when role separation is enforced, the members of the local Administrators group no longer have the ability to administer the CA. (They retain the ability to back up and restore CA keys.) Until you assign members to the new administrative groups, no one will be able to manage the CA. In addition, if the administrator is a member of both CA administrative groups, she will not be able to administer the CA because of role separation. In fact, a common mistake is to make the local Administrator account the only member of both groups and then enforce role separation. The result is that the administrator must first disable role separation, remove the Administrator account, and then properly define membership in these groups.

In spite of the ability to provide and enforce role separation, if administrators are not trustworthy, the benefits of role separation can be removed. A rogue administrator could, for example, establish fake user accounts and assign each one to only one of the important CA administration roles. He then could log on as one and then the other using runas, or log off and then back on again using different accounts, and thereby gain full control of the CA. As in any security process, audit of activity on the CA should be required, and someone who is not an administrator on the system should independently review audit records.

Certificate Services Processing

PKI components, both those on clients such as certificate stores and certificates and those on the CA, interoperate to provide public key technologies as part of network operations. Many operating system processes and applications use these services. Many of these processes, such as the use of certificates by IPSec policies and VPNs, are detailed in other chapters. Others, such as certificate enrollment and revocation, that are part of the certificate lifecycle and certificate chaining, which is key to certificate validation, are described in this section.

Certificate Lifecycle

The certificate lifecycle consists of several events:

- Enrollment
- Renewal
- Usage
- Recovery
- Revocation
- Expiration

Certificate Enrollment

The Certificate Enrollment function consists of a request, approval, and distribution or rejection. Requests may be made either manually or automatically. The process for requests made to an Enterprise CA follows these steps:

1. The request is made for a specific certificate type and is sent to the CA.
2. The user must be authenticated or the request is denied.

3. The requesting identity must have the Enroll permission on the certificate template or the request is denied.
4. If the requesting identity is both authenticated and has Enroll permission on the template, the process continues.
5. The requesting computer generates the encryption keys.
6. The public key of the key pair is transferred to the CA.
7. The private key is stored in the user's profile.
8. The public key and the credentials of the user along with specific template information are combined to create a certificate.
9. If the CA or the certificate type is configured to automatically approve the request, the certificate is issued and can be downloaded to the certificate store of the computer from which the request was received.
10. If the CA or the certificate type is configured to require approval, the certificate is held by the CA until approved, rejected, or expired.
11. If approved, the requesting identity can download the certificate to the certificate store.

TIP: Use Web Enrollment to Obtain V2 Certificates
A Windows 2000 computer cannot request a V2 certificate using the `Certificates` console. However, any computer using IE 5.01 or later can use web-enrollment methods and an ActiveX control to request and download V2 certificates. The ActiveX control can only be downloaded to the computer by a member of the Administrators or Power Users group. V2 certificates downloaded to a Windows XP Professional or a Windows Server 2003 computer can also be exported and then imported to a Windows 2000 computer.

Using the Certificates Console to Request a Certificate Use of the `Certificates` console to request a certificate does not require any special permission if the certificate request is for a certificate for the current user. If the request is for a different entity, such as a computer or a service, administrative privileges are necessary.

The `Certificates` console cannot be used in the following circumstances:

- A standalone CA is the issuing CA.

- You cannot select options you need from the `Certificate Console Certificate Request Wizard`. Some options are not available from this wizard, such as the following:
  - Marking keys as exportable.
  - Choosing the hash algorithm.
  - Saving the request as a PKCS# 10 file.
- Windows does not generate the certificate subject name.
- You are requesting a CA certificate from a Windows 2000 CA.

In these circumstances, you must use the certificate enrollment pages. These pages are located at *http://servername/certsrv*. These pages must also be used to download certificates that require approval.

TIP: DSS Certificates

If you require a *Digital Signature Standard* (DSS) certificate from an enterprise CA, select the `User Signature Only` certificate template from the wizard certificate page. This certificate uses the *Digital Signature Algorithm* (DSA) standard for its signature algorithm and the SHA-1 message hash algorithm. DSA can be used only for signatures, not for encryption.

To request a personal certificate, follow these steps:

1. Open a `Certificates` console by adding the `Certificates` snap-in to an MMC, or by opening a console created earlier and saved.
2. Right-click the `Certificates`, `Personal` folder, select `All Tasks`, and then select `Request New Certificate` and then click `Next`.
3. In the `Certificate Request Wizard`, as shown in Figure 12-17, check the type of certificate required.
4. If an `Advanced` option or certificate type is required, click the `Advanced` button and enter information, as shown in Figure 12-18, for the following optional items:
   a.) The CSP.
   b.) A key strength.
   c.) Check the `Enable strong private key protection` box. Checking this box will require that a password be entered each time the private key is used. Do not select this unless necessary, and do not select this for computer certificates. Computers have no way to respond to a request for a password before the private key can be used.

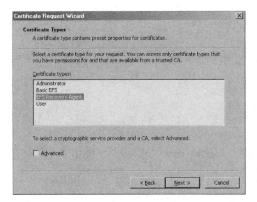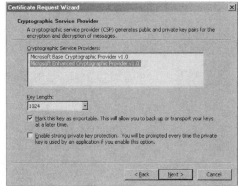

Figure 12-17 Check the certificate type required.

Figure 12-18 Use the Advanced Options page to change defaults for some items.

5. Click Next, and if more than one CA exists, choose the CA that you are required to use.

6. Click Next, enter a friendly name for the certificate, and then click Next. Click Finish.

7. Click OK when the popup The certificate request was successful appears.

Using the Web Enrollment Pages to Request a Certificate Web enrollment pages are located at *http://servername/certsrv*, where *servername* is the name of the Windows Server 2003 computer that is hosting web enrollment. This can be either the CA or the RA. Web enrollment pages must be used when the CA is a standalone CA. Additionally, you can also use the web enrollment pages to

- Check the status of a pending certificate request
- Download a CRL
- Retrieve a CA certificate from a CA
- Submit a request using a PKCS #10 or PKCS #7 file
- Request a smart card certificate on behalf of another user

To request a certificate, follow these steps:

1. Enter the `http://servername/certsrv` address in the browser.
2. When prompted, enter your user name and password.
3. Click `Request A Certificate`.
4. Click `User Certificate` or click `Advanced Certificate Request`, as shown in Figure 12-19. Selecting an advanced certificate request allows you to select
   a.) Certificate Template (enterprise CAs).
   b.) Intended purpose (standalone CA).
   c.) Cryptographic Service Provider (CSP). (The code that performs authentication, encryption, decryption, and other cryptographic processing through CryptoAPI. They create keys, destroy them, and use them to provide different cryptographic operations. Different CSPs exist to provide different types of key strength or to fit the requirements of a specific hardware vendor.)
   d.) Key size.
   e.) Hash algorithm.
   f.) Key use, such as *exchange*, *signature*, or both. The exchange usage means the key can be used to encrypt data. The signature key usage means the key can be used to digitally sign. If both usages are required, both selections should be made.
   g.) Use an existing key set or create a new key set.
   h.) Enable strong private key protection.
   i.) Mark keys as exportable.
   j.) Use the local machine store. This should be selected when the key must be available to other users or when the key is provided for the use of the computer.
   k.) Save the request to a PKCS #10 file. Use this option if the CA is not available online.

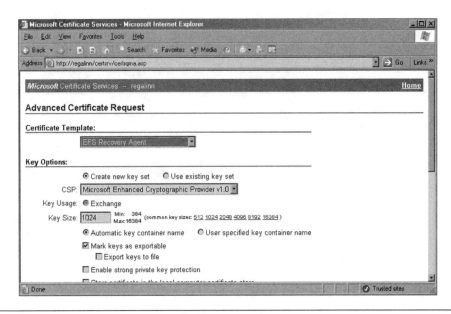

Figure 12-19   Check the certificate type required.

5. If the Advanced request Create and submit a request to this CA is selected, use the Certificate Template drop-down list to select the type of certificate required. Complete any other information required and then click Submit, followed by Yes twice to confirm your request.

6. If you are an authenticated user and this is an enterprise CA, the statement No further identifying information is required. To complete your certificate, press submit, as shown in Figure 12-20, may be present. Click the Submit button or click More Options to complete the request. If you click More Options, enter the information for optional items:

   a.)   Enter the CSP.

   b.)   Enable the use of strong private key protection.

7. If the CA is online, the certificate may be immediately issued. If this is the case, click the Install this certificate link and then click Yes to agree to let the web site install it. A confirmation should appear.

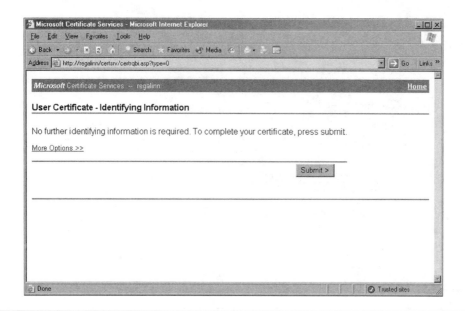

Figure 12-20   Submit the request when prompted.

8. If the certificate requires approval, the `Certificate Pending` page appears. You have to return to the web site to check status and, if the request is approved, retrieve the certificate. If the certificate can be automatically approved and is, click `OK` to download the certificate.

If certificates must be approved, you may be asked to return later to obtain the certificate. To check on a pending certificate, follow these steps:

1. Enter the `http://servername/certsrv` address in the browser.
2. Click `View the Status Of a Pending Certificate Request.`
3. If there are no pending requests, a message will state so.
4. If there are requests, the certificates will be listed.
5. Click a certificate to see its status. Its status may be one of the following:
   a.) Still pending. Your only choice here is to remove the request or continue to wait.
   b.) Issued.
   c.) Denied.
6. If the status is approved, select `Install This Certificate`.

Request a Certificate Using a PKCS #7 or PKCS #10 File If the CA is offline or is online but unreachable from the client, a certificate request may be saved in a file. To complete the request and obtain the certificate, you must take the request and access the CA either from its console or from a computer that can reach it online. To do so, follow these steps:

1. Enter the CA's address in Internet Explorer: `http://server-name/certsrv`.
2. Click `Request a Certificate`, and then click `Advanced Certificate Request`.
3. Check `Submit a certificate request using a base-64-encoded CMC or PKCS #10 file, or submit a renewal request by using a base-64-encoded PKCS #7 file`, as shown in Figure 12-21.
4. Click `Browse For A File To Insert`.
5. Browse for the file. When you locate it, click `Open`.
6. On the web page, click `Read!` to paste the contents of the file into the scroll box.
7. If necessary, select the template for the certificate type required. The subordinate CA certificate is the default template type.
8. Add additional information into the `Additional Attributes` section as necessary.
9. Click `Submit`.
10. If approval is required, you have to check the pending request later.
11. If approval is automatic, download the certificate chain to a removable disk.
12. Use the certificate import function to import the certificate into the certificate store.

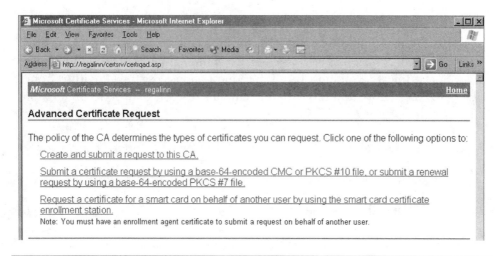

Figure 12-21   Identify the file type.

Command-Line Options for Requesting Certificates   The `certreq` command can be used to request a certificate. This tool is part of the support tools available on the Windows Server 2003 installation CD-ROM. To use the tool, use the syntax as described at `http://www.microsoft.com/resources/documentation/WindowsServ /2003/standard/proddocs/en-us/Default.asp?url=/resources/ documentation/windowsserv/2003/standard/proddocs/en-us/ sag_cs_certreq2.asp`.

For example, request a certificate from the regalinn CA installed on the server regalinn by using this command:

```
Certreq -config regalinn\regalinn
```

Then, enter the name of the certificate request file you have prepared.

Certificate Distribution and Automatic Enrollment

Reading about and requesting a single certificate makes the distribution part of the enrollment process seem effortless, as indeed it can be. When large numbers of users must individually request certificates, and when certificates must be manually requested for computers, however, the process is not so easily accomplished. Many users will have difficulty with the procedure, and the time that might be spent helping them or requesting certificates for them can be substantial. In addition, if an administrator must manually request every computer certificate, this too can become tedious.

Automatic enrollment can be used to solve these problems. Windows 2000 can be configured to automatically enroll computers, but not to provide automatic enrollment for user certificates. Windows Server 2003 offers automatic enrollment for user and computer certificates. Autoenrollment can reduce the cost of implementing and managing PKI. Certificate renewal, superseding of certificates, and multiple signature requirement certificate requests can also be automatically enrolled. In some cases, the process may require some user intervention and may provide user notification. For example, when smart card certificates are required, the user will be prompted to insert a smart card. Examples of the types of certificates that can be automatically enrolled include the following:

- Smart card logon
- EFS
- Secure Sockets Layer (SSL)
- Secure/Multipurpose Internet Mail Extension (S/MIME)
- User
- Computer

Certificate autoenrollment is based on Group Policy settings and the use of V2 certificates. V2 certificates can use autoenrollment or can require a request. Autoenrollment is only possible if the requestor is registered and authenticated as a user or computer in Active Directory. In addition, the following operating system–specific requirements must be met:

- Windows Server 2003 schema and Group Policy updates
- Windows Server 2000 Service Pack 3 or later domain controllers
- Windows XP or Windows Server 2003 clients
- Windows Server 2003 Enterprise Edition or Datacenter Edition Enterprise CA

TIP: V2 Certificate Client Enrollment

Only Windows XP and Windows Server 2003 computers can participate in the V2 certificate client enrollment process, and *only* a Windows Server 2003 Enterprise Edition or Datacenter Edition CA can develop the V2 certificate templates.

NOTE: Auto Download

Auto download of CA certificates and CTL can also be provided by the autoenrollment service.

The NTAuth store is created during the setup of Enterprise CA. The store designates CAs that can issue certificates for use in smart card logon and use the enroll `on behalf of` right. It can be added to using the `DSSTORE` command in Windows 2000 and the `certutil` command for Windows XP and Windows Server 2003.

Group Policy is used to manage autoenrollment. The user configuration container is used for user certificates, and the computer configuration container for computer certificates. Once configured, autoenrollment is triggered by logon, at boot for computers, and at logon for users. Policy is refreshed every eight hours, and this timeframe can be configured in Group Policy. Once configured, the autoenrollment process proceeds as follows:

1. Autoenrollment is triggered by winlogon or by Group Policy refresh.
2. The client OS requests any components necessary from Active Directory, such as the root CA certificate, the CTL, cross-certification certificates, NTAuth container, or certificate temples.
3. The list of certificate templates is cached in the registry.
4. If the user certificate attribute is set, expired certificates (present in the AD) are removed if a new certificate for the same purpose is present.
5. If the user certificate attribute is set, revoked and superceded (obsoleted) certificates (present in the AD) are removed automatically.
6. The list of templates is processed, looking for the Autoenroll and Read ACEs set for the current user or computer on the certificate.
7. The user's personal store is reviewed, looking for expired certificates, revoked certificates, or certificates without private keys. If any are found, they are added to the request list.
8. If a valid certificate is found in the certificate store, the certificate name is removed from the list.
9. If required and configured, the Active Directory will be searched for valid copies of the user certificates on the request list.
10. Pending requests can be retrieved, if approved, from the CA.
11. Template supercede requests are evaluated and, if found, are added to the request list.

12. The AD is searched for a CA that can supply the certificates requested. (Only Windows Server 2003 Enterprise Edition or DataCenter Edition CAs may issue V2 certificates.)

13. A security context for authentication is provided through the Distributed Component Object Model (DCOM). The CA enforces certificate profile and enrollment security as identified in the certificate.

14. A certificates revocation check for the issuing CA's entire certificate chain is done to ensure that the certificates have not been revoked. If revoked, the CA will not be used. Revocation will not occur if the CDP for the CRL is not in the certificate or if the certificate revocation status is offline.

15. If certificates are issued, they are stored in the user or computer personal store.

16. If certificates are pending, the request is stored in the Request store.

17. If user action is required, the UI balloon appears to notify the user.

TIP: Certificate Requests via Terminal Server

Many certificate requests, including autoenrollment requests, can be made through a Windows Server 2003 terminal server if the Windows Remote Display Protocol (RDP) 5.1 client is used. Enrollment agent requests cannot be made through a terminal server session.

Certificate Renewal

A certificate renewal request can be made from the web enrollment pages, or it can be configured to occur automatically by configuring a V2 certificate template. The information on the current certificate creates the renewal certificate. New keys can be generated or the existing keys can be renewed. Automatic certificate renewal can occur when the autoenrollment process is triggered and when the certificate has reached 80 percent of its lifetime, or by the certificate renewal period set on the certificate. (The default is six weeks, but it can be changed.) Revoked certificates cannot be automatically renewed. A new manual request is required after a certificate is revoked.

Enrollment can be forced for all V2 autoenrollment certificates by updating the version number of the certificates. The version number is checked during the autoenrollment process, and if the number has changed, the certificate is added to the request list. To force autoenrollment, follow these steps:

1. Add the `Certificates Templates` snap-in to an MMC or open a `Certificates Template` console saved previously.
2. Right-click the template.
3. Choose `Reenroll All Certificate Holders`. It may take 10 minutes or more before a template is updated.

Superceding Certificates

New certificate templates or revised templates can be specified to supercede existing templates. This allows V2 certificates to supercede existing ones. For example, to take advantage of key archival for EFS certificates, a new V2 template can be created and configured to supercede the existing EFS certificates. Likewise, to use autoenrollment to renew certificates, create a V2 certificate template and set it to supercede the existing certificate. A new certificate will be issued. This illustrates using superceding to move users from V1 to V2 certificates; other uses of superceding include the following:

- Changing certificate lifetime
- Changing key size
- Adding extended key use of application policy
- Correcting enrollment policy errors

The Supercede attribute is set in the certificate template on the Superceded page. Clicking the `Add` button displays a list of certificates to select from. Figure 12-22 shows that the new V2 template for EFS will supercede the EFS certificate.

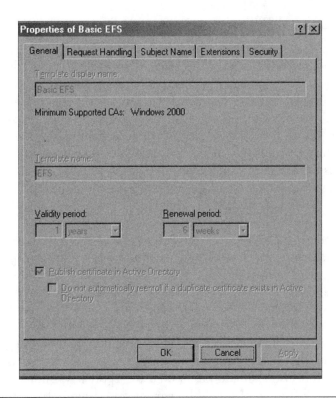

Figure 12-22   A superceded certificate will be replaced by a new template if the new template is configured to do so.

Certificate and Key Recovery and Archival

Certificates can be exported to a file with or without the associated private key. This method is often used to enable the use of a certificate and private key on another computer or as a form of backup. If the certificate and private key are exported, the file can be used to recover the certificate and private key. Additional methods for recovery exist.

Copies of certificates may be stored in the Active Directory. If they are, they may be recovered from the AD. Private keys are not stored in the Active Directory, so recovering a certificate from AD may be useless.

Private keys are stored in the user's profile. If the user has a roaming profile, when she logs on to a new computer, a copy of the profile and keys are downloaded to the computer.

If an EFS recovery agent policy is configured and a recovery agent certificate granted, and the certificates public key is used when a file is encrypted, the recovery agent can recover the file (decrypt it) and deliver it to the owner for encryption using a new key pair. In this case, the original keys are not recovered, but this is not necessary.

Windows Server 2003 Enterprise Edition Enterprise CA can establish key archival. *Key archival* is a new technique that can be used to archive private keys in the CA database. A special key recovery agent must be assigned, and V2 certificates must be used. This process allows the recovery of private keys. The process of establishing key recovery is detailed in Chapter 13.

Exporting Certificate and Private Key   Exporting a certificate and private key provides a simple backup solution. This is especially critical for certificates where creating a new key pair would remove the user's ability, for example, in the case of EFS certificates where key archival is not used. Exporting keys can also create a security issue. If users export certificate and key to a floppy disk, protect it with a weak password, and leave the disk easily available, it is subject to theft and might be used to attack the system and, in the case of EFS, to decrypt sensitive files. Whether users should be allowed to export keys should be a management decision and should be part of your organization's security policy. The ability to export keys can be technically constrained by selecting an attribute on the certificate. To export a certificate, follow these steps:

1. Open the Certificates console.
2. Right-click the certificate that you want to export.
3. Select All Tasks, and then select Export.
4. Click Next on the welcome page.
5. Select Yes, Export The Private Key, select No, Do Not Export The Private Key.
6. Click Next.
7. Select the format from those shown in Figure 12-23, and then click Next. If a format cannot be used, it will be grayed out. Formats and reasons why they might be used are listed in Table 12-4.

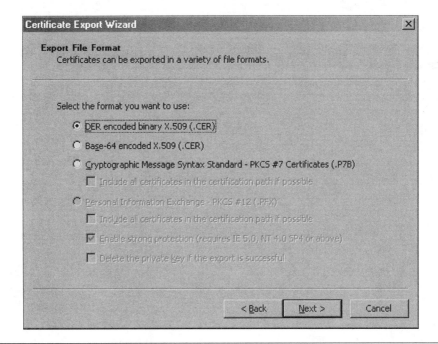

Figure 12-23 Select a file format.

8. Enter a file path and name or browse to a location and enter a file name.
9. Click Next, and then click Finish to export the certificate or certificate and private key.
10. Click OK.

Table 12-4 Certificate Format Uses

Functionality Required	Choose
Platform independence. Interoperability Application requires DER encoding.	DER encoded binary X.509 (.CER)
S/MIME.	BASE-64-encoded X.509 (.CER)
Need for countersignatures associated with signatures, use of signing time and authentication of signing time and message content. Preserves the chain of certificate authorities.	Cryptographic Message Syntax Standard—PKCS #7 Certificates (.P&B)

Table 12-4   Certificate Format Uses Continued

Functionality Required	Choose
Include all certificates in the path.	Cryptographic Message Syntax Standard—PKCS #7 Certificates (.P&B) or
	Personal Information Exchange—PKCS #12 (.PFX)
	and (in both cases)
	Select `Include all certificates in the certification path` if possible.
EFS export. Export of the private key.	Personal Information Exchange—PKCS #12 (.PFX)
Enable strong protection.	Personal Information Exchange—PKCS #12 (.PFX) and check the box `Enable strong protection` (Requires IE 5.0, NT 4.0 SP 4, or above.)
Delete the private key if the export is successful.	Personal Information Exchange—PKCS #12 (.PFX) and check the box `Delete the private key if the export is successful.`

Certificate Chaining and Certificate Revocation

Certificate chaining is the process of completing the path from the end-use certificate back to the root of its trust and includes the validation of each certificate in the chain. The process is carried out by a chaining engine (a process running on the local computer) and includes the following steps:

1. Creating the request list:
   a.) The chaining engine looks in memory and in the certificate cache for recently cached certificates. The location of the cache is the Documents and Settings\username\Local Settings\Temporary Internet Files folder.

b.) The chaining engine examines the certificate stores (trusted root certification authorities, Enterprise Trust, Intermediate Certification Authorities, Third-Party Root Certification Authorities, personal) on the current computer. The engine can be configured to check other stores, such as restricted root, restricted trust, restricted other, and additional stores. Additional stores are stores created by applications. More than one chain can be built when certificates are renewed or if complex cross-certification exists. For example, in a CA hierarchy with one CA, the certificate chain will be two certificates deep: the end certificate and the CA certificate. In Figure 12-24, this type of chain is displayed. Certification paths for actual certificates are displayed in the Certification Path page of a certificate, as shown in Figure 12-25. Figure 12-26 displays the details of the certificate itself. By viewing the Certification Path page and selecting the CA certificate in the path, then clicking View Certificate, you can view the CA certificate, as shown in Figure 12-27, which displays the certificate of the CA. Note how the issuer information in Figure 12-26 matches the subject information of the CA certificate in Figure 12-27. This is the information used to build the certificate chain. If the CA certificate has been renewed, it is possible that two chains will exist, each one using the different CA certificate.

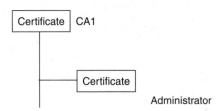

Figure 12-24   A simple certificate chain.

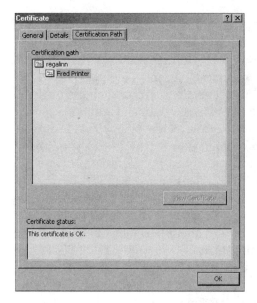

Figure 12-25   The certification path of the Certificate displays its certificate path.

Figure 12-26   The issue information on this certificate will match the subject information on the issuer certificate.

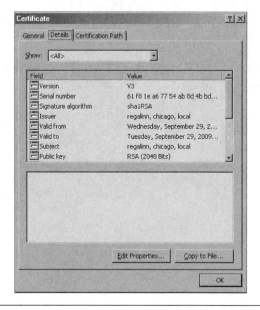

Figure 12-27   The issue information in the certificate in Figure 12-26 will match the subject information on this issuer certificate.

2. Assign Certificate status. Each certificate is assigned a status code based on characteristics such as time valid, revoked, expired, etc. The status is determined during the following processes:

    a.) Revocation checking is performed during chain building in Windows 2000 after the chain is built and, in Windows XP, while it is being built. Windows uses a CRL list as the default mechanism for revocation checking. If the certificate is on the list specified by the certificate, the certificate is noted as revoked. (The CA that signed the certificate must sign the CRL in order for the CRL to be used by the chaining engine.)

    b.) Third-party revocation provided can be registered with CryptoAPI and hence perform other methods of revocation checking, such as OCSP.

    c.) Path Validation. For each chain, *path validation* is the process of finding a valid path from the presented certificate to its root CA. First, the issuing CA is determined, and then the CA that issued the CA a certificate, and so on until a self-signed certificate is reached, the root CA certificate. A *valid certification path* is a leaf, or end-use certificate that chains to a trusted root CA. A certificate can be determined to not be trusted because it is time invalid, does not conform to the x.509 V1–3 standard, information in the certificate is invalid or incomplete, the digital thumbprint and signature fail an integrity check (the certificate has been tampered with or is corrupt), the root CA is not in the Trusted Root Certification Authorities Store, the certificate is not valid for the intended use as identified in a CTL, or the certificate includes a critical extension not understood by the application.

NOTE: Path Validation

During path validation, it is assumed that the application is responsible for validating and understanding an extension and the certificate is not rejected as long as the application does so. However, a CRL will be evaluated for critical extensions and will be rejected by Crypto API if the extension is not recognized.

d.) AKI checking. If the certificate has the Authority Key Identifier (AKI) field defined with the issuer's name and serial number, only certificates that match this information will be identified.

e.) Constraint validation. Possible constraints are checked. Basic constraints serve to identify the certificate as an end-use certificate or a CA certificate and can also limit the path length that is valid. For example, a path length of 0 means the CA can issue only end-use certificates. Name constraints identify namespaces that are permitted to be trusted— for example, a name constraint permitting the tailspintoys.com name space would validate certificates from tailspintoys.com CA but not those provided by a newyork.tailspingtoys.com CA. Policy constraints allow specification of when and where a certificate may be issued. Policies are implemented using OIDs. A certificate without the proper OID would not be considered valid, for example. Application constraints also use OIDs but identify whether the certificate can be used for a specific function in an application. For example, spending levels in accounts payable might be technically constrained using an application constraint. Different OIDs would identify spending limits. If a clerk attempted to purchase something over her spending level, the certificate would be rejected.

NOTE: Windows 2000 Doesn't Check All Constraints
Windows Server 2003 and Windows XP check all constraints. Windows 2000 only checks Basic constraints.

---

3. Each chain is assigned a status based on the status of the certificates in the chain.
4. The chains are ordered based on their status.
5. The chains are evaluated to determine if a valid path is found. If it is, the certificate can be accepted. If it is not, the certificate is rejected.

How Are Certificate Stores Populated?

One place that the certificate chaining engine looks for certificates is the certificate stores. How are the certificate stores populated?

- Certificates defined in Group Policy are added when the computer joins the domain and are refreshed every 8 hours. The root CA certificates from the Computer Configuration\Windows Settings, Security Settings\Public Key Policies, Trusted Root Certification Authorities Policy, and any other certificate in Group Policy are downloaded.

- NTAuth store certificates are added to the local machine store, and the NTAuth store is rechecked every 8 hours for new certificates.

- If the personal certificate store contains a certificate not issued by these CAs, then the root CA certificate from that chain will be downloaded from the AIA extension of the certificate if the certificate is not revoked or expired.

- Certificates referenced by cross-certificates are downloaded every 8 hours.

- If the Update Root Certificates component is added, then updated root certificates are added periodically as well.

- During certificate enrollment and certificate validation, all subordinate and root CA certificates are downloaded to the computer or user personal store.

Cross-Certification and Qualified Subordination

Qualified Subordination is a characteristic of Windows Server 2003 CAs that allows cross-certification of CA certificates and provides precise control of certificate trusts. *Cross-certification* is the process of creating a certificate trust between two CA hierarchies. *Certificate trusts* are created when cross-certification certificates from two different CA hierarchies are traded. If a certificate trust is created, certificates from either CA hierarchy can be trusted if the root CA certificate of one hierarchy is available.

For example, if two companies want to share documents between researchers at both companies, they must implement some form of authentication to make sure only the right individuals can access the documents. If each company has implemented PKI using their own in-house root CA, certificates from each may be presented as part of the authentication process. Because neither company has a copy of the root

CA certificate of the other, how can trust be established? It's always possible to provide a copy of the root CA certificate from each company to the other, and then import that certificate into the certificate stores of any computer in the extra net. This may be unwieldy if many computers must import the CA certificate and if Group Policy cannot be used. If each CA hierarchy provides a cross-certification certificate to the other, holders of either root CA certificate will trust certificates from either CA hierarchy.

In addition to providing basic trust, the trust can be constrained by rules established when the certificates are created. For example, certificates from a specific CA can be excluded from the trust, or specific certificate purposes can be trusted or not trusted. If, for example, IPSec certificate purpose was excluded from the trust, a computer certificate that can be used for domain authentication and for IPSec will be restricted and will only be useful for domain authentication.

Two typical places for installing the cross-certification certificate are with the root CA, as shown in Figure 12-28, and with a subordinate CA, as shown in Figure 12-29. When cross-certification is created at the root, and the certificate trust is not restricted by qualified subordination, every certificate issued by one CA is trusted by the other. On the other hand, if the trust is created at a subordinate CA level and is not restricted, only the certificates issued from the subordinate CA or its children are trusted by the other CA. In Figure 12-29, the CAs trusted by Regalinn are circled in the Motorinn Hierarchy.

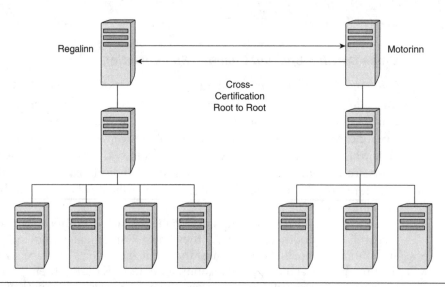

Figure 12-28   Cross-certification at the root extends trust throughout the hierarchy.

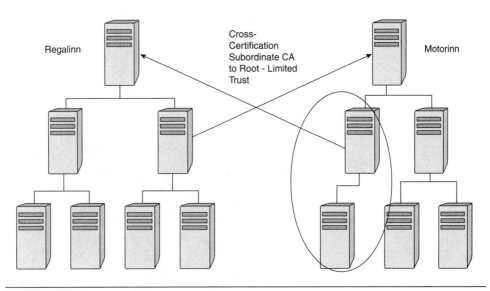

Figure 12-29   Trust at the subordinate CA level extends trust from the subordinate CA and below.

Cross-certification only creates a trust relationship between two CA hierarchies. This trust is not transitive. That is, if CA hierarchy A and CA hierarchy B are cross-certified, and CA hierarchy B and CA hierarchy C are cross-certified, there is no trust relationship between CA hierarchy A and CA hierarchy C. You can create that trust relationship by cross-certifying A and C. If many CA hierarchies are involved, this can become difficult to manage. Sometimes, something more is needed. When multiple trust relationships between multiple CA hierarchies are required, a bridge CA can be used.

Bridge CA   A *bridge CA* provides an easy way of creating trust relationships between multiple CA hierarchies. In this scenario, a CA serves as the managing hub or bridge for the trust relationships, as illustrated in Figure 12-30. All that is necessary is for each CA hierarchy to cross-certify with the bridge CA. This type of trust is not meant to combine multiple unrelated organizations with each other. However, it is extremely useful for large organizations composed of independent entities, such as a decentralized governmental organization.

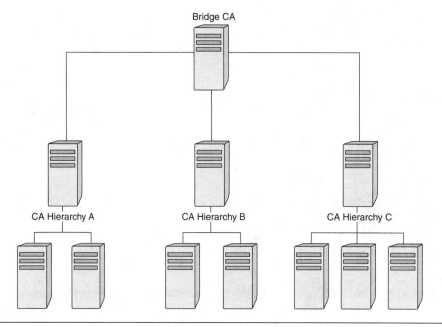

Figure 12-30   A bridge CA can establish trust relations between multiple CAs.

Summary

Many components and processes must be understood to implement a secure and successful PKI. Part of the planning process should include the development of a certificate practice policy that defines how the PKI will be used. This can ensure that the PKI remains worthy of the trust placed in it. The first step in creating a secure PKI is understanding the basic information described in this chapter. The second step is the creation of a test PKI, which is covered in Chapter 13.

Implementing a Secure PKI

Before you can implement public key infrastructure (PKI), you must educate yourself and staff on the technology, plan implementation, and develop policies. After all this, implementation is still a complicated process. Product documentation and many excellent articles on the Microsoft web site explain implementation. However, it is easy to get lost in the details. Installing a simple two-tier CA hierarchy with appropriate security is not a daunting task, yet the first time you must wade through all the details can be confusing.

Implementing a two-tier hierarchy is described in the following sections. First, instructions for installing and configuring a secure, offline root CA are provided, and then steps for installing and configuring a single enterprise subordinate CA are detailed. In this example, a Windows Server 2003 Enterprise Edition member server is used as the subordinate CA so that examples of configuring V2 templates can also be discussed. If you want to use a Windows Server 2003 Standard Edition member server as the subordinate CA, you may; however, V2 templates will not be available. The Windows Server 2003 forest must also be in Windows Server 2003 functional mode to customize the templates.

Your PKI implementation may be more complicated. You may decide or require another tier. You may install multiple issuing CAs, and you may need to provide cross-certification with another hierarchy. You can use the information in this chapter to begin. In addition to providing best practices for a simple two-tier hierarchy, many of these practices can scale to a larger implementation. This example can also serve as a simple test PKI implementation in which to learn how to deploy an offline root CA, configure an Enterprise CA, and work with templates.

The following steps are part of the implementation plan:

1. Use an offline root CA and provide extra physical protection for it.
2. Configure the offline root CA to support the hierarchy.
3. Install an enterprise subordinate CA.
4. Configure the subordinate CA to support users.
5. Customize templates.

Install an Offline Root CA

An offline root CA should be used to anchor the hierarchy. The offline root CA is easier to protect because it can be locked in a vault or another secure area. It needs no connection to the network. The offline root CA can be restricted to issuing subordinate CA certificates, a process that can easily be manually done. Little maintenance is required, and you can limit the number of people who have contact with it.

The offline root CA, however, must be carefully prepared and installed, or additional CAs and the PKI may not function correctly. To correctly install a root CA, prepare the server and then perform the CA installation offline.

Server Preparation

The server should be prepared before installing certificate services. Specifically:

- The server should be in a secure area. If the area cannot be locked, you should not leave the server during installation.
- The server should not be connected to any network. Ever.
- The installation of the standalone Windows Server 2003 should be done on a newly NTFS-formatted drive.
- The latest service pack and security patches should be installed.
- The server time should be manually synchronized with the Active Directory network.
- A capolicy.inf file should be prepared and added to the %systemroot% folder on the server.

Most of these steps are well known and well documented. Two topics require a little more explanation: time synchronization and the use of a capolicy.inf file.

Manually Synchronize the Time

Synchronizing the standalone server time may seem like an unusual step. After all, the server will not be connected to the network. Authentication will be local, and there will never be any drive mapping or any obvious reason to be concerned about time. However, every certificate has a *validity period*. A certificate's validity period is the time between the time at which it becomes valid for the use it has been configured for (the Valid From date), and a time at which it is no longer valid (the Valid To date). Typically, the Valid From date is the date on which the certificate is issued, and the Valid To date is calculated by adding the certificate lifetime to the Valid To date.

If the clock of the standalone CA is not manually synchronized with the Active Directory time, the certificates may be of no use at all. This is probably rather unlikely because it is doubtful that the clock setting during installation would be off by days or years. It is more likely that the clock is off perhaps by an hour or so, or perhaps by a few minutes. Small differences in time may not cause any problems, especially because the only certificates that will be issued from the offline CA will be other CA certificates. A CA certificate request from an offline CA must be carried on a floppy or other removable media to the offline CA and the issued certificate returned to the subordinate CA in the same manner. If the clocks on the offline CA and the subordinate CA differ by a few minutes, that amount of time may elapse before the certificate is installed. If, however, the time on the offline CA is ahead of the time on the subordinate CA, and an attempt to install the certificate is made before the subordinate CA catches up, the certificate will be rejected as invalid. More information on this phenomenon is provided in the sidebar "Time Differences" later in this chapter.

Use a Capolicy.inf File

The capolicy.inf file, if present, is read during the CA installation and during the CA certificate renewal, and the parameters set in the file are applied. It is not necessary to use a capolicy.inf file to install a CA, but a capolicy.inf file must be used when installing an offline root CA. The file is used to ensure that the root CA certificate is produced with an empty Authority Information Access (AIA) and Certificate Revocation List (CRL) Distribution Point (CDP) location. If you do not use the file for this purpose, the root CA certificate will list AIA and CDP locations on the local computer. Because the computer will always be offline, it will be impossible for applications and clients to locate the CDP, and revocation checks will fail. Likewise, applications and clients might need to download a copy of the AIA and fail.

The AIA and CDP locations must still be present in certificates that the offline root CA will issue, but you will configure the location after the CA is installed but before it issues any certificates. You will enter an available network location in the properties of the CA and then manually place a copy of the root CA certificate and the CDP at these network locations. This preparation will allow revocation checking to occur and will make available a copy of the root CA certificate.

Many sections and parameters can be placed in the capolicy.inf file; however, to keep the AIA and CDP locations from being added to the root CA certificate, only a couple are necessary. Two sets of data in the file are important. First, several renewal items are listed. These should match their counterparts entered during the CA installation. They will be used during CA certificate renewal. Second, the file is configured to prevent the AIA and CDP entries in the root CA certificate. Table 13-1 describes each entry in the file.

NOTE: BEST PRACTICES

The example file given here comes from examples provided in the document "Best Practices for Implementing a Windows Server 2003 Public Key Infrastructure," which can be downloaded from `http://www.microsoft.com/technet/prodtechnol/windowsserver2003/technologies/security/ws3pkibp.mspx`.

Table 13-1 capolicy.inf

Setting	Description
`[version]`	Section head.
`Signature= "$Windows NT$"`	Identifies operating system version.
`[Certsrv_Server]`	Section head.
`RenewalKeyLength=4096`	The key length for the CA keys. Leave the capolicy.inf file on the root server, and the key length will remain the same when the certificate is renewed. The key length can be changed at renewal but should never be smaller than the current key length. If changing the key length, you should also ensure that applications are able to use the larger key size.

Setting	Description
`RenewalValidityPeriod=Years`	The validity period for a CA certificate is calculated in years.
`RenewalValidityPeriodUnits =20`	The validity period units determine the number of years.
`[CRLDistributionPoint]`	Section title. By entering this section title and leaving the section blank, no CDP will be set for the root CA certificate.
`[AuthorityInformationAccess]`	Section title. By entering this section title and leaving the section blank, no AIA will be set for the root CA certificate.

Create the capolicy.inf File

To create the basic file, follow these steps:

1. Create the file in Notepad and enter the following information:
   ```
   [version]
   Signature= "$Windows NT$" [Certsrv_Server]
   RenewalKeyLength=4096
   RenewalValidityPeriod=Years
   RenewalValidityPeriodUnits=20
   [CRLDistributionPoint]
   [AuthorityInformationAccess]
   ```
2. Save the file to the `%systemroot%` of the computer on which the CA will be installed.

Installations Instructions for an Offline Root CA

The following instructions assume an Active Directory domain, tailspintoys.com with established servers and domain controllers. An additional computer, Computer1, is installed as previously detailed (including the addition of a capolicy.inf file). It will serve as the root CA. Additional sections in this chapter further configure the CA and detail the installation of a subordinate Enterprise CA:

1. Log on as a local administrator of the server.
2. Open `Start`, `Settings`, `Control Panel`, `Add or Remove Programs`, `Add/Remove Windows Components`.
3. Select the `Windows Certificate Services` check box.

4. Click Yes when prompted, as shown in Figure 13-1, and then click Next. Once a computer takes on the role of CA, you cannot change its name or domain membership. Because this computer will be kept separate from the network anyway, it should not be a domain member, and its name should be established before certificate services are installed.

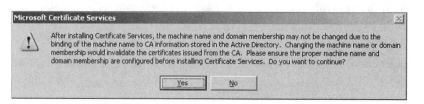

Figure 13-1   The computer name cannot be changed after installation.

5. Click Details and view the components Certificate Services CA and Certificate Services Web Enrollment Support (see Figure 13-2). Click OK, and then click Next. Although IIS will not be installed on this computer, and web services won't be used for certificate enrollment, you cannot delete the Web Enrollment Support component. This component creates the file structure necessary to support web-based certificate requests and meets the needs of default locations for CDP and AIA.

6. Click OK and then click Next.

7. Select stand-alone root CA. (While an Enterprise Root CA could be implemented on a member server, it would then be integrated with Active Directory. It would not be advisable to then remove that computer from the network. Removing such a computer permanently from the network would mean excess processing and errors as the member server keeps trying to find its domain controller.)

8. Select the Use Custom Settings To Generate The Key Pair And CA Certificate check box and click Next.

9. Leave the default Cryptographic Service Provider(CSP)– Microsoft Strong Cryptographic Provider. Vendors provide special CSPs so that their devices will work with certificate services. By default, three third-party CSPs (Schlumberger cryptographic service provider, Infinean SICRYPT Base Smart Card CSP, and Gemplus GemSAFE card CSP v1.0) are available, but vendor CSPs can be added as needed.

10. Leave the default integrity algorithm as the SHA-1 hash algorithm.

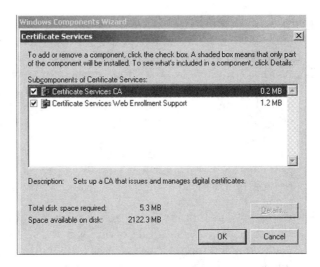

Figure 13-2   It is not necessary to install IIS on the offline root CA, but the web component parts are installed.

11. Select a 4096-bit key, as shown in Figure 13-3. The default key size is 2049, but a longer key length is advised. In general, you must weigh the increased security of a larger key with the longer time that will be taken when the key is used for encryption or signature. The root CA will only issue subordinate CA certificates, and the time difference taken by a 4096-bit key versus that of a 2049-bit key is insignificant when it is used only a few times.

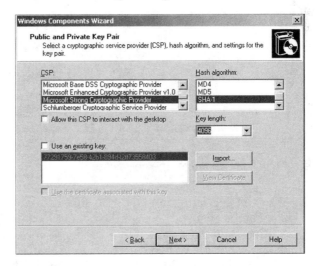

Figure 13-3   The default settings for CSP, hash algorithm, and key size can be changed.

12. Note that there is an option to use an existing key pair, and then click Next. If you need to recover or rebuild a CA, you can install the CA and import an existing key pair.

13. Enter a common name for the certification authority; the name rootA is used here for ease of identification in later exercises. In a production environment, use a name that identifies the certificate. The common name is the name that will be visible, for example, in the Trusted Root Certification Authorities store. The CA common name does not have to be the same as the computer name. However, the common name, validity period, location of the certificate database, log, and shared folder cannot be changed after setup.

14. Enter 20 years for the validity period, as shown in Figure 13-4, and click Next. The default time period is 5 years. The time period is made longer simply for convenience. If there is some reason to renew the certificate and generate new keys before that time period, it can easily be done. Certificates issued by CAs in the hierarchy cannot have a longer validity period than the CA certificate.

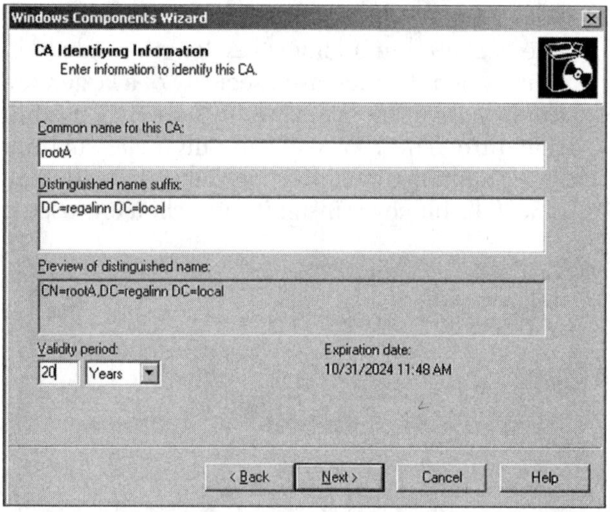

Figure 13-4   Select a validity period for the certificate.

15. After the keys are generated, the storage location for the database can be changed. Accept the default location for the storage locations and click Next. On a production system, it is a good idea to have at least two hard disk drives and place the database log on a different drive than the database. This may improve performance.

16. Wait while the system configures the CA components, and then click OK at the IIS warning message. A message will note that IIS is not installed and that Certificate Services Web Enrollment will not be available until IIS is installed. IIS is not needed on the root CA. There will not be many requests for subordinate CAs, and those can be managed manually from the Certification Authority console. (The CA will not be online; therefore, any web-based requests would be local, and the extra service is just not necessary.)

17. If prompted, enter or browse to the path for the Windows Server 2003 installation disk.

18. When installation is finished, click Finish.

19. Go to Start, Administrative Tools, Certification Authority and note that the CA service has started, as evidenced by a green check mark on the CA.

20. Select File, Exit to close the Certification Authority console.

Standalone Root CA Post Installation Configuration

After installation, but before it is used to issue subordinate CA certificates, the root CA keys should be archived and the CA configured.

Back Up the CA Keys

CA keys can be backed up from the CA console, from the local machine's certificate stores console, or by using the certutil command. To do so, export a copy of the root CA certificate and include a copy of the private key. The result can be placed on a floppy disk or other removable media and must be protected.

Use certutil to Back Up CA Keys

Use the certutil command to back up CA keys. It can also be used to restore them. To back up the keys for the rootA offline root CA using the password tiab34T* to a PKCS #12 (.pfx) format file and place it on a floppy diskette in the A drive, use this command:

```
Certutil -backupkey -config name_of_server\rootA -p tiab34T*Y
A:
```

Figure 13-5 shows the command and result.

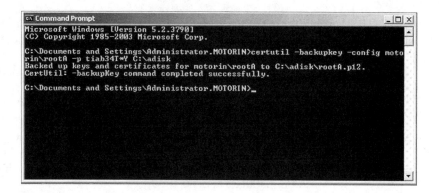

Figure 13-5 Use certutil to back up the keys.

Use the Certificates Console to Back Up CA keys

To use the local machine's certificate store, follow these steps:

1. Open an MMC console.
2. Click the File menu and select Add/Remove Snap-in.
3. Click Add, and then select Certificates from the Add Stand-alone Snap-in dialog.
4. Click Add, select Computer Account, click Next, click Finish, Close, and then click OK.
5. Expand the Certificates (Local Computer), Personal folder and then select the Certificates folder.
6. In the detail pane, right-click the CA certificate and select All Tasks, Export.
7. Click Next on the Welcome to the Certificate Export Wizard page.
8. Select Yes, export the private key, as shown in Figure 13-6, and then click Next.
9. Do not change the Export File Format page, as shown in Figure 13-7; instead, click Next.

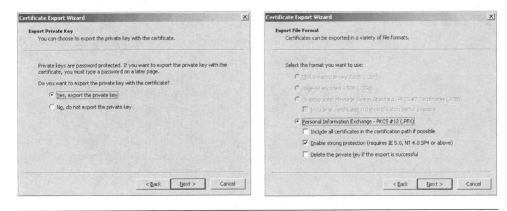

Figure 13-6 Export the private key when backing up the CA keys.

Figure 13-7 The Enable Strong Protection... setting ensures that the keys are password protected.

10. Enter and confirm a password. This password helps protect the keys. It must be entered before the keys can be imported into a certificate store. A maximum 32-character password can be used. The CA will be compromised if unauthorized individuals obtain the keys. The media should also be protected, and a strong password should be used. Because you may never have to use the password, it is unlikely that you will remember it, and you might not be present when it's needed. To ensure key recoverability, write down the password and store it in a safe place, separate from the media on which the key file exists.
11. Browse to the location for file storage, enter a file name, and click Next, and then click Finish.
12. If the export is successful, click the OK button.

Configure CDP and AIA on the Root CA

The root CA certificate will not include an AIA or CDP location. The Root CA should provide, however, an AIA and CDP location. This will be added to all the certificates that it issues. This is necessary primarily so that clients can do certificate validity processing by validating the signature of the root CA and locating the root CA CRL. The first step is to confirm that the root CA certificate does not include a CDP or AIA. Next, configure CDP and AIA network location information on the root CA.

Confirm No AIA or CDP

To confirm that the root CA certificate does not include an AIA or CDP location, follow these steps:

1. Open the `Certification Authority` console.
2. Right-click the CA and select `Properties`.
3. Click the `View Certificate` button on the `General` page.
4. Click the `Details` page of the certificate. Scroll down through the details, as shown in Figure 13-8, and confirm that the certificate does not include the `CRL Distribution Points` or `Authority Information Access` fields.
5. Click `OK` to close the certificate.

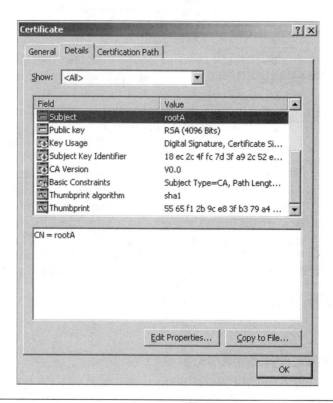

Figure 13-8   Always verify that the root CA certificate does not include the AIA and CDP field.

Configure Network Locations for CDP and AIA on the Root CA

For certificates issued by the CA to contain CDP and AIA locations, you must add those locations to the Extension Property page of the CA properties.

TIP: Syntax for AIA and CDP Extensions

The syntax for the AIA and CDP extensions is not well displayed in the interface. Worse, if you make an error, you must delete the error and re-enter the entire path. It's best if you have reviewed the syntax before attempting to create these paths. The article "Windows 2000 Certificate Servers" provides the syntax; this article is at

`http://www.microsoft.com/technet/prodtechnol/windows2000serv/`
`deploy/depopt/2000cert.mspx`.

---

1. If the property pages for the CA are not open, open the Certification Authority console and select the certification authority by clicking the CA.
2. Select `Properties` from the `Action` menu.
3. Click the `Extension` tab, click the `Select Extension` drop-down box, and then click `Authority Information Access (AIA)`. AIA specifies the location where clients may download a copy of the CA certificate. The AIA default location is on the CA computer. Because this CA will be offline, you must change the publication location of the AIA to the network so that it is accessible by clients. This must be done before certificates are issued because the AIA location is published on the certificate.
4. Note the syntax of the configured AIA extension locations. Click `Add` and enter the new web location. The following location (also shown in Figure 13-9) is where the certificate only (not the certificate and related private key) will be stored on a chicago.local server. In the URL, the enclosed variables `<CaName>` and `<CertificateName>` will be interpreted as rootA:
`http://chicago.local/CertEnroll/regalin_<CaName>`
`<CertificateName>.crt`

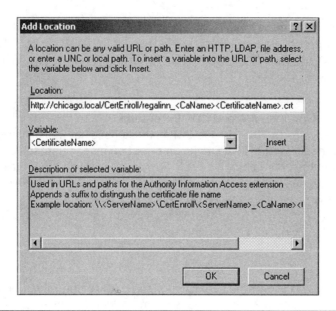

Figure 13-9   Modifying the AIA publication location URL.

5. When complete, click OK.
6. On the Extensions page, which is shown in Figure 3-10, make sure the new URL is selected and click the Include in the AIA extension of issued certificates check box. Do the same for the new file location if it is created. Don't forget this step! The location of the AIA must be available, and for it to be used, the information must be published on the certificate.
7. Click the default URL for the location of the AIA, the one pointing to a local IIS server, and click Remove.
8. Note the default location where you can find a copy of the CA certificate to copy to this location on the IIS server on the CA computer. The default location is `<systemroot>\System32\CertSrv\CertEnroll\motorin_rootA.crt`.
9. If desired, note the syntax for the file location for AIA and create a file location where the root CA certificate may be located. The following syntax is used for Tailspin Toys:

   `File://\regalin.chicago.local\CertSrv\CertEnroll\<CAName><CertificateName>.crt`

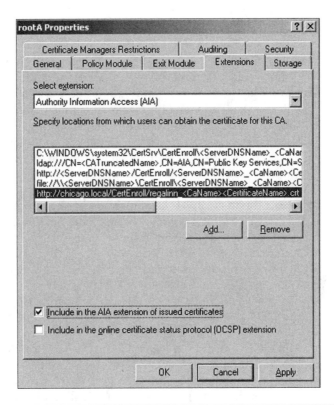

Figure 13-10   Check the Include instruction.

10. Click the Add button to add an LDAP location. The root CA certificate should be made available in the Active Directory. Don't forget to publish the certificate in the Active Directory. Use this syntax:

```
ldap:///CN=rootA,CN=AIA,CN=Public Key Services,CN=Ser-
vices, CN=Configuration,DC=chicago,DC=local?cACertifi-
cate?base?objectclass=certificationAuthority
```

11. Select the new LDAP entry and check the box Include in the AIA extension of issued certificates.

12. Select the default LDAP location and ensure that the Include in the AIA extension of issued certificates check box is not selected. The default LDAP location on a standalone server that is not a member server will not have this item checked, as it makes no sense for that server. (The root CA will not be available to the network, so publishing the local file location for the root certificate is unnecessary.)

13. In the `Select extension` drop-down box, select the extension CRL Distribution Point (CDP).

14. Select the LDAP location and make sure no boxes are checked. Again, no LDAP directory is available to a standalone server.

15. Click the `Add` button and add a new LDAP path for the chicago.local domain. Later, you'll publish this information to the directory. The syntax for the `ldap` entry is as follows:

    ```
    ldap:///CN=roota,CN=regalinn,CN=CDP,CN=Public Key
    Services,CN=Services,CN=Configuration,DC=chicago,DC=lo
    cal?certificateRevocatinoalLilst?base?objectlass=cRLD-
    istributionPoint
    ```

16. Select the new LDAP location and check the boxes `Include in all CRLs`, `Specifies where to publish in the Active Directory when publishing manually`, and `Include in the CDP Extension of Issued Certificates`.

17. Select the file location and click `Include in the CDP extension of issued certificates` to deselect it. The root CA will not be accessible to computers, so publishing the file location in the CDP extension of certificates is useless. The `Publish CRLs to this location` check box should remain checked. The published CRL must be retrieved from this location in order to publish it on the network where it can be located.

18. Click `Add` and enter a new `http` location. A new `http` CDP location must be added because the CA will not be online. The new CDP must be at an online location. Use this syntax:

    ```
    http://chicago.local/CertEnroll/<CaName><CRLNameSuf-
    fix><DeltaCRLAllowed>.crl
    ```

19. Click `OK` to return to the `Extensions` page.

20. With the new `http` entry selected, click the `Include in the CDP extension of issued certificates` check box, and then click `OK`.

21. Select the default `http` CRL location, click `Remove`, and then click `OK`.

22. Note that the default location for the publication of the CRL is the same as that for the root certificate. You need to copy both of these files to removable media so that you can make them available for publication to Active Directory and the web site of the CA.

23. Click `Apply` to save settings. Click `No` when asked if you want to stop and restart certificate services at this point.

24. Click the `Policy Module` tab and then click `Properties`.

25. Note, as shown in Figure 13-11, that `Set the certificate request status to pending` is checked. Requests for CA certificates should always be manually approved. Standalone CAs cannot use the Active Directory to authenticate the user and determine if it's OK to issue certificates to users or computers. When certificate requests are marked as "pending," the CA administrator has to approve them.

26. Click `Cancel` to close the `Policy Module` property pages, and then click `OK` to close the root CA property pages.

27. Right-click the `Revoked Certificates` node and select `Properties`.

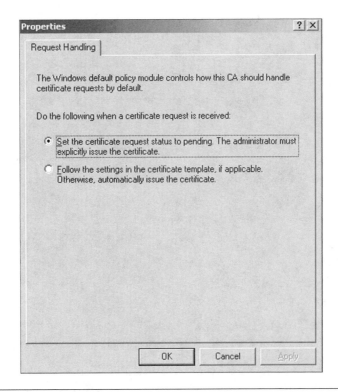

Figure 13-11   The Certificate Manager must approve certificate requests by default on the root CA.

28. In the CRL Publication Interval box, enter 6, use the drop-down box to select Months, and then click OK (see Figure 13-12). The CRL will be published to the file system of the rootA CA. After each publication, you need to copy it and manually ensure it is published to the Active Directory and the network-accessible locations, in this case, on the computer2 web server. The first CRL, an empty CRL, is published to the file system. You can manually publish a CRL at any time and manually locate it at the proper locations. Setting the timeframe at six months means you must manually retrieve each new root CA CRL and manually publish it to the network locations.

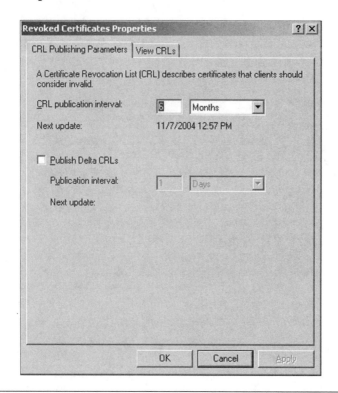

Figure 13-12   Change the CRL Publication period.

29. Click the View CRLs tab to see that the CRL has been published, as shown in Figure 13-13. Then, click the View CRL button and click the Revocation List tab. Note, as shown in Figure 13-14, that a CRL has been published and is empty, as you would expect.

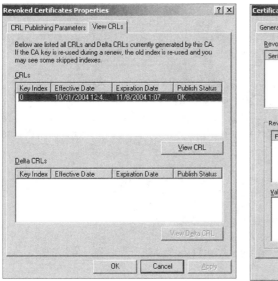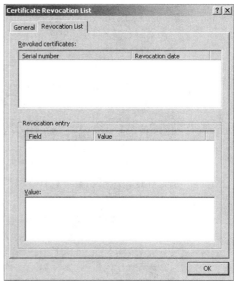

Figure 13-13   A CRL has been published.

Figure 13-14   The CRL is empty, as it should be.

30. Click OK twice to close the Property pages.

31. Stop and start the certificate service.

32. The current CRL does not contain the new http and ldap entries that you have created. Publish a new CRL manually by right-clicking the Revoked Certificates node, selecting All Tasks, and then click Publish.

33. Click File, Exit to close the Certification Authority console.

34. Open Windows Explorer, browse to <windir>\system32\ CertEnroll, and copy the CRL and certificate files (rootA.crl and motorin_rootA.crt files in this example) to removable media.

Add the Root CA Certificate and CRL to Network Locations

The Root CA certificate and CRL must be placed on the web server, and the certificate must be published in the Active Directory. To add them to the web server, simply copy the files roota.pfx (from the backup file) and rootA.crt from the removable media that contains them to the server (in this case, to %windir%\system32\certsrv\certenroll).

To publish them in the Active Directory, use the certutil command.

Publish Certificate and CRL to Active Directory

To add the certificate and CRL for the Tailspin Toys domain root CA to the Active Directory, follow these steps:

1. Log on to regalinn as a member of the Domain Admins group.
2. Publish the CA certificate to Active Directory by using the `certutil` command. This adds the standalone root CA certificate to the Active Directory. It must be accessible to the certificate verifiers:

   ```
   Certutil -dspublish -f motorin_rootA.crt
   ```
3. Publish the CRL to the Active Directory by using the `certutil` command:

   ```
   Certutil -dspublish -f rootA.crl
   ```

Figure 13-15 shows the command and the result.

Figure 13-15   Use certutil to publish the CRL and the certificate.

Distribute the Root CA Certificate Via Group Policy

The Root CA certificate must be available to clients. By publishing the certificate to Active Directory, you make the certificate available; however, for clients to trust certificates issued by a CA in the hierarchy, a copy of the certificate must be in the Trusted Root Certification Authorities certificate store. Users can download a copy of the certificate by using the web enrollment pages; however, this process should be automated by distributing the certificate via Group Policy.

To provide a copy of the root CA certificate to clients and place it in their Trusted Certification Authority store, you must obtain a copy of the certificate and then do the following:

1. Log on as a member of the Domain Admins group.
2. Open a GPO linked to the domain.
3. Select the `Computer Configuration`, `Windows Settings`, `Security Settings`, `Public Key Policies` node.
4. In the details pane, right-click the Trusted Root Certification Authorities policy, click `Import`, and then click `Next`.
5. Browse to the root CA certificate file (a copy is in `<systemroot>\system32\certsrv\certenroll`).
6. Select the file, click `Open`, and then click `Next`.
7. Click `Place All Certificates in the Following Store`, select the Trusted Root Certification Authorities store, and then click `Next`.
8. Review the summary and click `Finish`.
9. In the GPO, note that the certificate is now listed.

Configure Auditing on the Root CA

By default, some CA errors will be recorded in the application log. However, to ensure that the details required to audit the CA operation are recorded, configure CA auditing for the root CA. This is a two-step process. For many of the audit functions to work, Object auditing for the computer must be turned on. For audit records to be created, auditing must be configured in the CA properties. Enable other local auditing to meet your security policy. The following example provides extensive audit trails of activity on the CA.

A security log review process should be established for CAs. Collection of audit records is an exercise in futility if records are not reviewed.

Enable Auditing for the Local Computer

To turn on auditing for the local computer, use the Local Security Policy:

1. Log on to the root CA computer `Administrative Tools`, `Local Security Policy` console. On a standalone computer, object auditing must be enabled locally. Computer accounts for CAs that are member servers should be in their own OU, and a GPO can be used to turn on object auditing for all Enterprise CAs.
2. Browse to `Local Policies`, `Audit Policy`.

3. Double-click on `Audit Account Logon Events` and click the `Failure` box to select it. (The `Success` box is already selected.) Click `OK`.

4. Repeat for the `Audit Logon Events` category.

5. Open `Audit Account Management`, select `Success` and `Failure`, and then click `OK`.

6. Repeat for `Audit Object Access`, `Audit Policy Change`, `Audit Privilege Use`, and `Audit System Events`. It is critical to monitor all CA operations. Changes also need to be made to the event log policy to accommodate the collection of events and ensure the retention of logs.

7. Close the `Local Security Policy`.

8. Open the `Start`, `Administrative Tools`, `Event Viewer` console.

9. Right-click the `Security` node and select `Properties`.

10. Note the default log size and select the `Do Not Overwrite Events (Clear Log Manually)` button to select it. Establish requirements for the security log file. No audit policy is complete without specifying parameters for the management of the security log file. Even though the initial project is small, auditing settings will collect extensive information. The size of the log should be set large and monitored for growth. Before the project is expanded, size history should be evaluated and a larger file designated to ensure adequate space.

11. Click `OK` to close the property pages and then close the Event Viewer console.

Configure CA Auditing

Specific auditing choices can be made in the properties pages of the CA:

1. Open the `Certification Authority` console, right-click the CA, and then select `Properties`.

2. Select the `Auditing` page.

3. Select all the audit events by checking all the event boxes (see Figure 3-16). Note the message when the `Start and Stop Certificate Services` selection is made. It indicates that a cryptographic hash is made of the database when the service is stopped or started and warns of a time delay. This could become a performance issue for issuing CAs; however, the database will not be large on the root CA, and the root CA will not often be stopped and started again.

4. Click `OK`.

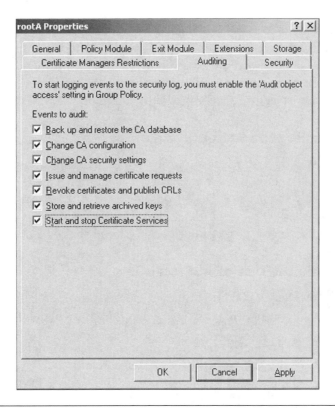

Figure 13-16   Selecting CA audit events to monitor.

Install and Configure a Subordinate CA

After the root CA is prepared, the subordinate CA must be installed. The following example installs and configures an enterprise subordinate CA. A standalone subordinate CA could also be installed but would not have the flexibility that an Enterprise CA has. In this example, the subordinate CA of the root CA will be the issuing CA for chicago.local. However, best practices indicate that a middle layer of intermediary subordinate CAs, which may or may not be kept offline, should be created. This layer provides flexibility, especially when organizations are large, when organizations anticipate cross-certification with partner CA hierarchies, or when the certificate usage will be large. However, it is not necessary, especially for smaller organizations, and providing instructions for the configuration of this layer would add little to this chapter. If you require a broader CA hierarchy, extensive information is available in the "Best Practices for Implementing a Windows Server 2003 Public Key Infrastructure" paper previously mentioned in this chapter.

Installing the Subordinate CA

To install the enterprise subordinate CA, a certificate request file must be generated on the subordinate CA computer. This request is used to manually obtain a certificate from the root CA. The certificate must then be installed on the subordinate CA. If the subordinate CA will also perform the Registration Authority role, IIS must also be installed.

Enable the Use of ASP on IIS

Windows Server 2003 IIS installs in a locked down configuration. You must enable the use of ASP pages for the CA Web Enrollment pages to work:

1. Open the Internet Information Services Manager console.
2. Select the Web Services Extension folder.
3. Right-click the ASP pages button and select Properties.
4. Select the Requires Files page.
5. Select the file asp.dll and click Allow.
6. Confirm that ASP extensions are now "Allowed," as shown in Figure 13-17.

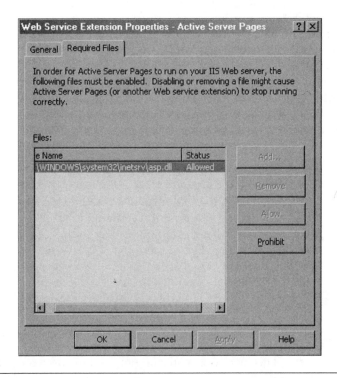

Figure 13-17   Confirm that ASP pages may be used on the CA web server.

Start the Installation

The first step of the subordinate CA installation adds the files and registry keys and creates the certificate request file. If the CA that will provide the certificate is online, the CA certificate can be requested online, but that is not the case with the root CA. To start the installation and obtain a certificate request file, follow these steps:

1. Log onto the subordinate CA server computer regalinn as a member of the Domain Admin group.
2. Go to `Start`, `Settings`, `Control Panel`, `Add or Remove Programs`, `Add/Remove Windows Components`.

TIP: Don't Install the CA on a Domain Controller

In our examples, we've used the DC regalinn, but this is not necessary and, in fact, it is not a good idea to place the subordinate CA on a DC. Placing a CA on a domain controller offers it easy access to Active Directory and hence makes authentication of the certificate requests and publication of the CRL more efficient. However, it may degrade performance in a large enterprise. It will also be more difficult to limit administrative authority on the machine because all members of the Domain Admins group have default administrative control. It is not a good idea to install a CA on a DC.

3. Select the `Windows Certificate Services` check box.
4. At the dialog warning that the computer name cannot be changed and that the computer cannot be joined to or removed from a domain, click `Yes` and then click `Next`.
5. Click `Enterprise subordinate CA`, as shown in Figure 3-18. Intermediate and issuing CAs in a CA hierarchy must be subordinate CAs. When integration with Active Directory is desired, an Enterprise CA role should be selected. However, no rule says intermediate CAs have to be Enterprise CAs. They also can be standalone CAs and receive stronger protection, even offline status. This increases management but improves security.

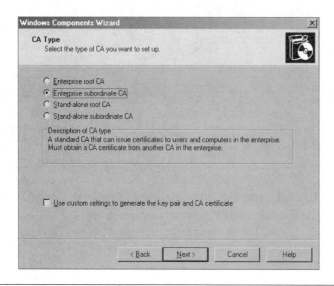

Figure 13-18   Selecting an enterprise subordinate CA.

6. Select the Use custom settings to generate the key pair and CA certificate check box, and then click Next.
7. Change the key length to 4096, and then click Next.
8. Enter the common name for this CA (in our example, SubCA), as shown in Figure 3-19, and then click OK. Note that the Distinguished name suffix, DC=chicago, DC=local is added for you, and the entire Distinguished name, CN=SubCA, DC=chicago, DC=local, is displayed. The figure shows that the validity period is determined by the parent CA.
9. Click Next.

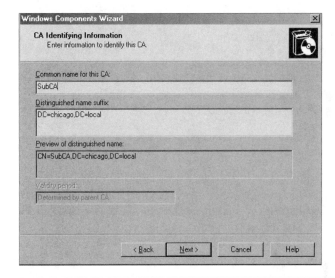

Figure 13-19   Adding the common name for the CA.

NOTE: Keys Are Generated by the Computer
The keys are generated at this point. Note that this computer generates the keys. The certificate will be produced by the root CA, but the keys are created locally on the local CA.

10. Accept the default database and log locations and click Next.
11. Click the Save the request to a file radio button, as shown in Figure 13-20, and then click Next.

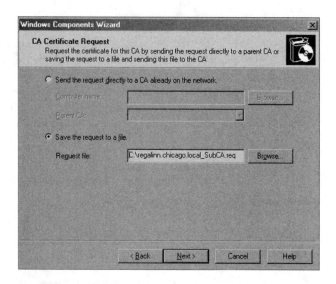

Figure 13-20   Saving the certificate request.

12. When prompted to stop IIS, click Yes. Then, wait while components are configured.
13. Click OK at the message reminding you that the certificate request file must be used to obtain a certificate from the parent CA.
14. Finish the installation of the CA. The installation will complete, but the service will not start until a CA certificate is obtained and installed.
15. Copy the regalinn.chicago.local_subCA.req file to a floppy disk.

Obtain a Root CA Certificate from the Root CA

The certificate request file must be transported manually to the root CA and used to request a CA certificate. The certificate will be added to the Pending folder of the CA:

1. Log on to the root CA as the Administrator.
2. Insert the floppy or other media that includes the certificate request file.
3. Open the Certification Authority console.
4. Right-click the root1, click All Tasks, and then select Submit New Request.
5. Enter the path or browse to A:\ regalinn.chicago.local_ subCA.req and click Open. The request is processed.

6. Select the Pending Requests folder to see the CA certificate request, as shown in Figure 13-21. Note the Request ID, which is 2. The Request ID will also be shown in the Issued Certificates node and is required to request a copy via the command line of the certificate.

7. Right-click the request, click All Tasks, and then select Issue.

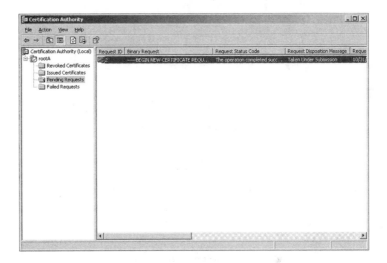

Figure 13-21   Viewing the Certificate Request.

Inspect the Subordinate CA Certificate and Obtain the Request ID

The new subordinate CA certificate should be inspected to ensure the correct CDP and AIA locations are present:

1. In the Certification Authority console, select the Issued Certificates node.

2. In the detail pane, note the Request ID for the subordinate CA certificate. In this example, the Request ID is number 2.

3. Double-click the certificate to view it.

4. Select the Details page and select the CRL Distribution Points field. Confirm that the distribution point is correct in both location and syntax. An example is shown in Figure 13-22.

5. Select the Authorities Information Access field and confirm that the location is correct both in location and syntax. An example is shown in Figure 13-23.

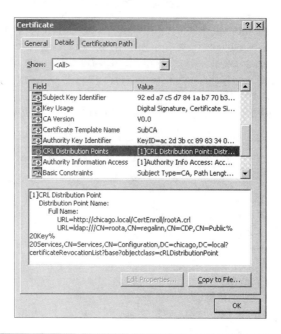

Figure 13-22   Verify the CDP.

6. Click OK to close the certificate view.

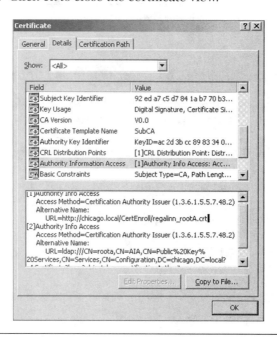

Figure 13-23   Verify the AIA.

Use certreq to Retrieve a Copy of the Certificate

The CA certificate is issued to the root CA database. To complete the installation of the subordinate CA, the certificate must be placed in a file and installed on the subordinate CA. To obtain a copy of the CA certificate for the regalinn CA, use the `certreq` command. The root CA computer, CA name, Request ID, and a file path must be listed:

1. From a command prompt, issue the following command:
   ```
   certreq -retrieve -config motorin\rootA 2 subcert.p7b
   ```

Install the CA Certificate

The CA certificate file is then used to install the CA certificate at the CA console:

1. Log on to the subordinate CA and open the `Certification Authority` console.
2. Right-click the CA node, click `All Tasks`, and then select `Install certificate`.
3. Browse to the floppy disk with certificate file and click `Open`.
4. The CA node should turn green to indicate that the service is started.

NOTE: CA Certificate Automatic Publishing

Because the subordinate Enterprise CA is integrated with Active Directory, the CA certificate will be automatically published to the Active Directory.

Time Differences

Recently, I assisted a client in setting up a PKI in a test network. All went smoothly until we went to install the subordinate CA certificate. The error indicated that the validity period was not correct. When the certificate was inspected, the Valid From time on the certificate was 10 minutes ahead of the current time on the subordinate CA. When the CA certificate is not valid, it cannot be installed. To be valid, the certificate must not be expired, and its Valid From time must already have passed on the CA to which it will be installed. In this case, because the time difference was slight, we simply waited 10 minutes, then tried again and were successful. We did manually synchronize the time on the root CA with the Active Directory.

Configure a Subordinate CA

After the enterprise subordinate CA is installed, but before it issues certificates, the following tasks should be completed:

1. Back up the CA keys.
2. Establish the CRL and delta CRL publishing schedules.
3. Set auditing in the Active Directory and for the CA (see setting auditing for the rootCA).
4. Set permissions on all the templates.
5. Establish role separation.
6. Configure autoenrollment and other Group Policy for PKI.

Steps 1 and 2 can be done in the same manner as they were done for the root CA. Setting auditing in Active Directory is similar to setting auditing in the Local Security Policy. It should be done in the OU in which the CA member server resides. The CRL and delta CRL publishing schedule is set by default, but you need to modify it to fit.

Restrict Certificate Usage by Setting Permissions

Certificate templates are stored in the Active Directory and are managed outside of the CA. Even if some templates will not be used, permissions should be set for all templates. Many certificates can be autoenrolled and others can be requested and obtained without any need to validate the request. If a user or computer can authenticate, and the certificate is not restricted, the certificate will be issued. Restrict certificates by setting the Enroll permission on the template, by removing certificate templates from the CA console, and for V2 templates, by requiring approval before the requested certificate is issued. Information on configuring V2 templates is provided in the section, "Use Custom Templates to Configure Key Archival for EFS."

Set Template Permissions

To set permissions on certificate templates, follow these steps:

1. Open the `Certification Authority` console.
2. Right-click the `Certificate Templates` node and select `Manage`. The `Certificate Templates` console opens.
3. Double-click a template and then select the `Security` tab.
4. Use the object picker to select the group that should have permission to request the template.
5. Select this group and give them the `Read` and `Enroll` permissions.

6. Select Domain Users, or any other group that has been given the Enroll permission and shouldn't have it, and then click the `Enroll` permission to deselect it.

7. Click `OK` to close the certificate.

8. Repeat for each certificate template.

9. Close the `Certificate Templates` console.

Restrict Certificate Usage by Limiting the Certificates the CA Can Issue

Just as the root CA and any intermediary CAs should issue only CA certificates, the issuing CA should issue only those certificates they are authorized to issue. The certificates each CA should issue are a matter of security policy and CA hierarchy design, but no issuing CA should issue CA certificates. Removing the certificates listed in the `Certificates Template` node of the CA can prevent the CA from issuing them. However, any administrator with the proper privileges can add them back in. Removing the certificates, however, will prevent accidental issuance of these certificates. Audit the Enterprise CA to confirm compliance.

Limit the Certificates the CA Can Issue

1. Open the `Certification Authority` console.

2. Select the `Certificate Templates` node.

3. Right-click the subordinate CA certificate template and click `Delete`.

4. Click `Yes` to confirm the deletion.

5. Repeat until all certificates templates that you do not want this CA to issue are removed.

TIP: Templates Are Persistent

Removing templates from the Certificate Templates node does not remove the certificate templates; it simply prevents the CA from issuing certificates of this type.

Establish Role Separation for the Subordinate CA

Role separation is the process of dividing the CA administration duties among several people. To delegate administrative responsibilities, assign permissions on the CA to different custom Windows groups. To prevent an individual account from becoming a member of both groups and thus hinder role separation, enforce role separation.

Role separation can be configured and enforced for all CAs. For the offline root, use local computer groups. For an Enterprise CA, use global computer groups. In an environment where a large number of certificates will be issued, you may want to further divide the role of Certificate Manager. To do so, create multiple Certificate Manager groups. Then, use the Restrict Certificate Manager CA property page to assign each group the responsibility of managing groups of users and computers.

Separating Administrative Roles

1. Use Active Directory Users and Computers and create three new groups: CA Administrator, Certificate ManagerA, and Certificate ManagerB.

2. Add authorized users to the appropriate groups. Make sure that no account is added to both CA Administrators and either of the Certificate Manager groups. Each authorized user account must only be added to one group. Remember, once role separation is enabled, if a user has both privileges, he will not be able to use either.

3. Log on to the CA as the Administrator.

4. Open the `Certification Authority` console.

5. Right-click the CA node and select `Properties`.

6. Select the `Security` tab.

7. Click `Add`, then enter or use the object picker to add the CA Administrator group, and then click `OK`.

8. Select the CA Administrator group and click the `Manage CA` permission.

9. Click `Add`, then enter or use the object picker to add the Certificate Manager group, and then click `OK`.

10. Select the `Certificate Manager` group and click the `Issue and Manage Certificates` permission, as shown in Figure 13-24. This creates the two CA roles. You can name the groups whatever you please when you assign the security permission that provides them the ability to perform the role.

11. Select the local Administrators group and clear the `Issue and Manage Certificates` and `Manage CA` permissions. To provide role separation, the local Administrators group cannot have either permission. If role separation will be enforced, make sure that these permissions are removed before role separation is enforced.

12. On the CA computer, make the new groups members of the local Administrators group.

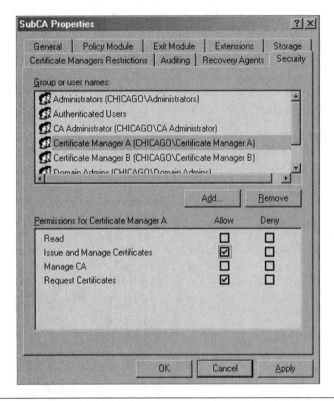

Figure 13-24   Configuring CA roles.

Enforce Role Separation

If role separation is not enforced, an individual account could be a member of both groups and therefore have full control of the CA. To enforce role separation, follow these steps:

1. Open a command prompt on the CA and enter the following command. (The `setreg` switch adds the information to the registry, and `ca\RoleSeparationEnabled` is the registry key that controls role separation. When it has a value of 1, role separation is enabled.)

```
certutil -setreg ca\RoleSeparationEnabled 1
```

2. To verify that role separation has been applied, enter the following command:

```
certutil -getreg ca\RoleSeparationEnabled
```

3. Stop and start certificate services:

```
Net stop certsvc
Net start certsvc
```

TIP: Remove Role Separation

If you have incorrectly enabled role separation and need to remove it, enter the following command:

```
certutil -delreg ca\RoleSeparationEnabled
```

Restrict Certificate Managers

To limit certificate managers by Windows group, follow these steps:

1. Open the Certification Authority console.
2. Right-click the CA and select Properties.
3. Select the Certificate Manager Restrictions page.
4. Select Restrict Certificate Managers.
5. Use the drop-down box to select a Windows group that has been given the permission Issue and Manage Certificates.
6. Use the Add button to add Windows groups that this certificate manager group should have responsibility for, as shown in Figure 13-25.

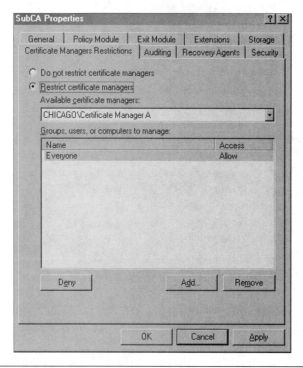

Figure 13-25   Restrict Certificate Managers by assigning them management of specific Windows groups.

Configure Autoenrollment

The process by which a user or computer certificate is issued can be broken into three parts:

- **Request**—A certificate is requested by some manual action, such as by using the web enrollment pages or the certificates snap-in. A certificate request may also be automatically issued when a user or computer authenticates to Active Directory.
- **Issue**—A certificate request is approved, and the certificate is created.
- **Distribution**—The certificate is installed in the certificate stores of the computer.

Autoenrollment, which is the performance of these activities without user intervention can be configured in many cases. In other cases, user intervention is required. Autoenrollment is configured in three places:

- On the Policy property page of the CA, as shown in the configuration sections of both the offline root CA and the enterprise subordinate CA. There are two choices: certificates may require a Certificate Manager approval, or they may be issued automatically. If the CA is a Windows Server 2003 Enterprise Edition Enterprise CA, certificates may be issued according to configuration of the V2 certificate.
- In the certificate template.
- In Group Policy.

For more information on capabilities for `certutil`, check `http://www.microsoft.com/resources/documentation/WindowsServ/ 2003/standard/proddocs/en-us/Default.asp?url=/resources/ documentation/WindowsServ/2003/standard/proddocs/en-us/sag_ cs_certutil2.asp`.

Configure Autoenrollment Using Certificate Templates

The `Certificate Templates` console displays the certificates and basic information about them. A column is provided for autoenrollment status. Each certificate, as shown in Figure 13-26, is marked as either autoenrollment Allowed or autoenrollment Not Allowed. In the figure, the Key Recovery Agent certificate is marked as Allowed. This does not mean the certificate is automatically issued; in this case, it just means that the certificate can be installed without user intervention. Double-click the certificate to view it, and on the `Issuance Requirements` page, note that the box CA Certificate Manager Approval is checked (see Figure 13-27). If an authorized individual requests the certificate, and the CA Certificate Manager issues the certificate, the certificate is automatically installed in the user's Personal certificate store.

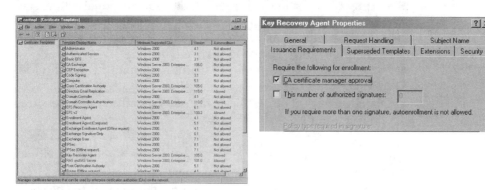

Figure 13-26 Certificate templates are marked autoenrollment Allowed or Not Allowed.

Figure 13-27 The Key Recovery certificate issuance requires CA Certificate Manager approval.

Template configuration sections on several template property pages can have an impact on autoenrollment. Select these settings, as described in Table 13-2, to configure templates for autoenrollment. While only a Windows Server 2003 Enterprise Edition CA or a Windows Server 2003 Datacenter Edition CA can be used to configure the properties of the certificates, autoenrollment is possible based on template defaults and Group Policy configuration no matter which Windows CA is used.

Table 13-2 Autoenrollment Certificate Template Settings

Property Page	Setting	Description
Request Handling	Enroll subject without requiring any user input	Users won't know that a certificate is being installed.

Property Page	Setting	Description
Request Handling	`Prompt the user during enrollment`	The user is notified and may need to take an action, such as inserting a smart card.
Request Handling	`Prompt the user during enrollment and require user input when the private key is used.`	During enrollment and during use, the user must take some action.
Request Handling	`CSP selection`	A number of CSPs that can be used by the template are listed. The user is given a choice.
Subject Name	`Supply in the request`	Disables autoenrollment of certificates based on this template because the user must be prompted to enter a subject name.
Issuance Requirements	`This number of authorized signatures`	If a number greater than 1 is entered, autoenrollment based on this template is disabled. If a 1 is entered, the user must have a valid signing certificate in his certificate store. The valid certificate is specified in the Application Policy and Issuance Policies section of this page.
Issuance Requirements	`Valid existing certificate`	If configured, the subject may not need to supply a valid signing certificate for certificate renewal of a valid certificate based on this template.
General	`Validity period and renewal periods`	Autoenrollment will not renew a certificate unless 20 percent of the certificate lifetime has expired (prevents autoenrollment based on improper configuration—short validity periods that overlap with renewal periods).

Certificate Template Permissions can also impact autoenrollment. The permissions are as follows:

- **Read**—Discover the template in Active Directory.
- **Enroll**—Request and receive the certificate.
- **Full Control**—All actions.
- **Autoenroll**—Automatically enroll. This new permission is only present on v2 templates. Templates customized by duplicating v2 templates will also have the permission. A user must have the Enroll and Autoenroll permission.
- **Write**—Modify templates.

TIP: Check Permissions

The Enterprise CA must also have Enroll permission on the template. Typically, the Enterprise CA gets this permission because it is a member of the Authenticated Users group. If you remove the Enroll permission for the Authenticate Users group, be sure and add the Enterprise CA and provide it permissions if you want autoenrollment to occur.

Configure Autoenrollment in Group Policy

Group Policy PKI settings are configured in the `Computer Configuration`, `Windows Settings`, `Security Settings`, `Public Key Policy` and in the `User Configuration` path. Policies that can be configured are as follows:

- Encrypting File System
- Automatic Certificate Request Setting
- Trusted Root Certification Authority
- Enterprise Trust

At the root of the Public Key Policy folder, in the details pane, there is also an Autoenrollment policy. This policy turns on or turns off autoenrollment, as shown in Figure 13-28, for this GPO. To enable autoenrollment for users and computers, you must enable enrollment in both `User Configuration` and `Computer Configuration` paths.

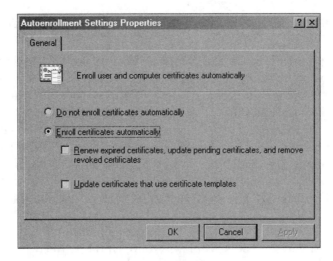

Figure 13-28   Turn autoenrollment on or off for a GPO.

The Automatic Certificate Request Setting policies configure autoenrollment of computer certificates. Right-clicking the policy and selecting New allows the selection of a computer certificate from a wizard page, as shown in Figure 13-29, to automatically enroll authorized computers. Each policy can include only one certificate type.

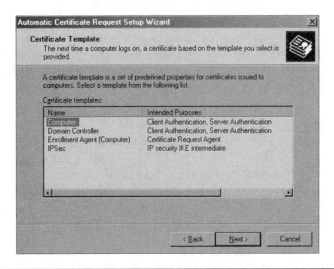

Figure 13-29   Configure autoenrollment of computer certificates.

Use Custom Templates to Configure Key Archival for EFS

Chapter 6, "EFS Basics," detailed the basics of EFS and warned of the problems that damaged and missing private EFS keys can cause. One way to mitigate this risk is to use PKI to replace the use of self-signed EFS certificates with CA-provided EFS certificates and to provide multiple recovery agents. This can be implemented in either a Windows 2000 CA PKI or a Windows Server 2003 PKI. However, in a Windows Server 2003 forest in Windows Server 2003 functional mode, a Windows Server 2003 Enterprise Edition Enterprise CA can also be used to establish key archival. The following steps must be taken:

1. Create a EFS Key Recovery Agent custom template.
2. Create a new Windows group, EFS Key Recovery Agents.
3. Give the new group Read and Enroll permissions on the template.
4. Add users to the new Windows group and have them request Key Recovery Agent Certificates.
5. Enable Key archival on the CA and add the Key Recovery Agent Certificates.
6. Create a new EFS template that allows key archival.
7. Give those users who are allowed EFS permission the Read and Enroll permissions on the new template.
8. Replace or issue new EFS certificates.

Steps 2 and 4 are not described because they represent common administrative tasks. Step 3 is performed during template creation, and step 8 is managed by setting Autoenroll and Supercede permissions while configuring the custom EFS template.

Create Key Recovery Agent Template and Add to the CA

The first step is to create a custom template:

1. Open the `Certificate Templates` console by right-clicking the `Certificate Templates` node in the `Certification Authority` console and clicking `Manage`.
2. Right-click the Key Recovery Agent certificate and select `Duplicate template`.

3. Name the certificate template EFS Key Recovery Agent or some other descriptive name.
4. Click OK.
5. Double-click the template to open it.
6. Select the Issuance Requirements Page and select CA certificate manager approval, as shown in Figure 13-30.

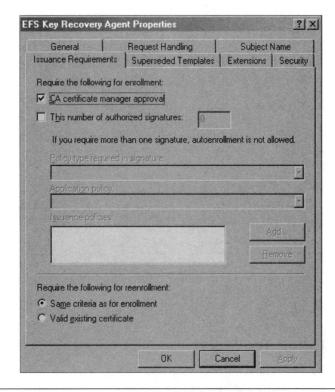

Figure 13-30   Make sure that the Key Recovery Agent Certificate is NOT automatically published.

7. Select the Security page and use the Add button to add the EFS Key Recovery Agent Group, as shown in Figure 13-31.
8. Click OK to return to the console.
9. Select the EFS Recovery Agent group and give it Enroll and Autoenroll permissions.

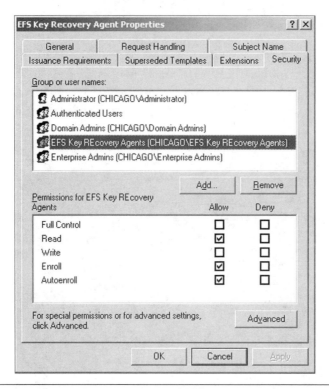

Figure 13-31   Add the Recovery Agent group to the certificate template.

10. From the CA console, right-click the Certificate Templates node, select New, and then Certificate Template to Issue.

11. In the Enable Certificate Templates box, as shown in Figure 13-32, select EFS Key Recovery Agent and click OK.

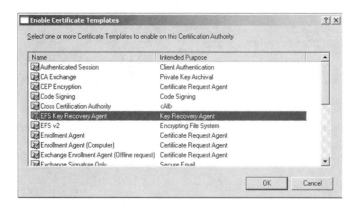

Figure 13-32   Add the EFS Key Recovery Agent certificate to the CA.

Issue Key Recovery Agent Certificates

Before Key archival can be enabled, at least one Key Recovery Agent Certificate must be issued, and a new EFS template must be created that allows key archival:

1. Add the users who have been granted key recovery permission to the new Windows group. A good practice is to create accounts for use as key recovery agents. These accounts are only used to obtain the key recovery certificate

2. Log on using an account that has been given key recovery rights.

3. Open a `Certificates` console by adding the snap-in to an MMC.

4. Right-click the `Personal\Certificates` store and select `All tasks`. Request a new `Certificate`.

5. Click `Next` on the `Request a New Certificate Wizard` welcome page.

6. Select the EFS Key Recovery Agent certificate.

7. Enter a friendly name, click `Next`, and then click `Finish`.

8. Open the `Certification Authority` console.

9. Right-click the `Pending Requests`, and select the certificate just requested.

10. Right-click this certificate and click `Issue`.

Create Key Archival EFS Certificate

Certificates must also be set with the key archival extension. To do so, create a custom template:

1. Open the `Certificate Templates` console by right-clicking the `Certificate Templates` node in the `Certification Authority` console and clicking `Manage`.

2. Right-click the Basic EFS certificate and select `Duplicate template`.

3. On the `General` page, name the certificate template EFS Archival or some other descriptive name.

4. On the `Request Handling` page, select `Archive Subject's Encryption Private Key`, as shown in Figure 13-33, and then click `OK`.

5. On the `Superceded Templates` page, select `Supercede` and select the EFS certificate.

6. Select the `Security` page, add those groups who will be allowed to use EFS, and then give them Read and Enroll permissions on the template.

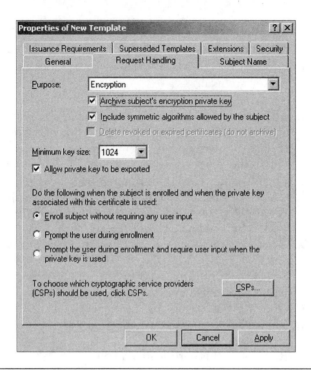

Figure 13-33 The certificate won't be marked as good until the process is complete.

7. Click OK to return to the console.
8. From the CA console, right-click the Certificate Templates node and select New, then Certificate Template to Issue.
9. In the Enable Certificate Templates box, select EFS Archival and click OK.

Enable Key Archival on the CA

Key archival is not enabled by default. To enable it, do the following:

1. Open the Certificate Authorities console.
2. Right-click the CA and select Properties.
3. Select the Recovery Agent page.
4. Select Archive the Key.
5. Enter 1 for the Number of Recovery Agents.
6. In the Key Recovery Agents Certificates box, as shown in Figure 13-34, select an account that has been issued a certificate.

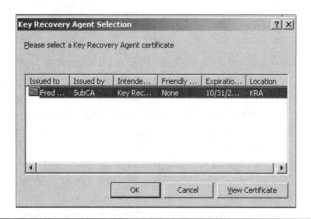

Figure 13-34   Select the Key Recovery Agent certificate.

7. Select the agent and click OK. The certificate will be x'd, as shown in Figure 13-35. After certificate services are restarted, the x will disappear, as shown in Figure 13-36, to indicate that it is accepted and that key archival has been configured. (On the screen, the x is red and the unx'd certificate is green.)

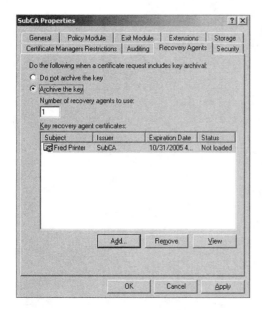

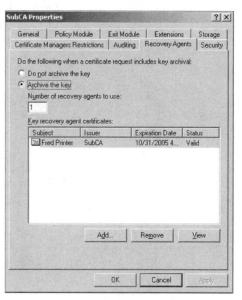

Figure 13-35   The certificate won't be marked as good until the process is complete.

Figure 13-36   After certificate services are stopped and started, the certificate will be approved.

Summary

Deploying a secure PKI is not difficult if you plan and practice the steps. Using a root offline CA is part of that strategy, but a number of steps are required in order to use it as the base for an Active Directory–integrated CA hierarchy. In addition to basic installation and configuration techniques, customized templates can be used and their use can be secured.

Securing PKI is necessary because it serves as the basis for trust within the organization. Even if passwords for user authentication are not slated for replacement by smart cards or other devices that require certificates, certificates are being increasingly used to support secure transactions. Many functions, such as VPNs, IP Security policies, secured web sites, and secure wireless networks are based on certificates. The following chapters describe how to use them in these circumstances.

PART V

Securing the Virtual Network

CHAPTER 14

Securing Remote Access

Remote access is often defined as a connection to computers on one private network from another network. However, remote access is also the ability to connect to and use the resources of a computer without sitting down to the console to log on. Therefore, a better definition for remote access is any access to computer resources that is not made directly from the computer console. It includes the use of dial-up services, VPNs, wireless access points, web sites, file shares, and administrative applications. Some of these processes are directly addressed in other chapters, such as file shares in Chapter 6, "EFS Basics," and remote recovery tools in Chapter 18, "Auditing." This chapter covers the traditional remote access portals, Microsoft Routing and Remote Access Service (RRAS), Microsoft Internet Authentication Service (IAS), and web-based access to internal resources using Internet Information Server (IIS).

Securing Traditional Remote Access Portals

Remote access portals are those created by using specific devices, protocols, and techniques to facilitate trusted access to internal resources from outside the network. *Trusted access* is defined as approved access by employees, contractors, partners, and customers. It is typically protected by authentication requirements and may be restricted by conditions and protected via encryption. Windows Server 2003 provides several types of remote access through its Routing and Remote Access Services (RRAS) and Internet Authentication Services (IAS). RRAS provides

- Dial-up access via the public telephone network
- Virtual Private Network (VPN) connections over the dial-up connection
- VPN connections over private Wide Area Networks (WANs)
- VPN connections over the Internet
- Remote Access Policies to manage and control access
- Selection of encryption protocols
- Selection of authentication protocols

IAS, Microsoft's implementation of RADIUS, provides additional functionality. RADIUS, or Remote Authentication Dial-In User Service, is a remote authentication, authorization, and accounting service often implemented on a server to manage remote access to a network. It provides

- **Additional constraints**—Authorization for connections is judged against more conditions than RRAS alone can provide, and authorized connections can be further constrained by additional profile attributes.
- **Centralized authentication, accounting, and authorization services**—IAS can manage these services for many RRAS servers. The servers are established as RADIUS clients of the IAS server. When this is so, only Remote Access Policies on the IAS server will be in effect.
- **RADIUS proxy**—The RADIUS server can proxy connection requests to the organization's ISP and forward them to an IAS server on the organization's network.
- **Network Access Quarantine Control**—Each client connection can be quarantined until the client proves compliance with security policy.
- **802.1x authentication services**—Wireless client authentication and key management is provided.

To manage and secure remote access, configure:

- **Authorization**—Identify which users and computers can connect to the network remotely and what they can do once they are connected. This includes the configuration of Network Access Quarantine Control, a new service provided by Windows Server 2003 IAS.
- **Authentication**—Specify how users and computers can prove they are the accounts authorized for remote access.
- **Accounting (auditing)**—Configure what events and details will be recorded about the remote access connection.
- **Communication Protection**—Set encryption for dial-up connections and/or configure VPN protocol choices.
- **Wireless Communication Security**—Configure 802.1x authentication and security for wireless access.

The use of IAS to configure 802.1x authentication is discussed in the section "Securing Wireless Access Using IAS"; the rest of these topics are included here after brief instructions for the secure installation of Windows Server 2003 RRAS and IAS and the configuration of client-side remote access connections.

Secure Installation of Windows Server 2003 RRAS and IAS Preparation

The first step in providing secure remote access services is to plan a secure installation. No amount of hardening or secure procedures will matter if the machine is compromised before being used for remote access. Management should provide an organizational Remote Access Policy; however, you may be required to provide services without one. You should insist on management approval for

- The plan
- The groups of individuals allowed to remotely access the network
- Provisions for the proper purchase of equipment and software
- Time necessary to provide secure remote access

You cannot create a plan for remote access deployment until you know the remote access capabilities and the security provisions available. Use the information in this chapter, your knowledge of your networks, policies, and procedures, and your knowledge of the technologies to create that plan. The processes described next provide the details necessary for the second step—secure installation of the services. Before installing them on a production network, you should create your plan; however, to examine the configuration information discussed in future selections, you may want to install them on a test network.

Before installing RRAS or IAS, install a secure Windows Server 2003 computer. To do so, provide the necessary hardware (modem or additional network interface cards) and use the usual precautions:

- Install the operating system isolated from the network and the Internet.
- Apply the most recent service pack and security hotfixes before connecting the system to a test network.
- Follow your organization's security baseline for new servers. If the security baseline includes disabling RRAS and other related remote access services, enable them after using the security baseline during the installation. (By default, RRAS is installed but not started.)
- Determine which type of remote access portal you will use.
- Install RRAS or IAS as detailed in the following section. IAS and RRAS can be installed on the same computer, but IAS can also be installed on its own server.

NOTE: Baseline Info
Chapter 11, "Securing Infrastructure Roles," has recommendations for developing a security baseline and provides information on ways to manage this across multiple systems.

Install and Configure RRAS

To use RRAS as a remote access portal, you must configure the type(s) of access it will provide. Your choice will depend on the type of remote access you need to provide. The choices are

- Dial-up
- Client/Server VPN
- Demand-Dial (Router-to-Router) VPN

Dial-up access is provided via ordinary phone system connections and uses the point-to-point communications protocol (PPP). You can supplement authentication and communications protection by also configuring and requiring the use of a VPN. A *Virtual Private Network* (VPN) provides a simulated point-to-point connection between two networks across a third. When a VPN connection is used, the logical connection appears to be directly between the two networks. A dial-up connection may actually travel through many telephone system switches and even across multiple systems owned by different companies. A VPN connection across a private WAN or across the Internet may start with a connection to the ISP and travel over many networks to reach the VPN server. In both cases, it appears to the user and the computer that the connection is simply between the computer and the VPN server. The VPN logical connection and real network route is illustrated in Figure 14-1.

The previous VPN example is the one most commonly understood and is known as the client/server VPN. A client computer running client VPN software connects to a VPN server. If configured, data is both tunneled and encrypted as it travels from the client to the server. Note, as shown in Figure 14-2, that once the data leaves the VPN server, unless connections have been figured for encrypted communications, the data is not encrypted.

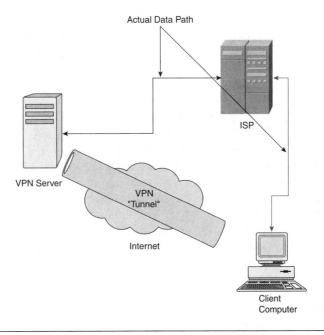

Figure 14-1   The VPN connection simulates a PPP connection.

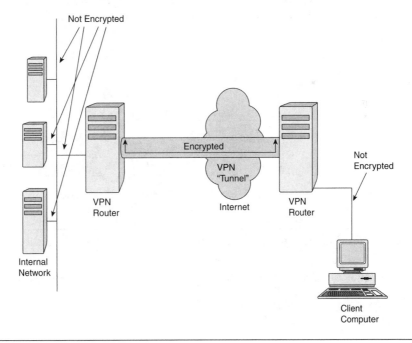

Figure 14-2   The client/server VPN tunnels and encrypts data as it travels from the client to the VPN server.

The *demand-dial* or router-to-router VPN, another type of VPN, can also be configured between two Window Server 2003 VPN servers. This type of VPN connection provides a tunneled and encrypted communications path between two networks over a third but does not require the client computers on either network to install a VPN client or participate in the VPN connection. Instead, if data leaving the local network for the remote network is routed through the VPN server on the local network, it will automatically use the tunnel and be encrypted.

Don't let the name "demand-dial" confuse you. The connection can be configured to occur on demand and can be used to connect two VPN servers over the telephone network. However, a demand-dial VPN can also be configured to use the Internet and to remain always connected (a persistent connection). Figure 14-3 illustrates a demand-dial VPN. In the figure, a client computer on the branch office network can communicate with the network at headquarters by using VPN server branch office. A demand-dial connection exists between the branch office VPN router and the headquarters VPN router. Note that data from the computers on the branch office network to the branch office VPN server will not be encrypted or tunneled. Likewise, data from the headquarters VPN server to any computers on the headquarters network will not be encrypted or tunneled. If protection for data between the computers on either network and the VPN server is required, IPSec policies or other encryption could be provided for these connections, as shown in Figure 14-3.

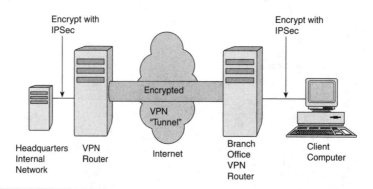

Figure 14-3   Provide alternative encryption to create an end-to-end solution.

If the connection will not be available at all times, configure the connection as demand-dial. In this case, when data must be sent from one network to the other, the VPN server initiates the connection to the other VPN server. To illustrate this action, consider the following process:

1. John Doe is working at the branch office and needs to access a file on a file server on the Headquarters network. He uses the `Windows Explorer, Tools, Map Network Drive` tool to enter the IP address, 192.168.10.15, of the server and the share name.
2. The branch office network is configured to route requests for resources on the 192.168.10.0/24 network (a headquarters network subnet) to the branch office VPN server.
3. The branch office VPN server receives the data and recognizes the destination address as one on the network it is configured to connect to.
4. The VPN server requests a connection to the remote VPN server. Configured connection parameters must be fulfilled for the connection to occur.
5. The connection is made.
6. The request for the drive mapping is evaluated at the remote server in the headquarters network. If authorized, John is connected to the server and can access its resources as if his computer were on the network at headquarters.

Enabling RRAS and Configuring RRAS for Dial-Up and VPN Connections

To install RRAS on a prepared Windows Server 2003 server, follow these steps:

1. Add the computer account to the RAS and IAS Server security group in Active Directory. (If you are a domain administrator, this is not necessary, because the account will be added automatically when you enable RRAS.)
2. At the console of the server, open the `Start, Administrative Tools, Routing And Remote Access Services` console.
3. Right-click the server icon in the console, select `Configure and Enable Routing and Remote Access`, and then click `Next`.
4. Select `Remote Access (Dial up and VPN)` and click `Next`.
5. Select `VPN` and click `Next`.
6. Select the network interface that is connected to the Internet.
7. Select `Enable security on the selected interface by setting up static packet filters. Static packet filters`

allow only VPN traffic to gain access to this server through the selected interface and click Next.

8. If network address assignment for clients will be via an established DHCP server, click Automatic or click From a specific range addresses, and then click Next.

9. If the property From a specific range of address was selected, use the New button to enter the address range. Click OK, and then click Next.

10. If Routing and Remote Access will be used for authentication, as shown in Figure 14-4, click Next, and then click Finish.

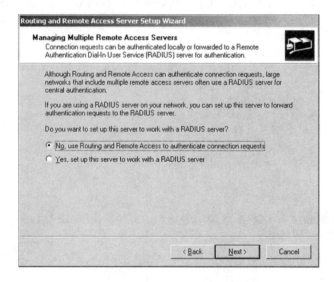

Figure 14-4   Configuring RRAS for authentication.

11. If RADIUS will be used for authentication:
In the Managing Multiple Remote Access Servers page, click Yes, setup this server to work with RADIUS, and then click Next.
Enter the name of the primary and secondary RADIUS server and enter the shared secret. Click Next, and then click Finish.

12. If prompted, click OK to start the RRAS service.

13. Expand the server in the RRAS console and view the folder, as shown in Figure 14-5. If you selected RADIUS as the authentication provider, the Remote Access Policies container will not be present.

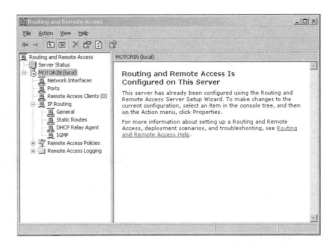

Figure 14-5   Viewing the RRAS console.

When Routing and Remote Access is selected for authentication, the RRAS server will use its local user database or, if it is joined in a domain, the Active Directory database to authenticate users. If the centralized services of an IAS server will be required, you have to configure IAS as the authentication and/or accounting source.

Each configuration made using the wizard can be modified later. The use of RADIUS or Windows for authentication and/or accounting and the client IP addressing selection are configured from the Property pages (right-click the server and select `Properties`). Additional PPTP and/or L2TP/IPSec ports, as well as network interface selection, are configured from the RRAS console Ports and Network Interface containers, respectively.

Configuring RRAS as Demand-Dial VPN

It is not difficult to configure a demand-dial VPN, but it can be confusing. Several pieces of information must be configured, and some of them must match their counterparts on the other server. To make it easier to do so, keep these two key pieces of information in mind. First, the name of the interface becomes the name of the user account necessary to access that interface. The account will be created for you if the option is selected during the configuration process. This account becomes the dial-in account name referenced in the setup wizard. Second, the user account, the dial-out account requested in the setup wizard, which will be used to make a connection to the opposite VPN server, is the dial-in account name of the opposite VPN server. To configure a demand-dial VPN, follow these steps:

1. Create a table and enter the configuration parameters for both servers. Table 14-1 is an example of such a table. The parameters entered in the table are examples used to illustrate these steps. They should be replaced with your own data. The parameters in the table will be referenced in these instructions to make them more understandable.
2. Make the table available to both VPN server administrators.
3. Configure the Motorin router by opening the Routing and Remote Access console and expanding the server.
4. Select the `Network Interface` container and select the Internet interface in the detail pane.
5. Right-click the `Network Interface` container, select `New Demand-Dial Interface`, and then click `Next`.
6. Enter the interface name DD_NewYork, as shown in Figure 14-6, then click `Next`. The DD_NewYork interface name is the name of the interface on the motorin VPN server.

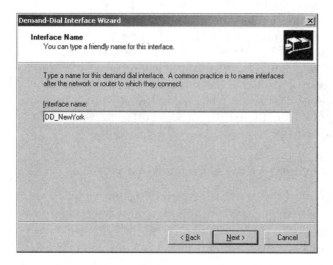

Figure 14-6 Enter an interface name.

7. Select `Connect Using Virtual Private Networking (VPN)` and click `Next`.

8. Select the protocol to be used and click Next.
   If L2TP is selected, IPSec certificates can be used for VPN computer authentication in addition to the user account. However, each computer must be able to validate the certificate presented by the other. If a different CA issues the certificate for each computer, a copy of the root CA certificate for each CA must be placed in the computer certificate store.
9. Enter the IP address for the external interface from the table, 207.209.66.50. Click Next. (This IP address is the external interface of regalinn, the other VPN server.)
10. Select Add a user account so a remote router can dial in, as shown in Figure 14-7, and click Next. (The account will be added for you.)
11. Add static routes, in this case, for the 192.168.10.0/24 network, the internal network for regalinn. Then, click Next.
12. Complete the dial-in credentials in adding and confirming a password for the account created in step 10. These will be the credentials used by the regalinn router to connect to this router. The name of the interface entered in step 6 is shown as the user name, as shown in Figure 14-8, and cannot be changed. Click Next.

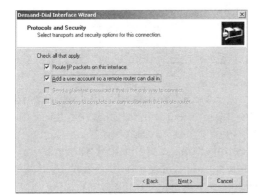 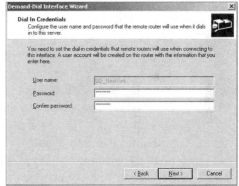

Figure 14-7 Add a User Account so the other VPN can authenticate its connection.

Figure 14-8 The name of the interface is used to name the user account.

13. Enter the dial-out credentials, the user name domain, the password for the user account at regalinn, and then click Next. Click Finish.

14. Repeat the process on the regalinn computer, using the information from Table 14-1. (The interface name for regalinn must match the user name entered in step 13, and the dial-out credentials must match the information entered for the motorin computer.)

15. When the configuration is complete, test the connection by right-clicking the interface and selecting `Connect`.

Table 14-1 Demand-Dial VPN Configuration

Parameter	Network One Atlanta	Network Two New York
Router Name	Motorin	Regalinn
IP Address of the opposite router external interface	207.209.66.50	208.147.68.50
Interface name	DD_NewYork	DD_Atlanta
User name for the account in the dial-out interface	DD_Atlanta	DD_NewYork
IP network of the internal interface	192.168.10.0/24	192.168.5.0/24

After the wizard is complete, you can configure additional settings to meet specific needs and to secure the connection. Settings relate to callback, encryption, authentication, and other restrictions. For example, you may want to change the connection to Persistent (always connected), configure encryption, and set allowed authentication methods and secure the connection by requiring callback to use the phone number of the other VPN router.

Persistence and Restrictions

Demand-dial connections can be configured to provide connection over IP networks and telephone networks. When configuring connections over IP networks, you may want the connection to stay up at all times. In this case, configure the connection to be persistent by double-clicking the demand-dial interface in the `Network Interfaces` node of the RRAS server to open the Property pages, selecting the `Options` page, as shown in Figure 14-9, and then clicking to select the `Persistent connection` radio button.

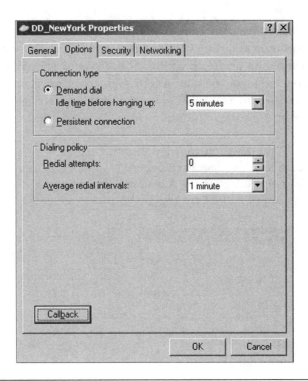

Figure 14-9   Configure persistence from the Options Property page.

Use the other options on this page to restrict idle time and set the dial policy for redial attempts and redial intervals.

Callback

Requiring callback for a demand-dial connection can prevent connections from non-authorized computers. Callback can be configured in a Remote Access Policy, or on a standalone router, it may be configured in the Property pages of the demand-dial interface. To configure callback in the Property pages, follow these steps:

1. Double-click the interface in the `Network Interface` node of the `Routing and Remote Access` console.
2. Select the `Options` page.
3. Click the `Callback` button.
4. Use the `Add the phone` button to identify the modem to use and the phone numbers approved for callback. These are the numbers answered by the peer router.
5. Click `OK` to close.

Encryption and Authentication

Encryption and authentication are set by default to use a secure password and to require encryption. The strongest encryption should always be used, although you may need to reduce the encryption strength if you must connect to a down-level version of the operating system. To change these settings, follow these steps:

1. Open the demand-dial Property pages.
2. Select the `Security` page.
3. Click to select the `Advanced (custom settings)` radio button and click the `Settings...` button, as shown in Figure 14-10.

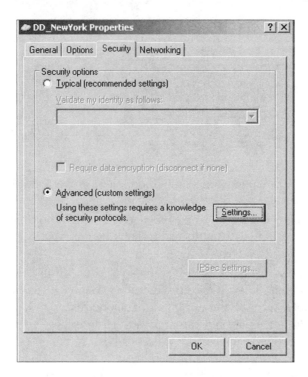

Figure 14-10 Customize authentication and encryption from the Security page.

4. Configure encryption using the `Data encryption` drop-down list, as shown in Figure 14-11. The choices are as follows:

   `No encryption allowed (server will disconnect if it requires encryption)`
   `Options encryption (connect even if no encryption)`

```
Require encryption (disconnect if server declines)
Maximum strength encryption (disconnect if server
declines)
```

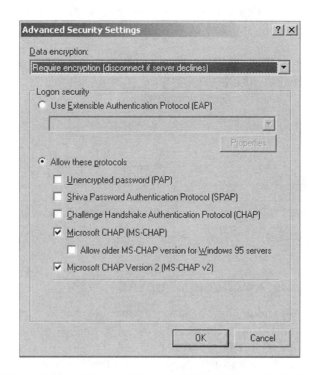

Figure 14-11   Select the strongest possible encryption and authentication.

5. Configure authentication in the Logon security box.
6. If certificates will be used, click to select Use Extensible Authentication Protocol (EAP) and select Smart Card or other certificate (encryption enabled).
7. If certificates or MD5 challenge are not used, always select the strongest possible authentication choices from the Allow these protocols area. By default, MS-CHAP and MS-CHAPv2 are selected. Click to deselect MS-CHAP; demand-dial connections between any combination of Windows 2000 servers and Windows Server 2003 servers are capable of using MS-CHAPv2.
8. Click OK to complete.

If L2TP/IPSec is configured for the demand-dial connection, configure the pre-shared key password for this connection by clicking the IPSec

Settings button from the Security Property page. The entered password is in clear text, as shown in Figure 14-12, and hence is visible to anyone with the ability to review the Property pages of the demand-dial connection. Don't forget to enter the same password on the other router's configuration pages.

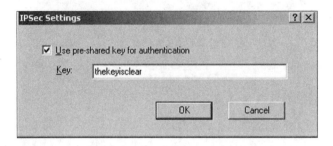

Figure 14-12   The L2TP/IPSec pre-shared key is clearly visible in the configuration pages.

Installing and Configuring IAS

Installing and configuring IAS requires several steps, including installation, configuring a connection request policy, and configuring RRAS servers to act as RADIUS clients.

To install IAS on a prepared Windows Server 2003 server, follow these steps:

1. Open the Start, Setting, Control Panel, Add or Remove Programs applet and double-click the Add/Remove Windows Components option.
2. Click Networking Services and click Details.
3. Select Internet Authentication Service, click OK, and then click Next.
4. If prompted, insert the Windows Server 2003 installation disc.
5. When the installation is done, click Finish and click Close.

To configure the connection for each RADIUS client, follow these steps:

1. Open the Start, Administrative Tools, Internet Authentication Service console, as shown in Figure 14-13.

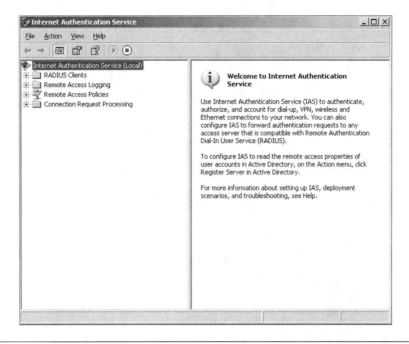

Figure 14-13   The IAS console provides access for configuring RADIUS clients.

2. Right-click the RADIUS Client container and select New RADIUS
   Client.
3. Enter a friendly name for the client, as shown in Figure 14-14.

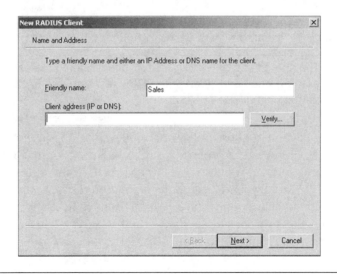

Figure 14-14   Add the RRAS server as a RADIUS client.

4. Enter the client computer (the RRAS computer) name or IP address.

5. If a name was entered, click the `Verify` button and the `Resolve` button to resolve the name into an IP address.

6. Click `OK`, and then click `Next` to continue.

7. Enter and confirm the shared secret for this RADIUS client, as shown in Figure 14-15.

8. Click `Request must contain the Message Authenticator attribute`. (See the sidebar "Best Practices for IAS and RRAS Security" for an explanation of this attribute.)

9. Click `Finish`.

10. Repeat steps 2 to 9 for each RADIUS client.

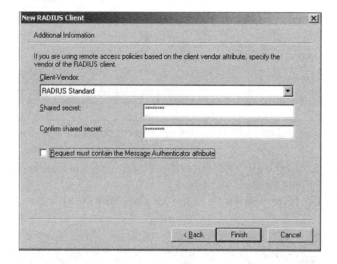

Figure 14-15   The shared secret for the RADIUS client should match the one entered when configuring the RRAS server to use RADIUS for authentication.

A connection request policy is a policy that IAS uses to manage the requests from RRAS servers or a RADIUS proxy or to configure the IAS server to forward requests to another RADIUS server for authentication (be a RADIUS proxy). A default connection request policy is configured to authenticate connection requests from a RRAS server-based VPN connection or from a direct dial to the IAS server. You can customize this connection request by making selections from its Property pages, or you can create your own customized connection request using the wizard. To use the wizard, follow these steps:

1. Expand the `Connection Request Processing` folder in the `Internet Authentication Service` console.
2. Right-click the `Connection Request Policies` container, select `New Connection Request Policy`, as shown in Figure 14-16, and then click `Next`.

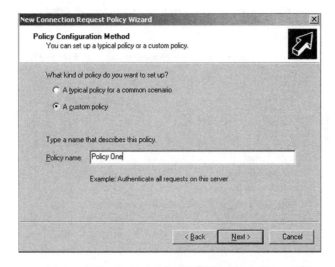

Figure 14-16   Configure a custom connection request policy.

3. Select `A custom policy`.
4. Add a name for the policy and click `Next`.
5. Click the `Add` button to add policy conditions.
6. Select attributes such as Day-and-Time Restrictions, Tunnel Type, and so forth. Attributes are described in the section "Configure Clients to Use Remote Access," later in this chapter.
7. Click `Add` to add the attribute, select the constraints for the condition, and click `OK`.
8. Add additional policy conditions if required. When you are done, click `Next`.
9. Use the `Edit Profile` button to add additional attributes (conditions and constraints) to this request, such as changing the RADIUS server for Accounting.
10. Click `Next` and click `Finish`.

To configure a RRAS server to use RADIUS for authentication follow these steps:

1. Open the Routing and Remote Access console.
2. Right-click the server and select Properties.
3. Select the Security tab.
4. Use the Authentication provider: drop-down box, as shown in Figure 14-17, to change to RADIUS authentication.

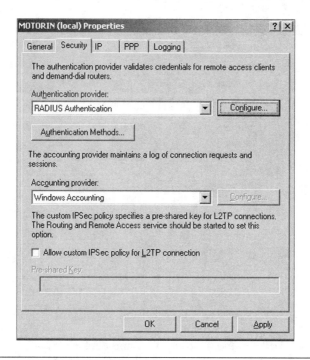

Figure 14-17   Change to RADIUS authentication.

5. Click the Configure... button.
6. Click Add to add the RADIUS server name.
7. Click the Change button to add the shared secret, as shown in Figure 14-18. The shared secret must match that configured at the RADIUS server for this client.
8. Select the Always use message authenticator check box.
9. If multiple RADIUS servers will be used, indicate the score, as shown in Figure 14-18. The RADIUS servers will be queried in order from highest to lowest.

10. Click OK.

11. Add additional RADIUS servers in the same manner.

12. Click OK twice when you are done.

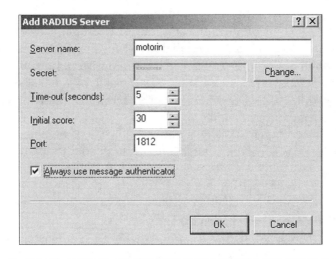

Figure 14-18   Set the shared secret.

RADIUS Ports for Firewall and IPSec Policy Configuration

The typical placement of the RADIUS server that will be used by Internet connections and the VPN server is behind the firewall on the Perimeter network. To allow access, you may need to configure VPN protocol ports and/or RADIUS ports on the firewall. In addition, if IPSec policies are configured between RADIUS clients, proxies, and servers, the filters must be configured for RADIUS traffic. Table 14-2 lists the RADIUS ports and indicates how they are used.

Table 14-2   RADIUS Ports

RADIUS Messages	Standard Port	Optional Port
Authentication	UDP 1812	UDP 1645
Accounting	UDP 1813	UDP 1646

Configure Clients to Use Remote Access

Clients can be individually configured to use remote access connections. However, this makes managing clients difficult. To manage clients, use the Connection Manager Administration Kit (CMAK) to create client profiles. The Connection Manager (CM) profile is a self-executing file that installs a preconfigured dialer and any provided scripts on the client computer. Creating profiles ensures consistency in configuration for each Windows OS. In addition, custom actions, such as the running of a Network Access Quarantine Control script, can be configured for each phase of the connection.

In addition to a dialer, a Phone Book can be created, which will provide traveling users with a listing of the phone numbers for every location. The Phone Book can be updated online from an FTP server configured as a Phone Book server.

TIP: CMAK on Installation CD

The CMAK is provided on the Windows Server 2003 installation CD-ROM but is not installed by default. You can install this tool by running the adminpak.msi program from the I386 folder on the installation CD-ROM. To create a profile, run the Connection Manager Administration Kit program from `Start, Administrative Tools`. A tutorial on setting up a Connection Manager profile can be downloaded at http://www.microsoft.com/downloads/details.aspx?FamilyID=93fd20e7-e73a-43f6-96ec-7bcc7527709b&DisplayLang=en Authorization.

Regardless of technology, you must grant authorization for remote access before any remote access can occur. You may need to configure both account dial-in permissions and Remote Access Policy.

Configure User Account Properties for Remote Access

By default, remote access authorization is not granted to any account. Access is set on the user's dial-in Property page to deny access. However, if the RRAS server is a standalone remote access server, or when a Windows Server 2003 domain is raised to Windows Server 2003 functional mode, the dial-in page of new accounts will indicate that access depends on Remote Access Policies, as shown in Figure 14-19. This option will still deny the user remote access by default because the default Remote Access Policy is set to deny access, as shown in Figure 14-20. To manage user accounts in an efficient manner, use Remote Access Policies.

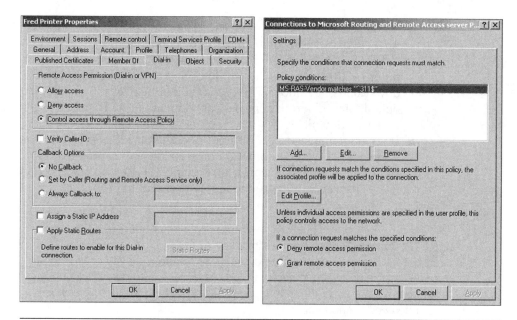

Figure 14-19   RRAS servers in a Windows Server 2003 functional mode domain refer remote access permissions to Remote Access Policies.

Figure 14-20   The default Remote Access Policy denies remote access.

TIP: Servers as Clients to Switches

Windows Server 2003 computers can also be configured as remote access clients. One of the computer account Properties pages is a dial-in page. This feature might be used so that an 802.1x Ethernet client could use EAP-TLS and a computer certificate to authenticate to an authenticating Ethernet switch.

The dial-in Property page selections `Deny`, `Allow`, and `Control Access Through Remote Access Policy` have the following impact on remote access:

- If an account is configured to Deny remote access, a connection attempt will be denied. However, if the IAS profile constraint that ignores user dial-in properties is set, access might still be granted.

- If an account is configured to Allow remote access, Remote Access Policies can still terminate the connection.
- If RRAS is installed on a Windows Server 2003 standalone computer or after you raise a Windows Server 2003 domain to Windows 2000 or Windows Server 2003 functional level, new account default dial-in permissions become dependent on Remote Access Policy by default.
- If access is managed via Remote Access Policies, the connection is controlled by a combination of account dial-in properties and Remote Access Policy constraints unless the Remote Access Policy settings are configured to ignore user dial-in properties.

NOTE: Control Access Permissions
By default, no account has authorization to remotely dial-up or VPN to the network. The first step in securing remote access is to carefully control this permission. Require management approval before granting any user remote access capability.

In a simple remote access scenario, accounts are granted remote access permissions by individually configuring each account approved for access. Once the selection `Allow Access` is made, the choices, as displayed previously in Figure 14-19 and as described in Table 14-3, can be configured. Some of these choices add no additional security.

Table 14-3   Dial-In Account Configuration

Setting	Description
Verify Caller-ID	Before using this feature, verify the following:
	All parts of the dial-up connection, including the caller, the phone system between the caller and the remote access server, and the phone system between the remote access server and the call answering equipment, provide Caller-ID services.
	The call answering equipment can provide the remote access server with the number called from, and the phone number from which the user may call may be entered here.
	If your systems meet these conditions, and this feature is desired, enter the number the user will use to dial-in. The user will be denied access if he places a call from another number.

Setting	Description
No Callback	RRAS will not disconnect a connection and attempt to dial the user's computer.
Set by Caller (Routing and Remote Access Service only)	At connection, an authorized user can request dial back to a phone number he enters. This offers no real security benefit. It is not available if IAS is used to manage RRAS connection requests.
Always Callback to	Enter a phone number in the user's dial-in Property page. RRAS will dial the number entered after the user's connection is authorized. This feature may prevent unauthorized use of the user's credentials, if the person using them does not also have access to the phone line represented here. This can be an effective security measure, but it restricts the user to one location and one phone line.
Assign a Static IP Address	In the typical configuration, RRAS assigns an internal network address to the connection, either by using a network accessible DHCP server or from an address pool configured on the server. Using an assigned IP address may provide greater accountability because the user's network access can be tracked by IP address and by user account. If auditing is configured, it is also possible to link IP addresses to user accounts by reviewing the records.
Apply Static Routes	It may be necessary to identify static routes, routes that are needed for this specific account. When an account configured with static routes makes a connection, the routes are added to the RRAS server.

It is important to provide dial-in Property page configuration to manage specific accounts; however, if the user will use multiple remote access methods, such as dial-in and wireless, a conflict may occur. For example, wireless access does not use a phone number; therefore, setting the callback feature on the user's dial-in Property page may prevent a wireless connection. Wireless and dial-up connections can be made from the same user account if IAS Remote Access Policies are used. If correctly configured, an additional constraint can block the use of dial-in page settings when wireless access is requested.

Remote Access Policies

Remote Access Policies are used both to make management of remote access simpler and to provide additional access restrictions based on Windows groups, the type of connection, time of day, and by profile constraints that apply to the authorized connection. If the authentication choice for a RRAS server is set to Windows Authentication, the Remote Access Policies configured on the RRAS server are used to manage the connection. However, if authentication is configured to use RADIUS, and a Windows IAS server is designated as the RADIUS server, remote access policies on the IAS server are used to manage the connection. Table 14-4 lists the items that can be configured via Remote Access Policies. You can only configure some Remote Access Policy constraints if you are using IAS, and they are marked in Table 14-5 as (IAS only).

Table 14-4   Remote Access Policy Restrictions RRAS and IAS

Attribute	Description
Authentication Type	Identification of the authentication type that is used. Authentication types are CHAP, EAP, MS-CHAP or MS_CHAPv2, and so forth.
Called Station ID	The phone number of the network access server (NAS) or RRAS server that is acting as the RADIUS client. The server must support passing the called ID.
Calling Station ID	The phone number used by the client accessing the NAS or RRAS server.
Day and Time Restrictions	The day of the week and the time of day of the connection attempt. The RRAS server day and time are used.
Tunnel Type	The requesting client tunnel type. Types include Point-to-Point Tunneling Protocol (PPTP) and Layer Two Tunneling Protocol (L2TP). This attribute can also specify profile settings, such as authentication method or encryption strength.
Windows Groups	The name of the Windows group to which the user or computer account belongs.

Table 14-5 Remote Access Policy Restrictions (IAS Only)

Attribute	Description
Client Friendly Name (IAS only)	The name of the RADIUS client that is requesting authentication. Configure this in the Friendly Name on the `Setting` tab of the RADIUS client properties in IAS (IAS only).
Client IP Address	The IP address of the RADIUS client (the RRAS or NAS) or the RADIUS proxy.
Client Vendor	The NAS vendor (the NAS requesting authentication).
Framed Protocol	The framing type of the incoming packets—for example: PPP, SLIP, Frame Relay, and x.25 (IAS server only).
NAS Identifier	The name of the NAS (IAS only).
NAS IP Address	The IP address of the NAS (the RADIUS client) that sent the message (IAS only).
NAS Port Type	The access client media type used, such as analog phone line (async), ISDN, tunnels, VPNs, (virtual), IEEE 802.11 wireless, and Ethernet switches.
Service Type	The type of service requested—for example; framed (a PPP connection) or login (Telnet connection).

If the connection request meets the conditions set by an RRAS or IAS Remote Access Policy, RRAS or IAS evaluates the Allow or Deny authorization property of the Remote Access Policy or the dial-in Property page. RRAS or IAS will evaluate the Remote Access Policy profile properties if the setting is Allow. The Remote Access Policy profile properties can further constrain or deny the connection. The constraints configured in the profile will only affect connections that meet the conditions set by the Remote Access Policy. Table 14-6 lists and describes these items.

Table 14-6   Profile Properties

Property Page	Description
Dial-in constraints	Sets idle time, connection limit, days and times, specified number, and specific media (async, ISDN, virtual, or 802.11).
IP	Specifies client IP address assignment and, optionally, IP packet filters. IP address assignment choices are as follows:
	Access server supplies the address.
	Client requests an IP address.
	Address assignment is specified by the access server.
	Profile lists a static IP address.
	An IP address in the user account Dial-in Property page will override the profile setting unless the dial-in properties are ignored.
	IP packet filters defined on this page apply to remote connection traffic.
Multilink	Sets the number of ports a multilink connection can use and specifies Bandwidth Allocation Protocol (BAP) policies. (The RRAS server must have multilink and BAP enabled for these to work.)
Authentication	Enables authentication types. Authentication types are configured in the Property pages of the RRAS and IAS server, but settings on the authentication page overrides those settings when this Remote Access Policy is used. This page also determines if users are allowed to change their passwords by using MS-CHAP. (This setting must match the settings for RRAS.)
Encryption	Defines encryption choices. The client and the server negotiate the encryption that will be used; this specification indicates the choices the server may accept. The choices are as follows:
	No encryption
	Basic (dial-up and PPTP connections use 40-bit key MPPE. L2TP/IPSec connections use 56-bit DES)
	Strong (PPTP connections use 56-bit MPPE, L2TP/IPSec connections use 56-DES)
	Strongest (PPTP connections use 128-bit MPPE, L2TP/IPSec connections use 3DES)

Property Page	Description
Advanced	Provides the ability to define RADIUS attributes. The IAS server will use these attributes to constrain an authorized connection between the RADIUS server (IAS) and the RADIUS client (RRAS). Configure the Ignore User Dial-in Properties attribute here.

Configuring Remote Access Policies

To configure a simple Remote Access Policy, follow these steps:

1. Open the `Routing and Remote Access` console if Windows authentication is used or the Internet Authentication Service if RADIUS authentication is used.
2. Right-click the `Remote Access Policies` container, select `New Remote Access Policy`, and then click `Next`.
3. Enter a name for the policy, as shown in Figure 14-21, and click `Next`.

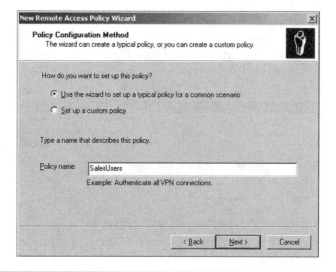

Figure 14-21   Enter a name for the policy.

4. Select the access method, as shown in Figure 14-22, such as VPN, and then click `Next`.

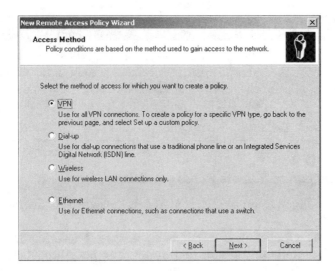

Figure 14-22   Select the access method that will trigger this policy.

5. Use the Add button and the object picker to select the Windows groups that will be affected by this policy. Add as many groups as you require and click Next.

6. Choose the authentication methods that will be allowed by selecting or deselecting check boxes, as shown in Figure 14-23. If smart cards or EAP is selected, the server certificate must be available for selection.

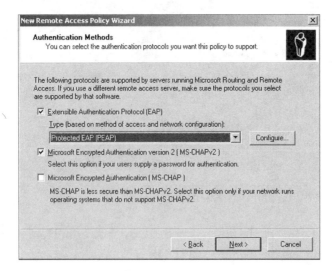

Figure 14-23   Select authentication methods.

7. If Extensible Authentication Protocol (EAP) is selected, choose `Protected EAP (PEAP)` or `Smart Card or other certificate` in the `Type` drop-down box. After selection, use the `Configure` button to select the server certificate, as shown in Figures 14-24 (for smart cards) and 14-25 (for PEAP).

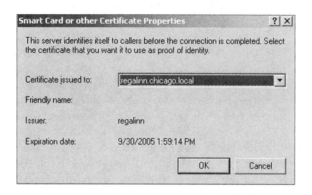

Figure 14-24   Select the server certificate.

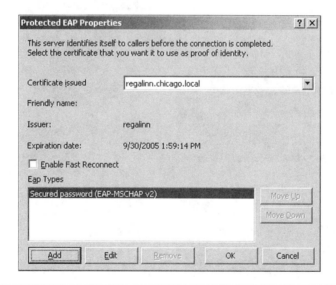

Figure 14-25   Select the server certificate for PEAP.

8. Click `Next`.
9. Select the encryption level desired, and then click `Next` and `Finish`.

To configure a custom policy and edit the profile, follow these steps:

1. Open the `Routing and Remote Access` console if Windows authentication is used or the Internet Authentication Service if RADIUS authentication is used.
2. Right-click the `Remote Access Policies` container, select `New Remote Access Policy`, and then click `Next`.
3. Select `Set up a custom policy` and click `Next`.
4. Use the `Add` button and select a condition from the `Select Attribute` page, as shown in Figure 14-26.
5. When you have configured the conditions, close the `Select Attribute` page by clicking `OK`, and then click `Next`.
6. Chose `Deny Remote Access Permission` or `Grant Remote Access Permission`. Click `Next`.
7. Click the `Edit Profile` button to edit the `Remote Access Policy` profile.
8. Select the `Dial-in Constraints` page to configure session settings, as shown in Figure 14-27.

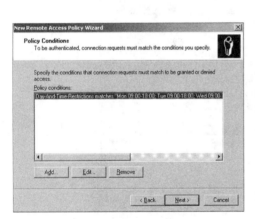

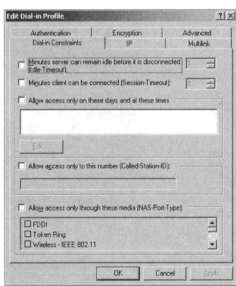

Figure 14-26   Select a condition that this policy relates to.

Figure 14-27   Set dial-in constraints.

9. Select the IP tab, as shown in Figure 14-28, and configure how IP address assignment will occur. This page is also used to add input and output protocol filters.

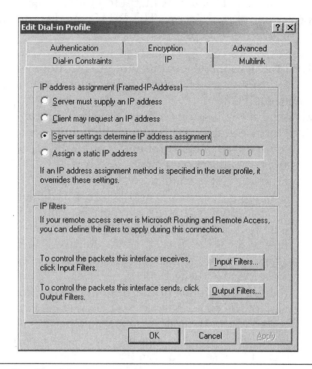

Figure 14-28 Set IP address assignment and configure protocol filters.

10. Select the Advanced tab and use its Add button to configure additional attributes. This is where the Ignore User dial-in constraints attribute is configured.
11. Click OK to close the profile, then click Next, followed by Finish.

The Remote Access Connection Process

When an RRAS server receives a request, authentication is evaluated according to the RRAS server settings, which is discussed in the section "Authentication." However, regardless of the authentication setting, the remote access connection request is evaluated by the RRAS or IAS server by considering the account dial-in Property pages and Remote Access Policies.

A default Remote Access Policy specifies that `unless` individual access permissions are specified in the user profile, this policy controls access to the network. The default policy also specifies Deny remote access permission. This means that setting individual user dial-in properties can control user access. The RRAS and IAS default connection process follows these steps:

1. If the account is not configured to use Remote Access Policies, the `Deny` or `Allow` setting determines if remote access can be attempted.
2. If the account setting is `Deny`, remote access is denied.
3. If the account setting is `Allow`, the remote access is allowed subject to the constraints set in the properties and, of course, additional constraints on network resources.
4. If the account is configured to use Remote Access Policies and no Remote Access Policy exists, access is denied.
5. If the account is configured to use Remote Access Policies and Remote Access Policies exist, the connection attempt is evaluated against the first Remote Access Policy conditions. (A default Remote Access Policy denies connection any time of the day, any day of the week.)
6. If all the conditions of the Remote Access Policy are met, the value of the `Ignore-User-Dial-in-Properties` attribute (configured in the Remote Access Policy profile) is checked. If it is set to true, any dial-in page constraints are ignored. If it is not set or is set to false, any dial-in Property page settings are evaluated.
7. If all the conditions of the Remote Access Policy are not met, the next Remote Access Policy is evaluated. (Remote Access Policies are evaluated in the order listed in the `Remote Access Policies` node. The order can be changed.)
8. If no Remote Access Policy matches the connection attempt, the connection attempt is rejected.
9. If the connection is allowed, it is constrained by the profile settings of the Remote Access Policy.

If a Remote Access Policy is evaluated, these steps are followed:

1. The dial-in Property page of the user account is checked.
2. If the account setting is `Allow`, the process continues. Remote Access Policy conditions are checked, and Remote Access Policy profile constraints may be applied. If all conditions are met, the connection is accepted. If they are not, any remaining Remote Access Policies are checked.

3. If the account setting is Deny, the connection attempt is rejected.

4. If the user account setting is Control Access Through Remote Access Policy, the remote access permissions setting of the policy is checked. If it is Deny, the connection is rejected. If it is Allow, processing will continue.

5. The account dial-in Property page constraints and the Remote Access Policy profile constraints are evaluated.

6. If all connection settings in the policy and the user dial-in page are met, the connection is accepted.

7. If some connection setting is not met, the connection is rejected.

Configure Authentication and Auditing for RRAS and IAS

Authentication and Auditing (often called accounting in RADIUS discussions) is a very important part of your RRAS and/or IAS configuration. Standalone RRAS servers are each configured separately. In the typical Windows Server 2003 IAS implementation, Authentication and Auditing are configured on the IAS server. This provides centralized management of these features. Configuring one server manages Authentication and Auditing for all the remote access servers that act as RADIUS clients for the IAS servers.

Authentication

The first authentication consideration when configuration RRAS is the selection of Windows authentication or RADIUS authentication. By default, both use the local Windows Server 2003 account database of a standalone RRAS server or the domain account database if the RRAS server is a member server. However, Windows authentication provides a local selection of PPP remote access authentication protocols and the use of local Remote Access Policies. Multiple RRAS servers can exist independently on the network. Synchronization of their configuration and Remote Access policies can only be manually done if Windows authentication is selected. If RADIUS is selected as the authentication mechanism, the RRAS server acts as a RADIUS client and forwards authentication, accounting, and auditing requests to the IAS server. In this case, only the Remote Access Policies configured at the IAS server are used.

The second authentication consideration is the selection of authentication protocols. Table 14-7 lists and describes the possible remote access authentication protocols.

To configure authentication protocols, follow these steps:

1. Open the `Routing and Remote Access` console.
2. Right-click the server and select `Properties`.
3. Select the `Security` tab and click the `Authentication Methods` button. Figure 14-29 displays the initial authentication configuration screen for remote access services.

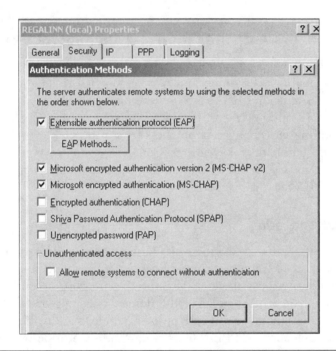

Figure 14-29 Selecting remote access authentication protocols.

Table 14-7 Remote Access Authentication Protocols

Protocol	Description
Password Authentication Protocol (PAP)	A plaintext password is sent across the network. PAP is rarely used, but might be required to accommodate some legacy clients.

Protocol	Description
Shiva Password Authentication Protocol (SPAP)	Employs a proprietary reversible encryption mechanism supported by Shiva remote access servers. This is more secure than PAP but less secure than CHAP. Microsoft Point-to-Point Encryption cannot be used with SPAP.
CHAP	The MD5 hashing protocol encrypts challenge strings. The user name, but not the password, is transported across the network in plain text. The server, however, must store a plaintext copy of the password, or store the password using a reversible encryption algorithm. CHAP may be required to accommodate some UNIX clients.
MS-CHAP	The MD4 hash is used, and the server can store a hashed version of the password. The protocol can provide more sophisticated error messages than CHAP, including a password expired error code that allows the user the ability to change the password during the authentication phase of the connection. The client and server independently create the encryption key based on the user's password. MS-CHAP may be required if Windows 95 clients must connect to the remote access server.
MS-CHAPv2	*Mutual authentication*, a process in this case where both the client and server prove that they have knowledge of the client password, and other improvements over the MS-CHAP protocol are provided. Still, because the encryption key is based on the user's password, the protection is only as strong as the user's password.
Extensible Authentication	An extension to PPP that provides Protocol (EAP) for a choice of authentication protocols, known as *EAP types*. EAP types are dynamically negotiated during the authentication phase of PPP. Because EAP is modularly designed, it provides for the introduction of new authentication types without requiring that the EAP protocol be rewritten. The currently available EAP types in for Windows Server 2003 are as follows: EAP-TLS—Enables mutual authentication between clients and severs. The dial-in server validates the client certificate, and the client validates the server's certificate.

Table 14-7   Remote Access Authentication Protocols Continued

Protocol	Description
	EAP-TLS can be used with PPTP and L2TP/IPSec. When EAP-TLS is used, client computer certificates are not required. (This will always be the case when PPTP is used.) A server certificate is required, however. User certificates may be either installed on client computers or smart cards.
	EAP-MD5—Can only be used with L2TP/IPSec. VPNs and dial-up access usage is allowed but not PPTP or wireless VPNs. A password is used by the user, and no certificates are required. This is less secure than EAP-TLS. A reversibly encrypted password must be stored in the account database, which weakens password security as well.

Accounting (Auditing)

Logging for both RRAS and IAS consists of entries in the Windows event logs as well as RRAS- and IAS-specific logs. By default, connection requests are not logged, and only service start and stop events are recorded in the event logs. You should configure additional logging in order to record information for troubleshooting and security events. Logging connection attempts and successes is useful for troubleshooting but also can assist in tracing remote access as well as attempted and successful attacks. The service-specific logs, if configured, include information about each connection request. Logging can also be redirected to a Microsoft SQL server or to a named pipe. A *named pipe* is a pipe that has been given a name. Pipes are a form of *interprocess communication* (sharing of information between processes). *Pipes* are a one-way or duplex connection point to a running process, and they might be used to send information to another computer. When RADIUS accounting is selected, and IAS is used as the RADIUS server, the logging from all

RRAS servers can be collected on the IAS server. To configure the location for accounting, select the accounting provider from the `Security` page of the RRAS properties, as shown in Figure 14-30. If RADIUS Accounting is selected, the `Configure...` button can be used to enter the name of the RADIUS servers that are available.

Configure additional event logging on the `Logging` tab of the RRAS server properties. (Right-click the server in the `Routing and Remote Access` console, select `Properties`, and then click the `Logging` tab.) Log all events to capture information related to access events, as shown in Figure 14-31.

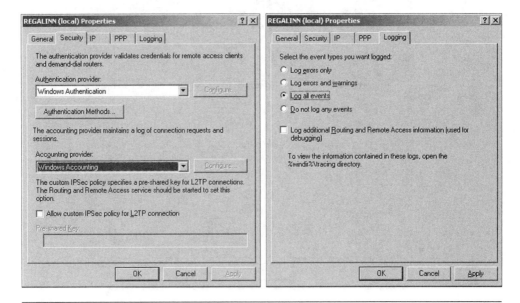

Figure 14-30   Use the Security Property page of the RRAS server to select the Accounting method.

Figure 14-31   Configure event logging on the Logging Property page.

To configure request logging, select the Remote Access Logging folder
in the `Routing and Remote Access` console, double-click the log file
type in the detail pane, and select boxes for accounting and authentication requests, as shown in Figure 14-32. If RADIUS accounting has
been configured for the RRAS server, use the Remote Access Logging
folder in the IAS server console. The Property pages will look the same.

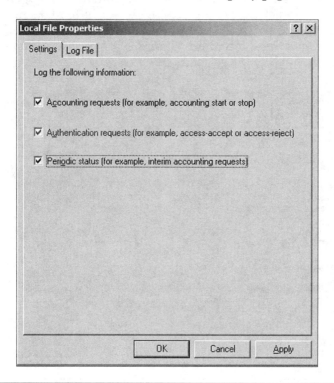

Figure 14-32   RRAS Access attempts are logged in a special log file or SQL server if
configured.

The `Log File` tab, as shown in Figure 14-33, can be used to change the
location for the log file, the log file format, or the frequency of new log
file creation.

When additional log file recording is configured, the following information is recorded:

- The name of the Remote Access Policy that accepted or rejected
  the connection attempt
- The RRAS server IP address
- User name

- Record date
- Record time
- Service name
- Computer name
- Attribute value pairs, which specify items such as routing information, IP address configured for the user, tunnel information, and reason codes (such as success or a reason for the rejection)

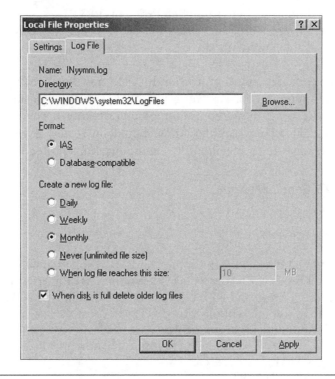

Figure 14-33   Log file location and frequency are configured on the Log File tab.

TIP: Find More Attribute Definitions
A full list of attributes is provided in the product documentation and can be located online in the article "Interpreting IAS-Formatted Log Files" at `http://www.microsoft.com/technet/treeview/default.asp?url=/t echnet/prodtechnol/windowsserver2003/proddocs/standard/sag_i as_log1a.asp.`

VPN Protocol Consideration

Communication protection is provided both by the selection of protocol and by its configuration. Dial-up connections can be protected by encryption if configured to do so; however, using a VPN provides more control and protection. Three protocols may be defined for use in a Windows Server 2003 VPN:

- Point-to-Point Tunneling Protocol (PPTP)
- Layer 2 Tunneling Protocol over IP Security (L2TP/IPSec)
- IPSec tunnel mode

Each provides sound protection for data traveling across a VPN. However, some protocols are more suitable in some circumstances than others, and some cannot be used in certain situations. The following PPTP and L2TP/IPSec considerations should be reviewed before selection and configuring a specific VPN communications protocol.

PPTP Considerations

PPTP was developed by Microsoft but is an IETF standard. It can tunnel and encrypt multiprotocol traffic across an IP network. Additionally:

- PPTP provides the tunnel and Microsoft Point-to-Point Encryption (MPPE) provides encryption. MPPE uses the RSA/RC4 algorithm and 40-bit, 56-bit, or 128-bit encryption keys.
- To use encryption with PPTP, you must use one of the following authentication protocols:
  Microsoft Challenge-Handshake Authentication Protocol (MS-CHAP).
  MS-CHAPv2.
  Extensible Authentication Protocol-Transport Level Security (EAP-TLS).
- The PPTP tunnel negotiates authentication, compression, and encryption.
- The initial encryption key is generated during user authentication and is periodically refreshed.
- PPTP encrypts only the data payload. Figure 14-34 shows the PPTP packet and identifies the encrypted area.
- PPTP and L2TP/IPSec support dynamic assignment of client addresses.

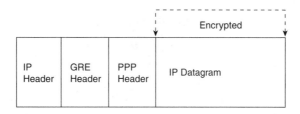

Figure 14-34   Only the data portion of the PPTP packet is encrypted.

L2TP/IPSec Considerations

L2TP is a combination of Cisco Layer 2 Forwarding Protocol (L2F) and Microsoft PPTP. In addition:

- L2TP can tunnel data across any network that transports PPP traffic, such as IP, Frame Relay, and Asynchronous Transfer Mode (ATM) networks.
- L2TP uses User Data Protocol (UDP) over IP messages for tunnel management.
- L2TP sends encapsulated PPP packets over UDP, and payloads can be encrypted and compressed.
- IPSec Encapsulating Security Payload (ESP) encrypts L2TP VPNs by using an automatically generated IPSec policy that uses IPSec in transport mode.
- IPSec ESP encryption encrypts more than the data payload portion of the packet. Figure 14-35 illustrates the packet and identifies the encrypted portion.
- L2TP/IPSec VPNs require user and mutual computer authentication. Computer authentication for VPNs requires computer certificates.
- L2TP/IPSec is generally considered more secure and does offer additional security beyond what PPTP offers.
- L2TP/IPSec may not work behind a Network Address Translation (NAT) server.

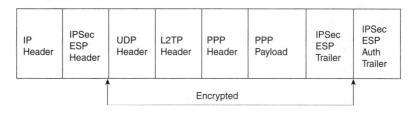

Figure 14-35   A large portion of the L2TP/Ipsec packet is encrypted.

IPSec in Tunnel Mode Considerations

IPSec tunnel mode has limited use as a VPN on a Windows Server 2003 network. Consider the following:

- IPSec in tunnel mode is usually used to connect a Windows Server VPN server with a device, such as a router, that does not use L2TP.
- In IPSec tunnel mode, IP packets are encrypted using IPSec and tunneled across an IP network.
- IPSec in tunnel mode can be used for a demand-dial or client/server VPN.
- However, its use for user remote access VPN is not supported.
- The use of IPSec filters to allow or block communications using specific protocols or ports is not supported in IPSec tunnel mode.

L2TP/IPSec, NAT, and NAT-T

The original L2TP/IPSec standard is incompatible with a NAT server. During processing, a NAT server replaces the IP address of the source computer in outbound packets. This does not cause a problem for most traffic because any responses are delivered to the NAT server, and the NAT server can match the response with the original source and deliver the packets. It does cause a problem for IPSec encrypted packets, however. The standard includes a requirement that the encrypted IPSec protected packets include a checksum calculated over much of the packet and including the IP address of the original source computer. This checksum is used when the packet is received to determine if the packet has been changed during transport. Guaranteeing the integrity of the packet is one of the strengths of IPSec. Because the IPSec encryption occurs before the NAT processing, and NAT cannot decrypt and then re-encrypt the packet with a new checksum, the packet is dropped on receipt because it fails the checksum test. The IPSec decryption process cannot tell the difference between a modification made by a NAT server and an attack.

If IPSec is implemented to match the standard, as it was in Windows 2000, IPSec or L2TP/IPSec VPNs cannot operate behind a NAT server. Windows Server 2003 solves this problems by adopting a new standard, NAT-Traversal (NAT-T). NAT-T uses UDP encapsulation of the IPSec packet. The NAT changes are not made to the IPSec packet; it passes through the NAT server intact. When received and decrypted, there is no suggestion of tampering, and the packet is not dropped.

A Windows Server 2003 VPN server can operate behind a NAT server if the NAT server implements NAT-T. Internet Key Exchange (IKE), a component of the IPSec implementation, can detect NAT-T and then use UDP-ESP encapsulation. More information about IPSec and NAT-T is in Chapter 15, "Protecting Data in Flight." Windows clients must also be NAT-T compliant. The following updates and clients are available:

- Windows XP and the L2TP/IPSec update
- Windows 2000 and the L2TP/IPSec update
- Windows NT 4.0 and the L2TP/IPSec VPN client
- Windows 98 and the L2TP/IPsec VPN client

NOTE: NAT-T Issue
A Windows 2000 server can be a NAT-T client, but a Windows 2000 VPN server cannot utilize NAT-T.

Firewall Ports for VPN Protocols

The following tables list the ports used by VPN protocols. The firewall must be configured to allow these ports if these protocols must traverse the firewall.

Tables 14-8 and 14-9 provide input and output port information for PPTP.

Table 14-8 PPTP Input Filters: Packets That Should Not Be Dropped

Interface IP	Subnet Mask	Destination Port	Purpose
Internet interface VPN router	255.255.255.255	TCP 1723	PPTP tunnel maintenance
Internet interface of router	255.255.255.255	Protocol ID 47	PPTP tunneled data to router
VPN router Internet interface	255.255.255.255	TCP source port 1723	Only for the calling router

Table 14-9   PPTP Destination Output Filters: Packets That Should Not Be Dropped

Source Interface IP	Subnet Mask	Source Port	Purpose
Internet interface VPN router	255.255.255.255	TCP 1723	PPTP tunnel maintenance
Internet interface of router	255.255.255.255	Protocol ID 47	PPTP tunneled data to router
VPN router Internet interface	255.255.255.255	TCP source port 1723	Only for the calling router

Tables 14-10 and 14-11 provide configuration specifications for L2TP/IPSec.

Table 14-10   L2TP/IPSec Input Filters: Packets That Should Not Be Dropped

Destination Interface IP	Subnet Mask	Destination Port	Purpose
Internet interface VPN router	255.255.255.255	UDP 500	Internet Key Exchange (IKE)
Internet interface of router	255.255.255.255	UDP 4500	IPSec NAT-T (if necessary)
VPN router Internet interface	255.255.255.255	UPD 1701	L2TP traffic

Table 14-11   L2TP/IPSec Destination Output Filters: Packets That Should Not Be Dropped

Source Interface IP	Subnet Mask	Source Port	Purpose
Internet interface VPN router	255.255.255.255	UDP 500	IKE traffic
Internet interface of router	255.255.255.255	UDP 4500	IPSec NAT-T (if required)
VPN router Internet interface	255.255.255.255	UDP 1701	L2TP traffic

Network Access Quarantine Control

Network Access Quarantine Control is a new process that can be configured on a Windows Server 2003 computer running RRAS or IAS. When configured, Quarantine Control encourages secure practices by the users of the client computers attempting to remotely access the network. If client computers do not meet the conditions defined by policy and tested by a script, they are prevented from making full, authorized remote access. Instead, they may be directed to a site that describes what they must do to meet policy conditions. Conditions might require the computer to be up-to-date with security patches, running updated and approved anti-virus software, and so forth.

Network Access Quarantine Control may help prevent some forms of attack by providing the support that Remote Access Policies do not. Remote Access Policies set conditions and constraints on remote access connections. Remote Access Policies can require some client connection and communication configuration specifics such as authentication, encryption, and communications protocols. However, the security status of the client system is not checked. VPNs and encryption do not inspect the traffic that they protect. Indeed, an encrypted, authenticated, and authorized connection can transport a virus, Trojan horse, or other malicious code. In addition, a compromised client computer might be used to attack the network over the protected remote access connection. If a determined attacker has access to authorized credentials, Network Access Quarantine Control will not prevent his directed attacks from being successful. However, Network Access Quarantine Control can require that a client connecting remotely has security configuration in place, which may prevent the spread of virus infection and automated Trojan horse attacks. Clients that are up-to-date with security patches will also be less likely to be compromised.

For Network Access Quarantine Control to be used, both a quarantine-compatible remote access client and a compatible remote access server must be available. Clients can be configured by developing a Connection Manager (CM) profile using the Connection Manager Administration Kit (CMAK), which is provided with Windows Server 2003. Compatible clients are as follows:

- Windows Server 2003
- Windows XP Professional
- Windows XP Home Edition
- Windows 2000
- Windows Millennium Edition
- Windows 98 Second Edition

A compatible remote access server is a Windows Server 2003 Routing and Remote Access Service and a listener component (rqs.exe). The listener component listens for messages from the clients. If Windows authentication is configured, a RADIUS server is not required. If RADIUS authentication is configured, a Quarantine Control–compatible RADIUS server, such as IAS, is required.

When a connection is made and the client is placed in quarantine, Network Access Quarantine Control has the following restrictions:

- **Quarantine packet filters**—Restricts the traffic that can be sent to and from a quarantined remote access client.
- **Quarantine session timer**—Restricts the amount of time a client can be connected in quarantine mode.

When a Network Access Quarantine Control Remote Access Policy is added to an RRAS server, the process works like this:

1. An authorized connection attempt is received by the remote access server. If the client is authenticated and authorized to make a remote access connection, the connection is made, but the client is subject to the quarantine restrictions.
2. The client runs a network policy requirements script (the script is included in the CM profile).
3. The script evaluates the client computer according to specified controls such as anti-virus product, security patch level, and so forth. (The script can be a simple batch file of commands or a custom executable file.)
4. If the client script successfully runs (the client has met the conditions of the script), a notifier component (rqc.exe from the Windows Server 2003 resource kit or a custom notifier) runs to notify the remote access server.
   A listener component on the server (rqs.exe from the resource kit or a custom listener component) receives the message and removes the quarantine restrictions from the remote access connection. Appropriate access is granted to the user.
5. If the script does not execute successfully, it directs the remote access client to a quarantine resource that describes how to install the components required for network policy compliance.

If a client is not configured with the CM profile and therefore cannot run the script, and the Remote Access Policy that specifies the use of the process is the only Remote Access Policy, the client is placed in quarantine and cannot complete its remote access connection.

TIP: Some Clients Are Not Compatible With Network Access Quarantine Control
Network Access Quarantine Control cannot be used with wireless clients and authenticated switch clients. However, these clients must have a domain account for computer authentication; therefore, configure a network policy compliance script to run as part of the computer's startup and logon sequence.

Configuring Network Access Quarantine Control

Network Access Quarantine Control is configured after the IAS server is installed and configured for normal usage. Then, the following steps are taken:

1. Designate quarantine resources. Quarantine resources are those that a quarantined client can access, such as DNS servers, DHCP servers, file servers, and web servers. These services will be used by the quarantined client to view instructions for policy compliance and to download programs required for compliance. Existing resources can be utilized by setting packet filters for each resource in the MS-Quarantine-IPFilter attribute of the Remote Access Policy, such as setting a packet filter allowing port 53 traffic to the IP address of a specific DNS server. Alternatively, you might deploy quarantine resources and only quarantine resources on a single subnet just for this purpose. A single input/output packet filter can then be configured. Figure 14-36 illustrates this arrangement and shows the location of the quarantine resources, the quarantine-compatible servers and clients, and other network elements.

2. Create a script to validate client configuration. This script can be a simple batch file (*.cmd or *.bat) or a custom program. The script performs tests and must complete with a call to the notifier or, in the case of failed compliance, to a web page that includes instructions on how to comply.

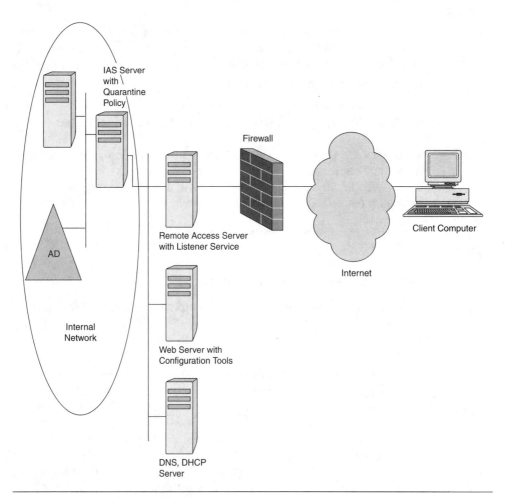

Figure 14-36   If special quarantine resources are set up, you can limit client access to a single subnet.

NOTE: For More Info
An example script is provided in the article "Network Access Quarantine Control in Windows Server 2003" and can be downloaded at
`http://www.microsoft.com/windowsserver2003/techinfo/overview/quarantine.mspx`.

3. Install the Remote Access Quarantine Agent service (rqs.exe) on all Windows Server 2003 remote access servers.

4. Create a Quarantine CM profile with the Windows Server 2003 CMAK. This is a normal profile with a couple of additions. You need to use the `Custom Actions` page of the CMAK wizard to add a post-connect action to run the script and add the notification agent to the profile using the `Additional Files` page of the CMAK wizard.
5. Distribute the CM profile to Remote Access Client computers.
6. Configure a Quarantine Remote Access Policy. If Windows authentication is used, configure the policy on the RRAS server. If RADIUS authentication is used, configure the policy on the IAS server.
7. Start the Remote Access Quarantine Agent Service.

To install the Remote Access Quarantine Agent Service, use other Network Access Quarantine Control items and install the Windows Server 2003 Resource Kit tools on the remote access server:

1. Open the Program Files\Resource Kit\rqs_setup.bat file in Notepad.
2. Use Edit\Find to search on Version1\0 and replace the string with the information from the script created in step 2 of the previous list.
3. Close and save the file.
4. From a command prompt, run the setup file using the following command:
   ```
   rqs_setup/install
   ```

To configure the Quarantine Remote Access Policy, follow these steps:

1. Follow steps 1 to 6 of the custom Remote Access Policy procedure to configure a custom Remote Access Policy and name it Quarantine VPN remote access connections or something similar. Specify Windows groups to indicate the group of users authorized to make remote access connections.
2. Click the `Edit Profile` button to edit the `Remote Access Policy` profile.
3. Select the `Advanced` tab and click the `Add` button.
4. In the `Attribute` list, click MS-Quarantine-Session-Timeout and click `Add`.
5. In the `Attribute information` dialog box, enter the quarantine session time, as shown in Figure 14-37, and then click `OK`. The MS-Quarantine-Session-Timeout setting is the time, in seconds, that the session can remain in the restricted state before being disconnected.

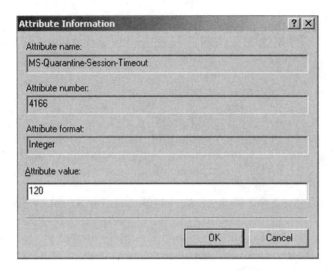

Figure 14-37   Configure session timeout in the profile attribute.

6. Click Add, and in the Attribute list, click MS-Quarantine-IP Filter. Then, click Add.
7. Click Input Filters.
8. In the Inbound Filter box, click New to add a filter.
9. Click Destination Network and add the IP address and subnet mask of the server where the notification message should be received.
10. For Protocol, click TCP. For Destination port, enter 7250 (this port is used to receive the notification message from the quarantined remote access clients), and then click OK.
11. Click to select Permit only the packets listed below.
12. Repeat steps 8 to 11 for each packet filter that you need in order to allow access to quarantine resources.
13. When you finish adding filters, click OK to save the filter list.
14. Click OK to save the attributes and click OK to close the profile.
15. Click OK twice to complete the Quarantine Remote Access Policy.

Securing Wireless Access Using IAS

Access to your network via 802.11 wireless access points (APs) should be considered as a form of remote access. Unlike wired LANs and WANs, the wireless network boundary can easily and unintentionally extend beyond your organization's perimeters and, by default, is also available to anyone visiting your organization that has a wireless access card and appropriate computing device. Laptop computers and PDAs now come with wireless network cards, and for those that do not have a card, many inexpensive cards are available.

By default, little to no security is imposed on wireless network APs; thus, wireless networks can pose serious threats to the security of wired networks. There are security features provided with most APs, including authentication and encryption; however, in many cases, there are ways around these features, and in most cases, they are not configured at all. There are three possible ways to improve wireless security.

Native 802.11 Security Features

The first step to securing wireless is to understand the features offered by existing wireless APs and use them. The features usually available are as follows:

- **Encryption**—Wireless Equivalent Privacy (WEP) is the encryption process provided for 802.11 networks. The implementation of WEP in most APs is flawed, and tools exist that can discover encryption keys and thus read messages if the tools are allowed to capture enough packets. Still, for most implementations, the benefits of using encryption are like the benefits of locking one's house or car. Tools exist that can get past the locks, but most people do not have nor have a desire to use the tools, and a lock, or in this case encryption, does what it is supposed to do. In addition to its vulnerability to sophisticated technical attacks, WEP does not provide key management. In order to change keys, which could lessen the threat of successful attack, the AP and all clients must be reconfigured. This is not easily done in a network of any size.

What's All the Fuss?

WEP can be cracked, or so they say. Researchers at Berkeley first documented possible attacks on WEP, and their research has been supported by others. Tools exist today, such as AirSnort, that can be used to crack WEP. A large number of packets must be captured, which might take longer than the intruder cares to wait. However, in a busy network, 15 minutes might be all that is required. Still, not every network is monitored all the time, and more recent WAPs include WEP algorithms that appear resistant to these types of attacks.

- **Authentication**—Authentication is either Open System, in which no authentication is required, or Shared Key authentication, in which the client must manually enter the key used by the AP. There is no key management for the shared key. The same key is used by every client. In addition, it may be more secure to use Open System. In many wireless implementations, the shared key for authentication is the same as the encryption key. Shared key authentication uses a challenge and response mechanism that may be susceptible to attack. If the authentication key is obtained, it can be used to decrypt encrypted wireless messages.
- **MAC address filtering**—The Media Access Control (MAC) address of the network card is stored on the AP, and only those computers whose MAC address is present can connect. Because MAC addresses can be spoofed, this security is not foolproof. However, it does add some protection from the casual interloper.
- **No SSID broadcast**—The SSID is the network name for the wireless network. It is broadcast by default, and many devices are programmed to automatically connect to available SSIDs. Turning off the broadcast discourages casual access once again, but the SSID is part of wireless communications that is not encrypted, and thus a sniffer can determine the SSID. In addition, the SSID is entered in clear text in the wireless network configuration of the clients, so the SSID can be easily discovered by visiting with authorized users or possibly by looking over their shoulders.
- **Secure AP use of SNMP**—Many wireless APs automatically configure the Simple Network Management Protocol (SNMP) to provide remote administration of the AP. However, few provide any security. Common default community names such as public and comcomcom are implemented. Community names are used by SNMP to provide access to administrator. They can be used to

find information about the AP and modify its configuration. If SNMP must be used for administration, modify the community names. Take the time to verify that the SNMP agent has been patched to correct the flaw exploitable by the PROTOs tool developed by the University of Oulu. If SNMP is not needed, turn it off.

- **Secure administration tools**—Many APs have web-based administration tools that can be accessed over the wireless network. Change the password for these tools to a long, strong password before the AP is placed on the network.

WiFi Protected Access (WPA)

WPA is an interim standard that follows the proposed 802.11i wireless standard. 802.11i uses the Temporal Key Integrity (TKI) algorithm. TKIP rekeys (changes) the key used for every frame. WPA specifies synchronization of keys between client and server. If a RADIUS server is available, the standard supports the use of EAP for authentication; otherwise, a shared key can be used. A technique called Michael provides integrity. An 8-byte Message Integrity Code (MIC) is included with the data, and the Integrity check value used by 802.11. Some network APs are now available that use WPA, and some current 802.11 APs and wireless network cards may be upgradeable. An upgrade for Windows XP Professional implements the WPA architecture.

Using a VPN

Typical 802.11 wireless networks can be provided additional security by requiring a VPN connection to the network where wireless APs are used. When VPN connections are required, Windows accounts can be used for authentication, and the encryption can be provided by the VPN. Figure 14-38 illustrates this arrangement. The wireless AP is connected to the external interface of the VPN server, and the internal network is connected to the internal interface of the VPN server. To connect to the internal network, the wireless client must authenticate to the VPN server and make a VPN connection.

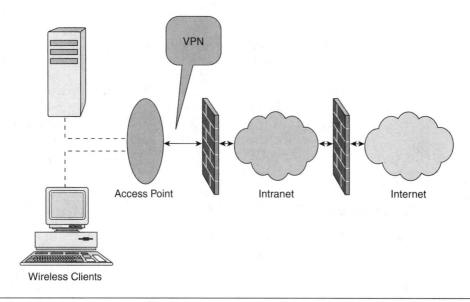

Wireless Clients

Figure 14-38 VPN protection can be added between the wireless network and the internal network.

Using 802.1x

802.1x is a new standard for 802.11 network authentication. This standard requires wireless APs and wireless network cards that meet the standard and a RADIUS server. A Windows Server 2003 IAS server can be used as that RADIUS server. Figure 14-39 illustrates the network topology. Clients request a connection to the wireless access point, which in turn acts as a RADIUS client. The RADIUS server uses Active Directory or its own account database for authentication and Remote Access Policies to determine if the access is authorized. This solution can also solve the key management problem; encryption keys can be automatically issued to authorized clients and changed frequently without manual intervention. In addition, clients can be required to have computer certificates. When clients must use certificates to authenticate to the IAS server, many unauthorized attempts at connection can be rejected.

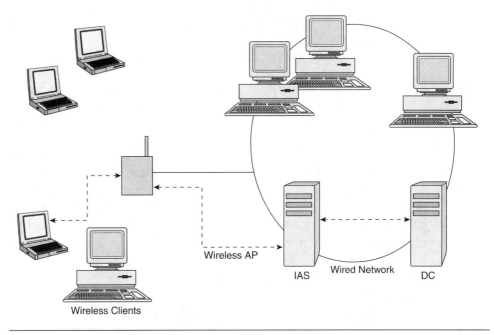

Figure 14-39 VPN protection can be added between the wireless network and the internal network.

NOTE: Downlevel Systems

An upgrade for Windows 2000 is available to allow a Windows 2000 IAS server to be used as the RADIUS server for 802.1x authentication. An 802.1x client is available for Windows 2000. Additional clients are available to Microsoft customers with a support agreement for Windows 98, Windows Millennium Edition, and Windows NT 4.0.

Security Improvements with 802.1x and WPA

There are two major security improvements: improved authentication methods and dynamic key assignment.

Instead of relying on simple AP identification, 802.1x provides a choice of authentication methods:

- **Protected Extensible Authentication Protocol (PEAP) EAP-MSCHAPv2**—Passwords are protected by Transport Layer Security. The IAS server must have a certificate, but client computers do not. Users can use their Windows account passwords.

- **EAP-TLS**—Certificate-based mutual authentication. Both client computers and IAS must have certificates.
- **EAP-MD5**—No certificates at all are required. Authentication is not mutual. This choice is not considered secure because the user provides an account and password using the MS-CHAP protocol. Unlike the PEAP EAP-MSCHAPv2, EAP-MD5 is susceptible to dictionary attacks.

Unlike earlier wireless standards that provide no key management and rely on WEP, WPA (and some implementations of 802.1x, such as Microsoft's) provides key management and encryption. *Dynamic key assignment* or rekeying is used to distribute keys to the client automatically and to change the keys frequently when certificates are used for authentication (when EAP-TLS is used). 802.1x can be implemented with either WPA or 128-bit WEP. When Windows XP clients are used with IAS, key assignment is performed during certificate authentication and is protected. Keys can be refreshed periodically by forcing Windows XP to re-authenticate to the server every 10 minutes.

Implementing 802.1x Security Using IAS

To configure IAS to support 802.1x authentication for wireless APs, follow these instructions:

1. Configure the AP as a RADIUS client by using the instructions given previously for configuring an RRAS server as a RADIUS client in the IAS interface.
2. Configure the wireless AP according to the manufacturer's instructions.
3. Create a Remote Access Policy for wireless clients.
4. Create a Connection Request Policy. Remote Access Policies are created to define and constrain user connections. A Connection Request Policy is used to constrain RADIUS clients. They can be used to restrict a RADIUS client to dates, times, and so forth.
5. Configure wireless clients via Group Policy.

Create a Remote Access Policy for Wireless Clients

Use the Remote Access Policy Wizard to create a policy for wireless clients. The following custom configuration should be made:

■ To identify incoming requests from wireless clients, use the Condition NAS-Port Type and select `Wireless - Other` or `Wireless-IEEE 802.11` policy, as shown in Figure 14-40.

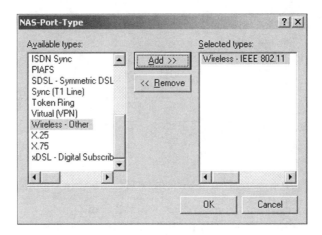

Figure 14-40   Use the Wireless - Other or Wireless-IEEE 802.11 NAS port type in the Remote Access Policy.

■ Configure other parameters as required. For example, restrict wireless access to certain groups of users, for certain times of day, and so forth.
■ Set the profile attribute `Ignore Users-Dial-in` to `True` to ensure that settings such as Callback are not sent to wireless APs.
■ Set the `Advanced` profile attribute `Terminate Action` to `RADIUS-Request`, as shown in Figure 14-41, to ensure that when XP clients re-authenticate, wireless APs don't disconnect them.

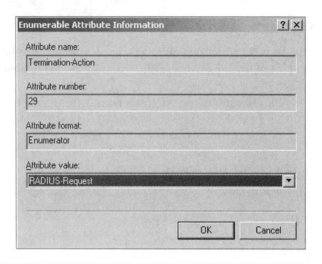

Figure 14-41   Set Terminate Action to RADIUS-Request.

Configure 802.1x Authentication for Clients Using Group Policy

Windows XP clients can be individually configured to use 802.1x; however, you can do so more efficiently and consistently by using Group Policy. To do so, follow these steps:

1. Select the Computer Configuration, Windows Settings, Security Settings, Wireless Network (IEEE 802.11) Policies, as shown in Figure 14-42, and double-click the policy that you want to configure. If the policy does not exist, create one by right-clicking the Wireless Network Policies and selecting Create New Policy.

2. On the General tab, as shown in Figure 14-43, use the Network to access drop-down box to select Access point (infrastructure) networks only.

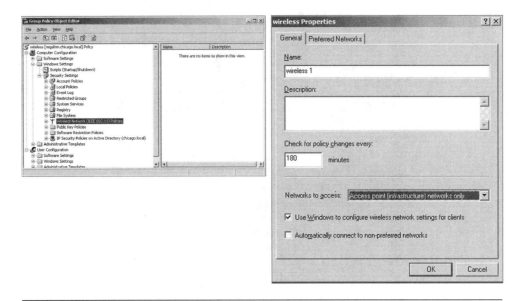

Figure 14-42   Find the wireless policy in Group Policy.

Figure 14-43   Select infrastructure networks.

3. On the `General` tab, select the `Use Windows to configure wireless network settings for` to set a preference for Windows configuration over a third-party wireless client loaded on the client computer.

4. Do not select `Automatically connect to non-preferred networks`. (It is cleared by default.) Checking this box allows clients to automatically attempt to connect to any wireless network. This is not a good policy for environments where rogue wireless networks may exist. Connecting to them may subject the client computer to attack.

5. On the `Preferred Networks` tab, click the `Add` button to configure the organization's AP information including, SSID and WEP, as shown in Figure 14-44, Repeat for each AP.

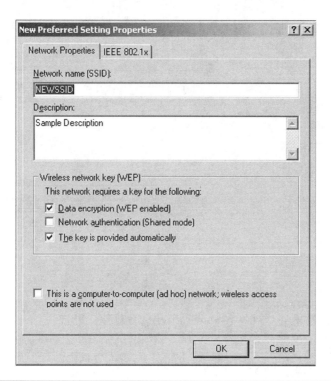

Figure 14-44   Add wireless network information on the Network Properties tab.

6. For each network, use the `Network Properties` tab to configure the SSID.

7. Do not select `Shared Mode` for network authentication. Open mode is required to allow 802.1x authentication.

8. Enable WEP and select `The key is provided automatically` to allow dynamic key exchange.

9. Select the `IEEE 802.1x` tab, as shown in Figure 14-45, to configure 802.1x-specific properties. `Enable network access control using IEEE 802.1x` is enabled by default.

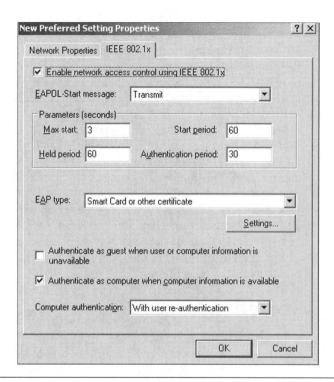

Figure 14-45 Configure 802.1x authentication.

10. In the EAPOL-Start message, specify any parameters for transmitting EAP over LAN (EAPOL) start messages. These must match the configuration at the AP. Choices are Transmit, Do Not Transmit, and Transmit per IEEE 802.11x. Specify the parameters (seconds).

11. Select the EAP types to be used with the wireless network. This will match that selected in IAS.

12. If Smart Card or other certificate is selected, click Settings... and
Select Use My Smart Card if smart cards are to be used
or
select Use a Certificate On This Computer if a certificate in the certificate store on the computer should be used for authentication.
Verify that the server certificate is valid by selecting the Validate Server Certificate box, then click Connect to These Servers and specify the server or servers that client computers should automatically connect to. Specify the trusted root certification authorities.

To allow users to use a different name than the user name associated with their smart card or certificate (in case this name is not the same as their domain user name for the domain in which they wish to log on), select the Use A Different User Name for the Connection box.

13. If PEAP is selected in the EAP type, then

Select the Validate Server Certificate check box to validate that the server certificate is still valid. Click the Connect to These Servers check box and specify the server or servers that clients should automatically connect to. Specify the trusted root certification authority.

Use the Select Authentication Method area to select the authentication method that clients can use within PEAP.

If Secured Password (EAP-MSCHAPv2) is selected, in its properties, specify if the user name, password, and domain that users normally use should be used.

If Smart Card or other certificate is selected, configure as specified in step 6.

If Fast Reconnect is desired, check the Enable Fast Reconnect check box.

PEAP Fast Reconnect allows roaming users to maintain connectivity when traveling between APs on the same network if each AP is configured as a RADIUS client of the same IAS server. Both wireless client and RADIUS server must be configured for fast reconnect.

14. If client computers should attempt to authenticate when user information or computer information is not available, select Authenticate as Guest When User or Computer Information Is Unavailable.

15. If client computers should attempt to authenticate when users are not logged on, check the Authenticate as Computer When Computer Information is Available. In Computer Authentication, click an option to specify how. The options are as follows:

- User Authentication—Computer credentials are used and will continue to be used even when the user logs on. If a different AP is accessed, and the user is logged on, his credentials will be used.

- With User Re-Authentication (Recommended)—Computer credentials are used when the user is not logged on, and user credentials are used when the user logs on. When the user logs off, the computer credentials are used again.

■ `Computer only`—Authentication always uses the computer credentials, never the users.

Allowing computer authentication using any of these methods is useful in order to maintain client connections when users are logged off. On the other hand, it might allow an attack to go unnoticed, as computers may connect to the network when users are not logged on, and in the first and latter case, it may allow unauthorized users to obtain wireless access.

How Does 802.1x Authentication Work?

802.1x authentication specifies the following physical infrastructure:

■ **A supplicant**—This is the wireless client.

■ **A wireless AP with two ports**—One port is the uncontrolled port and any client can connect and begin to negotiate a connection with the uncontrolled port. The controlled port grants access to authenticated and authorized clients to the network.

■ **A RADIUS server or authenticator**—This serves as the control agent.

■ **An authenticating server**—This validates client credentials.

Figure 14-46 illustrates this arrangement; in the figure, a client has requested access but has not been authenticated, so the controlled port is not available to it.

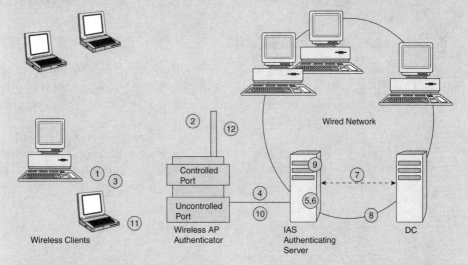

Figure 14-46 802.1x requires access to the controlled port be authenticated and authorized.

As implemented using IAS, access is negotiated in the following manner:

1. The supplicant, the wireless client, requests a connection.
2. The AP requests identity information.
3. The supplicant returns the information.
4. The AP creates a RADIUS access request message that includes the supplicant's credentials and sends it to the authenticator. (In our case, the IAS server.)
5. IAS checks its Connection Requests Policies to see whether the AP is approved and whether the request meets any constraints.
6. If the AP is approved and constraints are met, IAS checks its Remote Access Policies to see whether the client is authorized.
7. If the client is authorized, the credentials from the access request message are forwarded to the domain controller (the authenticating server) for validation.
8. If the client is authenticated, confirmation is returned to IAS.
9. IAS checks its Remote Access Policies for any constraints that must be applied to the connection.
10. Notice of accepted authentication and authorization is returned to the AP in a RADIUS accept message.
11. The AP generates the WEP keys and passes them to the client.
12. The client is allowed access to the network through the controlled port.

Securing Wireless Clients

Securing wireless clients is another important aspect of wireless security. Compromised clients pose a threat to servers and other clients. Mobile wireless clients are often exposed to viruses, Trojan horses, and other attacks when they connect to public networks.

Client security should be maintained by hardening clients, including the use of personal firewalls, anti-virus software, and by only connecting to protected wireless networks. When 802.1x authentication is not in place, clients should be configured to use a VPN for access to the network.

Best Practices for Wireless Access

- Use Group Policy to set Client Settings.
- Use 802.1x.
- Use SSL, SSH, or another secured connection when remotely managing APs to prevent capture of configuration data.
- Manage APs from the wired network.
- Use IAS Remote Access Policies to control client authorization, encryption, IP packet filters, and static routes.
- Use IAS Connection Policies to validate APs and restrict their access.
- Use PEAP-EAP MS-CHAPv2 when computers are not domain members and when certificate infrastructure is not in place.
- Do not use PEAP-MD5. The password is not protected against dictionary attacks.

Best Practices for IAS and RRAS Security

- If you must use passwords, use strong passwords. Strong passwords are those that are 8 or more characters long and are composed of uppercase and lowercase characters, numbers, and special characters. Strong passwords make password-cracking attacks more difficult.
- If possible, require smart cards for remote authentication.
- Where MS-CHAP will be allowed for authentication, require MS-CHAPv2 authentication. MS-CHAPv2 updates are available for most Windows versions that are not able to use MS-CHAPv2 by default.
- Disallow the use of MS-CHAP. If you cannot, change the value of the Allow LM Authentication to 0 at the following location. This prevents the use of LM authentication that is allowed by default when MS-CHAP is used. Be sure to configure clients by adding, if necessary, the AD client and configuring the clients to use NTLMv2 for authentication:

  `HKLM\SYSTEM\CurrentControlSet\Services\RemoteAccessPolicy`

- Configure the highest level of encryption and authentication that clients can use.
- When RADIUS is selected as an authentication and/or accounting method, use a long shared secret (22 characters or more) composed of a random sequence of letters, numbers, and punctuation and change it often. This helps protect the password from dictionary and brute-force password attacks.

- The shared secret is also used to provide message integrity.

- Use the Message Authenticator attribute to protect RADIUS from spoofed IP addresses. The IP address of the RADIUS client is configured in the IAS properties and is used to determine whether or not to consider a connection request. Because IP addresses can be spoofed, the Message Authenticator attribute can be used to provide further protection. It is an MD5 hash of the entire RADIUS message that uses the shared secret as a key. If the feature is used, RADIUS messages can be verified as coming from a client or server with knowledge of the shared secret. Messages that do not pass this test are dropped. If the Message Authenticator attribute is required and not used, the message will also be dropped.

- Use a different shared secret for each RADIUS client and RADIUS server pair, and for each RADIUS proxy and RADIUS server pair, unless you specify RADIUS clients by IP address range, in which case you must use the same shared secret for each RADIUS client in that group.

- Use IPSec to secure the entire RADIUS message by creating a policy for use by communication between the RRAS and IAS servers. This is especially important where the threat environment may be high.

- Enforce strong password policies on the network if smart cards cannot be used.

- Be cautious if you decide to use account lockout policy for remote access. If a dictionary or brute-force attack is run against accounts, it can lock out both the attacker and the legitimate user. (Note that account lockout for remote access has nothing to do with the account lockout policy configured in Group Policy.)

- If you locate the logs to a different place from the default location, configure the ACLs on the log files to allow only the local system account and the Administrators group access.

- If you redirect logging to SQL server, ensure control of who can access database. Secure the SQL server and the connection and transport of log data.

- Configure auditing to track who accesses the log files.

- Do not move log files to a server on which access controls cannot be set on the files.

- Establish encrypted communication between the RRAS or IAS server and the SQL server if log files are published to the SQL server. The log data is sent in plain text and should be encrypted to protect it. See the SQL server documentation for help in configuring the encrypted communication.

- Use terminal services to administer RRAS and IAS remotely. Communications are 128-bit encrypted.

Securing Web Server–Based Access to Internal Resources

Many IT pros think of the web server as a server that presents resources to the public, such as information and e-commerce. They therefore consider its security and that of its applications as a separate security domain. While one group of individuals administers and is responsible for securing the network, IT often delegates the administration of the web server and its security to a different group. The web server is a unique entity and should be administered by those who know it best. However, if web server security is divorced from mainstream network consideration, no one wins. In fact, if web server activities are not reviewed against the general security policies of the network, this can introduce additional vulnerabilities into the network.

This is because many web server applications require support from network resources and are administered from network computers. Intentionally or not, web servers have become remote access portals—another way in which access is provided to the internal network. This section identifies general web server and web application security issues and addresses the use of the web server as a remote access portal. It does not pretend, however, to be a complete guide to web server and web application security.

Web Server Security Basics

Securing a web server starts with a secure implementation and hardening of the Windows Server 2003 computer on which it will be deployed. By default, web services are not installed on the Windows Server 2003 Enterprise and Standard Edition computers during installation, and they should not be installed at that time. Instead, install Windows Server 2003, install the latest service pack and security patches, and harden the server according to your organization's security policy and practices. Chapter 11 provides a methodology for securing domain member computers using security templates developed from those provided by Microsoft.

A default installation of IIS 6.0 can only serve static web pages. In fact, many services and extensions that you may require for web applications are not available, not installed, or not enabled. The first IIS security lesson is to remember to determine only what you need and enable that. Do not blindly turn everything on. When selecting applications, require vendor specification of the minimal IIS support that is required so that you will only have to enable the least number of items. When internally developed web applications will be used, ensure that developers have been trained in secure web application development and understand IIS 6.0.

The following steps should be taken to secure IIS 6.0:

- Consider disabling services that are often enabled for other servers. Specifically, the following services, which may provide services critical to other servers, should be considered as possible candidates for disabling on web servers:

    Automatic Updates —This service may be used to provide automatic updates either via the Windows Update site or by using a Software Update Services server. Disable this service if you will perform manual updates for the web server.

    Background Information Transfer Service (BITS)—This service is used by Automatic Updates download patches using background processes. If Automatic Updates is disabled, disable BITS as well.

    Remote Registry Service—This service is used by many administration tools to allow administrators to administer the computer. Consider using alternative administrative tools or administer the web server at the console.

    Terminal Services—Do not install terminal services in application mode. If terminal services is required for administration, it is available in administrative mode as the Remote Desktop. You do not want ordinary users to obtain terminal service access to the web server.

    Simple Mail Transfer Protocol (SMTP) Service—If a web application requires SMTP services to provide email services, this service may be required. However, if applications do not require it, disable it. If it is used, configure it securely by assigning SMTP operators (users who can configure or manage SMTP) and preventing relay. (Uncontrolled relay can result in spam that may both close your servers and network as well as others.)

NOTE: Preventing Relay

Knowledge Base articles 324285 (`http://support.microsoft.com/default.aspx?scid=kb;en-us;324281`) provide instructions on preventing relay. An article on securing IIS 6.0 SMPT virtual servers can be found at `http://www.microsoft.com/resources/documentation/IIS/6/all/techref/en-us/iisRG_CFG_39.mspx`.

- When web servers must also serve other purposes, ensure protection of these services and applications. Do not allow weak security of these other applications to compromise the web server, and do not allow weak security of the web server or its applications to compromise other applications and resources.
- Use ACLs and identities to isolate web sites and web applications and to protect server resources. Applications can be isolated by using application pools. *Application pools* are groups of web sites and applications that use the same worker process. Application pools are isolation boundaries, and applications running outside the application pool have no access to the process or web site running inside the application pool.
- Design authentication to meet the needs of the web site. Enable only those forms of authentication that are necessary. See the sidebar "Design Web Site Authentication" for more information.
- Locate web server content on a separate disk or volume from the operating system to prevent directory traversal attacks. In a directory traversal attack, the attacker gains access to some minor data area of the web site and uses an attack to move about the directory on the disk and gain access to sensitive areas, such as operating systems files and commands.
- Set the root access permissions on the web server content disk to administrators and SYSTEM Full Control. Grant access elsewhere on the disk as required by the applications.
- Use a single top-level folder for web sites and applications, but provide a unique subfolder for each web site and web application.
- If anonymous accounts are used to access public web site data, ensure that the accounts are not granted access elsewhere on the site or server.
- If Windows accounts are given access to parts of a web site, ensure that they only have the type of access that they require.
- Set correct ACLs on all folders and files to support the protection and proper functions of web applications and data.
- You can enable the use of all unknown (not specifically defined for this web server) ISAPI extensions in the `Web Services Extension` node of the `Internet Information Services (IIS)` Manager console. Do not change the status of the `Allow All Unknown ISAPI Extension` web service extension to `Allowed` from `Prohibited`, as shown in Figure 14-47. Instead, only allow those ISAPI extensions that are required and that have been reviewed to determine if they can be safely used.

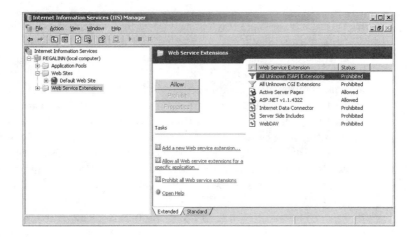

Figure 14-47   Do not blindly allow ISAPI extensions.

- Secure the use of the following web site roles:

  IUSR_*servername*—This account is used for anonymous access.

  IWAM_*servername*—This account is provided for compatibility with IIS 5.0. IIS 5.0 could be run in isolation mode, a different construct than the IIS 6.0 worker process isolation mode. When applications are run in IIS 5.0 isolation mode, they are run in the context of the privileged local systems account. Applications run out-of-process in IIS 5.0 run under the context of the IWAM_servername account, which has fewer privileges on the server.

  Process identity—The account that a process runs under. When anonymous access is allowed, the IUSR_*servername* account is the process identity.

  Application pool identity—The user account that is the process identity for a worker process that services an application pool. Each application pool should have a separate application pool identity. You restrict and grant access to resources based on this identity.

  IIS_WPG group—A default group added when IIS is installed. The group has default access to write log files, access to the metabase, and access that is required for IIS applications to run. Instead of applying the proper access rights and permissions to each new user account created as an application pool identity, add them to this group.

- Use web site permissions. Web site permissions are used by IIS to determine what type of access is allowed to a web site or virtual directory. Web site permissions are not used instead of NTFS permissions. If both web permissions and NTFS permissions are used, the most restrictive permission will be applied. Web site permissions, however, only affect those who visit the web site. NTFS permissions affect all visitors to the data. NTFS permissions should always be used to protect files and folders. Web site permissions are

  Read view the content and directory and file properties—If all content is scripted, such as ASP pages, the Read permission is not required and can be removed. Do not combine Read and Script Source Access on the same folder. Visitors might find sensitive information in script files such as passwords.

  Write—Change the content and properties of files and folders. Do not combine Write and Execute permissions on the same folders. To do so would allow a visitor to add a script or program to the web site and then execute it with potentially disastrous results.

  Script Source Access—Permits access to source files. If Script Source Access and Read are set on the same folder, visitors to the web site can read scripts, and if Write is set, they can modify the source files. Script Source Access is required when WebDAV is used.

  Directory Browsing—View file lists.

  Log Visits—A log entry for each visitor is added. Enable logging. Having information on who visited the web site and at what time may help determine the source of an attack.

  Index this resource—Permits the indexing service to index the resources so that searches can be made.

  Execute—Has three different levels of access: None—no scripts or executables can run; Scripts Only—only scripts can run; Scripts and Executables—scripts and executables can run on the server.

- Keep different file types in different folders and set appropriate permissions on the folders.
- Back up web site data and the metabase. The metabase is the structure that store IIS configuration.

Design Web Site Authentication

One of the best ways to make it easy for attackers to compromise a web site is to allow authentication processes that are weak and then to have weak account policies. If, for example, basic authentication is allowed, passwords will traverse the network in the clear and might be captured. On the other hand, if Windows integrated authentication is allowed, passwords do not traverse the network in plaintext, but the credentials are subject to known attacks. If the passwords are weak, the attacks may succeed. If password policy is strong, such as requiring long, complex passwords and preventing the use of LM password hashes, attacks are less likely to succeed. The ultimate solution, however, may be to provide SSL encryption of the entire message, including the transfer of authentication credentials and/or the use of certificates for client authentication. The following additional authentication requirements should be considered:

- Use Windows integrated authentication on the local intranet where risk of credentials being captured may be less.

- Use digest authentication only if all clients are members of the same domain as the IIS server and only if other authentication techniques cannot be used. Digest authentication is another form of challenge/handshake authentication but is weaker than Windows integrated authentication.

- Use anonymous authentication for public access. No user will need to provide credentials.

- Use certificate authentication when highly secure access is required and a secure mechanism for certificate distribution and management is present.

- Use SSL to secure basic authentication.

In addition, remember that, in general, when multiple authentication methods are available, IIS will use the most secure method first; however, if anonymous access is provided, and anonymous access is allowed to a resource, it will be used. If .NET passport authentication is chosen as the authentication method for a web site, no other form of authentication will be available.

Remote Access Considerations

Many of the security considerations listed previously will also help to protect the internal network. If the web server is compromised, its authorized connections to internal resources can turn it into a backdoor to the network and enable compromise:

- Restrict access from the web server to internal resources. Instead of simply allowing the web server access to the network, reduce that access to specific servers only. For example, an internal firewall between the web server on the perimeter network and the internal network can allow access to specific ports on specific servers by the web server.

- Consider the protection of data as it leaves and comes to the web server. E-commerce transactions are often protected with Secure Sockets Layer (SSL), but these are not the only communications processes that should be considered. Both customer transactions and communications between the web server and backend servers, such as databases, may need protection. Consider SSL or IPSec as possible communication protection options. SSL, for example, can be used to secure communications between the web server and Internet Security and Acceleration (ISA) server, and between the web server and Microsoft SQL server. IPSec can also be used to secure communications between the web server and resources it needs to access.

- Consider protection for administrative access to web servers. Consider isolating administrative access to specific administrator computers and protect communications with IPSec.

- Do not install the Remote Administration (HTML) Tool. This tool provides remote administration via a web browser. Port 80 access to administration tools is not a good idea because port 80 will always be open to the Internet if a web server is used.

- Consider the use of terminal services for administration from the LAN. Terminal services communications are encrypted, and the user is authenticated.

- Require VPN access for administration across the WAN if such access is allowed.

- Protect the process of content management. Not only should an approval process exist, but you also should require authenticated access to the server and use ACLs to ensure that only authorized individuals can change content.

- Provide additional change control management to ensure appropriate and timely addition of service packs and security patches as well as equipment updates.

- Restrict access to intranet sites. Use the web site Directory Security Property page and its IP address and name restrictions button to limit access by specifying domain names and IP addresses. This may prevent remote access or access from unauthorized computers. Remember, however, that IP addresses can be spoofed. To restrict access, click the `Denied access` radio button and then use the Add button to enter the IP address or domain name of the approved computers. Figure 14-48 shows the configuration to only allow access from computers joined in the chicago.local domain.

WARNING: Performance Issue
Using domain names to restrict access to web sites requires the use of a reverse lookup for each attempted request. This can hamper performance.

- Use FTP user isolation when access by multiple, diverse populations to FTP services is required. When multiple FTP sites are established on the same server, it is difficult to configure FTP and the server to keep malicious users from obtaining access to other sites. Directory traversal attacks are used to gain access. FTP user isolation solves this issue. When FTP user isolation is used, each FTP site appears to be at the root of the FTP server, and directory traversal attacks cannot be used to gain access to other sites. A user with credentials for one site cannot access the resources on another. For more information, see KB article 816525 at http://support.microsoft.com/default.aspx?scid=kb;en-us;816525.

Figure 14-48   Restricting access by IP address.

Summary

Securing remote access to networks is a broad subject. First, the use of tools such as RRAS and IAS must be considered, and their role as remote access portals must be explained. Next, and equally important, is the security of these devices. Improper configuration of these services can negate any security that they provide. New uses for these servers, such as using Network Access Quarantine Control to place security requirements on clients that connect to the remote access servers and the implementation of VPNS and 802.1x authentication to protect network access via wireless networks, are also critical to the protection of network. Finally, to complete an understanding of remote access, consider barriers to network access that result from the use of and connection to the internal network by web servers and the applications that run on them.

CHAPTER 15

Protecting Data in Flight

Data traveling from network to network can be secured via VPNs and Secure Sockets Layer (SSL). Data that travels across the internal network must also be secured. VPNs can be configured for this purpose, as can SSL, but other technologies designed specifically for communications between two hosts on the same network or for specific Windows Server 2003 communications can also be used. This chapter describes the following technologies in addition to SSL:

- Server Message Block signing
- Session Security for NTLM
- IPSec
- SSL
- LDAP Signing and other Active Directory Access Security Mechanisms

Use Server Message Block Signing

The server message block (SMB) protocol is used for communications between Windows computers. SMB signing is a process that ensures that the communication received by a computer was actually sent by the computer referenced as the source. This is an important security setting because even if authentication is established between domain member computers, after the session start, communications may be vulnerable to man-in-the-middle attacks. When SMB signing is required, the Windows computer signs each message it sends. The Windows computer that receives the message can and does check to ensure that the source of the communication is valid. SMB signing is enabled by default on Windows Server 2003. SMB signing is very resource-intensive and can significantly impact performance by up to 30 percent.

TIP: Legacy Systems Can Be Configured to Do SMB Signing
Windows 2000, Windows Server 2003, and Windows XP Professional can
be easily configured to do SMB signing using Group Policy. Knowledge
Base article 555038 explains how Windows NT 4.0 and Windows 98 can
be configured to do SMB signing (`http://support.microsoft.com/
default.aspx?scid=kb;en-us;555038`).

Four Security Options are used to configure SMB signing in Windows
Server 2003, two for the client and two for the server. The `Security`
`Options` are as follows:

- `Microsoft Network client: Digitally sign communications
  (always)`
- `Microsoft Network client: Digitally sign communications
  (if server agrees)`
- `Microsoft Network server: Digitally sign communications
  (always)`
- `Microsoft Network server: Digitally sign communications
  (if client agrees)`

Message signing is negotiated during the connection request. If the
server or client must (always) do message signing, and its counterpart
cannot, communications will not be permitted. Because this setting is
enabled by default on Windows Server 2003, Windows 2000 and legacy
clients will not be able communicate with Windows Server 2003 computers. If you must provide these systems with access to Windows Server
2003, you will have to configure them to use SMB signing or disable the
Security Option in Windows Server 2003. If at all possible, retain the
default settings.

Use Session Security for NTLM

NTLM session security has been available since Service Pack 4 of Windows
NT 4.0. This option allows the configuration of integrity (the messages
received are exactly the same as those sent) and confidentiality (encryption). Two Security Options are available to configure session security:

- `Network Security: Minimum session security for NTLM SSP
  based (including secure RPC) clients.`

- Network Security: Minimum session security for NTLM SSP based (including secure RPC) servers

Each Security Option can be configured with the following options:

- Require message integrity
- Require message con dentiality
- Require NTLMv2 session security
- Require 128-bit encryption

Check one or more of these options to set the requirements for NTLM session security. Session security is negotiated at session start.

Use Internet Protocol Security Policies

The original TCP/IP standard had as its goal the development of a bullet-proof protocol. TCP/IP's designers, however, did not add any requirements for confidentiality. They may not have been particularly interested in keeping people from reading the information contained in the communications packets because, at that time, it was difficult just to get computer systems to talk. Basic communication between diverse systems was difficult because many computer systems of the day had their own proprietary communications. In addition, few organizations, let alone individuals, had access to computer systems, and fewer had access to the network that was being built between governments and universities.

Today, the opposite is true: It is possible to obtain 24×7 connectivity to the rest of the world at very little cost. With that, unfortunately, comes the problem that data can be captured as it transits the network and read by those that shouldn't be reading it. One way to control access to data is to encrypt and protect it during transit by using Internet Protocol security (IPSec). IPSec was developed as part of a newer version of the TCP/IP protocol, IPv6. IPSec, however, is built into the TCP/IP stack of Windows Server 2003, Windows 2000, and Windows XP and is available as an add-in for other operating systems. It is also widely used as a VPN security protocol, either alone or as the encryption protocol for L2TP tunnels.

The use of IPSec in VPNs was described in Chapter 14, "Securing Remote Access." This chapter details IPSec's ability as a security protocol to block or permit communications with a server or to negotiate secure communications between two computers. IPSec can also be used to secure communications between a Windows 2003 Server and a device such as a Cisco router. This type of communication follows the same pattern as those described in the following section, though not all IPSec devices will be compatible with each other. You will need to determine interoperability and follow the instructions provided by the device manufacturer.

NOTE: FYI

The article "Simple Certificate Enrollment Protocol (SCEP) Add on for Certificate Services" (`http://www.microsoft.com/downloads/details.aspx?FamilyID=9f306763-d036-41d8-8860-1636411b2d01&displaylang=en`) provides information and a downloadable tool that can make it easy for a Cisco router to download a certificate from a Windows Server 2003 CA. "Windows Virtual Private Network Connectivity to a Cisco PIX Firewall" (`http://support.microsoft.com/default.aspx?scid=kb;en-us;249576`) and other articles provide interoperability information.

To use IPSec to secure communications between Windows computers, including Windows 2000, Windows XP, and Windows Server 2003, write IPSec policies. To do so, you must understand how the protocol works, as described in the section "How IPSec Works" and how to write the policy, as detailed in the section "Writing IPSec Policies." It is also important to be able to monitor and troubleshoot IPSec, as described in the section "Monitoring and Troubleshooting IPSec," after the policy is assigned.

IPSec Implementation in Windows Server 2003

IPSec is implemented as the IPSec driver within the TCP/IP protocol stack, and as a Windows service (IPSec services) in Windows Server 2003. Although the service is enabled by default, no IPSec protection is available until a policy is written and assigned. The protocol and the policies are complex, and the best way to understand IPSec is to write and test a few policies in a test environment. Windows Server 2003 IPSec components are illustrated in Figure 15-1 and described in Table 15-1. In Figure 15-1, the shaded rectangles represent the components, and those that are built into the TCP/IP protocol stack are illustrated as such. The unlabeled rectangles at the physical layer of the stack represent the capabilities of the IPSec driver to offload encryption to TCP/IP cards that are capable of doing so. The IPSec components can be broken down into parts, which are further defined in the process description in the section "How IPSec Works."

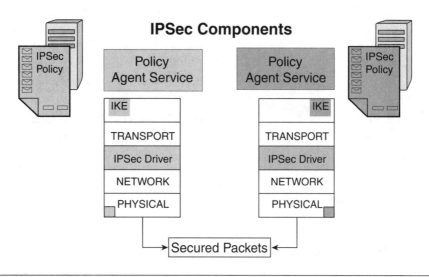

Figure 15-1   IPSec components.

Table 15-1   IPSec Components

Component	Action
IPSec Policy Agent (IPSec Services)	Retrieves policy information and passes it on to the other components. Obtains the policy from Active Directory or from the local registry of the computer. Polls for policy changes. Passes policy information to the IPSec driver.
IPSec driver	Matches inbound and outbound packets with filters in the IPSec policy and responds according to filter action defined in the policy. Receives policy information (filter list) from the IPSec Policy Agent. Compares each inbound and outbound packet against the list. Responds according to the filter action defined in the policy.

Table 15-1   IPSec Components Continued

Component	Action
Internet Key Exchange (IKE)	Negotiates and manages communications between two computers. Negotiates Security Associate (SA) or agreement on how to protect and exchange information between two computers. Centralizes SA management. Generates and manages secret keys.
IPSec Policy	When active, sets the response for all inbound and outbound TCP/IP communications. Defines the filters and responses. Defines security protocols and security settings for negotiated communications.

How IPSec Works

IPSec monitors inbound and outbound traffic. When IPSec policies are assigned (made active), they are used only when IP traffic, either inbound or outbound, meets the IPSec filter requirements. The IPSec filter is a combination of source and destination IP addresses, protocols, and ports defined in one of the policies' rules. Rules are a policy part composed of a list of filters, filter actions, and other settings. If a packet matches a filter, this triggers a filter action associated with the filter's rule. A *filter action* specifies what happens to the packet.

Three possible filter actions are as follows:

- **Block**—Do not allow traffic to pass; packets are dropped.
- **Permit**—Allow traffic to pass.
- **Negotiate**—Agree on security protocols, key settings, and other secure configurations and securely exchange traffic if authenticated.

For example, if an IPSec policy filter identifies inbound port 23 traffic from any source address and the filter action is block, all inbound traffic to port 23 will be dropped. If, however, in addition to this filter and filter action, another rule in the policy has a filter that specifies that inbound port 23 traffic from a specific IP address is allowed (the filter action is Allow), only inbound port 23 traffic from that address will be allowed.

Here's how the IPSec components work together on inbound and outbound traffic:

1. The IPSec Policy Agent monitors for changes in policy and passes that information on to the IPSec driver.
2. The driver attempts to match every inbound and outbound packet against the filters in the active policy.
3. If a packet does not match any filter, or if it matches a filter with a Permit filter action, it is passed back to the TCP/IP driver.
4. If a packet matches a filter with the Block filter action, the packet is dropped.
5. If packets match a filter with the Negotiate filter action, the IPSec Policy Agent queues the packet, notifies IKE, and then IKE negotiates the inbound and outbound Security Association (SA). SA and IKE negotiation are detailed in the section "IKE Negotiation."
6. If negotiation fails, the packet is dropped.
7. If negotiation for outbound packet is successful, the IPSec Policy Agent does the following:
   Receives SA with session key from IKE.
   Inserts a Security Parameters Index (SPI) in the protocol header (either the ESP or AH protocol header—see the section, "IPSec Protocols").
   Signs, encrypts if required.
   Sends packet onto IP layer for forwarding.
   Stores quick mode SA information in a database. (Quick mode is discussed in the section "IKE Negotiation.")
8. If an inbound secured packet matches the filter, the IPSec Policy Agent does the following:
   Receives SPI, SA, and session key from IKE.
   Uses the Security Parameters Index to match a packet with the SA in its database.
   Decrypts if necessary.
   Checks the signature.
   Checks the packet against the filter to make sure that nothing but what was negotiated was received.
   Sends the packet to the TCP/IP driver to pass on to the application.
9. If the unsecured packet is received, checks filters. If the packet should be secured, discards it.

IPSec Protocols

IPSec is composed of two protocols: Authentication Header (AH) and Encapsulated Security Protocol (ESP). An IPSec policy can specify the use of one or both of them. Both protocols provide authentication, integrity, and anti-replay; however, AH cannot provide confidentiality (encryption) but provides superior integrity protection. The AH packet is pictured in Figure 15-2. Note that the IP header, the AH header, and the IP payload are signed by AH. In contrast, the ESP packet, shown in Figure 15-3, signs only the ESP header and trailer and the IP payload. This means that the IP header, because it is not signed, is not necessarily protected from modification. The IP payload and ESP trailer are encrypted.

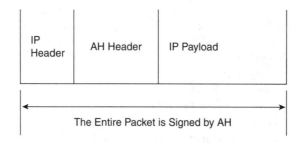

Figure 15-2   AH provides superior integrity by signing the entire packet.

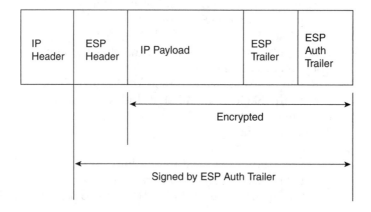

Figure 15-3   ESP does not sign the IP header.

What Is an IPSec Policy?

The IPSec policy defines the elements that decide what traffic is allowed, blocked, or negotiated and, if negotiated, what protocols and what type of protection is used. An administrator can create an IPSec policy locally, distribute it via Group Policy, or copy it from one computer to another. A policy is not active until it is assigned. Only one policy can be active on a specific computer at a time. Policy parts are defined in Table 15-2.

Table 15-2   IPSec Policy Parts

Element	Description
Rules	A policy includes one or more rules. Rules are collections of filters and can contain multiple filters. Each rule can have only one filter action. If a policy requires more than one filter action (it must block some packets, for example, while allowing or negotiating others), multiple rules must be defined.
Filter List	A collection of filters that belong to a single rule.
Filter Action	Specifies what happens when an inbound or outbound packet matches a filter.
Negotiation Specifications	Details that specify the elements that are required and that may be negotiated if the filter action is negotiate.

Setup of policies that only specify block or allow filter actions is straightforward, and these policies act like simple gateways, either dropping or passing packets to the TCP/IP driver. Policies whose rule(s) specify a filter action of negotiation are more complex. In addition to filter lists, many other specifications must be defined. In order for negotiation to be successful between two IPSec Policy Agents on the respective computers, the specifications in both policies must be compatible. Table 15-3 lists and describes these specifications.

Table 15-3 IPSec Policy Specifications

Item	Description
Authentication	Communication must be authenticated. Three choices are Kerberos, Shared secret, and Certificates.
Integrity	Integrity is provided to ensure that the data is not changed when it travels from one computer to another. Integrity can be provided either by ESP or AH protocols, and either MD5 or SHA1 algorithms can be selected.
Confidentiality	Confidentiality is provided by ESP encryption. DES or 3DES may be selected.
Diffie-Hellman Group	Used to determine the base prime number (numbers used as key material) length. The strength of the keys derived from the DH exchange depends on the strength of the DH group. Each group uses a different length. Group 1 has 768 bits of keying material, while Group 2 has 1,024 bits. Group 3 (only available with Windows Server 2003) has 2,048 bits. DH groups must be matched across IPSec peers.
Perfect Forward Secrecy	Determines how a key is generated rather than when. It ensures that keying material and keys used to protect a transmission in either mode cannot be used to generate new keys. Master key PFS requires reauthentication as well and is therefore resource-intensive. A new main mode negotiation is required for every quick mode negotiation. Session PFS does not require reauthentication but does require a new DH exchange to generate new keying material.
Key lifetime	Determines when a new key is generated (Dynamic keying or rekeying or key regeneration). Setting key lifetime allows you to force key regeneration after a specified interval. The SA is also renegotiated. Changing keys frequently ensures that less information is available should a single key be deduced.
Session key refresh limit	Session keys are keyed off the Diffie-Hellman shared secret. Therefore, a session key refresh limit can be imposed. Setting the session key refresh limit to 1 is the same as setting master key perfect forward secrecy (PFS).

IKE Negotiation

Internet Key Exchange (IKE) negotiation is used to create the Security Agreement or Security Association (SA) between two computers (also known as IPSec peers). During the negotiation, an agreement is reached on how to exchange and protect information. Both sides must be able to agree, and neither side can agree on some configuration that is not present. Negotiations are divided into two phases: Phase I (main mode) and Phase II (quick mode).

During main mode:

1. A secure, authenticated channel is established.
2. Encryption (DES or 3DES), integrity (MD5 or SHA1), Diffie-Hellman group (1, 2, or 3) and authentication method (Kerberos, preshared key, or certificates) is negotiated.
3. Diffie-Hellman exchange of public values and master key generation. No actual keys are exchanged, just keying material that is required by the Diffie-Hellman key determination algorithm. Both computers generate the master key. The DH exchange must be authenticated or no communications can proceed.
4. The sender presents an SA to the receiver, who cannot modify it but can accept or reply with an alternative.

If main mode is successful, during quick mode, the negotiation process is protected by the main mode SA:

1. Policy negotiation of IPSec protocol (ESP or AH), hash algorithm for integrity (MD5 or SHA1), and encryption (DES or 3DES). If a common agreement can be reached, two quick mode SAs are established: one for inbound and one for outbound communication.
2. Session key material refreshes or is exchanged. IKE refreshes keying material, and new shared keys are generated for packet integrity, authentication, and encryption.
3. The IPSec Policy Agent generates a SPI.
4. SAs keys and SPI are passed to the driver.

Writing IPSec Policies

Policies may be written using either the GUI policy wizard or the command-line tool `netsh`. If the wizard is used, it can be initiated via a Group Policy Object (GPO) (IP Security Policy on Active Directory) linked to an Active Directory object via the IP Security Policies on the Local Computer in the Local Security Policy, or by adding the IP Security Policy Management snap-in to an MMC. The wizard works the same way no matter where it is started. Both options, GUI or command line, can produce the same policy, with the exception of the a special policy, which can be activated before the IPSec Policy Agent service is started during system boot. This type of policy must be created and assigned using `netsh`.

How to Write Policies Using the IPSec Policy Wizard

To understand how policies work, create policies and make them work. Do this on a test network between two servers. A good way to do so is to first work with one computer, creating a blocking rule and testing it. Then, in the same policy, create a permit rule and test it. Finally, change the permit rule to a negotiate rule, and create a policy with its counterpart at another server. Make the policy simple. For example, block a single protocol, then allow that protocol—but only if its source address is a single computer. Then, turn that rule into a negotiated policy.

By writing the policy bit by bit, you gain experience and find that troubleshooting is easier if something goes wrong. One area of policy definition that often causes problems is authentication. You can eliminate this as an initial problem:

1. Configure your test policies to use a preshared secret for authentication.
2. If the policy does not work (and you confirm that both IPSec computers are using the same preshared secret), the problem lies elsewhere (not with authentication), most likely in your protocol configuration.
3. When the policy works, you can change the authentication to Kerberos or certificates, whichever you require, and test the policy again.

If your goal is to use IPSec policies for many computers that are joined in an Active Directory domain, test the policy between two computers before including the policy in a GPO. Once tested between two computers, a policy should be tested in a test Active Directory domain and only then implemented in production.

To create and test a policy via the GUI, do the following:

- Create a console by adding the IPSec Management snap-in to an MMC.
- Write a blocking rule and test it.
- Write and test a Permit rule.
- Change the allow rule to a Negotiate rule and test it.

Create an MMC Console

The first step is to create a console:

1. Open an MMC by clicking `Start`, `MMC`.
2. From the File menu, click `Add/Remove Snap-in` and click `Add`.
3. From the `Add Standalone Snap-in`, select `IP Security Policy Management`, and then click `Add`.
4. From the `Select Computer or Domain` dialog, accept the default `Local computer` selection and click `Finish`, as shown in Figure 15-4, then `Close` and click `OK`.

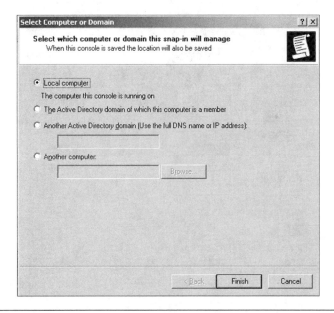

Figure 15-4   Test policies first by using the local computer. Do so by adding the IP Security Management snap-in to an MMC.

5. From the `File` menu, click `Save As`, enter the file name IP Security Policy Management, and click `Save`.

Create and Test a Blocking Rule

Next, take the easy way—configure and test a blocking rule:

1. In the IP Security Policy Management console, right-click the IP Security Policies on Local Computer container, select Create an IP Security Policy, and then click Next.
2. Name the policy Telnet, enter a brief description, and click Next.
3. Uncheck the default response rule. If the default response rule is left active, insecure communication could occur if the IPSec policy rule fails.
4. Click Next, and then click Finish.
5. In the new policy's Properties page, as shown in Figure 15-5, uncheck Use Add Wizard and click Add.

NOTE: To Use or Not Use Add Wizards

Although wizards are useful tools, the Add Wizard in IPSec configuration is not useful in this circumstance.

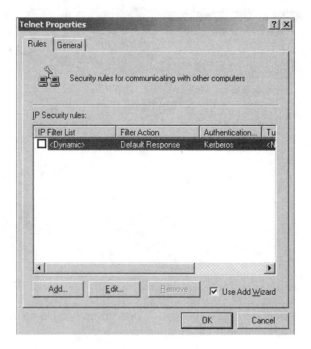

Figure 15-5 Deselect the Add Wizard.

6. In the IP Filter List tab, as shown in Figure 15-6, click Add to create the filter list.

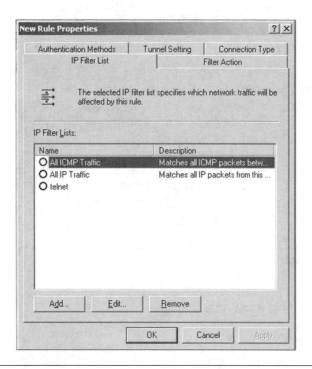

Figure 15-6   Adding a filter list.

7. Enter Blocking all Telnet to name the filter list.
8. Uncheck the Use Add Wizard box and click Add to add a filter.
9. In the Source address drop-down list, select Any IP Address. (You want to block all traffic arriving for this port.)
10. In Destination address, select My IP Address, as shown in Figure 15-7, and then click the Protocol tab.
11. In the Select a protocol type box, select TCP.
12. In the Set the IP protocol port field, as shown in Figure 15-8, click To this port, enter 23, then click OK.

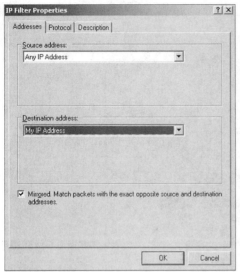 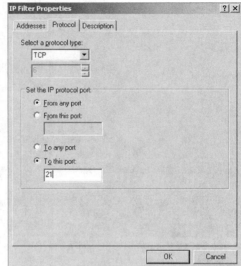

Figure 15-7   Creating the filter.

Figure 15-8   Defining filter ports.

13. Click OK to close the IP Filter List page.
14. In the IP Filter lists box, select the Blocking all Telnet entry, and then click the Filter Action tab.
15. Deselect the Use Add Wizard button and click Add to add a Filter Action.
16. In the Security Methods tab, as shown in Figure 15-9, select Block.
17. Click the General tab, enter Block for the filter's Name, and then click OK.
18. On the Filter Action Property page, click the Block filter action button, as shown in Figure 15-10, and then click Close.
19. On the New Rule Properties page, click Close.
20. Click OK to close the policy.

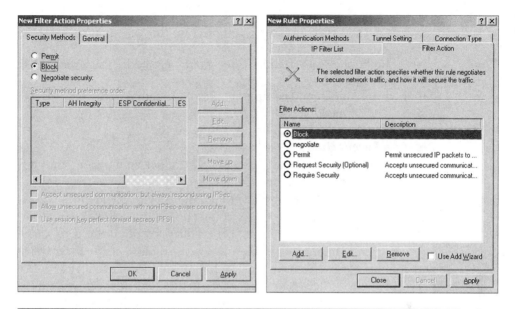

Figure 15-9 Creating the Blocking filter action.

Figure 15-10 Select the filter you created.

It is only necessary to create a blocking policy on one computer. To test the policy, follow these steps:

1. Open the Services console and set the startup status of the telnet service to automatic. Then, start the service.
2. Open a command prompt on a second computer.
3. On this computer, enter the command telnet *ipaddress*, where *ipaddress* is the address of the computer on which you created the Telnet policy.
4. Because the IPSec policy has not been activated, the computer at that *ipaddress* should respond. It asks for an account and password, and then provides a command prompt. If it does not, troubleshoot this connection before moving on. When a connection is made, close it. This test demonstrates that telnet was started on the first computer and that you can connect to it from a second computer using the telnet command.

5. On the first computer, open or go to the IP Security Policy Management console.
6. Right-click the Telnet IPSec policy created earlier and select Assign.
7. From the second computer, attempt to telnet to the first.
8. The connection will not be successful.

Create a Permit Rule

The blocking rule blocks all attempts at a telnet connection from any computer. However, if a more specific rule, such as one that identifies a specific computer, permits telnet traffic, the specifically identified computer will be able to make a telnet connection and use telnet in the normal manner. This is because the IPSec Policy Agent attempts to match packets against the more specific rules first, so packets from the specified computer are accepted because they match the Permit rule, while packets from all other computers won't match that rule, but will match the generic Block rule. You create the Permit rule in the same IPSec policy because only one IPSec policy can be active on the computer at a time:

1. On the first computer, open or go to the IP Security Policy Management console.
2. Right-click the Telnet IPSec policy and select un-assign.
3. Double-click the policy to open it.
4. In the policy's Properties Rules page, click Add to add a rule.
5. On the IP Filter List page, click Add to create the filter list.
6. Name the filter list Permit Computer Two.
7. Click Add to add a filter.
8. In the Source address drop-down list, select A Specific IP Address.
9. Enter the IP address of computer B, as shown in Figure 15-11.
10. In the Destination address, select My IP Address, and then click the Protocol tab.
11. In the Select a protocol type box, select TCP.
12. In the Set the IP protocol port field, click To This Port and enter 21, and then click OK.
13. Click OK to close the IP Filter List page.
14. In the IP Filter lists box, select the Permit Computer Two entry, and then click the Filter Action tab.
15. Click Permit.
16. Click Close, and then click OK.

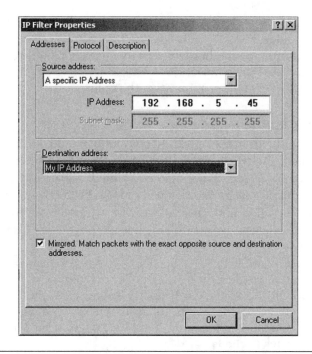

Figure 15-11   Specify a computer address to make a more specific rule.

To test the new rule, you first need to show that an attempt from the specified computer will be successful. However, you should also check that when the IP address does not match that identified in the policy, the telnet connection will be dropped.

1. On the first computer, open or go to the IP Security Policy Management console.
2. Right-click the Telnet IPSec policy created earlier and select Assign.
3. From the second computer, attempt to telnet to the first.
4. The first computer should respond and request a userid and password. If this is not the case, troubleshoot the policy.
5. Enter the required information, and the connection should be made.
6. Close the connection.
7. Change the IP address of computer B.
8. Attempt to telnet to computer A.
9. The request will be dropped.

10. Change the IP address of computer B back to the original IP address.
11. Attempt another telnet connection. It should be successful.
12. Close the connection.
13. On computer A, unassign the policy.

Change the Allow Rule to Negotiated

If the traffic from the approved computer should also be protected, and it should, the rule should be given a Negotiate filter action, and the specifics for negotiation should be defined. The creation of a Permit rule first is not necessary. It is detailed only in this section to demonstrate the Permit function and make it easier for those new to IPSec to create rules. To change the rule, follow these steps:

1. Open the `IP Security Policy Management` console and double-click the `Telnet` policy to open it.
2. On the `Policy s` Property pages, click the `General` tab, and then click `Settings` to locate the `Key Exchange Settings`.
3. On the `Key Exchange Settings` page, as shown in Figure 15-12, click `Methods`.

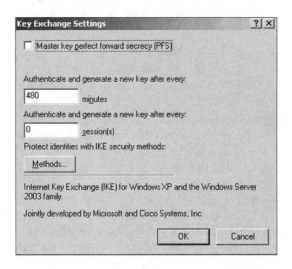

Figure 15-12   Inspecting key exchange settings.

4. Examine the Key Exchange Security Methods page, which is shown in Figure 15-13. For greater security, select the fourth (last) default security method (it uses DES and MD5) and click the Remove button. Select the last (formerly the third) method (it specifies DES and SHA1) in turn and remove it as well. Two methods, both of which specify 3DES, which is a stronger encryption protocol, remain. When a connection attempt occurs, the only possible security methods that can be used are those that exist here. If the other computer cannot use these security methods, the connection will fail. If the additional methods are left in the policy, the communication may be less protected. You can prevent possible compromise by removing the security methods that allowed the weaker encryption algorithm, DES, to be used. Only a client who can negotiate 3DES and SHA1 or MD5 using Diffie-Hellman group 2 can negotiate a connection. The Diffie-Hellman group could also be changed to High to improve security, but this limits limit connections to Windows Server 2003 computers only.

Figure 15-13   Reducing the number of security methods.

5. Click OK twice to return to the General page, and then select the Rules page.
6. Double-click the Permit rule to modify it.

7. Click the `Tunnel Setting` page and note that by default, no tunnel is checked.

8. Click the `Connection Type` page and note that by default, the `All network connections` button is selected.

9. Click the `IP Filter List` page.

10. Double-click the `Permit` filter. Change the name of the `Filter` to `Negotiate`, and then click `OK`.

11. Click the `Filter Action` page.

12. Click the `Require Security` button, and then click `Apply`. (If this step is not taken, you cannot add an authentication method because the policy still has a Permit filter action, which does not require authentication.)

13. Click the `Authentication Methods` tab.

14. Click the `Add` button.

15. Select `Use this string (preshared key)`.

16. Enter the word `test` in the text box, as shown in Figure 15-14, and click `OK`. In a production environment, use certificates or Kerberos if both computers are in the same domain or in trusted domains. Using preshared keys is very insecure but makes a good test methodology.

17. Click `OK` and then click `Close` to close the rule.

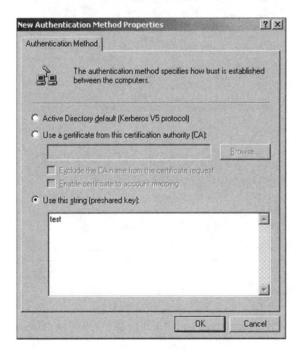

Figure 15-14   Use a shared key to test the policy.

To test the rule, the second computer must also have a policy assigned. This policy needs only one rule, a Negotiate rule, that matches the one written for the first computer. That is, it must have the same security methods and shared key that the other policy does for this rule:

1. Create a policy on the second computer that has a single Negotiate rule.
2. This rule should have a single filter that uses the `From My Computer` and `from any protocol` as the source IP address and source protocol and uses the IP address of computer A and port 21 as the destination IP address and port. Alternatively, the source and destination address could be `Any` as well as the port, and the policy would still work. If this computer needed to connect to many different computers using many different computers and yet be required to negotiate the connection, you would adjust it as necessary.
3. This rule should also have the identical security methods and authentication via the "test" preshared key. In other words, this rule matches the one on the first computer.
4. From the second computer, attempt to telnet to computer A. Negotiation should fail.
5. Assign the policy on the second computer.
6. From the second computer, attempt to telnet to the first. Negotiation should succeed.
7. Close the connection.
8. On the second computer, unassign the policy and attempt the connection again. The connection should fail.
9. Unassign the policy on computer A.

TIP: Stop and Start IPSec Policy Agent Service
If IPSec policies are not working as you expected after you have made changes, you may want to force a policy refresh by starting and stopping the IPSec Policy Agent service. The agent does periodically poll the policy database to see if changes have been made, but stopping and starting the Policy Agent service quickly clears and resets any policy information.

If you have problems implementing this test IPSec policy, use the information included in the section "Using netsh to Monitor IPSec" as an aid in troubleshooting.

How to Write Policies Using netsh

IPSec policies for the local computer can be created by using `netsh` at the command line. The `netsh` command is a complex command that offers much more functionality than the GUI. The `netsh` IPSec commands described here are for Windows Server 2003.

NOTE: FYI

A complete list of `netsh` IPSec commands is in Windows Server 2003 help. You can locate them in the `%system root%\Help\ntcmds.chm::/netsh_ipsec.htm` file.

Another guide to the `netsh` commands that can be used to configure policies and manage IPSec can be found at "Netsh commands for Internet Protocol Security" (`http://www.microsoft.com/technet/treeview/default.asp?url=/technet/prodtechnol/windowsserver2003/proddocs/standard/netsh_ipsec.asp`).

Because many individual commands may be necessary, a more efficient method is to create the command lines in a batch file or script and then run the batch file or script. Using this method allows you to easily add a policy to another computer by simply placing a copy of the file on the computer and running it. You can also use this file as part of a boot script.

netsh IPSec commands can be executed in either static or dynamic mode. When you work in static mode, it's like creating policies using the GUI: nothing you do actually changes the use or non-use of IPSec on the computer because the IPSec Policy Agent is not aware of them. You must issue a command to assign the policy. Dynamic mode netsh IPSec allows you to make immediate changes to IPSec policy; however, if the Policy Agent service is stopped, the dynamic changes are discarded. Dynamic IPSec should be used only if you must make immediate changes to IPSec processing. Be careful, however, because you will have no warning and no opportunity to discover a mistake in your command. If you create a valid command that does not do what you want, it will still run.

Before creating IPSec policies or changing them, enter the IPSec context by entering `netsh ipsec` at the command line, and then enter the word `static` or `dynamic` to select the mode. Alternatively, you can enter all three words at the same time: `netsh ipsec static`.

To create and assign the policy, you follow steps similar to those out-lined for the GUI interface. You add the information for IKE configuration and add rules that are composed of filter lists, filter actions, and other configuration parameters. You can create blocking, permitting, and negotiation rules and do things such as monitor IPSec and create special types of IPSec policies that cannot be created with the GUI.

To make the policy make more sense, we'll use the computer names Andy and Betty. To create your own policy, substitute your own computer names. The first netsh policy will create an IPSec policy that blocks telnet access from all computers except from computer Betty. Then, the Negotiate rule will be added. If you are creating your own policy, enter lines in a text file and save it as a batch file using the extension .bat. Using a text file helps when policies are longer, like this one. After you test the first step (the blocking policy), you can re-open the text file and add the commands for the second rule (the Negotiate rule). You run a .bat batch file by entering its name at the command line. You will also be able to use it on another computer with slight adjustments. You can also enter each line at the command line, and when you press the Enter key, it will be executed. If your syntax is correct, a new command prompt will be made available.

TIP: Erasing netsh Mistakes

If you make mistakes or need to remove the policy, do so by using the delete policy command. Here's an example using the policy name:

```
Delete policy name=telnet
```

To create policies, first create a policy for computer Andy that will block all telnet but negotiate telnet from computer Betty. In this example, the IP address of computers on a test network is used so that you can see the complete syntax of the command. When you create your test, substitute the actual IP address of the computer used in the test. Remember that the policy on Andy will require two rules. Table 15-4 lists and defines some of the netsh command parameters that are not obvious from their name.

Table 15-4   IPSec netsh Command Parameters

Parameter	Description
mmsecmethods	The main mode security methods information
Srcaddr	Source address
Dstaaddr	Destination address
Srcmask	The number of bits in the subnet mask of the source address that are non-zero
Dstmask	The number of bits in the subnet mask of the destination address that are non-zero
Srcport	The port used by the source address
Dstport	The port used by the destination address
qmsecmethods	Quick mode security method
qmpfs=no	Indicates perfect forward security is not used
Inpass=no	Insecure communication is not allowed

1. Enter IPSec static mode:

   ```
   netsh ipsec static
   ```

2. Create the policy on computer Andy:

   ```
   add policy name="telnet" description="block all
   telnet except Betty" activatedefaultrule=no
   mmsecmethods="3DES-MD5-3"
   ```

3. Create the filter that identifies computer Betty. It adds the IP address of computer Betty in the policy written on computer Andy:

   ```
   Add  lter  lterlist="telnet Betty"
   srcaddr=192.168.5.3 dstaaddr=Me
   description="Betty telnet to Andy" protocol=TCP
   mirrored=yes srcmask=24 dstmask=32 srcport=0
   dstport=23
   ```

4. Add a Negotiate filter action:

   ```
   Add  lteraction name="negotiate Betty telnet"
   qmpfs=no inpass=no soft=no action=negotiate
   qmsecmethods="ESP 3 DES,MD5
   ```

5. Add the rule for negotiation. Note how the filter action is identified by name, as is the policy and the filter list. The rule statement ties these important parts together:

```
Add rule name="telnetN" policy="telnet" l-
terlist "telnet Betty" lteraction="negotiate
Betty telnet" Kerberos=yes description="this
rule negotiates telnet if the source address is
computer B"
```

6. Create the second rule, the blocking rule. First, create a filter:

```
Add lter lterlist= blocktelnet srcaddr=Any
dstaddr=Me description= block all telnet to
Andy protocol=TCP mirrored=yes srcmask=24 dst-
mask=24 srcport=ANY dstport=23
```

7. Add the filter action:

```
Add lteraction name="block telnet" inpass=yes
action=block
```

8. Add the rule:

```
Add rule name="telnet Betty" policy="telnet" l-
terlist "blocktelnet" lteraction="block tel-
net" Kerberos=yes description="this rule blocks
all telnet"
```

Next, create a policy on computer Betty. This policy only needs a single rule, the Negotiate rule. The easiest way is to copy the policy created for computer A and delete the block rule. Then, if necessary, you can adjust the statements. A copy of the policy written in the previous list is shown in the following code with the adjustment made to the filter. The change is necessary to switch the source and destination addresses:

```
netsh ipsec static
add policy name="telnet" description="block all telnet except
computer Betty" activatedefaultrule=no mmsecmethods="3DES-MD5-3"
Add lter lterlist="telnet computer Betty" srcaddr=Me
dstaddr=192.168.5.50 description="computer Betty telnet to
computer Andy" protocol=TCP mirrored=yes srcmask=32 dstmask=24
srcport=0 dstport=23
Add lteraction name="negotiate computer Betty telnet" qmpfs=no
inpass=no soft=no action=negotiate qmsecmethods="ESP 3 DES,MD5
Add rule name="telnetN" policy="telnet" lterlist "telnet
computer Betty" lteraction="negotiate computer Betty telnet"
Kerberos=yes description="this rule negotiates telnet if the
source address is computer Betty"
```

The final step is to assign the policy. Remember to add this line to both batch files:

```
Set policy name=telnet assign=yes
```

Using Group Policy to Implement IPSec

IPSec policies can also be created as part of a Group Policy Object (GPO) and will be distributed to the computers whose accounts are impacted by the GPO. These policies can be created by right-clicking the IP Security Policies on Active Directory node of the GPO, selecting Create IP Security Policy and following the wizard, or by importing a saved policy into the IP Security node of the GPO. When creating IPSec Group Policy-based policies, be sure to do the following:

- Always create and test the policy in a test network between two computers.
- Use an OU in a test forest and create a new GPO for the test. The OU should contain computer accounts from representative computers, such as Windows 2000, Windows XP, and Windows Server 2003 if all these operating systems will be assigned the policy in the production network.
- Test the policy using a shared key until it is working correctly.
- Change the authentication method to Kerberos or certificates and test again.
- When the policy is working as expected, add the policy to the production domain but assign it at first to a small test OU. Perhaps this OU can temporarily hold a few computers belonging to IT staff.
- After testing, assign the policy to larger groups of computers in the production domain.

TIP: DCs and IPSec
Be careful when implementing IPSec policies that will impact domain controllers. It is easy to block communications between domain controllers or between domain controllers and member computers, and it is more difficult to reverse the effect.

Special IPSec Policy Operations

The `netsh` command can also be used to perform special IPSec operations, such as Oakley (IKE) logging (useful for diagnostic purposes), changing driver modes, creating persistent policies, and requiring strong CRL checking (ensures protection from the use of revoked certificates for computer authentication of IPSec policies). Driver modes and persistent policies are discussed in the following sections.

Even IPSec protected systems may be vulnerable to attack during times when the IPSec policy is not in affect. This may occur during boot (after the IPSec driver starts but before the IPSec Policy Agent service starts) or if polices are implemented through Group Policy and Group Policy is for some reason unable to distribute the policy. Group Policy IPSec policies are cached in the local computer registry and can be used when a domain controller is not available at computer boot; however, no changes to Group Policy and therefore to IPSec policy will be downloaded. To ensure protection for these potential gaps in coverage, use persistent policies and configure IPSec driver mode.

IPSec Driver Modes

The IPSec driver modes are computer startup, operational, and diagnostic. When the operating system boots, the IPSec driver is loaded in computer startup mode, which is used until the IPSec Policy Agent can set the IPSec driver into operational mode. (Diagnostic mode can be set using a `netsh` command.) There are three computer startup modes:

- **Permit**—No IP packets are processed. When no IPSec policy has ever been assigned, Permit mode is the default computer startup mode. It is the default mode when the IPSec Policy Agent service is disabled or set to Manual startup mode and selected if the service is automatic but no IPSec policies have ever been assigned.
- **Block**—All inbound and outbound IP packets are dropped unless they match filters configured to be used during Block mode, or they are DHCP traffic (so that a computer can obtain an IP address). To configure Block mode, use the `netsh ipsec dynamic set con g bootexemptions` command.

- **Stateful**—All outbound traffic is allowed, and inbound permit filters are created in response to outbound traffic. All other inbound traffic is dropped, including unicast, broadcast, and multicast. If an IPSec policy is assigned to a computer and the IPSec Policy Agent service is set to automatic startup, the computer startup mode of the IPSec driver will be stateful mode.

The computer startup mode can also be modified by using the `netsh ipsec static set con g bootmode` command.

Once the IPSec Policy Agent service starts, the IPSec Policy Agent sets the IPSec driver to operational mode. Any computer startup mode filters are discarded. You cannot change operational mode via any commands. Operational modes are

- **Secure**—IPSec policy filters are enforced. If a persistent policy is configured, it will be applied first, then the agent sets the driver into secure mode and then applies the Active Directory IPSec policy or local policy if one is assigned. If no persistent policy is assigned, Secure mode does not protect the computer until the Active Directory of the local policy can be applied.
- **Permit**—No IP packets are processed, and no IPSec protection is provided. Permit operational mode is active when the IPSec service is manually stopped.
- **Block**—All inbound and outbound traffic is dropped. If filters are configured for computer startup mode, they are not applied here. Block mode is active if a persistent policy is configured but cannot be applied.

Diagnostic mode is used to record all inbound and outbound dropped packets and other packet-processing errors in the System Event log. Diagnostic mode is disabled by default. To enable it, use the command `netsh ipsec dynamic set con g ipsecdiagnostics value=`, where the value equals a number from 0 to 9, with 0 meaning disabled, which is the default.

Creating Protection for Computer Startup

During computer startup, three periods of time must be considered to ensure complete protection. The time periods, protection requirements, and solutions are listed in Table 15-5.

Table 15-5 Complete IPSec Protection

Time Period	Need for IPSec Protection	Solution
From power on until the IPSec driver is started	No network access is available. The TCP/IP driver and IPSec driver start at the same time.	N/A
From IPSec driver start until the IPSec Policy Agent service starts	Conceivably, an attack could occur before IPSec protects the system. The computer can receive network traffic.	Force computer startup mode to be Stateful by assigning an IPSec policy, or set it to be Block using netsh and create filters if some traffic should be permitted.
After the Policy Agent service starts but before it can apply the local or domain configured IPSec policy	Conceivably, an attack could occur before IPSec protects the system. The computer can receive network traffic. Also, something could block the application of IPSec domain or local policy.	Set a persistent policy. If a policy is assigned, the operational IPSec mode will be secure, and the persistent policy will be loaded.
After the domain or local IPSec policy is applied until the service is stopped	The system should be protected by the applied IPSec policy.	N/A

To set the computer operation mode to Block and apply a filter that will allow the use of the remote desktop connection during startup, use the netsh command:

```
netsh ipsec dynamic set con g bootexemptions
value=tcp:0:3389:
inbound
```

Make a policy persistent by doing the following:

1. Create the policy using netsh. For example, a simple policy named "telnet" that blocks all telnet to computer A was listed earlier.

2. Assign the policy using `netsh`:

   ```
   set policy name=telnet assign=yes
   ```

3. Make the policy persistent by using `netsh`:

   ```
   set store location=persistent
   ```

Monitoring and Troubleshooting IPSec

Many IPSec problems are due to configuration errors, and many of these can be easily discovered by reviewing the policy configuration. Common errors are IP addresses that are entered incorrectly, mismatched encryption or integrity algorithms, and so forth. However, the IPSec protocol and policy configuration are complex enough that additional troubleshooting may be required. In addition, by monitoring IPSec, you can confirm that encryption is taking place.

Two tools can be used to monitor and troubleshoot IPSec on Windows Server 2003: `netsh show` commands and the IP Security Monitor snap-in loaded in an MMC console.

Using netsh to Monitor IPSec

The `netsh show` command can be used to obtain policy information on the current IPSec session and to obtain diagnostics and logging information. If you can obtain the information using the GUI IP Security Monitor, you can obtain it using `netsh`.

To display the current IPSec policy, use the `netsh ipsec static show all` command. This will list all the information on the current policy. To narrow down the range of information displayed, you can use variations such as the following:

- Show the filter list: `show  lter list name=filterlist`
- Show a specific rule: `show rule name`
- Display a specific policy: `show policy name=policy name`

To find diagnostic information, use the `netsh ipsec dynamic set con g` commands, such as the following:

- Set diagnostic logging from level 0 (disabled) to level 7 (for all logging): `ipsecdiagnostic value=`
- Turn on or off IKE (Oakley) logging: `Ikelogging value=`
- Disable CRL checking (0), fail certificate validation if the certificate is revoked (1), or fail if any CRL check error occurs (2): `strongcrlcheck value=`

Diagnostic logging levels and IKE logging are two different things. IKE logging is enabled or disabled using a 1 or 0, respectively. When IKE logging is enabled, the information is added to the systemroot\ Debug\Oakley.log. Diagnostic logging results are added to the system log. Diagnostic levels are defined in Table 15-6.

Table 15-6   Diagnostic Logging Levels

Log Level	Records
0	Disabled, no events are recorded.
1	Bad SPI packets, IKE negotiation failures, IPSec processing failures, invalid packet syntax, hashing errors, and other errors.
2	Inbound per-packet drop events.
3	Level 1 and Level 2 levels are recorded.
4	Outbound per-packet drop events.
5	Level 1 and level 4.
6	Level 2 and level 4.
7	All levels.

Several `show` commands provide miscellaneous information:

- Resolve DNS or NetBIOS computer names associated with an IP address (helpful in determining if the policy impacts the correct computers): `show all resolvedns=yes`
- Display information on the IPSec main mode SA: `show mmsas`
- Display quick mode SAs: `show qmsas`
- Display IKE main mode and/or IPSec quick mode statistics: `show stats`

TIP: Use of Netdiag Differs for Windows Server 2003
`Netdiag` is a command-line tool that is used to display IPSec information and test and view network configuration for Windows 2000 computers. However, though the command can be used to test and view network configuration of Windows Server 2003 computers, the `netdiag /test:ipsec` option is not available. The `netsh` command provides this information.

Using the IP Security Monitor to Monitor IPSec

The IP Security Monitor is available as an MMC snap-in for Windows XP and Windows Server 2003 computers. It cannot be used to monitor Windows 2000 IPSec. Use the tool to monitor the active IPSec policy. Policy configuration information, quick mode and main mode statistics, and information on active SAs can be obtained. To use the monitor, add it to an MMC and expand its node when IPSec policies are active. You can add additional Windows Server 2003 computers to the console, which is useful for diagnosing problems or monitoring activity on communications between two computers. Although some policy information is straightforward, some of the information on IPSec main mode and quick mode statistics is not. Some of them will only make sense if they are collected and monitored over time because they must be considered in context. For example, whether the number of pending requests or messages queued represents a problem (perhaps few are being serviced) may depend on the amount of processing normally done on this computer. Other policy statistics are almost self-explanatory. For example, if there are a large number of authentication failures and failed connections, it probably means that authentication is misconfigured (or it could mean an attempt is being made from an unauthorized computer). An explanation of main mode statistics is listed in Table 15-7.

Table 15-7   Main Mode Statistics

Statistic	Definition
Active Acquire	Number of pending requests for IKE negotiation between IPSec peers.
Active Receive	Number of IKE messages queued for processing.
Acquire Failures	Number of outbound establish SA requests that have failed since IPSec service started.
Receive Failures	Number of errors in received IKE messages since the IPSec service started.
Send Failures	Number of errors during IKE.
Acquire Heap Size	Number of successive outbound requests to establish SAs.
Receive Heap Size	Number of IKE messages in IKE receive buffers.

Statistic	Definition
Authentication failures	Number of failed authentication failures since the start of the IPSec service. If connections are failing, check to see if authentication failures increase when you try to make a connection. If the authentication failures increase, authentication is most likely the problem. Check to see if preshared secrets match, peers are members of the domain, and certificates are available and correct.
Negotiation failures	The number of main mode and quick mode negotiation failures. If connections are failing and negotiation failures increase when they are attempted, security methods, or possibly authentication is mismatched.
Invalid cookies received	Cookies are values in receive IKE messages and are used to help identify the corresponding main mode SA. (SPIs are used to identify quick mode SAs.) Total acquire—Number of request submitted to IKE (including those resulting in soft SAs).
Total get SPI	Requests to driver for SPI.
Key addition	Number of outbound quick mode SA additions.
Key updates	Number of inbound quick mode SAs added by IKE.
Get SPI failures	Failed request for a unique SPI.
Key addition failures	Failed outbound quick mode SA addition request submitted by IKE.
Key update failures	Failed inbound quick mode SA addition request.
ISADB List Size	Number of main mode state entries including successful main modes, main modes in negotiation, and those that have failed or expired but have not been deleted.
Connection list size	Number quick mode negotiations in process.
IKE main mode	Number of successful SAs in main mode.
IKE quick mode	Total SAs in quick mode.
Soft associations	SAs with computers who haven't done main mode negotiation. These communications are insecure. They are not encrypted.
In valid packets received	Number of invalid IKE messages. Can be the result of invalid header fields, payload lengths, and incorrect values. Check to see if the preshared key is matched in the peer configuration. This may also be the result of retransmitted IKE messages.

IPSec Quick Mode Statistics are listed in Table 15-8.

Table 15-8   Quick Mode Statistics

Statistic	Definition
Active Security Association	Number of quick mode SAs. (Though two SAs are used during quick mode, only one of them will be shown here.)
Offloaded Security Association	Number of quick mode SAs offloaded to hardware.
Pending Key Operations	Number of key exchange operations.
Key Additions	Number of keys added for quick mode SAs since the computer started.
Key Deletions	Number of keys quick mode SAs that have been successfully deleted since computer started.
Rekeys	Number of successful rekey operations for quick mode.
Active Tunnels	Number of active tunnels.
Bad SPI Packets	Number of packets with incorrect SPI. This may mean that the SPI expired and an old packet just arrived. If rekeying is frequent and/or there are a large number of SAs, this number may be higher but mean nothing. It might also indicate a spoofing attack.
Packets Not Decrypted	Number of packets not decrypted. Packets are not decrypted if they fail a validation check.
Packets Not Authenticated	Might indicate IPSec packet spoofing or modification attack or corruption by network devices.
Packets with Replay detection	Number of packets that contain an invalid sequence number. Watch for increases which might mean network problems or replay attacks.
Confidential bytes sent	Number of encrypted bytes (those sent using ESP protocol).
Authenticated bytes sent	Number of bytes authenticated using AH or ESP.
Transport bytes sent	Number of received bytes using IPSec transport mode.
Bytes sent in Tunnels	Bytes sent using IPSec tunnel mode.
Bytes received in Tunnels	Bytes received.
Offloaded bytes sent	Number of bytes sent that use the hardware offload.
Offloaded bytes received	Number of bytes received using hardware offload.

IPSec Best Practices

■ Configure and assign a persistent policy to protect computers during startup.

■ Do not use preshared keys for authentication.

■ In mixed Windows XP, Windows 2000, and Windows Server 2003 networks where IPSec will be used on all operating systems, test all policies before implementation for compatibility. Several Windows Server 2003 IPSec features are not available in earlier Windows systems.

■ Assign IPSec policies as high in the Active Directory hierarchy as possible to reduce configuration and administrative time; however, remember that IPSec policies are never merged, and policies assigned at the lower level of Active Directory will supplant those assigned at a higher level.

■ When certificates are used for authentication, test the certificate enrollment process and deploy certificates a day or two before applying IPSec policies that need them. (The time lag is not necessary in smaller Active Directory implementations.)

■ Unassign Active Directory–based IPSec policies at least 24 hours before deleting them. Policies deleted before being unassigned may remain in effect.

■ Use caution when setting key lifetimes. If different settings are configured for master and session keys, a quick mode SA might be left in place after the main mode SA has expired.

■ Use default security methods where possible to avoid overhead and confusion. They provide a medium level of security. For higher security, modify the settings. Make sure to continue to match settings between IPSec peers. That is, if you eliminate the 3DES methods on one peer and eliminate the DES requirements on the other, they will not be able to communicate.

Use Secure Sockets Layer

Secure Sockets Layer (SSL) was devised by Netscape Communications Corporation as a communications protocol that could provide identification of a secure web server and the ability to encrypt communications between a web browser client and a web server. For many years, its main use was just that: to provide secure communications for secure web servers, primarily for e-commerce. Today, however, SSL is used to protect Outlook Web Access (OWA) email access and communications between Microsoft SQL Server and Internet Information Server, between Microsoft Internet Security and Acceleration (ISA) server and IIS, and between ISA and browser clients. It is also used to protect other types of web-based applications, such as web services and even entries on a web form, and it is being offered in dedicated SSL VPN servers. Transport Layer Security (TLS), an industry standard implementation of SSL that works in a similar fashion, is the basis for protection in many Internet-based operations. It is, for example, implemented as an EAP type. This section describes the basic SSL process and provides straightforward implementation instructions for using SSL with IIS.

In many implementations, SSL implementation consists of installing a certificate on the web server and then requiring SSL at specific web sites that are based on the server. The web applications specify where SSL should be required.

How SSL Works

SSL uses a combination of public key and symmetric key encryption. Symmetric key encryption is used to encrypt the data because it is faster, while public key encryption is used to protect the pre-master key (material used to generate the symmetric session key) and to authenticate the server to the client.. The pre-master key is generated by the client, encrypted using the server's public key, and passed to the server during the SSL handshake. An SSL certificate and associated private key are installed on the server. It is also possible to require client authentication, in which case the client must have an SSL certificate and associated private key. When a connection is requested to the SSL protected server, the following steps make up the SSL handshake or connection:

1. The client sends the server information that the server will need to communicate with the client. This information includes the client's SSL version number, encryption settings, and other information. For example, if the client is only authorized to use SSL 3.0, it would communicate this information to the server, and if the server only has an SSL 2.0 version certificate, the connection will be terminated.

2. The server sends the client the information the client will need to communicate with the server, such as a copy of the server's certificate. If the client is attempting to access a resource that requires client authentication, the server will request the client certificate at this time.

3. The client uses the server information to authenticate the server. The following information is checked:

   Is today's date within the validity date of the certificate?

   Is the issuing CA a trusted CA (does the Distinguished Name (DN) of the issuing CA match the DN of a CA on the client's list of trusted CAs)?

   Does the issuing CA validate the issuer's digital signature? (The public key from the CA's certificate, found in its list of trusted CAs, is used to validate the CA's digital signature on the server certificate that is presented.)

   Does the domain name of the certificate match the domain name of the server? (Validation of this step is not part of the SSL protocol, but can be used to prevent a man-in-the-middle attack because it verifies that the server is on the network address specified by the domain name in the server certificate.)

4. Authentication can fail and the session can be dropped during any of the tests in step 3. However, if the server cannot be authenticated, the client is warned and, depending on the implementation, the user may be able to accept the certificate even if the authentication process finds a problem with it. The normal browser to web server SSL negotiation process gives the user this option. If the server can be authenticated (or is accepted by the user), the session handshake proceeds.

5. The client creates the pre-master secret for the session and encrypts it using the server's public key (obtained with the certificate in step 2). The client sends this encrypted pre-master secret to the server.

6. If the server has requested the client's certificate, the client signs some bit of data only known to the server and the client, and sends that, along with its certificate, to the server.

7. If required, the server attempts to authenticate the client. It follows a similar process as that outlined in step 3. However, because a user does not monitor the process, an authentication failure cannot be simply accepted, and the session handshake will be terminated. If the client can be authenticated, the session continues.

8. The server uses its private key to decrypt the pre-master key sent by the client. This pre-master key material generates the master secret.

9. The client uses the pre-master key material and the same algorithm as the server to generate the master secret.

10. Client and server use the master secret they have generated (which is the same) to generate the session key. The session key will be used to encrypt the data sent between the server and the client and to verify the integrity of the data.

11. The client informs the server that all future messages will be encrypted.

12. The client sends an encrypted message telling the server that the client part of the handshake is done.

13. The server informs the client that it will encrypt all future messages using the session key.

14. The server sends an encrypted messages telling the client that the server part of the handshake is done.

15. The session begins. All data sent between the client and the server is encrypted using the session key. Because each party has its own session key, and this key is identical, each is able to decrypt the messages sent by the other.

Implementing SSL in IIS

The first step in implementing SSL in IIS is to obtain an SSL certificate either by purchasing one from a third party or by obtaining one from Windows certificate services. Windows certificate services is not installed by default and should not be installed without proper planning. If certificate services is available, however, consider if an SSL certificate produced internally is a proper choice. For example, SSL used by your commercial web site should use a public CA certificate to ensure that the certificate can be validated by any customer on the Internet. To obtain a certificate, follow these steps:

1. Open `Internet Services Manager`, right-click the web site that the certificate will be used for, and click `Properties`.

2. Select the `Directory Security` tab, as shown in Figure 15-15, select `Server Certi cate`, and click `Next`.

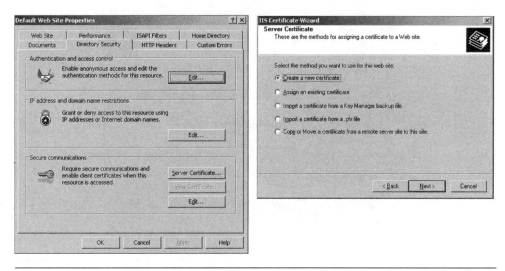

Figure 15-15   To request a certificate, run the wizard by clicking the Server
Certificate button.

3. In the wizard, click Create a new certi cate, as shown in Fig-
    ure 15-16, and click Next.

Figure 15-16   Create a new certificate.

4. Click Prepare the request now, but send later, and then
    click Next. (If the certificate will be supplied by your Enterprise
    CA, you can choose to submit the request online.)
5. Accept the name for the certificate (taken from the web site
    name, as shown in Figure 15-17, or enter a new name). Change
    the key strength (recommended) and, if necessary, change the
    CSP, and then click Next.

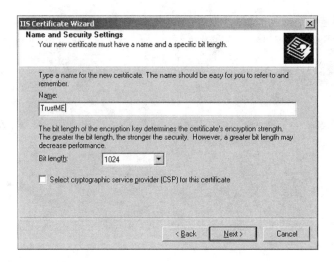

IIS Certificate Wizard

Name and Security Settings
Your new certificate must have a name and a specific bit length.

Type a name for the new certificate. The name should be easy for you to refer to and remember.

Name:

| TrustME |

The bit length of the encryption key determines the certificate's encryption strength. The greater the bit length, the stronger the security. However, a greater bit length may decrease performance.

Bit length: | 1024   ▼ |

☐ Select cryptographic service provider (CSP) for this certificate

< Back   Next >   Cancel

Figure 15-17   Modify name, key strength, and CSP.

6. Enter or accept the organization name and OU and click Next.
7. Enter the common name, as shown in Figure 15-18 (this should be the FQDN of the web server that will be using the certificate if the web server will be available on the Internet, but it can be the NetBIOS name if the computer will only be available on your intranet), and then click Next.
8. Enter the city, state, and country information. Click Next.
9. Browse to a location to save the certificate request file, click Next twice, and click Finish. A certificate request will be saved in a file called certreq.txt. You can view the file in Notepad, as shown in Figure 15-19.

Figure 15-18   The common name should be the FQDN of the server.

Figure 15-19   Viewing the certificate request contents.

After obtaining the certificate request file, you must submit it to a CA to obtain the certificate. If you are using a third-party CA, follow the instructions that it has given you. If using a Microsoft Windows CA, use the following instructions to obtain the certificate:

1. Use Internet Explorer to browse to the CA's web site. For example, if you will do so at the CA console, use `http://local-host/certsrv`.
2. Click `Request a Certi cate`.
3. Click `Advanced Certi cate Request`.
4. Click `Submit a certi cate request by using a base-64-encoded CMC or PKCS # 10  le, or submit a renewal request by using a base-64-Encoded PCKS #7  le`, as shown in Figure 15-20.

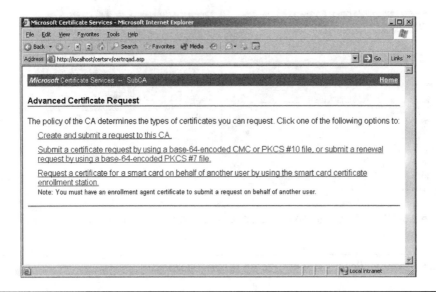

Figure 15-20   Select the advance certificate request using a file.

5. Click Browse for a le to insert and browse to the saved file, then click Read to enter the information in the text box, or instead of using the browse option, open the file in Notepad, select its entire contents, and cut and paste the information in the text box on the screen, as shown in Figure 15-21. When the browse option is selected, the pages accessed must all be identified individually or as part of a trusted site in IE. If the pages are not trusted and you attempt to use the browse option, the browser's security settings will warn that they are preventing the web page from accessing the local disk. You should decide whether you want to follow the instructions to allow this to happen. To do so, you add this site to the trusted sites for the browser.

Figure 15-21   Security settings may prevent file access.

6. Use the Certi cate Template drop-down list to select Web Server, as shown in Figure 15-22, and then click Submit to submit the request.

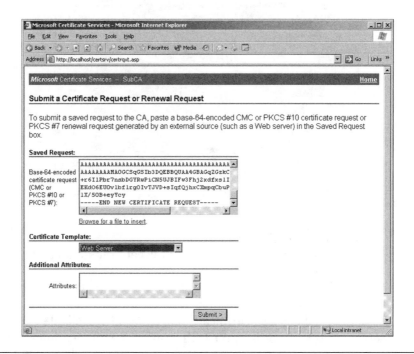

Figure 15-22   Use the cut and paste method to obtain the certificate request.

7. If the CA requires the certificate be approved, a warning will be issued. If you have authority, use the CA console to approve the request. You will need to return later using IE to check the pending request and download the certificate.
8. If the certificate is issued, choose one of the encoding schemes (DER or base 64) and click Next.
9. Select Download certi cate and browse to a location to store the certificate file.

When the certificate is received, it must be installed on the server:

1. Open the Directory Security page of the web site and click Server Certi cate.
2. Click Process the pending request and install the certi cate, as shown in Figure 15-23, and then click Next.

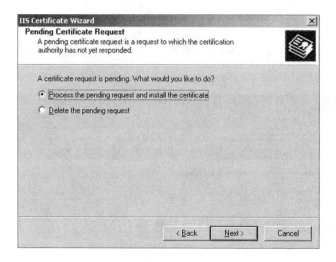

Figure 15-23   Process the request.

  3. Browse to the certificate file.
  4. Specify the SSL port to use or accept the default 443, and then click Next.
  5. Review the information, click OK, and then click Finish.

Finally, installing the certificate makes it SSL available on the web server. In other words, both HTTP and HTTPS communications can occur. To ensure that all communications use SSL, you must require it:

  1. From the Directory Security Property page of the web site, click the Edit button.
  2. Click Require secure channel (SSL), as shown in Figure 15-24.
  3. If all clients are capable of using 128-bit encryption, click Require 128-bit encryption.
  4. If you also will require client certificates, click that statement.
  5. Click OK to close the page.

Figure 15-24 To ensure that all communications use SSL, you must require its usage.

Use LDAP Server Signing

LDAP is an industry standard protocol used to query and update information in a directory service, and it is the primary access protocol used with Active Directory. Many Windows Server 2003 administrative tools sign and encrypt all LDAP traffic by default, including the following:

- Active Directory Users and Computers
- Active Directory Sites and Services
- Active Directory Domains and Trusts
- Active Directory Schema
- ADSI Edit
- Server resource kit utilities

However, you can require that LDAP traffic always be signed by using the Security Option `Domain Controller: LDAP Server Signing Requirements`. The `None` setting does not require LDAP signing, but the DC will support it if the client requests it. The setting `Require Signature` requires a signature.

Don't forget to set the client security setting `Network Security: LDAP client Signing Requirements`. If the server is set to `Require`, and the client is not set, the LDAP connection will be lost. The following options are available:

- `None`—LDAP traffic is issued with the requirements of the caller (the application).
- `Negotiate`—If SSL/TLS is already being used, the LDAP request is issued with the requirement of the caller. If SSL/TLS is not used, the LDAP BIND request (binding is the process where the client authenticates to the server) includes the LDAP signing requirement in addition to the caller requests.
- `Require`—Same as negotiate except if that the server cannot BIND, request fails.

LDAP requests are issued using `ldap_bind` statements. The `ldap_simple_bind` and `ldap_simple_bind_s` statements are not capable of requiring signing or encrypting. These functions pass the user ID and password in the clear and should not be used unless an encrypted session using SSL/TLS is set up. If signing is required and `ldap_simple_bind` or `ldap_simple_bind_s` are used, the request will be rejected. To ensure security, programs that use LDAP should authenticate (to identify who is making the request), sign (to guarantee the integrity of the message, ensuring that it has not been changed during transport), and encrypt (to keep confidential the contents including the users id and password) LDAP communications. Windows Server 2003 does, as does Windows 2000 Service Pack 3 and above.

LDAP communications used by Windows Server 2003 are authenticated, signed, and encrypted by default. Applications developed for Windows Server 2003 should also meet these requirements. It is possible to do so in one of three ways. The programmer can require the use of Simple Authentication and Security Layer Protocol (SASL) or TLS. The SASL requirement does not require certificates while TLS does. If TLS is required, certificates must already be available on the client and on the server. These settings are incorporated by the programmer when writing applications, but the concept of securing traffic between client and server when manipulating Active Directory information is also relevant to administrators who may write scripts. These scripts will more commonly use the Active Directory Service Interfaces (ADSI), but must also bind to the AD. ADSI is a set of COM interfaces used to interface with the Active Directory, and security can be established by specifying either Kerberos or TLS. Like LDAP, use of ADSI with TLS requires computer certificates.

When an Enterprise CA is installed, its CA certificate is set as the default certificate for SSL validation. Use the autoenrollment feature of Group Policy to enroll server and client computers.

Summary

Protecting data while it traverses the network is important, whether the network is the Internet or the internal network. Several strategies can be employed depending on the nature of the data that must be protected. Active Directory access should be protected by using LDAP signing where LDAP is used and, where appropriate, by requiring SASL or TLS. Other secured communications, such as logons, can be secured via Security Options to ensure that they are signed and/or encrypted. SMB sessions are secured by default using SMB signing. Where web servers and other servers configured for SSL are part of the communication, SSL should be appropriately configured. Finally, where communications need to be blocked, specifically permitted, or negotiated between two computers, IPSec policies can be configured to provide computer authentication, integrity, and encryption. Many of these security strategies require computer certificates, and if Microsoft certificate services have been implemented, computers may be configured for automatic enrollment.

PART VI

Maintenance and Recovery

CHAPTER 16

Maintenance Strategies and Administrative Practices

Hardening systems and operations, providing protection for data, and applying security principles can build a solid security foundation. However, nothing stands still. New defensive operations and products are discovered, vulnerabilities are uncovered, and today's perfect security infrastructure becomes weaker over time. To ensure that security remains strong, you should review new discoveries, but the first step is to have sound maintenance strategies and management practices as part of the overall security plan.

Security maintenance is not the application of a new security technology, nor is it the hardening process itself. Security maintenance is a combination of managing changes to security policy and managing updates, such as patches and service packs. Secure administrative practices support this process by ensuring that even minor changes to operating systems and applications do not reduce security, and that the actions of administrators do not increase the likelihood of system compromise.

TIP: Patch Management Guides

Microsoft's patch management site at (`http://www.microsoft.com/ technet/security/topics/patchmanagement.mspx` provides the details of creating and implementing a change management infrastructure for security maintenance, and information about Microsoft and third-party products for patch management can be found in the "Microsoft Guide to Security Patch Management"(`http://www.microsoft.com/downloads/ details.aspx?familyid=73ac38b7-5826-421d-99e8-cdcc608b8992& displaylang=en`).

895

Maintenance Strategies for Change Management

Change management is the process that formalizes and appropriately organizes the response to necessary changes. Patch management is one form of change control, albeit a potentially more volatile one. Change management, however, encompasses all potential changes, even those that are not security-related. It includes system upgrades, release changes to existing software packages, and new programs, hardware, and systems. Another part of change management, security configuration maintenance, must be a part of change control as well. Security configuration maintenance is the process of keeping security configuration and practices in place. Over time, security practices may be modified due to performance, temporary requirements, or some legitimate change to the system, which may weaken security.

NOTE: Changes Can Mean New Threats

Changing from passwords to smart cards for authentication is a change that, at face value, improves the security of the network, but if not handled properly, can have the opposite effect. For example, if the process required to obtain a smart card does not include proof that the requestor has a current account on the system or is approved for a new account, unauthorized individuals may obtain credentials that permit them to access the system. The attacker does not have to break the increased security that smart cards provide because he has legitimate credentials. Other changes, such as the addition of PDAs that interface with the network, may not appear to be security-related at all and yet bring with them the potential to impact security. PDAs might be lost and, if not correctly configured, might offer unrestricted access to the organization's network to anyone who finds the PDA or access to sensitive data on the PDA. In addition, PDAs configured for wireless communications might become infected with a virus and spread it to the network. Each change, therefore, should be evaluated for the impact on security before and after the change is made.

Although testing and troubleshooting is not usually considered part of change management, these processes can have a significant impact on security. While testing should be done in a lab or test environment, not in production, it doesn't always happen this way. Security settings may be relaxed in order to tell if they are the reason for a problem or because the person performing the tests knows that they have the potential for causing a problem. If the security configuration is not returned to its previous state, a permanent reduction in security may result. In some cases, the security change is not reinstituted because it will prevent some required new functionality or reinstate something required that was removed when a security configuration was made. In either case, the reason for the security configuration change should be determined, not simply left as a decision made by the troubleshooter.

Security Policy Maintenance

Security policy maintenance is the process of ensuring that security settings, policies, and practices remain in place. In an Active Directory domain, security settings established in Group Policy will automatically be refreshed, as described in Chapter 7, "Active Directory's Role in Domain Security." In addition, Group Policy is reapplied during computer startup and user logon. However, if there is no policy and procedure in place to manage changes to Group Policy or to authorize administrators who can change Group Policy, security settings might be arbitrarily changed, and what once was a strong security framework might become weakened or perverted over time. Ensure the proper administration of GPOs by training, approving, and auditing administrators. Do this and manage the permissions on GPOs, and you ensure the maintenance of these policies—as long as Group Policy is operating correctly. If Group Policy fails, security settings will not be refreshed.

Be aware that other Group Policy settings outside of domain-based Group Policy must also be maintained. Other management processes must be established for these settings. These settings include the following:

- Those established on standalone computers
- Those established directly in local Group Policy for individual computers (and not overridden by domain-based policy)
- Those that are established outside of any Group Policy

Two ways to ensure the maintenance of security configuration are the normal reapplication made when the security settings of Group Policy are applied, and the use of security audits to determine that settings that are being applied in compliance with your organization's security policy. Security Settings, a section of Group Policy, are reapplied every 16 hours whether or not changes to Group Policy are made. Security Settings do not encompass every security configuration that might be made with Group Policy but do include those made in Account Policy, Local Policy,

Event Log, and so on, as shown in Figure 16-1. It does not include security settings made in the Administrative Templates sections of User or Computer Configuration.

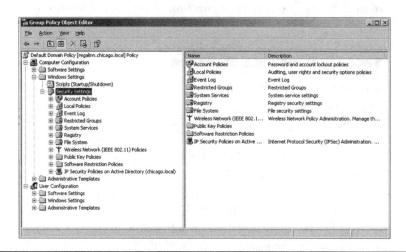

Figure 16-1 Security Settings areas that are automatically refreshed.

Security audits can and should encompass manual and automatic techniques and can uncover any non-compliance with current security. Automated methods for security audits include the use of the Security Configuration and Analysis tool, the Security Baseline Analyzer, and third-party tools. More information on security audits is in Chapter 18, "Auditing."

As part of your maintenance strategies, establish a periodic review of security settings. Just as an IT auditor might review your current security settings against your organization's security policy and information security best practices, you should review the actual security settings to ensure that they remain the way they are supposed to. There are numerous ways to do so. Steps that should be part of your security maintenance plan are as follows:

- Ensure that Group Policy is working. If Group Policy is not working, cached Group Policy will be applied to the computer. However, problems with Group Policy mean problems for any new changes to Group Policy. Part of security maintenance should include verification that Group Policy is working.

- Directly test application of security settings by analyzing different classes of computers using Security Configuration and Analysis (SCA). Use a template that accurately reflects the security for the computer tested and that is added to the system to be tested just for the test, not a local copy of the template that might have been subject to modification. A good practice is to keep a template copy in a secure location. SCA will point out differences between the actual security on a system and the security that is supposed to be applied. Because the "actual" security is tested against a known security policy, you can be sure of discovering any problems due to unauthorized changed in Group Policy, or the movement of computer accounts to OUs where the proper security for this specific computer is not linked. SCA can also be used to test stand-alone computers.
- Use Resultant Set of Policy to determine the security in place when a specific type of user is logged on. RSoP will also show the impact of administrative templates, which SCA cannot do.
- Periodically review OU locations of user and computer accounts. If an account is not in the proper OU, it may not be getting the appropriate security applied.
- Ensure that change control practices are designed to consider the impact of changes on security. Changes to security may improve security and mitigate risk or they may weaken security and increase risk. Ensure that the design is implemented in written policies and procedures and audit their use. If proposed changes do not indicate security changes, review security after changes are made to ensure that this is so. If proposed changes will impact security, ensure that management properly reviews this impact.

Updating Security

Security updates can be both reactive and proactive. Reactive security updates are responses to announcements of security vulnerability and, in most cases, are accomplished via patch management. Proactive security updates are the result of either the acquisition of new security information (you learn, for example, that you can reduce exposure by limiting permissions on some critical resource or by disabling some unnecessary service and do so) or new security policy. Reactive security updates are undertaken as the result of the public notice of some new vulnerability, sometimes after an exploit that takes advantage of the vulnerability is already circulating. Security patch installation may be reactionary; it may also become mostly proactive if a well-designed patch management program is in place. Because service pack installations provide security updates as well as other fixes and feature changes and are not usually provided as critical updates, they can be either proactive or reactive. On one hand, they are usually applied after much testing and planning, which may be part of the patch management program. On the other hand, if systems are long overdue on a service pack update, installation may be reactionary as it applies multiple security patches at one time.

Methods for performing updates vary. Proactive security updates may require manual configuration, changes to Group Policy, or the development of scripts. They may also include the slipstreaming of service packs and patches into new operating system installs. Reactive updates often use well-established methods such as Windows Update, Automatic Update, Software Update Services (SUS), or third-party products. However, these patch installation methods may also be part of a well-planned and operated patch management program.

Implementing Proactive Updates

Manual changes are described throughout this book, and modification of Group Policy is described in Chapter 7. Information on developing scripts is amply covered in the "Microsoft Windows 2000 Scripting Guide," which can be downloaded from `http://www.microsoft.com/technet/scriptcenter/guide/default.mspx`. The guide includes a basic tutorial on script writing. Many additional sample scripts can be found at the Script Center Repository at `http://www.microsoft.com/technet/scriptcenter/scripts/default.mspx`.

New systems should always be updated before being put into production. This means that service packs and security patches should be slipstreamed during the installation process or applied right after installation. In prior editions of Windows, the application of multiple updates potentially required multiple reboots or the use of the qchain.exe utility. This ensured that the most recent version of updated software was retained. All Windows Server 2003 updates have this functionality built in when the /z switch is used with the security patch update.exe executable.

Slipstreaming updates during an installation requires some initial setup but can save time by automating the process for multiple installations. The process outlined here is further discussed in the article "Guide for Installing and Deploying Updates for Microsoft Windows Server 2003 and Windows XP 64-Bit Edition Version 2003" (`http://www.microsoft.com/technet/security/topics/patch/hfde ploy.mspx`). To prepare a network server installation point with slip-streamed security patches, follow these steps:

1. Create and share a folder on a file server that will be used for server installs. You can name the folder and the share as you wish; in this example, the name W2K3 is used. Give the Administrators group or selected administrators full control of this folder. Provide users authorized to install servers with the Read and Execute permissions.

2. Copy the installation files for Windows Server 2003 from the installation CD-ROM and the updates to the shared distribution folder. Use xcopy to do so. In this example, the folder name C:\W2K3\I386 is used.

3. Open and edit the file dosnet.inf. This file can be found in the C:\W2K3\I386 folder.
   If necessary, create the section [OptionalSrcDirs] in the file.
   Add the word svcpack to this section.

4. Create the subfolder C:\W2K3\i386\svcpack.

5. Copy each update to the new subfolder.
   Rename each update from the longname format to an 8.3 format, KB######.exe, where ###### is the KB number of the update.
   Copy each update to the subfolder.

6. Expand each update to its own temporary folder, one at a time.

7. Ignore the contents of the rtmqdr folder created by the expanded update.

8. From the rtmqfe folder, copy the catalog file (KB######.cat) to the svcpack folder.

9. Evaluate and then copy if necessary the update binary files (.exe, .dll, or .sys) from the temporary folder to the C:\W2K3\i386 folder.
   Examine the version number of the update. (Right-click the file, click Properties, click the Versions tab, and examine the File version entry.)
   Find the same file in the i386 folder and examine its version number.
   If the version number in the i386 folder is later than the update, do nothing.
   If the version number on the update is later than that in the i386 folder, copy the update to the i386 folder.
   If there is no matching file in the i386 folder, copy the update file to the folder.

10. Each file copied in step 9 should be listed in the dosnet.inf [Files] section in the format d1,*filename*. If it is not, add an entry using the same syntax.

11. Delete the svcpack.in_ file in the i386 drive.

12. Create an svcpack.inf file. In the file, add the section [version] and enter the following lines:

```
[Version]

Signature="$Windows NT$"

MajorVersion=5

MinorVersion=5

BuildNumber=3790

[SetupData]

CatalogSubDir="\WS2003\i386\svcpack"
```

13. Add the section [ProductCatalogsToInstall]. For each catalog file, add an entry; for example:

```
[ProductCatalogsToInstall]

KB######.cat
```

14. Add the section [SetupHotfixesToRun] and, for each update, add the update executable. The options suggested are /Q for quiet, /N for not backups, and /z for do not restart. A sample section might look like this:

```
[SetupHotfixesToRun]

KB######.exe /Q /N /Z
```

To install the server, connect to the share and run winnt.exe or winnt32.exe from the i386 folder.

Implementing Reactive Updates

Some very creative people, both those interested in protecting systems and those interested in destroying them, are hard at work searching for vulnerabilities or weaknesses in computer software. No matter who finds the problem, the end result is the same. If you are responsible for the security of computer systems on which the vulnerable software is running, you must take steps to ensure that the systems are protected from any attack that might exploit the new vulnerability. Those organizations that follow sound security principles may already have in place controls that might prevent or mitigate the impact of such an attack. However, even if this describes your organization, each new discovery should be investigated and properly addressed.

Unfortunately, many organizations install security patches willy-nilly in response to imminent attacks. They download the patch and install it individually on computers using the patch's update executable, use Windows Update, or frantically write scripts in hopes of speeding application over multiple systems or of multiple patches. When the next worm or exploit becomes known, the process starts again. This reactionary fiasco can be turned into a managed process. Although there may still be times when emergency patches must be quickly deployed because of the announcement of an exploit at the same time as a patch, most updates can be carried out as part of normal maintenance.

Maintenance Strategies for Patch Management

Patch management should be a part of your organization's formal change control process but should have its own set of rules and processes. Patch management should be defined separately because it is much more time-dependent than most change requirements. A new software upgrade often has some flexibility in its implementation plan. However, an announced vulnerability is often followed by an attack that uses it. The timeframe allowed for the application of security patches is the time between the patch availability and the attack. However, no one knows when an attack will occur, and the timeframe is getting increasingly shorter. Patch management should include processes to update all servers, devices, and applications on your network; however, the tools described here are native Windows tools that can be used to update Windows Server 2003.

Patch Management Process

Many products and software processes can be used to update Windows Server 2003 with security patches. However, the process of patch management is not just patch application. The process of patch management can be split into three steps:

1. Monitor
2. Evaluate
3. Act

Monitor

The first step is gaining knowledge by monitoring security sites and lists. Sign up for Microsoft security bulletins at `www.microsoft.com/technet/security/default.asp`. When a new vulnerability and solution is announced, the information will be emailed directly to you with links to additional information and the location where the patch can be downloaded. You should also subscribe to other security lists, such as the `ntbugtraq.com` and `securityfocus.com` lists. ntbugtraq automatically adds a Microsoft vulnerability bulletin notice to the list when one is made available. This is useful because bulletin emails may be lost or incorrectly removed by anti-spam agents, so the ntbugtraq notice can serve as a backup. In addition, you may find and offer feedback on successes and problems observed during testing and implementation of security patches. Both lists also accept vulnerability notices from individuals. This does not mean that the vulnerability has been verified, merely that someone thinks there is one. This can sometimes serve as early warning, but it may also be countered by information from another list member. All this information can help you in your evaluation of a security patch or security configuration application.

When you receive email notifications of security issues, immediately follow best practices and evaluate the notice to ensure that it comes from a trusted source. For example, Microsoft security email notifications do not include attachments, so any security bulletin claiming to be from Microsoft that includes an attachment can be safely disregarded.

Periodic evaluation of patching status is also a good idea. Products such as Microsoft Baseline Security Analyzer (MBSA) can be used to determine if systems are up-to-date on patches. The use of MBSA is described in Chapter 18.

Best Practices for Managing Security Vulnerability Announcements

1. Verify the source. For example, Microsoft bulletins never include attachments. Microsoft bulletins are signed using Pretty Good Privacy (PGP). You can download the Microsoft Security Bulletin key from `www.microsoft.com/technet/security/bulletin/notify.asp`. You need PGP software to verify the authenticity of the PGP bulletin signature, but PGP software can be obtained for free.

2. Paste links within publications in a browser instead of clicking them directly. This helps ensure that the links direct you to a Microsoft or other site that you trust.

3. If you have any questions, visit the Microsoft web site and read the bulletin there.

4. Always locate and read any supporting documentation that will help you understand the nature of the potential vulnerability.

5. Monitor security lists for any discussions of the vulnerabilities, including problems with patches, workarounds, etc.

6. Seek understanding of the vulnerability and the possibility of workarounds, external protection, or other circumstances that may extend the time available to consider the need for the change.

7. Consider the impact of the vulnerability. Not all vulnerabilities are rated the same.

8. Consider the recommendation. If vulnerabilities are severe or if there is a greater likelihood for exploitation, advice on immediate installation will be included.

Evaluate

Whether or not you should make a change or apply a patch is based on a number of factors, including your organization's policy on security maintenance. In general, the decision of whether and when is based on evaluating the following issues:

- Does the security issue apply to your systems? For example, a change that should be made to Windows 2000 systems is of no concern if Windows 2000 computers are not part of your network. Nor is change for Microsoft Office of interest to you if your only responsibilities are Windows Server 2003 servers, unless these servers in some way are responsible for the security of desktops that run Microsoft Office, such as if Group Policy–based Microsoft Office administrative templates are used to assist in the lockdown of Office applications, and the modification is related to those administrative templates. Any reported Windows Server 2003 operating system vulnerabilities and applicable patches or configuration changes, however, must be evaluated.

- Will the recommended change or patch cause other problems? The change, for example, may recommend disabling a specific service. However, you may rely on that service for critical operations. There is also no guarantee that a patch will not cause a new problem or issue. Although patches are thoroughly tested, it would be impossible to guarantee that no conflict or possible problem will result from the application of the patch. To determine if a patch is safe for use across all servers, test them on servers configured in the same manner.

- How immediate is the need for the patch? In most cases, the announcement of vulnerability is based on research into the possibility of an exploit, not the existence of attacks in the wild. This means that although there is a need to respond, there is time to evaluate, test, and make the change as part of a regularly scheduled change process, instead of a knee-jerk reaction. In addition, many recommended changes or patches will be rated and a distinction made between a critical patch that needs to be made quickly and a patch or change that has less immediacy.

Zero-Day Attacks

A zero-day attack is one in which the attack code is used to attack systems either before or on the same day that the vulnerability is announced. A patch may or may not be ready. Therefore, there is no time to test a patch. The risk of possible patch issues must be weighed against the risk of a successful attack. The risk may be mitigated by other security practices.

- What additional protective measures or workarounds can be put into place? In many cases, firewalls can protect systems from an external attack. This does not mean that the recommended change or patch should not be applied; instead, it means that the other protection can buy time while the change is appropriately researched.

In addition to these considerations, if it is decided that the patch should be applied, before you apply it in a production environment, test its application and function on test computers configured similarly to your production systems.

Act

Patches and changes always will need to be made before any action is required, although you should determine how the changes will be made and put into place in any necessary infrastructure. Several possible methods exist for each type of change in:

- Direct application to a single machine by running the executable provided
- Using Windows Update site
- Using Automatic Updates
- Using Software Update Services
- Using Systems Management Server (SMS) to apply the patch

Should You Update Computers That Are Not Exposed to the Internet?

Some will ask why updates are important on a network that is not exposed to the Internet. Updates correct software errors that might be exploited, thereby compromising the computer. They may also simply prevent annoying problems with software, problems that might cause a reboot or cause some software to fail. For these reasons alone, it may be desirable to apply applicable updates after testing. However, there is another reason for applying updates: the source of an exploit might not be the Internet.

Patching Processes

Part of your security maintenance plan should be the establishment of policy and procedures for applying patches.

Directly Applying Patches

You can directly apply a single patch to a single machine or create your own scripts for applying multiple patches. In most cases, applying a single patch is accomplished by double-clicking the patch executable. Patches can be obtained by visiting the Windows Update site or by visiting the Microsoft Download Center. To obtain a patch from the download center, follow these steps:

1. Enter the URL for the download center or select Download from the menu on the Microsoft home page.

2. In the `Keywords` box, enter the Knowledge Base (KB) number from the article that describes the patch. Alternatively, you can select the product from the `Product/Technology` drop-down list and click `Go` to see a list of the available downloads.
3. Click the software update desired.
4. Click the download link or follow the instructions on the download page.

Using the Windows Update Site

The Windows Update Site is a reasonable solution for small businesses with a couple of Windows Server 2003 computers. However, these businesses will have to schedule a time when they manually request the updates. The site allows an individual to automatically have a single system evaluated for the need to update and then, with a click of a button, have the updates downloaded and applied. The major advantages of Windows Update are that additional updates and drivers are also identified and that you can select which updates to apply. The disadvantage is that you must manually request the scan, which is a time-consuming operation if more than a couple of servers must be updated. Other drawbacks include the fact that the user must have administrative privileges on the computer, the user must be knowledgeable about his systems to consider which changes should be made, and no local testing is done.

To use Windows Update, follow these steps:

1. If necessary, adjust the security settings in IE. You may need to add the Windows Update site `*`.windowsupdate.com to the `Trusted Zone`. You may need to adjust the Custom settings for the `Trusted Zone` to accommodate this. Specifically, to use the Windows Update site, the use of an ActiveX control is necessary (by default, the `Trusted Zone` allows this).
2. Use the Internet Explorer `Tools` menu and click `Windows Update`.
3. Click `Scan For Updates`. After the scan is complete, a list of critical updates (security patches), Windows Server 2003 updates (updates to operating system utilities such as DirectX), and drivers is shown. To review the list, click the `Review and install updates` arrow, and they will be displayed, as shown in Figure 16-2.

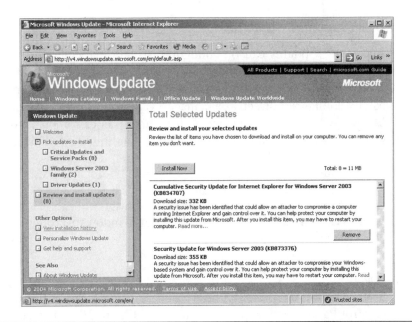

Figure 16-2   The results of a Windows Update scan can be reviewed before installation.

4. Click `Review and install updates`.
5. Review the proposed updates and click `Remove` to prevent the installation of any updates that you do not want to apply at this time.
6. Click `Install Now` to install the updates.
7. Review any supplemental EULAs presented and click `Accept`. (If you do not agree with the EULA, do not click `Accept`, but the update will not be installed.)
8. Review any additional drivers or software updates and install if desired.
9. When the update process is complete, close IE.

Using Automatic Updates

Automatic Updates can be configured to automatically download and install new updates to Windows Server 2003 from the Microsoft web site or from a local SUS server. Automatic Updates for Windows Server 2003 can be configured directly or managed via Group Policy. In fact, Group Policy can be used to manage Automatic Updates for many Windows systems if they are joined to the domain, including, the following:

- Windows Server 2003
- Windows XP Professional
- Windows 2000 Service Pack 3 and above
- Windows 2000 Service Pack 2 and Windows Automatic Update client

Manual Configuration

Manual configuration is via the Automatic Update Property page of the Control Panel System applet, as shown in Figure 16-3. The choices are as follows:

- Turn on or turn off automatic updating.
- Notify the logged on user when updates are available and notify before installing.
- Automatically download updates and notify when they are ready for installation.
- Automatically download and install updates according to a selected schedule.

If the last option is selected, updating is totally automatic. You should, however, audit the application of updates. Periodic use of a tool such as Microsoft Security Baseline Analyzer should be used.

Automatic updating of servers, however, may not be a perfect solution. Although most patches do not cause problems, there will be occasional problems that may result in system downtime. This is not a good idea, especially if the servers involved are running mission-critical services or applications. It is always wise to test the addition of any patch on test systems before applying it in a production environment. However, in smaller organizations where test staff and systems do not exist, the risk of downtime due to malware or attacks that may take advantage of unprotected systems is far greater than the risk of downtime due to a problem with a patch.

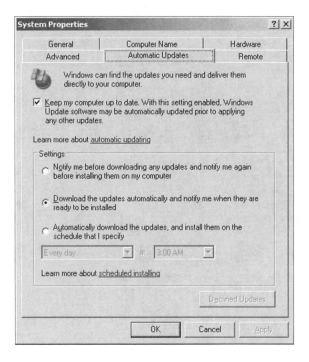

Figure 16-3   Manually configure a single server for Automatic Updates using the Control Panel.

Group Policy Configuration

The Group Policy Windows Update configuration is located in the `Computer Configuration`, `Administrative Templates`, `Windows Components`, `Windows Updates` section, as displayed in Figure 16-4.

NOTE: SUS and Windows 2000

If Windows 2000 is used as the host for SUS, the wuau.adm administrative template must be added to the Group Policy to use these settings.

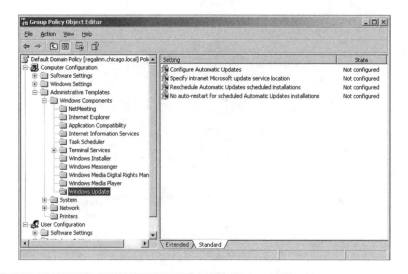

Figure 16-4   Group Policy offers four categories of update configuration

Each section is described in Table 16-1, which is followed by screenshots of each option.

Table 16-1   Windows Update Group Policy Configuration

Selection	Explanation
Configure automatic updates	If enabled, select one of three options: 1—Notify before download and before install 2—Download and notify before install (the default) 3—Automatically download and install according to entered schedule
Specify intranet Microsoft update service location	This option is used to point computers to an intranet location of a SUS server. If configured, the computer will use the SUS server to automatically download updates. If not configured, the computer will use Microsoft's update site for automatic updating.

Selection	Explanation
Reschedule Automatic Updates scheduled installations	If enabled, and a scheduled update is not completed, the computer will attempt another update the number of minutes after reboot specified in this setting. If not configured or disabled, missed updates will be attempted at the next scheduled update. (If updates are not scheduled, this setting has no effect.)
No auto-restart for scheduled Automatic Updates installations	Some updates require reboots. This setting can be used to prevent an automatic restart. The computer will need to be manually restarted to complete the installation of the update. (If updates are not scheduled, this setting has no effect.)

Configuring Automatic Updates is displayed in Figure 16-5, SUS server location in Figure 16-6, updating missed updates in Figure 16-7, and preventing auto-restarts in Figure 16-8.

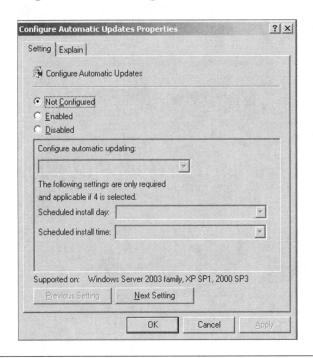

Figure 16-5   Configure Automatic Updates.

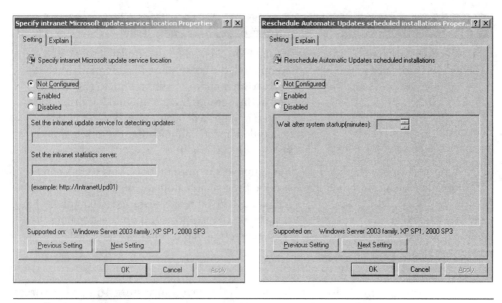

Figure 16-6   Change to a SUS server as the location for updates.

Figure 16-7   Update missed scheduled updates.

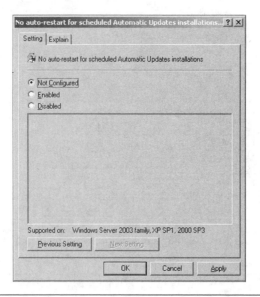

Figure 16-8   Prevent auto-restarts after scheduled updates.

Using SUS

Software Update Services (SUS) is a free security patch updating system that offers the best features of automatic updating and yet provides the opportunity to select which updates will be applied. Using SUS can also reduce bandwidth requirements for Internet access because only one computer needs to download patches over the Internet. In its simplest form, a single SUS server exists as a locally approved source of official Microsoft operating system security patches that can be used by configured clients for automatic updates. Windows XP, Windows 2000, and Windows Server 2003 computers can be updated. Organizations with complex, large, or geographically dispersed networks can use multiple SUS servers to meet their needs. It is possible to link SUS servers in SUS hierarchies and manually transfer approved updates to a SUS server that exists within an isolated network (a network with no Internet connectivity).

TIP: SUS Only Applies MS Updates

SUS cannot be used to apply configuration changes or to apply software updates that are not provided by Microsoft. All updates are signed. If you attempt to manually add an update to the SUS server, the update will not be applied to clients.

The basic scenario works like this:

1. SUS server software is installed on a Windows Server 2003 (or Windows 2000 server) computer and configured to download Microsoft security patches and service packs.
2. After the initial download in which all current patches and service packs are downloaded via the Internet (a choice of languages is provided), the SUS server can be scheduled to automatically download all security updates from Microsoft as they become available or set for manually update only. An administrator can sign up for email notification of new downloads.
3. An administrator selects which security patches and service packs the SUS server will allow clients to obtain. (Updates should be tested via the organization's normal test process before they are approved for the production network.)
4. An administrator configures clients for automatic updating and points them to the SUS server using either the local Control Panel configuration or Group Policy.

5. Clients connect to the SUS server and download and apply updates.
6. An administrator must develop a way to audit whether patches are being applied.

Using SUS Hierarchies

SUS hierarchies are collections of SUS servers that are linked together to better serve an organization's update requirements. The root or parent SUS server downloads the security patches from Microsoft. Other SUS servers use this server as their source for updates. Each server can be configured to provide a different set of security patches or can simply provide alternative local locations for obtaining patches. Group Policy can be used to point the computers with accounts in different OUs to different SUS servers, thus distributing the download load. A simple SUS hierarchy is displayed in Figure 16-9.

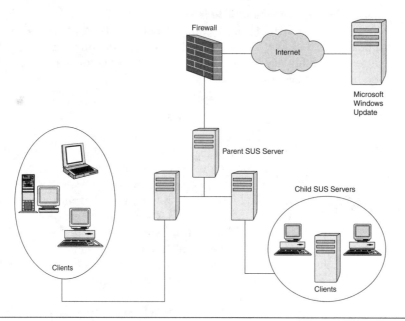

Figure 16-9 A SUS hierarchy can be used to provide multiple locations for local patch downloads.

Figure 16-10 illustrates another use for a SUS hierarchy. In this figure, a parent SUS server downloads patches from Microsoft while two child SUS servers offer updates to either a test network or the production network. The test network SUS server is used to make available patches for the clients on the test network. After the patches are tested, they are approved for download on the production network SUS server. This arrangement allows automatic updating of multiple test clients that match production configuration. Patches can be tested on many different configurations automatically, thus making the testing process more efficient.

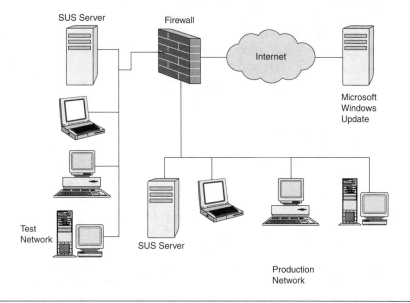

Figure 16-10   Use a SUS hierarchy when a large test network is used.

Securing the SUS Server

The SUS server should be secured to prevent possible compromise or simple accidental misuse. In addition to keeping the SUS server behind a firewall and hardening it in the normal fashion, three specific operations should be considered.

- **Limit the number of administrators**—Only those administrators who are members of the local SUS server Administrators group can administer SUS. Because the Domain Admins group is a de facto member of the local Administrators group, consider removing it, and in its place, add a custom local group to which you add approved SUS administrators. Don't forget to add the new group to the local Administrators group.

■ **Don't host other web sites on the SUS server**—The SUS server is the source of your approved patches, and access to this server should be restricted. When additional web sites are authorized on this server, users will have the right to log on locally, anonymous access may be provided, and the risk of compromise increases.

■ **Use SSL to protect the update process**—Using SSL ensures that the server is authenticated. Because clients are configured to use a specific SUS server, if SSL is required, the SUS site cannot be spoofed, and clients will not download updates from a SUS server that cannot provide the proper credentials. Obtain an SSL certificate for and add to the local IIS. Do not require SSL for the web site; instead, require SSL for access to the following directories:

\autoupdate\administration
\autoupdate\dictionaries
\Shared
\Content\EULA
\Content\RTF

Installing and Configuring SUS

SUS is not difficult to install and configure. The software can be downloaded for free from the Windows download site for use on a licensed server. Before installing SUS, check to ensure that the server meets SUS requirements. The requirements are as follows:

■ A minimum of a Pentium 700 MHz or equivalent.
■ 512 MB RAM.
■ Network adapter.
■ NTFS partition of at least 100 MB free space for SUS installation.
■ Minimum of 6 GB storage for updates.
■ Microsoft Windows 2000 Server service pack 2 or later or Windows Server 2003. The server can be a member server, a domain controller, or a Windows Small Business Server.
■ Microsoft Internet Information Services.
■ Microsoft Internet Explorer 5.5 or later.

TIP: SUS Demo

You can watch a demo of the SUS installation at `http://www.microsoft.`
`com/seminar/shared/asp/view.asp?url=/Seminar/en/20030925TNT1_`
`95d1/manifest.xml.`

To install SUS, follow these steps:

1. Turn off anti-virus software during the installation of SUS software.
2. If the SUS server will be a domain controller, promote the computer to domain controller before installing SUS. (Otherwise, you will not be able to uninstall SUS should this become necessary.)
3. If you do not want the default web site to host the SUS server, disable or remove the default web site and create a site to host SUS. The SUS server should not host another web site.
4. Double-click the SUS software executable. After a couple of minutes, the Welcome screen of the installation wizard appears. Click Next.
5. Read the license agreement if you agree, check I accept the terms in the License Agreement, and then click Next.
6. Chose Typical or Custom installation and click Next. The custom installation process allows you to select the location for installation SUS and SUS updates or direct SUS clients to a Microsoft Windows Update Server, as shown in Figure 16-11. (You can still indicate which security patches clients should download and install.)

Figure 16-11   Select a custom installation in order to change SUS installation location or redirect clients.

7. Choose the languages of the patches that you want to download, as shown in Figure 16-12. If you do not specify, all updates in all languages will be downloaded by default. Choices are English, all languages, or specifying the languages to download.

8. Click Next.

Figure 16-12   Choose the language of software updates to download.

9. Select Update approval settings, either automatically approve new versions of previously approved updates or require manual approval of new versions of approved updates.

10. Review the download URL. Client computers should use the URL to download updates; typically, the name is http://*name of the SUS server.*

11. Click Install to install SUS. Installation may take several minutes.

12. At the completion screen, click Finish, and Internet Explorer opens to the SUS site on the SUS server at http://localhost/SUSAdmin/, as shown in Figure 16-13.

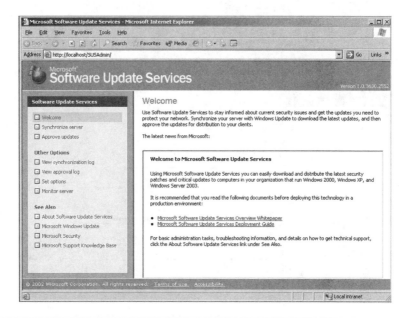

Figure 16-13   The SUS Administration site.

To configure SUS, follow these steps:

1. Open IE and use the URL `http://localhost/SUSAdmin`.
2. Click `Set Options` to review and configure settings.
3. If required, configure proxy settings, as shown in Figure 16-14. By default, SUS is set to automatically detect proxy server settings. You may also click `Do not use a proxy server to access the Internet` if you do not use a proxy server.
4. In the `Select which server to synchronize content from:` area, check the computer name that clients will use in their automatic update configuration.
5. Scroll down if necessary and, if required, point the SUS server to another SUS server.
6. Check language settings.
7. Click the `Apply` button if settings have been changed. A popup confirms that settings have been saved. Click `OK`.

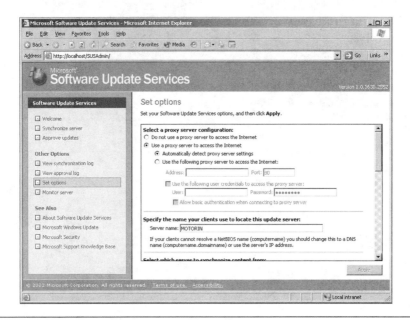

Figure 16-14   Review settings and modify as necessary.

8. Click `Synchronize server`, and then click the `Synchronization Schedule` button.

9. Create a schedule for downloading patches or set SUS to `Do not synchronize on a schedule` as shown in Figure 16-15, and then click `OK`.

10. Click the `Synchronize Now` button to download the current security patches. Because this is the first download, this process can take a long time.

11. Test updates.

12. After testing specific updates, use the `Approve Updates` section and click to select the updates that clients should download and install.

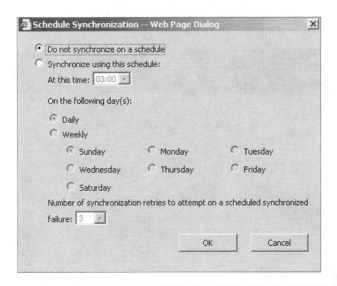

Figure 16-15   Set a schedule, or no schedule, for downloading updates.

WARNING: Choose the Language for SUS Downloads   Microsoft produces updates in many languages. The default setting for SUS is to download all updates in all languages. To reduce the time it takes to download changes, and to reduce the disk space necessary for updates, download only the languages that you need.

Configure Clients for SUS Automatic Updates

Windows XP Professional and Windows Server 2003 have Automatic Update clients installed as part of the OS, but earlier versions do not. A version of the client for Windows 2000, however, is available for download. SUS service pack 1 requires updates to some original Automatic Update clients. Table 16-2 lists Windows clients that can receive automatic updates via SUS and those that may need an additional update when SUS SP1 is used. If Windows systems have been kept updated with service packs, no download is required.

Table 16-2   Client Requirements for SUS and SUS SP1

Client	Automatic Update for SUS	Automatic Update for SUS SP1
Windows 2000	Download available when SUS released	Windows 2000 clients with out service pack 2 need the new client download.
Windows XP Professional	Built into OS	Windows XP without SP1 need the new client download.
Windows Server 2003	Built into OS	Built into OS.

If Automatic Update clients are up-to-date, configure them to point to SUS. You need the wuau.adm administrative template file. This file is installed in the %systemdrive%\inf folder when Automatic Updates is installed.

In a managed environment, update clients are configured using Group Policy. However, the Local Group Policy object can be used in test or non-Active Directory environments. To use the Local Group Policy object, open it in the Group Policy console. In an Active Directory environment, create and link a GPO to the OU where computer accounts to be updated live:

1. From Start, Run enter gpedit.msc to load the Group Policy console. (Alternatively, use the Group Policy Property page of the OU in Active Directory or the Group Policy Management console to work in an Active Directory domain.)
2. Expand the Computer Configuration node and right-click Administrative Templates.
3. Click Add/Remove Templates and click Add.
4. Enter the path for the wuau.adm file (%systemdrive%\ %windir%\inf\wuau.adm).
5. Click Open and click Close to load the file.
6. Navigate to the Windows Components container under Administrative Templates and select the Windows Update node.
7. The settings for each policy are defined in Table 16-1. Set the download options as defined in Table 16-2. If this policy is configured, Automatic Update settings on the client are disabled. If this policy is disabled, automatic updates cannot occur, and updates must be added in another manner.

8. Open the `Specify intranet Microsoft update service location` policy and enter the URL for the SUS server in the `Set the intranet update service for detecting updates:` and `Set the intranet statistics server:` text boxes. (Statistics are logged in the IIS logs of the designated statistic server. This can be a different server than the SUS server, but it must be running IIS. If multiple SUS servers are used, you may want to point them all to a single IIS server for centralized logging.)

If Active Directory will not or cannot be used to set update configuration, registry entries can be used. You need to manually create the RegDWORD keys, shown in Table 16-3, at the location `HKEY_LOCAL_MACHINE\Software\Policies\Microsoft\Windows\WindowsUpdate\AU`.

Table 16-3 Registry Keys for Updates

Key	Description	Range
RescheduleWaitTime	Enter the time in minutes to wait before beginning an installation after the scheduled time for the installation has passed.	1–60
NoAutoRebootWith LoggedOnUsers	Offers logged on users a choice.	Set to 1 to allow them a choice in rebooting or not.
NoAutoUpdate	Enable or disable AutoUpdates.	1 = disabled; 0 = enabled
AUOptions	Downloading options.	2 = Notify of download and installation; 3 = Automatically download and notify of installation; 4 = Automatic download and schedule installation
ScheduledInstallDay	Set a day for installation.	0 = Every day; 1 to 7 = Day of week from Sunday = 1 to Saturday = 7.
ScheduledInstallTime	Set a time for installation.	Time of day in 24 hour format.
UseWUServer	Enable use of SUS server entered in the Windows Update section.	1 = enabled.

To set the location of the SUS server, two keys at `HKEY_LOCAL_MACHINE\` `Software\Policies\Microsoft\Windows\WindowsUpdate` must be set:

- The URL of the SUS server should be entered in the key `WUServer`.
- The URL of the SUS statistic server should be entered in the key `WUStatusServer`.

Preparing and Using an Offline SUS

An offline SUS server is a SUS server with no connection to the Internet. This SUS server does not require IIS and is configured to use updates provided by a content management server. This server can be used to provide update access to clients on a network that is not connected to the Internet. To configure such a server, follow these steps:

1. Prepare a content management server by installing IIS 5.0 or later. The content management server acts as a SUS distribution point. It is a server that will run IIS 5.0 or later, but not necessarily SUS.
2. Create an IIS virtual directory named Content. (Create a \Content folder on a drive and use this for the virtual directory. The drive should have sufficient space for the updates.)
3. Copy the following content from a running SUS server to the content management server's \Content folder.
   From the root of the SUS web site, copy the autocatalog.cab, approveditems.txt, and aurtf.cab files.
   From the SUS web site, copy files and folders from the \Content\cabs folder.
4. Install a SUS server on the isolated network.
5. On the `SUSAdmin` page, click `Set options`, and scroll to the `Select which server to synchronize content from` area. Enter the name of the content management server, as shown in Figure 16-16.
6. Configure computers on the isolated network to obtain their updates from the SUS server located on the isolated network.

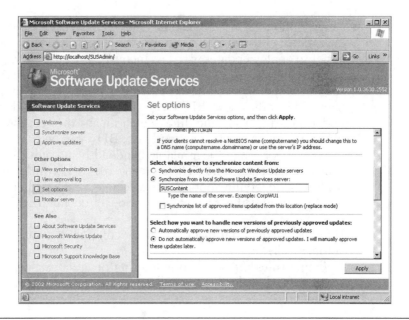

Figure 16-16   Point the isolated SUS server to the content management server.

WUS—An Improved SUS

A new version of SUS called Windows Update Services (WUS) will soon be available. It offers more functionality and the ability to provide patches for more Microsoft applications.

Changes to Client Patch Management Strategies with Windows XP SP2

Although this book is about Windows Server 2003, many of its features work best with Windows XP, and changes announced and released for Windows XP in SP2 will probably be available in SP1 for Windows Server 2003. Patch management via SUS is enhanced with Windows XP SP2, although many features cannot be used until the release of WUS. The following new features are part of Windows XP SP2:

- Windows updates for drivers and other applications are supported.

- A new option, `Install updates and shutdown option to the Shut Down Windows and Turn off Computer` dialog box, makes it easier to deploy updates with less inconvenience for users.
- Improvements to Background Intelligent Transfer Service (BITS), which is used during patch download, means improved bandwidth efficiency. BITS can be configured to download updates during a specific time, which means they can be scheduled for periods of lower network use. BITS can be configured to use only a portion of the available bandwidth and only the part of a file that has changed. BITS can recover from network failures.
- Additional scheduling options are available, such as administrator notification and the receipt of previously declined and hidden updates.
- Updates to the Automatic Updates components can be done automatically.
- Updating rules provide better filtering of updates, such as preventing the download of an update meant for a different version of the OS.

These new update configurations are represented by new registry key changes and updates to Group Policy. For a complete list of registry keys and values for these settings, see the document "Changes to Functionality in Microsoft Windows XP Service Pack 2" at `http://www.microsoft.com/technet/prodtechnol/winxppro/maintain/sp2maint.mspx`. There are four changes configurable by using Group Policy: three new policies under the Windows Components\Windows Update folder, and one in the Network\Background Intelligent Transfer Service node. The new Windows Updates policies are listed in Figure 16-17. Registry keys and Group Policy settings are only applicable for Windows XP SP2 computers.

`Do not display "Install Updates and Shut Down" option in Shut Down Windows dialog box` determines if this new options appears when the Shut Down box is displayed. When this option is enabled, the new shut down option is not displayed; if disabled or not configured, the option is displayed.

`Do not adjust default option to "Install Updates and Shut Down" in Shut Down Windows dialog box` controls what shut down option is the default. If this option is enabled, the user's last shutdown choice is the default; if disabled, the `Install Updates and Shut Down` option is the default.

`Enable client-side targeting` determines the update group assigned to the client. If enabled, the update group can be included, as shown in Figure 16-18. The client update group is only used if the WUS is installed and configured to use update groups. Update groups enable targeting of clients for specific updates.

The `Maximum network bandwidth that BITS uses` policy enables configuration of bandwidth management, as shown in Figure 16-19.

Figure 16-17   Three new Windows XP SP 2 Group Policy options for Windows Update.

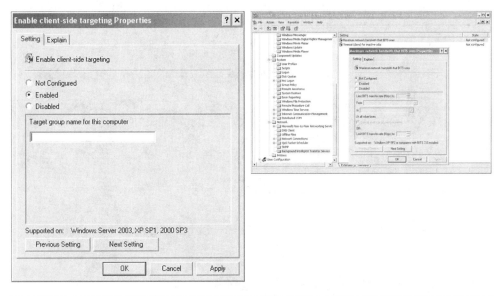

Figure 16-18   The client update group is only used if WUS is installed.

Figure 16-19   Manage update bandwidth utilization using BITS.

Using SMS

SMS 2003 adds and improves upon the patch management features made available for SMS 2.0 in the Software Update Services Features Pack. The feature pack added security patch management capability to the Microsoft Systems Management Server 2.0 server. Security patch management is integrated with SMS inventory and software distribution and provides automated deployment of Microsoft Office and operating system software updates and is integrated with SUS. Administrators must still test and approve patches. The Microsoft Baseline Security Analyzer (MBSA) can also be distributed via SMS, as can the client for patch downloads. The command-line version of MSBA is used by the client to do a patch inventory (using the list approved by SMS administrators) and provide that information to SMS. The SMS client can be used to download and install the appropriate patches. Only authorized updates will be applied. The status of updates, including successful and failed updates, is also reported. The advantage of using SMS for patch management is that SMS provides patch inventory information. This information allows the administrator to see which computers need which patches, but it also allows him or her to discover problems. If patches are not being installed, the inventory will still show unpatched systems, even though the patches have been approved.

Best Practices for Service Pack and Security Patch Application

- Consider risk. The risk of applying the service pack or security patch should be less than the risk of not applying it. In most cases, the risk is greater if they are not installed; however, you should test patches and service packs in your organization before deploying them.
- Devise and follow a change control practice.
- Read all documentation.
- Apply updates as needed. Evaluate whether all products need the updates.
- Test.
- Have a plan for recovering in case there are problems. Understand how to uninstall the patch or service pack and, in worse cases, how to recover the system from a backup.

- Ensure consistency across domain controllers; in other words, if there is some reason for *not* applying a service pack or update on one domain controller, do not apply it on others. You should follow this practice to eliminate possible replication and synchronization problems.
- Where possible, provide consistency across member servers and domain controllers.
- Schedule backups of systems before patch application.
- Warn help desks and user groups of potential server downtime.
- Make patch and pack management proactive. Schedule service pack and patch maintenance as a regular part of network administration, not as a reactive process.
- Target non-critical servers first after testing. However, keep in mind that when a large number of servers must be updated, and the risk of compromise is high, servers at higher risk may need to be updated before those at less risk, even though at-risk servers may be critical servers. Again, weigh the risk of applying the patch against the risk of not applying it.
- Ensure that security patches are applied to servers that already have the correct service pack deployed. Security patches are eventually included as part of a service pack—if the service pack has been installed, there is no need to install the patches. The reverse is true as well—security patches may assume that a specific service pack has been installed. They should not be installed if the service pack has not been. In most cases, if you attempt to install patches when they are not necessary or when the requisite service pack is not installed, you will be warned, and the installation will fail. However, you should do your part.
- When possible, install service packs instead of multiple security patches, but do not wait for service packs when security patches are announced. Evaluate the need for their application.

Management Practices

Administrative practices are also important to security. One example, change management, was introduced earlier in this chapter. This section introduces the best practices for securing administrative practices, including the use of administrative tools.

Adopt Secure Administration Practices

Administrators are entrusted with the security of the network, and yet few controls are placed on administration activity. Although administrators must have elevated privileges to do their job, many controls can be used to limit them to "just" the activities they need to do. There are ways to monitor their activity and to protect the process and lessen the possibility of account compromise. Monitoring administrative practice is discussed in Chapters 18 and 19. The other controls are described in this section.

Limiting Administrative Power

The security principles of separation of duties and limiting user rights and permissions to those needed to do their job also apply to Administrators. The first step is to realize that not every administrator needs to be able to do everything. To do so, examine default Windows Server 2003 administrative roles and create new roles where it is practical.

Default Administrative roles in Windows Server 2003 are described in Table 16-4.

Table 16-4 Windows Server 2003 Administrative Roles

Role	Description	Tip
Enterprise Admins	Have administrative rights in entire forest.	Should have few members. Some activities require membership in this group, and limiting its membership controls inadvertent or unauthorized activity.
Domain Admins	Have administrative rights in the domain.	Should have limited membership. Some activities require membership in this group, and limiting membership restricts access to these activities.

Role	Description	Tip
Schema Admins	Can modify schema.	Should have no members when schema modification activity is not necessary. Membership can be added when schema modification is necessary. By requiring a membership addition before schema changes are made, you prevent many inadvertent, unauthorized, or otherwise rash modifications to schema.
Local Administrators	Administrative rights are only available on the local computer.	Limit membership. The Domain Admins group is automatically a member if the server is joined to the domain. If necessary, remove the Domain Admins group and replace it with a limited number of administrators. Add accounts to this list if users require the ability to administer the server but do not need and should not have domain administrative rights. A good example is a database administrator who may need local server administrative authority.
Account Operators	Can manage accounts, except administrators.	Many individuals given membership in Domain Admins have the management of users as a primary responsibility. If they should manage users throughout the domain, membership in Account Operators is a better choice. If, however, they should manage

Table 16-4   Windows Server 2003 Administrative Roles Continues

Role	Description	Tip
		accounts in some subset of accounts, an OU should be and may already be created to host these accounts, and users who should administer these accounts should be given privileges on the OU, not at the domain level.
Server Operators	Can manage servers.	Manage this group like you do Account Operators. That is, if users should manage all servers in the domain, grant them membership in this group; otherwise, delegate privileges within a specific OU or OUs.
Backup Operators	Can back up data.	Manage this group by assigning it membership in selective local Backup Operator groups.

Custom groups can be used as administrative groups. These groups obtain their administrative rights via delegation, using the Delegation of Control Wizard or by assigning the group specific user rights. By using these methods, you can ensure that users only have the administrative rights they need over the user and computer accounts that they are authorized to manage. For example, a sound recommendation is to leave the membership of the Backup Operators group empty and create two groups, a Backup group and a Restore group, then give them the Backup or Restore privilege, respectively. This provides a way to separate those functions, thus fulfilling the separation of duties security principle.

In addition to limiting administrative users by assignment of rights and permissions, separation of duties is partially obtainable, if not completely enforceable, by technical controls. Two types of administrators should be defined: service administrators and data administrators. Data administrators are responsible for managing users, computers, databases, printers, and so forth. Service administrators manage the infrastructure of the Active Directory network. Service administrators are members of Domain Admins, Schema Admins, Enterprise Admins, and other groups created to manage infrastructure. Data administrators are members of other groups restricted to specific data tasks or to limited administrative roles, such as local administrator.

Data administrators, because of the groups that they are members of, do not have service administrator rights. Do not provide them with these rights. Service administrators, however, by default do have data administrator rights, and must even use some of them in day-to-day operations. Service administrators, for example, should administer their own group membership and the accounts of service administrators. There would be more risk if data administrators were able to manage service administrator accounts and groups than can be gained by separating the privilege of user management. If data administrators could manage administrator accounts and groups, data administrators or others might be given elevated privileges. To assist in maintaining this separation, place administrative accounts in special OUs and, when giving user and group management duties to data administrators, either give data administrators membership in the Account Operators group or use delegation and only give them account management rights in OUs where no service administrator accounts or groups exist.

NOTE: FYI

For more information on service and data administrators, read the article "Design Considerations for Delegation of Administration in Active Directory" at `http://www.microsoft.com/technet/treeview/default.asp`
`?url=/technet/prodtechnol/ad/windows2000/plan/addeladm.asp`.

Protecting the Administrative Process

Securing the administrative process is a combination of securing administrative account, securing administration tools, securing the administrative workstations, and securing communications between administrative workstations and computers that are being remotely administered.

In addition to hardening the computer used as an administrative workstation, additional security can be gained by putting these computers on a separate, protected subnet and by providing additional physical security along with limiting the use of remote administration tools and connections to servers to the administrative workstations. Connections to servers can be limited by creating IPSec policies. Policies on servers should be configured to only accept remote administration tool connections from administrative workstations.

Protecting Administrative Accounts

All administrative activity, no matter how carefully assigned and limited, can be subverted if administrator accounts are compromised. Fortunately, when all administrative accounts are only given the admin rights necessary to perform required duties, the impact of an account compromise might be less of a disaster. However, administrative account access should be protected. Because many security breaches occur when an unauthorized individual gains control of an account by learning its password, passwords for administrative accounts should be stronger than the general domain account password policy. Although you cannot provide different technical controls (the same password policy is used throughout the domain), you can require that administrators use longer passwords or provide them with smart cards or other authentication devices. The actual use of long passwords can be verified by using a password cracker. Don't forget to obtain written management approval before using a password cracker even on your own network for this purpose.

Hardening Remote Administrative Tools

In addition to the administrative tools present on the console, native Windows Server 2003 tools exist that can be used for remote administration. These tools can also be used to administer Windows XP. Remote administration tools include the Remote Desktop Connection for Windows Server 2003 (known as Terminal Services in Administrative Mode in Windows 2000) and Remote Assistance.

Remote Desktop Connection for Windows Server 2003

The Remote Desktop Connection for Windows Server 2003 was called Terminal Server in Remote Administration Mode in Windows 2000. (Terminal services in application mode, the other terminal services mode that allows clients to connect and run applications, is simply called Terminal Server in Windows Server 2003.) Remote Desktop does not require the installation of a terminal server. However, terminal services, a Windows Server 2003 service, is enabled and started by default. The Remote Desktop application must be enabled in order to use the service. Remote Desktop is not meant to be used as an application provider. Its only purpose is to provide support for remote administration. Using Remote Desktop, an administrator can administer the server using the server's local administration tools. Like terminal services, screen displays and keystrokes are the only data transferred between the administrator's desktop and the remote computer. All data is encrypted by default. 128-bit encryption is the default; however, this can be reduced if legacy clients must be used for administrative purposes. There is no computer authentication; however, only authorized administrators can use the service. If further security—including mutual authentication—is desired, it can be added by using IPSec.

Additionally, Remote Desktop provides roaming disconnect support—that is, an administrator can start a lengthy task and disconnect, and then come back later. The Remote Desktop client is part of Windows Server 2003 and Windows XP. It can be installed on Windows 98, Windows Me, and Windows 2000 SP2 and above.

NOTE: FYI

Download the Remote Desktop client for earlier versions of Windows from `http://www.microsoft.com/downloads/details.aspx?FamilyID=a82 55ffc-4b4a-40e7-a706-cde7e9b57e79&DisplayLang=en`.

Configuration Options for the Client

The Remote Desktop client provides a console where connections can be defined. Once defined, the connection can simply be clicked to start the connection process. Multiple connections can be stored. Each connection is configured with connection information (user name and password, server address), and each connection can be set up to allow connection to the local drives during the session and to either connect to the console or start a specific program. The drive connection option is actually giving permission for the connected server to access the local drives and ports. Although this option makes it convenient, as files can easily be transferred, it also makes the local system more vulnerable to an attack that originates at the server.

The drive connection and program start features are configured from the Property pages of the connection, as shown previously in Figure 16-17. These properties can be configured on the server and in Group Policy. Settings in Group Policy override local server and Remote Desktop connection settings. Server settings override Remote Desktop connections.

To create a connection, follow these steps:

1. Select the `Start`, `All   Programs`, `Accessories`, `Communica-tions`, `Remote Desktop Connection` program.
2. Click the `Options` button.
3. Enter the computer name that you want to access and your user name, password, and domain, as shown in Figure 16-20. Do not select `Save my password`.

Figure 16-20   Enter server and logon credentials for the connection.

4. Use the Property pages to configure settings for this connection. Options are displayed in Table 16-5.
5. Click the `Save As` button and name the connection. You will be able to select the connection and use it later.

Table 16-5 Remote Desktop Connection Settings

Page	Setting	Description	Comment
Display	Remote Desktop Size	Set the default size of the desktop.	Configure for your convenience.
Display	Colors	Set requested settings for display colors. The remote computers settings may override.	Configure for your convenience.
Display	Display connection bar	Display or don't display connection bar.	The bar helps identify that the window is a remote connection and allows you to change the size of the Window.
Local Resources	Remote computer sound	Hear sounds, don't hear sounds, or don't play sounds that will be played on the remote computer when using this connection.	Sound played on the remote computer may help you in administration if redirected to your client.
Local Resources	Apply Windows key combinations	Determine if these key combinations will affect the remote computer or the local computer.	Use In full screen mode only setting. This makes it convenient; you can manipulate the remote computer. It also protects you from accidentally using something on the local system (such as Ctrl+Alt+Del and shutdown) during a remote administration session.

Table 16-5 Remote Desktop Connection Settings Continued

Page	Setting	Description	Comment
Local Resources	Connect automatically to these local devices when logged on to the remote computer	Have access to local drives, printers, and serial ports during a remote administration session.	Malicious code running on the remote computer might have access to local resources. Uncheck these resources to prevent possible successful attacks.
Programs	Enable and enter the name and path of program to run upon connecting	Start any program when connection is made.	Use to start up a custom MMC that contains the administration tools this user requires. This can help limit administrators, especially those who have been delegated limited administration privileges.
Experience	Choose connection speed	Set the connection to use the speed that matches the capability of the connection hardware.	Configure for your environment.
Experience	Allow the following	Select options such as background, menu animation, etc.	Configure for your convenience. Appropriate configuration can aid performance when using slow links.

6. Click `Connect`. If the connection is successful, the desktop of the remote connection will be displayed on the local desktop, as shown in Figure 16-21. Note in the figure that the title bar tells you that this is a remote connection and which server it is located on.

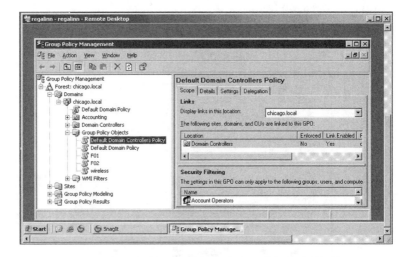

Figure 16-21 The Remote Desktop is display on the local machine.

7. Select `disconnect`, `Log Off`. If you close the window, the connection remains open, and any software running will continue to run. You can connect to the session again; however, because there are limited remote connections when terminal services is used for administrative purposes, you should only do this when you need to continue some process.

Configuration Options on the Server 2003 Computer

Windows Server 2003 Remote Desktop connections can be controlled by

- Configuring the `Remote` tab in the `System` applet in Control Panel
- Enabling or disabling the Terminal Services service
- Setting local server options in Terminal Services Configuration
- Using the Terminal Services settings in Group Policy

You can effectively block all terminal services connections, including Remote Desktop connections from administrators, either by disabling the Terminal Services service or by deselecting the Remote Desktop Allow users to connect remotely to this computer check box, as shown in Figure 16-22. If your policy is to disallow connections via terminal services, do both.

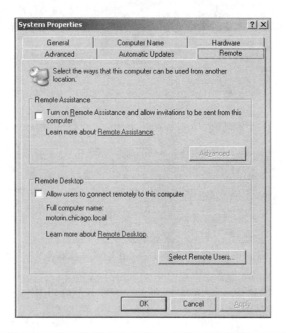

Figure 16-22 Disable Remote Desktop connections by removing that option in the System applet.

Local Terminal Services Configuration settings are managed by opening the Terminal Services Configuration console, as shown in Figure 16-23, and setting properties for the RDP-TCP protocol. To access the properties, right-click the RDD-Tcp node in the detail pane and select Properties. There are four important security considerations.

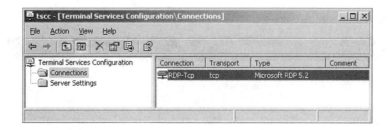

Figure 16-23   Remote Desktop Server controls are set in Terminal Services Configuration.

■ **Encryption level**—The General tab, shown in Figure 16-24, provides the option to change the encryption strength in the Encryption level drop-down box. Set encryption to High or FIPS compatible. The object here is to ensure the best encryption. If clients cannot match the High or FIPS compatible encryption setting, a different client should be used for administrative purposes. Encryption settings are detailed in Table 16-6.

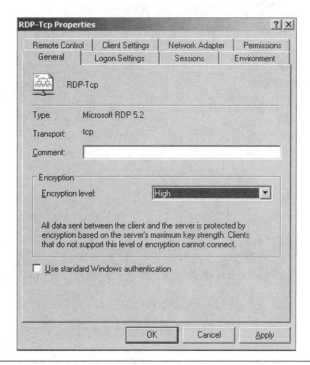

Figure 16-24   Leave encryption strength at High if possible.

Table 16-6 Terminal Services Encryption Levels

Encryption Level	Description
High	128-bit encryption.
Low	56-bit encryption.
Client Compatible	Encryption is negotiated depending on what the client is capable of.
FIPS	Compliant United States federal standard encryption algorithms are used.

■ **Resource redirection**—Override user settings by disabling resource redirection on the Client Settings tab, as shown in Figure 16-25. To disable any use of local resources during a Remote Desktop session, uncheck Use connection settings from user settings. To disable the use of a specific resource, use the Disable the following: section and check the resource.

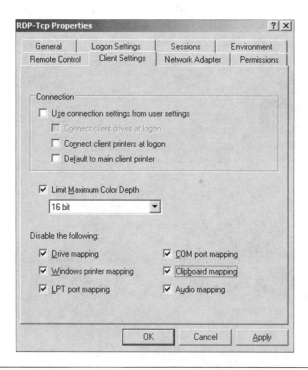

Figure 16-25 Set server connection properties for program start or drive redirection.

- **Override User Program Requests**—Use the `Environment` tab to override any user request to start a program on connection. It is important to control access to server resources.
- **Permissions**—By default, Administrators have Full Control, and Remote Desktop Users (a configurable group that does not include all users) are given User Access and Guest Access, as shown in Figure 16-26. User Access only allows viewing (query, connect, logon). If this is not necessary (the only users who should be able to use the terminal services connection should be administrators), you may delete the Remote Desktop Users selection. You may also want to grant or restrict access to a subset of the Administrators group. You can create a unique group, add administrator or delegated administrators accounts to it, and then assign the new group appropriate permissions.

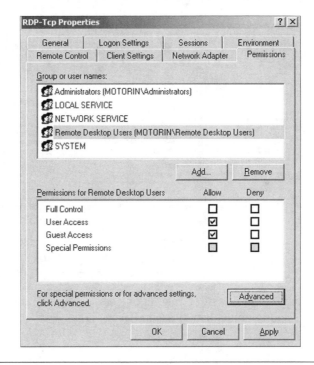

Figure 16-26   Manage permissions using the Permissions tab of the Properties page.

Group Policy Configuration Options

Group Policy settings for Remote Desktop connections are configured in the Terminal Services section of Computer Configuration, Figure 16-27, and User Configuration, Figure 16-28, under the Administrative Tools, Windows Components sections. Use a GPO linked to an OU to manage different servers differently. For example, you may want to insist on 128-bit encryption when administering more sensitive servers, but modify that setting for others.

Allowing client compatibility for encryption settings when terminal services will be used for administrative purposes is a bad idea. Doing so would mean that you want administrators to be able to use Windows 98, for example, to remotely administer servers. Windows 98 cannot be secured, and you should secure administrative workstations. Always use the best security you can when performing remote administration.

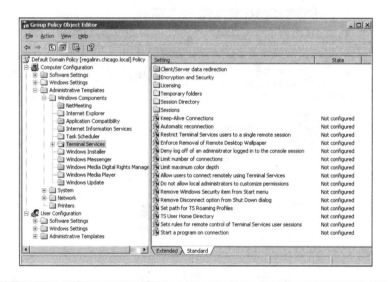

Figure 16-27   Most Remote Desktop restrictions can be made in the Computer Configuration section of Group Policy.

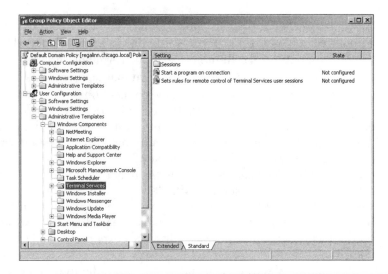

Figure 16-28   Use the User Configuration section to configure basic session information.

Use Non-Standard TCP/IP Port for Remote Desktop

An additional security configuration for Remote Desktop connections is to change the TCP/IP port to a non-standard one. An attacker cannot connect without knowledge of the port and cannot determine the presence of terminal services by scanning for port 3389, which is the default port. To change the port, a registry edit is required. The `PortNumber` value can be changed from 3389 to any non-standard port number. The client must then connect to terminal services using the IP address followed by the port number, such as 192.168.5.150:3150 if 3150 is the new port specified. The registry key location for `PortNumber` is

```
HKEY_LOCAL_MACHINE\System\CurrentControlSet\Control\Termi-
nalServer\WinStations\RDP-Tcp\PortNumber
```

Remote Assistance

Remote Assistance is different from Remote Desktop. Remote Assistance is designed to offer selected users, even users who do not have domain logons, to remotely control a Windows desktop. The Remote Assistance feature was introduced with Windows XP and can be used to offer repair, troubleshooting, and instruction to users of Windows XP and Windows Server 2003. Unlike Remote Desktop, connection with or without remote control is not possible unless a user is logged on to the remote computer. Like Remote Desktop, Terminal Services Configuration and Group Policy settings for terminal services can be used to prevent or manage Remote Assistance connections.

Although primarily a feature designed for use by help desk employees in their job as first-level response to user PC problems, Remote Assistance can be used to provide administrative assistance to those empowered to manage Windows Server 2003 servers. In large organizations, branch offices and other locations may require servers, but justification for a full-time staff of Windows experts may not be present. Instead, IT pros with less experience or personnel with other duties may be responsible for the operation of the servers. Remote Assistance may be the ideal way to offer these individuals expert assistance when they need it.

Group Policy settings can and should be configured to securely manage Remote Assistance. If it is not managed, it may be possible for unauthorized persons to obtain administrative access to XP or Windows Server 2003 computers. Users of Remote Assistance, both the novice requesting help and the expert providing help, should receive training in how to use Remote Assistance. Two strategies are outlined here: first, how to use Remote Assistance in a secure manner, and second, how to absolutely prevent its use. Your implementation of Remote Assistance may be a combination of both strategies, securing remotes assistance for some computers but not for others. You can manage Remote Assistance using Group Policy to provide this option.

Using Remote Assistance

To use Remote Assistance,

- The novice must have available either Windows Messenger or a Messaging Applications Programming Interface (MAPI) compliant email program, such as Microsoft Outlook or Outlook Express.
- Both the novice and expert computers must be connected to the Internet (or a TCP/IP network if email is used).
- The `Turn on Remote Assistance and allow invitation to be sent from this computer` option in the System\Remote Property page in Control Panel must be checked.

- The `Allow this computer to be controlled remotely` check box in the `Advanced` page of the Remote Property page in Control Panel must be checked if remote control is desired (see Figure 16-29).
- Any firewalls between the novice and expert computer must be configured to allow Remote Assistance traffic. Port 3389 is used by the novice's computer to accept Remote Assistance communications. Or, the Remote Desktop Web connection must be deployed.
- Remote Assistance must be configured and not blocked by Control Panel settings or security settings in Group Policy. Do not rely on a firewall or the use of a NAT device to prevent a Remote Assistance connection. If you do not want to allow Remote Assistance, disable it. Using Remote Assistance through a NAT device is possible if the NAT device supports Universal Plug and Play (UPnP). For example, the Windows Internet Connection Firewall does support UPnP, and a Remote Assistance connection can be used as long as both novice and expert computers are not behind NAT devices.

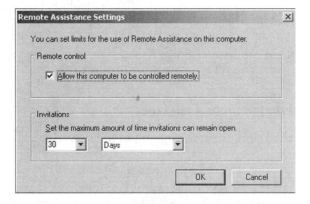

Figure 16-29 Remote Assistance can be granted without granting remote control.

In addition to using the Remote Desktop connection client, a Remote Desktop Web Connection option is available for use when the IIS Remote Desktop Web Connection subcomponent of IIS is installed. The client can then use Internet Explorer to download and install the ActiveX control. This control can then be used to use Remote Desktop services and Remote Assistance.

Remote Assistance is configured either directly in Control Panel or through Group Policy. By default, it is enabled. The Remote Assistance process can be divided into four parts:

- First, the novice requests Remote Assistance by sending a Windows Messenger instant message or an email to another individual. (An option to create an invitation in a file and send it as part of an email message is also provided.)
- Second, this individual accepts the request.
- Third, the novice is asked to accept the expert's connection to their computer.
- Finally, if novice authorizes it, the remote connection is established.

After the connection is established, the expert can then provide the following assistance:

- View the desktop of the remote computer in real time.
- Chat with the novice.
- If given approval, take remote control of the novice's desktop by clicking the `Take Control` button. (This ability is disabled by default and must be approved by the novice.)
- Send and receive files.

Requesting Remote Assistance

To use the Windows Messenger option, follow these steps:

1. Connect to the Internet and sign into Windows Messenger.
2. Check to see if the expert is online. If the expert is not online, the operation will not work (see step 7).
3. Click `Start`, and then click `Help and Support`.
4. Under `Support Tasks`, click `Support`.
5. Click `Get Remote Assistance`.
6. In the `Detail` pane, click `Invite someone to help you`.
7. If Windows Messenger is running, any of your Windows Messenger contacts that are online will be displayed. Select the Windows Messenger contact to invite, select email, or select to save the invitation as a file.
8. Wait for a response.

Windows Messenger will show the following message: "Inviting *person-you-invited* to connect to your computer. Please wait for a response." This message is followed by "Invitation Is Accepted."

9. Click `Yes` to respond to the message: "*person-you-invited* has accepted your Remote Assistance Invitation and is ready to connect to your computer. Do you want to let this person view your screen and chat with you?"

To use email, follow thses steps:

1. Click `Start`, and then click `Help and Support`.
2. Under `Support Tasks`, click `Support`.
3. Click `Get Remote Assistance`.
4. In the `Detail` pane, click `Invite someone to help you`, as shown in Figure 16-30.

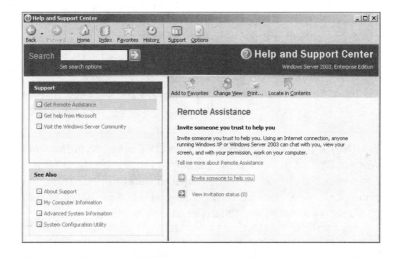

Figure 16-30   Use Help and Support to request assistance.

5. Scroll to the `or prepare an e-mail invitation` section and enter the name of the user you want to invite. Click `Continue`.
6. Set the invitation expiration time. It is always a good idea to make sure an invitation will eventually expire. This limits the time an attacker may have to use the Remote Assistance connection if he discovers its existence.

7. Check the box `Require the recipient to use a password`, enter and confirm the password to be used. Always do so because leaving an unprotected invitation provides an opening that an attacker can use to gain control of the server. Never include the password in the email invitation. Instead, communicate the password via telephone or other communication.

WARNING: Require a Password

If no password is required, anyone who can obtain the URL from the invitation can connect to the computer. Because the request to allow the connection will specify the name entered in the email message, the connection will probably be accepted by the user, as will a remote control request. This is a highly dangerous situation that can be prevented using Group Policy to prevent "buddy" connections. Buddy connections are those that do not require a user account on the computer and instead are approved by the simple use of a password. If buddy connections are not allowed, you can control Remote Assistance connections by including user accounts in the Remote Desktop Users group. (Administrators have the ability to connect without being added to this group.)

---

8. Click `Create Email Invitation`.
9. Enter the email address to send the message to, add any personal message, and click `Send`.

WARNING: Users Should Not Include the Password in the Invitation!

Warn users not to include the password for the session in the message. The password should be communicated via other means, such as a telephone call. If the password is included in the message, any person who can obtain the message can make the connection.

---

10. Enter the name of the intended recipient in the `To:` box of the email message, as shown in Figure 16-31. Add an additional message if required and then click `Send`.
11. Click `Yes` in response to the message in Figure 16-32 if the invitation was mailed or use the page to manually create an email.

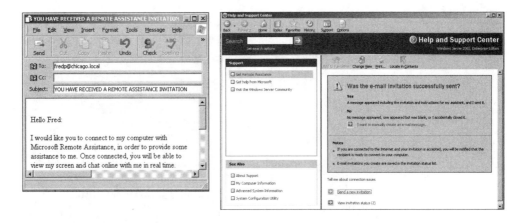

Figure 16-31 A Remote Assistance invitation, when answered, can be refused or accepted.

Figure 16-32 Use the confirmation page to manually create a message if necessary.

12. If you receive the message "*person-you-invited* would like to share control of your computer to help solve the problem," and you want the expert to remotely control your computer, click Yes.

Offering Remote Assistance

Remote Assistance can also be offered without an invitation if the following is present:

- The Administrative Templates, System, Remote Assistance, Offer Remote Assistance setting in Group Policy, as shown in Figure 16-33, must be enabled and configured on the user's computer.
- The user offering assistance must be listed as a Helper in the Offer Remote Assistance policy or a member of the Administrators group on the computer. The Helper list is configured by clicking the Helpers: Show button.
- The Solicited Remote Assistance Policy, as shown in Figure 16-34, must be enabled.

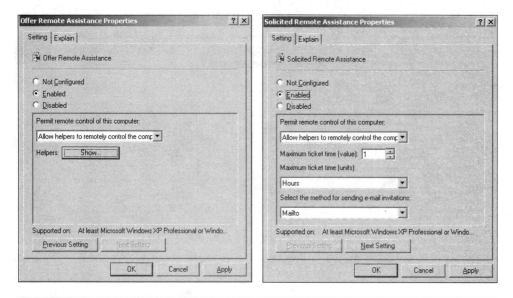

Figure 16-33   Click the Show button to list user that may offer assistance.

Figure 16-34   Configure the Solicited Remote Assistance Policy if you want administrators to offer assistance without an invitation.

The user must give permission before the assistance can see the user's desktop. The user must also give permission before remote control can proceed. To offer assistance, the expert should do the following:

1. Click `Start`, `Help and Support`.
2. Click `Support Tasks`, `Tools`.
3. Click `Tools`, `Help and Support Center Tools`.
4. Click `Help and Support Center Tools`, `Offer Remote Assistance`.
5. Enter the IP address or the name of the computer to connect to and click `Connect`.
6. The user on the remote server still has the option to accept or not accept the offer of assistance.

Configuring Remote Assistance for Security

Create a Remote Assistance policy that specifies who will classify computers that are allowed to request Remote Assistance, and who can actually offer assistance. Then, configure computers either directly or in Group Policy.

To control Remote Assistance locally, follow these steps:

1. Open `Control Panel`, `System`.
2. Click the `Remote` tab.
3. Click `Allow this computer to be controlled remotely` or click to deselect this option to prevent Remote Assistance.
4. To allow a Remote Assistance connection but to prevent remote control, click the `Advanced` button.
5. Uncheck the box `Allow this computer to be controlled remotely`.
6. To limit the time invitations are allowed to remain open (regardless of the user settings in the invitation), use the `Invitations` section of the `Remote Assistance Settings` page to indicate the number of hours or days allowed.
7. Click `OK` twice to close the `System` Properties box.

To control Remote Assistance via Group Policy, follow these steps:

1. Open the GPO in the `Group Policy Editor`.
2. Navigate to the `Computer Configuration`, `Administrative Templates`, `System`, `Remote Assistance` node.
3. In the `Solicited Remote Assistance Group` policy, if enabled, the following items should be configured:
   Select the type of control that is permitted in the `Permit remote control of this computer` drop-down box. Choices are `Allow helpers to remotely control this computer` or `Only allow helpers to view this computer`. `Permit remote control of this computer` should not be checked for sensitive computers. It should be checked for computers for which a plan for Remote Assistance has been approved. For example, you may want to prevent remote control of the payroll database server and all domain controllers, but allow remote control of desktop systems and perhaps some file or print servers or servers at remote locations where no local assistance is available.
   `Maximum Ticket Time` and `Maximum Ticket Unit` controls the time for which a request is valid and the number of times it can be used, respectively. To secure Remote Assistance, this time should be short, and the number of uses should be set very low.

(This is not the time that an established connection can be maintained; rather, it is the time for which a request can be successfully answered.)

4. If the Offer Remote Assistance policy will be enabled, use the Show button to add the user account names for those users who will be allowed to offer Remote Assistance.

Prevent Remote Assistance

To prevent employees from using Remote Assistance, especially to prevent Remote Assistance on servers, use the Group Policy Solicited Remote Assistance. This policy is located in the Computer Configuration, Administrative Templates, System, Remote Assistance area of Group Policy. If this policy is enabled, a user can request help and another user can connect to the computer. If the setting is disabled, no user can solicit help, and no user can assist using Remote Assistance. (If the setting is not configured, local requirements can be set.)

TIP: Terminal Services Setting

The Terminal Services service is installed and enabled by default. However, this does not make the Windows Server 2003 server a terminal server that can be used to allow users to run applications on the terminal server. Instead, this service is used to provide Remote Desktop and Remote Assistance tools. If this service is disabled, these tools cannot be used.

Summary

Management of change control and administrative practices is important to ensure that security continues during production. Hardening servers and networks is part pre-production preparation and part maintenance. Security maintenance is both proactive and reactive. If enough proactive steps are taken, less reactive activity will be necessary. Components of security maintenance and administration are change control, security configuration refresh, patch management, and securing administrative tools and practices.

CHAPTER 17

Basics of Data Backup and Restore

Every server will fail. Sooner or later, some emergency, natural event, fire, or simple accident will make the data on the server unavailable. Are you ready to recover? The recovery techniques described in this chapter for recovering data, services, and servers, as well as the more mundane restoration of files, require some preparation before recovery is possible. This chapter covers the basics of native Windows Server 2003 backup and recovery processes, including the following:

- Ntbackup, the Windows backup and restore application supplied for use in ordinary backups and for backing up system state data.
- Automated Systems Recovery, a tool that makes a backup of the system drive and saves configuration information that can be used for system recovery.
- Volume Shadow Copy service, a new utility that makes snapshot copies of volumes enabling both the backup of open files by ntbackup and the online recovery of previous versions of files.
- Miscellaneous Operations, which include special tools and processes that can back up configuration data for special operating system services, such as DHCP and EFS.
- IIS Backup, tools Iisback.vbs, a script that can be customized to back up IIS 6.0.
- Certutils backup functions, used for backing up a Windows Server 2003 certification authority.
- Restoring Active Directory

Best Practices for Backup

- Back up system state in addition to performing a full backup.
- Schedule backups to occur at regular intervals.
- Keep copies of backups in a safe place on location for quick restorations of critical files and servers.
- Keep copies of backups offsite in case a disaster destroys the data center or the local backup media as well as server drives.
- Review system logs of backups to ensure scheduled backups are occurring.
- Keep a manual log of backups that records when they occur, which tapes or other media were used, where they were stored, and by whom. Be sure to have anyone who handles the backup media sign the log and keep records of where and when backup media is taken offsite.
- Provide a secure offsite location miles away from your site. This ensures that a local disaster, such as flood, hurricane, or tornado, does not destroy your site and the offsite backup location.
- Back up the system files after system files are changed or new drivers are added. You can do this when backing up system state by using the advanced options.
- Develop backup procedures and test them.
- Train backup operators on how to back up and how to determine whether the backup or scheduled backup is working, and regularly hold drills in which a new server is built and backups are restored.
- Make the following types of backups:
  Automated System Recovery (ASR) backup
  Complete backup
  System state backup
  Data backups of critical configuration data
- Secure backup devices and media as well as storage locations.
- Do not disable volume shadow copy.
- To back up clusters, perform an ASR backup of each node in the cluster, each cluster disk, and each individual application running on the nodes.
- When backing up critical or sensitive servers, consider making backup media accessible only to the owner of the files or members of the Administrators group.

■ Use separation of privileges to manage backups of critical or sensitive data and servers. This can be done by not adding members to the Backup Operators group and creating custom groups. One group is given the Backup privilege, while the other group is given the Restore privilege. Because administrators have both rights by default, you may need to restrict them as well by removing or denying privileges. Remember that administrators can give themselves back these rights and audit for its abuse.

Backup Policy, Standards, and Procedures

A backup policy provides the information detailing the what, who, when, and where of information system backups. Standards designate the current approved backup programs and methodologies that will be used. Procedures detail the steps that must be taken to fulfill the policies and meet the standards. Refer to your organization's policy, standards, and procedures to determine what must be done accordingly. You should also be knowledgeable of the specifics of Windows Server 2003 backup and restore. You must ensure that your organization's documentation and practices fulfill the requirements stated by Microsoft for full data recovery, and you must also test the procedures to ensure that when you need to recover, you can.

Should Third-Party Backup Software Be Used?

Many organizations use third-party backup software instead of the native backup software included with Windows Server 2003. They say they do so because the features they require are not available with the native backup software. This may be true, but I have found that many organizations purchase third-party software without even knowing what they can do without it, and they only use features that are readily available in the native software.

It is also true that sometimes their knee-jerk reliance on third-party software gets them into trouble when it is not Active Directory–aware. Things appear to work just fine until they must restore Active Directory.

Finally, knowing what needs to be backed up and the native tools that are available to do so leads to better purchasing decisions because the right software will be purchased and better backup processes because the requirements of the operating system and the organization are known. If native tools do not fulfill the requirements, third-party software should be purchased.

More specifically, if your documentation does not include instructions on backing up system data for Windows systems, especially domain controllers and specialized services, you need to do so. In the interim, you should ensure the correct backup of this data.

Active Directory-Specific Backup Basics

The backup of the Active Directory database and the associated files that are needed to restore Active Directory are included in a system state backup. But the requirements of restoring Active Directory also dictate how old of a backup can be used in a restore. An Active Directory restore requires that the backup used be no older than the Active Directory tombstone lifetime.

An Active Directory tombstone is created when an object in the Active Directory is deleted. This tombstone is replicated throughout the domain and takes the place of the object. This ensures that the change is replicated throughout the domain, and yet prevents use of the object on those domains that have received the change. The tombstone eventually is deleted based on the tombstone lifetime. In a perfect world, the tombstone lifetime would exactly match the period that extends from the moment the object is deleted on one DC to the moment when every DC receives the replicated change. Although it is possible to determine how long it takes for changes to replicate throughout a specific Active Directory environment, this period may vary over time and therefore cannot be accepted as the time it will always take. Therefore, the tombstone lifetime should be set longer than the longest time it takes for changes to the Active Directory to be replicated, and any major change will require an adjustment. The tombstone lifetime is set to 60 days by default.

The tombstone lifetime attribute is part of the enterprise-wide DS config object and is located at `CN=Directory Service,CN=Windows NT,CN=Services,CN=Configuraiton,DC=domainname,DC=domainextension`. To change the tombstone lifetime, you need to use adsiedit.msc, ldp.exe, or an ADSI script.

If a backup older than the tombstone lifetime must be used in an Active Directory restore, the replica will have objects in its database that no other DC will have. An administrator would have to manually delete each object on the restored DC.

In most environments where a regular backup plan is adopted and enforced, a backup of Active Directory is usually made more frequently than every 60 days. Take care to see that the Active Directory tombstone lifetime is not adjusted arbitrarily or shortened without ensuring that the backup/restore procedures will provide a backup that can be successfully used in an Active Directory restore.

The Part Backup Plays in an Organization's Business Continuity Plan

In addition to operating system and Windows Server 2003 applications and services, a complete backup program includes provisions for all applications and data. A backup program is but one part of a disaster recovery program, which in turn is part of a business continuity plan. A disaster recovery program creates plans and recovery practices for major disasters, such as a flood, fire, system or network compromise, or other major events. It should include provisions for offsite storage of backups as well as plans for recovering information systems at an alternative location. Disaster recovery includes plans for recovery of other critical business systems as well. Business continuity plans include this process and dictate how to return the business from recovery to a continuation of the business in a more normal operational mode, such as rebuilding and returning to the business location or moving to a new one, restoring less essential services such as access to cafeteria lunch menus, and so forth. The book *Network Security: The Complete Reference* (published by McGraw-Hill Osborne, 2003) contains a good introduction to disaster recovery and business continuity.

How to Use Ntbackup

The ntbackup tool can be used for all basic backup processes, including the following:

- Immediate or scheduled backup of files to disk, tape, or optical disc
- System state backup, the backup of important system files and configuration data
- Restore from backup
- Restore systems state data
- Automated Systems Recovery

Automated Systems Recovery (ASR) is detailed in the section "Automated Systems Recovery" later in this chapter. ntbackup can be used via the backup GUI or at the command line. Backup can be scheduled or scripted. Backup over the network can be configured, but the system state backup must be done locally.

Many excellent third-party products extend the functionality of ntbackup, and you should be sure that the companies that create them understand how Windows Server 2003 operates to ensure that they are able to back up and restore critical system data.

Back Up Files and Folders

To back up files without having the Read, Modify, Full Control, or Owner permission, a user must be a member of either the Administrators or Backup Operators groups or be granted the Backup Files and Folders permission. A member of the Backup Operators group in the domain can back up files on any computer in the domain. Backup rights can be granted to other custom groups, and users with the following rights can also backup a file: Read, Read and Execute, Modify, or Full Control. Administrators and members of the Backup Operators group also have the right to restore backed up data. You can restrict access to specific backups by using the `Allow only the owner and the administrator access to the backup data` option in the `Backup Job Information` dialog box before the backup is made.

To do an immediate complete backup of all information on the computer follow these steps:

1. Open the ntbackup utility—`Start`, `All Programs`, `Accessories`, `System Tools`, `Backup`, and then click `Next`.
2. Click `Backup files and settings`.
3. Click `Next`.
4. Select `All information on this computer` and click `Next`.
5. Or, select `Let me choose what to backup`, expand the directory in the left-hand pane, and select the folders or use the detail pane to select files to back up, as shown in Figure 17-1.
6. Select the backup type if multiple ways to back up are available, such as tape and disk. (If you back up to disk, make sure the disk can be accessed if there is a system failure such as a writeable CD-ROM, or plan to transfer the backup to an offline disk that can be.)
7. If the backup type is file, select the location to store the backup.
8. Enter a name for the backup and, if the backup is to disk, read the warning that you will need a floppy disk for system recovery information, and then click `Next`.
9. Click `Finish` to start the backup.

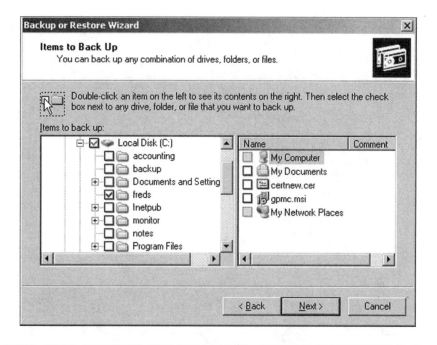

Figure 17-1   Select the folders to back up.

For additional options, such as scheduling a backup, you must start Backup in Advanced mode. To do so, follow these steps:

1. Go to `Start`, `All Programs`, `Accessories`, `System Tools`, `Backup` and do *not* click `Next`.
2. On the `Welcome` page, click `Advanced Mode` and click `Next`.
3. Click the `Backup Wizard (Advanced)` button and click `Next` to start the wizard. You can also use the `Backup` tab, as shown in Figure 17-2, to perform a simple immediate backup. If you also attempt to add a new job on the `Schedule Jobs` page, the advanced wizard will run and allow you to use these selections or change them.
4. On the wizard `Welcome` page, click `Next`.
5. Select `Backup everything on this computer` or select `Backup selected files, drives or network data`.
6. If `Backup everything on this computer` is selected, skip to step 8.

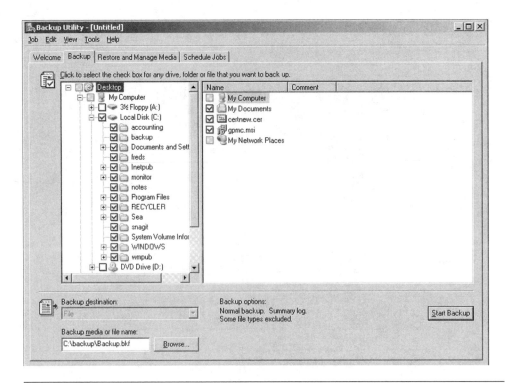

Figure 17-2 In advanced mode, files and folders are selected from the Backup tab.

7. Expand the directory in the left pane and select the folders or use the detail pane to select files to back up.

8. If necessary, select a backup destination, provide a name for the backup, and then click Next.

9. Select the type of backup. Backup types are described in Table 17-1.

10. If Remote Storage has been configured, click Backup migrated Remote Storage data if desired.

11. Click Next.

12. Select Verify data after backup to ensure that a good backup was made.

13. Click Disable Volume Shadow Copy if you prefer not to have Shadow Copy made before your backup and click Next. Volume Shadow Copy is a utility that makes a snapshot copy of the disk and enables backup-to-backup open files. In general, you want it to be enabled since you will get a more comprehensive backup. If you are just backing up a few files, you can save time by disabling it. (You cannot disable Volume Shadow Copy if you are backing up the system stage. See the section "Volume Shadow Copy Service" for more information.)

Table 17-1 Backup Types

Type	Description	What Is Necessary to Restore?
Normal	Copies all files selected and marks the files copied as backed up. Often used to create a complete backup of a disk.	The most recent copy of the backup file or tape to restore all the files as of the date the normal backup was made.
Copy backup	Copies all the selected files but does not mark each file as having been backed up. A good "interim" backup because it does not mark files as being backed up.	The most recent copy of the backup file or tape.
Daily backup	Copies all files selected that have modified on the day the daily backup is made. Files are not marked as backed up.	A normal or copy backup and a daily backup from every day. If one day is not available, a complete restore is not possible.
Differential backup	Copies files that have been created or changed since the last normal or incremental backup. Does not mark files as having been backed up.	If normal backups and differential backups are used, the normal backup and the last differential backup are all that is necessary to restore.
Incremental	Backs up only those files that have been created or changed since the last normal or incremental backup.	If only normal and incremental backups are used, the last normal backup and all the incremental backups since then are necessary.

14. Select whether to `Append this backup to the existing backups` or `Replace the existing backups`, as shown in Figure 17-3, and then click `Next`.

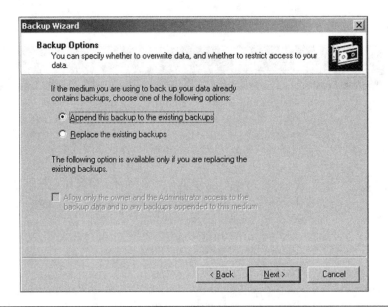

Figure 17-3   Select backup options.

15. Chose to run the backup Now or Later. If Later is selected, enter a job name for the backup and use the Set Schedule button, as shown in Figure 17-4, to enter a schedule for the job. If required, select a schedule for running the backup, and then click Next.
16. Enter an account, password, and password confirmation to run the backup, click OK, and then click Finish.
17. If running the backup now, a Backup Progress dialog appears and provides information on the estimated time of completion of the backup and its progress.
18. When backup is complete, click Report to view the report log. Backup logs are stored in the profile of the user doing the backup (at Local Settings, Application Data, Microsoft, Windows NT, ntbackup, data, bacupxx.log, where the xx is a two-digit number).

One of the most common backup strategies is to make a normal backup on a Sunday, and then either incremental or differential backups every day of the week. If a restore is necessary and incremental backups were made, the normal backup from Sunday and all the incremental backups must be applied to perform a restore. If a restore is necessary and differential backups were made, the Sunday backup and the last differential backup are necessary. This difference is illustrated in Figures 17-4 and 17-5. The backup tapes used for incremental or differential backups are rotated each week, but the normal Sunday backups are usually kept for

30 days, and an end-of-month tape is kept for a year. Tapes that are reused should be periodically replaced with new tapes. Check the manufacturer's instructions to determine the correct replacement timeframe.

NOTE: Incremental or Differential?

Differential backup is often selected because of its convenience—fewer tapes are necessary for a restore. However, if change is volatile, it may take too long to back up all changes every day. In this case, incremental backups are better.

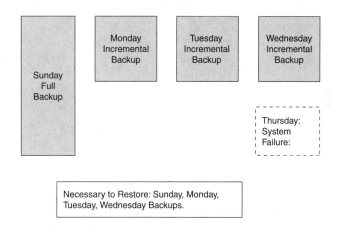

Figure 17-4 Restore from incremental backups requires the use of all incremental backups.

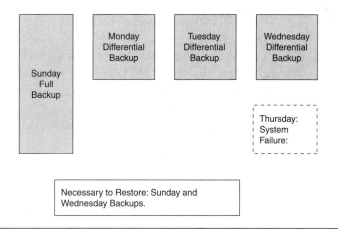

Figure 17-5 Restore from differential backups requires the use of only the last differential backup.

Default Backup options are set from the Tools, Options pages of Backup. The menus are displayed when ntbackup is started in Advanced mode. Table 17-2 lists the advanced backup options.

Table 17-2   Advanced Backup Options

Option	Description
Disable volume Shadow Copy	A volume Shadow Copy is not made.
Backup type	Determines how data is backed up.
Back up data that has been moved to remote storage	If remote storage has been set up, files that have not been used for some time may have been moved to remote storage. They ordinarily would not be backed up.
Verify data after backup	Checks to see that backed up data is the same as original data.
Compress backup data	Saves space on the backup media.
Backup system protected files with the system state.	Backs up system files in the systemroot directory in addition to the boot files included with the system state data. Adds substantially to the size of backup but is a good idea after system files have been changed or new drivers added.

System State Backup

In addition to backing up applications and files, you must ensure that system state data is backed up. System state backup backs up critical system files and configuration data. These files are necessary to recover a server and must be restored in a certain order. Do not attempt to use a normal file backup to manage system state backup. The following items are always backed up when a system state backup is made:

- Registry
- COM+ Class Registration database
- Boot files
- System files that are under Windows File Protection

In addition, the components in Table 17-3 are backed up if the requisite service or application is installed.

Table 17-3   Optional Components Backed Up

Component	Is Backed Up If
Certificate services database	The server is a certification authority.
IIS metadirectory	If IIS is installed.
Active Directory database (ndts.dit)	If the server is a domain controller.
SYSVOL directory	If the server is a domain controller.
Cluster service information	If the server is within a cluster.

To make a system state backup, follow these steps:

1. Open the ntbackup backup utility.
2. Click `Advanced Mode`.
3. Select `Backup Wizard (Advanced)` and click `Next`.
4. Select `Only back up the System State data`, as shown in Figure 17-6, and then click `Next`.

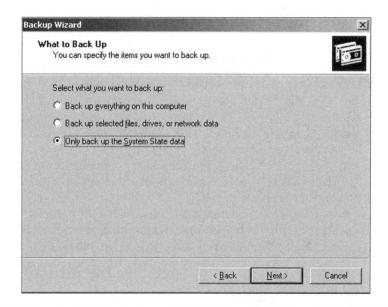

Figure 17-6   The main difference in the advanced backup wizard and the standard wizard is the opportunity to select a system state backup.

5. If necessary, select a backup destination and provide a name for the backup, and then click Next.

6. To make an immediate backup of the system state, click Finish. Otherwise, click the Advanced button and follow the previous backup instructions to complete the backup.

The system state data is critical, sensitive information that might allow an attacker to compromise the system. Always ensure the safe storage of the system state data.

NOTE: Skipped File During System State Backup May Be Ok
After backing up the system state, an error may report that some files were skipped. Examine the backup report. If the backup report includes only the error: Warning: unable to open "C:\windows\sysvol\domain\ DO_NOT_REMOVE_NtFrs_PreInstall_Directory", the integrity of the backup is OK according to Microsoft (see KB article 822132). It seems that this file should not be backed up, but under some circumstances, backup may attempt to do so.

Backup Defaults and Configuration Options

It is not necessary to use the backup wizard; instead, many options can be set manually. Select individual tabs to configure the backup:

- Welcome **tab**—Choose the Backup Wizard (Advanced), Restore Wizard, or ASR Wizard.
- Backup **tab**—Select the files to back up. Back up system state data. Select the Tools menu, then select options to open the backup Property pages.
- General **tab**—Change defaults, as shown in Figure 17-7.
- Backup Type **tab**—Change default backup type, as shown in Figure 17-8. (Backup types were detailed in Table 17-1.)

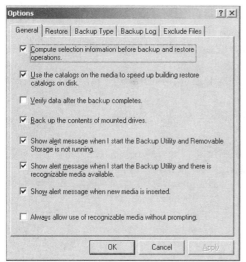 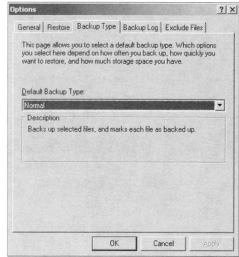

Figure 17-7   Change defaults on the General tab.

Figure 17-8   Change backup types on the Backup Type tab.

■ `Backup Log` **tab**—Change how much information is added to the log, as shown in Figure 17-9.

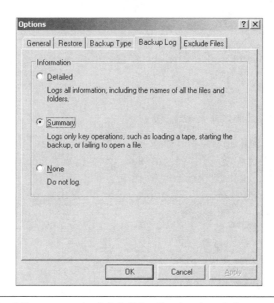

Figure 17-9   Select the amount of detail for the backup tab.

- `Exclude Files` **tab**—Remove files listed to not be backed up. Add files to skip, as shown in Figure 17-10. Excluded files include those that run the volume copy shadow service, pagefile.sys, and so on.
- `Restore and Manage Media` **tab**—Restore files and folders from backup.
- `Schedule Job` **tab**—Change or add schedules.

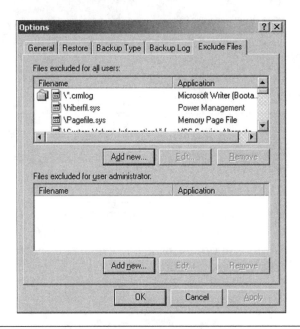

Figure 17-10   Remove or add files to the "not to be backed up" list.

Command-Line Backup

ntbackup can be used to back up at the command line or within a script. You cannot restore files from backup using the `ntbackup` command. Any option that is not specified in the command line defaults to those set in the backup program. The general form for the command is

```
Ntbackup backup logical_disk_path_and_file_name /J
name_of_the_job /F
or_/Tand_the_filename_or_tape_name_to_put_backup_on
```

Any options left off the command default to those configured in the backup program.

To create a normal backup named Backup job 2 that backs up the system state data to the D:\systemstate.bkf file, use

```
Ntbackup backup systemstate /M normal /J "backup job 2" /F
"D:\systemstate.bkf"
```

To set advanced options such as verifying data, using hardware compression or volume shadow copy, use the following syntax. For an explanation, see Table 17-4:

```
ntbackup backup /V:{yes|no} /HC:{on|off} /SNAP:{on|off}
```

A complete `ntbackup` command syntax is located in the local Windows Server 2003 help files.

Here's a sample command that would create the backup job "Backup 1", back up data on drive E:\ to the file D:\mybackup.bkf, and verify the data:

```
ntbackup backup E:\ /J "Backup 1" /F "D:\mybackup.bkrf"
/V:yes
```

TIP: An Easy Way to Write Backup Commands
To quickly and accurately create a backup command, create a scheduled backup job and then open the `Scheduled Tasks` control panel. The full command line is displayed in the control panel—copy this command into a batch file and modify if necessary.

Table 17-4 ntbackup Advanced Options

Value	Option	Description
/V:	Yes | No	Verify data or do not verify data
/HC:	On | Off	Use hardware compression or not
/SNAP:	On | Off	Use volume shadow copy or not

Restore Files and Folders

The backup program can also be used to restore files and folders from a backup. To restore individual files or folders, follow these steps:

1. Open the Backup program from `Start`, `All Programs`, `Accessories`, `System Tools`, `Backup`.
2. Click `Advanced Mode`.
3. Click the `Restore Wizard (Advanced)` button and click `Next`.
4. Select `Items to restore` and click `Next`.
5. If you want to use the default restore settings, click `Finish` and skip to step 10; if not, click the `Advanced` button and continue.
6. Select the destination for the restored files and folders. Choices are the original location, an alternate location, or a single folder; click `Next`. If an alternate location is selected, the `Browse` button and an alternate location text box will be added to the page for your use.
7. Select whether to leave or replace existing files, as shown in Figure 7-11, and then click `Next`.
8. Select advanced restore options, as shown in Figure 7-12, and then click `Next`.

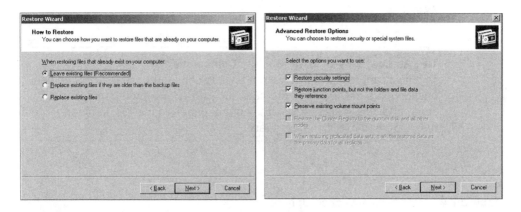

Figure 17-11   Select what to do with any existing files.

Figure 17-12   Select advanced restore options.

9. Click Finish to start the restore.
10. Click the Report button to view a report of the restore.

Alternatively, the Restore and Manage Media tab can be used to restore files and folders:

1. Click the Restore and Manage Media tab.
2. Click the media to restore, and click the check boxes next to the drives, folders, and/or files to restore.
3. Use the Restore files to: drop-down box to specify the location to restore the files, either to the Original location (where files were located when they were backed up), to an Alternate location, or to a Single folder, as shown in Figure 17-13.
4. If you select Alternate location or Single folder, enter the location where the data should be restored or browse to that location and click OK.
5. To change restore options, click the Tools menu, click Options, and then click the Restore tab, as shown in Figure 17-14. After selecting restore options, click OK.

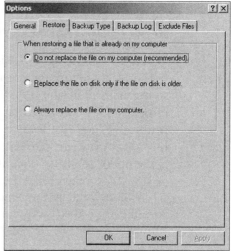

Figure 17-13   Use the Restore and Manage Media tab to restore files and folders.

Figure 17-14   Select the restore options.

6. Click Start Restore.
7. A popup dialog can be used to select advanced options, as shown in Figure 17-15. If advanced options are required, click Advanced and set options, and then click OK.

Figure 17-15   Select the advanced restore options.

8. Click OK to start restore.
9. A Restore Progress dialog appears, which tracks the restore progress. When it is complete, click Report to view the report or click OK to close the window.

Restore System State Backup

When you restore system state data, you can restore it to the same location or to an alternative location. If you restore to a different location, some data will not be restored. Specifically, only registry files, SYSVOL directory files, cluster database information, and system boot files are restored. When restoring the system state data to the original location, the current system state data is erased, and the backup is restored. This is the opposite of the default for file backup, which does not overwrite existing files unless the default has been changed.

Although the system state can be backed up while Active Directory is online, to restore the system state on a DC, Active Directory cannot be running. To restore the system state on a DC, reboot, select F8 during the boot, and then select the advanced startup option Directory Services Restore Mode. You must select Primary, Authoritative, or Normal restore. These modes of restore are discussed in the section "Active Directory Restore."

Automated Systems Recovery

The Automated Systems Recovery (ASR) process replaces the Windows 2000 Emergency Repair process. The Emergency Repair process allows restoration of corrupt system files without a format, whereas ASR does not. When ASR is initialized, it copies the system folders to backup media and critical startup information, such as the disk configuration to a floppy disk. It only copies system files that would be necessary to restart the computer: the boot volume and the system volume. It does not copy data files. (You can choose to back up all data on the computer, and this option backs up data and ASR data. You will need a floppy disk at the end of the backup to create the ASR disk.) Instead of restoring a failed system by reinstalling the OS and then applying a backup tape, ASR automates the process. The disk and the media can be used to recover a system when a system dies. The installation CD-ROM will also be necessary. An ASR set (files on backup media and floppy) should be kept in a secure place. Like system state backup, an ASR set might allow an attacker to compromise your system. It also might allow him or her to set up a rogue server and spoof your server, thereby collecting important or sensitive information from other servers and users. Keep the floppy and media set together; you must have matched floppy and backup media in order to use them to recover a server.

To make an ASR set, follow these steps:

1. Start the `Backup Wizard (advanced)`.
2. Select the `Automated System Recovery Wizard` and click `Next`.
3. Enter a name for the backup file, select a location for backup, and then click `Next`.
4. Information about the system is collected, and then the progress wizard displays the estimated time the backup will take and its estimated size.
5. When the backup is complete, a prompt to insert a floppy disk appears.
6. Insert the disk and click `OK`.
7. After the floppy is made, click `Close` to close the `Backup Progress` window.
8. Determine if specialized drivers for your mass storage driver are necessary and obtain a copy to store with the ASR recovery set.

To use an ASR set to recover, you must have the ASR recovery set (the matched floppy disk and media produced by performing an ASR backup) and the Windows Server 2003 installation disks. You may need specialized drivers for your mass storage driver if driver files on the installation disks cannot be used. The time to find this out is not during the restore. When ASR is run, it inspects the ASR floppy for disk information and restores the disk signatures and volumes that are used by the system to boot. These volumes are known as the critical volumes. Other volumes, such as the normal volumes, are not backed up as part of an ASR backup and are not restored. After critical disks are created, a simple installation of Windows Server 2003 is performed, and then a backup from the backup media is performed.

WARNING: Data Files Stored on System Volumes Will Be Lost
If data files are stored on the critical volumes, they will be lost. A format is done of the boot volume and may be done of the system volume before the restore.

An ASR restore can be done to a different computer than the one it was created on as long as the computer is the same as the previous computer with the following exception: The number of disks must be the same as or more than are needed to restore critical volumes. Hard disks, video cards, and network adapters can differ, but the number and volume of disks must be the same as or greater than the original computer.

1. Insert the installation CD-ROM into the CD-ROM drive.
2. Restart the computer. If prompted to press a key to start from the CD, do so.
3. Install any special drivers if necessary by pressing F6 when prompted.
4. Press F2 during the text mode part of setup when prompted to start the ASR recovery.
5. When prompted, insert the ASR floppy disk.
6. Follow the instructions.
7. During restart, you may need to use F6 and the special driver disk again.

Volume Shadow Copy Service

The volume shadow copy Service is used for two purposes. First, the service makes a snapshot disk copy at the start of ntbackup, and then ntbackup backs up the selected files and folders from the copy. When volume shadow copy is used, even open files can be backed up. Second, the service is used to provide users the opportunity to recover deleted files or earlier versions of a current file. This is called User Based File Recovery in technical documents and Previous Versions in end-user documents.

When Shadow Copy is used during backup, it does not need to be configured and is turned on by default. However, User Based File Recovery must be configured and client software distributed before it can be used. User Based File Recovery is configured on Windows Server 2003 shares; however, once configured, all shares on the volume are backed up. You can configure it for one volume and not another, but you cannot selectively choose shares within a volume and have some backed up and others not.

A Shadow Copy Client is required in order to recover files protected by Shadow Copy. The client must be added to Windows 2000 or Windows XP. The client is located on the <%system folder%>\system32\clients\x86\twsclient.exe. It can also be downloaded from `http://www.microsoft.com/downloads/details.aspx?FamilyID=e38 2358f-33c3-4de7-acd8-a33ac92d295e&displaylang=en`. The client can be distributed via Group Policy or placed on a share. Double-clicking the client executable installs the client without any other necessary interaction.

Best Practices for Shadow Copies of Shared Folders

- Use a storage location other than the disk of the volume that will be shadow copies. This may improve performance.

- Set appropriate NTFS file permissions. Do not give unauthorized users the ability to modify data in this way. If users can access previous versions of files, they can restore them and might inappropriately replace current data with older data. Instead of a tool that helps users recover inadvertently deleted data, the use of shadow copies can cause problems with data integrity. Restoration of old data may not be detected immediately, especially by the users of the files, and old data could be used. The integrity of data is dependent, as it always is, on the people who have access to files.

■ Do not use shadow copies of shared folders where the risk that some-one might restore old data without an approval process is considered too high. Keep backups of previous versions for historical reference.

■ Do not use shadow copies of shared folders to replace regular backup processes. There are too many ways that previous versions of the files could be lost.

■ Do not schedule shadow copies to happen more frequently than once every hour. Each shadow copy degrades system performance, and frequent shadow copies may do so to an unacceptable level. Frequent shadow copies can also fill up the disk too quickly, or reach the 64 Shadow Copy limit too quickly.

■ Adjust the schedule of shadow copies of shared folders to meet the needs of users. By default, no shadow copies are made on the weekend, for example, and you may have users that work on these days.

■ Delete Shadow Copy tasks before deleting a volume that is being shadow copied. Otherwise, the task will fail and could fill the event log with errors.

■ Use an allocation unit size of 16 KB or larger when formatting a volume on which shadow copies of shared folders will be enabled. Defragging volumes allocated with smaller units can result in the loss of previous versions of files.

■ Do not enable shadow copies on volumes that use mount points. Mounted drives will not be included when shadow copies are made.

■ Do not use shadow copies of shared folders on dual-boot computers.

Once a volume is configured for Shadow Copy, older versions of files can be located and recovered by any users authorized to read the current version of the file. Take care to set user expectations. Shadow copies are scheduled, and files created and deleted between backups cannot be recovered.

To Create Shadow Copy Volumes

Creating the volumes is easy, and there are only a few configuration options. To create the volume and make the first Shadow Copy volume, follow these steps:

1. Open Computer Management, and then right-click the Shared Folders folder, as shown in Figure 17-16.
2. Select All Tasks, and then click Configure Shadow Copies.
3. In the Shadow Copies dialog, select the volume to prepare, as shown in Figure 17-17.

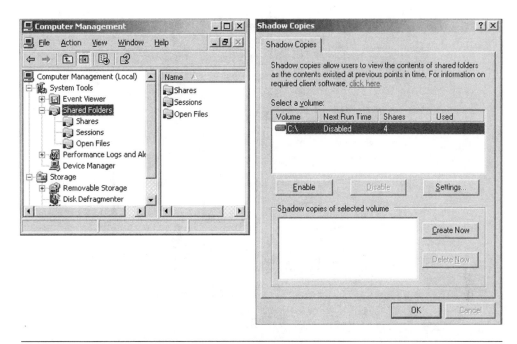

Figure 17-16 Open Computer Management and locate Shared Folders.

Figure 17-17 Shadow copies are set by the volume, not the share.

4. Click settings to change the volume on which the Shadow Copies will be stored, as shown in Figure 17-18. By default, shadow copies will be stored on the same volume as the share. If you are not using RAID volumes, it is a good idea to place the shadow copies on another volume. This way, the shadow copies will not fill the original disk, and on servers with a high I/0 load, it can make a real difference in performance. Remember, if you have to change the storage location of the shadow copy, you will have to delete the shadow copy. All old versions of the files will be lost.

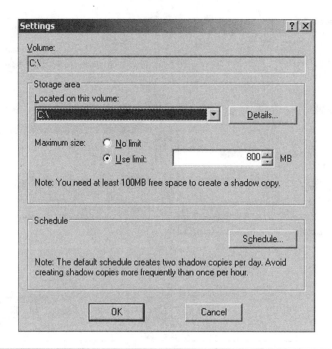

Figure 17-18   Change the location for the shadow copy storage.

5. Click Details and view the available disk space. Click OK.
6. Set the amount of space to allocate to the shadow copies. By default, 10 percent of the available space is allocated. When the allocated space is gone, older shadow copies are deleted. Also, a maximum of 64 shadow copies can be recorded. At that point, older copies are deleted before new ones are saved.
7. Click Schedule to set the times when a shadow copy will be made, as shown in Figure 17-19. By default, a shadow copy will be made at 7 A.M. and 12 P.M. You will want to adjust this schedule to meet your needs. For example, if you have people working on weekends or from different time zones, you may want to add additional times. Microsoft recommends that you do not schedule shadow copies less than one hour apart.
8. Click OK to close the schedule page and click OK to close the Settings page.
9. On the main page, shadow copies are enabled. Click Create Now to create the shadow copy, as shown in Figure 17-20. A shadow copy is made. View the Details page to see how much space was required.

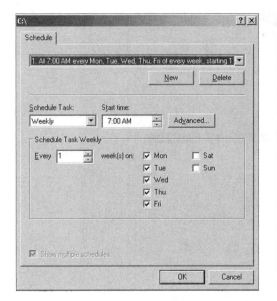 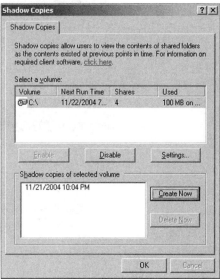

Figure 17-19   Set the shadow copy schedule that fits the way users work.

Figure 17-20   After enabling, you'll be able to view the shadow copies and space used on the drive.

10. Click OK to close the Shadow Copies page.

WARNING: Shadow Copy Location

Determine the best location for shadow copies before enabling them. You will have to delete any shadow copies in order to move the location where they will be saved.

Alternatively, open the Local Disk Properties for an NTFS volume and select the Shadow Copies tab, as shown in Figure 17-21.

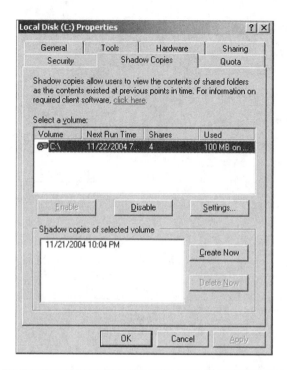

Figure 17-21   The Shadow Copies Property page is used to create shadow copies.

Restoring from Shadow Copies

Users must install client software before they can view or restore previous versions. They will be able to view file content before restoring files, but they will not be able to modify the previous version. After they restore the file, if they have permission, they can modify the file.

NOTE: Permissions Maintained
Shadow copies maintain permission settings. If a user does not have permission to read the file, he will not be able to read the Shadow Copy file.

Files can be viewed and restored from the Previous Versions tab of the shared folder properties, as shown in Figure 17-22, using a network connection. When the View button is selected, as shown in Figure 17-23, each file can be opened for read only. The Restore button restores the older version.

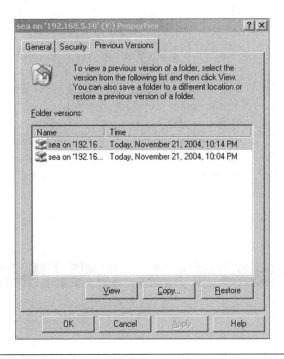

Figure 17-22   Previous versions are viewed through the Previous Version tab on the shared folder.

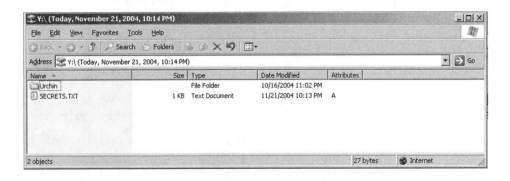

Figure 17-23   When the files are viewed, the version is specified next to the shared drive letter in the address file.

Command-Line Shadow Copy Administration

The vssadmin tool can be used at the command line to manage shadow copies. Vssadmin is provided for Windows XP and Windows Server 2003. The Windows XP version provides only a few commands and is mostly useful for management of previous versions of files from the user's perspective. Some useful examples of using vssadmin on Windows Server 2003 are listed in Table 17-5. A complete syntactical reference is located at http://www.microsoft.com/technet/treeview/default. asp?url=/technet/prodtechnol/windowsserver2003/proddocs/sta ndard/vssadmin.asp.

Table 17-5   Vssadmin

Command	Function
Vssadmin add shadowstorage /for=D:\research /or=e:\	Creates Shadow Volume for D:\ on the E:\ drive. D:\ must be a local volume or mount point.
Vssadmin create shadow /for=D:\	Creates a new shadow copy.
Vssadmin list shadows	Lists all shadow copies on the system.
Vssadmin list shadows /for=D:\	Lists all shadows for volume D:\.
Vssadmin list shadowstorage /for=D:\	Lists all associate shadow copies on any volumes for volume D:\.

Miscellaneous Backup Tools

While you should create both system state backups and data backups, many functions and services provide tools for backing up their critical data, thus allowing recovery of their functions without restoring the entire computer. Some of these functions are user-oriented, such as the password reset disk and EFS import and export functions, whereas others are relevant to the user or computer, such as registry backup. Nevertheless, they may have meaning and use on servers when account profiles may be stored there or where standalone servers are used. Other backup functions are provided to assist in the recovery of network services, such as DHCP, DNS, and WINS.

Backup Critical User Functions

On a standalone server, local accounts may be used for administration of the server and its services, or provided for special operations, such as database administration, or file backup and management. These accounts can be managed by local administrator accounts, and passwords can be reset using Computer Management. When local accounts on a standalone server are reset, it is possible to lose data (for example, if the local accounts have been used to encrypt files or if the server has recorded an Internet password). If the user of a local account forgets his or her password, instead of having an administrator reset the password, the user should use a password reset disk. The disk must be made before the password is reset.

If an administrator has already reset the user's password, thus preventing them from accessing encrypted files, the user can use his backup of EFS keys to regain access to them.

Password Reset Disk

When a local account is created on a standalone server, a password reset disk should be made. (This option is also viable for Windows XP computers that will not be joined to a domain.) A public and private key pair is created when a password reset disk is created. The private key is stored on the password reset disk; the public key is used to encrypt the local user account password. If a user forgets their password, the password reset disk can be used. The Forgotten Password Wizard uses the private key on the disk to decrypt the local password, and the user is prompted to enter a new password.

Password reset disks should be stored in a safe place, as an unauthorized individual could use them to gain access to the computer. In some environments, password reset disks should not be made in order to reduce risk. In these environments, the type of data that is at risk may also be disallowed or alternative recovery methods can be put into place.

To create a password reset disk, follow these steps:

1. Press Ctrl+Alt+Del.
2. Click `Change Password`.
3. Enter the user account name for which to create a password reset disk.
4. Click the computer name in the `Log on to` box.
5. Click `Backup`. The password reset disk starts.

To use the password reset disk, follow these steps:

1. At the Log on prompt, enter your user name, then click OK.
2. The logon fails because you did not enter a password. When the Logon Failed dialog appears, click Reset.
3. Insert the password reset disk.

It is not necessary to create a new password disk after changing the account.

EFS Import and Export Functions

EFS encrypted files use a public/private key pair to protect the symmetric key used to encrypt the files. The public/private key pair is stored in the user's profile. If something happens to the keys, such as if the profile is destroyed or if a local computer account user's password is reset, it will not be possible for the user to decrypt the encrypted files. If the keys have been exported, they can be imported into a user profile, and the files can be accessed. Alternatively, if key archival has been configured, the keys can be recovered. (For more information on how EFS works and how to export and import keys, see Chapter 6, "EFS Basics," and for information on key archival, see Chapter 13, "Implementing a Secure PKI.")

Backup and Restore Registry Keys

The registry is backed up when you back up the system state data. Nevertheless, when modifying registry keys, it is a good idea to back up or export the key that you are changing a value in before you change it.

To export a registry key, follow these steps:

1. Click Start, and then click Run.
2. Type regedit in the Open box and click OK.
3. Locate and then select the key to export.
4. From the File menu, select Export.
5. In the Save In box, select a location to save the registry entries, enter a file name, and then click Save.

To restore the registry key, double-click the .reg file to which you exported the key.

Backup Network Services and Other Server Utilities

Network services information is backed up when a complete backup is made. In addition, much of the information may be duplicated on other servers of the same type that are established as secondary servers (DNS) or replication partners (WINS), and local back ups of configuration data may be made.

DNS Backup

DNS secondary servers are usually deployed to provide alternative and redundant sources of DNS databases. When DNS data is stored in the Active Directory, secondary servers can be established, but it is not necessary because each domain controller will have a copy of the data. A backup of the DNS zone file is saved the <%systemroot%>\ DNS\backup folder. If DNS is integrated with Active Directory, the backup files are not updated.

To recover a zone from the backup, follow these steps:

1. Copy the backup DNS Zone file from the backup folder to the <%systemroot%> \DNS folder.
2. Open the DNS console.
3. Right-click the server and select Create a new zone file.
4. Point to the zone file in the folder as the zone file for the new zone.

DHCP Backup

The DHCP database is backed up automatically every 60 minutes to <%systemroot%>\DHCP\backup. You can also use the backup command from the DHCP console or the Backup program. (You do not need to stop the DHCP service to make a backup.) When the database is backed up from the DHCP console, all scopes, reservations, leases, options, registry keys, and other configuration settings, such as audit log settings and folder location settings if configured in DHCP property pages, are backed up. Dynamic update credentials, such as user name, domain, and password used when registering DHCP client computer with DNS, are not backed up.

Changing DHCP Backup

Change the default DHCP database backup interval at this registry location:

HKEY_LOCAL_MACHINE\SYSTEM\CurrentControlSet\Services\DHCPSer
ver\Parameters\BackupInterval

To restore the database, use the Restore command from the Action menu of the DHCP console.

WINS Backup

WINS database backups are not made by default. If you want to back up the database, you must set the database backup path and perform a backup. To change the WINS database backup path, follow these steps:

1. Open the WINS console from Start, Administrative Tools.
2. Select the WINS server on which to change the database backup path.
3. Click the Action menu, and then click Properties.
4. On the General tab, select Database Backup, select the Default Backup Path, and then type the path desired, or use the Browse button to browse to the location.
5. Click OK.

To back up the WINS database, follow these steps:

1. Open the WINS console from Start, Administrative Tools.
2. Select the WINS server to back up.
3. Click the Action menu, and then click Back Up Database.
4. If you have not created a default backup location, browse to a backup location.
5. Click OK.

TIP: Database Location is Important
The WINS database must be restored from the same location it was backed up to.

To restore the WINS database, follow these steps:

1. Open the WINS console on the WINS server that you need to restore to. You cannot restore the WINS server remotely.
2. If the WINS server is not stopped, stop the server. If necessary, refresh the console. The restore option is only available if the WINS service is stopped.
3. Select the WINS server to restore.
4. Click the Action menu, and then click Restore Database.
5. If necessary, browse to the location where the backup was saved and click OK.

Remote Storage Data

When removable storage or remote storage is used, back up the following files on a regular basis. This makes it possible to restore remote storage and removable storage data:

- <%systemroot%>\System32\Ntmsdata
- <%systemroot%>\System32\remotestorage

If you need to restore remote-storage files, you cannot do so to a different folder.

Reanimating Users from the Deleted Objects Store

In a Windows Server 2003 domain, it may be possible to recover deleted users from the Deleted Objects Store using the support tool ldp.exe. This process is called reanimating. Reanimation is not supported if a Windows Server 2003 DC has been upgraded from a Windows 2000 DC. User objects in the undeleted object stores only retain their SID, ObjectGUID, LastKnownParent, and SAMaccountName attributes, so you have to reset passwords, profiles, home directories, and group memberships after reanimating the account. The reanimated user account has the same SID. The SIDHistory attribute is not preserved.

1. Click start, Run, and then type ldp.exe. Click OK.
2. Use the Connection menu to connect and bind to the Windows Server 2003 domain controller.
3. From the Options menu, click Controls.
4. Click the Load Predefined list Return Deleted Objects.
5. In Control Type, click Server, and then click OK.
6. From the View menu, select Tree and enter the distinguished name path (the DN path, cn=deleted Objects,dc=domainname,dc=domainextension) of the delete object container in the domain where the deletion occurred, and then click OK.
7. Double-click the deleted objects container.
8. Double-click the object to be undeleted or reanimated.
9. Right-click the object to reanimate and then click Modify.
10. In the Edit Entry Attribute box, type isDeleted and leave the values box blank.
11. Click the Delete Option button, and then click Enter.

12. In the `Attribute` box, type `distinguishedName`.
13. In the `values` box, type the new DN path for the reanimated object:

    ```
    Cn=delteduser,ou=usersou,dc=domainname,dc=doma
    inextension
    ```

14. Alternatively, append the value of the deleted object's `Last-KnownParent` attribute to tie CN value and past the full DN path in the `values` box.
15. In the `Operation` box, click `REPLACE`.
16. Click `Enter`.
17. Click to select the `Synchronous` check box.
18. Click to select the `Extended` check box.
19. Click `RUN`.
20. Click `options` followed by `Controls`, click to clear `Return Deleted Objects`, and then click `OK`.
21. Reset user account passwords, profiles, home directories, and group memberships for the reanimated user.
22. Enable the reanimated account in `Active Directory Users and Computers`.
23. Clean up the account and reconnect it with any Active Directory integrated application. For example, if Microsoft Exchange is used for email, remove Exchange attributes and reconnect the user to his Exchange mailbox.

WARNING: Reanimation Should Not Be the Default Backup Strategy
Reanimation may or may not work. It should not be the only strategy in place to recover from deletions.

Active Directory Restore

Part of a successful Active Directory restoration is the planning and fulfillment of adequate directory backup, the selection of the proper type of restore, and practice in a complete restore. Even the smallest Active Directory implementation cannot survive a complete operational failure or disaster without the availability of appropriate backup and planning. As detailed in the section "System State Backup," it is not enough to simply copy the database file ntds.dit. Instead, you must have a complete system state backup. To restore, you must restore the system components. System components must be restored in a specific order. When ntbackup is used to restore the system state files backed up by ntbackup, this order is followed. Do not assume that every backup product understands what files need to be backed up for a system state backup, nor the order in which they must be restored.

Files must be restored in the following order:

1. Boot files
2. SysVol, Certificate Server, Cluster database, and COM+ class registration database (as applicable)
3. Restore Active Directory
4. Restore the registry

In addition to running ntbackup to restore system state, you must determine what kind of Active Directory restore is necessary:

- Primary restore is necessary when restoring the first DC in a domain, or the only working server or a replicated data set. In this case, all the DCs in the domain are lost, and you are working from backup.
- Normal (non-authoritative) restore is done to restore a replica of the directory that does not need to propagate any of its differences at the time of restore to the other DCs. Instead, changes that occurred since the backup are replicated to the restored DC from other DCs in the domain.
- Authoritative restores a deleted object. A replica is restored from a backup created before the object was deleted, and this object in the restored replica is given precedence over the other domain replicas. That is, the object is replicated to the other DCs in the domain. (The restored replica receives all other changes from the existing DCs via replication.) The end result is simply that the deleted object is restored.
- Authoritatively restore an earlier version of Active Directory. A replica is restored from a backup, and the restored replica is given precedence over the other domain replicas. The end result is a return to the Active Directory state of the replica.
- Restore from backup older than the Active Directory tombstone lifetime. Although this is not recommended and will not be a complete solution, it may provide a better solution than reloading the entire domain or Active Directory infrastructure from scratch.

Normal Restore

In a normal restore, the restored DC's objects have their update sequence number, which is used to determine if an object needs replicating. Because objects in the Active Directory may have been changed since the backup was created, the objects that are not up-to-date in the restored replica will appear to be old, and the new changes will be replicated to the restored DC in the normal manner. If the reason for the restore is to undelete or recover from changes made to Active Directory, a normal restore will not work because this information will be changed during the next replication and never replicated to other DCs. To replace objects or recover from changes, an authoritative restore must be done.

Authoritative Restore

During an authoritative restore, ntdsutil is used to change the update sequence number of an object to be higher than any other update sequence number in the Active Directory replication system. Objects and subtrees can be restored from an archived Active Directory database. The impact of authoritative restore depends on the type of object restored. For example, trust and computer account passwords are negotiated every 30 days by default. (Computer account password negotiation can be turned off by an administrator, but trust password negotiation cannot.) When performing a partial authoritative restore (only some objects will be restored), restore only the necessary objects. For example, rather than restoring the entire domain-naming context in which trust information, trust passwords, and computer passwords are stored, restore only those objects necessary. User accounts are another object that, if they must be restored, require additional work to return their status to the way it was. The section "Recovering Deleted User Accounts: An Example of a Complex Authoritative Restore" illustrates the authoritative restore process and details the impact the object to be restored can have on the process. Before performing an authoritative restore at the object level, you must understand the implications of such an object restore. Examples of issues that you may encounter during authoritative restore are

- Resetting the offline administrator password
- Recovering from an authoritative restore's impact on computer accounts and trusts

- Recovering deleted user accounts
- Restoring using a backup older than the Active Directory tomb-stone lifetime

Resetting the Offline Administrator Account Password

The offline administrator account is also referred to as the authoritative restore administrative account, and it is created and its password is entered during dcpromo. The password for this account can be reset using the setpwd command-line command on a DC in online mode on a Windows Server 2003 DC or a Windows 2000 DC Service Pack 2 and later. On Windows Server 2003, use the set dsrm password command in ntdsutil.

To reset the offline administrators account, follow these steps:

1. At Start, Run, enter ntdsutil and click OK.
2. Type set dsrm password.
3. If the DC console is the one on which the password should be reset, type reset password on server null.
4. If the DC console is not the DC on which the password should be reset, type reset password on server *servername*. *servername* is the DNS name for the server on which you want to set the password.
5. Enter the new password.
6. Type q to quit the dsrm command.
7. Type q to quit ntdsutil.

Recovering from the Impact of Authoritative Restore on Computer Accounts and Trusts

If the trust passwords that are restored do not match the current trust password, communication with domain controllers in the trusted domain will be blocked. If a computer account password is restored and no longer matches that known to the computer, the member computer will not be able to communicate with its domain. In either case, the solution is the same as that required if these passwords ever get out of synch. (Passwords might get out of synch, for example, if a member computer cannot communicate with the domain during the time at which the password should be renegotiated.) To recover a trust relationship, the trust should be removed from both sides and then recreated. If many trusts must be removed and recreated, use the Netdom utility and do them as a batch. To recover communications between a domain computer and its domain, the computer can be removed from the domain and then rejoined.

Recovering Deleted User Accounts: An Example of a Complex Authoritative Restore

If user accounts are accidentally deleted, there are many ways to recover them:

- New accounts can be added, but all previous group memberships and privileges will also have to be recreated. Accounts cannot simply be recreated as new users. If they are, they will receive a new SID, and therefore, any permissions granted to the old account will be invalid. If all permissions are assigned according to group membership, the old status can be recovered by adding the user account as a member of the appropriate groups. Any objects owned by the old account will not be owned by the new account. If it is necessary to return ownership of these objects to the user, an administrator can take ownership of the objects and give the user ownership privileges. In a small environment, if one or few accounts have been deleted, this may be an acceptable solution. In other cases, a more efficient way of recovering from deleted user accounts is to do an authoritative restore of the deleted account.
- Perform an authoritative restore of the deleted user account, and then the account can be manually added to the appropriate groups.
- Perform an authoritative restore of the deleted account and the groups the account was a member of. To do so, you must use a GC domain controller backup from the domain in which the account was deleted. This is because only this GC stores Universal group membership information. The drawback to this method is that if it is used, the additions to security groups prior to the backup used in the restore will be lost and must be manually entered.
- In a Windows Server 2003 Active Directory domain, you may be able to use the Repadmin method to authoritatively restore users, groups, and computers without having a backup. To do so, the following conditions must be true: You must have a latent global

catalog DC (a GC that has not yet replicated and deleted the accounts); the forest must be at the Windows Server 2003 or Windows Server 2003 Interim forest functional level; only user or computer accounts must have been deleted; and the deleted accounts must have been added after the move to Windows Server 2003 level. If all these things are true, the group membership links can be rebuilt with the outbound replication after the authoritative restore.

- In a Windows Server 2003 domain, you may be able to reanimate deleted user accounts.

When authoritative restore is used and the user account contains attributes such as managedBy and memberOf, you may need to do additional work after the restore. This is because these attributes are *back links* to other objects in the directory. Back links and *forward links* are attributes that link objects together; for example, the memberOf attribute is a back link in the user account that links the user account to a group account. The member attribute of the group is a forward link that links the group to user accounts. If you must restore an object with a forward link attribute, you must first make sure that the object containing its back link exists within Active Directory. If you must restore user accounts and groups, you cannot restore groups until all of its member accounts exist in Active Directory. (Member accounts may be user accounts, computer accounts, or the accounts of other groups.) This is why authoritative restore of user accounts and the groups they are members of must be done twice—once to restore the accounts and once to restore the groups.

The process of authoritative restore requires you to restore the most recent backup of the DC or stop the latent GC DC from replicating and then, in both cases, use ntdsutil to authoritatively restore the deleted objects. This is not a trivial undertaking, and your first attempt should be in a test forest. If you must restore deleted user accounts and group memberships, the Microsoft Knowledge Base article 840001, "How to Restore Deleted User Accounts and Their Group Memberships in Active Directory," provides detailed instructions on the process, including command syntax and pointers to more information. The process is outlined next.

To restore user accounts, computer accounts, or security groups, follow these steps:

1. If a global catalog domain controller exists that has not replicated any part of the deletion, stop it from replicating the deletion by using the following `Repadmin` command at the command line. This DC will be referred to as the recovery DC. (If you cannot immediately issue this command, remove the DC from the network until you can issue the command, and then immediately return the DC to the network.)

   ```
   Repadmin /options recoverydcname +DISABLE_INBOUND_REPL
   ```

2. Temporarily stop making changes to user accounts, computer accounts service accounts, security groups, and attributes on these.

3. Create a new system state backup in the domain where the deletion occurred.

4. If a GC in the domain replicated the deletion, back up its system state.

5. Start the recovery domain controller in Dsrepair mode by pressing `F8` during startup. You will need to know the offline administrator account password.

6. Log on to the console using the offline administrator account.

7. If the recovery domain controller is a latent global catalog domain controller, do not restore the system state; instead, go to step 8. If you are creating a recovery domain controller using a system state backup, restore the most current system state backup.

8. Authoritatively restore the deleted user accounts, the deleted computer accounts, or the deleted security groups by using the `ntdsutil` command tool to increment the version numbers of these objects. Order is important here. First, restore the domain name path for each deleted user account, computer account, or security group. Restore the OU or Common-Name (CN) containers that host the deleted user accounts or groups. Repeat for any peer OU that hosts deleted accounts. The `ntdsutil` command uses the following syntax for authoritative restore:

   ```
   ntdsutil "authoritative restore" "restore
   object objectDNpath" q q
   ```

9. Remove network cables from the recovery domain controller unless it was a latent GC DC whose inbound replication has already been disabled. Restart the recovery domain controller in normal Active Directory mode.

10. If the recovery DC is *not* a latent GC DC whose inbound replication has already been disabled, issue the following command to do so and then re-enable network connectivity:

```
Repadmin /options recoverydcname
+DISABLE_INBOUND_REPL
```

11. Use the following command to perform outbound replication and replicate the authoritatively restored objects:

```
repadmin /syncall /d /e /P recoverydcname
```

12. If the forest does not meet the conditions necessary for automatic rebuilding of group memberships, wait until the user accounts have replicated to all DCs and all GCs, and then add users or computers back to the groups. Ldifde.exe or Addgroup.exe, which are available from Microsoft Product Services, can be used to automate this task.

Restore from Backup Older than Active Directory Tombstone Lifetime

If other DCs in the domain exist, restore the old backup, and the changes to Active Directory will replicate to the DC. You will have to make other system changes unique to this DC that are not integrated in Active Directory.

If all DCs have been destroyed, restore one server from the old backup and create new DCs. The data from the old, restored DC will replicate to the new DCS.

Manually Deleting Objects Restored from an Outdated Backup

If a backup older than the Active Directory tombstone lifetime must be used to restore Active Directory, objects may exist on the restored replica that do not exist on the other DCs in the domain. Although using such a backup is not recommended, it may still be preferable to recreate the domain from scratch. If the backup is used, these objects must be manually deleted. The deletion process will depend on the object that needs to be deleted. It may be possible to use one of the GUI administration tools to delete the object, or you may need to use the adsitedit.exe support tool or some combination of tools to complete the deletion.

For example, if you must delete a DC object from Active Directory and the DC no longer exists, use the information in KB article 247393 (http://support.microsoft.com/default.aspx?scid=kb;en-us;247393). It may be possible to complete the deletion by removing the object from Active Directory Sites and Services, or you may have to use ntdiutil and Adsiedit as detailed in KB article 216498 (http://support.microsoft.com/kb/216498/EN-US/).

IIS Backup Process

In addition to backing up web content files and associated databases, the IIS metabase (MetaBase.xml) and the metabase schema (MBSchema.dll) should be backed up. An automated backup of the IIS metabase and schema is made when changes are made or IIS is restarted. An administrator can use the IIS console or the iisback.vbs script file to do so. The script file can be modified. The script creates backup copies of IIS configuration—the metabase and schema—which can be used locally or remotely and can also be used to restore IIS configuration. To use the script, follow these steps:

```
Iisback /backup /b IISbackup1 /e urtHv8c /s computer1
```

This command line will back up IIS on computer1 and give it the backup name IISbackup1. The password urtHv8c will be used to protect a generated session key used to encrypt the secure properties. You can read the backup copy and delete the file, but to restore the backup to IIS, the password is required. This can prevent an inadvertent or malicious restore of an older metabase and schema. The complete syntax for `iisback` is in the server help files. To restore the backup made previously, use this command:

```
Iisback /restore /b IISbackup1 /e urtHv8c /s computer1
```

To back up the metabase and schema from the console, follow these steps:

1. Click `Start`, `Administrative Tools`, `Internet Information Services`.
2. Right-click the name of the IIS server to back up, click `All Tasks`, and then click `Backup/Restore Configuration`.
3. Click `Create Backup` and enter a name for the backup.

4. To create a backup that can be securely moved to another server, click `Encrypt Backup Using Password`, and then enter and confirm a password, as shown in Figure 17-24 (only letters and numbers can be used). The secure data in the metabase is encrypted.

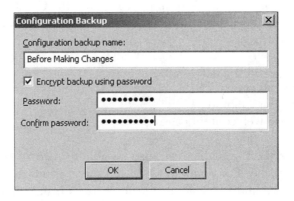

Figure 17-24   Enter a password to protect the backup.

5. Click `OK`. The backup is made to the systemroot\system32\inetsrv\MetaBack folder.
6. Click `Close`.

To restore the IIS metabase and schema, follow these steps:

1. Click `Start`, `Administrative Tools`, `Internet Information Services`.
2. Right-click the name of the IIS server to back up, click `All Tasks`, and then click `Backup/Restore Configuration`.
3. Select the file name of the backup to restore and click the `Restore` button.
4. Enter the password, if necessary, and click `OK`.
5. Click `OK` to close the warning, which alerts you to the time restore may take.
6. Click `OK` after receiving the success OK popup.

TIP: Metabase History on by Default
The Metabase history feature is on by default in IIS 6.0. This feature tracks changes to the metabase and metabase schema files and saves a copy of the file in the history folder. You can roll back the files from the history using the console Backup Restore Configuration option.

Certification Authority Backup

To recover a certification authority (CA), you should have a complete backup of the entire server made with the native ntbackup program. The complete backup should include system state data. (Note that the IIS metabase backup is required to restore the CA, and the system state data backup will back this up.) In addition to this backup, consider separate backups of

- Certificate database
- CA keys
- IIS metabase
- IIS web content pages

If this data is available, you may be able to recover certificate services more quickly. For example, if the IIS server is intact, you might be able to remove and reinstall certificate services using the existing CA keys and then restore the certificate database. You also might be able to do so if a standby server is ready to be put into place but requires the database and/or keys in order to replace the original server.

The CA console can be used to back up the private key and certificate as well as the certificate database. The IIS console can be used to back up the metabase. Backup should be used to back up the web content pages. Alternatively, IIS could be reinstalled and the certutil.exe -vroot command used to reconfigure IIS to support CA web pages.

To back up the database and CA keys, follow these steps:

1. Open the Certification Authority console.
2. Right-click the CA, click All Tasks, and then click Backup CA.
3. Click Next at the wizard welcome screen.
4. Select whether to back up the database, the keys, or both, as shown in Figure 17-25.
5. Enter or browse to the location for the backup, and then click Next.
6. If backing up the keys, enter a password, confirm the password, and then click Next. The password will be required to restore the keys.
7. When the backup is done, click Finish.

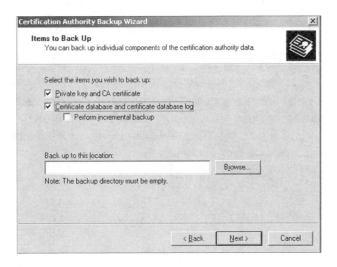

Figure 17-25 Keys, database, or both can be backed up.

The certutil.exe command can also be used to back up the database:

```
Certutil -backup -config cacomputername\caname
```

In this command, *cacomputername* is the name of the computer on which the CA is installed, and *caname* is the name of the CA itself. A password can be used to protect the backup. For complete syntax, see the CA help file.

When restoring the CA, do not delete the database logs if they are present. During the restore process, the logs will be replayed, and the certificate database can be brought up to date. (Database logs are, by default, stored at <%systemroot%>\system32\certlog.)

To restore database or keys using the CA console, follow these steps:

1. Open the Certification Authority console.
2. Right-click the CA, click All Tasks, and then click Restore CA.
3. Click Next at the wizard welcome screen.
4. Click OK to stop certificate services.
5. Select whether to restore the database, the keys, or both.
6. Enter or browse to the location for the backup, and then click Next.
7. If restoring the keys, enter a password used during the key backup, and then click Next.
8. When the restore is completed, click Finish.

Summary

Sooner or later, you will have to restore files, recover servers, and respond to disasters where multiple servers, services, and critical files have been corrupted or lost. The only way to ensure successful recovery is to have a disaster recovery plan. The first requirement of any disaster recovery plan is to have a good backup plan, which includes backups of data, service database, and system state data.

PART VII

Monitoring and Audit

CHAPTER 18

Auditing

Ask someone in IT what auditing is, and you may be told that it's running a vulnerability scanner from outside your network to assess its security weaknesses, configuring the audit policy on the Windows Server 2003 computer so that it records security events, or even performing a penetration test (pen test) from outside your network. IT auditors, on the other hand, may view auditing as checking the security configuration of systems and the exercise of IT operations against your organization's security policy and against legislative requirements to determine if IT systems are in compliance.

Both viewpoints are correct but don't go far enough. Auditing is a process that improves security not just because it finds known vulnerabilities or exposes variances from security policy or legislative requirements, but also because it points out weaknesses in the current security architecture. You should incorporate this approach into Windows Server 2003 security configuration and maintenance. You should also support auditing by non-IT employees or outside auditors. Many auditing functions should be done by IT, but regular audits by individuals who are not from IT are imperative if you want to maintain and improve the security of your information systems.

Auditing Versus Intrusion Detection

Auditing is not synonymous with intrusion detection. Even so, when the audit policy is configured, the security-related events collected can be used for intrusion detection. The information collected also can and should be used to

- Monitor usual and unusual activity
- Detect intrusion attempts and successes
- Provide forensic evidence that may be used to support prosecution or to determine what occurred

The monitoring and intrusion detection process is described further in Chapter 19, "Monitoring and Assessment." This chapter provides information on audit policy, interpreting audit records, and using tools to determine vulnerability status and security policy compliance.

It's management's job to dictate and ensure the proper implementation of controls that provide the confidentiality, integrity, and availability of information used during the conduction of business operations. Only management can set the security policy and enforce it. In addition to security policy, management provides for both internal and external audits that document where IT practices deviate from stated policy and/or established IT security best practices. The IT administrator should base security implementation on management-dictated security policy. It's time that IT administrators took more responsibility for helping management define a security policy and for auditing its adherence to stated policy and best practices.

This book provides information on the security technologies and best practices available for Windows Server 2003. Auditing implementation and practice for Windows Server 2003 networks consists of

- Implementing the Audit Policy functionality available in Group Policy for both domain controllers and member computers.
- If standalone Windows systems are part of the network, setting auditing controls as available locally, such as setting an audit policy in Local Security Policy.
- Setting auditing controls in implemented server services, such as certificate services and remote access server services.
- Setting auditing controls in Windows Server 2003–based applications implemented on the network.
- Verifying that technical security controls are in place, for example by using Security Configuration and Analysis, Microsoft Security Baseline Analysis, and/or third-party vulnerability assessment tools and perhaps penetration testing.
- Reviewing and verifying that physical security controls are in place.
- Reviewing and verifying that security policy, standards, and procedures are in place and meet best practices as defined in accepted standards and by well-known auditing associations.
- Reviewing the "people" part of security, including the security awareness and practice of good security by employees.

- Understanding and using log contents to differentiate the normal from the abnormal, document incidents, determine what happened, and potentially detect intrusions happening in real time or ones that may have happened in the past.
- Reviewing customer, partner, and vendor IT relationships with respect to technical and other controls where communications and connections exist, and if it is determined that the security practices of the other party may influence the security of your organization, reviewing their security policies, standards, procedures, and practices.

This chapter does not address all these points. It does not address issues specific to server applications such as SQL server, Exchange, or other Microsoft or third-party applications that may exist on your network. It does not address third-party vulnerability testing products, nor include pen testing specifics or intrusion detection techniques beyond those useful in evaluating the logs produced by Windows Server 2003. All these things are important, but they simply fall outside the scope of this book.

Information on IT auditing that is not Windows Server 2003–specific can be found on the web site of the Information Systems Audit and Control Association (ISACA) at `www.isaca.org`. ISACA is composed of over 35,000 members from over 100 countries, and its members are IT auditors, consultants, educators, IS security professionals, CIOs, and CSOs. The Certified Information System Auditor (CISA) certification is sponsored by ISACA. Start by reading the proposed IT auditing standards document, `http://www.isaca.org/Template.cfm?Section=Standards&Template=/TaggedPage/TaggedPageDisplay.cfm&TPLID=29&ContentID=6707`. An audit glossary is also on the site (`http://www.isaca.org/Template.cfm?Section=Glossary&Template=/CustomSource/Glossary.cfm&char=A&TermSelected=635`).

Establishing a Windows Server 2003 Audit Policy for the Forest

An audit policy is more than the configuration of a Group Policy Audit Policy and associated logs. Because Group Policy automates the implementation of security event collection, designing and implementing such a policy is a good first step in building a more comprehensive audit policy for your enterprise. Audit Policy is a part of the Security Settings section of Group Policy and, therefore, can be quickly configured and implemented across an entire domain. Learning the basics of configuration and interpretation of the events collected can help you determine what else is needed while you are benefiting from what you have quickly and easily implemented.

WARNING: Don't Configure Audit Policy Blindly

Use caution when implementing Audit Policy. You can easily collect more data than can easily be reviewed, and if you have not properly configured the Security Event Log and your policies for managing events, this data collection can overwhelm or even halt a system's operation. Audit Policy, like many Windows Server 2003 security features, can be quickly implemented, providing you with excellent benefits or with complete disaster. Spend some time learning about what you are doing and planning how the system will operate and how the data will be used.

Audit Policy is configured by default for Windows Server 2003 domain controllers. (Auditing is not turned on by default in previous releases of Windows.) An audit policy capable of producing comprehensive security log data has been available since the beginning of Windows NT. Although it may be argued that the collection of an audit trail is by itself not a sound security practice (you have to use the data in order for it to be effective), the default collection of this data is valuable in the following ways:

- After an intrusion or other security incident, the existence of audit records may be useful to determine what happened.
- Audit records may provide prosecutorial evidence of fraud, theft, or other illegal activities.
- Audit records may provide internally acceptable proof of non-compliance to organization policy.
- Because IT personnel are trained in the use of computer logs for monitoring and troubleshooting performance and other production issues, the availability of security-related information can assist them in these efforts (for example, in troubleshooting logon issues).
- Curiosity on the part of IT personnel who may examine log information can inadvertently bring to light security issues or evidence of intrusion, and better security practices can be developed as risks to operation are exposed.

Audit Policy Basics

In a Windows Server 2003 domain, Audit Policy settings are configured in the `Computer Configuration, Windows Settings, Security Settings, Local Policies, Audit Policy` section of a GPO. When this policy is configured, it applies to the computers whose accounts are within the container to which the GPO is linked. Security events are logged to the Security Event Log of the computer within which the event occurred. The Audit Policy in the Default Domain Controller GPO, as shown in Figure 18-1, is configured by default. However, there are no settings for the Default Domain GPO. Therefore, while some audit information is logged to the security event log on each DC, events are not logged for other computers joined to the domain.

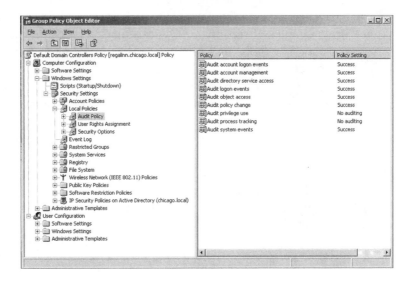

Figure 18-1 The default Audit Policy for the domain controller's OU.

To configure Audit Policy for the domain, do the following:

- Determine which computers need to have auditing turned on.
- Determine which Audit Policy settings are relevant for different computers.
- Configure an audit policy for adoption by domain members.

- Configure an event log policy. Event logs are unusual files; they cannot infinitely grow until all disk space is consumed. Instead, a maximum event log size is configured along with instructions on what to do when the event log reaches maximum size.
- Configure other audit and event log-related Security Options in Group Policy.

Determining Which Computers to Audit and Which Events to Collect

It is easy to suggest that you should turn on auditing for all computers, but in most environments, this is impractical. Certainly, all domain controllers, all servers, and those workstations in sensitive areas or where sensitive data is stored or from which it is accessed should have auditing tuned on. Examples of sensitive servers are mail servers, firewalls, web servers, database servers, and other servers that are part of critical or sensitive operations. For example, if an n-tier application (an applications whose components are spread across multiple computers) such as an e-commerce, customer relationship management, or distribution application is in operation, all computers involved in the application should be audited. Before blindly enabling auditing on these computers for full event collection, you should, of course, consider the impact on performance and on default user rights and permissions set by these applications. For example, auditing account logon events on Exchange servers may produce so many events that it has a very bad impact on performance.

Determine and Configure Audit Policy

The default Domain Controllers policy does have auditing configured, but is it right for your organization? What other policies need to be configured? The default Domain Controllers policy should be adjusted to meet your auditing needs for DCs. In addition, when you have decided which events should be collected at various servers and workstations, configure those policies within a GPO linked to the OU within which the computer account resides. Although it's possible to configure the Audit Policy for all computers in the domain by configuring the Audit Policy in a GPO linked to the domain object, this may not be practical either because security log entries will be so numerous as to never be reviewed, or because Audit Policy settings need to be configured differently for computers that play different roles on the network. If standalone computers are part of your organization, you must configure a local audit policy within the Local Security Policy console or by using the Group Policy snap-in.

On a standalone Windows Server 2003 computer, Audit Policy settings can be set to

- Success
- Failure
- Success and failure
- No auditing

In a GPO, Audit Policy settings can be one of the following:

- Not configured
- No auditing
- Success
- Failure
- Success and failure

Normal GPO hierarchical rules apply. A setting of Not configured means no selection. An Audit Policy set higher in the OU hierarchy or at the site or domain level will be unaffected by a GPO that specifies Not configured. No auditing, on the other hand, explicitly turns off auditing, and if the GPO within which it is located is closer to the computer account, it will override earlier settings. To change settings, double-click the policy to open its Property page and select or deselect the desired option. Audit policies are listed and described in Table 18-1.

Table 18-1 Audit Policies

Audit Policy	Purpose
Audit account logon events	To record logon events at the DC. Kerberos events are also recorded.
Audit account management	To record changes to user, group, and computer accounts. Records account creation and deletion, password changes, and group membership changes.
Audit directory service access	To enable logging of Active Directory object access. Some objects are already configured. Configure settings on specific objects in the Active Directory. To record those events in the Security log, you must turn object auditing on at this policy.
Audit logon events	To record logon events at the console where logon occurs. When IPSec negotiate policies are used, IKE events are also recorded, as are SID filtering events.
Audit object access	To enable logging of access to files, folders, registry keys, and printers if specific objects are configured for auditing.
Audit policy change	To record changes to the audit policy and Kerberos policy as well as to user rights, trust relationships, and the IPSec agent.
Audit privilege use	To record privileges added to the user's access token, and the use of these privileges. Multiple events may be recorded for each privilege use.
Audit process tracking	To record processing activity including process creation and exit, access to objects, backup and recovery of the data protection master key, installation of services, and creation of scheduled jobs. In most environments, this policy should not be set because it can generate massive amounts of events. In a development environment, this can be a useful policy because it can help the developer see what his code is actually doing.
Audit system events	To record startup and shutdown events, loading of authentication packages, clearing the audit log, and changes to the system time.

Table 18-2 provides recommendations for Audit Policy settings for domain controllers. Note that it varies from the default in most instances by adding the `Failure` setting. You should consider if this is right for you. The rationale for setting `Failure` is to generate those events that may aid in detecting attacks. For example, if failed logon events are captured, they may be simple user forgetfulness or fumble fingers; still, a larger number of failed logon events may mean an attack. Some recommend recording only failure events; after all, who wants to review successful logons? However, if successful logons are not recorded, and a large number of failure events are recorded but then stop, how will you determine if an attacker gave up or was successful in compromising the account? Another reason for recording successful logon is to be able to determine the timeframe within which a specific user was logged on. If you are trying to determine who might have performed some action on a system, knowing that an individual was or was not logged on is very useful.

Audit Policy, like many security settings, should be considered for each computer role on the network. Although it may be impractical to collect and examine all the possible audit records on all computers, an appropriate policy for each computer role should be developed. Settings for other member computers may need to be adjusted according to the sensitive nature of the data or computer role on the network. For example, developer computers may want to set `Audit process tracking`.

Table 18-2 Audit Policy Recommendations

Audit Policy	Default	Recommendation
Audit account logon events	Success	Success, Failure
Audit account management	Success	Success, Failure
Audit directory service access	Success	Success, Failure
Audit logon events	Success	Success, Failure
Audit object access	Success	Success, Failure
Audit policy change	Success	Success, Failure
Audit privilege use	No Auditing	No Auditing or Not Configured
Audit process tracking	No Auditing	No Auditing or Not Configured
Audit system events	Success	Success, Failure

Interpreting Audit Policy Events

After Audit Policy is configured, a lot of information will be collected. To be of value, it must be used. If security logs are reviewed in real time, they can provide evidence of an ongoing attack or can reveal a weakness that requires immediate correction. Archival records of activity on the server can provide evidence and establish accountability after the fact. Some activity may only be noticed when reviewing activity in the logs over time. By looking at the events over a period of hours or days, a pattern may emerge, or you may find a more sinister reason for some seemingly innocent behavior. The first step in learning how to use log data is to be able to understand the events that are being recorded there. Table 18-3 provides a list of security events that may be found in the security event log and how they might be interpreted.

Table 18-3   Suspicious Account Events

Event ID	Description	Possible Interpretation
675	Pre-authentication failed.	User entered an incorrect domain account password.
644	A user account was automatically locked.	A user incorrectly entered his password too many times, or an attack against user accounts is/was underway. What is the number of failed attempts necessary to generate the lock? (What is the account lockout policy?) If the account lockout policy requires a large number of failures before the lockout, it's more likely that this event indicates an attack. Check the number of these events. A large number of these events may indicate an automated password cracking attack.
529	Logon failure. Unknown user name or bad password.	Depending on the number and frequency of these events, they may indicate a password cracking attack. Are there a large number of these events for specific accounts and for a large number of accounts? If so an attack is the likely explanation.

Event ID	Description	Possible Interpretation
530	Logon Failure. Outside allotted time.	This might simply be the result of a workstation whose clock is not synchronized with the forest. It also could be an attack on Kerberos credentials.
531	Logon Failure. Disabled account.	Check the age of the account. If the account is disabled because it was just created, it might just mean that a new employee is attempting a logon. If the account is disabled because an employee left the company, this event could represent a possible attack.
532	Logon Failure. Expired account.	Check the status of the assigned owner of the account. If this is an account assigned to a temporary worker, is that worker still working? Expiration dates are usually set for temporary workers to ensure that the account is disabled after they have finished their assignment. The expiration date may be an estimate or the worker may have been assigned to a new project. It is typical that IT is not notified of these types of changes, and this could just represent that type of failure. It could also represent an attack.
533	Logon Failure. Account cannot logon at this computer.	Accounts can be restricted to logon at specific computers. If the policy is correctly communicated (letting users know which computers they can use to log on), this event represents an attack or a violation of security policy.
534	Logon Failure. Password type not allowed.	Password type in this instance refers to user rights such as `Access this computer from the network`, `Logon locally`, and so forth used to restrict logon at sensitive computers. If the policy has been communicated correctly (letting users know which computers they can use to logon and which computers they can access), this is an attack, a misconfigured application, or a violation of security policy.

Table 18-3 Suspicious Account Events Continued

Event ID	Description	Possible Interpretation
535	Logon Failure. Expired password.	May indicate simple user error or an attack on an account that is rarely used.
539	Logon Failure. Account lockout.	A large number of these events indicates the continuation of a cracking attack.
643	A domain policy was modified.	Be advised of changes to policy.
564	Object deleted.	Compare this event to authorized maintenance that may have required the deletion of a sensitive file.

Configure Auditing for File, Folder, Registry, and Printer Objects

To configure auditing for files, folders, registry, and printer objects, you must configure the Audit object access policy and configure auditing directory on the object. Setting auditing on the object adds an access control entry (ACE) to the object's system access control list (SACL). To configure auditing on files or folders, follow these steps:

1. Right-click the object and select Properties.
2. Select the Security tab and click the Advanced button.
3. Select the Auditing tab.
4. Click the Add button.
5. Use the object picker to select the group whose access you want to audit.
6. Select the permissions to audit, as shown in Figure 18-2, and then click OK.

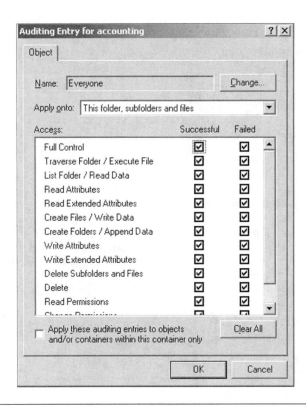

Figure 18-2   Select specific permissions to audit.

To configure auditing of registry keys, follow these steps:

1. Right-click the key and select `Permissions`.
2. Click the `Advanced` button.
3. Select the `Auditing` tab.
4. Click the `Add` button.
5. Use the object picker to select the group whose access you want to audit.
6. Select the permissions to audit, as shown in Figure 18-3, and then click `OK`.

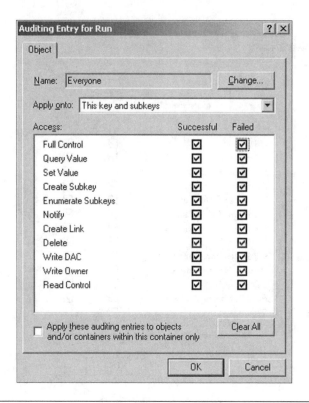

Figure 18-3   Select registry key permissions to audit.

To configure auditing for printers, follow these steps:

1. Right-click the printer in the `Printers and Faxes` window and select `Properties`.
2. Click the `Security` tab.
3. Click the `Advanced` button.
4. Select the `Auditing` tab.
5. Click the `Add` button.
6. Use the object picker to select the group whose access you want to audit.
7. Select the permissions to audit, as shown in Figure 18-4, and then click `OK`.

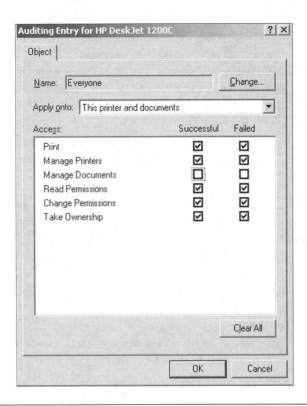

Figure 18-4   Select printer permissions to audit.

If ACEs are set, events are logged to the event log. Like ACEs for DACLs, ACEs for SACLs are composed of a user group or user name and a permission. SACL ACEs are set for success and/or failure, not Allow or Deny. When SACL ACEs are set, any access that meets their conditions will result in a record in the Security Event Log. Which of these objects should you audit? Auditing access to all objects would be of little value. Who cares, for example, if a user is reading documents that they created? A good way to determine what access should be audited is to use the classic approach to data protection: Classify data by its sensitivity and act accordingly. If data is already classified in your organization, you may be able to use this information; if not, using this method requires that you learn from the data owners which data they consider sensitive and to what degree. You can make some educated guess to help you in your discussions with them. For example, you may want to audit access to printers used to print checks, or other printers that have restricted access.

Don't forget to apply the same thought process to data that IT owns, such as system files. It's useful, for example, to audit access to the %WINDIR%\system32\config folder on the domain controller. This folder holds the event log files and registry files. Access to the SAM file stored here might mean the DC has been started in restore mode since the SAM is offline on a DC. Access to other files might also bear investigation. By default, only the Administrators group and the system have access to these files, so auditing for permission changes would be wise.

Configure Auditing of AD Objects

Configuring auditing of AD objects is similar to configuring auditing for files and folders permissions. Like other object access, a policy in audit policy as well as specific object settings must be in effect. Some AD objects already have SACL ACEs set. When you configure the Audit Directory Service Access audit policy and these objects are access, audit records will be recorded in the Security Event Log. Just as a limited number of permissions on objects other than directory objects makes setting access controls on these objects easier, the large number of permissions on directory objects makes them difficult to audit. To get started, examine the settings that are preconfigured, and do not make changes or add auditing to additional objects until you have done so.

Until you understand the current settings, you cannot decide if they should be reduced or increased. You must determine the information that they will produce in the security event log and understand why that information would be valuable. To do so, consider the following:

- Which objects are preconfigured for audit? What information is sought?
- Which groups are audited?
- What permissions are audited?

To get started, look at important objects. Start with the obvious. For example, examine the auditing settings for the domain object. You can do so by examining the Auditing Properties page, as displayed in Figure 18-5, of the object. To examine the settings, right-click the domain object in Active Directory Users and Computers and select Properties, then select the Security tab, and use the Advanced button to get to the Auditing page.

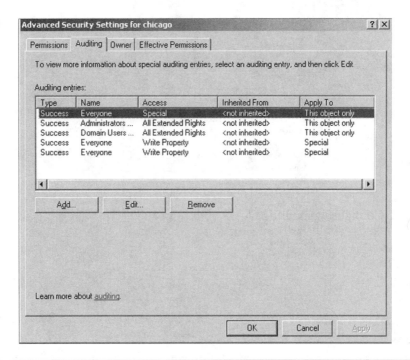

Figure 18-5   Audit settings on the domain object are preset to record access.

Note that access by Everyone, Administrators, and Domain Users is recorded. Note, too, that these auditing settings are not inherited. Auditing settings can be inherited, just like permissions. Also note that the permission sets for each group are not set to record every type of access but are restricted. Finally, note that some settings are only applied to the domain object, while others are more narrowly defined.

Select a group and click the Edit button to examine the specific audit settings. The Special settings for the group Everyone are displayed in Figure 18-6. (Two other Everyone entries in the table must also be looked at to catalog the audit settings for the group Everyone.) Table 18-4 lists the settings for each group.

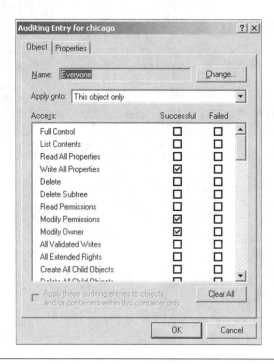

Figure 18-6   Review the specifics of auditing settings for each group.

Table 18-4   Audit Settings on the Domain Object

Group	Access	Apply Onto	Access Task	Type
Everyone	Special	This object only	Write all proper ties, Modify Permissions, Modify Owner	Success
Everyone	Write Property	Special	Write gPLink	Success
Everyone	Write Property	Special	Write gPOptions	Success
Administrators	All Extended Rights	This object only	All Extended Rights (therefore, all extended rights for this object are also checked)	Success
Domain Users	All Extended Rights	This object only	All Extended Rights (therefore, all extended rights for this object are also checked)	Success

GPLink is a property that holds the list of linked GPOs and includes information on the GPO's Enforced (No Override) and Disabled options. The other write property audit, gPOptions, contains the Block Policy Inheritance options. Auditing additions and changes to GPLink (Write Property) and gPOptions provides information of changes to Group Policy. It's easy to see how valuable this knowledge can be. You can check any recorded changes and determine if they are the result of authorized changes by authorized individual or possible attacks. By default, only a successful change is recorded. In sensitive environments, consider also auditing for failed attempts.

Extended Rights and the rights themselves can be viewed from the Object page of the Auditing entry. In addition to those rights exposed in the GUI, additional rights on the domain object exist, such as Change Password (the user can change their password) and User Force Change Password (some can reset the password). The use of these extended rights is also audited. For the domain object, only some objects are displayed by default. Figure 18-7 displays most of these, and Table 18-5 describes them. For a more comprehensive listing, see a listing of Active Directory Schema Extended Rights in the Platform SDK (http://msdn.microsoft.com/library/default.asp?url=/library/en-us/adschema/adschema/r_ds_replication_get_changes.asp).

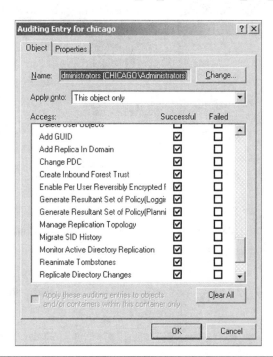

Figure 18-7 Extended Rights are defined per object and listed on the Object page.

Table 18-5 Extended Rights Audit Settings on the Domain Object

Extended Rights for the Domain Object	Description
Add GUID	Add an object with a specific GUID, such as a domain controller, GPO.
Add Replica in Domain	Add a new DC to the domain.
Change PDC	Transfer or seize the PDC emulator operations master.
Create Inbound Forest Trust	Create a trust that provides access to domain objects from another forest.
Enable Per User Reversibly Encrypted Password	Enable or disable the reversible encrypted password setting. (Enabling this option drops protection on passwords.)
Generate Resultant Set of Policy (Logging)	RSoP logging performed.
Generate Resultant Set of Policy (Planning)	RSoP planning performed.
Manage Replication Topology	Make changes to replication, replication links.
Migrate SID History	This permission can be used to migrate SID History—Permissions from another domain are retained by migrated users to this domain. Can be granted to non-administrative users.
Monitor Active Directory Replication	Allows replication data, such as replication status and metadata. Replication activity is being monitored.
Reanimate Tombstones	A deleted object is recovered.
Replicate Directory Changes	Replication has occurred.
Replicating Directory Changes All	Replication of all domain data.
Replication Synchronization	Ability to synchronize replication.
Unexpire Password	Restore a password for a user object.
Update Password Not Required Bit	Enable or disable the "password not required" setting for user objects.

To successfully use the information generated by Active Directory object auditing, become familiar with the events generated during normal usage. AD object auditing events always are identified as Event ID 566 but provide information on the object, the type of access, and the user name. For example, linking a GPO to the domain container produces several events that document access to gPLink, writing a display name to the Group Policy container, gPCFileSysPath (true or false information about indexing, GC location, and other parameters), version number, and gPCFunctionalityVersion (the version of the Group Policy Editor that produced the write). Figure 18-8 displays one of these events.

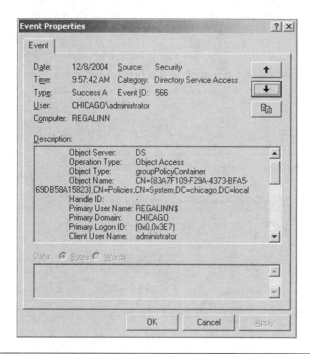

Figure 18-8   AD object access events indicate the access and user as well as DC.

Configure Event Log Policy

There are three Windows Server 2003 default logs: System, Application, and Security. Other logs are created depending on the computer role. For example, Windows Server 2003 DNS servers have a DNS event log, while domain controllers have a Directory Service event log and a File

Replication Service event log. All logs can be viewed from the Event Viewer, as shown in Figure 18-9. The properties of the event logs can be displayed by right-clicking the log and selecting Properties, as shown in Figure 18-10. Event log properties may be set in Group Policy for the three default logs, as shown in Figure 18-11. Therefore, consistency across servers for these logs is possible. Properties for all other logs must be set directly on the log. Setting properties for these logs requires manual work or a custom script.

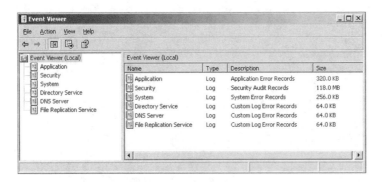

Figure 18-9 Events are viewed in the Event Viewer.

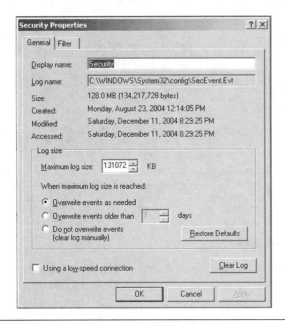

Figure 18-10 Event log properties can be configured directly on the event log.

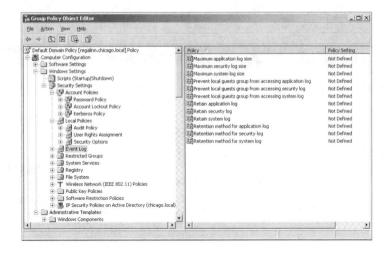

Figure 18-11   Event log properties for the three default logs can be set in Group Policy.

Set log properties according to the amount of auditing configured, the level of activity, and the frequency of archive. Table 18-6 lists and describes event log settings and provides some recommendations.

Table 18-6   Event Log Properties

Setting	Description	Recommendation
Maximum log size	Event logs, unlike normal files, do not grow infinitely bounded only by disk space. Instead, they can only grow as large as the size specified here.	Event logs in Windows Server 2003 are set by default to a reasonable size for a newly initialized server. Adjust this size to accommodate the activity depending on server role and to meet the needs of your audit policy. Your audit policy includes an archival period and a policy for what to do if the security event log becomes full. Plan on monitoring log size. A larger log can mean less frequent archival, while smaller logs may have to be archived more frequently.

Table 18-6 Event Log Properties Continued

Setting	Description	Recommendation
Retention Method (In individual log properties titled as "When Maximum log size is reached")	Choices are Overwrite events as needed Overwrite events older than x days (also known as "Retain" x days) Do not overwrite events (clear log manually)	Set to "overwrite events as needed." In this case, if the event log is large enough and is archived frequently, no events will be lost. In times of heavy event logging or slow administrator response, only the older events will be lost.
Prevent local Guests group from accessing application log	The Guests group cannot access the log. By default, only administrators and the system can access the Windows Server 2003 event logs	Enable
Prevent local Guests group from accessing security log	The Guests group cannot access the log. By default, only administrators and the system can access the Windows Server 2003 event logs.	Enable
Prevent local Guests group from accessing system log	The Guests group cannot access the log. By default, only administrators and the system can access the Windows Server 2003 event logs.	Enable

Configure User Rights

Two user rights are directly related to the auditing function:

- Generate security audits—Accounts with this right can be used to add events to the security log. By default, the Local Service and Network Service accounts are included in the Default Domain Controllers Policy. This user right might be added to a service account to enable its application to add events to the security log. Best practices state that the application should be written, where possible, to use the Local Service or Network Service account for this purpose.

■ `Manage auditing and security log`—By default, only the Administrators group has the right to modify the audit policy and manage the security event log. Create a custom Windows group for auditors and provide that group this right. This allows auditors to review the security log without having full administrator rights. Consider the implications of giving them the right to manage the log. This allows auditors, who are often defined as "observers," the ability to change the systems they are auditing.

TIP: Third-Party Exchange Applications Failure Mystery Resolved

Changes and upgrades made to Microsoft applications can have adverse affects on applications that use broad permissions on Active Directory objects. When Microsoft changes default permission settings, this can have an impact on these applications. For example, some third-party applications work by granting the service account used by their application membership in the Exchange Domain Servers group. The forestprep utility, which must be run prior to installing or upgrading to Exchange Server 2003, places a Deny access control entry (ACE) on the Active Directory Servers container. This change is made to help improve messaging system security, but it may cause the third-party application to fail. To fix the problem, determine the access the service accounts really need, create a group, give that group access on the appropriate Active Directory objects, and then add the third-party application service accounts membership in that group.

Another utility, domain prep, must be run prior to installing or upgrading to Exchange Server 2003. This utility gives the Exchange Enterprise Servers group the `Manage auditing and security log` user right in the Default Domain Controller policy in order to allow this group to read the SACLs on mailboxes. This permission is necessary to enable mailbox auditing. If you have implemented user rights in other GPOs that might affect the use of this right, you need to add this user right in those policies or ensure that their implementation doesn't modify this user right for the Exchange Enterprise Servers group. Failure to do so can prevent the Exchange messaging stores from mounting and therefore stop Exchange from working. For more information on permissions and Exchange Server 2003, see Chapter 3 of "Introduction to the Working with Active Directory Permissions in Exchange Server 2003 Guide" at `http://www.microsoft.com/technet/prodtechnol/Exchange/guides` `/E2k3ADPerm/52821d76-9941-4eb2-8384-ca4fe790e38e.mspx`.

Configure Security Options

In addition to a formal audit policy, several Security Options can be set that affect auditing. The security options are as follows:

- `Audit: Audit the access of global system objects`—Global system objects are objects such as mutexes (used for thread synchronization), events, semaphores (locking objects), and DOS devices. If this policy is enabled, these objects are created with a default SACL, and access to them is audited. By default, this option is not enabled.
- `Audit: Audit the use of Backup and Restore privilege`—Setting this option generates a large number of events during any backup and restore. The backup of each file is recorded. Modern backup programs create logs that can provide this information in a more manageable format.
- `Audit: Shut down system immediately if unable to log security`—If the Retention method in the security event log is `Do not overwrite events (Clear log manually)` and this Security Option is set, processing on the computer will be stopped if the security log is full. An administrator will have to archive and clear the log, then reset this option before users are able to log on. A stop error `C0000244{Audit failed}` is generated. Do not set this Security Option unless ensuring a complete log (no events lost) is more important than production and unless an administrator is available at all times to recover from a full log.

Auditing the Standalone Windows Server 2003 Computer

Audit policy for a standalone Windows Server 2003 computer can be set in its local security policy, as shown in Figure 18-12. Don't forget to consider user rights and Security Options as described later in the sections "Configure User Rights" and "Configure Security Options." Exactly which audit settings should be applied will depend on the role the server plays on the network and your organization's audit policy. Event log policies are set from the Event Viewer.

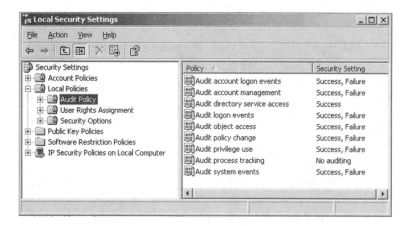

Figure 18-12   The Local Security Policy Audit Policy.

Auditing Server Applications and Services

Server applications and services may post events to the Application and System log or to special log files specific to them. Although much of this information may be more helpful for troubleshooting network, OS, or application operation, rather than auditing, some security-specific data may be present, especially if the application or service is configured to do so. A good rule of thumb is to expect that some configuration may need to be done in order to produce audit information and take a good look at documentation and administration tools. Fortunately, Microsoft and others are cognizant of audit requirements and are building opportunities for event collection as well as providing more documentation on them. Information is provided here for more common services.

Network Services Auditing

Network services such as DNS, WINS, and DHCP typically generate a range of events that are logged to the DNS, application, and system logs.

DNS

Several types of logging can be configured, including debug logging, event logging, and object events. Debug logging for DNS is set from the DNS server `Debug Logging` tab of the Property pages of the DNS server, as shown in Figure 18-13. Click to select `Log packets for debugging` and then select a packet direction, a transport protocol, and other options. Set up file location and maximum size. Note that debug logging is not turned on by default and may produce enough events to seriously impair performance.

Event logging is configured on the `Event Logging` tab of the server Property pages and provides information on errors, errors and warnings, or all events, as shown in Figure 18-14. It can also be turned off. Event logging records events in the DNS event log. You can also set auditing on the Property pages of specific DNS objects, such as zones and individual records, to record events related to zones and DNS registration.

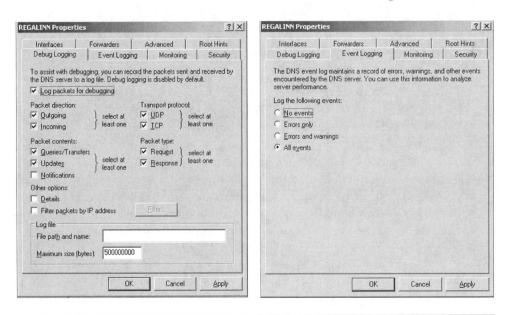

Figure 18-13   Set Debug Logging for DNS in the server Property pages.

Figure 18-14   Set Event Logging for DNS in the server Property pages.

DHCP

DHCP audit logging is enabled on the General Property page, as shown in Figure 18-15. Logs are saved at %windir%\System32\dhcp and this can be edited on the Advanced Property page, as shown in Figure 18-16. The DHCP service checks the file system to make sure that there is adequate space for the audit log file after every 50 events it writes to the log file and when the date changes on the server. Log entries include general service information such as start, stop, and authorization, as well as information on the MAC address of the client and the IP address of the client when noting lease assignments and releases. This information provides a history of lease assignments and can aid in tracing which machine had which IP address at a specific time.

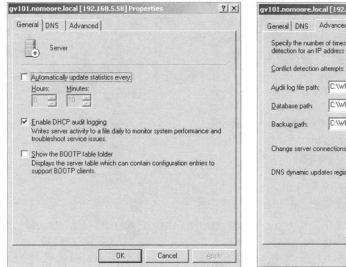 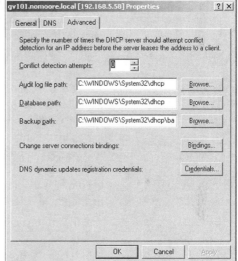

Figure 18-15   Configure audit logging from the General Property page.

Figure 18-16   Configure log location from the Advanced Property page.

Several registry entries located at HKLM\SYSTEM\CurrentControlSet\ Services\DHCPServer\Parameters control audit logging. Pay attention to their defaults or configure them to suit you. If not set correctly, or if disk space is not adequate, audit logging will stop. If you are trying to keep an audit trail of IP address assignment, monitor for warning event log messages and monitor disk space availability. Registry parameters are shown in Table 18-7.

Table 18-7   Registry Parameters

Parameter	Description	Type	Default
ActivityLogFlag	When set to 0, audit logging is not used. When set to 1, it is.	REG_DWORD	0
DhcpLogDiskSpace CheckInterval	Indicates how many events are recorded in the log before a disk space check is made.	REG_DWORD	0x32 (50)
DhcpLogFilePath	The loation for the audit logs. If this entry is changed, DHCP will move the logs.	REG_SZ	%Windir %\system 32\dhcp
DhcpLogFiles MaxSize	The maximum combined file size (DHCP generates a new log file for each day of the week) for one week's worth of audit logs. The default is 7 MB. If the size is exceeded, DHCP stops writing log file entries until space becomes available. (The logs are deleted or archived.)	REG_DWORD	0x7 (7 MB)
DhcpLogMinSpace OnDisk	The minimum remaining space on the disk required in order for DHCP logging to continue. If this space is not available, logging stops.	REG_DWORD	0x14 (20 MB)

WINS

WINS records error and informational messages to the system log. The level of information recorded is managed by settings on the Advanced Property page of WINS. To change them, select the log detailed events box on the page. When set, in addition to errors, WINS will also log warning and informational messages.

IPSec Auditing

Success or failure of IKE negotiations will be recorded in the Security Event Log if Audit Logon Events is set for Success and Failure. More detailed IKE logging can be configured, and events will be recorded in the %systemroot%\Debug\oakley.log file. A registry entry can be used, or logging can be controlled dynamically by using netsh.

To dynamically turn on IKE logging, use this command:

```
netsh ipsec dynamic set config ikelogging 1
```

To stop logging, use this command:

```
netsh ipsec dynamic set config ikelogging 0
```

The IKE logging registry key is located at HKEY_LOCAL_MACHINE\ System\CurrentControlSet\Services\PolicyAgent\Oakley\.

To enable logging, add the REG_DWORD value EnableLogging, set it to 1, and then use the command net stop policyagent followed by net start policyagent. Using the registry key is the only way to enable IKE logging for Windows XP and Windows 2000. To stop logging, remove the value or set it to 0, and then stop and start the policy agent service.

Certification Authority Auditing

Auditing for the certification authority is set on the Auditing Property page of the CA, as shown in Figure 18-17. Object auditing must be turned on in the Audit Policy for the server in order for events to be collected. Check all boxes to prepare an audit trail of changes to settings, backup, certificate issuance and revoking, and key archival.

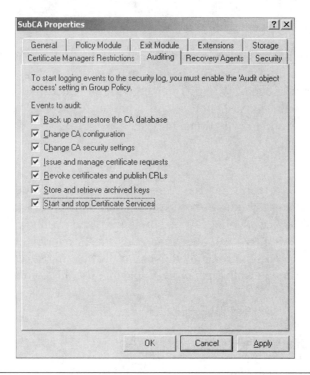

Figure 18-17   Configure CA auditing on the Auditing Property page.

If role-based administration is enforced, only someone with the auditor role can change these settings. The auditor role is created by creating a Windows custom group and assigning it the user right `Manage auditing and security log`. User accounts added to this group will assume the CA auditor role. For more information on CA role-based administration and role separation, refer to Chapter 12, "PKI Basics."

VPN Auditing

Routing and Remote Access Service (RRAS) logging consists of event logging and authentication and accounting logging. Event logging is configured on the `Logging` page of the server properties in the `Routing and Remote Access` console, as shown in Figure 18-18. Event logging is primarily meant to assist troubleshooting connections but can be useful for recording remote access activity for auditing purpose. Authentication and accounting information is recorded locally if Windows authentication and/or Windows accounting is enabled. Events are logged to the %windir%\system32\logfiles folder and can be used to track remote access usage and connection attempts.

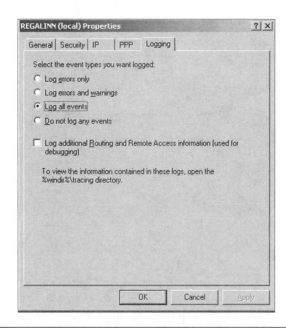

Figure 18-18   Configure event logging for RRAS.

Authentication and accounting logging is configured by expanding the `Remote Access Logging` node of the server, as shown in Figure 18-19. Double-click the logging method (Local File or SQL Server) in the detail pane to select options. Figure 18-20 displays the `Settings` page for Local File properties, while the `Log File` page is displayed in Figure 18-21. If Windows authentication is not configured, the Remote Access Logging folder is not displayed.

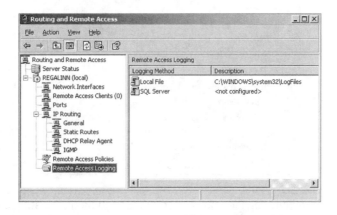

Figure 18-19   Configure authentication and accounting logging.

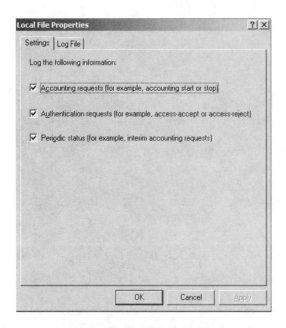

Figure 18-20 Specify log configuration for authentication and accounting logging.

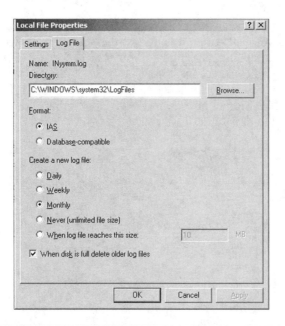

Figure 18-21 Configure log file information and schedule for creating a new log file.

When Internet Authentication Service (IAS) is used to coordinate remote access authentication and accounting, authentication and accounting events can be centrally logged for those RRAS servers that use it. Configure logging using the Remote Access Logging folder from the IAS console.

In addition to manual review of the logs, you can use the `netsh` command to collect log information from a specific time period and dump the information to a file. For example, the command `netsh ras diagnostics show logs type=file destination=c:\ras.htm hours=4 verbose=enabled` creates the ras.htm file in the temp directory that includes events from the tracing logs, modem logs, connection manager logs, IP Security log, remote access event logs, and security event logs. Figure 18-22 displays the first part of this report.

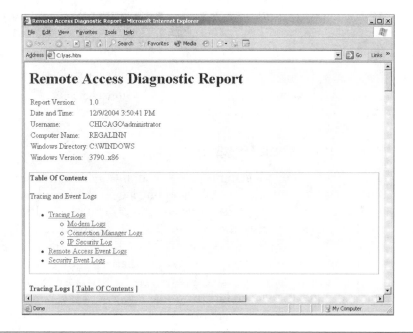

Figure 18-22   Use netsh to compile a report of relevant remote access information.

Authorization Manager Auditing

Authorization Manager auditing can be configured to provide information on runtime events and authorization store changes at the authorization store, application, and scope levels. The level of auditing available depends on whether the authorization store is based on Active Directory or XML. Table 18-8 provides the details. The two levels of auditing are

- **Application runtime**—Success and failure as defined by policy in the authorization store on items such as client contexts and access checks.
- **Authorization store change**—An audit record is produced if the authorization store is modified. For all events, success or failure is recorded.

Table 18-8   Authorization Manager Auditing

	XML	Active Directory
Authorization store	Runtime and store change	Runtime and store change
Application	Runtime	Runtime and store change
Scope	None	Store change

Net Logon Debug Logging

If Net Logon debug logging is enabled, an intruder can more easily be tracked on the network. Net Logon debug logging is turned on by using the `nltest /dbflag:flag` at a command prompt. The *flag* is a hexadecimal number that represents the level of logging required. Flags for Net Logon debug logging are documented in KB article 109626, "Enable Debug Logging for the Net Logon Service" (`http://support. microsoft.com/default.aspx?scid=kb;en-us;109626`). You can combine the flags with control bits to get the data you want. Because debug logging produces a plethora of events, you may want to limit events produced by requesting timestamps (control bit 0x20000000) and just the logon processing events (flag 0x00000004). The command to enter then is

```
nltest /dbflag:0x20000004
```

Once enabled, events are logged to %windir%\debug\netlogon.log.

TIP: Examine the Use of Net Logon Debug Logging
An article on using Net Logon debug logging to track intruders on a Windows network is available online at the United States Department of Energy Information Bridge site (`http://www.osti.gov/dublincore/gpo /servlets/purl/821123-32MRSo/native/`). The article was written by Christina S. Davis, Principal Network Engineer at Westinghouse Savannah River Company. Sample logs and their interpretations are published in the article.

Auditing Security Controls: Policy Compliance, Vulnerability Assessment, and Pen Testing

Determining security policy and implementing the technical controls that support it is not a trivial task. Keeping controls in place is harder. There are many reasons for this:

- Security policy can change. Although this is not usually a rapid process, when a change is made, it can mean that a lot of configuration changes or procedural changes are needed. Security policy changes can result from legislative changes, internal or external audits, a better understanding of the technology or the risks inherent in its use for a specific purpose, or even management's acceptance of a proposed change from you.
- Required changes to operating systems and applications (patches and upgrades) may reset configurations, return settings to their defaults, or require additional controls to be added.
- New applications and OSs require additional controls or impact current systems. Controls may be weakened because these new implementations will not work with current controls in place. Replacement OSs and applications may not have the controls made available by others. New OSs and applications may also lack appropriate controls or may just be unfamiliar to staff and therefore require more work.
- Tests and troubleshooting efforts may "temporarily" remove or change controls. (Someone may forget to change them back.)

■ Administrators authorized to make changes to technical controls make mistakes. Configuring security controls can be complicated, and sometimes vendor documentation and the language in the user interface can be confusing. For example, many security controls contain double negatives, such as when you "Enable" the "Disable ..." setting in order to disable the setting. If you "Disable" the setting, you actually "Enable" what you may want to "Disable."

■ Many security controls rely on complex technologies to deploy, implement, or maintain them. The result is that a problem with these technologies, such as network communications, DNS, or Group Policy, means that the security control is not deployed or does not produce the desired result.

Keeping controls in place requires diligence, training, proper procedures, service, and application monitoring. To ensure that controls are in place, plan to periodically test for policy compliance, perform vulnerability assessment, and perform pen tests. Although all these things may come under the heading of proper network maintenance and appear to be part of your job description, be sure to acquire written authority, especially if you are scanning systems on your network or attempting to hack into systems. Also, be sure to thoroughly understand any tool that you use. Some vulnerability testing programs, scanners, and other tools may have adverse affects on systems simply by being used. For example, some control equipment for factory equipment or for use by utilities is now being managed over TCP/IP. Some simple scans of these products can cause them to fail, shutting down business-critical operations or interfering with critical infrastructure.

Auditing Security Configuration Using Security Configuration and Analysis

This book emphasizes the use of Group Policy to implement security settings across the Windows network. Optional ways of securing stand-alone systems using local Group Policy controls and/or Security Configuration and Analysis have also been discussed. To ensure that changes to these settings have not occurred, audit current settings against required settings. Manual inspection is possible, but a far easier way to audit policy settings is available: the "analyze" function of the Security Configuration and Analysis console.

To use the tool, you must have a security template prepared that matches the official security policy for the computer you are testing. Such templates may have been created if you used this method to define security when creating role-based security models. If this is not the case, you can still create a security template for use in analysis. It's not a good idea to use a template stored on a production server as this may be out of date or altered in some way. Instead, use a copy of the security template originally produced and stored in a safe place. In either case, make sure that the template used does match your policy by manually checking the template settings against your organization's current security policy. After you have the template, you can perform an analysis:

1. Add the `Security Configuration and Analysis` snap-in to an MMC console. Start by clicking `Start`, `Run`, enter `mmc`, and click the `OK` button.
2. Select the `File` menu, and then select `Add/Remove Snap-in`.
3. Click the `Add` button.
4. Select `Security Configuration and Analysis`, click `Add`, and then click `Close`.
5. Click `OK`.
6. Expand the `Security Configuration and Analysis` node.
7. Right-click the `Security Configuration and Analysis` node and select `Open database`.
8. Enter a name for the database and click `Open`.
9. Browse to the security template file and then click `Open`.
10. Right-click the `Security Configuration and Analysis` node and select `Analyze computer now`.
11. Browse to a location to record an error log, and then click `OK`. By default, the log is saved to the My Documents\Security\Logs*name_of_database*.log file.
12. Click `OK`.
13. When the analysis has completed, expand the `Security Configuration and Analysis` node and view the detail pane. If there are differences between the database setting (your security policy as entered into the security template selected in step 9) and the computer setting, a white x in a red circle will identify it, as shown in Figure 18-23.

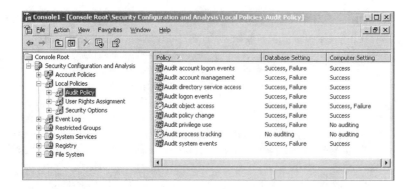

Figure 18-23 Any variances from policy will show up as a white x within a red circle.

You can also use the `secedit` command to perform an analysis, but to review the report, you have to load the results in the Security Configuration and Analysis tool. To do an analysis, use this command:

```
secedit /analyze /db filenameofdatabaseforanalysis.sdb [/cfg
securitytemplatename] [/overwrite] [/log nameforlogfile]
[/quiet]
```

In the command, the `/overwrite` switch will overwrite any existing file by the same name, and the `/quiet` switch will not echo any information to the screen. If you have already created a database file by importing a security template using Security Configuration and Analysis, and it includes the correct security template, you can leave off the `/cfg` switch.

TIP: Batch Analysis
Both Security Configuration and Analysis and the `secedit` command listed here will analyze only one computer at a time. You can create a script to use the `secedit` command on multiple computers and collect the results to a single location, such as a desktop PC, where it can later be analyzed and archived as proof of compliance or to create a list of systems that need to be updated.

Auditing Security Configuration for Specific Computers and Users

The use of Group Policy makes it possible to extend security configuration across the network to many Windows systems and to direct specific security settings for specific types of computers and users. You cannot assume that just because the settings are correctly defined, they are being correctly applied. Many things, such as network connectivity or Active Directory replication problems, can interfere. To audit these settings, you must inventory the applied settings on specific computers and for specific users. To do so, you can use RSoP in logging mode. This utility can reach out across the network and remotely examine the security settings for a specific user/computer combination.

To do RSoP logging, follow these steps:

1. Add the RSoP snap-in to an MMC console.
2. Click the Action Menu, select Generate Resultant Set of Policy, and then click Next.
3. On the Mode Selection page, select Logging mode, as shown in Figure 18-24, and click Next.

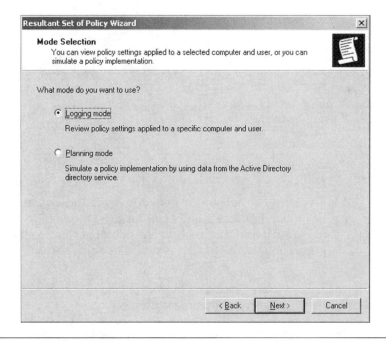

Figure 18-24   Select logging to create a report on the current settings.

4. Select a computer. The computer must be reachable.
5. Select whether to display computer and user settings or just user settings and click Next.
6. Select the user to display, as shown in Figure 18-25, or select not to display user results (display computer only) and click Next.
7. Review the selection and click Next.
8. When the wizard completes, click Finish.
9. Expand the report and review it. Note that only the items that are enabled are reported on.
10. Double-click the policy part to view its details, as shown in Figure 18-26, and compare with the required security policy on the computer for the selected user.

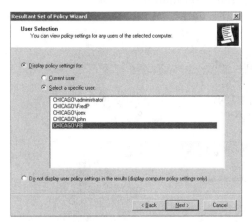 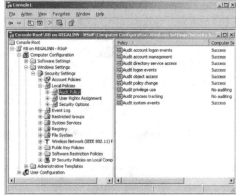

Figure 18-25   Select the user.

Figure 18-26   Examine RSoP results in the detail pane.

11. To save the results for review later, name and save the console. If desired, additional RSoP snap-ins can be added to the console and used to produce reports on additional combinations of computers and users. Reports may also be refreshed.

Scanning for Known Vulnerabilities

In the correctly configured and properly patched network, scanning for known vulnerabilities is a waste of time. After all, correct configuration and patching implies an appreciation of known vulnerabilities and an effort to mitigate them. In reality, you cannot know with certainty that mitigation efforts have actually been implemented. Even if you perform each mitigation step yourself, you must use software to do so, and the software itself may have errors or may not work correctly in some circumstances. The very fact that you must apply patches to correct software bugs should prevent you from trusting any software-based effort to correct them.

Assessing Vulnerabilities with Microsoft Baseline Security Analyzer (MBSA)

Therefore, you must audit system configuration looking for known vulnerabilities. Microsoft Baseline Security Analyzer can perform basic vulnerability checking and is available for free at `http://www.micro-soft.com/technet/security/tools/mbsahome.mspx`. This tool checks for major, well-known configuration vulnerabilities of Windows Server 2003, Windows 2000, Windows XP, and Windows NT 4.0. It also looks at IIS, SQL Server, Windows Media Player, and Exchange. Its primary purpose is to look for missing patches. Because patches are a response to vulnerability, a missing patch means the computer is vulnerable. Many fine third-party products go much further, providing extensive reporting capabilities that seek out evidence of the existence of known vulnerabilities. So, although MBSA's orientation is to provide information on which patches you need to add, many third-party products emphasize the specific vulnerability you need to protect the system against. To be fair, MBSA reports point to Microsoft documentation that describes what the patch protects you from, and many third-party products point to the Microsoft patch that will mitigate the vulnerability. By default, MBSA accesses an online database of patches that is kept up-to-date by Microsoft. If you use Microsoft Software Update Server (SUS) to provide patches tested and approved by your organization, you can point MBSA to the SUS server, and it will use its database of approved patches instead. If you do so, the audit will not report on missing patches that you have not yet approved for distribution to systems on your network. MBSA can be used to remotely scan multiple Windows systems, but there is a downside. MBSA is an agentless scanner—that is, no client-side software must be installed on clients in order to scan them. This means that MBSA requires that File and Printer Sharing be enabled on the client as well as the Remote Registry Service. Many security experts argue that these things should be disabled in order to protect the computer from possible compromise. Microsoft, however, has indicated that it believes having the ability to scan for missing patches far outweighs the risk posed by shutting down these remote access channels. You can mitigate your exposure by configuring IPSec to block access to these channels from all sources while allowing the computer used by MBSA to use them.

To use MBSA to scan computer(s), follow these steps:

1. Click `Start, Programs, Microsoft Baseline Security Analyzer`.
2. Click `Scan a computer` or `Scan more than one computer`.
3. If you select to `Scan a computer`, pick the computer by name or IP address, name the report, select options, as shown in Figure 18-27, and click `Start scan`.

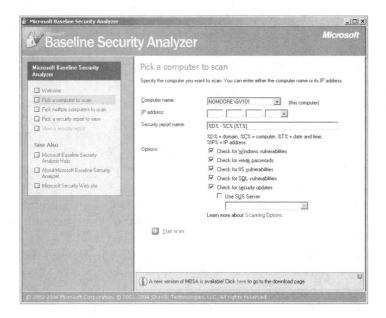

Figure 18-27   Select reporting options before starting the scan.

4. When the scan is complete, view the report and use its results to improve security on the system.
5. If you select to `Scan more than one computer`, select the computers by entering a domain name or an IP address range and select options, as shown in Figure 18-28, then click `Start scan`.

TIP: Review MBSA Screens for TIPs

When MBSA runs, it checks the version of its engine and checks for more up-to-date patches. Note that in Figure 18-28, MBSA is advising that a more recent version of MBSA is available. New versions of MBSA must be downloaded manually.

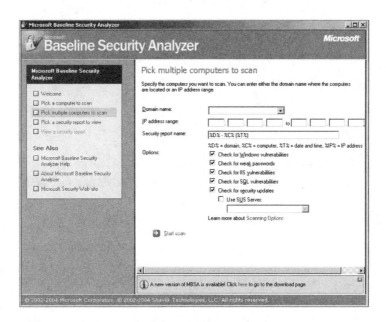

Figure 18-28   Scanning multiple computers requires entry of a domain name or IP address range.

6. The scanning process may take a while if many computers need to be scanned. You can stop the scanning process by clicking the `stop` button. A progress report bar and a record of how many IP addresses have been checked or scanned are displayed. Scanning problems are also reported, as shown in Figure 18-29.

7. When the scan is complete, select a report to review and review reports one at a time.

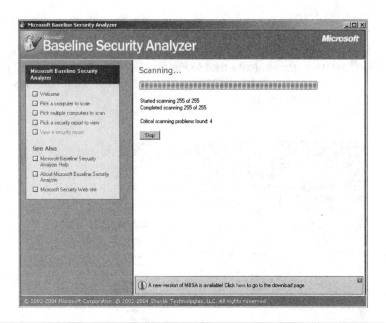

Figure 18-29   Scanning problems are reported at the end of a multiple computer scan.

MBSA reports are HTML-based files. It is not possible to examine a cross section of reports; they must be viewed one at a time. You can use a command-line version of the product to produce a text-based file. The text-based file will only include information on missing patches and not vulnerability assessment information. You can then import the files, one for each computer, into an Access or SQL Server database and use database queries to obtain information. For example, if you discover that patches are not being installed on some subset of computers, you can troubleshoot the patching problems by determining if the computers have anything in common, such as operating system and service pack level, computer role, location, and so on. You can also use a query to develop a list of computers that have not received specific patches and then use the list to get the job done.

To obtain a text file report on all the computers in the chicago.local domain and put it in the file scan1.txt, use this command:

```
Mbsacli /hf -d chicago.local -o tab -f scan1.txt
```

The /hf switch specifies that the HFNetChk syntax will be used. HFNetChk is the original tool developed by Shavlik (www.shavlik.com) for Microsoft. The /d indicates that a domain will be used for the search. The o specifies the output format, and the tab indicates a tab-delimited file. By asking for this type of format, the file will be easy to import into Access. The f specifies the file name. More information on command syntax and instructions on how to use mbsacli and Access to audit patch management are included in the article "Auditing Patch Management" published in Microsoft Certified Professional Magazine at http://mcp-mag.com/columns/article.asp?EditorialsID=531.

Toward a More Comprehensive Vulnerability Scan

MBSA is not a full-featured vulnerability scanner. It is a useful tool for auditing patch management and for finding some of the more egregious errors in configuration—the errors that make Windows systems vulnerable to attack. A number of products perform a more comprehensive test. Some of these products, such as NMAP (http://www.insecure.org/), look for vulnerabilities on other operating systems and can provide you with an enterprise-wide picture. You should obtain a product that can be used to scan for vulnerabilities and that can be regularly updated. Keep the following points in mind when evaluating the results of a vulnerability scan:

- Does the product offer advice on mitigation? In other words, does it tell you what to do to correct the error or reduce the chance that the vulnerability will be used to compromise your network?
- Does the product do an in-depth analysis? For example, instead of reporting that a specific service (such as IIS) creates a vulnerability for your network, does the tool examine your implementation of IIS by looking at the mitigation you may have already put into place, such as IIS hardening?
- Can you customize the product? You may want to add your own items that should be checked but that are not in the scanner's database.
- Is the scanner updatable? New vulnerabilities are discovered all the time. Can the scanner's database be updated?
- Is the scanner well known in the industry? Experienced scanner users may become important resources.

- Can the scanner be configured to restrict it to scanning only specific computers? It's important to be able to focus the scan on a certain area of the network or to exclude specific computers, such as those that a scan might damage.

Penetration Testing

Hardening and non-invasive scanning can go a long way in protecting your network. Taking these steps can protect systems from attackers if the mitigation you apply really does perform as advertised. If you use the advice and information provided by known authorities, you can be reasonably sure that what you have done will mitigate vulnerability. However, you cannot be 100 percent sure that

- In every case, on every machine, the "fix" is correctly applied.
- Audits and scans are correctly reporting the status of systems.
- Every system is properly evaluated.
- Some new vulnerability or new way to attack your systems was not recently developed and thus mitigation is unknown.
- You and your advisors know everything there is to know and everything there is to do.

These issues, of course, have no real solution. You will never be 100 percent secure, nor 100 percent sure that you have dealt with every issue. Still, you have to try every approach. Another way to detect flaws in your defenses is to perform (or have a third-party organization perform) a penetration test (pen test). Pen tests are active tests; they attack systems. Their goal is to compromise systems. Therefore, to get good results, make sure pen tests are performed by someone with no interest in proving that your organization's security is good. This is not to say that an authorized employee should not perform a pen test, but simply that she should not be the only one performing a test. Pen tests are now part of many audits performed by information security auditing firms. There are also many information security companies that also perform these tests. Carefully consider the experience and background of the organization and the individuals it uses to perform these tests.

WARNING: Do Not Perform Pen Tests without Written Authority
There is no way to determine "intent" when examining the results of an attack on a computer system. If you perform a penetration test, you are attacking a computer system. If you do not have written permission to test security in this way, you could easily find yourself accused of a crime.

Auditing Physical Security

All the best technical security defenses in the world may not work if an attacker can obtain physical access to computers or computing infrastructure. Physical security should be a major consideration when developing a computer security plan and should be audited. Although physical security is outside of the scope of this book, any discussion of security auditing would be incomplete without at least indicating the need to consider physical security. Specifically, when considering physical security for Windows Server 2003 systems, look for the following:

- The use of smart cards or other physical devices that may have been implemented. Although using these devices may not prevent an attacker with physical access from compromising the computer (he might boot to another OS, for example), they can help. If a smart card is required for logon, it will be more difficult to attack than if only an account and password are necessary.
- Removal of removable media drives, such as floppy and hard disk drives. This can thwart attacks that would boot to another OS and may also prevent data theft.
- Lack of or disabling of other access ports, such as USB ports and firewire ports, that might be used for data theft.

Auditing Policy, Standards, and Procedures

In addition to checking the status of server configuration and policy compliance, you should audit policy, standards, and procedures to ensure that they are up-to-date, meet needs, and are correct for the way your organization operates today. In many organizations, policy addresses security in a broad way, leaving others to define the technology and controls to be used to implement a policy. In these organizations, standards are written that state which technologies will be used and procedures to define how they will be configured. In other organizations, a policy may be specific as to technology and may even state procedural implementation steps. Other organizations may implement security policy using a mixture of these techniques.

In all cases, these written documents should be examined. At least consider the following questions about them: Do they address mobile computing issues such as remote access using PDAs or wireless networks? Do they reference technologies that no longer exist on your network or lack information on technologies you may have implemented? Do they address the current risks of the organization? (Are you doing more sensitive work and haven't updated risk assessments and mitigations?)

Windows Server 2003 mostly improved technologies introduced with Windows 2000, and you may find that your policy and documentation is current. However, many implementations are the direct result of a need to introduce newer technologies, so you should check to ensure that those technologies are addressed by security policies, standards, and procedures.

Reviewing Security Awareness

Security awareness is a state of consciousness in which individuals or groups are cognizant of security issues and what they need to do to mitigate threats. A different level of security awareness can be defined for different groups of people. That is, the ordinary computer user needs to know and practice different information security than the IT administrator. The user needs to have specific knowledge that will allow her to securely operate and use computer systems and manage sensitive information, including any information that might be used to compromise the organization's computer systems. The IT administrator, because she has more knowledge and more privileges on computer systems, needs to have the end user's knowledge plus much, much more. Other individuals within the organizations may also have different security awareness needs.

All members of the organization can benefit from security awareness training that is directed toward their needs. An audit of security awareness should judge the status of knowledge, review the security awareness program, and test the program both by observation (are passwords written on sticky notes and attached to computer monitors?) and by active attempts at social engineering (perhaps a phone call that attempts to obtain a password).

Auditing Outsiders: The Impact of Others on Your Organization's Information Security

In the past, computer activity was limited primarily to inside the organization's boundaries. There were few, if any, connections to the rest of the world. That is no longer the case. Windows Sever 2003 provides many technologies that can be used to provide connectivity both for employees of your own organization that are working from different locations and for your business partners, suppliers, and customers. An audit of the security implemented for those technologies should be a part of any audit. Another aspect of these connections should also be addressed in your audit. You should consider the security efforts practiced by those outsiders who interface with your network. Think about it—if you have established a Windows trust between your and a partner's Windows domain or forest, you have opened up a security boundary that could provide an avenue for attack. Although you can attest for the security in place on your side of the connection, what can you say about that of your partner?

Summary

Auditing is more than just determining compliance to policy, scanning for vulnerabilities, or setting up the Windows Audit Policy. Auditing is all of these. Effectively auditing Windows systems requires systems administrators and separate audit staff, as well as the proper use of native and third-party tools. When done properly, auditing merges with monitoring, which is the subject of the next chapter.

CHAPTER 19

Monitoring and Assessment

Security monitoring and assessment is the process of keeping tabs on the security status of the Windows Server 2003 system(s). Because it focuses on what is normal, it can also help you determine what is abnormal and then help you distinguish between failures and security incidents. Because security is dependent not just on security technologies but also on the availability and proper operation of components, security monitoring and assessment focuses on monitoring those components. The argument could be made that all network, operating system, and application operation can impact security, but security monitoring should concentrate on those items most likely to cause security problems. Security monitoring therefore concentrates on services such as Active Directory and DNS and on irregularities in any operations. Security monitoring is part intrusion detection, and part simply making sure that all security processes and processes that security depends on are functioning. Monitoring may use information collected via many tools including data from the event logs, results of diagnostic utilities, performance monitoring tools, network monitors, and third-party monitoring tools. Do not make the mistake of assuming that connecting a network monitor and digesting packets is the only monitoring and assessment you must do. Instead, take these steps:

- Establish baselines for normal operation
- Monitor services
- Monitor active directory
- Use live and archival data to detect intrusion
- Establish incident response procedures

Establish Baselines

You cannot determine which events require investigation as possible security incidents unless you know what is normal. Thus, the first step in detecting abnormality is establishing a baseline. If you know what is ordinary for your organization, it is easier to spot the unusual. For example, do you know how many logon failure events in the event log of a domain controller constitutes ordinary forgetfulness or error on the part of your users? Users will forget passwords and enter them incorrectly, so there will be failed logon events in the logs. If you know how many logon failures are typical, you won't be alarmed to see them but will correctly identify a sudden rise in logon failures as something to investigate immediately. If you have no idea what is normal, you might see a few events as a problem, or count large numbers of events as normal operations. The number of normal failed logons for a specific DC in your system is not a number that can be determined by examining some statistic recorded by another organization. Baselines for event log activity are not the only statistic to consider, either. Do you know the average time it takes to fully replicate changes to the Active Directory across your enterprise? Are spikes in network utilization normal for a specific day of the week, month, time of day, or do they represent a spreading worm?

Attack!

Early in my tests of Microsoft Internet Security and Acceleration (ISA) server, I reviewed the logs several times daily in order to become more comfortable with them. I set up all of its reporting features and thoroughly investigated its operation. Then, I had to travel for a bit. I left ISA in place, but I removed its connection to the internal test network. When I returned, I found the logs full of failed logon attempts. As I watched, more were added. My first instinct in such cases is usually wrong. Typically, I want to disconnect the system under attack from the Internet in order to protect the internal network. But this server's only connection was to the Internet. If the server were compromised, the only loss would be the server itself, and I might learn more by keeping it connected. I left the server connected to the Internet and started investigating.

As I continued to examine the logs, a pattern emerged. A single account was under attack, and the failed logon attempts were occurring with regularity. However, there was some time between them. It was either a sophisticated attack that was trying not to trigger an account lockout, or an individual working very slowly but precisely. The attack had been going on for a few days. What person could ever maintain that pace hour after hour, day after day? It had to be software.

Then, it hit me. The account under attack was an account I set up to be used by the reporting engine. The production of reports draws data from the ISA logs and cannot operate without authentication. Could this be a failure of the reporting engine and not an attack after all? Well, I was half right. It was not an attack. I had set the account password to expire and had not reset it. The password had expired, but the automated process had not. Everything was working as it should, except the system administrator. A quick password reset, the report program could log on, and the incident was over.

This security "incident" was not the result of an attack, but it does point out the need for understanding the systems we are required to protect and for understanding normal activity in the logs.

Many of these baselines may be tracked already as part of network operations. From a security perspective, your job may be simply to help interpret the variations. A number of resources can help, including a web sites such as the Information Technology Professionals Resource Center (ITPRC), which lists and describes products and provides whitepapers on network monitoring at `http://www.itprc.com/nms.htm`.

Other operations, such as monitoring Active Directory and Group Policy operation and interpreting Windows logs, may not be addressed by traditional network monitoring products and networking staff. They are addressed by a growing number of third-party and Microsoft products, such as Microsoft Operations Manager (MOM). The suitability of any specific product for your network is not within the scope of this book; understanding what to monitor and how to use built-in or resource kit tools is.

NOTE: Resource on Intrusion Detection

Using network monitors for intrusion detection and forensics is beyond the scope of this book. A good resource is *The Tao of Network Security Monitoring: Beyond Intrusion Detection* by Richard Bejtlich (Addison-Wesley, 2004). This book provides detailed analysis of network traffic captured using free and commercial network monitors.

Monitor Basic Services

Your Windows Server 2003 network may or may not incorporate every bit of functionality that it can provide. However, you should understand how to determine when the operations of these services can impact security and what to do about it. Many freely available Microsoft tools can be used to monitor these services and are discussed in this section. Sources of these tools are described in Table 19-1. Start the process by determining what services should be running on which machines, and then use tools and logs to determine if they are operating correctly. This chapter only covers services that provide or directly support the operation of security services.

Table 19-1   Tools for Monitoring Services

Source	Description	Available
Built-in command line tools	Many tools and utilities are executable files installed by default.	By default. Many of them are located in %windir%\system32.
MMC, browser-based, or other console-based tools	Many administrative tools are provided that can be snapped-in to a Microsoft Management Console, or loaded in IE.	Many are available directly from the Start\Administrative Tools folder. Others are added when a specific services is installed, or may be added by opening an MMC and using the File menu Add\Remove Snap-in selection.
Support tools	Support tools are additional utilities that are not installed by default.	Located on the Windows Server 2003 installation CD-ROM.
Resource kit tools	Tools provided as part of a server-specific resource kit. Resource kits are compiled technical references on a specific Microsoft product. They may or may not include utilities.	Purchase of the resource kit provides a copy of the tools. Some, if not all, tools may be downloaded from http://www.micro soft.com/downloads/ details.aspx?familyid= 9d467a69-57ff-4ae7-96ee-b18c4790cffd& displaylang=en.

Monitoring DNS and Network Connectivity

Proper DNS operation is critical to security services. DNS is used to determine the names and locations of domain controllers and services such as ldap, Kerberos, and global catalog servers (GCs). If DNS fails, or if its service records are not correct, basic security fails. Authentication, replication, Universal group membership, and other domain services cannot function without it. Testing and monitoring DNS can also provide confirmation of basic network connectivity.

TIP: Monitor Network Connectivity Using the Application and System Event Logs

Events 1058 and 1030 in the Application Event log can be indications of basic network connectivity problems. Event 1058 indicates that Windows cannot access the gpi.ini file that is necessary for applying GPOs. It may also indicate that the DC cannot be reached or that access is denied. Event 1030 "Windows cannot query for the list of Group Policy objects" and the System Event log event warning 11197 can indicate DNS issues but can be due to other problems.

To test DNS, you must test not only the ability of DNS to resolve computer names to IP address, but also the proper registration of domain services. DNS can be correctly configured and operating perfectly, but if domain services are not properly registered, security services will not work well or will not work at all. Use the following tests to verify DNS operation.

nslookup

Use `nslookup` to verify SRV records in DNS. These records locate AD services on the network and DCs use them to find replication partners:

1. Open a command prompt on the DNS server, type `nslookup`, and then press `Enter`.
2. Type `set type=all` and press `Enter`.
3. Type `ldap.tcp.dc._msdcs.domain_name` and press `Enter`. (*domain_name* should be the name of a domain in your Active Directory forest.) The LDAP SRV record, as shown in Figure 19-1, will be returned. While other SRV records must be present for proper operation, if `nslookup` does not return the LDAP SRV record for each DC, SRV records are not complete. Use `DNSLint` and/or `dcdiag` to check further or examine DNS records directly.

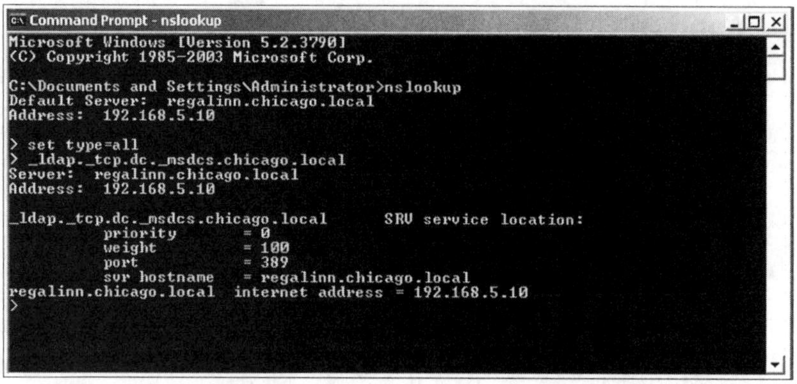

Figure 19-1   SRV records can be listed by using nslookup.

ipconfig

Check TCP/IP configuration on DCs using `ipconfig /all` to ensure that the DNS server listed is the appropriate one. (Each DC should point to a DNS server for its domain.) In the forest root domain, if DNS is integrated with Active Directory, make sure that DCs running the DNS service do not all point to themselves for DNS services. If they do, each may only record its own IP information. Replication between DCs may not occur because only one DC record will be in each DNS server. Instead of pointing each DC to itself, a good basic rule is to point all DCs to the same DNS server and point that DC to itself. (For more information, see KB article 275278.)

DNSLint

Use `DNSLint` to diagnose DNS errors. `DNSLint` can also be used to find replication errors. To diagnose DNS errors, run the `DNSLint` command. `DNSLint /d domain_name` looks on the Internet to find registered DNS domains. If your Active Directory domain is not registered, you must provide `DNSLint` with the IP address of a DC. Use the command `DNSLint /d domain_name /s ipaddressofdomain_nameDC`. This command will access the DNS records on the `ipaddressofdomain_nameDC` you provide. To produce a text file in addition to an HTML report, use the /t switch. DNSLint produces a report that includes this information:

- Domain authoritative DNS servers.
- Source of Authority (SOA) records.
- Host records for DNS servers.
- Mail server (MX) records for the domain.
- If multiple authoritative DNS records are located, DNSLint will compare the information provided looking for differences.

It will also document the following errors if present:

- **Lame delegation**—A DNS server delegates authority for a sub-domain to a DNS server that cannot be reached, does not exist, or is not configured to be authoritative for the sub-domain.
- **Missing glue records**—Glue or host records are needed for name resolution.
- **Non-authoritative DNS servers**—Provides the information needed to troubleshoot lame delegation issues.
- **Non-responsive DNS servers**—If DNSLint can't reach them, neither can clients.
- **Improperly configured TCP/IP**—The DNS server location in TCP/IP does not represent an authoritative server for the domain.
- **Missing CNAME or host (glue or A) record**—Records for DCs do not exist in DNS. Clients search for a DC by finding the DC's GUID and resolving this to the associated CNAME and finally obtaining an IP address from the host record.
- **Missing service location records**—Some or all SRV records are missing.

You can obtain more information and download DNSLint from http://support.microsoft.com/default.aspx?scid=kb;EN-US;321045. Table 19-2 lists and describes DNSLint parameters.

Table 19-2 DNSLint Parameters

Parameter	Description
/ad	Tests LDAP and SRV records.
/c SMTP	Checks for SMTP server records and check connectivity for POP, SMTP, and NNTP.
/no_open	Don't open the dnslint.htm file at the end of processing.
/s	Checks locally. Do not use a Internic whois command.
/t	Produces a text file.
/test_tcp	Tests the response of DNS to TCP port 53.
/v	Verbose reporting.

Figure 19-2 displays part of a DNSLint report.

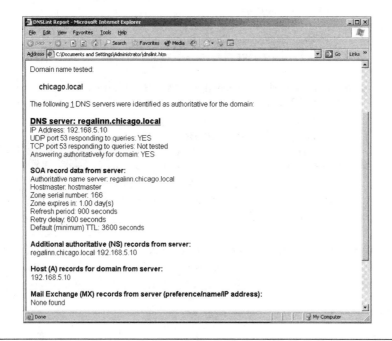

Figure 19-2 Use DNSLint to look for DNS issues.

dcdiag, netdiag, and portqry

Network connectivity problems can disrupt Active Directory and Group Policy function. `Dcdiag` is a general purpose DC and Active Directory diagnostic tool. It can also be used to test basic DNS and network function because if these services are not operating properly, many if not most dcdiag tests will fail. Use `dcdiag /test:DomainDNSzones` and `dcdiag /test:ForestDNSZones` to check DNS for proper domain SRV records.

If `dcdiag` tests fail, check network connectivity. Use `netdiag` to test network services related to Active Directory. Entering `netdiag` without any parameters performs a number of network function tests. To test DNS, use the command `netdiag /test:DNS`. This test checks DNS function and checks that DC information is properly registered in DNS. Other useful tests are `dclist`, which produces a list of DCs, and Kerberos, which checks Kerberos. Both `dcdiag` and `netdiag` have useful fix commands that may fix DNS domain registration problems.

Use `portqry` to determine if DCs are listening on appropriate ports. `portqry -n dc1.nomain_name.extension -p udp -e 53` will determine if the DC is listening on UDP port 53. Although `portqry` is a simple port tester and can be used to test if the DC is listening on specific ports, it is often unnecessary because this can be verified when other tests or tools are used. For example, if you can successfully use the utility ldp.exe to search and modify Active Directory on a specific DC, you already have proof that that DC is listening on an LDAP port. Ldpexe connects and binds to either LDAP port 389 or the LDAP SSL port 3268. There is no need to perform a separate test.

Monitor DHCP

DHCP automatically assigns an IP address and other TCP/IP configuration information to clients on the network. DHCP can also be used to register DNS information to DNS. When DHCP servers fail or run out of addresses and when rogue DHCP servers are able to interfere with your network operation, this can be a serious security problem as well as a network operation problem. A rogue DHCP server can direct clients to a DNS server that incorrectly resolves addresses and potentially directs clients to servers and sources where information of a sensitive nature goes to the wrong people, or incorrect information may be perceived by clients as correct. If clients cannot obtain an IP address, they cannot participate on the network. What if the client that cannot participate needs to do so to monitor security, to administer sensitive systems, or to otherwise communicate information that may protect the network and its resources?

The Product Operations Guide at `http://www.microsoft.com/ technet/itsolutions/cits/mo/winsrvmg/dhcppog/dhcppog3.mspx#E GAp` provides information on how to use System Monitor to monitor DHCP server performance. Monitoring performance and disk utilization for DHCP servers can provide early warnings of possible failure. It cannot provide information about rogue DHCP servers, however.

The DHCP logs should also be reviewed for information that may indicate performance issues or even attacks. In addition to using the DHCP logs and System Monitor to monitor DHCP function, the Windows Support tool, dhcploc.exe (the DHCP Server Locator Utility), displays active DHCP servers on a subnet. It can also alert you to unauthorized DHCP servers (it actually beeps and can send out messages). It can also be used to display packets from DHCP servers.

`dhcploc` does not rely on DHCP registration with Active Directory to determine which DHCP servers are authorized. Instead, you create a list of authorized DHCP servers, and `dhcploc` lets you know if DHCP servers that are not on the list are active on your network. Table 19-3 lists the parameters that can be used with the `dhcploc.exe` command.

Table 19-3   dhcploc Parameters

Parameter	Description
/p	Suppress display of packets from authorized DHCP servers as listed in your valid DHCP server list.
/a:"alertname"	Sends alert messages to the names in alertname, a list of user names.
/I:alertinterval	Alert interval is the alert frequency in seconds.
ComptuerIPAddress	The IP address on which you run dhcploc.exe. Specify the IP address of the adapter on the subnet on which you want to run the test.
ValidDHCPServerList	The IP addresses of authorized DHCP servers.

An example command that will run `dhcploc` on server 192.168.5.55 and produce alerts if rogue DHCP servers (those other than 192.168.5.100) are found and display packets from them is as follows:

```
dhcploc /p 192.168.5.55 192.168.5.100
```

Once dhcploc is running, type the letter d to display packets.

Packet information includes the time, IP address to which the DHCP offer is made, the server that made the offer, and the DHCP message (OFFER, NACK, ACK). Do not run dhcploc on a DHCP server because it will interfere with operations. To send an alert to the user Administrator, use the following command:

```
dhcploc /p /a:Administrator 192.168.5.55 192.168.5.100
```

Monitor PKI

If a public key infrastructure (PKI) is installed and used on your network, it is important to know that it is properly operating. If the PKI includes Microsoft enterprise certification authorities (CAs), use the PKI Health Tool (pkiview.msc) to monitor PKI health. PKI Health is an MMC snap-in that gathers information from each CA and reviews the status of their CA certificates to make sure they are working correctly. The utility can also be used to view CA root and issuing CA certificates, identify the AIA location (the locations from which the CA certificate can be downloaded), view cross certificates, display the CRL distribution point, and identify key recovery agent certificates. If you have many CAs in your organization that are integrated with Active Directory, pkiview can be used to collect information about all of them. Comparing this information can also help you discover any unauthorized CAs that may have been integrated with AD.

To use the tool, add the Enterprise PKI tool to an MMC console. (The tool is available from the Add/Remove Snap-ins command if resource kit tools have been installed on the computer.) When opened in a console, pkiview displays the CA hierarchy, providing a node for each CA, as shown in Figure 19-3. In the figure, the rootA CA is marked by an x'd circle. This means that pkiview has identified an error. Select the CA to view the error in the detail pane. In this case, pkiview has attempted to download certificates from AIA locations and has found that one location is inaccessible. Downloading certificates is necessary when checking certificate signatures and when adding the CA to the computer's trusted CAs.

The figure also shows a warning. In this case, opening the SubCA CA node, as shown in Figure 19-4, reveals that the delta CRL is nearing expiration. Reviewing errors in pkiview can help you see where problems may be or about to be that can cause problems with certificate services.

Figure 19-3   pkiview can identify errors in your PKI implementation.

Figure 19-4   Warnings can alert you to potential issues.

Monitor Routing and Remote Access

The Resource Kit tool RRAS Server Monitor (RASSrvMon.exe) is a GUI tool that can be used to review remote access service activity in detail. It can provide summary information on the server as well as individual connection information. Connection information for every connection includes user name, computer name, IP address, connection start time, duration, bytes transmitted, error count, and line speed. You can also configure alerts, for example, to warn if the remote access server is unreachable or non-responsive. Alerts can be configured to run a program, such as to send an email or a page.

RASSrvMon generates three files for each monitored RRAS server: a summary file, servername.webstatus; a user connection file, servername.userdetails; and a file used to generate the data dumps, servername.userlist.

To start the monitor, enter the command `rassrvmon    /s: servername_or_IP_address /t:TimeOffset` where `TimeOffset` is the length of time that the server has been running before the monitor was started. Because one of the purposes of RASSrvMon is to alert you if a RRAS server is not working, it is best to monitor the RRAS server from another computer. If you must run the monitor on the RRAS server, use the `/p:svchost_Pid` parameter instead of the `/s:` parameter. `svchost_Pid` is the process ID of the `svchost` process under which the remote access server is running. Because multiple `svchost` processes may be running, determine the one that is running the RRAS service by using the `tasklist /svc` command. The command produces a list of running processes, their PID, and the name of the service, as shown in Figure 19-5. Each svchost.exe process is listed along with the services it has loaded. Use `tasklist` on the RRAS server, identify the RRAS service, and record the PID. Then, use the PID with the `RASSrvMon` command.

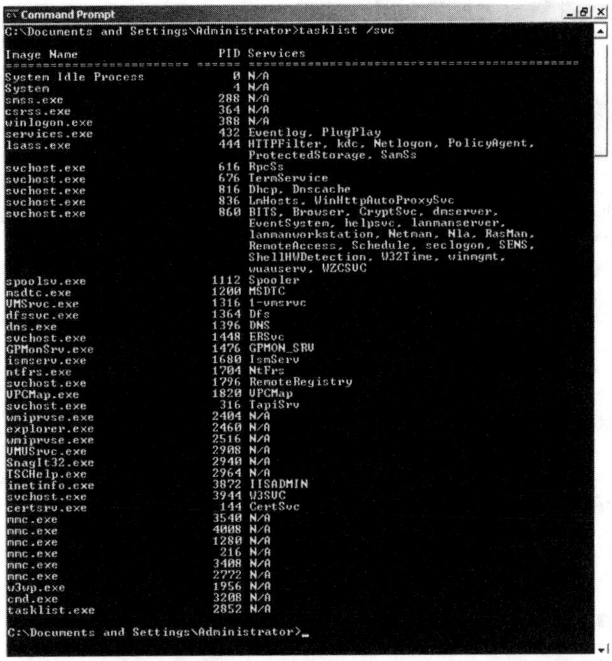

Figure 19-5 Use tasklist to determine which services a specific svchost process is running.

In the figure, PID 860 is the PID for the svchost running the Remote Access service. To start RASSrvMon, enter the command:

```
Rassrvmon /p:860 /t:TimeOffset
```

The RAS Monitor GUI is displayed. In Figure 19-6, the Monitor configuration page is displayed to show two important alert settings: MprAdminPortEnum Failure and No Incoming Calls. These settings, if configured to send an alert, can warn you of a non-functioning RRAS server. MprAdminPortEnum is a call to list the connections on the RRAS server ports. RASSrvMon can be configured to poll all ports. If the call fails, it may be an indication that the server is malfunctioning. If the server is in constant use and yet receives no calls over some time period you configure, this may also indicate that the server is down.

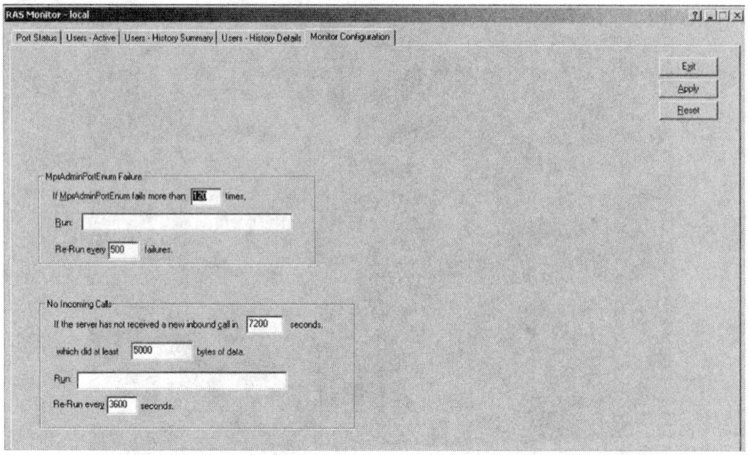

Figure 19-6   RAS Monitor Alert Settings.

Monitor Shares

In addition to monitoring access to sensitive files using object auditing, monitor server shares with the Server Share Check Tool (Srvcheck.exe). This tool lists non-hidden shares, as shown in Figure 19-7, and the permissions set on each. There are two uses for this information. First, if you keep a record of which shares should be available on the server, you can compare this information to ensure that only the proper shares are available. Second, you can compare the ACLs with those authorized for the shares. If you send the results of using srvcheck to a file, as shown in the following command, you can compare future results (also recorded in a file) and note differences:

```
Srvcheck \\server_name > shares.txt
```

Figure 19-7 displays the shares.txt file in Notepad.

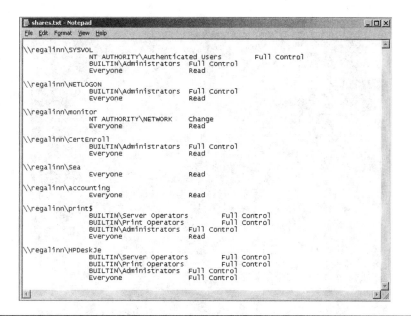

Figure 19-7   Srvcheck lists the non-hidden shares and their permissions.

TIP: Comparing Files
The GUI tool windiff.exe provided with Windows Server 2003 can be used
to compare two files. To compare two files from the command prompt,
enter the command `Windiff filepath1 filepath2`. Enter `windiff` at a
command prompt to open the tool. An included help file explains its use.

Monitor All Active Services

While monitoring tools for specific services exist, it's helpful to be able to
determine if the appropriate services for any particular server are up and
running and to determine if any new services have been added. The
Resource Kit tool srvinfo.exe can report services information on remote
servers. Use the command `srvinfo.exe` to display services and devices
and whether they are stopped or started. Other information is also displayed, such as forest information for this server and network configuration. Use the `-s` parameter to display shares. Compare this information
with what should be available on the server. Figure 19-8 displays partial
results from the use of the command `srvinfo \\motorin` from another
computer on the network.

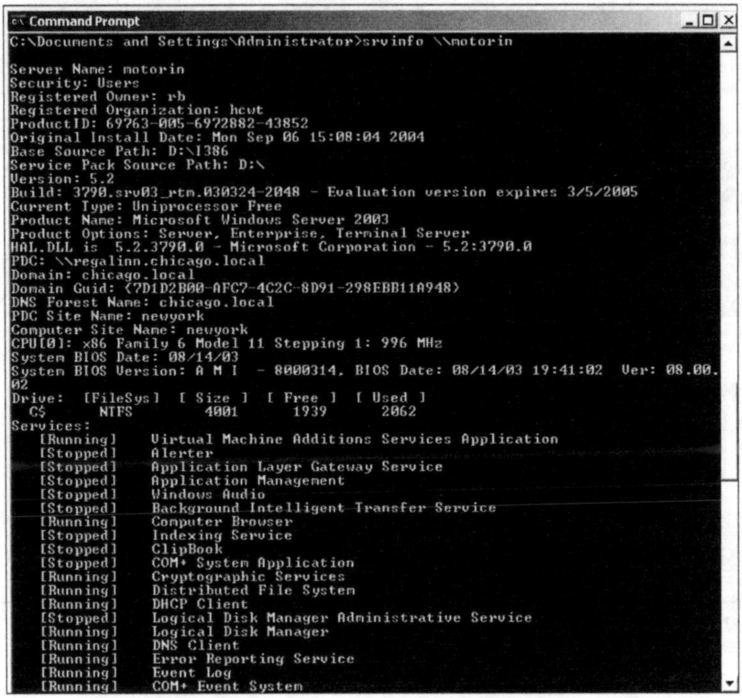

Figure 19-8 Use srvinfo to determine which services are running.

Monitor Active Directory and Group Policy

A healthy Active Directory and properly functioning Group Policy operations are critical to security for domain computers and users. A large number of security operations in every domain rely on them. Among the security functions of Active Directory, Group Policy, and their related services are

- Authentication. The AD database stores user, group, and computer accounts and passwords.
- The netlogon service is part of the authentication process. If netlogon fails, authentication fails.

- Special operational roles, such as the PDC emulator, are critical. If the PDC emulator is not available in the domain, account lockout is possible, and time synchronization may not occur. If the RID master is unavailable and the domain controller uses its supply of relative IDs, new accounts cannot be created.
- Security configuration. Security settings are configured in Group Policy objects. Some of the GPO data is stored in the AD and replicated via AD replication. (Additional data is stored in the folder and replicated using the File Replication Service [FRS]). If AD and the SYSVOL shared folder do not replicate properly, security policy can fail.
- If AD replication fails, new logon credentials are not available, and changes to account status such as deleted or disabled accounts will not be consistent across domains. If new accounts and credentials are not available, it may mean denial of service for legitimate users. If information on disabled and deleted accounts is not available, it can mean system compromise.
- Storage and protection of critical Windows network information. The Active Directory stores information on every computer and every user in the forest as well as site and subnet information.

To ensure smoothly functioning Active Directory and Group Policy operations, do the following:

- Monitor related services such as netlogon, DNS, Event Log, File Replication, KDC, Resultant Set of Policy Provider, and Server.
- Create a baseline by collecting data for a time period that covers peak and low usage, such as during peak logon times in the A.M. and through password change policy and month-end activity. Use the baseline as a judge of unusual activity. Create new baselines periodically.
- Monitor disk space on drives that contain the Active Directory database and log files. Low disk space can prevent replication from occurring and cause other problems. The performance monitor tool can be configured to watch and alert when disk space is low.
- Consider the use of specialized monitoring products such as Microsoft Operations Manager (MOM). These solutions can make monitoring a large enterprise a manageable task.

- Thoroughly learn built-in and freely downloadable Microsoft tools for monitoring. In many cases, these tools may do an adequate job, or may be able to gather enough information to show the value of the monitoring process so that a larger, more comprehensive tool or suite of tools can be justified. In addition, many of these tools are quick, operate at the command line, and can be used by anyone with the appropriate administrative operating systems privileges. Third-party tools should be and often are restricted to smaller groups of administrators, yet some information is valuable to a larger group.
- Develop a response plan. It's not enough to know that there is malfunction—you must know how to deal with it. It may be a simple networking or configuration error, or it might be the result of an attack. Without a planned approach, your response can be crippled by indecision, inactivity, or delegation of the problem to the wrong person for solution.

Use the following utilities to monitor its operation. In addition to general tests, be sure to monitor AD replication and the File Replication Service (FRS).

Use dcdiag for an Overall Health Report

dcdiag.exe is a Windows Support tool that is composed of many tests of domain controller operations. Information on using dcdiag for troubleshooting Group Policy is included in Chapter 9, "Troubleshooting Group Policy." This section provides an overall review of dcdiag for overall Active Directory health monitoring. You can use this tool to test specific DC functionality or as a baseline report on overall health. A good practice is to periodically use the tool to prepare a report from as many of its tests as possible. The command dcdiag.exe /a /v /c /f: dcreport.txt will run most dcdiag tests (all except dcpromo and RegisterInDNS) and place detailed results in the dcreport.txt file. Figure 19-9 displays a portion of the file produced by the command.

Figure 19-9   Use dcdiag for a comprehensive report on Active Directory function.

Table 19-4 lists and describes the tests performed. You can find an analysis of a sample report in Chapter 3 of my e-book "Five Key Lessons to Securing Active Directory" in the technical library at www.redmondmag.com.

Table 19-4   Dcdiag Tests

Test	Description	Use Results
Connectivity	Tests connectivity to directory services. Determines site information and which servers and DCs exist. Tests Light weight Directory Access Protocol (LDAP) services, Remote Procedure Call (RPC) services, and checks each DC's registration in DNS.	A connectivity test pass confirms both network connectivity and DC registration in DNS. Failure points to a specific area to check.

Table 19-4 Dcdiag Tests Continued

Test	Description	Use Results
Replication	Tests replication for errors.	Pass on all these tests means that AD replication is OK. Failures point to specific items to troubleshoot.
Topology	Tests topology configuration and integrity.	
CutoffServers	Determines if replication partners can be reached.	
NCSecDesc	Checks replication permissions.	
Netlogons	Check logon privileges for replication.	
Advertising	Can domain services be located? Domain services are DC, LDAP server, writeable directory, KDC, timeserver, GC (if applicable).	A pass here means that DC activity is normal. This test fails if the netlogon service has stopped working.
KnowsofRole Holders	Determines if each DC can locate the domain and forest FSMOs.	A pass means that all FMSOs are working. Failures point to items to troubleshoot.
RidManager	Binds with RID master and reports RID Pool numbers, RID master DC.	
MachineAccount	Tests to see if the machine account for each DC is registered and its services advertised.	A pass means that all normal DC services available. Two dcdiag switches can be used to attempt repairs if these tests fail. Use /RecreateMachineAccount to attempt a repair or run and /FixMachineAccount if machine account flags are reported to be incorrect. Rerun the /MachineAccount test.
Services	Tests operation of domain services such as dnscache, NtFrs, IsmServ, kdc, SamSs, LanmanServer, Lanman Workstation, RpcSs, w32time, and netlogon.	

Test	Description	Use Results
OutboundSecure Channels	This test will not run when `dcdiag /c` is entered. Run this test separately and include the domain name. When properly run, tests outbound secure channels.	A pass documents the proper for mation of outbound secure channels.
Objects Replicated other	Determines if domain account and DSA objects are replicated.	A pass confirms that domain information is replicating to DCs in the domain.
Frssysvol	Checks the status of SYSVOL.	A pass means basic FRS services are functioning.
Frsevent	Browses FRS event log for errors and reports.	
Kccevent	Checks operation of the knowledge consistency checker (KCC).	A pass means there have been no KCC errors in the last 15 minutes.
Systemlog	Checks the system log for errors.	A pass indicates no errors in the last 60 minutes
CheckSDRef Dom	This test will not run when `dcdiag /c` is entered. Run separately to determine if application directory partitions have security description reference domains. The security reference domain is the domain used to determine the default security descriptors for domain objects.	A pass means domain objects will have security descriptors defined based on the same reference.
VerifyReplicas	Tests to see that application directory partitions are complete on all replica servers.	Pass means FRS is OK.
CrossRef Validation	Checks validity of cross-references. Cross-references allow a DC to be aware of all directory partitions in the forest.	

Table 19-4   Dcdiag Tests Continued

Test	Description	Use Results
VerifyReferences	Checks system references for FRS and it replication infrastructure within a domain.	
VerifyEnterprise References	Checks system references for FRS and its replication infrastructure across all objects on each domain controller.	
Intersite	Checks site connections.	All sites have connections to another site.
FsmoCheck	Determines location of GC, timeserver, KDC, and PDC.	Reports locations.

Running `dcdiag` and getting back a pass on all tests provides a good indicator that all is well with Active Directory. It's also a reasonable indication that DNS is functioning and includes appropriate service resource records because DNS is used to locate domain services. Because both DNS and Active Directory can be presumed OK, the likelihood of Group Policy being operational is also good. However, note that the status of services can change over time and that Group Policy operations are not tested directly. `dcdiag` just allows you to conclude that the proper infrastructure for Group Policy is operational.

Monitor Active Directory Replication

By ensuring proper DNS operations, you eliminate a major contributor to AD replication problems. Before replication can occur, the DC must locate its replication partner(s) using the following method:

1. Find the GUID of the replication partner by looking in `CN=NTDS Settings, CN=name-of-server, CN=Servers, CD=Site_name, CN=Sites, CN=Configuration, DC=domain_name, DC=Domain_name_extension`. `DNSLint` finds these GUIDs and then does a DNS lookup for the CNAME and glue record. You can manually look up the GUID using ldp.exe, as shown in Figure 19-10.

2. Query DNS for the CNAME associated with the GUID. The CNAME is of the form guid.msdcs.forest.root and identifies the DC name, as shown in Figure 19-11.

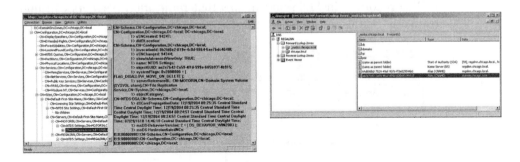

Figure 19-10   The GUID of the replication partner is the only AD information available.

Figure 19-11   A DNS query can obtain the CNAME from the GUID.

3. A second DNS query for the host record for the DC and its associated IP address is shown in Figure 19-12.

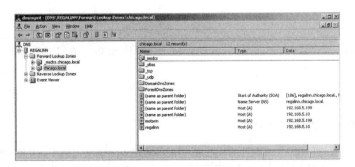

Figure 19-12   A DNS query can obtain the host record if the DC name is known.

Use DNSLint

You can use DNSLint to automatically make these inquires for all DCs. Figure 19-13 shows the result. A successful test documents that the GUID record is in DNS and means that replication partners can find each other—this must occur before replication can occur.

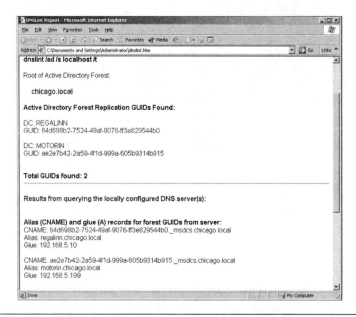

Figure 19-13 DNSLint finds the GUIDs in Active Directory and then does a DNS lookup.

Use replmon.exe

Use replmon.exe to display information about replication and replication partners. To use replmon.exe, follow these steps:

1. Open Windows Explorer and navigate to the Program Files, Support Tools folder.
2. Double-click replmon.exe.
3. Right-click the Monitored Servers node and select Add monitored server. Click Next.
4. Enter the name of the DC to monitor, click Next, and then click Finish.

5. Expand and select one of the nodes to see replication data in the detail pane, as shown in Figure 19-14.

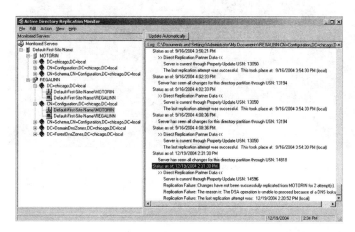

Figure 19-14   Information on replication can be observed by using replmon.

In the figure, a red circle with a white cross identifies an error. The screen has been scrolled to the error message in the detail pane. The error indicates that a replication attempt has failed and the reason for the failure as a DNS lookup. Because the server had recently been restarted, the `replmon` tool was used to request synchronization with the server's replication partner (right-click the node and select `Synchronize with this Replication Partner`), and then the `View` menu was used to refresh the data. This time, replication was successful, indicating that the failure was probably a result of the server being temporarily offline.

Use Replication Diagnostics Tool

Use the Replication Diagnostics Tool (repadmin.exe) to check replication links and latency. It also provides a summary of replication between partners. You can find out which replicated data has been received by which DCs and when they received it. Use the tool to generate a list of replicated objects and compare to find out if all DCs are receiving the information. If items are not being replicated to some DCs, use tools such as `dcdiag` and `DNSLint` to determine if network connectivity, DNS records, or the DC's operation may be the problem. Repadmin can also be used to force replication or to force KCC to run and select replication partners. Replication statistics are displayed using `repadmin /replsummary name_of_dc`, as shown in Figure 19-15.

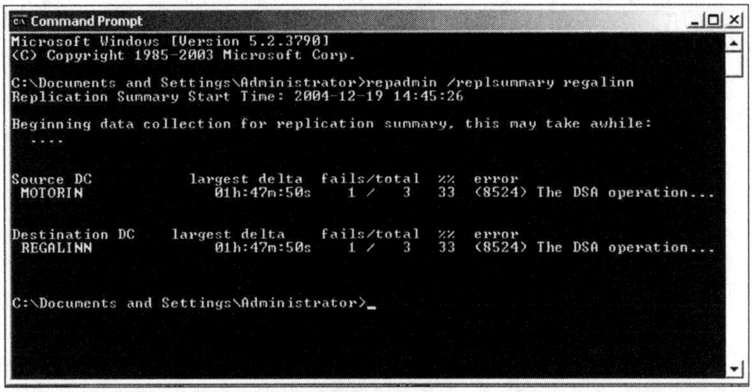

Figure 19-15 Information on replication can be observed by using replmon.

Use the Directory Services Utility

The Support Tool Directory Services Utility (dsastat.exe) is used to determine if domain controllers are up-to-date with each other. dsastat also checks the GC's information to ensure that it's up-to-date with DCs in other domains. When DCs are up-to-date, they present a consistent and accurate picture of their own domain. dsastat.exe can be used to test GCs to see if their information is consistent with DCs in each domain.

For example, to test consistency in the forest chicago.local, use the names of all child domains. The command `dsastat -s:regalinn; motorin -b:DC=chicago,DC=local —sort:true` compares the objects in the chicago.local domain across the two DCs: regalinn and motorin. By default, all objects are checked. You can specify objects, such as user groups, by using the `filter` parameter. Table 19-5 lists and describes the parameters used in the command as well as the additional parameters that can be used.

Table 19-5 Dsastat.exe Command Parameters

Parameter	Description
`-s:servername[portnumber]` `;servername[portnumber]...]`	A list of DCs in the domain by server name.

Parameter	Description
-b:*Searchpath*	The directory name for the part of the directory to search, such as an entire domain, or just an OU.
-qcattrs:all	In this case, lists all objects. You can specify the objects to list.
-sort:{TRUE|FALSE}	Sort results by object GUID. This can make the comparison slower in a statistical sort but faster in a full content comparison. It ensures object results are returned in nearly the same order from different servers.
-t:{TRUE|FALSE}	Perform statistics comparison or full content. A statistics comparison (set to true, the default) simply counts objects and ignores the qcattrs parameter. A full content comparison checks the attributes of objects including permissions.
-p:{1-999]	Pagesize (default is 64). Indicates the number of items to be returned per page for the ldap_search operation. Use a smaller page size if directory objects are large.
/loglevel:{INFO|TRACE|BOTH}	The extent of logging that can be requested. The default is INFO.
/output:{SCREEN|FILE|BOTH}	Location to report data. Default is screen.
/scope:{BASE|ONELEVEL|SUBTREE}	Extent of the scope for the search. Default is subtree.
/Filter:*LdapFilter*	The attributes to be returned. The default is "(objectclass=°)" indicating to return all objects.
/gcattrs:{ [LDAPAttributes [Attribute;Attribute...]] | [Objectclass] |auto] | [All]	Specifies attributes to be returned from the search. The use of "Objectclass" indicates no attributes should be returned. The use of "auto" specifies only those in the global catalog should be returned.
/U:*UserName*	Name of a user to use for the query.
/pwd:*password*	The user's password.
/d:*domain*	Domain to use for authenticating the user name.

The report lists each object checked and sums the information at the end. Figure 19-16 is a capture of the end of the report.

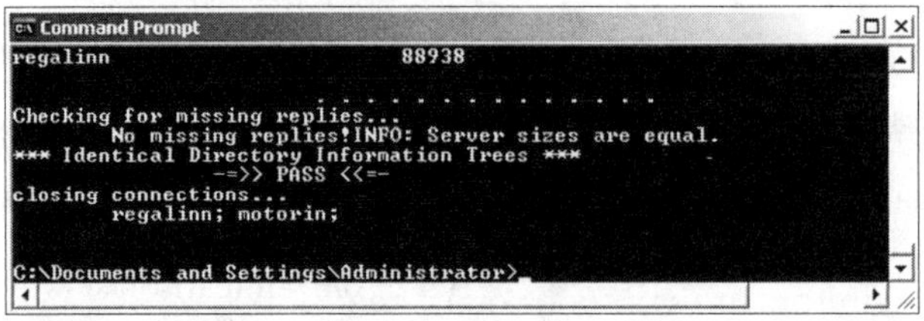

Figure 19-16   Information on replication can be observed by using replmon.

Use checkrepl

Use the Resource Kit tool checkrepl.vbs to view the replication topology of a specific DC. `checkrepl.vbs regalinn` lists the inbound and outbound replication neighbors and the date of the last successful replication. The property update number (the latest revision number) for each partition is listed, as is the protocol used for replication and the GUIDs of outbound partners. Running the command on other DCs in the domain provides information for comparison. Figure 19-17 displays the results of entering the following command:

```
Cscript checkrepl.vbs motorin
```

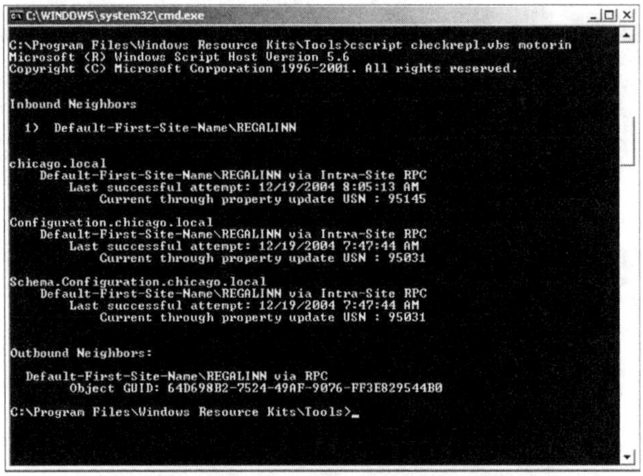

Figure 19-17   checkrepl reports replication topology for a DC.

Monitor FRS Replication

File Replication Service replicates the contents of the SYSVOL directory. Files in this directory are especially important to Group Policy, and this is also the location of logon and logoff scripts. FRS also can be used to replicate files unrelated to Active Directory. Two tools, FRS Health Check and FRS Diag, can be used to collect massive amounts of data relevant to FRS replication and Active Directory health. FRS Health Check runs a script, while FRS Diag presents a GUI interface. Other FRS monitors are gpotool, sonar, and ultrasound. Both sonar and ultrasound are monitoring tools that can be turned on and left to gather statistics during normal operation.

Use FRS Health Check

Use FRS Health Check (FRSHealth_CHk), a command-line support tool that monitors FRS, to retrieve FRS information from a specific DC or server. FRSHealth_CHk uses multiple support and resource kit tools as listed in Table 19-6 and collects FRS-related events from the Application, System, DNS, Active Directory and FRS event logs. Running FRSHealth_CHk against a selection of servers on a daily basis is a good monitoring option as it provides detailed information from a number of important tools. To select which servers to monitor, consider how FRS is used. To only monitor SYSVOL replication, select appropriate DCs, such as DCs used when changing Group Policy.

Table 19-6   Tools Used by FRSHealth_CHk

Tool	Purpose
connstat.cmd	Summarizes the status of FRS connections to and from a specific server using the results of ntfrsutil.exe.
dcdiag.exe	Checks DC status.
eventquery.vbs	Lists and filters events from event logs.
Iologsum.cmd	When the inlog, outlog, or idtable parameters are used with ntfrsutil.exe, information on pending inbound or outbound FRS change orders is collected in the inlog and outlog reports, respectively. Iologsum uses this raw data and creates a summary. This data can point out problems with FRS replication, such as changes not being replicated to all servers.

Table 19-6   Tools Used by FRSHealth_CHk Continued

Tool	Purpose
netdiag.exe	Diagnoses network connectivity problems.
ntfrsutil.exe	Analyzes events recorded during dcpromo as well as transaction and event details of FRS.
reg.exe	Used to add, change, import, and export registry subkeys.
repadmin.exe	Used to monitor AD health, view replication topology, force replication events, and view replication data.
topchk.cmd	Produces reports on topology and server replication partners using the results of the ntfrsutil command.

To issue the command, use the following:

```
Health_chk result_dir [target_computer]
```

As the tests are run, status information is reported. If no directory is specified in the command parameter result_dir, a default directory named for the server tested is created.

Use frsdiag

frsdiag.exe is a GUI-based tool that can provide much of the same information as FRSHealth_CHk. frsdiag produces a text file and a CAB file that can be sent to Microsoft for analysis. Tools and tests used by frsdiag are listed in Table 19-7.

Table 19-7   frsdiag.exe Tests and Tools

Tool	Description
DS Event Log	Checks the directory services event log for errors during the last 12 days.
ForceReplication	Forces replication.
FRS Debug Logs	Reports file replication errors.

Tool	Description
FRS Event Log test	Looks in the FRS event log and reports errors and warning from the past seven days. Also looks for 13508 warnings that are unmatched by 13509 events. 13508 indicates FRS problems, and 13509 indicates a resolution.
GUIDName	Builds a server GUID-to-name reference for a server.
Ntfrs_config Table	Checks free disk space. Checks FRS structure including the Sysvol folder, junction point, and the staging area folder.
Ntfrs_connstat	Warns when the number of backlog files is greater than 30. Reports an error when backlog files number greater than 100. Backlog files are files that need to be replicated.
Ntfrs_DS Services	Identifies broken or missing objects and object references.
Ntfrs_Replica Sets	Finds replication schedule issues.
Ntfrs_stage	Checks staging area size and warns when reaching limits.
Ntfrs_versions	Verifies FRS version requirements.
Propagation File Tracer	Checks current FRS replication consistency. Each server should have the same number of files and folders.
Registry dump	Dumps FRS Registry entries.
Repadmin/showreps	Looks for failed AD replication events.
Services and Shares	Tests NTFRS, W32Time, netlogon, server, workstation, and RPC services. Looks for Sysvol and netlogon shares.
Set Debug Logging Settings	Remotely changes or deletes NTFRS Debug Logging Registry values.

To use frsdiag.exe, follow these steps:

1. Open Windows Explorer and navigate to the Program Files\resource kit\frsdiag folder.
2. Double-click the frsdaig.exe file to open the GUI, as shown in Figure 19-18.
3. Select the local server or browse to another DC.
4. Review the information to be used and gathered in the interface or use the Tools menu to select tests to run. To run the tests, click GO. Log files are created with the results of the test. The pass/fail results of tests are displayed in the detail screen, as shown in Figure 19-19.

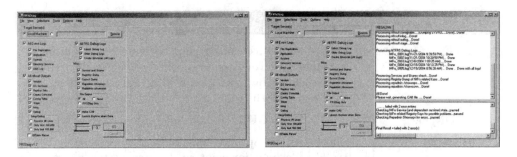

Figure 19-18   The FRSdiag tool allows selection of tests and tools to run.

Figure 19-19   Pass/fail results are displayed in the tool.

The results of tests can be logged to the FRSdiag folder for review.

Use GPOTool

Check the sysvol consistency with Active Directory replication using the Resource Kit tool GPOtool.exe. Group Policies are replicated in part by Active Directory and in part by FRS, so it is possible that if either replication process is not performing, GPO data can be inconsistent. Running gpotool.exe without any parameters lists the GPOs and the results of all tests. Sample output is displayed in Figure 19-20. The Group Policy Management console can also be used to display consistency information.

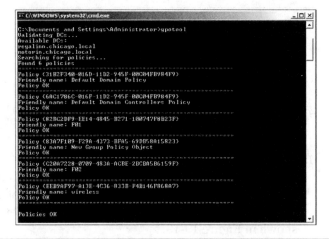

Figure 19-20   Use gpotool for a quick check of sysvol replication consistency with Active Directory Replication.

Use Sonar

Use sonar.exe to view the status of FRS. Traffic levels, backlog, and other statistics for replica sets are logged to a file and can be viewed in a special viewer. Sonar will also detect the sharing violations that can occur when a client leaves a file open. Open files cannot be replicated. To use the tool, follow these steps:

1. Start the tool from the Help and Support interface to load a window for configuration, as shown in Figure 19-21.

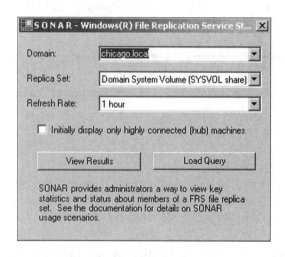

Figure 19-21   Start sonar to monitor FRS.

2. By default, the domain of the current computer and the SYSVOL share are configured for testing. Change this information using the drop-down boxes as appropriate. When first testing the tool, reset the refresh rate to one minute in order to view some results faster. Be sure to reset sonar to collect data more infrequently for production use.
3. Click the `View Results` button to display the Sonar—Windows File Replication Service Viewer.
4. From the `File` menu, select `Log` and use the popup shown in Figure 19-22 to start logging.

Figure 19-22   Start sonar to monitor FRS.

> **5.** As sonar refreshes, statistics are added, as shown in Figure 19-23.

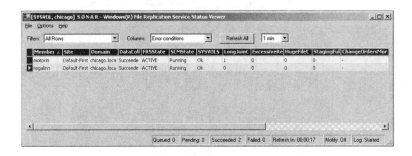

Figure 19-23   A quick visual of the statistics can be viewed.

A command line can also be used to start logging data.
To install the tool and start the log, enter this command:

```
Sonar /i /s configuration_file_name
```

To stop data collection, uninstall sonar using this command:
```
Sonar /u
```

Use Ultrasound

Use ultrasound to monitor and notify via email when replication problems are occurring. Ultrasound installs WMI providers on the replica set servers, centrally collects FRS replication data, and analyzes it looking for problems. Download ultrasound from http://www.microsoft.com/downloads/details.aspx?FamilyID=61acb9b9-c354-4f98-a823-24cc0da73b50&DisplayLang=en.

Monitor Group Policy Operations

If Group Policy operations fail, modified security settings will not be replicated to the computers and users. There are several options for confirming the health of Group Policy.

Use the Application Event Log

Application event log event 1704, displayed in Figure 19-24, indicates that Group Policy is applying security settings. This is scheduled to occur every 16 hours. Monitor for the presence of this event. If the event is not being written to the log, something is wrong with Group Policy operations.

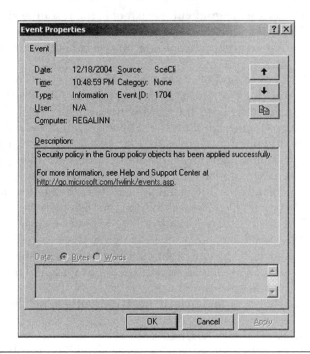

Figure 19-24   This normal event should appear every 16 hours in the application event log; if it doesn't, it's cause for alarm.

Use GPResult

GPResult can be used to list which GPOs were applied and when. To use the command to dump information to a text file, enter `gpresults /V > textfilename.txt` at the command line. You must run this command while logged on as the user you want to test policy for on the computer you wish to test policy for. It is more efficient to use the Group Policy Management console's Group Policy Results tool. However, gpresult is a good tool if you are sitting at the computer console of the computer you want to test. It can also provide validation for results obtained using the Group Policy Management console.

Use Gpmonitor

Use gpmonitor.exe to centrally collect and analyze Group Policy changes:

1. Locate the gpmonitor.exe tool in the resource kit directory.
2. Double-click the `gpmonitor.exe` tool.
3. When prompted, enter or browse to a location to extract the tool files to.
4. Use Group Policy software installation (use machine assignment for deployment type) to deploy the GP Monitor.msi to DCs. Also distribute the gpMonitor.adm files (you should then add gpMonitor.adm to the Default Domain Controller GPO as described in steps 6 to 10). All DCs must run the agent. The installed service, gpmonitor, automatically captures policy change information when Group Policy changes are made and uploads the information to a share defined using the gpmonitor.adm file. The service does not listen on the network.
5. Create a share for uploading the policy changes.
6. Open the `Default Domain Controller GPO`.
7. Navigate to and right-click the `Windows Settings`, `Security Settings`, `Administrative Templates` folder, and then select `Add/Remove templates`.
8. Click `Add` and select the GPMonitor.adm file, and then click `Open` followed by `Close`.
9. Expand the `Administrative templates` node and select to open the `Group Policy Monitor` folder. Double-click the `Group Policy Monitor` icon in the detail pane to display its `Settings` page.
10. Enter a UNC path to the share, as shown in Figure 19-25, that will be used for policy information uploads.

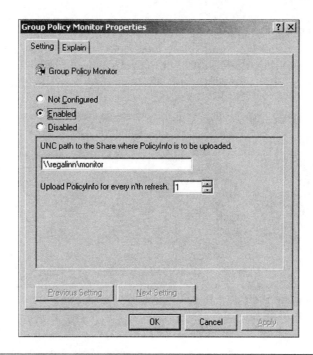

Figure 19-25 Enter a path for the share.

11. Accept or change the refresh number for policy change upload. Click OK.
12. At a command prompt, enter gpupdate to force a policy refresh.
13. Open a GPO in the Group Policy Editor and make some change to the GPO. (Never make arbitrary changes. Even in a test network, know the result of the change before implementing it.)
14. Open the Group Policy Monitor tool installed in the Administrative Tools folder to launch the user interface.
15. From the File menu, select New Query.
16. List machines to use in the query or leave the asterisk (°) in place to query all machines.
17. Enter the number of refreshes to display, as shown in Figure 19-26, and then click GO.

18. Right-click a Machine Policy Refresh by date, as shown in Figure 19-27, and select `Generate RSOP Report`. A refresh with a red mark denotes that the refresh included a policy change.
19. When complete, view the report to note the changes.

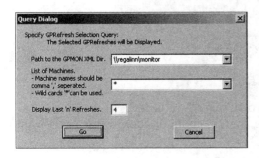 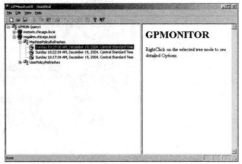

Figure 19-26 Define the query by entering computer names and number of refreshes.

Figure 19-27 An x within a circle indicates a policy change occurred during the refresh.

Use Performance Monitoring

Performance monitoring is not usually considered to be security monitoring. However, some data gathered by performance monitoring tools such as the built-in Windows Server 2003 Systems Monitor and Performance Logs and Alerts tools can be used in security monitoring. You can create logs and alerts using the Performance Logs and Alerts tool and view the results or create live monitors using Systems Monitor. Entering `perfmon` at a command prompt opens both tools in an MMC console. Examples of uses for performance monitoring data for security monitoring are as follows:

- Monitoring for low disk space on Active Directory database and log file disks
- Alerting on attack indicators

Use Performance Logs and Alerts to Alert on Low Disk Space

Low disk space can cause any number of programs to fail and may cause problems for virtual memory. The Active Directory database and log disks should be monitored to ensure that adequate disk space is available. Set an alert to warn you when disk space is getting critically low. To do so:

- Determine drives on which disk space issues can cause critical failures. For a domain controller, these disks are the database and log disks.
- Determine how much disk space is required.
- Set an alert using the System monitor tool to warn when disk space is low.
- Monitor for your practical usage and adjust this figure as necessary.

Determine Disk Space Required

A basic formula for requiring disk space is provided in the Microsoft Windows 2000 resource kit (`http://www.microsoft.com/resources/documentation/Windows/2000/server/reskit/en-us/Default.asp?url=/resources/documentation/Windows/2000/server/reskit/en-us/core/fnee_exa_skbl.asp`). It includes:

1. Start with 1 GB.
2. Add the size of all applications, including their database and/or log files. If you have isolated the logs or database on their own disk, the size of applications may be zero.
3. Add the size of the paging file if the paging file uses this disk. (General recommendations for paging file size are twice the amount of memory. Space on multiple disks may be allocated.) If no space is allocated, nothing needs to be added.

To this good start, add the following:

1. If this is the first DC, start with size of the installation database and log files. Double that size at least and add it in step 2.
2. If this is a new DC in an established domain/forest, use the current size of the database and logs.

3. Monitor the size of the database and/or logs periodically to estimate growth over time and adjust the size of the disk requirement according. Allow for rapid growth during initial installation of the forest and at peak times when large numbers of objects are added.

4. Then, as the resource kit indicates, multiply by 130 percent to allow room for expansion.

The total figure produced by these steps is the total disk space required. Since you need to alert when the "minimum" free space is left on the disk, subtract the amount estimated before multiplying by 130 percent (the amount after step 3 but before step 4) from the total disk space required. The result of this calculation is the minimum amount of free space that should always be present on the disk. Since the System Monitor alert is in %free space, calculate the percentage of the disk used for the AD database and logs that this figure represents. Be sure to periodically recalculate to obtain current requirements.

Set an Alert

Although you may want to establish many disk counters to measure disk performance, these instructions just detail how to set up a monitor to warn of disk space issues:

1. Install the logical disk counters by opening a command prompt, typing `diskperf -yv,` and then press `Enter.`
2. Restart the server to load LogicalDisk counters.
3. Click `Start, Run,` and then type `perfmon` and press `Enter.` This starts System Monitor.
4. Expand the `Performance Logs and Alerts` tree.
5. Right-click `Alerts` and click `New Alert Settings.`
6. Enter a name for the alert, and then click `OK.`
7. Enter a comment. "Monitors disk space on AD database drive X" is a good comment. X is the letter of the drive this alert is for.
8. Click `Add` to open `Select Counters.`
9. Click `Select Counters from computer` and click the DC in the list.
10. Select the `Performance object` drop-down box and select `LogicalDisk.`
11. Click `Select instances from list` and select the drive to monitor.
12. Click `Select counters from list` and click `% Free Space,` as shown in Figure 19-28.

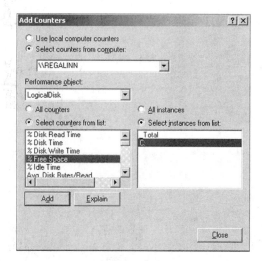

Figure 19-28   Select the DC and drive to monitor.

13. Click Add and then click Close.

14. On the General tab, in the Alert when the value is box, click Under and then set the Limit value, as shown in Figure 19-29, to at least the value you estimated as required for growth.

15. Adjust the Sample data every setting to something that makes sense for your environment and then click Apply.

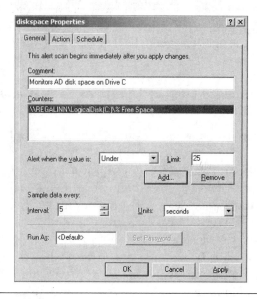

Figure 19-29   Set the value.

16. On the Action tab, click Log an entry in the application event log and configure other actions, such as sending a network message, starting a performance data log, and running a specific program, as shown in Figure 19-30. The latter choice may be used to send an email.

17. Click the Schedule tab and set the time to start the scan.

18. Click OK to save the alert.

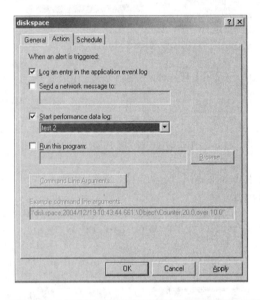

Figure 19-30   Set the action the event should trigger.

Use Performance Logs and Alerts as Early Warning Signs of Possible Attacks

Information in the event logs may help you identify problems, identify security incidents, and provide an audit trail for evaluation after the fact. Monitoring the event logs for this information in real time is not a chore for manual review. System Monitor can help. It can be used to alert you to unusual circumstances and provide information that may help you determine whether unusual activity is a troubleshooting issue or a security incident. For example, System Monitor can be used to focus on the number of failed logons and send an alert when they exceed some number. (Determine what is normal for your environment and set the alert for some number over that.) This can provide you with an early warning that there may be a possible password-cracking attack underway.

Some counters to monitor are

- Errors Access Permissions
- Errors Granted Access
- Errors Logon

Create a log of events over time to find the baseline for your environment, then create alerts to help you identify possible security incidents. Continue to log events as a record.

To log events, follow these steps:

1. Right-click the `Counter Logs` node.
2. Enter a name for the new log.
3. Click `Add Counters`.
4. Select the computer in the `Select counter objects from computer` or select `Use local computer objects`.
5. Select the `Performance Object`, such as server.
6. Select the counter from the list provided. Click `Add` to add the counter.
7. Repeat until you have added all the desired counters, and then click `Close`.
8. Adjust the sample interval and click `Apply`.
9. Use the `Log Files` tab to configure log files; for example, you may want to select a log file type of comma delimited in order to store data in a database for viewing, or select SQL server format if you want to log data directly to a SQL server database.
10. Use the `Schedule` tab to dictate when the recording should start.

Monitor Event Logs

Several of the tools described in this chapter poll events logs and report errors. A more comprehensive plan for event log monitoring is required to spot security incidents and determine what happened during them. MOM is a product that uses event log data, and many third-party products can be used to centrally collect and even manage events. A new tool is planned as part of an update to Windows Server 2003 that will automatically centralize and analyze event log information.

Meanwhile, two helpful tools, EventcombMT and lockoutstatus, can span servers to collect and help analyze events.

Use EventCombMT

EventCombMT can be downloaded from Microsoft.

To run the tool, follow these steps:

1. Type `EventCombmt` at a command prompt.
2. Review the sample instructions, as shown in Figure 19-31, and click OK.

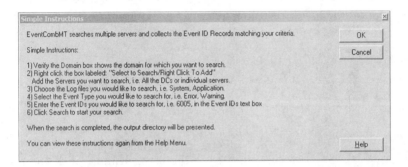

Figure 19-31   Most information needed to operate EventCombMT is in the sample instructions.

3. Right-click the `Select To Search/Right Click to Add` box and select `Get DCs` in domain or other listing such as GCs in the domain, all servers, all servers in a list, or select individual servers.
4. Use the `Searches` menu to select a built-in search such as `FRS health`, `account lockouts`, `Active Directory DNS registration failure`, and so forth.

   OR

   Customize the log files, event types, event IDs, and timeframe to search for, as shown in Figure 19-32. If several event IDs are entered, separate them with spaces.
5. Click the `Search` button. To view the results, open the text files recorded for each server monitored. The log files are saved to the temp directory, which is opened at the conclusion of the search. The motorin log is shown in Figure 19-33. (The search can take some time if many servers and large logs are a factor. In this example, event 643 was the only event identified; the search was to record any instances of an account policy being changed. The results found events.)

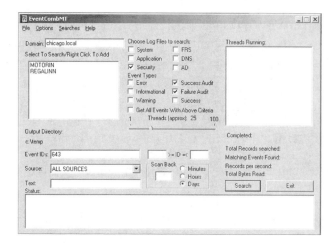

Figure 19-32   Customize the search using check boxes and text boxes.

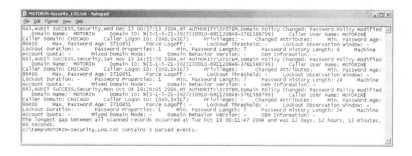

Figure 19-33   Review the results.

Use Lockoutstatus

Another tool, the Resource Kit tool lockoutstatus.exe, can help you troubleshoot account lockout issues. One of the benefits of setting the account lockout policy is that password-cracking attacks will lock out the account. In order to diagnose whether a lockout is due to an attack or user malfunction, and to determine which computer was used in the attack, you must review data from every domain controller in the domain. In a large domain, this can be time-consuming. The Lockoutstatus.exe tool can be used to display lockout information from all DCs in the domain. To display lockout information on the fredp account in the chicago.local domain, use this command at the command line:

```
Lockoutstatus /u:chicago.local\fredp
```

Alternatively the fredp@chicago.local account format is acceptable input for the /u: parameter. A GUI displays the results, as shown in Figure 19-34. Right-clicking a DC allows you to view its event log from which you can view logon events and determine the client the user used. The tool can also be used to list account status such as max password age and current age.

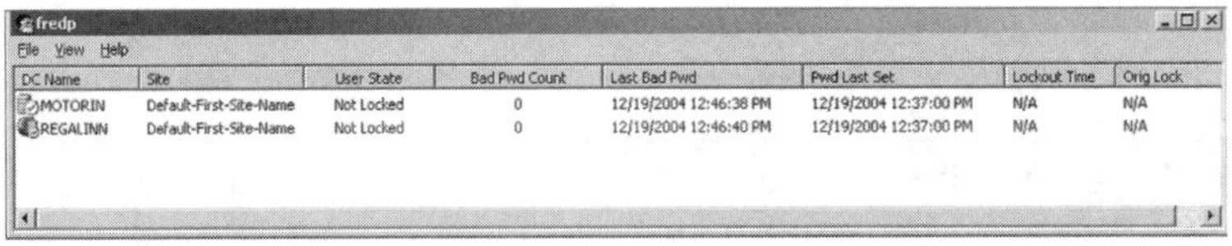

Figure 19-34 Use lockoutstatus.exe to help determine why the even occurred.

Introduction to Incident Response

Incident response is the collection of actions taken after an alleged security incident is identified. In many organizations, a formal incident response team coordinates response. Its members are drawn from IT, audit, security, human resources, legal, senior management, and other areas of the company. In many cases, only a few of these people are assigned to any incident, and additional employees as well as outside specialists may be recruited during specific incidents. In other companies, incident response is less formal. Teaching you how to create a crack team and detailing how to respond to every possible security incident is not the purpose of this section. Instead, its purpose is to help you identify action points that can be taken in order to formulate a response to incidents. If you already have an incident response team or process in place for incident response, your first task should be to contact them to understand what your role should be in reporting or working as part of their extended team. If you do not have any process in place, or want to review the process you do have in hopes of improving it, use the following guidelines.

The classic incident response process consist of sseven elements:

- Detect the incident.
- Respond to the incident with some action.
- Contain the incident; don't let it continue to grow or further compromise information systems.
- Recover systems.
- Resume normal operation.
- Review the what, when, why, who, and how the event happened and how it was dealt with.
- Improve by implementing steps to prevent future incidents and by developing a better response.

However, before you can follow this path, you must develop a plan. Here are some steps that can help:

- List possible security incidents. Security incidents can be as devastating as malware storms in which massive infections threaten to destroy network operations to suspected misuse or sharing of logon credentials. In addition to the incidents you may hypothesize from your familiarity with current attack vectors, be sure to include the results of threat modeling that may have been done on your network operations and specific applications. Another good source of possible incidents is reviewing the event logs and other data collected as the result of tools described in this chapter. When you know what is normal, can you identify the data that might mean simple operational failure and thus need troubleshooting, from that which might point to possible attack? Add those events to your list.
- Categorize incidents. You may want to use several types of categories. One good category is by type. For example, various malware infections may have similar vectors, as well as similar cleanup requirements, while directed attacks are very different. The advantage of categorizing is that you can estimate the number and type of individual who will be necessary for the response.
- Plan operations that might reveal various incidents in progress or from the data trail they produce in various logs.
- Determine the type of response for each type of incident. How many people will be needed? What needs to be done? Will specific department members need to be part of the team; for example, legal may need to advise you on what information needs to be shared with the public, when to call in law enforcement, or when and what to say to customers. Human relations may need to

be informed in order to work with employees in countering rumors with fact or in helping employees to deal with the affects of the attack such as finding uncompromised data and work sources, or preventing reinfection.

- Assign responsibility for starting and working the response process. Who takes the alleged incident, determines if it is a security incident, assigns a team, and monitors progress? Who keeps management and other team members not directly involved in the technical aspect of the response informed? Who documents activity?

- Plan for a post mortem. After an incident, collect all information and meet with incident response team members, both those involved with this incident and others. A lot can be learned from reviewing how the event was handled. Kudos can be given, and errors can be discussed leading to improved procedures and team efforts in the future.

Summary

Monitoring and assessment is a critical part of information security. It is useful both in keeping systems running and in dealing with security events. It can alert administrators to problems, identify attacks in progress, and provide information for use in dissecting events or provide information for legal prosecution after a security event has occurred. In order to effectively perform these chores, the administrator must be knowledgeable in the use of many tools and be given the time to evaluated their results. In the day-to-day operation of networks, both knowledge and review tasks are often ignored or trivialized in favor of just keeping systems running. Unfortunately, this chapter can only provide the knowledge part of the monitoring and assessment task. Organizations must be motivated to provide appropriate intellectual bandwidth for systems review of and action based on that review. If they do, they will be rewarded with systems that work better, faster, more efficiently, and longer. They will be able to do more than "just keep systems up and running."

Index

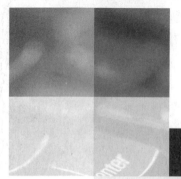